WONDER WOMAN
THE WORLD WAR II YEARS
1941–1945

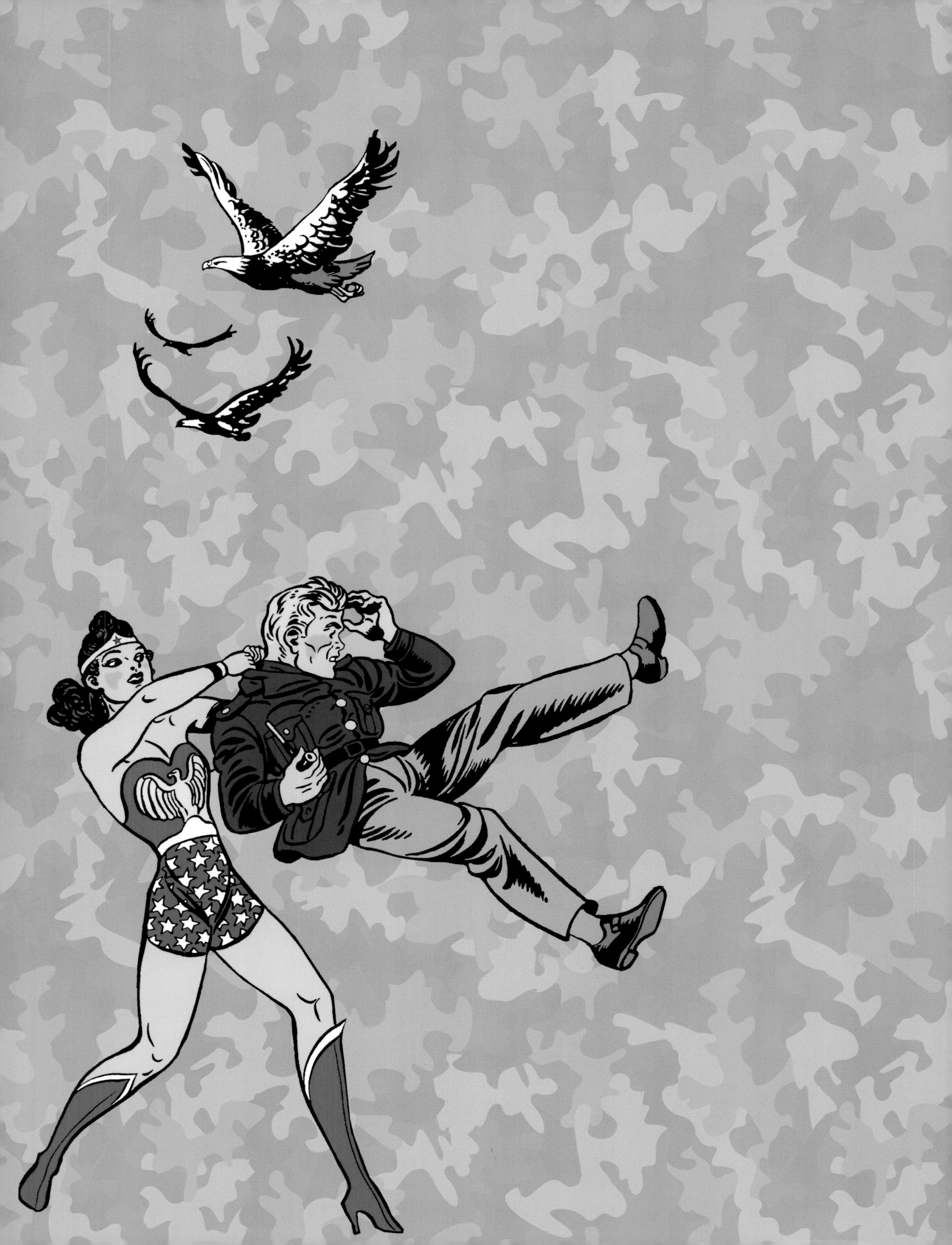

Wonder Woman

THE WAR YEARS
1941 – 1945

By Roy Thomas

CHARTWELL
BOOKS

EDITORS
Michelle Faulkner
Frank Oppel

EDITORIAL ASSISTANT
Jason Chappell

DESIGNER
Maria P. Cabardo

DESIGN ASSISTANT
Cheryl Smith

COVER DESIGNER
Rachael Cronin

This edition published in 2015 by Chartwell Books , an imprint of Book Sales, a division of Quarto Publishing Group USA Inc.
142 West 36th Street, 4th Floor, New York, New York 10018 USA

This edition published with permission of and by arrangement with DC Entertainment
4000 Warner Boulevard, Burbank, CA 91505 USA
A Warner Bros. Entertainment Company.

ISBN-13: 978-0-7858-3284-3   Printed in China   2 4 6 8 10 9 7 5 3 1   www.quartous.com

All identification of writers and artists made in this book utilized information provided by the Online Grand Comics Database.

Compiled by Roy Thomas

To Dann—the first woman ever
to have a writing credit
on Wonder Woman—
and a wondrous woman
in her own right.

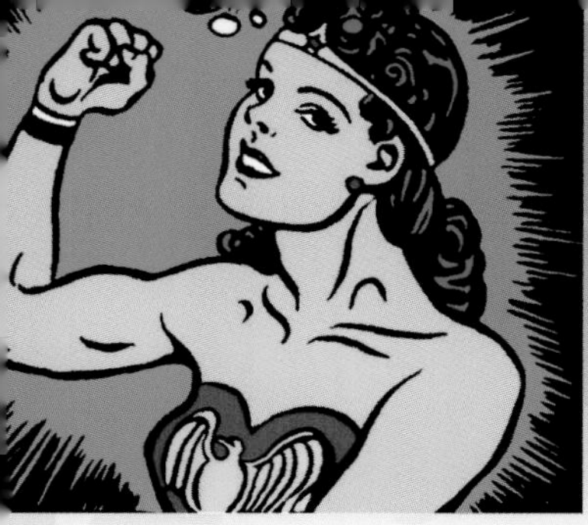

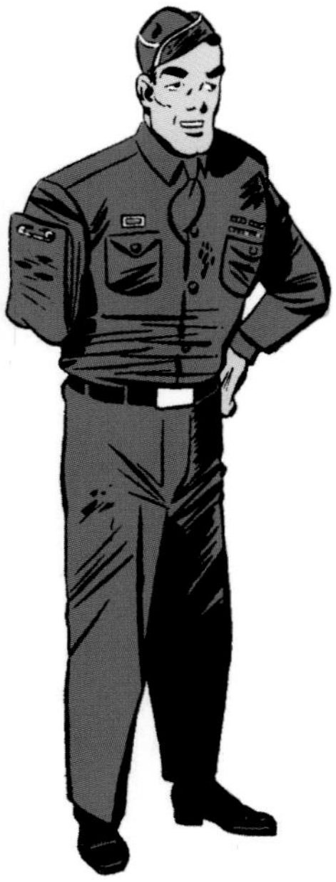

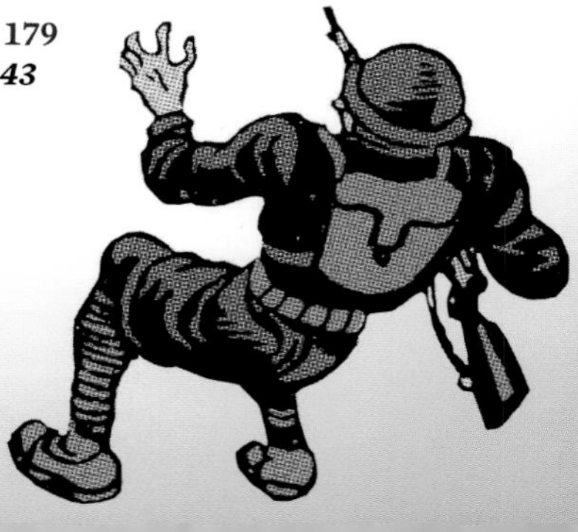

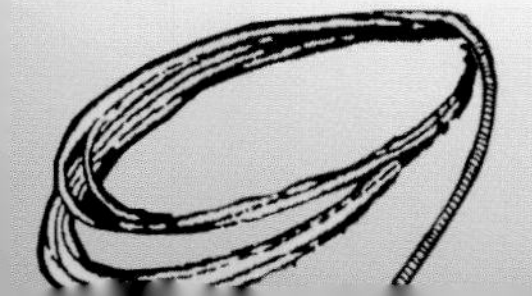

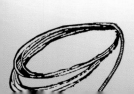

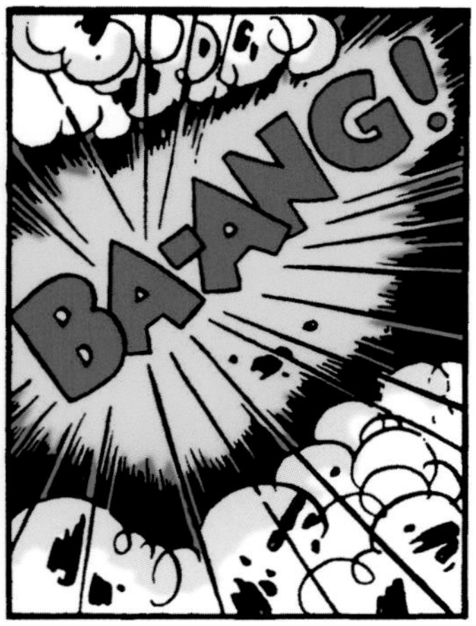
BA-ANG!

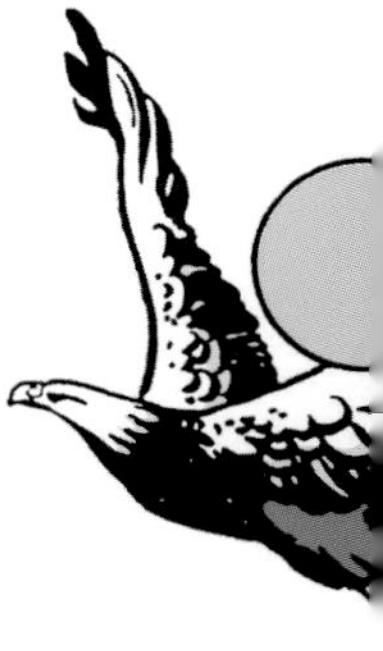

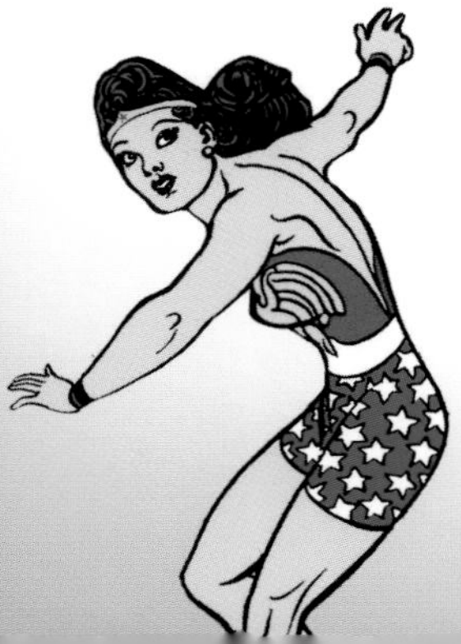

Some stories were untitled in the original comic books; for convenience, titles have been added on this contents page.

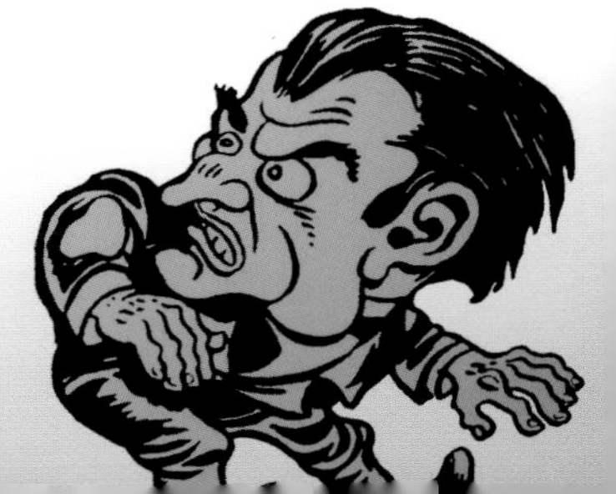

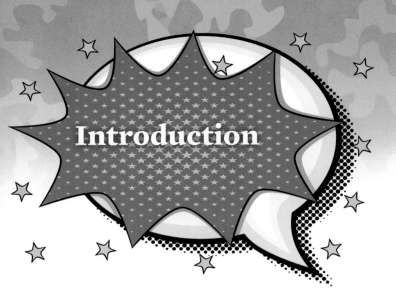

Introduction

BY ROY THOMAS

Wonder Woman.

When Wonder Woman made her debut near the end of 1941, she wasn't the first costumed heroine in comic books. Not even close. She'd been beaten into four-color print by the likes of Amazona the Mighty Woman, Astron the Crocodile Queen, the Black Cat, the Black Widow (in fact, by two different characters with that name, neither of them the one currently appearing in The Avengers movies), Miss America (no relation to any beauty queen), Miss Victory, Pat Parker/War Nurse, Pat Patriot, Phantom Lady, Red Tornado, the Silver Scorpion, Wildfire, and the Woman in Red, not to mention several jungle queens whose costumes were made from the hides of deceased leopards, tigers, or zebras.

Yet, of the above names, probably none rings a bell with more than a tiny, ever-shrinking portion of the general populace, while Wonder Woman is instantly recognized, even by people who haven't read a comic book (or seen a TV re-run) in years.

Princess Diana, to give Wonder Woman the name she bore among the hidden Amazon civilization of which she was a part, was dreamed up not, as Superman was, by a couple of young men with visions of super-strength dancing in their heads, but by a middle-aged psychologist who already had a string of accomplishments behind him . . . and who knew how to make the most of them.

Dr. William Moulton Marston was a 1915 Harvard graduate, married to the former Elizabeth Holloway. Both obtained law degrees, but practiced rarely, if at all. After serving in the "psychological division" of the U.S. Army during the First World War, William Marston earned a Ph.D. in psychology in 1921 and became—well, if he wasn't exactly the "inventor of the lie detector," as is often reported

(based on a paper he'd published in 1917 about how measurement of blood pressure could be used to identify deception), he has been called that device's "most enthusiastic advocate." He was adept at attracting media attention to himself with showboat-style events that utilized lie detectors and attractive young women. Secretly, he also had an unusual home situation, in that his assistant, Olive Byrne, became a sort of "second wife" to Marston, with himself, the two women, and their several children living happily together for many years. During the Great Depression, however, his opportunities as a college educator began to dry up, perhaps partly because other academics eyed his publicity-seeking activities with skepticism. Luckily, his (legal) wife had a good job with a life insurance company.

In the late 1930s Marston began to write articles and give interviews predicting that "women would take over the rule of the country, politically and economically." In other words, not just equality for women, but superiority.

And, before long, he got his chance to see his theories put into practice—at least in comic books. Landing a job as consulting psychologist for *Family Circle* magazine, he wrote a 1940 article titled "Don't Laugh at the Comics," which defended comic books in an era when they were beginning to come under attack as the cause of juvenile delinquency, bad reading habits, impaired eyesight, etc., etc., etc. In the piece, he particularly lauded M.C. Gaines, publisher of the All-American Comics Group (which was formally allied with DC Comics, with the two companies cross-advertising and both featuring the DC symbol on their covers). The article landed him a moonlighting position as a member of DC/AA's Editorial Advisory

Board . . . which he promptly used as a springboard to sell Gaines on his idea for a new super-hero.

Or rather . . . super-*heroine*.

According to a later statement by Marston, he proposed the notion that "America's woman of tomorrow should be made the hero of a new type of comic-strip." Years later, his wife claimed the sex of the new character was *her* idea. Gaines, Marston reminisced, was skeptical at first, since most comic books with female stars hadn't sold well. (Although *Jumbo Comics*, over at Fiction House, was doing fairly good business with Sheena, Queen of the Jungle.) Marston said that Gaines finally agreed to publish such a lead feature for six months, if Marston himself would write it. The psychologist agreed to do so, under the pseudonym "Charles Moulton," a combination of Gaines's and his own middle names.

As artist—but hired and paid by Marston rather than working directly for Gaines and his editor—they hired Harry G. Peter, a middle-aged cartoonist, to draw the feature. Born in 1880 and already older than forty in 1941, he had experience drawing newspaper illustrations, mostly in concert with his wife. His only comic book super-hero work prior to this had been a character called Man o' Metal for another company's magazine. Working at least in part from Marston's instructions, and in a time when the worsening world situation was bringing the nation's patriotism to the fore, Peter gave the heroine an America-centric red-white-and-blue costume with a golden eagle on her chest. Neither Marston nor his wife ever counted Peter as being a co-creator of Wonder Woman, but generations of readers and experts have made up their own minds on the matter.

Actually, though, she wasn't "Wonder Woman" right off the bat. The original title of the feature submitted to M.C. Gaines in February of 1941, according to comics historian Les Daniels in his book *The Complete History of Wonder Woman*, was "Suprema, the Wonder Woman." Gaines nixed the "Suprema" bit, probably as being too close to Superman. She was scheduled to make her debut in the first issue of a new AA title, *Sensation Comics*, with a cover date of January 1942, going on sale circa November of 1941. After studying some sample

comic scripts provided to him, Marston began to write and soon turned in his first script.

At the last minute, however, Gaines decided the best way to introduce Wonder Woman to comic book readers would be to have her appear in a story prior to *Sensation #1*. Thus, Marston's first script and Peter's accompanying art were printed as a one-time back-up feature in AA's already strongly-selling *All-Star Comics*. That title starred the Justice Society of America, a group of eight (male) super-heroes who had banded together to fight evil, and was a showcase for DC and AA characters not yet popular enough to have graduated to their own eponymous comic books, as had DC's Superman and Batman and AA's Flash and Green Lantern.

What most likely happened, based on evidence from surviving copies of the earliest scripts, is that the first two pages of Marston's initial script for a then-standard 13-page story were drawn in comics style by H.G. Peter—then a bloc of perhaps six pages' worth of script were compressed into two pages of typeset prose, studded with several drawings (really comics panels minus word balloons)—followed by the script's final five pages, once again drawn in straight comics style. The typeset mid-section was a flashback related by Wonder Woman's mother, Hippolyte, queen of the Amazons, about their all-female tribe's trials and tribulations (including a brief conquest by Hercules) that had forced them, many centuries earlier, to migrate from ancient Greece to the hidden Paradise Island, where they established a new world of their own, free from domination by men. The yarn "Introducing Wonder Woman" duly appeared in *All-Star Comics #8* (Dec. 1941–Jan. 1942). Gaines felt strongly enough about his marketing idea that he paid for that issue to have eight more pages than the preceding or succeeding ones.

Amusingly, the theme of *All-Star #8*'s up-front Justice Society adventure, heralded on its cover, was that "two new members win their spurs," replacing Green Lantern (who'd been bumped from the comic after he'd recently been awarded his own quarterly solo magazine) and Hour-Man, a character Gaines had decided wasn't worth keeping in the group mag. That pair were replaced by Starman, the new cover star of DC's *Adventure Comics*, and Dr. Mid-Nite, a new feature in *All-American Comics*. But Starman would vanish from comic books in early 1946, and Dr. Mid-Nite would disappear when *All-Star Comics* itself was discontinued at the turn of 1951—while Wonder Woman would remain in print and in steady, continuous publication from that day to this! Gaines was smart to bet on Wonder Woman. And Marston, for his part, had the courage of his convictions—or at least he put up a good bluff, making himself seem professionally accomplished and financially independent. When, a few issues later, Wonder Woman was formally inducted into the Justice Society as its first female member, he predicted she would prove more popular than any of the male super-heroes in the magazine. She did, eclipsing in comics sales not only Hawkman, Starman, the Spectre, and the rest of *All-Star's* cast, but even founding JSAers Flash and Green Lantern, both of whom had preceded her in being awarded their own magazines. As it would happen, all titles featuring solo stories of Flash and Green Lantern would be discontinued in the late 1940s, at a time when Wonder Woman was still starring not only in her own mag but also in *Sensation Comics* (as well as in *All-Star*, in which all three of them continued to appear for a couple more years).

Wonder Woman was a remarkable character, with a number of unique things about her besides her sex. She flew around in an invisible plane, the original stealth technology . . . she had a lasso which compelled anyone in its grip to tell the truth (a sort of lie detector in reverse) . . . she wore metal bracelets which, guided by her super reflexes, could repel bullets . . . and she was both "stronger than Hercules" and "swifter than Mercury." Between that and her costume that gave Timely's Captain America a run for his money as a patriotic ensemble, she swiftly eclipsed all DC/AA heroes except Superman and Batman in sales.

However, the remarkable Golden Age popularity of Wonder Woman would only last through the late 1940s, a time when readers' interest in super-heroes quickly waned in the post-World War II years. But, if stories going around can be believed, All-American (which in 1945 was purchased from Gaines by DC Comics) made a deal with Marston which specified that, if DC ever ceased publishing her adventures, rights would revert to the psychologist or his family . . . and the publisher didn't want that to happen. Marston himself died in 1947, but Elizabeth Marston lived well into her nineties.

So perhaps William Moulton Marston was right, at that—and the female of the species was indeed destined to conquer all!

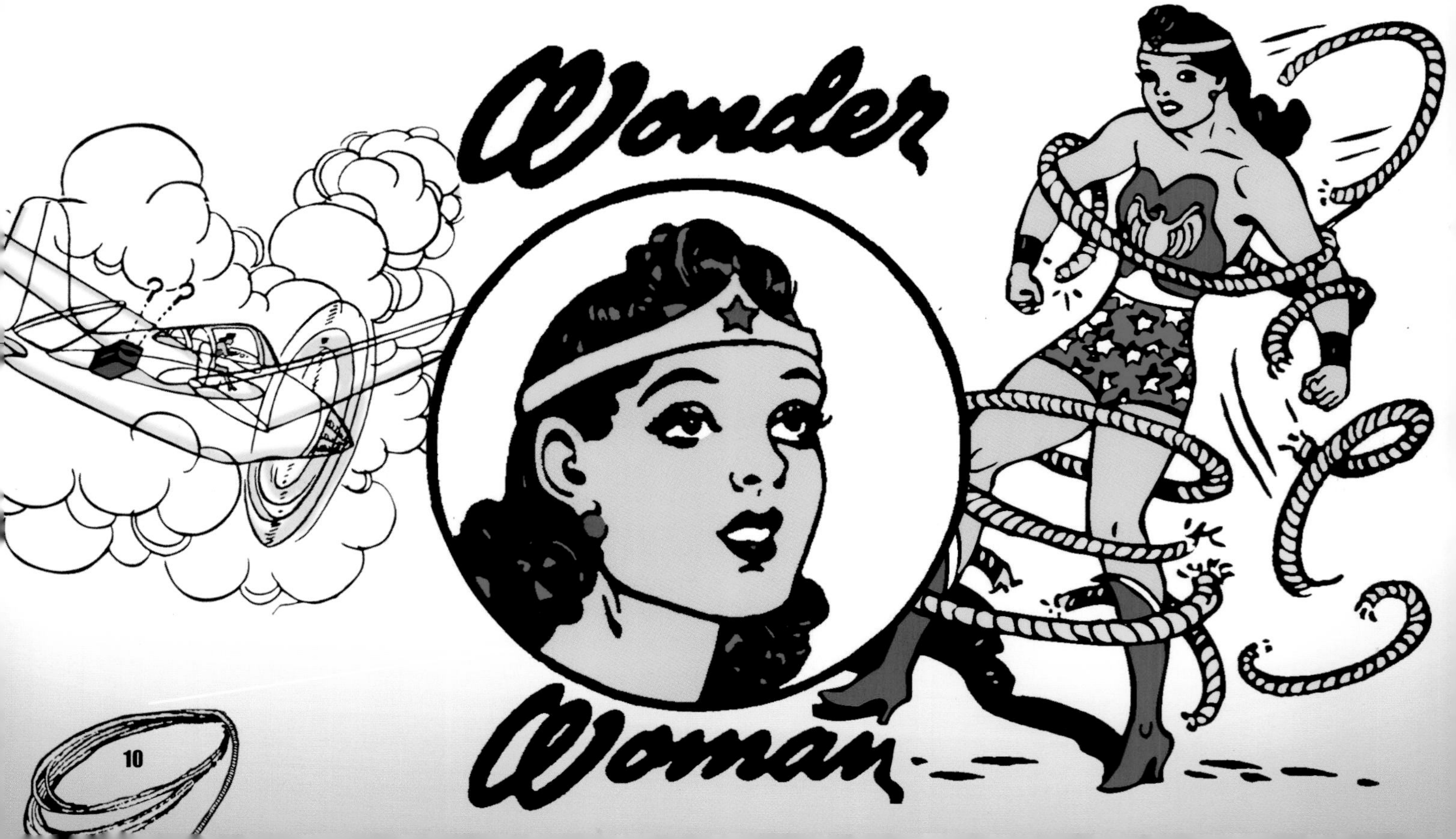

Wonder Woman

Part One

Wonder Woman came into existence in 1941—in a world largely at war— when the United States was walking a tightrope of official neutrality.

The War Comes to Paradise Island

Superman made his debut in Action Comics #1 in early 1938, at a time when the average American was still far more concerned with the ongoing Depression in the United States than with what the Nazis and Japanese were up to in Europe and the Far East. A year later, even Batman's first bow occurred before the British and French declared war on Adolf Hitler's Germany following the latter's invasion of Poland.

But Wonder Woman came into existence in 1941, in a world largely at war—even if the U.S.A. was still walking a tightrope of official neutrality. While, of course, those first Wonder Woman stories, in *All-Star Comics* #8 and *Sensation Comics* #2, came out within weeks of each other, both with cover dates that included January 1942, they had gone on sale a couple of months earlier, and had been prepared several months before that. And even in the spring or summer of 1941, an ever-diminishing proportion of the American populace really believed their country was going to be able to resist getting into the war, sooner or later. It didn't seem possible that Britain (even with the aid of its post-June 1941 ally, the Soviet Union) could defeat the German war machine. Even when the British prevailed against the Italians in North Africa, Hitler's Nazi troops were right there to bail them out and push the British back. And Japan? Who in America would've dreamed that it would be a Japanese action, rather than a German provocation, that would finally propel the "48 states" into congealing two wars in two separate hemispheres into one globe-encircling Second World War?

The primacy of American concerns about Germany rather than Japan is apparent even in the truncated Wonder Woman tale in *All-Star* #8, which devotes three of its nine pages to Captain Steve Trevor's bout against a spy ring. No home country for the foreign agents is identified, but they have names like "Fritz" and "von Storm," and they utter expressions like "Vas ist?" and "Nicht wahr?" and "Mein herr." They obviously aren't French! And, after the Amazon rescues a blond captain of U.S. Army Intelligence and returns with him to America, it is von Storm who is brought low by the end of the story in *Sensation* #1.

Oddly, the first collaboration between Wonder Woman and Captain Steve Trevor was given quite a different angle when it was retold in the early days of the Wonder Woman newspaper comic strip that debuted more than three years later. There, the spy ring Steve was trying to foil was Japanese, not German. (Princess Diana's comic strip didn't last nearly as long as Batman's, let alone Superman's. It ran from May 8, 1944, through December 1, 1945, only a little more than a year and a half—and there was never a color Sunday rendition. It seemed that, with her male counterparts having beaten her into the nation's funny-pages, there just wasn't room for a third super-hero strip in the nation's newspapers. Still, we wanted to give you a taste of that strip in this book.)

By the Amazon's third adventure, in *Sensation Comics* #2, she met her first costumed foe, who bore the unpleasant code name Dr. Poison. The good doctor's true identity would turn out to be a surprise, we suspect, to the great majority of readers. Since this story, too, was scripted prior to all declarations of war by the U.S., Poison's nationality is not revealed. If anything, this was a slight pulling-back from the first two stories, especially the one in *All-Star*, for Dr. Poison doesn't speak with a Germanic accent. Incidentally, in *Sensation* #3, Wonder Woman, in her secret identity as nurse Diana Prince, uses a blood-pressure lie detector on a suspected spy; Marston couldn't resist pushing his old theories.

It was left to the lead story in *Sensation* #4 to introduce a character who would become one of Wonder Woman's most noteworthy foes: the Baroness Paula von Gunther, head of a very Germanic spy ring this time, even if the Fatherland is never identified by name. Several years later, Paula would reform and become a scientist for the Amazons on Paradise Island.

By the fifth issue of *Sensation*, though, German accents are in evidence again, even if that tale's spies are still not identified as hailing from the Third Reich. This time, Wonder Woman is protecting a new U.S. submarine from being stolen by the foreign agents, who at least manage an "Ach!" or two between them. The date on this issue's cover is May 1942—meaning the tale would've been prepared shortly before the attack on Hawaii on Sunday, December 7, 1941. At this stage, submarines were a part of the national defense effort, but were not yet being deployed against any enemy.

That, however, would soon change . . .

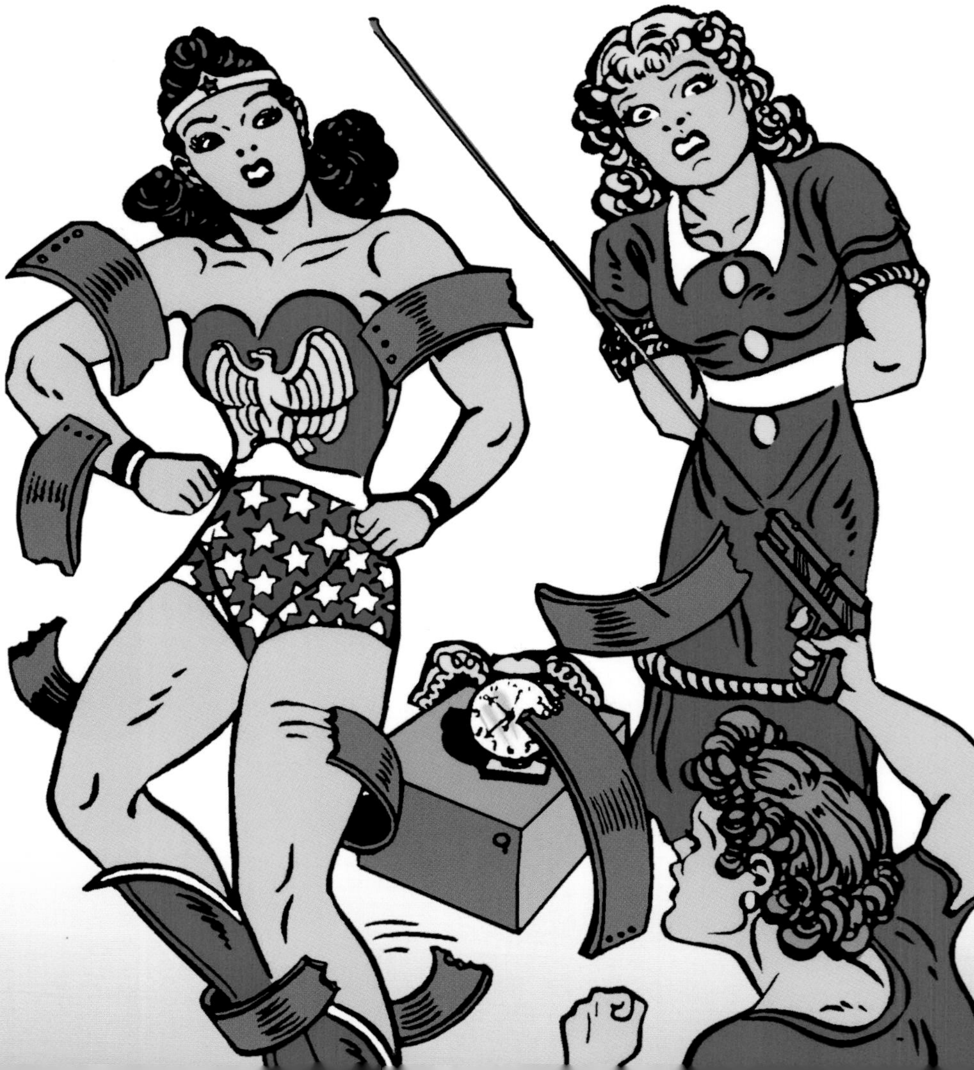

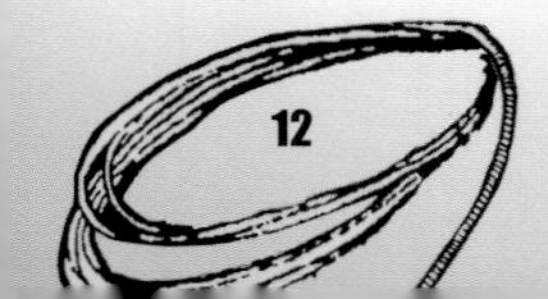

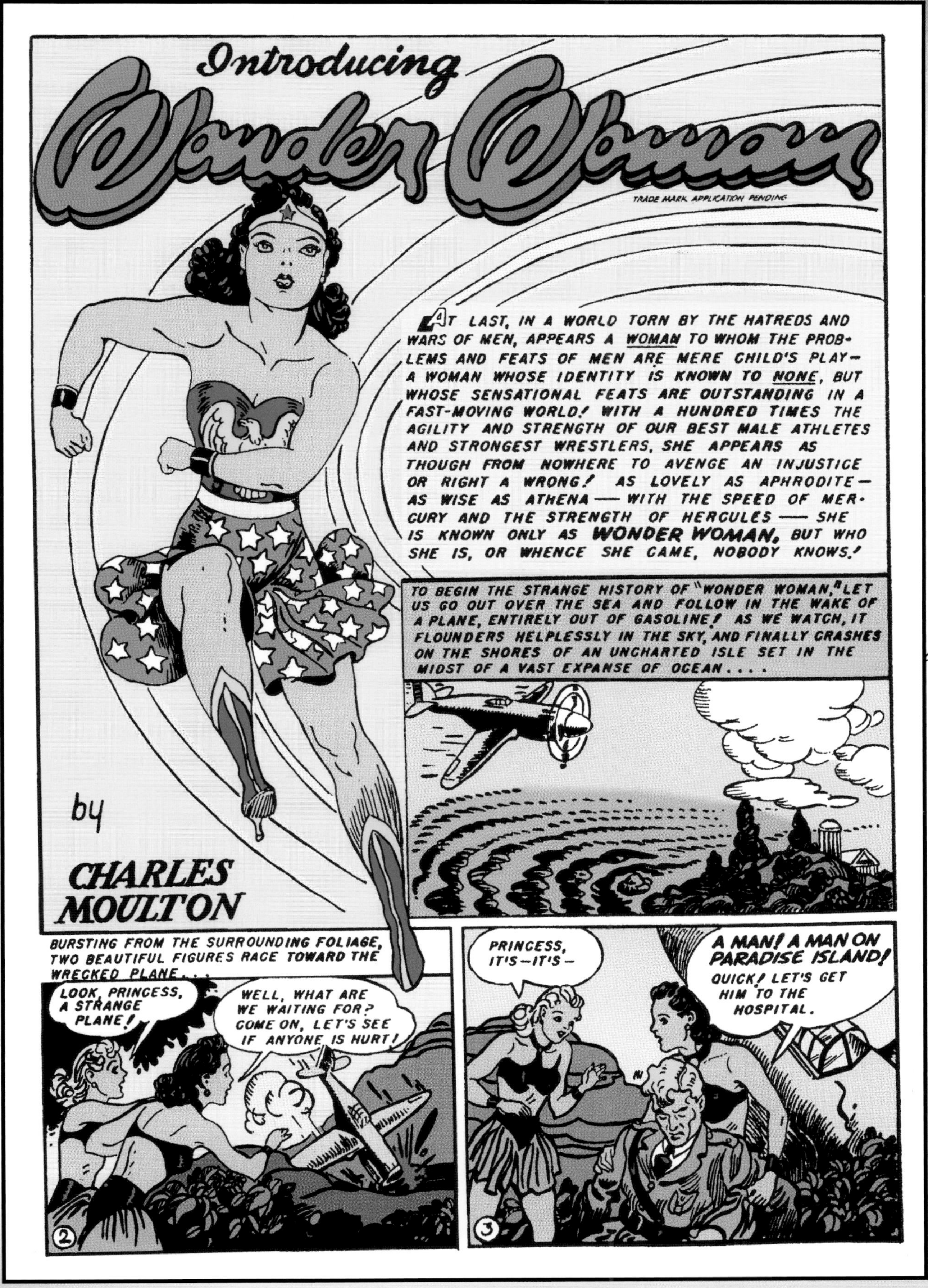
Introducing
Wonder Woman
TRADE MARK APPLICATION PENDING
AT LAST, IN A WORLD TORN BY THE HATREDS AND WARS OF MEN, APPEARS A WOMAN TO WHOM THE PROBLEMS AND FEATS OF MEN ARE MERE CHILD'S PLAY— A WOMAN WHOSE IDENTITY IS KNOWN TO NONE, BUT WHOSE SENSATIONAL FEATS ARE OUTSTANDING IN A FAST-MOVING WORLD! WITH A HUNDRED TIMES THE AGILITY AND STRENGTH OF OUR BEST MALE ATHLETES AND STRONGEST WRESTLERS, SHE APPEARS AS THOUGH FROM NOWHERE TO AVENGE AN INJUSTICE OR RIGHT A WRONG! AS LOVELY AS APHRODITE— AS WISE AS ATHENA — WITH THE SPEED OF MERCURY AND THE STRENGTH OF HERCULES — SHE IS KNOWN ONLY AS WONDER WOMAN, BUT WHO SHE IS, OR WHENCE SHE CAME, NOBODY KNOWS!
TO BEGIN THE STRANGE HISTORY OF "WONDER WOMAN," LET US GO OUT OVER THE SEA AND FOLLOW IN THE WAKE OF A PLANE, ENTIRELY OUT OF GASOLINE! AS WE WATCH, IT FLOUNDERS HELPLESSLY IN THE SKY, AND FINALLY CRASHES ON THE SHORES OF AN UNCHARTED ISLE SET IN THE MIDST OF A VAST EXPANSE OF OCEAN. . . .
by
CHARLES MOULTON
BURSTING FROM THE SURROUNDING FOLIAGE, TWO BEAUTIFUL FIGURES RACE TOWARD THE WRECKED PLANE . . .
LOOK, PRINCESS, A STRANGE PLANE!
WELL, WHAT ARE WE WAITING FOR? COME ON, LET'S SEE IF ANYONE IS HURT!
2
PRINCESS, IT'S—IT'S—
A MAN! A MAN ON PARADISE ISLAND! QUICK! LET'S GET HIM TO THE HOSPITAL.
3

All-Star Comics #8 (Dec. 1941–Jan. 1942) - script: William Moulton Marston - art: H.G. Peter

CARRYING THE FULL GROWN MAN AS IF HE WERE A CHILD, THE YOUNG WOMAN STEPS THROUGH THE FOLIAGE AND ENTERS THE STREETS OF A CITY THAT FOR ALL THE WORLD SEEMS TO BE BORN OF ANCIENT GREECE!

A MAN!

HOW DID HE GET HERE?

SOMEONE TELL THE QUEEN THERE'S A **MAN** ON PARADISE ISLAND!

AT THE HOSPITAL —

IS HE ALL RIGHT? WILL HE LIVE?

I DON'T KNOW. HE'S HAD A CONCUSSION. WE WON'T KNOW ANYTHING FOR DAYS. I WONDER WHAT THE QUEEN WILL DO WITH HIM. HE CAN'T BE MOVED.

SUDDENLY, HIPPOLYTE, THE QUEEN, ENTERS THE HOSPITAL ROOM...

MOTHER!

THE QUEEN!

I HEARD THAT THERE WAS A MAN HERE, BUT I COULDN'T BELIEVE IT. WHO IS HE?

HIS PLANE CRASHED ON THE BEACH OF THE ISLAND THIS MORNING. THE PRINCESS AND MALA BROUGHT HIM HERE. I FOUND THESE PAPERS IN HIS POCKET.

" CAPT. STEVEN TREVOR, U.S. ARMY INTELLIGENCE SERVICE." HMM. WE CAN'T LET HIM DIE. SEE THAT HE GETS THE BEST OF ATTENTION. KEEP HIS EYES COVERED SO THAT, IF HE SHOULD AWAKE, HE WILL SEE NOTHING! HAVE HIS PLANE REPAIRED, FOR HE MUST LEAVE AS SOON AS HE IS WELL! KEEP ME INFORMED OF HIS PROGRESS!

IN THE ENSUING DAYS, THE PRINCESS, THE QUEEN'S ONLY DAUGHTER, IS CONSTANTLY AT THE BEDSIDE OF THE UNCONSCIOUS MAN, HELPING — WATCHING —

YOU OUGHT TO GET SOME SLEEP, PRINCESS. YOU HAVE BEEN ON THE JOB NOW FOR FOUR- TEEN HOURS.

NEVER MIND ME. WE - WE MUST MAKE HIM WELL.

LEAVING THE PRINCESS TO WATCH OVER THE INJURED PILOT, THE DOCTOR SEEKS AUDIENCE WITH THE QUEEN . . . .

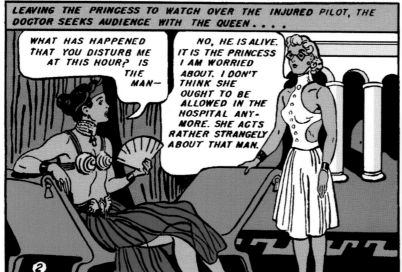

WHAT HAS HAPPENED THAT YOU DISTURB ME AT THIS HOUR? IS THE MAN —

NO, HE IS ALIVE. IT IS THE PRINCESS I AM WORRIED ABOUT. I DON'T THINK SHE OUGHT TO BE ALLOWED IN THE HOSPITAL ANY- MORE. SHE ACTS RATHER STRANGELY ABOUT THAT MAN.

SO SHE IS IN LOVE! I WAS AFRAID OF THAT! YOU ARE QUITE RIGHT, DOCTOR. I SHALL TAKE STEPS IMMEDIATELY.

THAT WOULD BE WISE. IT'S FOR THE CHILD'S OWN GOOD.

②

AND SO THE PRINCESS, FORBIDDEN THE PLEASURE OF NURSING THE ONLY MAN SHE CAN RECALL EVER HAVING SEEN IN HER LIFE, GOES TO HER MOTHER, HIPPOLYTE, THE QUEEN OF THE AMAZONS.!
BUT MOTHER — I DON'T UNDERSTAND— I MUST SEE HIM! I MUST KNOW WHO HE IS, HOW HE GOT HERE! AND WHY HE MUST LEAVE? I–I LOVE HIM!
I WAS AFRAID,DAUGHTER, THAT THE TIME WOULD SOME DAY ARRIVE THAT I WOULD HAVE TO SATISFY YOUR CURIOSITY. COME— I WILL TELL YOU EVERYTHING!

AND THIS IS THE STARTLING STORY UNFOLDED BY HIPPOLYTE, QUEEN OF THE AMAZONS, TO THE PRINCESS, HER DAUGHTER !

In the days of Ancient Greece, many centuries ago, we Amazons were the foremost nation in the world. In Amazonia, women ruled and all was well. Then one day, Hercules, the strongest man in the world, stung by taunts that he couldn't conquer the Amazon women, selected his strongest and fiercest warriors and landed on our shores. I challenged him to personal combat—because I knew that with my MAGIC GIRDLE, given me by Aphrodite, Goddess of Love, I could not lose.

And win I did! But Hercules, by deceit and trickery, managed to secure my MAGIC GIRDLE—and soon we Amazons were taken into slavery. And Aphrodite, angry at me for having succumbed to the wiles of men, would do naught to help us!

Finally our submission to men became unbearable—we could stand it no longer—and I appealed to the Goddess Aphrodite again. This time not in vain, for she relented and with her help, I secured the MAGIC GIRDLE from Hercules.

With the MAGIC GIRDLE in my possession, it didn't take us long to overcome our masters, the MEN—and taking from them their entire fleet, we set sail for another shore, for it was Aphrodite's condition that we leave the man-made world and establish a new world of our own! Aphrodite also decreed that we must always wear these bracelets fashioned by our captors, as a reminder that we must always keep aloof from men.

And so, after sailing the seas many days and many nights, we found Paradise Island and settled here to build a new World! With its fertile soil, its marvelous vegetation—its varied natural resources—here is no want, no illness, no hatreds, no wars, and as long as we remain on Paradise Island and I retain the MAGIC GIRDLE, we have the power of Eternal Life—so long as we do not permit ourselves to be again beguiled by men! We are indeed a race of Wonder Women!

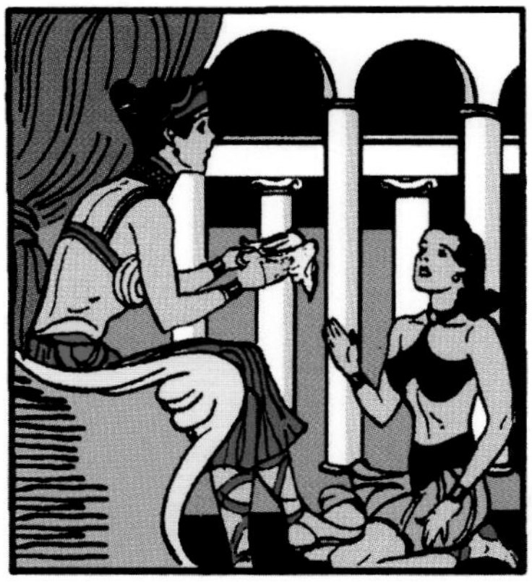

That was the promise of Aphrodite—and we must keep our promise to her if we are to remain here safe and in peace!

That is why this American must go and as soon as possible!

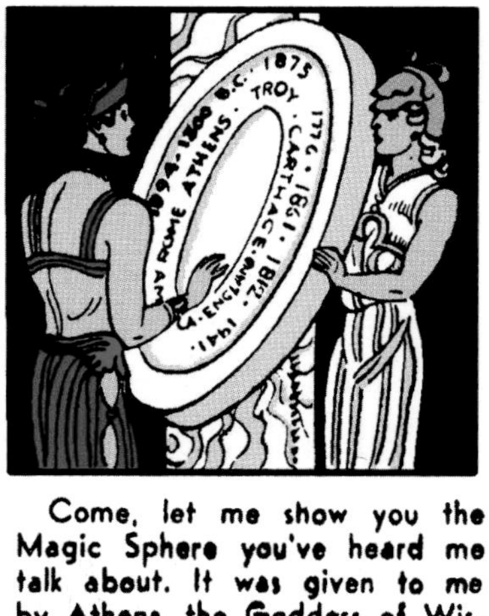

Come, let me show you the Magic Sphere you've heard me talk about. It was given to me by Athena, the Goddess of Wisdom, just after we conquered the Herculeans and set sail for Paradise Island! It is through this Magic Sphere that I have been able to know what has gone on and is going on in the other world, and even, at times, forecast the future!

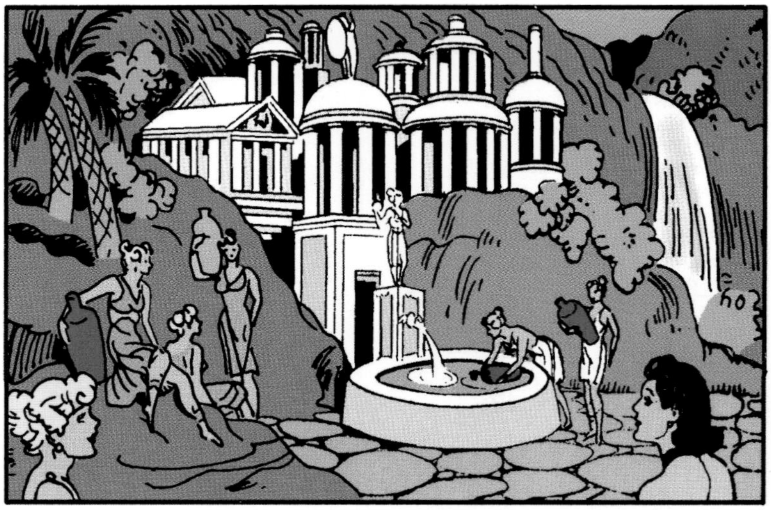

That is why we Amazons have been able to far surpass the inventions of the so-called man-made civilization! We are not only stronger and wiser than men—but our weapons are better—our flying machines are further advanced! And it is through the knowledge that I have gained from this Magic Sphere that I have taught you, my daughter, all the arts and sciences and languages of modern as well as ancient times!

But let us see where your American captain came from and how he got here. Watch closely—

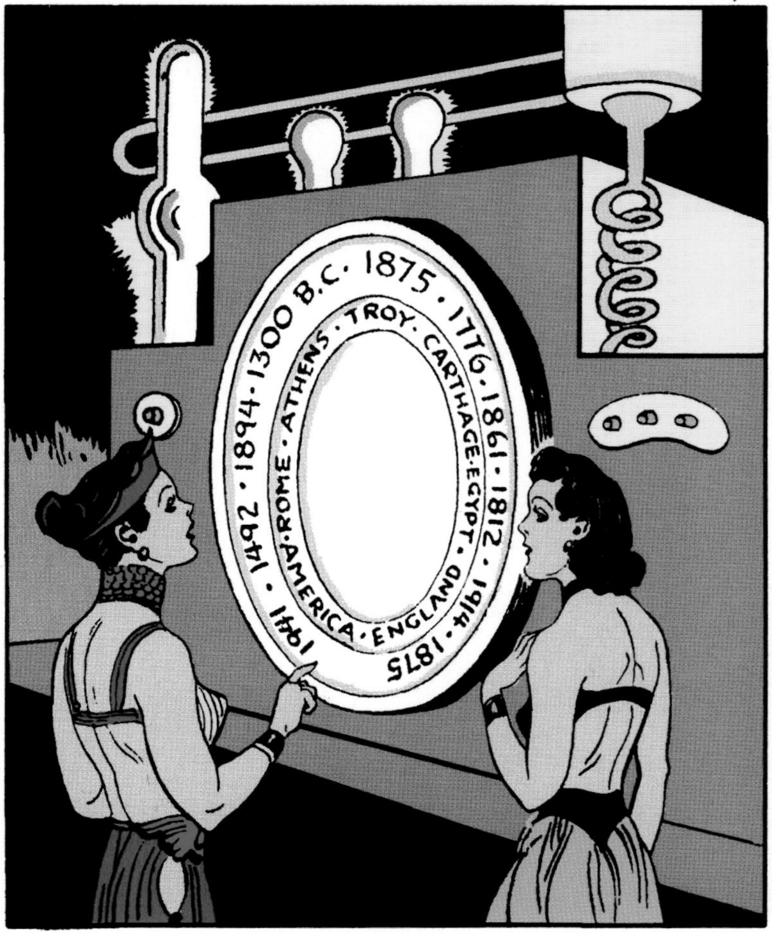

1300 B.C. · 1875 · 1776 · 1861 · 1812 · 1914 · 1875 · 1941 · 1492 · 1894 ·
TROY · CARTHAGE · EGYPT · ENGLAND · AMERICA · ROME · ATHENS

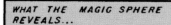
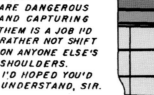

WHAT THE MAGIC SPHERE REVEALS...

SIR, I'VE COME TO REPORT THAT I HAVE AT LAST UNCOVERED INFORMATION AS TO WHO THE LEADERS OF THE SPY RING ARE. I'D LIKE PERMISSION TO CLOSE IN ON THEM PERSONALLY!

BUT THAT'S RIDICULOUS, CAPTAIN. YOU'RE THE MOST VALUABLE MAN IN THE ARMY INTELLIGENCE DEPARTMENT. WE CAN'T RISK LOSING YOU!

THAT MAY BE, SIR. BUT THESE MEN ARE DANGEROUS AND CAPTURING THEM IS A JOB I'D RATHER NOT SHIFT ON ANYONE ELSE'S SHOULDERS. I'D HOPED YOU'D UNDERSTAND, SIR.

HMM. I BELIEVE I DO, SON... I BELIEVE I DO.. GO TO IT, AND THE BEST OF LUCK TO YOU!

THAT NIGHT, STEVE TREVOR DRIVES TO A HIDDEN AIRFIELD NOT FAR FROM AN ARMY AIR BASE...

THOSE RATS HAVE THEIR PLANES HIDDEN HERE. VON STORM SHOULD DRIVE PAST HERE ANY MINUTE. IF I CAN CAPTURE HIM—THEIR LEADER—A CLEAN-UP JOB WILL BE SIMPLE.

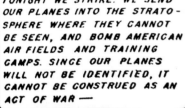

MEANWHILE IN ANOTHER CAR, APPROACHING STEVE'S HIDING PLACE...

TONIGHT WE STRIKE. WE SEND OUR PLANES INTO THE STRATOSPHERE WHERE THEY CANNOT BE SEEN, AND BOMB AMERICAN AIR FIELDS AND TRAINING CAMPS. SINCE OUR PLANES WILL NOT BE IDENTIFIED, IT CANNOT BE CONSTRUED AS AN ACT OF WAR —

SUDDENLY, AS THE CAR PASSES STEVE'S HIDING PLACE....

VAS IST?

JUST TAKE IT EASY, BOYS - YOU'VE GOT COMPANY!

IF YOU'LL BE GOOD ENOUGH TO STOP THE CAR AND STEP OUT QUIETLY, THERE WON'T BE ANY TROUBLE, GENTLEMEN—

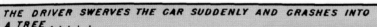

THE DRIVER SWERVES THE CAR SUDDENLY AND CRASHES INTO A TREE.....

GOOT WORK, FRITZ!

HA, GENTLEMEN! THE QUICK THINKING OF OUR DRIVER HAS NETTED FOR US AN AMERICAN OFFICER.

HE IS NOT HURT, JUST UNCONSCIOUS. HE WILL COME IN HANDY FOR OUR PLANS, NICHT WAR?

5

17

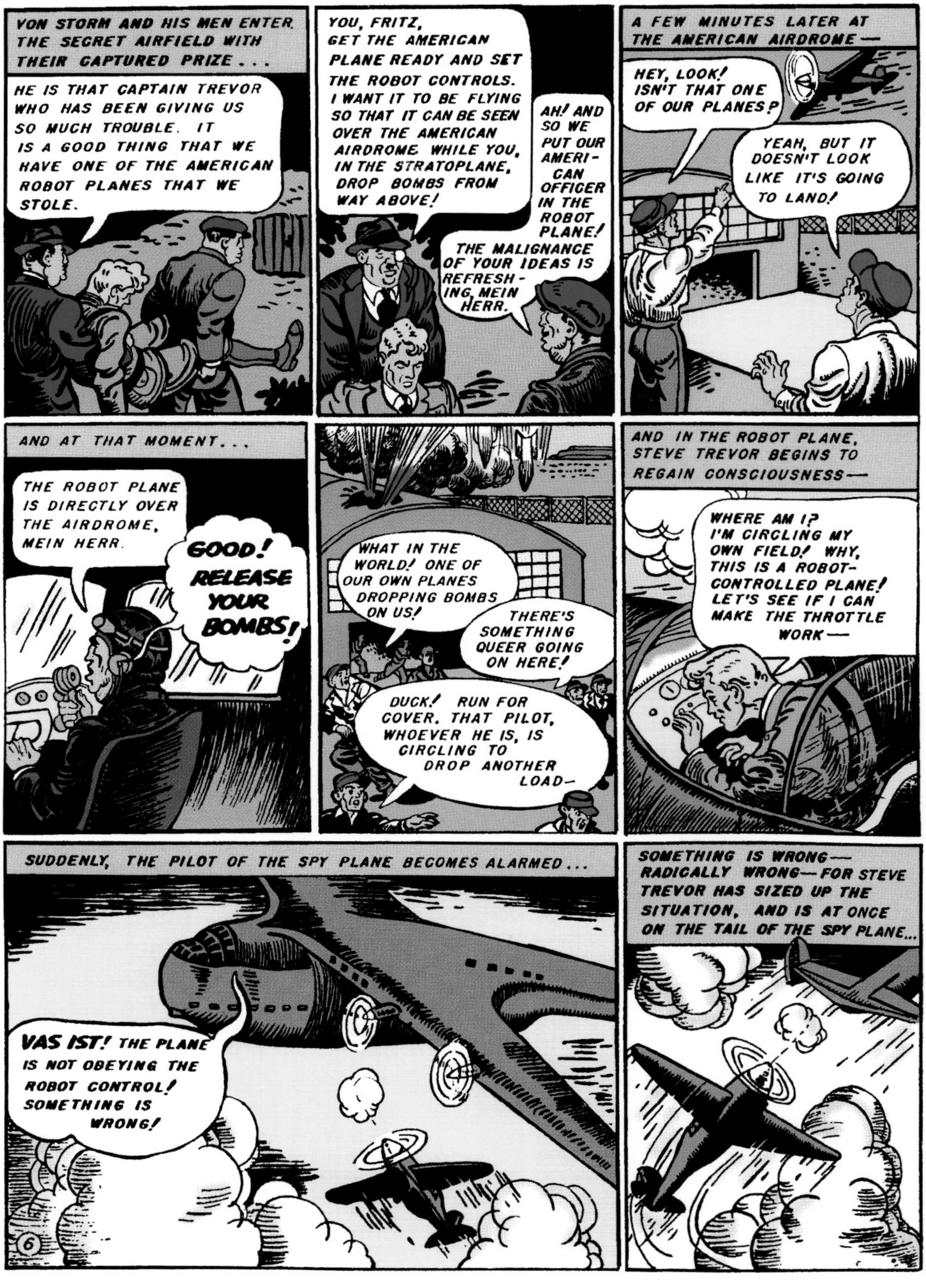

VON STORM AND HIS MEN ENTER THE SECRET AIRFIELD WITH THEIR CAPTURED PRIZE . . .
HE IS THAT CAPTAIN TREVOR WHO HAS BEEN GIVING US SO MUCH TROUBLE. IT IS A GOOD THING THAT WE HAVE ONE OF THE AMERICAN ROBOT PLANES THAT WE STOLE.
YOU, FRITZ, GET THE AMERICAN PLANE READY AND SET THE ROBOT CONTROLS. I WANT IT TO BE FLYING SO THAT IT CAN BE SEEN OVER THE AMERICAN AIRDROME WHILE YOU, IN THE STRATOPLANE, DROP BOMBS FROM WAY ABOVE!
AH! AND SO WE PUT OUR AMERI-CAN OFFICER IN THE ROBOT PLANE!
THE MALIGNANCE OF YOUR IDEAS IS REFRESH-ING, MEIN HERR.
A FEW MINUTES LATER AT THE AMERICAN AIRDROME—
HEY, LOOK! ISN'T THAT ONE OF OUR PLANES?
YEAH, BUT IT DOESN'T LOOK LIKE IT'S GOING TO LAND!
AND AT THAT MOMENT . . .
THE ROBOT PLANE IS DIRECTLY OVER THE AIRDROME, MEIN HERR.
GOOD! RELEASE YOUR BOMBS!
WHAT IN THE WORLD! ONE OF OUR OWN PLANES DROPPING BOMBS ON US!
THERE'S SOMETHING QUEER GOING ON HERE!
DUCK! RUN FOR COVER. THAT PILOT, WHOEVER HE IS, IS CIRCLING TO DROP ANOTHER LOAD—
AND IN THE ROBOT PLANE, STEVE TREVOR BEGINS TO REGAIN CONSCIOUSNESS—
WHERE AM I? I'M CIRCLING MY OWN FIELD! WHY, THIS IS A ROBOT-CONTROLLED PLANE! LET'S SEE IF I CAN MAKE THE THROTTLE WORK—
SUDDENLY, THE PILOT OF THE SPY PLANE BECOMES ALARMED . . .
VAS IST! THE PLANE IS NOT OBEYING THE ROBOT CONTROL! SOMETHING IS WRONG!
6
SOMETHING IS WRONG— RADICALLY WRONG— FOR STEVE TREVOR HAS SIZED UP THE SITUATION, AND IS AT ONCE ON THE TAIL OF THE SPY PLANE...

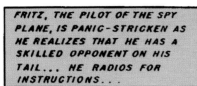
FRITZ, THE PILOT OF THE SPY PLANE, IS PANIC-STRICKEN AS HE REALIZES THAT HE HAS A SKILLED OPPONENT ON HIS TAIL... HE RADIOS FOR INSTRUCTIONS...

VON STORM! THE AMERICAN HAS RECOVERED CONSCIOUSNESS. HE IS TURNING THE ROBOT PLANE AGAINST ME. I CAN'T SHOOT HIM DOWN! WHAT SHALL I DO? HELLO VON STORM, DO YOU HEAR ME?

VON STORM IS FURIOUS AT THE WAY HIS PLANS ARE GOING—

YOU FOOL! DON'T LET HIM SHOOT YOU DOWN! THEY MUST NOT FIND OUT THIS PLAN! THEY MUST NOT KNOW YOU DROPPED THOSE BOMBS! GET HIM AWAY FROM HIS FIELD—

THE STRATOPLANE TURNS TAIL AND RUNS—— STEVE FOLLOWS...

HE'S TURNED TAIL, THE SKUNK! I'VE GOT TO SHOOT HIM DOWN, BUT HE KEEPS MOVING TOO HIGH FOR ME. I'LL CATCH HIM IF IT'S THE LAST THING I DO!

ALWAYS OUT OF SHOOTING RANGE, THE BLACK PLANE KEEPS STEVE FOLLOWING UNTIL THEY ARE FAR OUT AT SEA

I WONDER HOW LONG HE'S GOING TO KEEP THIS UP! WELL, AS LONG AS THERE IS GAS LEFT IN THIS CRATE, I'M GOING TO STAY WITH HIM—

HOURS PASS AND MANY MILES— HUNDREDS OF MILES— PASS WITH THEM, BUT STEVE KEEPS DOGGEDLY ON THE TRAIL OF THE ENEMY PLANE UNTIL FINALLY HIS GAS BEGINS TO RUN LOW —

RUNNING SHORT OF GAS! LOOKS LIKE HE HAS ME LICKED! WAIT! WHAT'S THAT BELOW? CAN IT BE AN ISLAND? IT SEEMS SURROUNDED BY CLOUD FORMATIONS!

19

WELL, DAUGHTER, THERE'S THE HISTORY OF YOUR CAPTAIN UP TO THE VERY MOMENT HIS PLANE CRASHED ON PARADISE ISLAND!

BUT MOTHER, HE MUST BE TAKEN BACK TO AMERICA TO FINISH THE JOB HE STARTED!

GETTING HIM BACK WOULD BE A PROBLEM. LEAVE ME ALONE, MY DAUGHTER. I MUST CONSULT WITH APHRODITE AND ATHENA, OUR GODDESSES. I MUST SEEK THEIR ADVICE!

YES, MOTHER.

IT WOULDN'T BE ANY TRICK AT ALL FOR ME TO FLY HIM BACK MYSELF, BUT MOTHER WOULD NEVER HEAR OF IT.

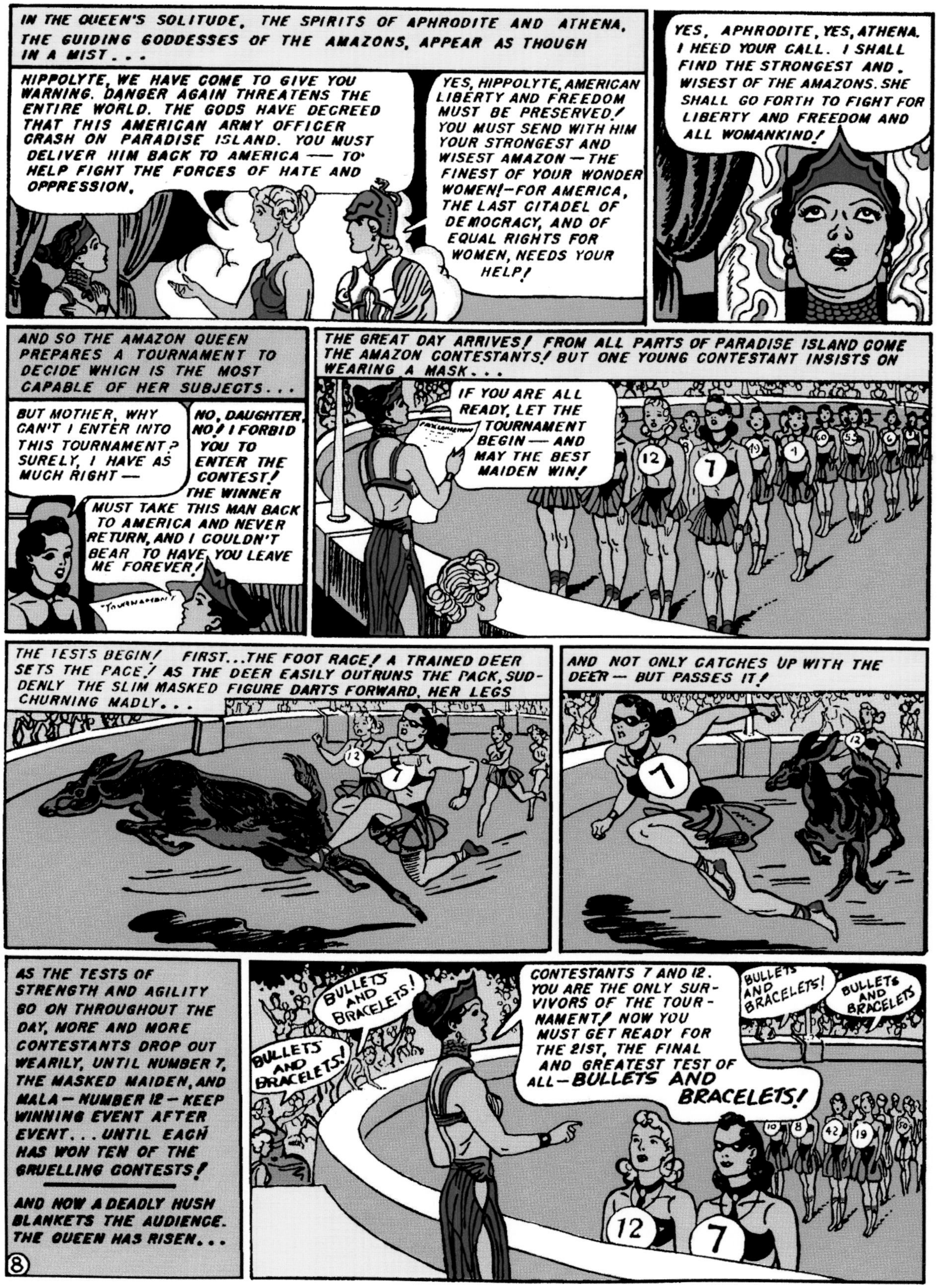
IN THE QUEEN'S SOLITUDE, THE SPIRITS OF APHRODITE AND ATHENA, THE GUIDING GODDESSES OF THE AMAZONS, APPEAR AS THOUGH IN A MIST . . .
HIPPOLYTE, WE HAVE COME TO GIVE YOU WARNING. DANGER AGAIN THREATENS THE ENTIRE WORLD. THE GODS HAVE DECREED THAT THIS AMERICAN ARMY OFFICER CRASH ON PARADISE ISLAND. YOU MUST DELIVER HIM BACK TO AMERICA — TO HELP FIGHT THE FORCES OF HATE AND OPPRESSION.
YES, HIPPOLYTE, AMERICAN LIBERTY AND FREEDOM MUST BE PRESERVED! YOU MUST SEND WITH HIM YOUR STRONGEST AND WISEST AMAZON — THE FINEST OF YOUR WONDER WOMEN! — FOR AMERICA, THE LAST CITADEL OF DEMOCRACY, AND OF EQUAL RIGHTS FOR WOMEN, NEEDS YOUR HELP!
YES, APHRODITE, YES, ATHENA. I HEED YOUR CALL. I SHALL FIND THE STRONGEST AND WISEST OF THE AMAZONS. SHE SHALL GO FORTH TO FIGHT FOR LIBERTY AND FREEDOM AND ALL WOMANKIND!
AND SO THE AMAZON QUEEN PREPARES A TOURNAMENT TO DECIDE WHICH IS THE MOST CAPABLE OF HER SUBJECTS . . .
BUT MOTHER, WHY CAN'T I ENTER INTO THIS TOURNAMENT? SURELY, I HAVE AS MUCH RIGHT —
NO, DAUGHTER, NO! I FORBID YOU TO ENTER THE CONTEST! THE WINNER MUST TAKE THIS MAN BACK TO AMERICA AND NEVER RETURN, AND I COULDN'T BEAR TO HAVE YOU LEAVE ME FOREVER!
"TOURNAMENT"
THE GREAT DAY ARRIVES! FROM ALL PARTS OF PARADISE ISLAND COME THE AMAZON CONTESTANTS! BUT ONE YOUNG CONTESTANT INSISTS ON WEARING A MASK . . .
IF YOU ARE ALL READY, LET THE TOURNAMENT BEGIN — AND MAY THE BEST MAIDEN WIN!
THE TESTS BEGIN! FIRST...THE FOOT RACE! A TRAINED DEER SETS THE PACE! AS THE DEER EASILY OUTRUNS THE PACK, SUDDENLY THE SLIM MASKED FIGURE DARTS FORWARD, HER LEGS CHURNING MADLY . . .
AND NOT ONLY CATCHES UP WITH THE DEER — BUT PASSES IT!
AS THE TESTS OF STRENGTH AND AGILITY GO ON THROUGHOUT THE DAY, MORE AND MORE CONTESTANTS DROP OUT WEARILY, UNTIL NUMBER 7, THE MASKED MAIDEN, AND MALA — NUMBER 12 — KEEP WINNING EVENT AFTER EVENT . . . UNTIL EACH HAS WON TEN OF THE GRUELLING CONTESTS!
AND NOW A DEADLY HUSH BLANKETS THE AUDIENCE. THE QUEEN HAS RISEN . . .
8
BULLETS AND BRACELETS!
BULLETS AND BRACELETS!
CONTESTANTS 7 AND 12. YOU ARE THE ONLY SURVIVORS OF THE TOURNAMENT! NOW YOU MUST GET READY FOR THE 21ST, THE FINAL AND GREATEST TEST OF ALL — BULLETS AND BRACELETS!
BULLETS AND BRACELETS!
BULLETS AND BRACELETS

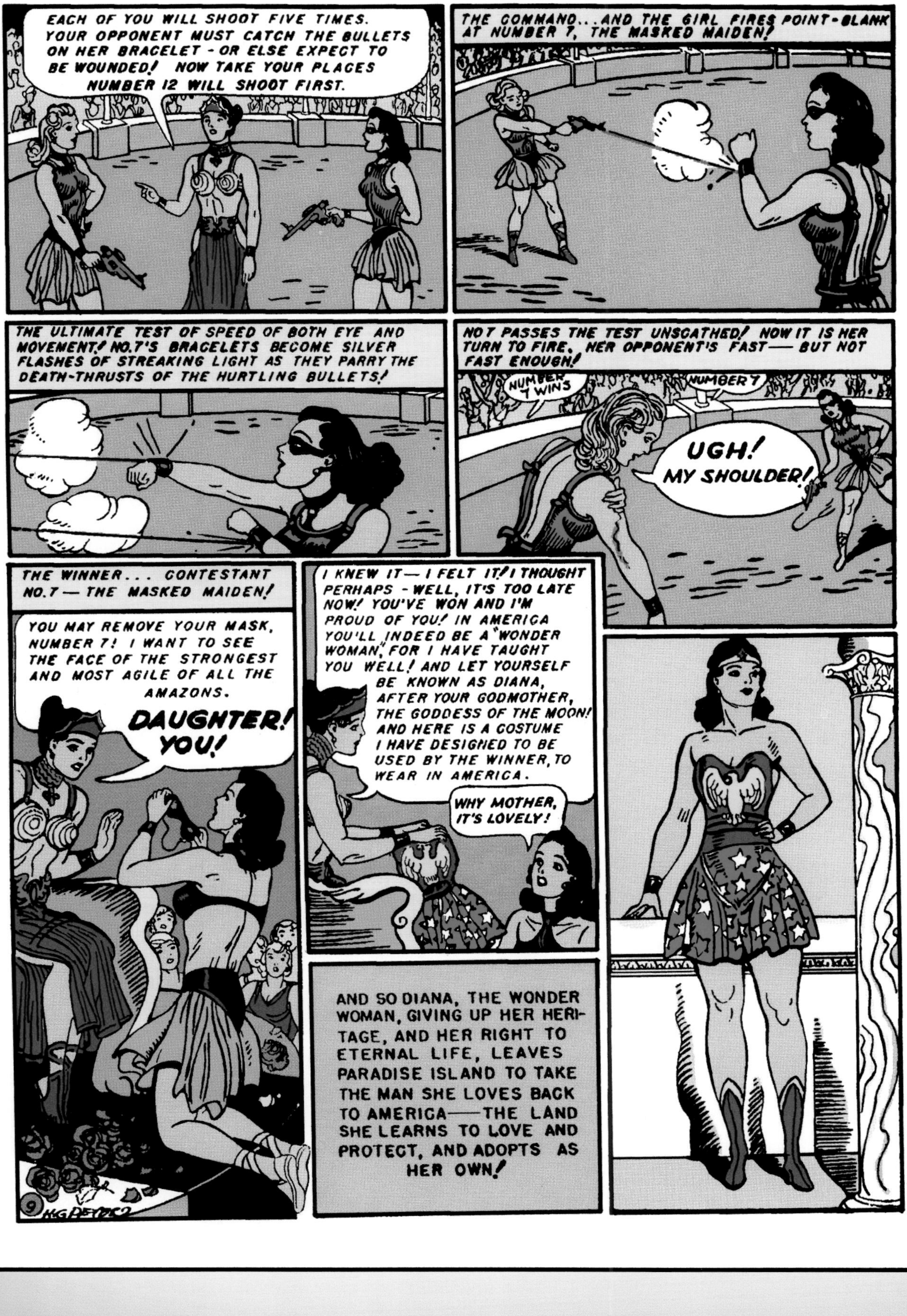
EACH OF YOU WILL SHOOT FIVE TIMES. YOUR OPPONENT MUST CATCH THE BULLETS ON HER BRACELET - OR ELSE EXPECT TO BE WOUNDED! NOW TAKE YOUR PLACES NUMBER 12 WILL SHOOT FIRST.
THE COMMAND... AND THE GIRL FIRES POINT-BLANK AT NUMBER 7, THE MASKED MAIDEN!
THE ULTIMATE TEST OF SPEED OF BOTH EYE AND MOVEMENT! NO.7'S BRACELETS BECOME SILVER FLASHES OF STREAKING LIGHT AS THEY PARRY THE DEATH-THRUSTS OF THE HURTLING BULLETS!
NOT PASSES THE TEST UNSCATHED! NOW IT IS HER TURN TO FIRE. HER OPPONENT'S FAST— BUT NOT FAST ENOUGH!
NUMBER 7 WINS
NUMBER 7
UGH! MY SHOULDER!
THE WINNER... CONTESTANT NO.7 — THE MASKED MAIDEN!
YOU MAY REMOVE YOUR MASK, NUMBER 7! I WANT TO SEE THE FACE OF THE STRONGEST AND MOST AGILE OF ALL THE AMAZONS.
DAUGHTER! YOU!
I KNEW IT— I FELT IT! I THOUGHT PERHAPS - WELL, IT'S TOO LATE NOW! YOU'VE WON AND I'M PROUD OF YOU! IN AMERICA YOU'LL INDEED BE A "WONDER WOMAN", FOR I HAVE TAUGHT YOU WELL! AND LET YOURSELF BE KNOWN AS DIANA, AFTER YOUR GODMOTHER, THE GODDESS OF THE MOON! AND HERE IS A COSTUME I HAVE DESIGNED TO BE USED BY THE WINNER, TO WEAR IN AMERICA.
WHY MOTHER, IT'S LOVELY!
AND SO DIANA, THE WONDER WOMAN, GIVING UP HER HERITAGE, AND HER RIGHT TO ETERNAL LIFE, LEAVES PARADISE ISLAND TO TAKE THE MAN SHE LOVES BACK TO AMERICA—THE LAND SHE LEARNS TO LOVE AND PROTECT, AND ADOPTS AS HER OWN!
9 H.G.PETER

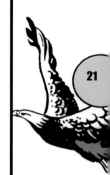

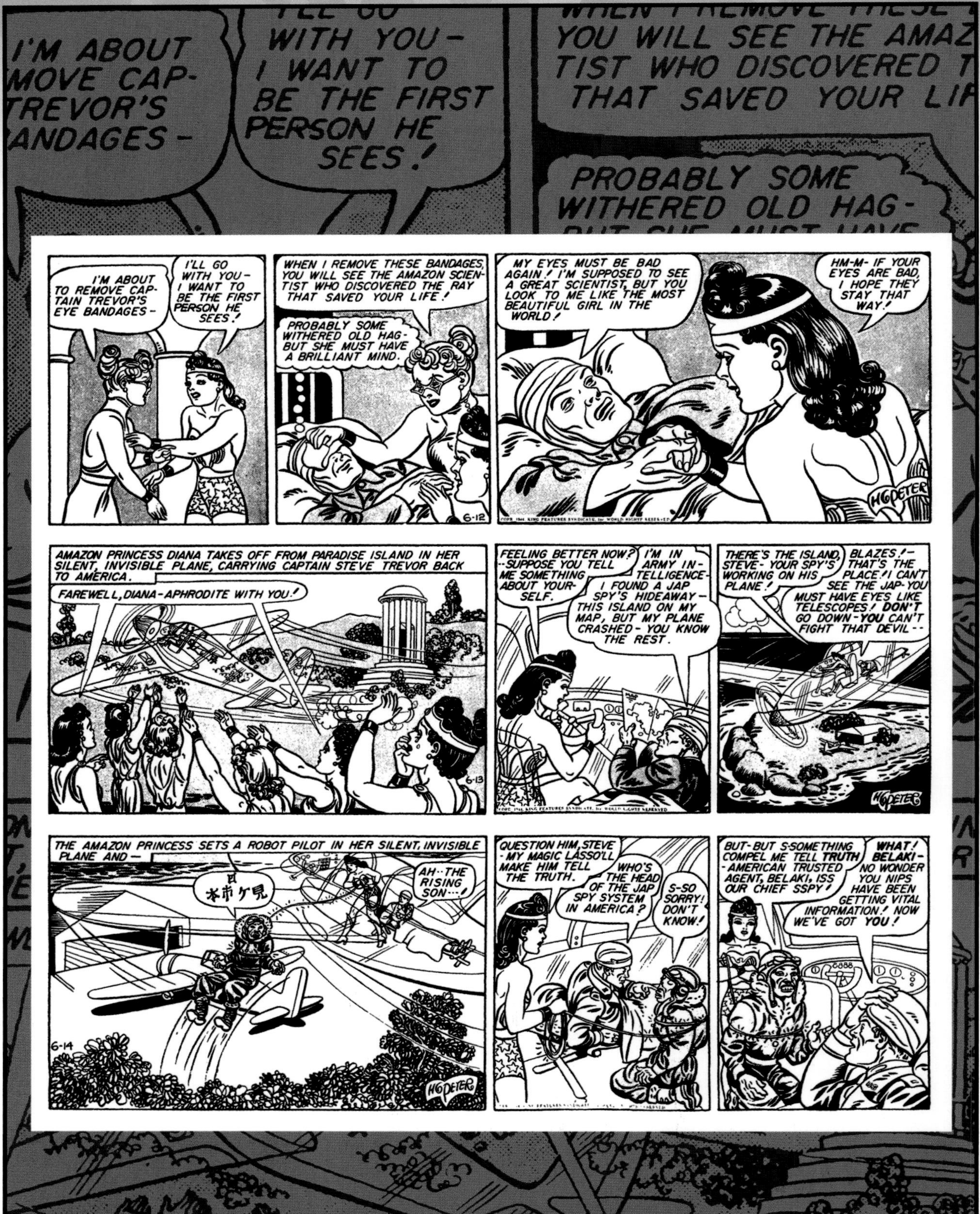
I'M ABOUT TO REMOVE CAPTAIN TREVOR'S EYE BANDAGES -
I'LL GO WITH YOU - I WANT TO BE THE FIRST PERSON HE SEES!
WHEN I REMOVE THESE BANDAGES, YOU WILL SEE THE AMAZON SCIENTIST WHO DISCOVERED THE RAY THAT SAVED YOUR LIFE!
PROBABLY SOME WITHERED OLD HAG - BUT SHE MUST HAVE A BRILLIANT MIND.
6-12
MY EYES MUST BE BAD AGAIN! I'M SUPPOSED TO SEE A GREAT SCIENTIST, BUT YOU LOOK TO ME LIKE THE MOST BEAUTIFUL GIRL IN THE WORLD!
HM-M- IF YOUR EYES ARE BAD, I HOPE THEY STAY THAT WAY!
H.G. PETER
AMAZON PRINCESS DIANA TAKES OFF FROM PARADISE ISLAND IN HER SILENT, INVISIBLE PLANE, CARRYING CAPTAIN STEVE TREVOR BACK TO AMERICA.
FAREWELL, DIANA - APHRODITE WITH YOU!
6-13
FEELING BETTER NOW? - SUPPOSE YOU TELL ME SOMETHING ABOUT YOURSELF.
I'M IN ARMY INTELLIGENCE - I FOUND A JAP SPY'S HIDEAWAY - THIS ISLAND ON MY MAP, BUT MY PLANE CRASHED - YOU KNOW THE REST.
THERE'S THE ISLAND, STEVE - YOUR SPY'S WORKING ON HIS PLANE!
BLAZES! - THAT'S THE PLACE! I CAN'T SEE THE JAP - YOU MUST HAVE EYES LIKE TELESCOPES! DON'T GO DOWN - YOU CAN'T FIGHT THAT DEVIL - -
H.G. PETER
THE AMAZON PRINCESS SETS A ROBOT PILOT IN HER SILENT, INVISIBLE PLANE AND -
AH - THE RISING SON - - !
6-14
H.G. PETER
QUESTION HIM, STEVE - MY MAGIC LASSO'LL MAKE HIM TELL THE TRUTH.
WHO'S THE HEAD OF THE JAP SPY SYSTEM IN AMERICA?
S-SO SORRY! DON'T KNOW!
BUT - BUT S-SOMETHING COMPEL ME TELL TRUTH - AMERICAN TRUSTED AGENT, BELAKI, ISS OUR CHIEF SSPY!
WHAT! BELAKI - NO WONDER YOU NIPS HAVE BEEN GETTING VITAL INFORMATION! NOW WE'VE GOT YOU!

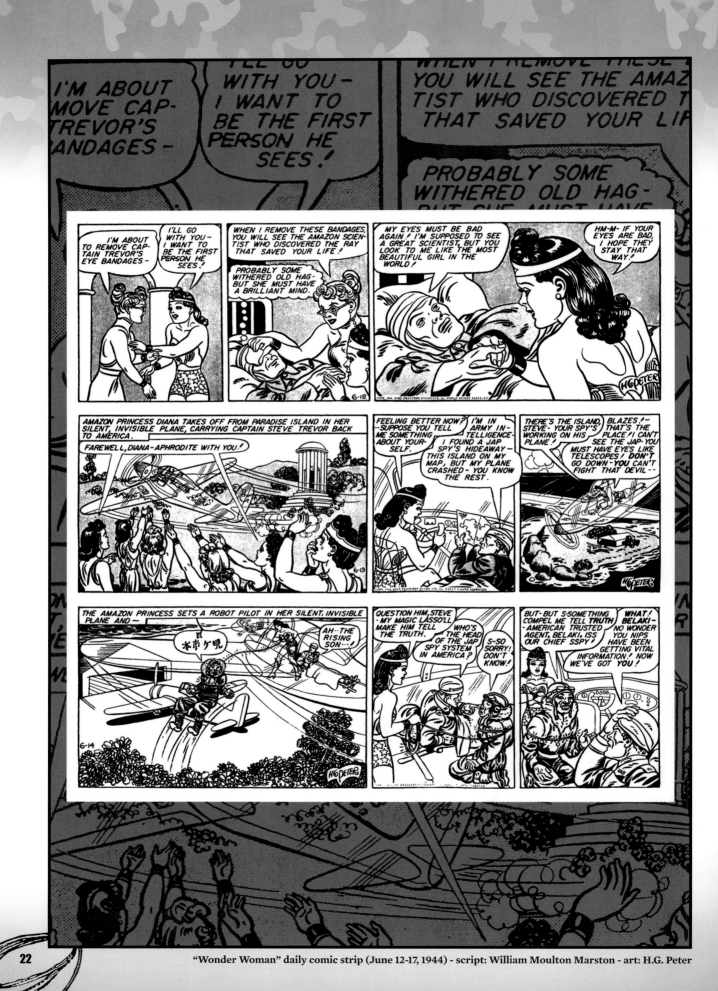

 "Wonder Woman" daily comic strip (June 12-17, 1944) - script: William Moulton Marston - art: H.G. Peter

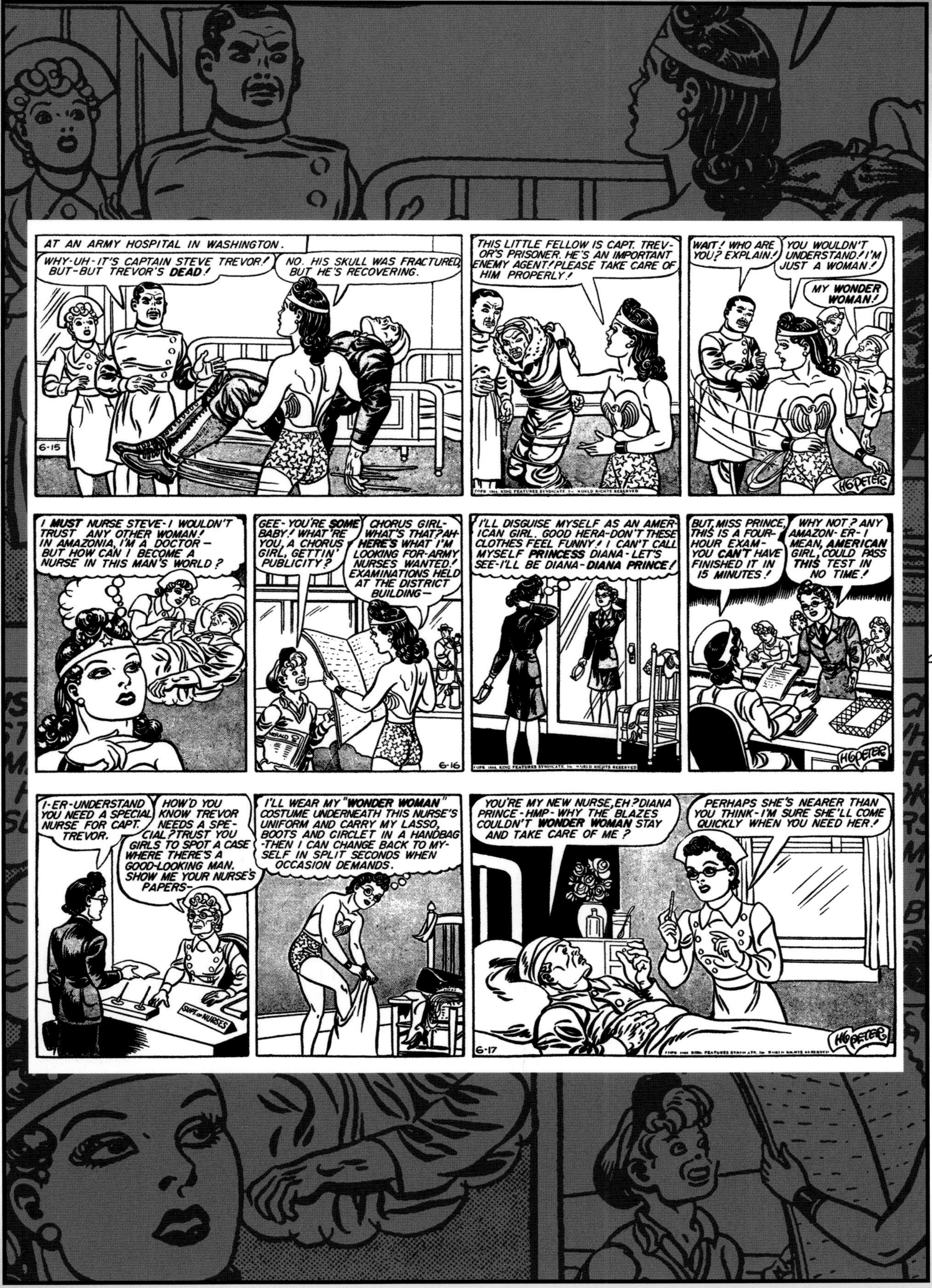
AT AN ARMY HOSPITAL IN WASHINGTON.
WHY-UH-IT'S CAPTAIN STEVE TREVOR! BUT-BUT TREVOR'S DEAD!
NO. HIS SKULL WAS FRACTURED, BUT HE'S RECOVERING.
6-15
THIS LITTLE FELLOW IS CAPT. TREVOR'S PRISONER. HE'S AN IMPORTANT ENEMY AGENT! PLEASE TAKE CARE OF HIM PROPERLY!
WAIT! WHO ARE YOU? EXPLAIN!
YOU WOULDN'T UNDERSTAND! I'M JUST A WOMAN!
MY WONDER WOMAN!
H.G.PETER
I MUST NURSE STEVE-I WOULDN'T TRUST ANY OTHER WOMAN! IN AMAZONIA, I'M A DOCTOR-BUT HOW CAN I BECOME A NURSE IN THIS MAN'S WORLD?
GEE-YOU'RE SOME BABY! WHAT'RE YOU, A CHORUS GIRL, GETTIN' PUBLICITY?
CHORUS GIRL-WHAT'S THAT? AH-HERE'S WHAT I'M LOOKING FOR-ARMY NURSES WANTED! EXAMINATIONS HELD AT THE DISTRICT BUILDING-
HERALD
6-16
I'LL DISGUISE MYSELF AS AN AMERICAN GIRL. GOOD HERA-DON'T THESE CLOTHES FEEL FUNNY! I CAN'T CALL MYSELF PRINCESS DIANA-LET'S SEE-I'LL BE DIANA-DIANA PRINCE!
BUT, MISS PRINCE, THIS IS A FOUR-HOUR EXAM-YOU CAN'T HAVE FINISHED IT IN 15 MINUTES!
WHY NOT? ANY AMAZON-ER-I MEAN, AMERICAN GIRL, COULD PASS THIS TEST IN NO TIME!
H.G.PETER
I-ER-UNDERSTAND YOU NEED A SPECIAL NURSE FOR CAPT. TREVOR.
HOW'D YOU KNOW TREVOR NEEDS A SPECIAL? TRUST YOU GIRLS TO SPOT A CASE WHERE THERE'S A GOOD-LOOKING MAN. SHOW ME YOUR NURSE'S PAPERS-
SUPT. OF NURSES
I'LL WEAR MY "WONDER WOMAN" COSTUME UNDERNEATH THIS NURSE'S UNIFORM AND CARRY MY LASSO, BOOTS AND CIRCLET IN A HANDBAG-THEN I CAN CHANGE BACK TO MYSELF IN SPLIT SECONDS WHEN OCCASION DEMANDS.
YOU'RE MY NEW NURSE, EH? DIANA PRINCE-HMP-WHY THE BLAZES COULDN'T WONDER WOMAN STAY AND TAKE CARE OF ME?
PERHAPS SHE'S NEARER THAN YOU THINK-I'M SURE SHE'LL COME QUICKLY WHEN YOU NEED HER!
6-17
H.G.PETER

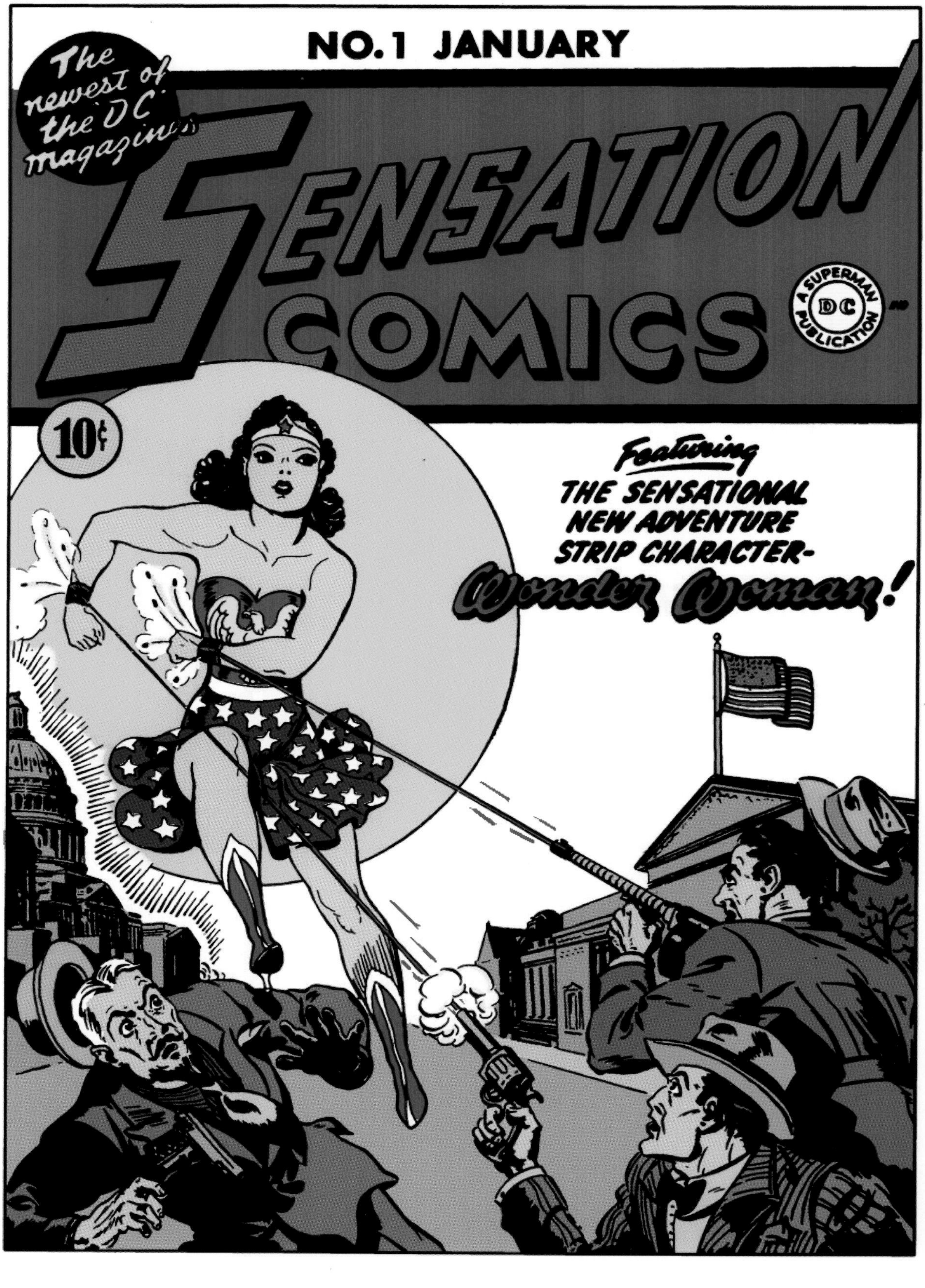
NO.1 JANUARY
The newest of the DC magazines
SENSATION COMICS
A SUPERMAN DC PUBLICATION
10¢
Featuring
THE SENSATIONAL
NEW ADVENTURE
STRIP CHARACTER-
Wonder Woman!

Sensation Comics #1 (Jan. 1942) - art: H.G. Peter & Jon Blummer

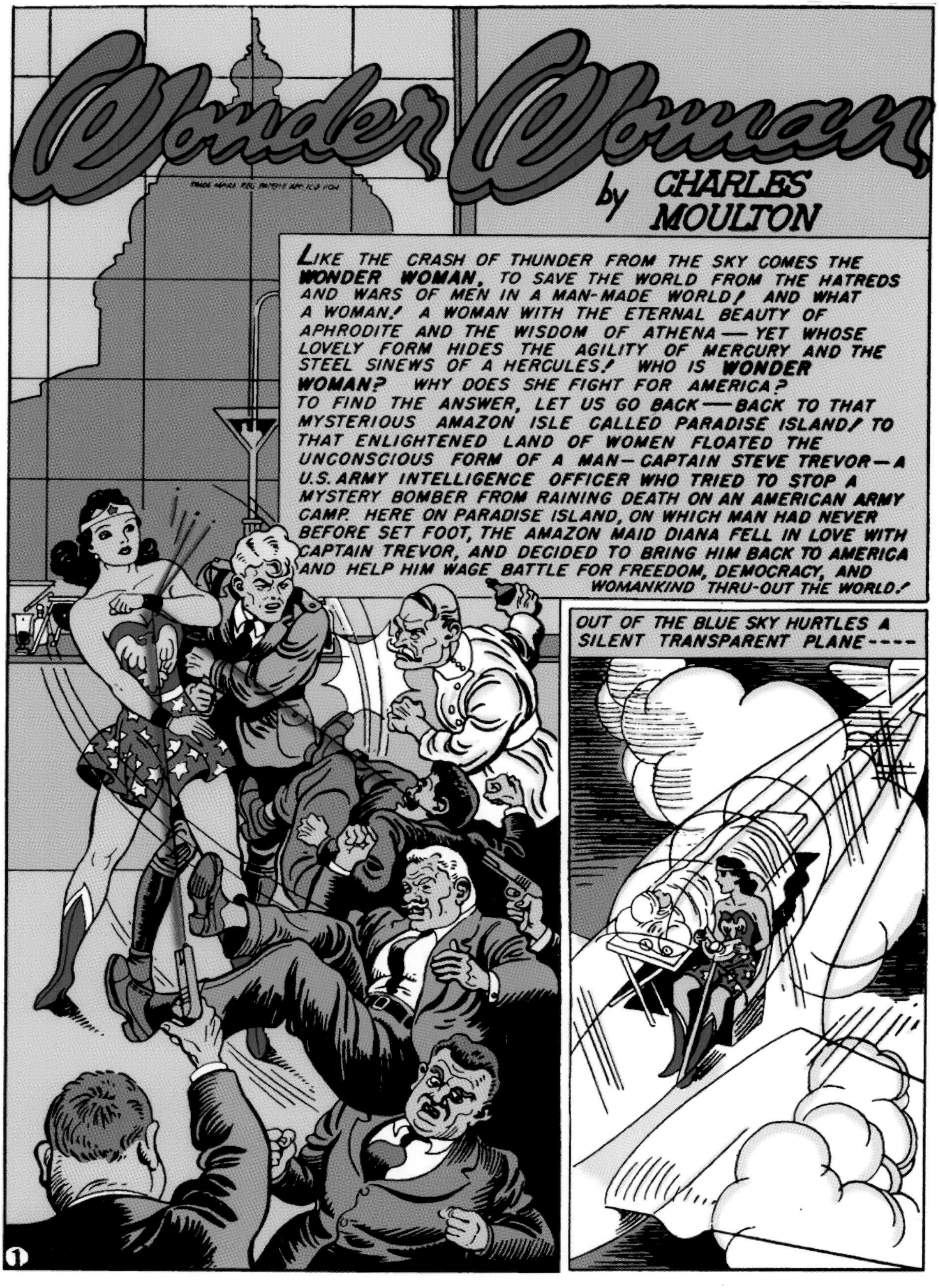
Wonder Woman
by CHARLES MOULTON
LIKE THE CRASH OF THUNDER FROM THE SKY COMES THE WONDER WOMAN, TO SAVE THE WORLD FROM THE HATREDS AND WARS OF MEN IN A MAN-MADE WORLD! AND WHAT A WOMAN! A WOMAN WITH THE ETERNAL BEAUTY OF APHRODITE AND THE WISDOM OF ATHENA — YET WHOSE LOVELY FORM HIDES THE AGILITY OF MERCURY AND THE STEEL SINEWS OF A HERCULES! WHO IS WONDER WOMAN? WHY DOES SHE FIGHT FOR AMERICA? TO FIND THE ANSWER, LET US GO BACK — BACK TO THAT MYSTERIOUS AMAZON ISLE CALLED PARADISE ISLAND! TO THAT ENLIGHTENED LAND OF WOMEN FLOATED THE UNCONSCIOUS FORM OF A MAN — CAPTAIN STEVE TREVOR — A U.S. ARMY INTELLIGENCE OFFICER WHO TRIED TO STOP A MYSTERY BOMBER FROM RAINING DEATH ON AN AMERICAN ARMY CAMP. HERE ON PARADISE ISLAND, ON WHICH MAN HAD NEVER BEFORE SET FOOT, THE AMAZON MAID DIANA FELL IN LOVE WITH CAPTAIN TREVOR, AND DECIDED TO BRING HIM BACK TO AMERICA AND HELP HIM WAGE BATTLE FOR FREEDOM, DEMOCRACY, AND WOMANKIND THRU-OUT THE WORLD!
OUT OF THE BLUE SKY HURTLES A SILENT TRANSPARENT PLANE----
1

Sensation Comics #1 (Jan. 1942) - script: William Moulton Marston - art: H.G. Peter

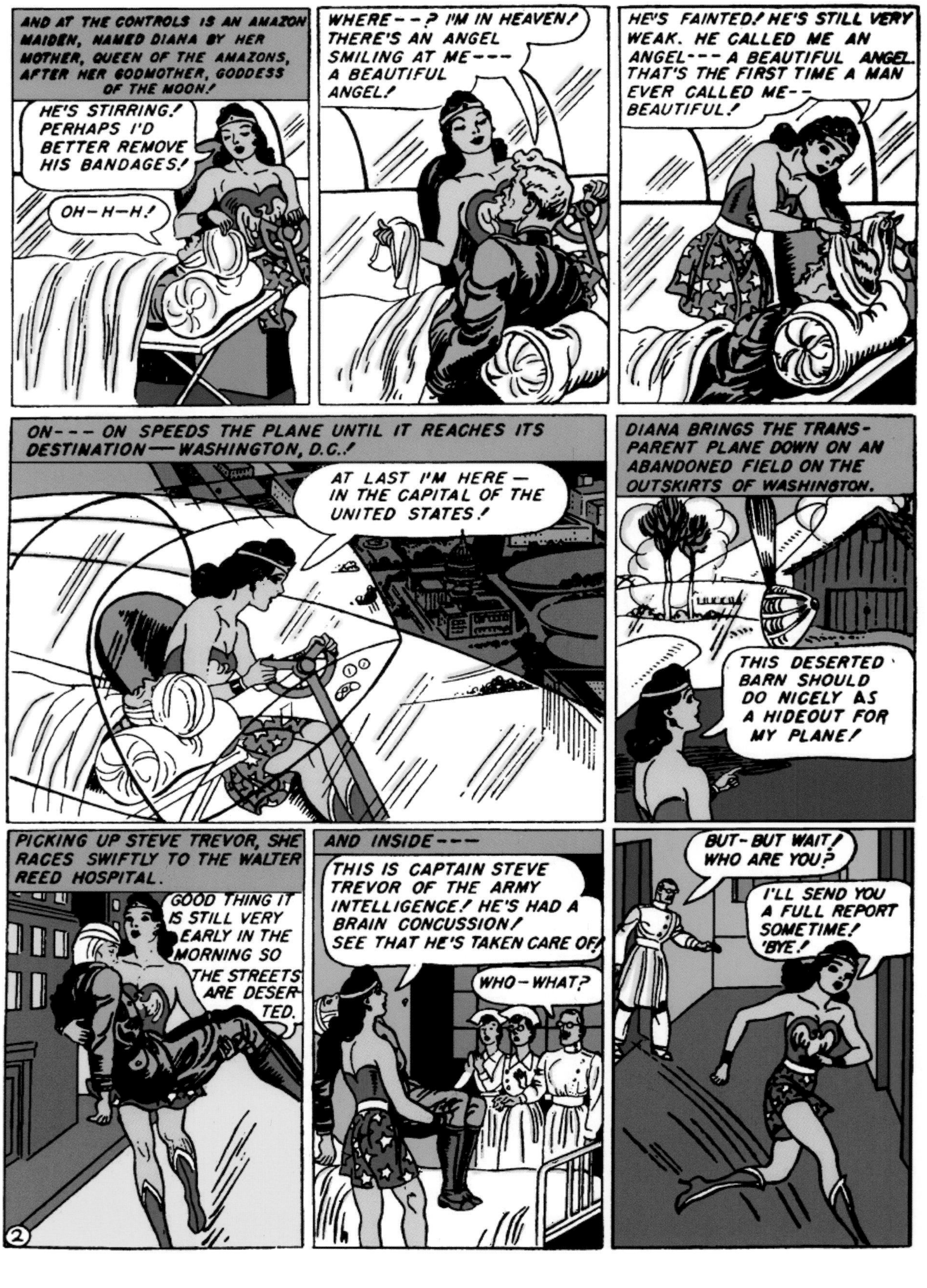
AND AT THE CONTROLS IS AN AMAZON MAIDEN, NAMED DIANA BY HER MOTHER, QUEEN OF THE AMAZONS, AFTER HER GODMOTHER, GODDESS OF THE MOON!
HE'S STIRRING! PERHAPS I'D BETTER REMOVE HIS BANDAGES!
OH-H-H!
WHERE--? I'M IN HEAVEN! THERE'S AN ANGEL SMILING AT ME--- A BEAUTIFUL ANGEL!
HE'S FAINTED! HE'S STILL VERY WEAK. HE CALLED ME AN ANGEL--- A BEAUTIFUL ANGEL. THAT'S THE FIRST TIME A MAN EVER CALLED ME-- BEAUTIFUL!
ON--- ON SPEEDS THE PLANE UNTIL IT REACHES ITS DESTINATION — WASHINGTON, D.C.!
AT LAST I'M HERE — IN THE CAPITAL OF THE UNITED STATES!
DIANA BRINGS THE TRANS-PARENT PLANE DOWN ON AN ABANDONED FIELD ON THE OUTSKIRTS OF WASHINGTON.
THIS DESERTED BARN SHOULD DO NICELY AS A HIDEOUT FOR MY PLANE!
PICKING UP STEVE TREVOR, SHE RACES SWIFTLY TO THE WALTER REED HOSPITAL.
GOOD THING IT IS STILL VERY EARLY IN THE MORNING SO THE STREETS ARE DESER-TED.
2
AND INSIDE---
THIS IS CAPTAIN STEVE TREVOR OF THE ARMY INTELLIGENCE! HE'S HAD A BRAIN CONCUSSION! SEE THAT HE'S TAKEN CARE OF!
WHO-WHAT?
BUT-BUT WAIT! WHO ARE YOU?
I'LL SEND YOU A FULL REPORT SOMETIME! 'BYE!

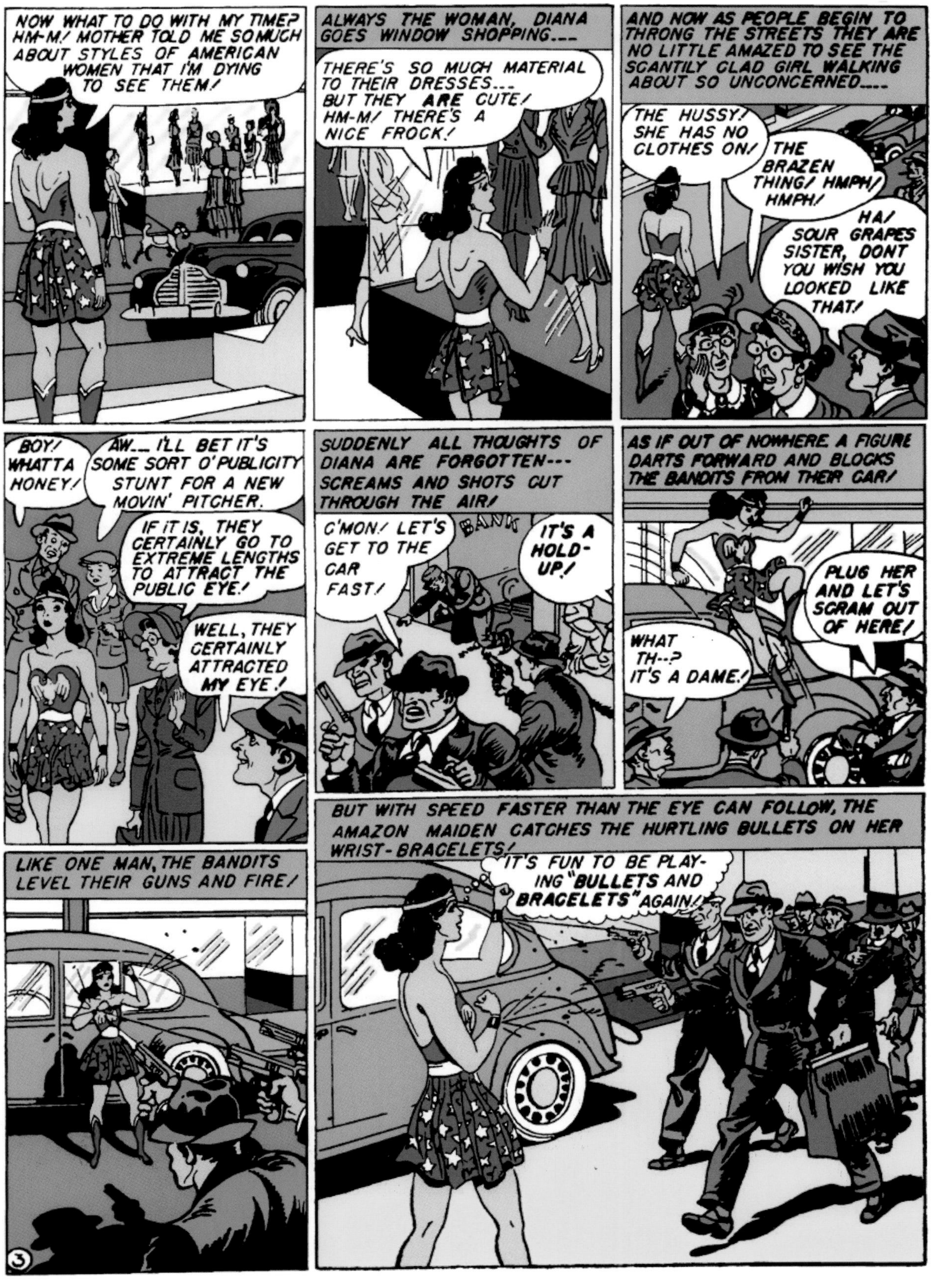
NOW WHAT TO DO WITH MY TIME? HM-M! MOTHER TOLD ME SO MUCH ABOUT STYLES OF AMERICAN WOMEN THAT I'M DYING TO SEE THEM!
ALWAYS THE WOMAN, DIANA GOES WINDOW SHOPPING---
THERE'S SO MUCH MATERIAL TO THEIR DRESSES--- BUT THEY ARE CUTE! HM-M! THERE'S A NICE FROCK!
AND NOW AS PEOPLE BEGIN TO THRONG THE STREETS THEY ARE NO LITTLE AMAZED TO SEE THE SCANTILY CLAD GIRL WALKING ABOUT SO UNCONCERNED----
THE HUSSY! SHE HAS NO CLOTHES ON!
THE BRAZEN THING! HMPH! HMPH!
HA! SOUR GRAPES SISTER, DONT YOU WISH YOU LOOKED LIKE THAT!
BOY! WHATTA HONEY!
AW--- I'LL BET IT'S SOME SORT O' PUBLICITY STUNT FOR A NEW MOVIN' PITCHER.
IF IT IS, THEY CERTAINLY GO TO EXTREME LENGTHS TO ATTRACT THE PUBLIC EYE!
WELL, THEY CERTAINLY ATTRACTED MY EYE!
SUDDENLY ALL THOUGHTS OF DIANA ARE FORGOTTEN--- SCREAMS AND SHOTS CUT THROUGH THE AIR!
BANK
C'MON! LET'S GET TO THE CAR FAST!
IT'S A HOLD-UP!
AS IF OUT OF NOWHERE A FIGURE DARTS FORWARD AND BLOCKS THE BANDITS FROM THEIR CAR!
PLUG HER AND LET'S SCRAM OUT OF HERE!
WHAT TH--? IT'S A DAME!
LIKE ONE MAN, THE BANDITS LEVEL THEIR GUNS AND FIRE!
BUT WITH SPEED FASTER THAN THE EYE CAN FOLLOW, THE AMAZON MAIDEN CATCHES THE HURTLING BULLETS ON HER WRIST-BRACELETS!
IT'S FUN TO BE PLAYING "BULLETS AND BRACELETS" AGAIN!
3

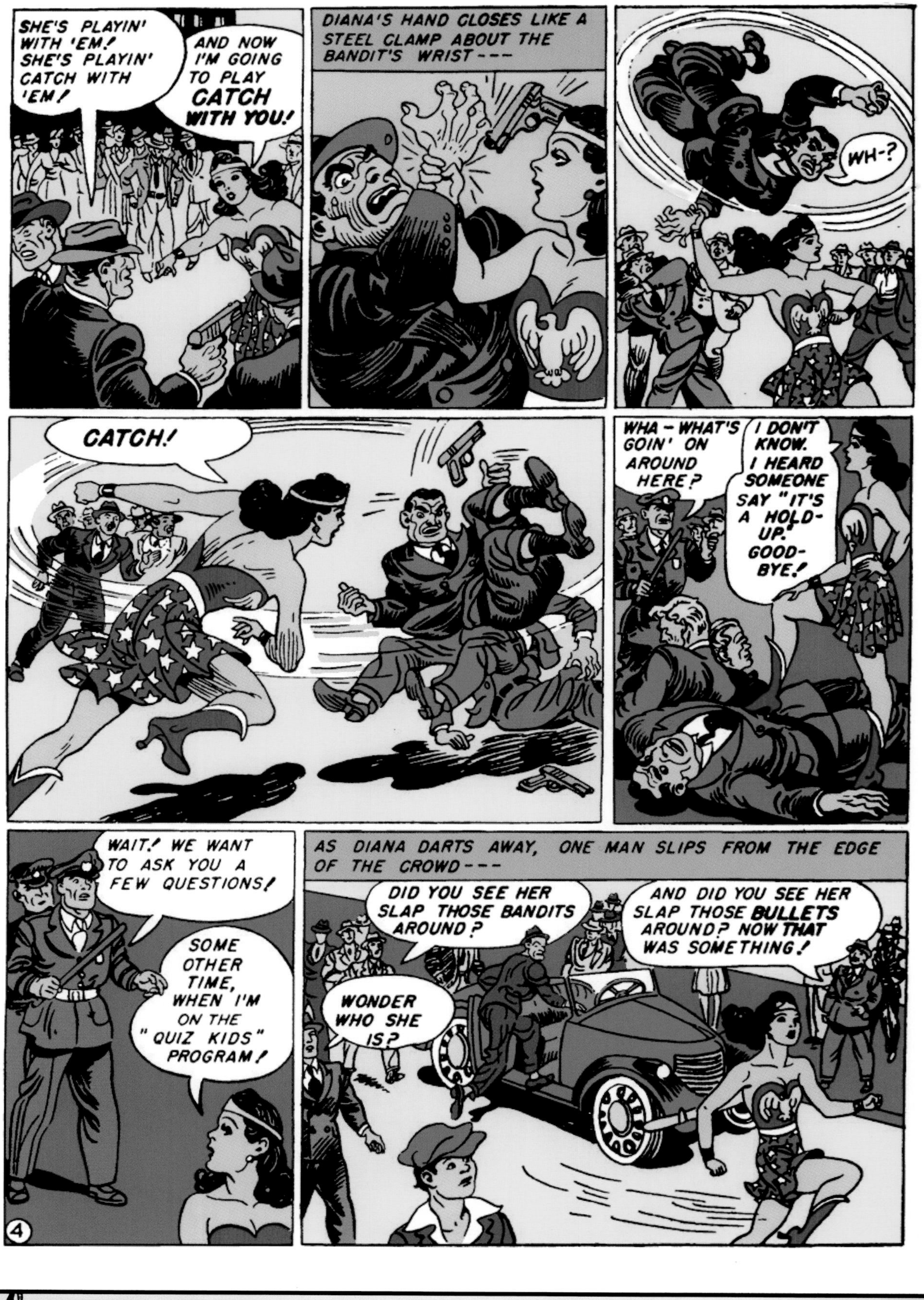
SHE'S PLAYIN' WITH 'EM! SHE'S PLAYIN' CATCH WITH 'EM!
AND NOW I'M GOING TO PLAY CATCH WITH YOU!
DIANA'S HAND CLOSES LIKE A STEEL CLAMP ABOUT THE BANDIT'S WRIST---
WH-?
CATCH!
WHA - WHAT'S GOIN' ON AROUND HERE?
I DON'T KNOW. I HEARD SOMEONE SAY "IT'S A HOLD-UP." GOOD-BYE!
WAIT! WE WANT TO ASK YOU A FEW QUESTIONS!
SOME OTHER TIME, WHEN I'M ON THE "QUIZ KIDS" PROGRAM!
4
AS DIANA DARTS AWAY, ONE MAN SLIPS FROM THE EDGE OF THE CROWD---
DID YOU SEE HER SLAP THOSE BANDITS AROUND?
AND DID YOU SEE HER SLAP THOSE BULLETS AROUND? NOW THAT WAS SOMETHING!
WONDER WHO SHE IS?

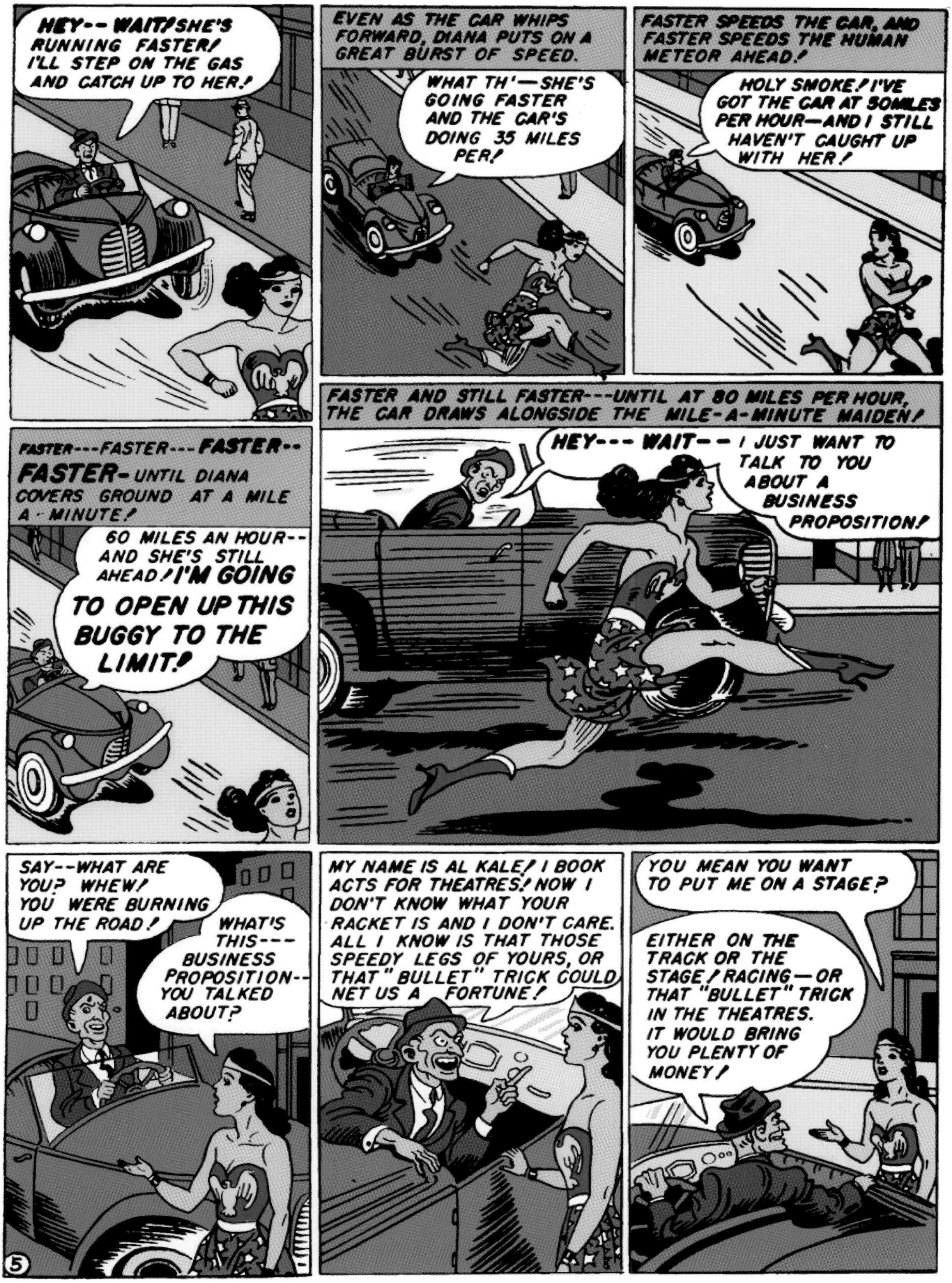
HEY-- WAIT! SHE'S RUNNING FASTER! I'LL STEP ON THE GAS AND CATCH UP TO HER!
EVEN AS THE CAR WHIPS FORWARD, DIANA PUTS ON A GREAT BURST OF SPEED.
WHAT TH'—SHE'S GOING FASTER AND THE CAR'S DOING 35 MILES PER!
FASTER SPEEDS THE CAR, AND FASTER SPEEDS THE HUMAN METEOR AHEAD!
HOLY SMOKE! I'VE GOT THE CAR AT 50MILES PER HOUR—AND I STILL HAVEN'T CAUGHT UP WITH HER!
FASTER---FASTER---FASTER-- FASTER- UNTIL DIANA COVERS GROUND AT A MILE A - MINUTE!
60 MILES AN HOUR-- AND SHE'S STILL AHEAD! I'M GOING TO OPEN UP THIS BUGGY TO THE LIMIT!
FASTER AND STILL FASTER---UNTIL AT 80 MILES PER HOUR, THE CAR DRAWS ALONGSIDE THE MILE-A-MINUTE MAIDEN!
HEY--- WAIT-- - I JUST WANT TO TALK TO YOU ABOUT A BUSINESS PROPOSITION!
SAY--WHAT ARE YOU? WHEW! YOU WERE BURNING UP THE ROAD!
WHAT'S THIS--- BUSINESS PROPOSITION-- YOU TALKED ABOUT?
MY NAME IS AL KALE! I BOOK ACTS FOR THEATRES! NOW I DON'T KNOW WHAT YOUR RACKET IS AND I DON'T CARE. ALL I KNOW IS THAT THOSE SPEEDY LEGS OF YOURS, OR THAT "BULLET" TRICK COULD NET US A FORTUNE!
YOU MEAN YOU WANT TO PUT ME ON A STAGE?
EITHER ON THE TRACK OR THE STAGE! RACING—OR THAT "BULLET" TRICK IN THE THEATRES. IT WOULD BRING YOU PLENTY OF MONEY!
5

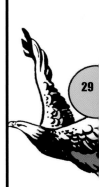

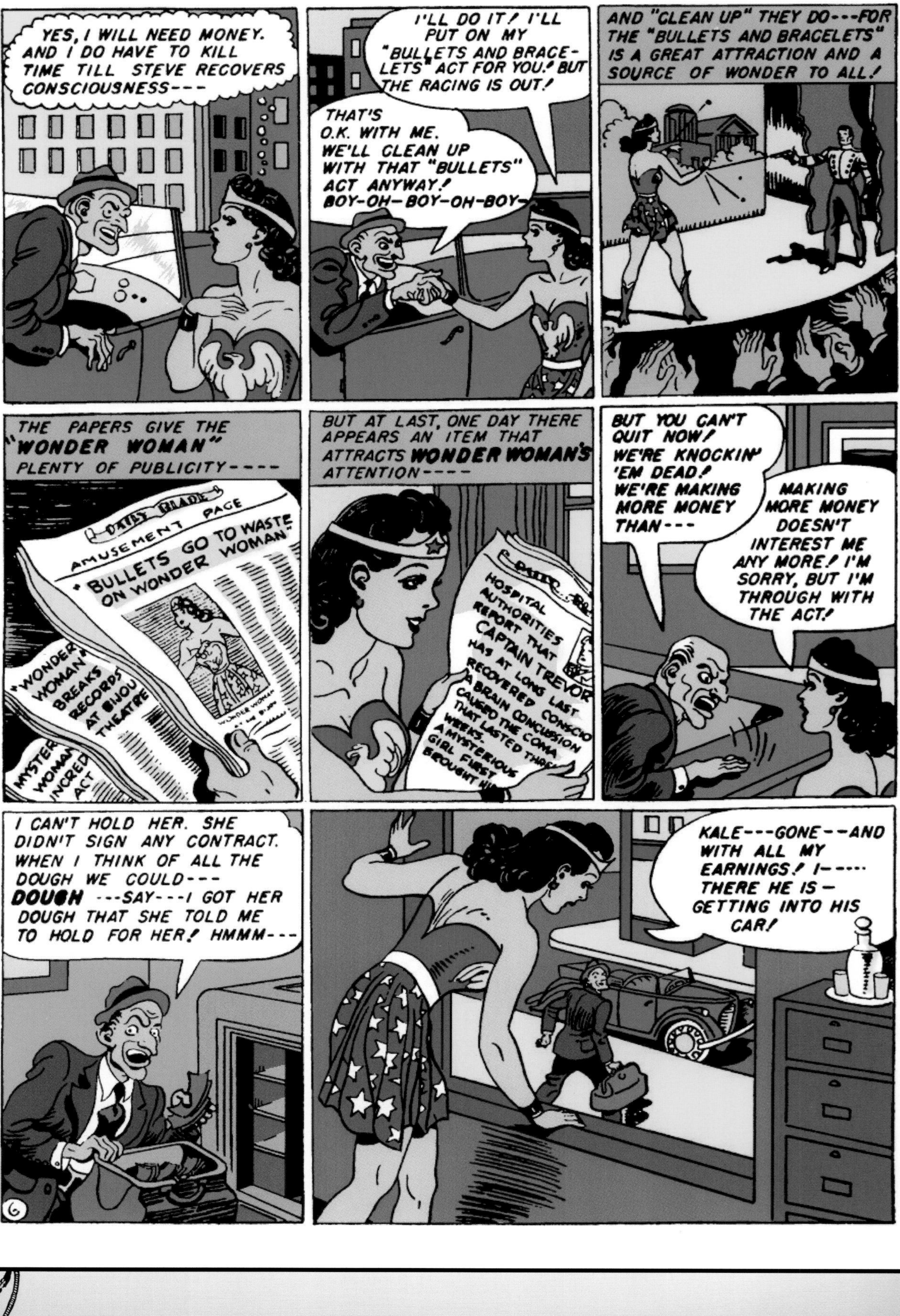

YES, I WILL NEED MONEY. AND I DO HAVE TO KILL TIME TILL STEVE RECOVERS CONSCIOUSNESS---
I'LL DO IT! I'LL PUT ON MY "BULLETS AND BRACELETS" ACT FOR YOU! BUT THE RACING IS OUT!
THAT'S O.K. WITH ME. WE'LL CLEAN UP WITH THAT "BULLETS" ACT ANYWAY! BOY-OH-BOY-OH-BOY-
AND "CLEAN UP" THEY DO---FOR THE "BULLETS AND BRACELETS" IS A GREAT ATTRACTION AND A SOURCE OF WONDER TO ALL!
THE PAPERS GIVE THE "WONDER WOMAN" PLENTY OF PUBLICITY----
AMUSEMENT PAGE
"BULLETS GO TO WASTE ON WONDER WOMAN"
"WONDER WOMAN" BREAKS RECORDS AT BIJOU THEATRE
BUT AT LAST, ONE DAY THERE APPEARS AN ITEM THAT ATTRACTS WONDER WOMAN'S ATTENTION----
HOSPITAL AUTHORITIES REPORT THAT CAPTAIN TREVOR HAS AT LONG LAST RECOVERED CONSCIO
BUT YOU CAN'T QUIT NOW! WE'RE KNOCKIN' 'EM DEAD! WE'RE MAKING MORE MONEY THAN---
MAKING MORE MONEY DOESN'T INTEREST ME ANY MORE! I'M SORRY, BUT I'M THROUGH WITH THE ACT!
I CAN'T HOLD HER. SHE DIDN'T SIGN ANY CONTRACT. WHEN I THINK OF ALL THE DOUGH WE COULD--- DOUGH ---SAY---I GOT HER DOUGH THAT SHE TOLD ME TO HOLD FOR HER! HMMM---
KALE---GONE--AND WITH ALL MY EARNINGS! I----- THERE HE IS— GETTING INTO HIS CAR!

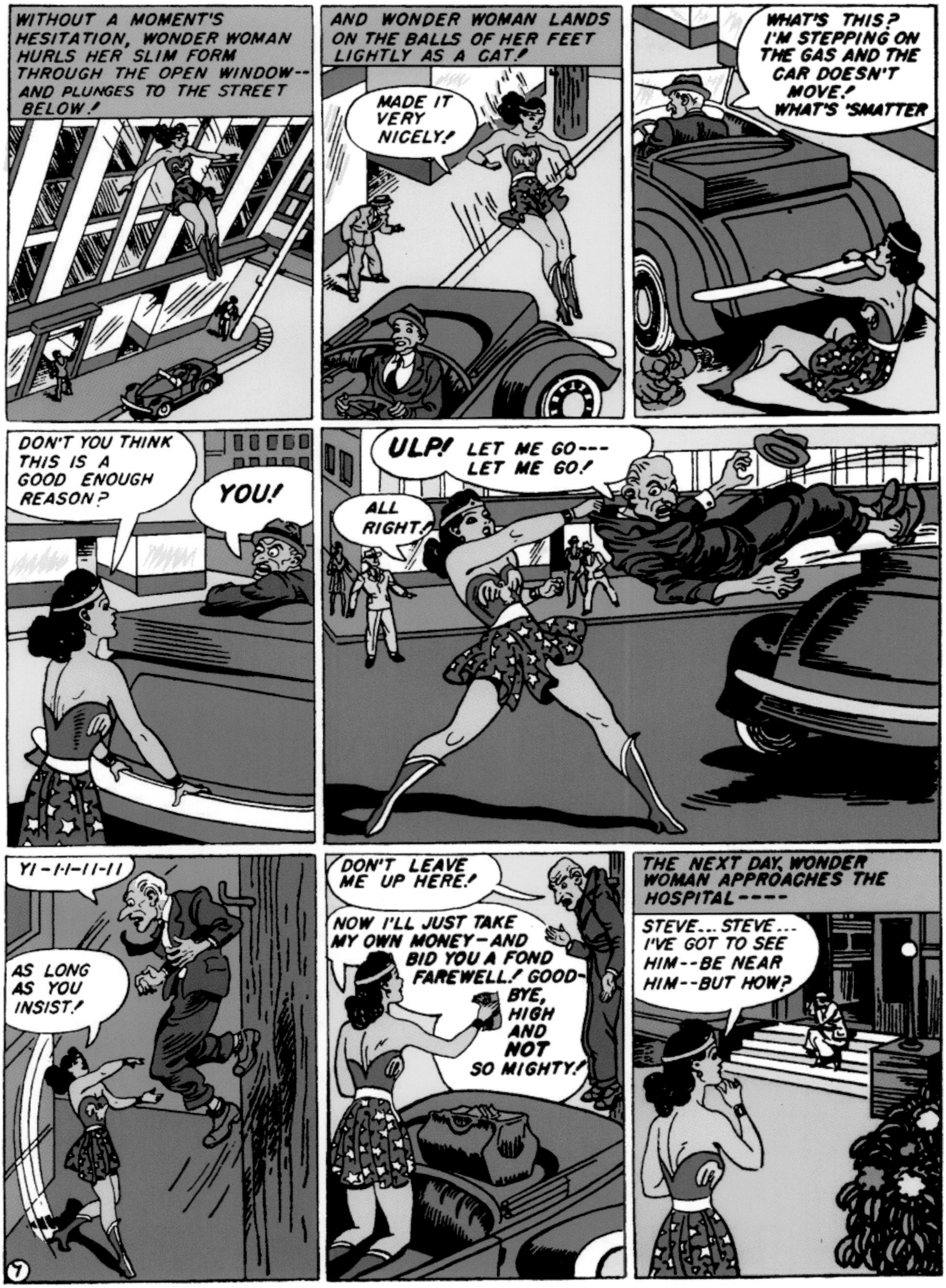
WITHOUT A MOMENT'S HESITATION, WONDER WOMAN HURLS HER SLIM FORM THROUGH THE OPEN WINDOW--AND PLUNGES TO THE STREET BELOW!
AND WONDER WOMAN LANDS ON THE BALLS OF HER FEET LIGHTLY AS A CAT!
MADE IT VERY NICELY!
WHAT'S THIS? I'M STEPPING ON THE GAS AND THE CAR DOESN'T MOVE! WHAT'S 'SMATTER
DON'T YOU THINK THIS IS A GOOD ENOUGH REASON?
YOU!
ULP! LET ME GO--- LET ME GO!
ALL RIGHT!
YI-I-I-II-II
AS LONG AS YOU INSIST!
7
DON'T LEAVE ME UP HERE!
NOW I'LL JUST TAKE MY OWN MONEY—AND BID YOU A FOND FAREWELL! GOOD-BYE, HIGH AND NOT SO MIGHTY!
THE NEXT DAY, WONDER WOMAN APPROACHES THE HOSPITAL----
STEVE... STEVE... I'VE GOT TO SEE HIM--BE NEAR HIM--BUT HOW?

AS SHE NEARS THE STEPS, **WON-DER WOMAN** SEES A GIRL HUD-DLED AND CRYING THERE---

I DON'T MEAN TO INTRUDE BUT CAN I HELP YOU?

NO ONE CAN HELP ME! BOO-HOO!

THE GIRL TELLS **WONDER WOMAN** THAT SHE IS AN ARMY NURSE JUST APPOINTED TO THIS HOSPITAL---

AND TODAY MY FIANCE JUST GOT A JOB IN SOUTH AMERICA, BUT HE CAN'T SEND FOR ME BECAUSE HIS SALARY IS TOO SMALL AT THE MOMENT!

THAT'S TERRIBLE, AND JUST THINK-- IT ALL WOULD WORK OUT RIGHT IF ONLY YOU HAD A LITTLE MONEY!

I JUST NOTICED -- WITH THESE GLASSES OFF, YOU LOOK A LOT LIKE ME! I HAVE AN IDEA! IF I GAVE YOU MONEY WOULD YOU SELL ME YOUR CREDENTIALS?

YOU--YOU MEAN YOU WANT TO TAKE MY PLACE HERE AT THE HOSPITAL? BUT- I CAN'T--- I MEAN--

LOOK-- BY TAKING YOUR PLACE I CAN SEE THE MAN I LOVE AND YOU CAN MARRY THE MAN YOU LOVE! NO HARM DONE, FOR I'M A TRAINED NURSE, TOO -- JUST A LITTLE MONEY AND A SUBSTITUTION--

AND WE'D BOTH BE HAPPY! I'LL DO IT! OH-- THIS IS WONDERFUL!

OH, BY THE WAY-- MY NAME IS DIANA. WHAT'S YOURS?

WHY, THAT'S AN AMAZING COINCI-DENCE-- I'M DIANA TOO! DIANA PRINCE! AND YOU'D BETTER REMEMBER THAT LAST NAME -- BECAUSE IT'LL BE YOURS FROM NOW ON.

AND SO THAT AFTERNOON----

AN ANGEL--- A BEAUTIFUL ANGEL!

OH, CAPTAIN TREVOR -- YOU FLATTER ME I'M JUST DIANA PRINCE, YOUR SPECIAL NURSE! HE REMEMBERED ME--- HE REMEMBERED!

DAYS PASS AND STEVE TREVOR RECOVERS RAPIDLY UNDER HIS NEW NURSE'S TENDER CARE---

YOU'RE PRETTY SWELL TO ME, DIANA! BUT I'M JUST WASTING AWAY HERE. I SHOULD BE BACK ON MY JOB!

I DON'T BELIEVE IT'S YOUR JOB. YOU WANT TO FIND THAT "BEAUTIFUL ANGEL" YOU WERE TALKING ABOUT-- THE ONE WHO BROUGHT YOU HERE! BE A GOOD BOY, NOW, AND KEEP QUIET---

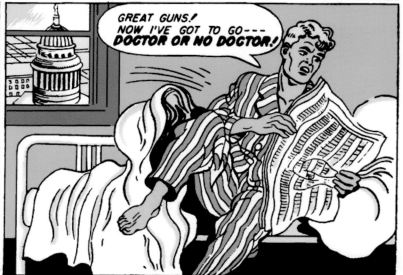

GREAT GUNS! NOW I'VE GOT TO GO--- **DOCTOR OR NO DOCTOR!**

BY THE TIME THEY NOTICE I'M GONE, IT'LL BE TOO LATE TO STOP ME!

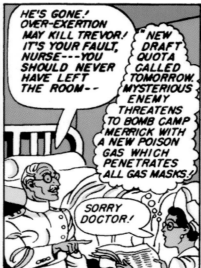

HE'S GONE! OVER-EXERTION MAY KILL TREVOR! IT'S YOUR FAULT, NURSE---YOU SHOULD NEVER HAVE LEFT THE ROOM--

"NEW DRAFT QUOTA CALLED TOMORROW. MYSTERIOUS ENEMY THREATENS TO BOMB CAMP MERRICK WITH A NEW POISON GAS WHICH PENETRATES ALL GAS MASKS!

SORRY DOCTOR!

THAT NIGHT, NURSE DIANA PRINCE DARTS TOWARD AN OLD DESERTED BARN ON THE OUTSKIRTS OF WASHINGTON----

I HOPE NO ONE'S FOUND THIS HIDEOUT WHILE I'VE BEEN NURSING STEVE TREVOR!

INSIDE THE BARN, THE GIRL TRANSFORMS HERSELF FROM DRAB DIANA PRINCE TO THE EXCITING AMAZON MAIDEN... WONDER WOMAN!

IT FEELS GRAND TO BE MYSELF AGAIN! AND NOW FOR CLEVER STEVE TREVOR... THE IMPETUOUS DARLING!

AT CAMP MERRICK, STEVE TREVOR REPORTS TO THE C.O.!

I'VE GOT AIR PATROLS COVERING THE ENTIRE COAST. BUT THIS MYSTERY BOMBER USES A STRATOSPHERE PLANE. HE'LL POWER-DIVE ON THE CAMP AND I'M GOING TO WAIT FOR HIM.

WE'RE DEPENDING ON YOU, CAPTAIN!

HIGH OVER CAMP MERRICK, STEVE TREVOR CIRCLES LIKE A BIRD OF PREY--WAITING FOR THE ENEMY!

33

THEN-- LIKE A DIVING, WINGED COMET--THE MYSTERY BOMBER!

WOW! HE MUST BE DOING 650 M.P.H.! I'VE GOT TO STOP HIM!

JUMPING BLUE BLAZES! THAT GUY'S GOT A FLYING FORT! I CAN'T EVEN DENT HIS POLISH!

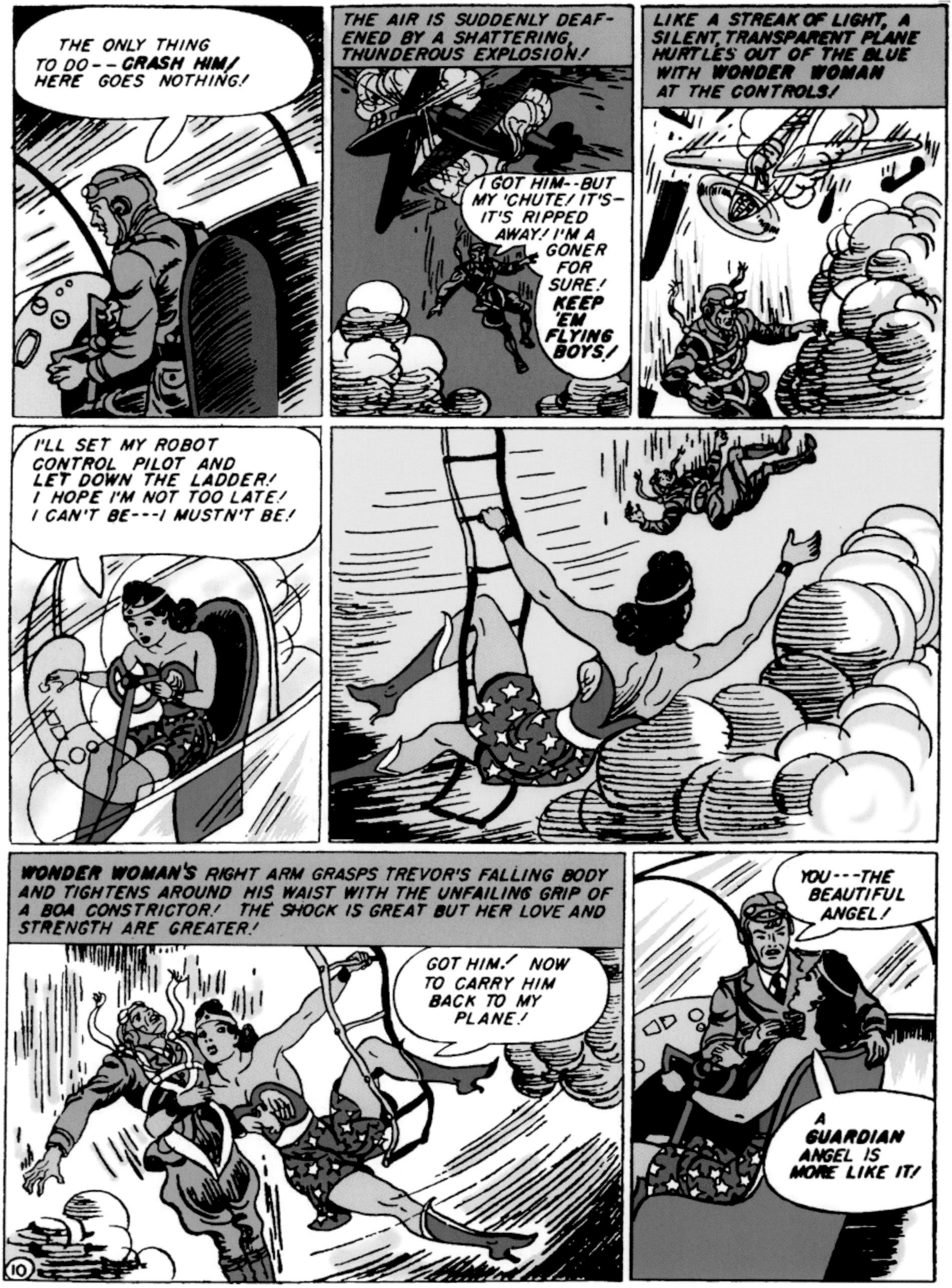
THE ONLY THING TO DO-- CRASH HIM! HERE GOES NOTHING!
THE AIR IS SUDDENLY DEAFENED BY A SHATTERING, THUNDEROUS EXPLOSION!
I GOT HIM--BUT MY 'CHUTE! IT'S-IT'S RIPPED AWAY! I'M A GONER FOR SURE! KEEP 'EM FLYING BOYS!
LIKE A STREAK OF LIGHT, A SILENT, TRANSPARENT PLANE HURTLES OUT OF THE BLUE WITH WONDER WOMAN AT THE CONTROLS!
I'LL SET MY ROBOT CONTROL PILOT AND LET DOWN THE LADDER! I HOPE I'M NOT TOO LATE! I CAN'T BE---I MUSTN'T BE!
WONDER WOMAN'S RIGHT ARM GRASPS TREVOR'S FALLING BODY AND TIGHTENS AROUND HIS WAIST WITH THE UNFAILING GRIP OF A BOA CONSTRICTOR! THE SHOCK IS GREAT BUT HER LOVE AND STRENGTH ARE GREATER!
GOT HIM! NOW TO CARRY HIM BACK TO MY PLANE!
10
YOU---THE BEAUTIFUL ANGEL!
A GUARDIAN ANGEL IS MORE LIKE IT!

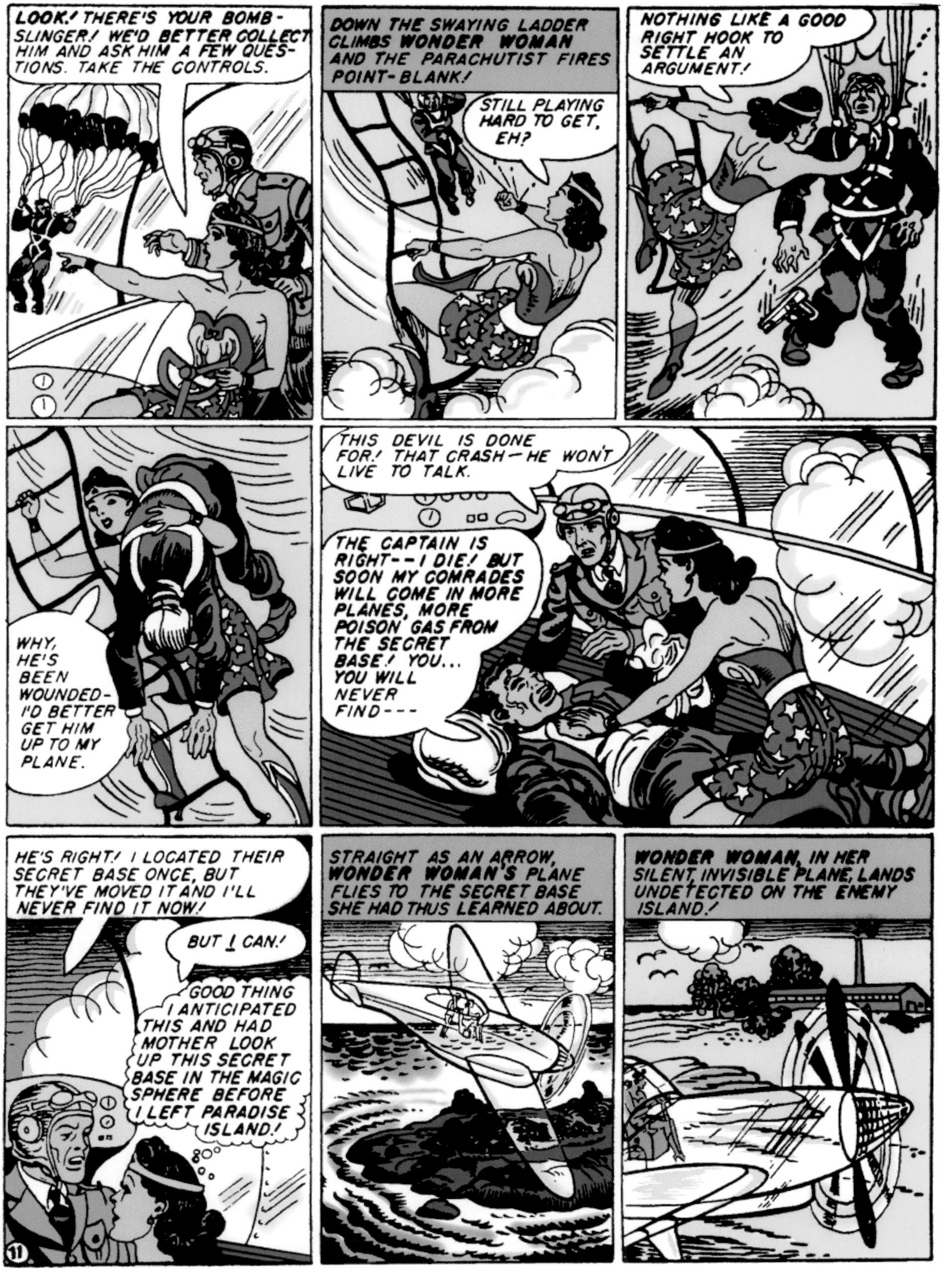
LOOK! THERE'S YOUR BOMB-SLINGER! WE'D BETTER COLLECT HIM AND ASK HIM A FEW QUESTIONS. TAKE THE CONTROLS.
DOWN THE SWAYING LADDER CLIMBS WONDER WOMAN AND THE PARACHUTIST FIRES POINT-BLANK!
STILL PLAYING HARD TO GET, EH?
NOTHING LIKE A GOOD RIGHT HOOK TO SETTLE AN ARGUMENT!
WHY, HE'S BEEN WOUNDED-I'D BETTER GET HIM UP TO MY PLANE.
THIS DEVIL IS DONE FOR! THAT CRASH—HE WON'T LIVE TO TALK.
THE CAPTAIN IS RIGHT--I DIE! BUT SOON MY COMRADES WILL COME IN MORE PLANES, MORE POISON GAS FROM THE SECRET BASE! YOU... YOU WILL NEVER FIND---
HE'S RIGHT! I LOCATED THEIR SECRET BASE ONCE, BUT THEY'VE MOVED IT AND I'LL NEVER FIND IT NOW!
BUT I CAN!
GOOD THING I ANTICIPATED THIS AND HAD MOTHER LOOK UP THIS SECRET BASE IN THE MAGIC SPHERE BEFORE I LEFT PARADISE ISLAND!
11
STRAIGHT AS AN ARROW, WONDER WOMAN'S PLANE FLIES TO THE SECRET BASE SHE HAD THUS LEARNED ABOUT.
WONDER WOMAN, IN HER SILENT, INVISIBLE PLANE, LANDS UNDETECTED ON THE ENEMY ISLAND!

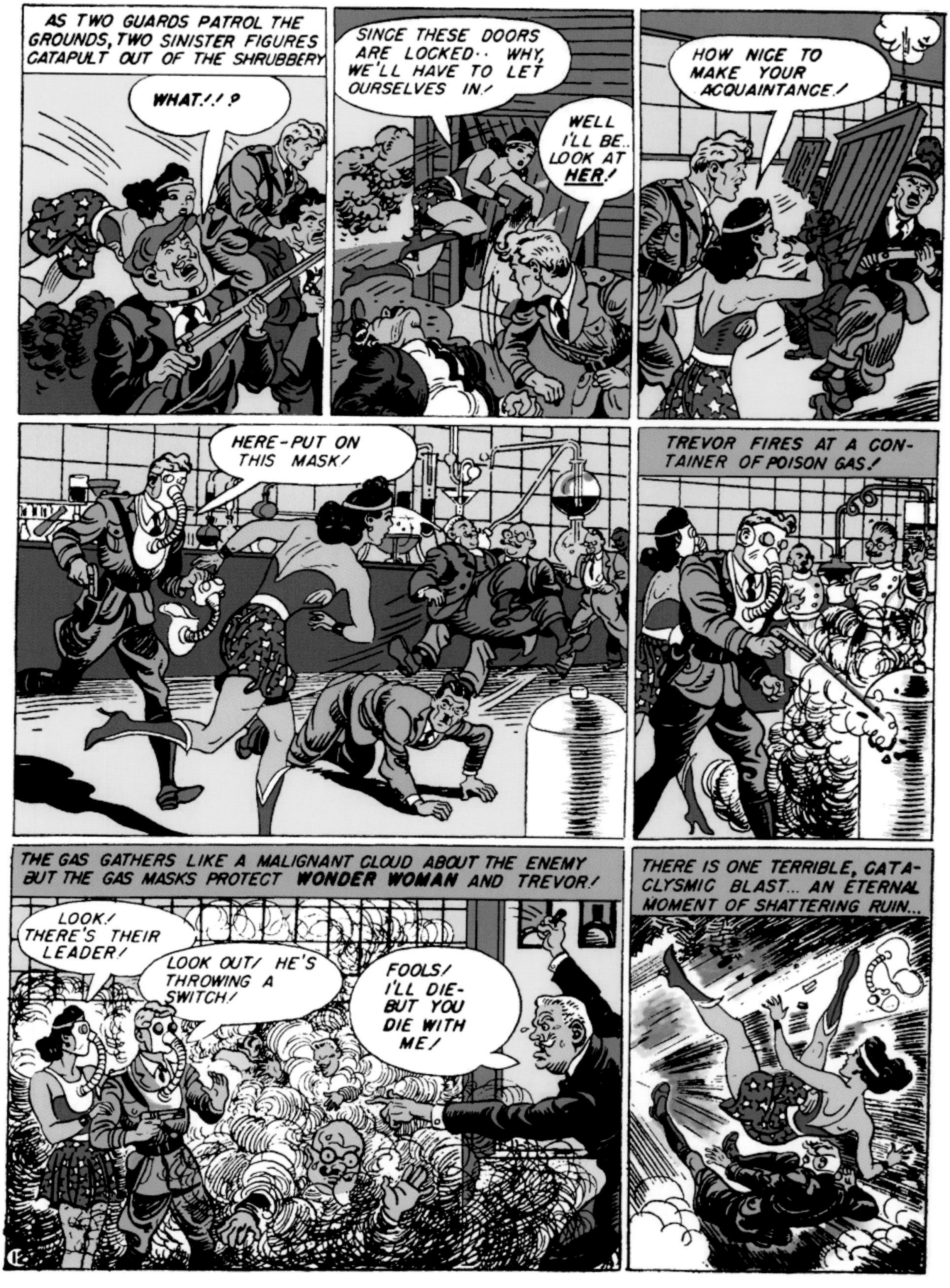

AS TWO GUARDS PATROL THE GROUNDS, TWO SINISTER FIGURES CATAPULT OUT OF THE SHRUBBERY
WHAT!!?
SINCE THESE DOORS ARE LOCKED.. WHY, WE'LL HAVE TO LET OURSELVES IN!
WELL I'LL BE.. LOOK AT HER!
HOW NICE TO MAKE YOUR ACQUAINTANCE!
HERE-PUT ON THIS MASK!
TREVOR FIRES AT A CONTAINER OF POISON GAS!
THE GAS GATHERS LIKE A MALIGNANT CLOUD ABOUT THE ENEMY BUT THE GAS MASKS PROTECT WONDER WOMAN AND TREVOR!
LOOK! THERE'S THEIR LEADER!
LOOK OUT! HE'S THROWING A SWITCH!
FOOLS! I'LL DIE-BUT YOU DIE WITH ME!
THERE IS ONE TERRIBLE, CATACLYSMIC BLAST... AN ETERNAL MOMENT OF SHATTERING RUIN...

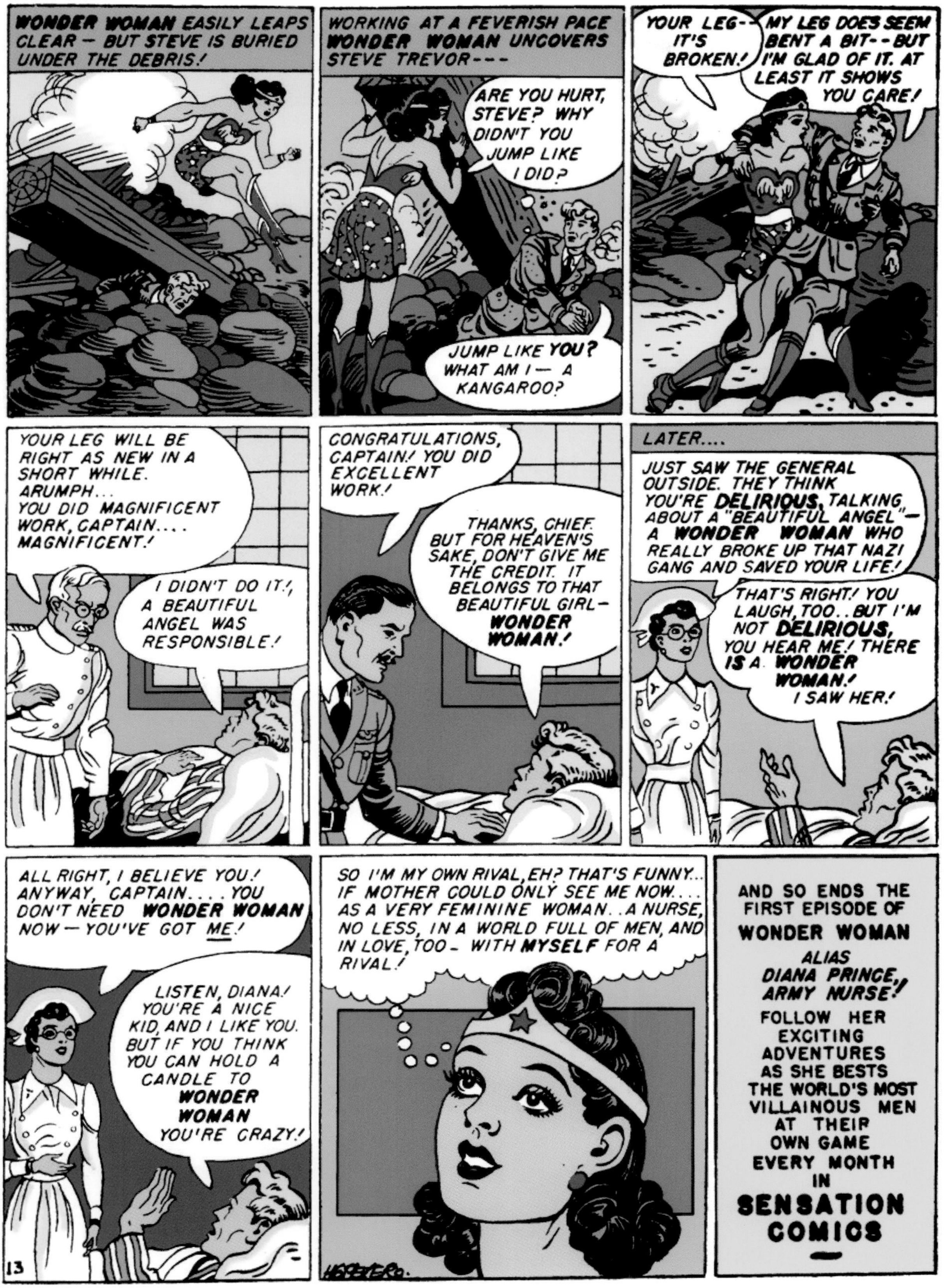
WONDER WOMAN EASILY LEAPS CLEAR — BUT STEVE IS BURIED UNDER THE DEBRIS!
WORKING AT A FEVERISH PACE WONDER WOMAN UNCOVERS STEVE TREVOR---
ARE YOU HURT, STEVE? WHY DIDN'T YOU JUMP LIKE I DID?
JUMP LIKE YOU? WHAT AM I — A KANGAROO?
YOUR LEG-- IT'S BROKEN!
MY LEG DOES SEEM BENT A BIT--BUT I'M GLAD OF IT. AT LEAST IT SHOWS YOU CARE!
YOUR LEG WILL BE RIGHT AS NEW IN A SHORT WHILE. ARUMPH... YOU DID MAGNIFICENT WORK, CAPTAIN.... MAGNIFICENT!
I DIDN'T DO IT!, A BEAUTIFUL ANGEL WAS RESPONSIBLE!
CONGRATULATIONS, CAPTAIN! YOU DID EXCELLENT WORK!
THANKS, CHIEF. BUT FOR HEAVEN'S SAKE, DON'T GIVE ME THE CREDIT. IT BELONGS TO THAT BEAUTIFUL GIRL— WONDER WOMAN!
LATER....
JUST SAW THE GENERAL OUTSIDE. THEY THINK YOU'RE DELIRIOUS, TALKING ABOUT A "BEAUTIFUL ANGEL"— A WONDER WOMAN WHO REALLY BROKE UP THAT NAZI GANG AND SAVED YOUR LIFE!
THAT'S RIGHT! YOU LAUGH, TOO.. BUT I'M NOT DELIRIOUS, YOU HEAR ME! THERE IS A WONDER WOMAN! I SAW HER!
ALL RIGHT, I BELIEVE YOU! ANYWAY, CAPTAIN.... YOU DON'T NEED WONDER WOMAN NOW — YOU'VE GOT ME!
LISTEN, DIANA! YOU'RE A NICE KID, AND I LIKE YOU. BUT IF YOU THINK YOU CAN HOLD A CANDLE TO WONDER WOMAN YOU'RE CRAZY!
13
SO I'M MY OWN RIVAL, EH? THAT'S FUNNY... IF MOTHER COULD ONLY SEE ME NOW.... AS A VERY FEMININE WOMAN.. A NURSE, NO LESS, IN A WORLD FULL OF MEN, AND IN LOVE, TOO - WITH MYSELF FOR A RIVAL!
AND SO ENDS THE FIRST EPISODE OF WONDER WOMAN ALIAS DIANA PRINCE, ARMY NURSE! FOLLOW HER EXCITING ADVENTURES AS SHE BESTS THE WORLD'S MOST VILLAINOUS MEN AT THEIR OWN GAME EVERY MONTH IN SENSATION COMICS

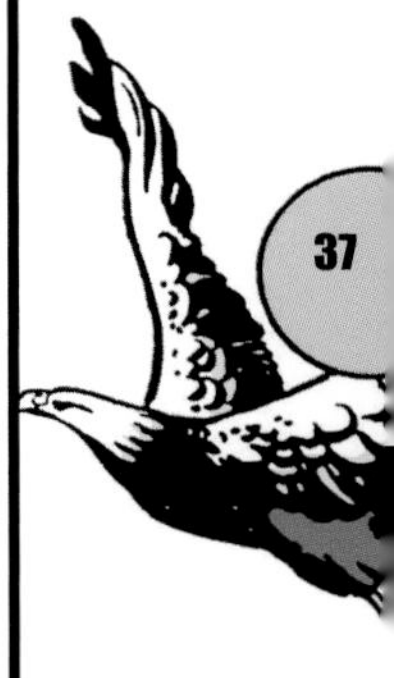

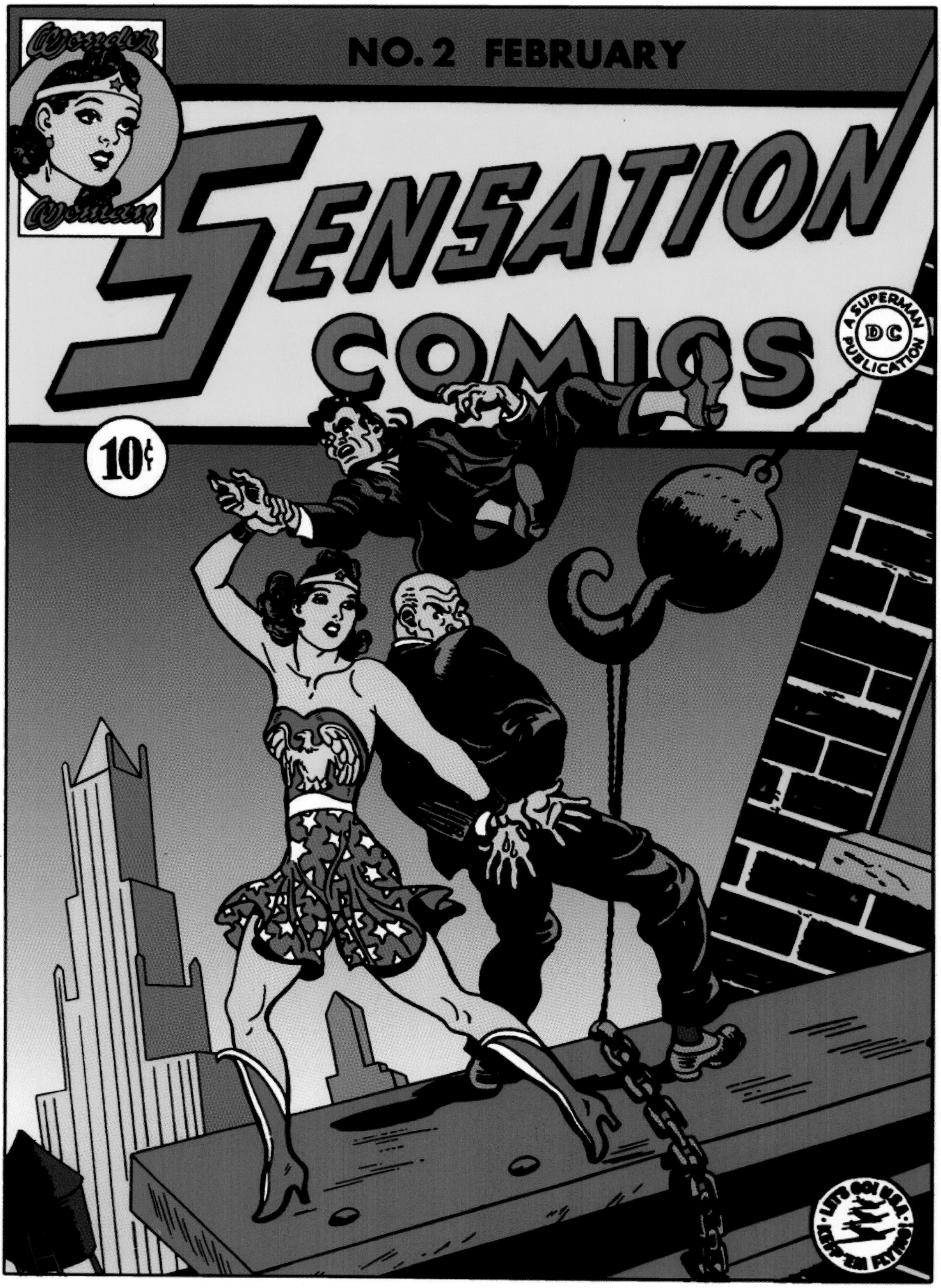
Wonder Woman
NO. 2 FEBRUARY
SENSATION COMICS
10¢
A SUPERMAN DC PUBLICATION

Sensation Comics #2 (Feb. 1942) - art: H.G. Peter

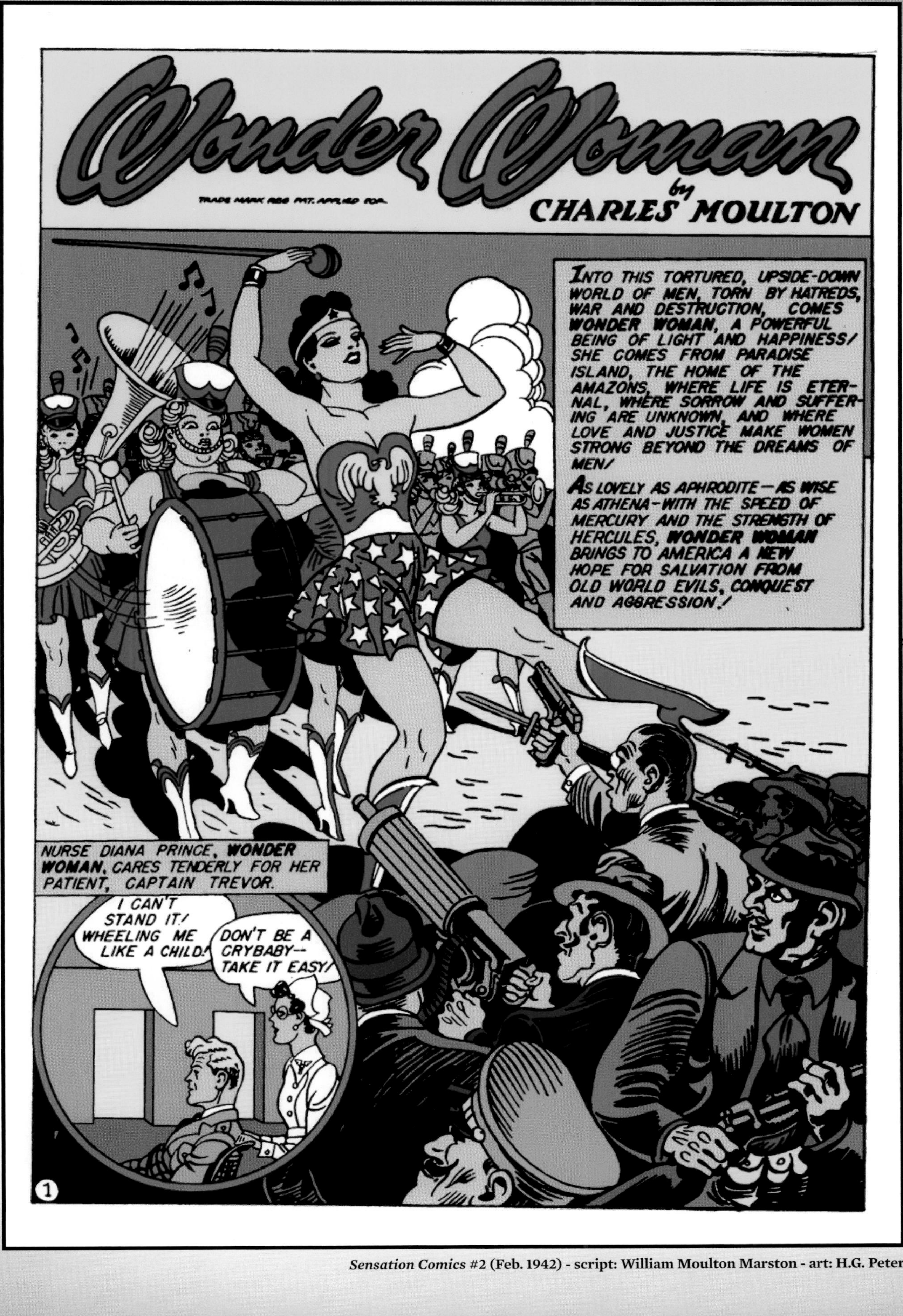
Wonder Woman
TRADE MARK REG PAT. APPLIED FOR
by CHARLES MOULTON
INTO THIS TORTURED, UPSIDE-DOWN WORLD OF MEN, TORN BY HATREDS, WAR AND DESTRUCTION, COMES WONDER WOMAN, A POWERFUL BEING OF LIGHT AND HAPPINESS! SHE COMES FROM PARADISE ISLAND, THE HOME OF THE AMAZONS, WHERE LIFE IS ETERNAL, WHERE SORROW AND SUFFERING ARE UNKNOWN, AND WHERE LOVE AND JUSTICE MAKE WOMEN STRONG BEYOND THE DREAMS OF MEN!
AS LOVELY AS APHRODITE—AS WISE AS ATHENA-WITH THE SPEED OF MERCURY AND THE STRENGTH OF HERCULES, WONDER WOMAN BRINGS TO AMERICA A NEW HOPE FOR SALVATION FROM OLD WORLD EVILS, CONQUEST AND AGGRESSION!
NURSE DIANA PRINCE, WONDER WOMAN, CARES TENDERLY FOR HER PATIENT, CAPTAIN TREVOR.
I CAN'T STAND IT! WHEELING ME LIKE A CHILD!
DON'T BE A CRYBABY-- TAKE IT EASY!
1

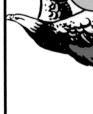

Sensation Comics #2 (Feb. 1942) - script: William Moulton Marston - art: H.G. Peter

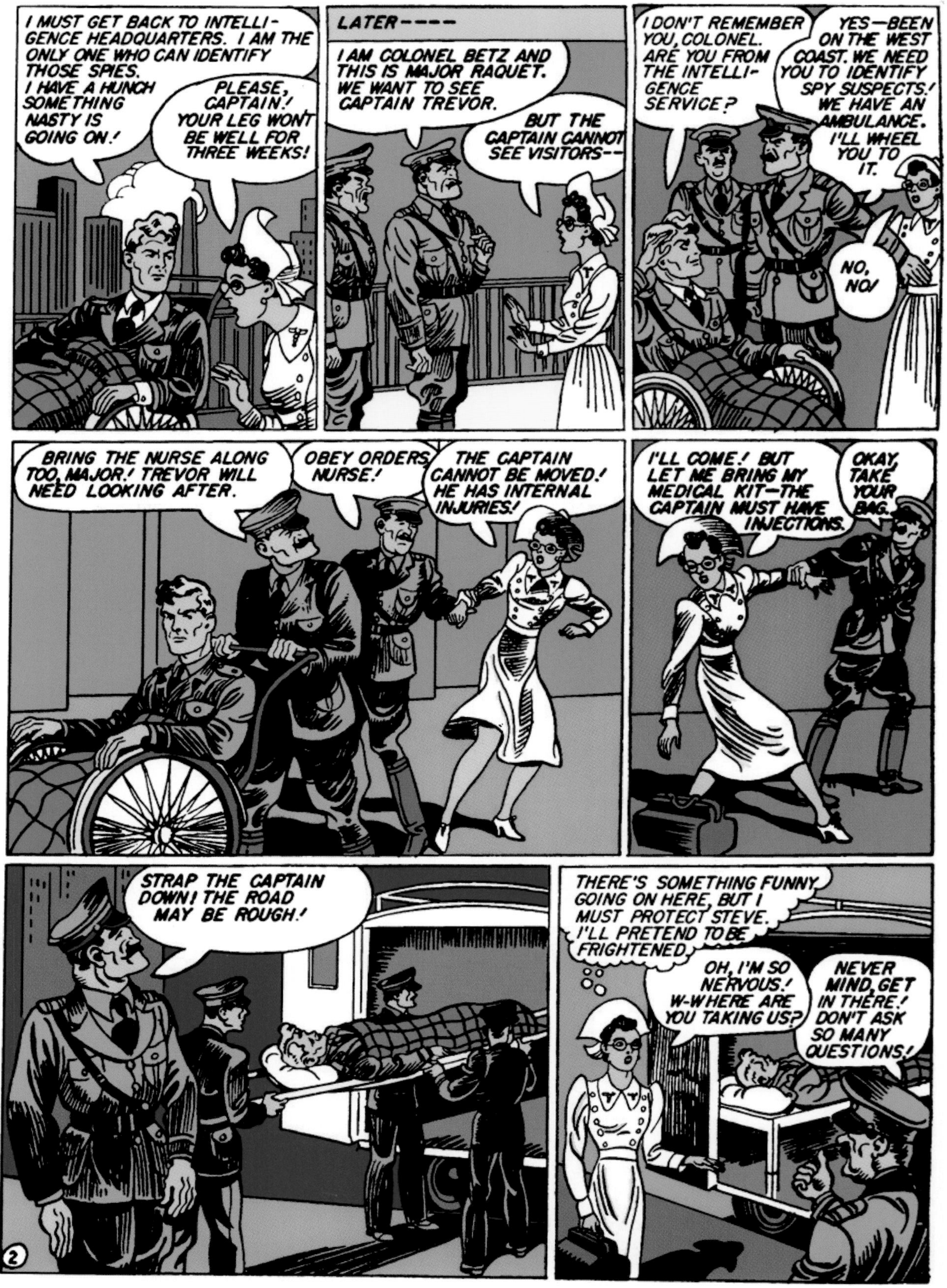

I MUST GET BACK TO INTELLIGENCE HEADQUARTERS. I AM THE ONLY ONE WHO CAN IDENTIFY THOSE SPIES. I HAVE A HUNCH SOMETHING NASTY IS GOING ON!
PLEASE, CAPTAIN! YOUR LEG WON'T BE WELL FOR THREE WEEKS!
LATER----
I AM COLONEL BETZ AND THIS IS MAJOR RAQUET. WE WANT TO SEE CAPTAIN TREVOR.
BUT THE CAPTAIN CANNOT SEE VISITORS--
I DON'T REMEMBER YOU, COLONEL. ARE YOU FROM THE INTELLIGENCE SERVICE?
YES—BEEN ON THE WEST COAST. WE NEED YOU TO IDENTIFY SPY SUSPECTS! WE HAVE AN AMBULANCE. I'LL WHEEL YOU TO IT.
NO, NO!
BRING THE NURSE ALONG TOO, MAJOR! TREVOR WILL NEED LOOKING AFTER.
OBEY ORDERS, NURSE!
THE CAPTAIN CANNOT BE MOVED! HE HAS INTERNAL INJURIES!
I'LL COME! BUT LET ME BRING MY MEDICAL KIT—THE CAPTAIN MUST HAVE INJECTIONS.
OKAY, TAKE YOUR BAG.
STRAP THE CAPTAIN DOWN! THE ROAD MAY BE ROUGH!
2
THERE'S SOMETHING FUNNY GOING ON HERE, BUT I MUST PROTECT STEVE. I'LL PRETEND TO BE FRIGHTENED.
OH, I'M SO NERVOUS! W-WHERE ARE YOU TAKING US?
NEVER MIND, GET IN THERE! DON'T ASK SO MANY QUESTIONS!

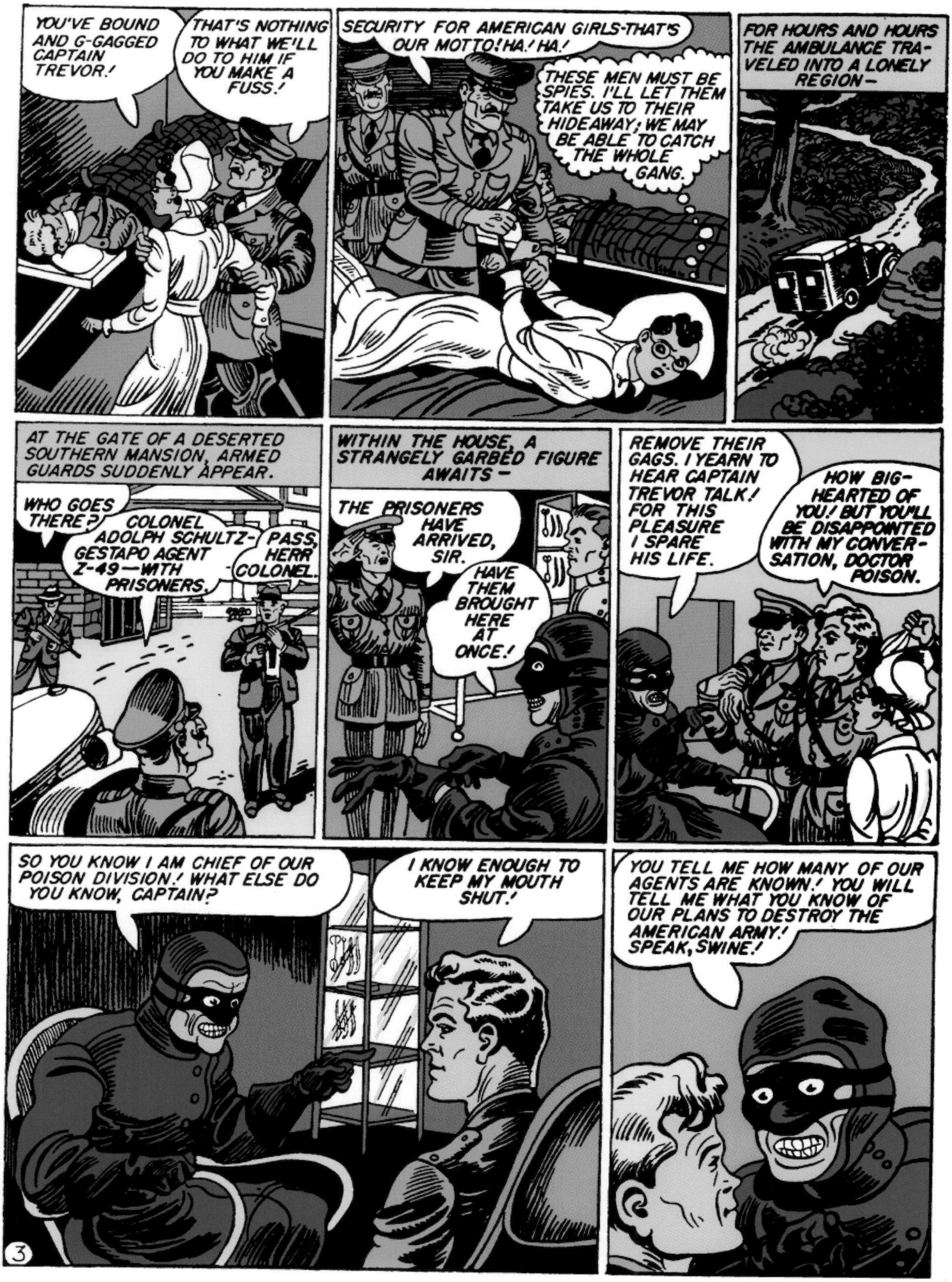
YOU'VE BOUND AND G-GAGGED CAPTAIN TREVOR!
THAT'S NOTHING TO WHAT WE'LL DO TO HIM IF YOU MAKE A FUSS!
SECURITY FOR AMERICAN GIRLS-THAT'S OUR MOTTO! HA! HA!
THESE MEN MUST BE SPIES. I'LL LET THEM TAKE US TO THEIR HIDEAWAY; WE MAY BE ABLE TO CATCH THE WHOLE GANG.
FOR HOURS AND HOURS THE AMBULANCE TRAVELED INTO A LONELY REGION—
AT THE GATE OF A DESERTED SOUTHERN MANSION, ARMED GUARDS SUDDENLY APPEAR.
WHO GOES THERE?
COLONEL ADOLPH SCHULTZ-GESTAPO AGENT Z-49—WITH PRISONERS.
PASS, HERR COLONEL.
WITHIN THE HOUSE, A STRANGELY GARBED FIGURE AWAITS—
THE PRISONERS HAVE ARRIVED, SIR.
HAVE THEM BROUGHT HERE AT ONCE!
REMOVE THEIR GAGS. I YEARN TO HEAR CAPTAIN TREVOR TALK! FOR THIS PLEASURE I SPARE HIS LIFE.
HOW BIG-HEARTED OF YOU! BUT YOU'LL BE DISAPPOINTED WITH MY CONVERSATION, DOCTOR POISON.
SO YOU KNOW I AM CHIEF OF OUR POISON DIVISION! WHAT ELSE DO YOU KNOW, CAPTAIN?
I KNOW ENOUGH TO KEEP MY MOUTH SHUT!
YOU TELL ME HOW MANY OF OUR AGENTS ARE KNOWN! YOU WILL TELL ME WHAT YOU KNOW OF OUR PLANS TO DESTROY THE AMERICAN ARMY! SPEAK, SWINE!
3

THE ONLY THING I'LL TELL YOU, POISON, IS WHERE TO GO.
THE CAPTAIN IS QUITE COCKY! BUT WE'LL MAKE HIM TALK! PUT HIM ON THE OPERATING TABLE!
THIS SYRINGE CONTAINS SCOPOLAMINE AND MORPHINE IN SUITABLE PROPORTIONS. YOU KNOW WHAT THAT IS?
TRUTH SERUM! YOU DEVIL!
DIANA, UNABLE TO RESTRAIN HERSELF, BURSTS HER BONDS—
DON'T YOU DARE GIVE THAT DRUG TO CAPTAIN TREVOR! IT MIGHT KILL HIM!
WOT HIT ME?
SHE'S NO NURSE! SHE'S A JACK DEMPSEY!
BUT THE SPY CHIEF SUBDUES DIANA BY THREATENING STEVE.
STOP! OBEY ME, NURSE. OR I WILL CUT YOUR PATIENT'S THROAT!
OH-H-H! I'LL OBEY YOU—
THEN STERILIZE THIS SYRINGE, NURSE!
YES, DOCTOR.
I ALMOST GAVE MYSELF AWAY THAT TIME—I'LL HAVE TO WATCH MY STEP!
DIANA SECRETLY CHANGES THE TRUTH SERUM FOR A SYRINGE OF HARMLESS SALINE SOLUTION IN HER MEDICAL KIT.
4
I CHANGED THE HYPODERMICS-- THIS INJECTION WON'T AFFECT YOU. PRETEND THAT TRUTH SERUM IS MAKING YOU TALK!
RIGHT! GOOD GIRL!
THE DRUG IS TAKING EFFECT--HE'LL TALK IN A MINUTE!
UG—WUG-- GRU! SPIES— PHLUT—KILL— ARMY—

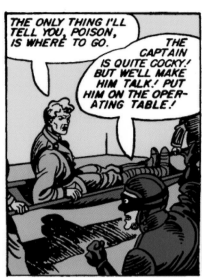

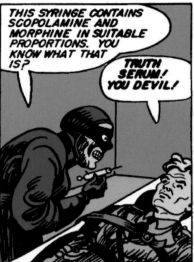

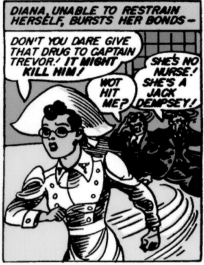

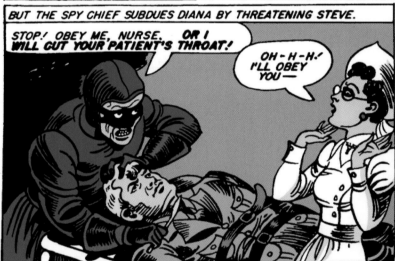

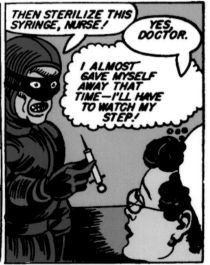

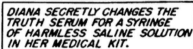

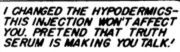

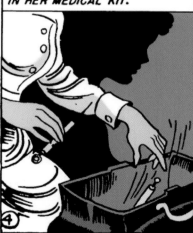

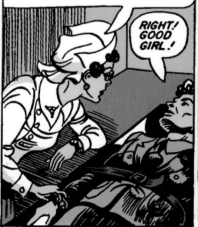

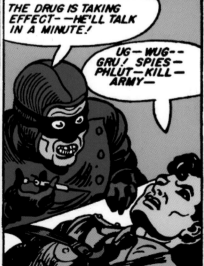

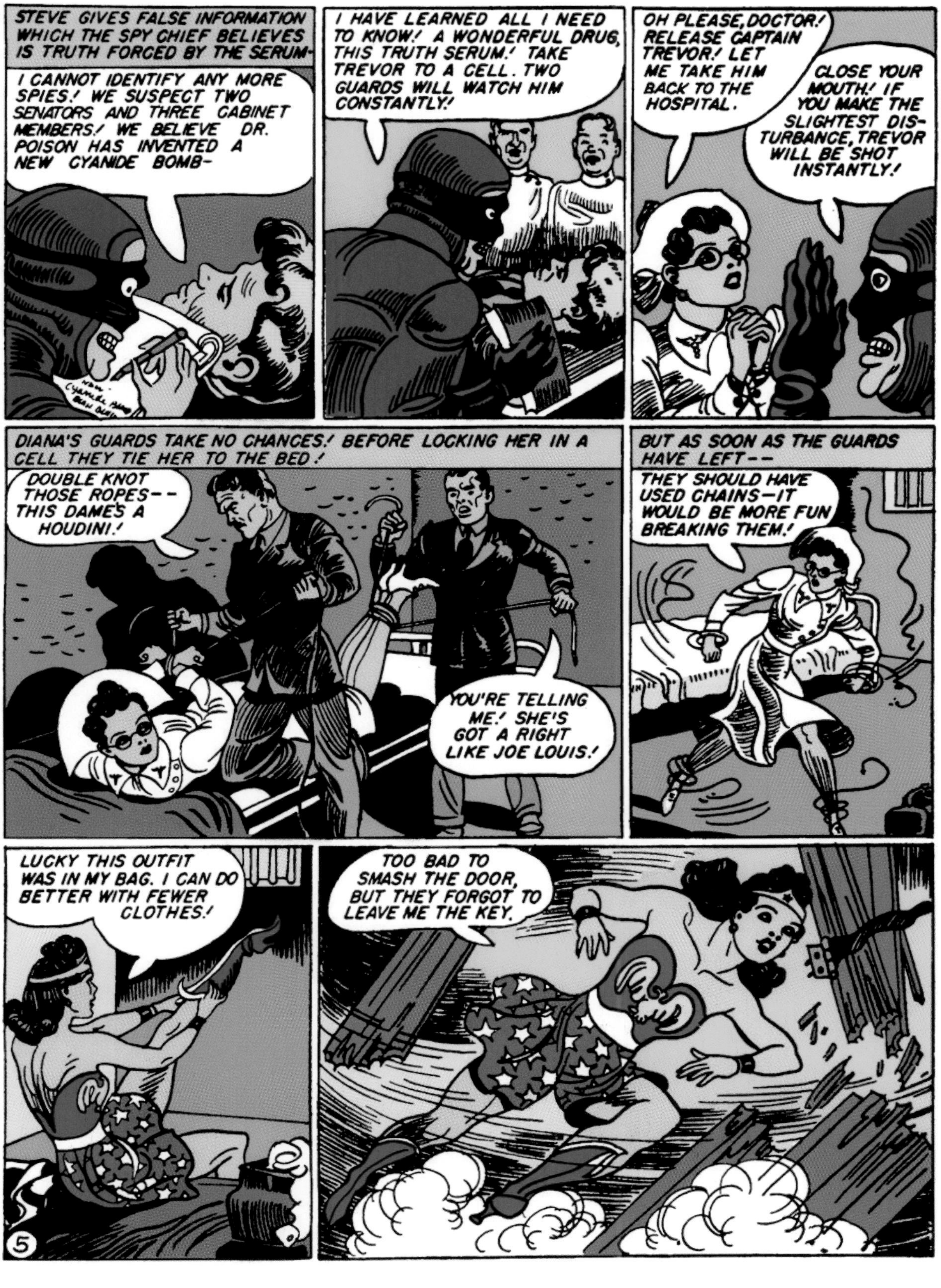
STEVE GIVES FALSE INFORMATION WHICH THE SPY CHIEF BELIEVES IS TRUTH FORCED BY THE SERUM-
I CANNOT IDENTIFY ANY MORE SPIES! WE SUSPECT TWO SENATORS AND THREE CABINET MEMBERS! WE BELIEVE DR. POISON HAS INVENTED A NEW CYANIDE BOMB-
I HAVE LEARNED ALL I NEED TO KNOW! A WONDERFUL DRUG, THIS TRUTH SERUM! TAKE TREVOR TO A CELL. TWO GUARDS WILL WATCH HIM CONSTANTLY!
OH PLEASE, DOCTOR! RELEASE CAPTAIN TREVOR! LET ME TAKE HIM BACK TO THE HOSPITAL.
CLOSE YOUR MOUTH! IF YOU MAKE THE SLIGHTEST DISTURBANCE, TREVOR WILL BE SHOT INSTANTLY!
DIANA'S GUARDS TAKE NO CHANCES! BEFORE LOCKING HER IN A CELL THEY TIE HER TO THE BED!
DOUBLE KNOT THOSE ROPES-- THIS DAME'S A HOUDINI!
YOU'RE TELLING ME! SHE'S GOT A RIGHT LIKE JOE LOUIS!
BUT AS SOON AS THE GUARDS HAVE LEFT--
THEY SHOULD HAVE USED CHAINS—IT WOULD BE MORE FUN BREAKING THEM!
LUCKY THIS OUTFIT WAS IN MY BAG. I CAN DO BETTER WITH FEWER CLOTHES!
TOO BAD TO SMASH THE DOOR, BUT THEY FORGOT TO LEAVE ME THE KEY.
5

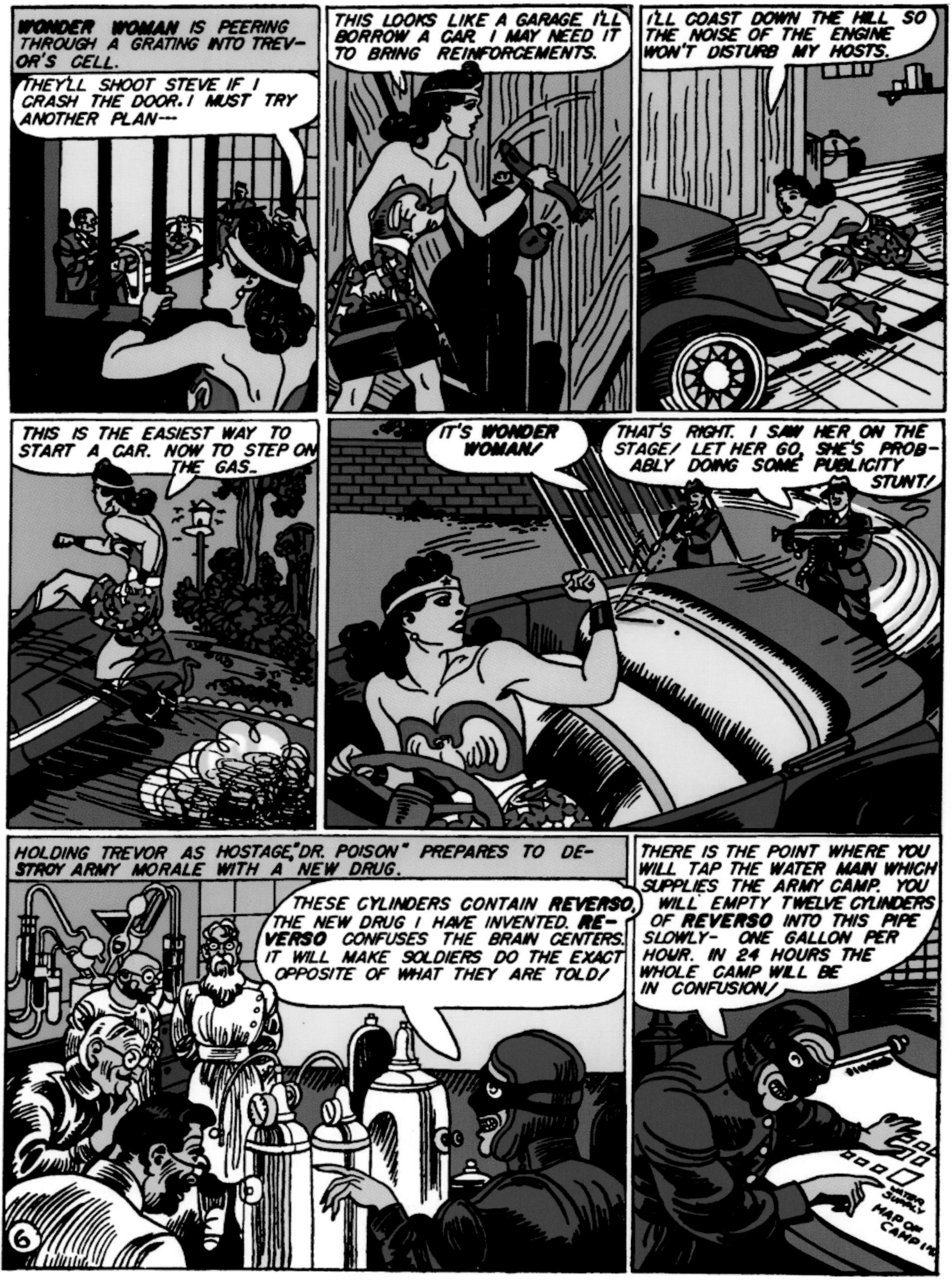
WONDER WOMAN IS PEERING THROUGH A GRATING INTO TREV-OR'S CELL.
THEY'LL SHOOT STEVE IF I CRASH THE DOOR. I MUST TRY ANOTHER PLAN---
THIS LOOKS LIKE A GARAGE. I'LL BORROW A CAR. I MAY NEED IT TO BRING REINFORCEMENTS.
I'LL COAST DOWN THE HILL SO THE NOISE OF THE ENGINE WON'T DISTURB MY HOSTS.
THIS IS THE EASIEST WAY TO START A CAR. NOW TO STEP ON THE GAS.
IT'S WONDER WOMAN!
THAT'S RIGHT. I SAW HER ON THE STAGE! LET HER GO, SHE'S PROB-ABLY DOING SOME PUBLICITY STUNT!
HOLDING TREVOR AS HOSTAGE,"DR. POISON" PREPARES TO DE-STROY ARMY MORALE WITH A NEW DRUG.
THESE CYLINDERS CONTAIN REVERSO, THE NEW DRUG I HAVE INVENTED. RE-VERSO CONFUSES THE BRAIN CENTERS. IT WILL MAKE SOLDIERS DO THE EXACT OPPOSITE OF WHAT THEY ARE TOLD!
THERE IS THE POINT WHERE YOU WILL TAP THE WATER MAIN WHICH SUPPLIES THE ARMY CAMP. YOU WILL EMPTY TWELVE CYLINDERS OF REVERSO INTO THIS PIPE SLOWLY- ONE GALLON PER HOUR. IN 24 HOURS THE WHOLE CAMP WILL BE IN CONFUSION!
6
WATER SUPPLY
MAP OF CAMP

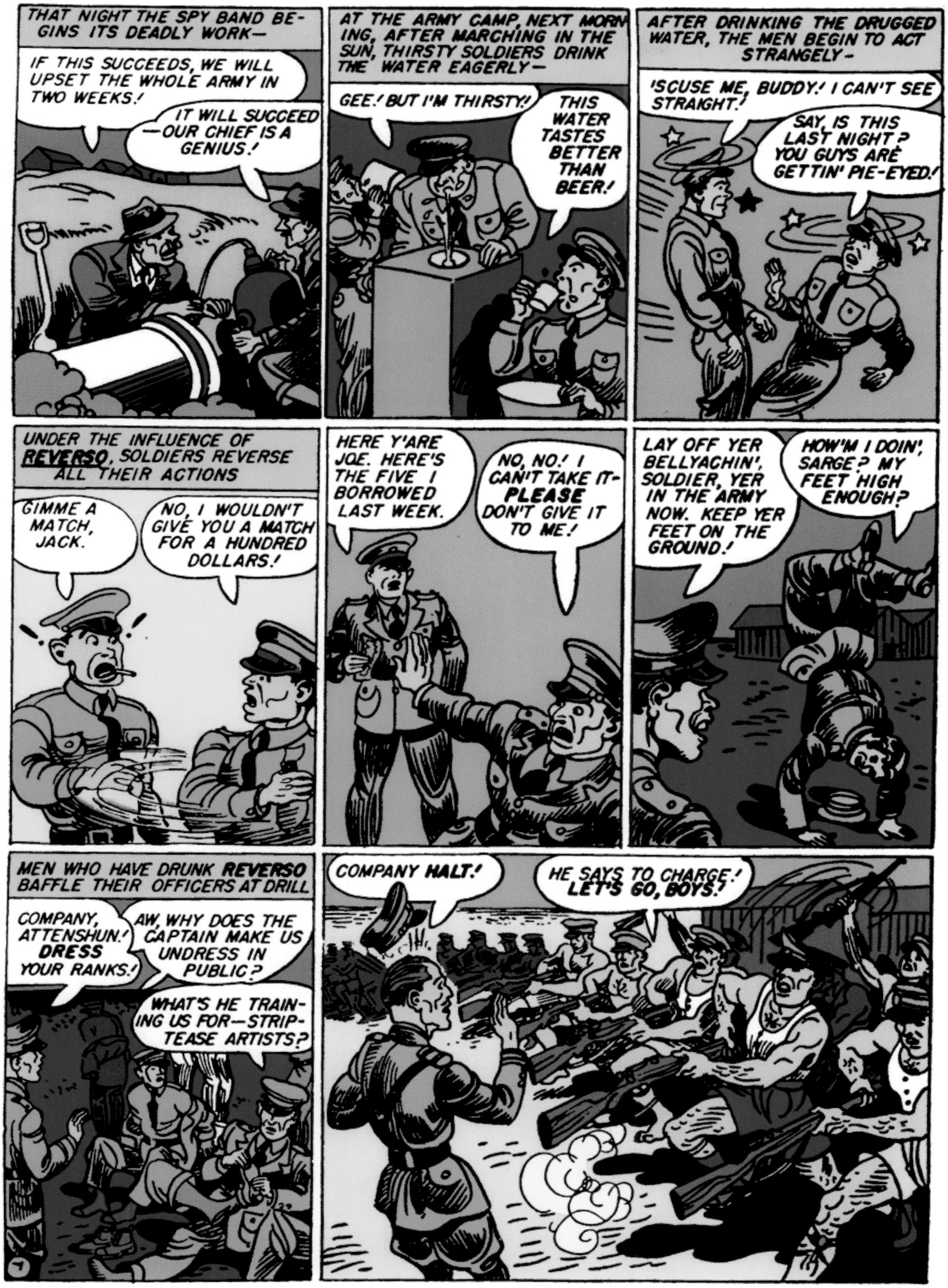
THAT NIGHT THE SPY BAND BEGINS ITS DEADLY WORK—
IF THIS SUCCEEDS, WE WILL UPSET THE WHOLE ARMY IN TWO WEEKS.!
IT WILL SUCCEED —OUR CHIEF IS A GENIUS.!
AT THE ARMY CAMP, NEXT MORNING, AFTER MARCHING IN THE SUN, THIRSTY SOLDIERS DRINK THE WATER EAGERLY—
GEE.! BUT I'M THIRSTY.!
THIS WATER TASTES BETTER THAN BEER.!
AFTER DRINKING THE DRUGGED WATER, THE MEN BEGIN TO ACT STRANGELY—
'SCUSE ME, BUDDY.! I CAN'T SEE STRAIGHT.!
SAY, IS THIS LAST NIGHT? YOU GUYS ARE GETTIN' PIE-EYED.!
UNDER THE INFLUENCE OF REVERSO, SOLDIERS REVERSE ALL THEIR ACTIONS
GIMME A MATCH, JACK.
NO, I WOULDN'T GIVE YOU A MATCH FOR A HUNDRED DOLLARS.!
HERE Y'ARE JOE. HERE'S THE FIVE I BORROWED LAST WEEK.
NO, NO.! I CAN'T TAKE IT- PLEASE DON'T GIVE IT TO ME.!
LAY OFF YER BELLYACHIN', SOLDIER, YER IN THE ARMY NOW. KEEP YER FEET ON THE GROUND.!
HOW'M I DOIN', SARGE? MY FEET HIGH ENOUGH?
MEN WHO HAVE DRUNK REVERSO BAFFLE THEIR OFFICERS AT DRILL
COMPANY, ATTENSHUN.! DRESS YOUR RANKS.!
AW, WHY DOES THE CAPTAIN MAKE US UNDRESS IN PUBLIC?
WHAT'S HE TRAINING US FOR—STRIP-TEASE ARTISTS?
COMPANY HALT.!
HE SAYS TO CHARGE.! LET'S GO, BOYS.!

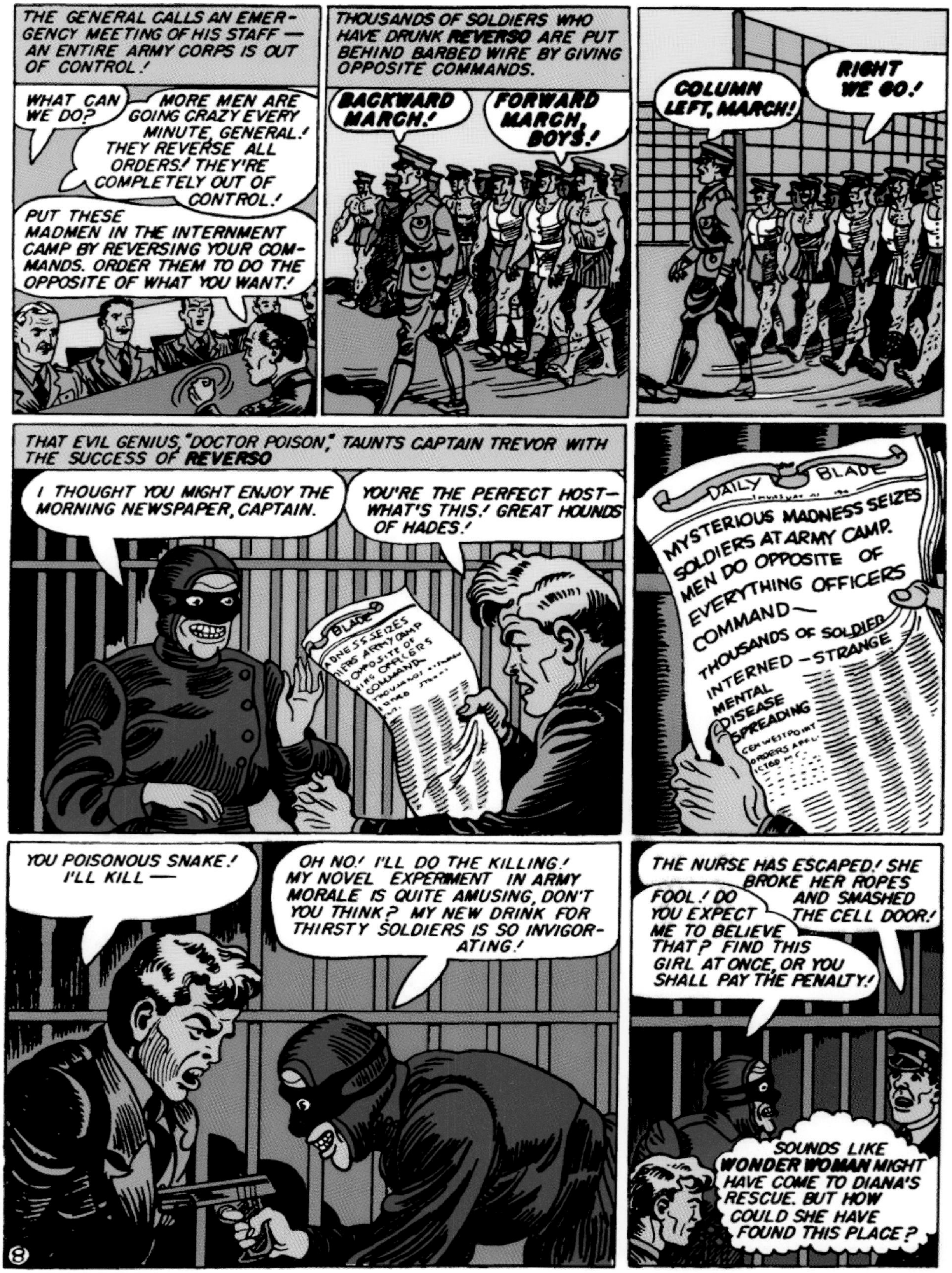

THE GENERAL CALLS AN EMERGENCY MEETING OF HIS STAFF — AN ENTIRE ARMY CORPS IS OUT OF CONTROL!
WHAT CAN WE DO?
MORE MEN ARE GOING CRAZY EVERY MINUTE, GENERAL! THEY REVERSE ALL ORDERS! THEY'RE COMPLETELY OUT OF CONTROL!
PUT THESE MADMEN IN THE INTERNMENT CAMP BY REVERSING YOUR COMMANDS. ORDER THEM TO DO THE OPPOSITE OF WHAT YOU WANT!
THOUSANDS OF SOLDIERS WHO HAVE DRUNK REVERSO ARE PUT BEHIND BARBED WIRE BY GIVING OPPOSITE COMMANDS.
BACKWARD MARCH!
FORWARD MARCH, BOYS!
COLUMN LEFT, MARCH!
RIGHT WE GO!
THAT EVIL GENIUS, "DOCTOR POISON," TAUNTS CAPTAIN TREVOR WITH THE SUCCESS OF REVERSO
I THOUGHT YOU MIGHT ENJOY THE MORNING NEWSPAPER, CAPTAIN.
YOU'RE THE PERFECT HOST— WHAT'S THIS! GREAT HOUNDS OF HADES!
DAILY BLADE
MYSTERIOUS MADNESS SEIZES SOLDIERS AT ARMY CAMP. MEN DO OPPOSITE OF EVERYTHING OFFICERS COMMAND—
THOUSANDS OF SOLDIER INTERNED — STRANGE MENTAL DISEASE SPREADING
YOU POISONOUS SNAKE! I'LL KILL —
OH NO! I'LL DO THE KILLING! MY NOVEL EXPERIMENT IN ARMY MORALE IS QUITE AMUSING, DON'T YOU THINK? MY NEW DRINK FOR THIRSTY SOLDIERS IS SO INVIGORATING!
THE NURSE HAS ESCAPED! SHE BROKE HER ROPES AND SMASHED THE CELL DOOR!
FOOL! DO YOU EXPECT ME TO BELIEVE THAT? FIND THIS GIRL AT ONCE, OR YOU SHALL PAY THE PENALTY!
SOUNDS LIKE WONDER WOMAN MIGHT HAVE COME TO DIANA'S RESCUE. BUT HOW COULD SHE HAVE FOUND THIS PLACE?
8

THE SPY BAND ENTRENCHES AGAINST POSSIBLE ATTACK —
DIG TRENCHES ACROSS THIS ROAD AND DEFEND THEM TO THE LAST MAN! I MUST HAVE TIME TO COMPRESS THE *REVERSO* FOR SHIPMENT. SHOULD THE GIRL WHO ESCAPED BRING SOLDIERS, TELL THEM TREVOR WILL BE SHOT IF THEY ATTACK!

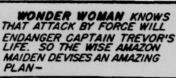

WONDER WOMAN KNOWS THAT ATTACK BY FORCE WILL ENDANGER CAPTAIN TREVOR'S LIFE. SO THE WISE AMAZON MAIDEN DEVISES AN AMAZING PLAN —

HOLLIDAY COLLEGE FOR WOMEN

I AM LOOKING FOR MY FRIEND, ETTA CANDY.

ETTA IS REHEARSING WITH THE BAND IN MUSIC HALL. AND IF THAT'S ONE OF THE NEW BAND COSTUMES YOU'RE WEARING, IT'S NO WONDER THE DEAN SAID YOU MUST TAKE THEM OFF!

REGISTRAR

THAT'S A DUCKY COSTUME, MY PET, BUT THE DEAN WON'T LET YOU WEAR IT! SHE INSISTS ON MORE ABOVE THE WAIST!

I AM NOT HERE TO JOIN THE BAND. I SEEK ETTA CANDY.

THIS IS ETTA CANDY.

OH, I'D NEVER HAVE KNOWN YOU, ETTA! ER-THAT IS-MY FRIEND, DIANA PRINCE, THE NURSE, SAID YOU WERE A THIN GIRL WHEN SHE KNEW YOU IN THE HOSPITAL.

I WAS THIN, ALL RIGHT, WHEN I WENT TO THE HOSPITAL. BUT AFTER THEY TOOK OUT MY APPENDIX, I COULD EAT ANYTHING-SO I DID! NURSE DIANA WAS SWELL TO ME-I'D DO ANYTHING FOR HER-EXCEPT DIET!

HELP ME SAVE THE MAN DIANA LOVES! I'LL TELL YOU ABOUT HIM---

47

SENTIMENTAL ETTA AGREES TO HELP A HANDSOME MAN IN DISTRESS —

BESIDES YOUR BAND, WE NEED A HUNDRED PRETTY GIRLS BRAVE ENOUGH TO CAPTURE DANGEROUS MEN!

SAY! IF YOU'RE OUT TO CATCH *MEN*, EVERY GIRL IN COLLEGE WILL BE GLAD TO HELP! WOO! WOO!

HUNDREDS OF GIRLS VOLUNTEER AND *WONDER WOMAN* PICKS THE PRETTIEST AND STRONGEST —

THIS RECRUIT FILLS OUR QUOTA!

AMERICA'S FIRST WOMEN'S EXPEDITIONARY FORCE! ONE HUNDRED BEAUTIFUL ATHLETIC GIRLS — LIKE ME!

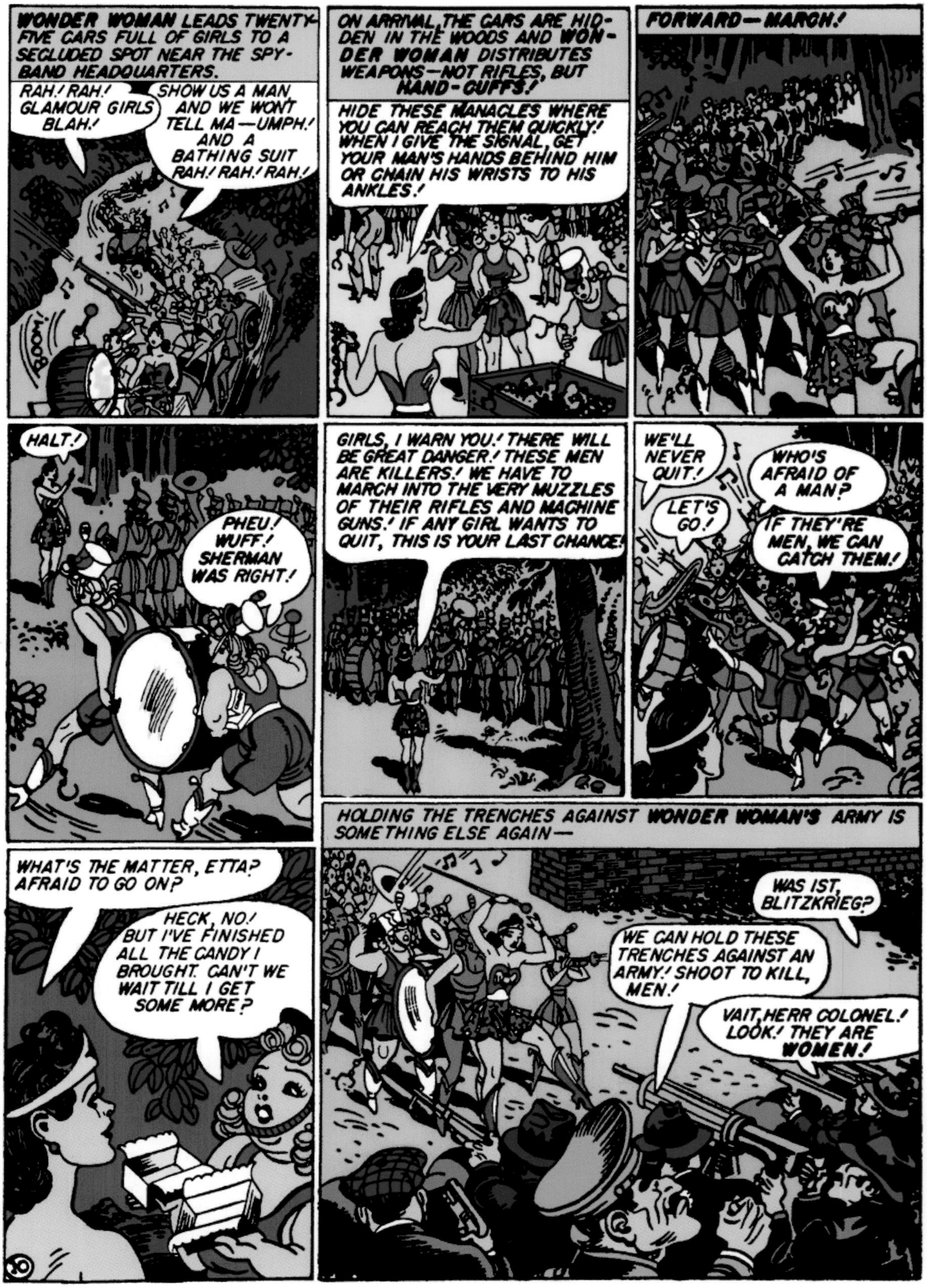
WONDER WOMAN LEADS TWENTY-FIVE CARS FULL OF GIRLS TO A SECLUDED SPOT NEAR THE SPY-BAND HEADQUARTERS.
RAH! RAH! GLAMOUR GIRLS BLAH!
SHOW US A MAN, AND WE WON'T TELL MA—UMPH! AND A BATHING SUIT RAH! RAH! RAH!
BOOM!
ON ARRIVAL, THE CARS ARE HIDDEN IN THE WOODS AND WONDER WOMAN DISTRIBUTES WEAPONS—NOT RIFLES, BUT HAND-CUFFS!
HIDE THESE MANACLES WHERE YOU CAN REACH THEM QUICKLY! WHEN I GIVE THE SIGNAL, GET YOUR MAN'S HANDS BEHIND HIM OR CHAIN HIS WRISTS TO HIS ANKLES!
FORWARD—MARCH!
HALT!
PHEU! WUFF! SHERMAN WAS RIGHT!
GIRLS, I WARN YOU! THERE WILL BE GREAT DANGER! THESE MEN ARE KILLERS! WE HAVE TO MARCH INTO THE VERY MUZZLES OF THEIR RIFLES AND MACHINE GUNS! IF ANY GIRL WANTS TO QUIT, THIS IS YOUR LAST CHANCE!
WE'LL NEVER QUIT!
WHO'S AFRAID OF A MAN?
LET'S GO!
IF THEY'RE MEN, WE CAN CATCH THEM!
WHAT'S THE MATTER, ETTA? AFRAID TO GO ON?
HECK, NO! BUT I'VE FINISHED ALL THE CANDY I BROUGHT. CAN'T WE WAIT TILL I GET SOME MORE?
HOLDING THE TRENCHES AGAINST WONDER WOMAN'S ARMY IS SOMETHING ELSE AGAIN—
WAS IST, BLITZKRIEG?
WE CAN HOLD THESE TRENCHES AGAINST AN ARMY! SHOOT TO KILL, MEN!
VAIT, HERR COLONEL! LOOK! THEY ARE WOMEN!
10

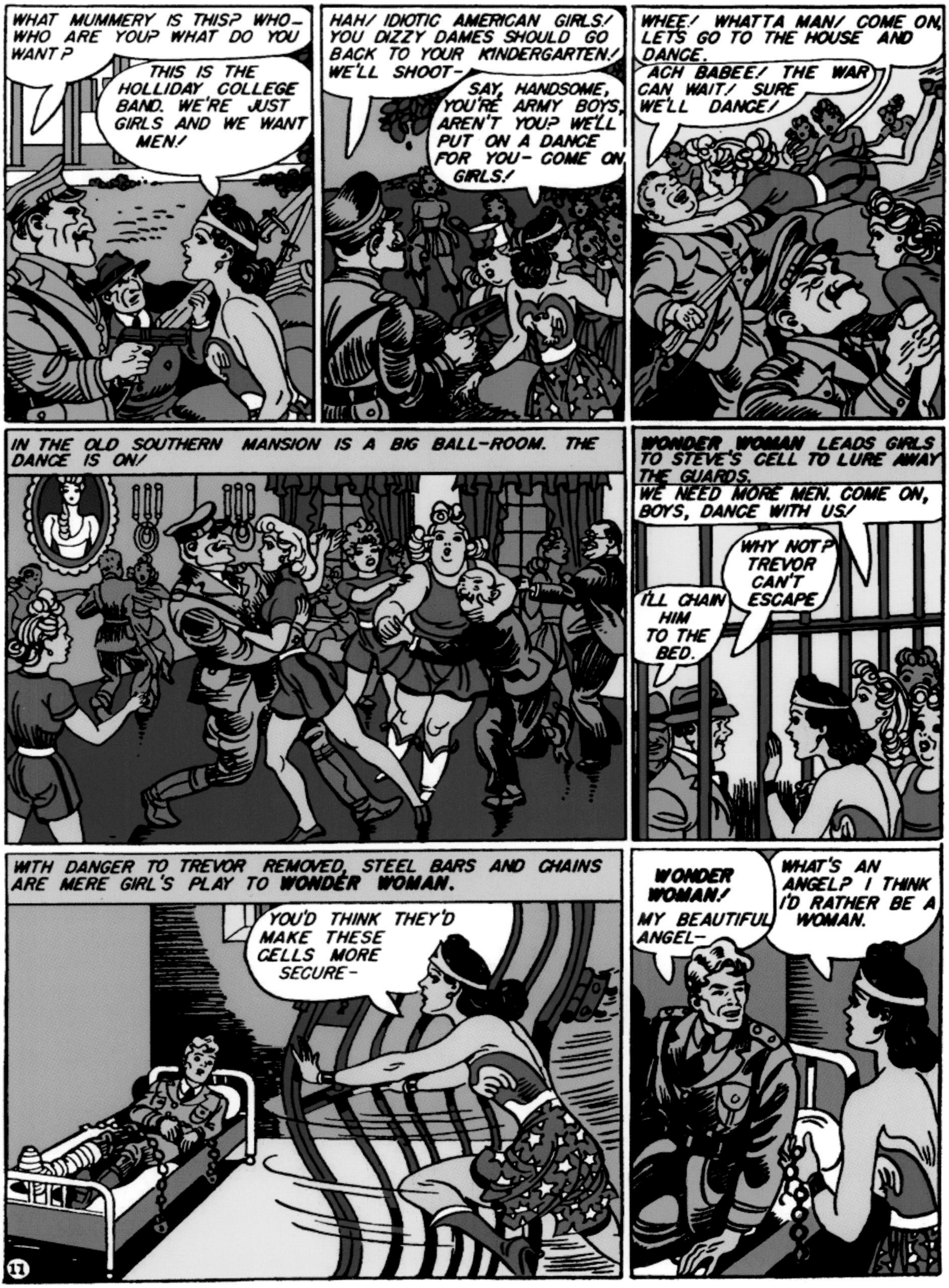
WHAT MUMMERY IS THIS? WHO-WHO ARE YOU? WHAT DO YOU WANT?
THIS IS THE HOLLIDAY COLLEGE BAND. WE'RE JUST GIRLS AND WE WANT MEN!
HAH! IDIOTIC AMERICAN GIRLS! YOU DIZZY DAMES SHOULD GO BACK TO YOUR KINDERGARTEN! WE'LL SHOOT-
SAY, HANDSOME, YOU'RE ARMY BOYS, AREN'T YOU? WE'LL PUT ON A DANCE FOR YOU- COME ON GIRLS!
WHEE! WHATTA MAN! COME ON, LET'S GO TO THE HOUSE AND DANCE.
ACH BABEE! THE WAR CAN WAIT! SURE WE'LL DANCE!
IN THE OLD SOUTHERN MANSION IS A BIG BALL-ROOM. THE DANCE IS ON!
WONDER WOMAN LEADS GIRLS TO STEVE'S CELL TO LURE AWAY THE GUARDS.
WE NEED MORE MEN. COME ON, BOYS, DANCE WITH US!
WHY NOT? TREVOR CAN'T ESCAPE
I'LL CHAIN HIM TO THE BED.
WITH DANGER TO TREVOR REMOVED, STEEL BARS AND CHAINS ARE MERE GIRL'S PLAY TO WONDER WOMAN.
YOU'D THINK THEY'D MAKE THESE CELLS MORE SECURE-
11
WONDER WOMAN! MY BEAUTIFUL ANGEL-
WHAT'S AN ANGEL? I THINK I'D RATHER BE A WOMAN.

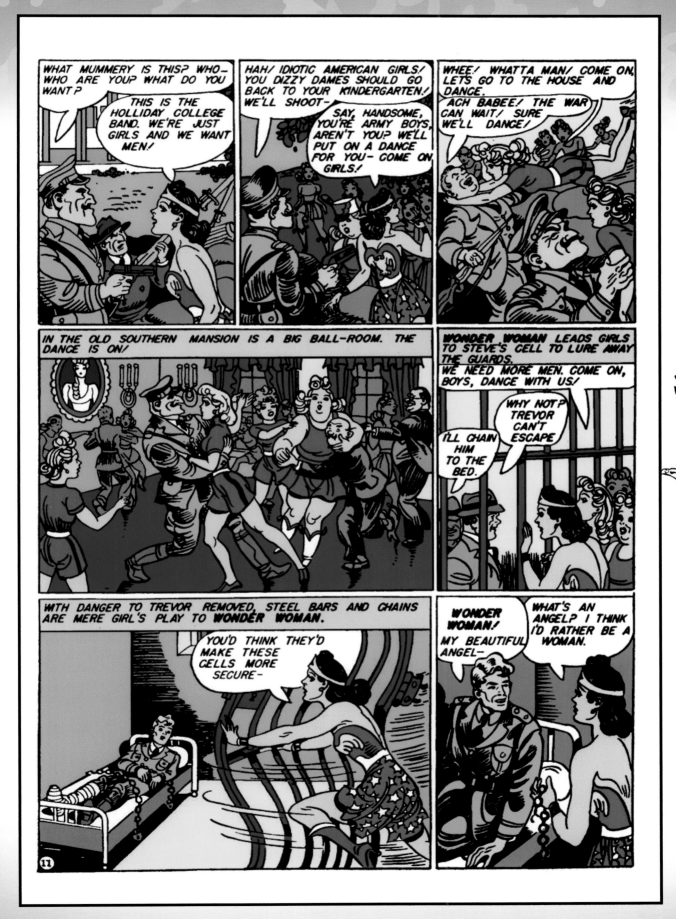

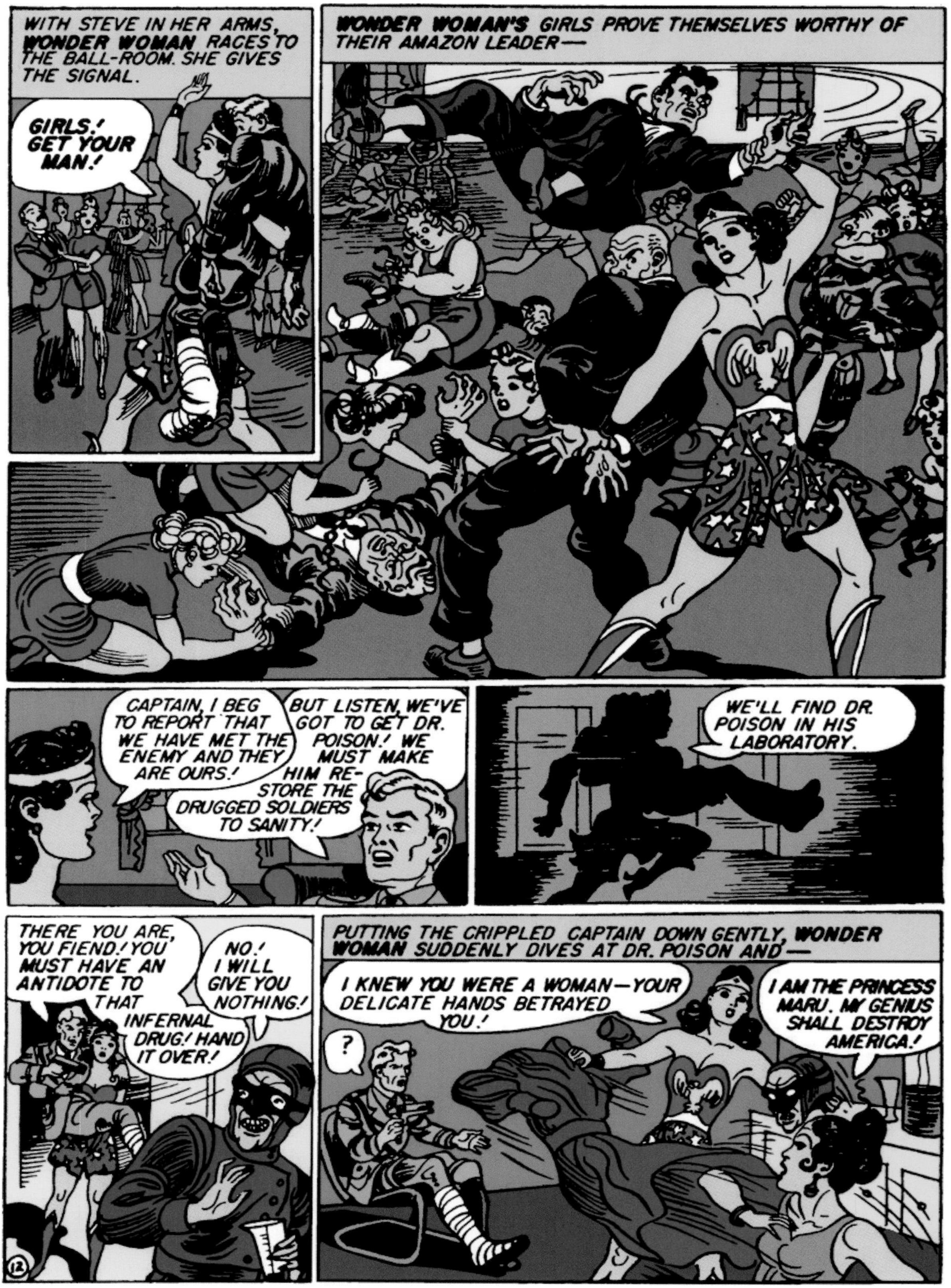
WITH STEVE IN HER ARMS, WONDER WOMAN RACES TO THE BALL-ROOM. SHE GIVES THE SIGNAL.
GIRLS! GET YOUR MAN!
WONDER WOMAN'S GIRLS PROVE THEMSELVES WORTHY OF THEIR AMAZON LEADER—
CAPTAIN, I BEG TO REPORT THAT WE HAVE MET THE ENEMY AND THEY ARE OURS!
BUT LISTEN, WE'VE GOT TO GET DR. POISON! WE MUST MAKE HIM RE-STORE THE DRUGGED SOLDIERS TO SANITY!
WE'LL FIND DR. POISON IN HIS LABORATORY.
THERE YOU ARE, YOU FIEND! YOU MUST HAVE AN ANTIDOTE TO THAT INFERNAL DRUG! HAND IT OVER!
NO! I WILL GIVE YOU NOTHING!
12
PUTTING THE CRIPPLED CAPTAIN DOWN GENTLY, WONDER WOMAN SUDDENLY DIVES AT DR. POISON AND—
I KNEW YOU WERE A WOMAN—YOUR DELICATE HANDS BETRAYED YOU!
?
I AM THE PRINCESS MARU. MY GENIUS SHALL DESTROY AMERICA!

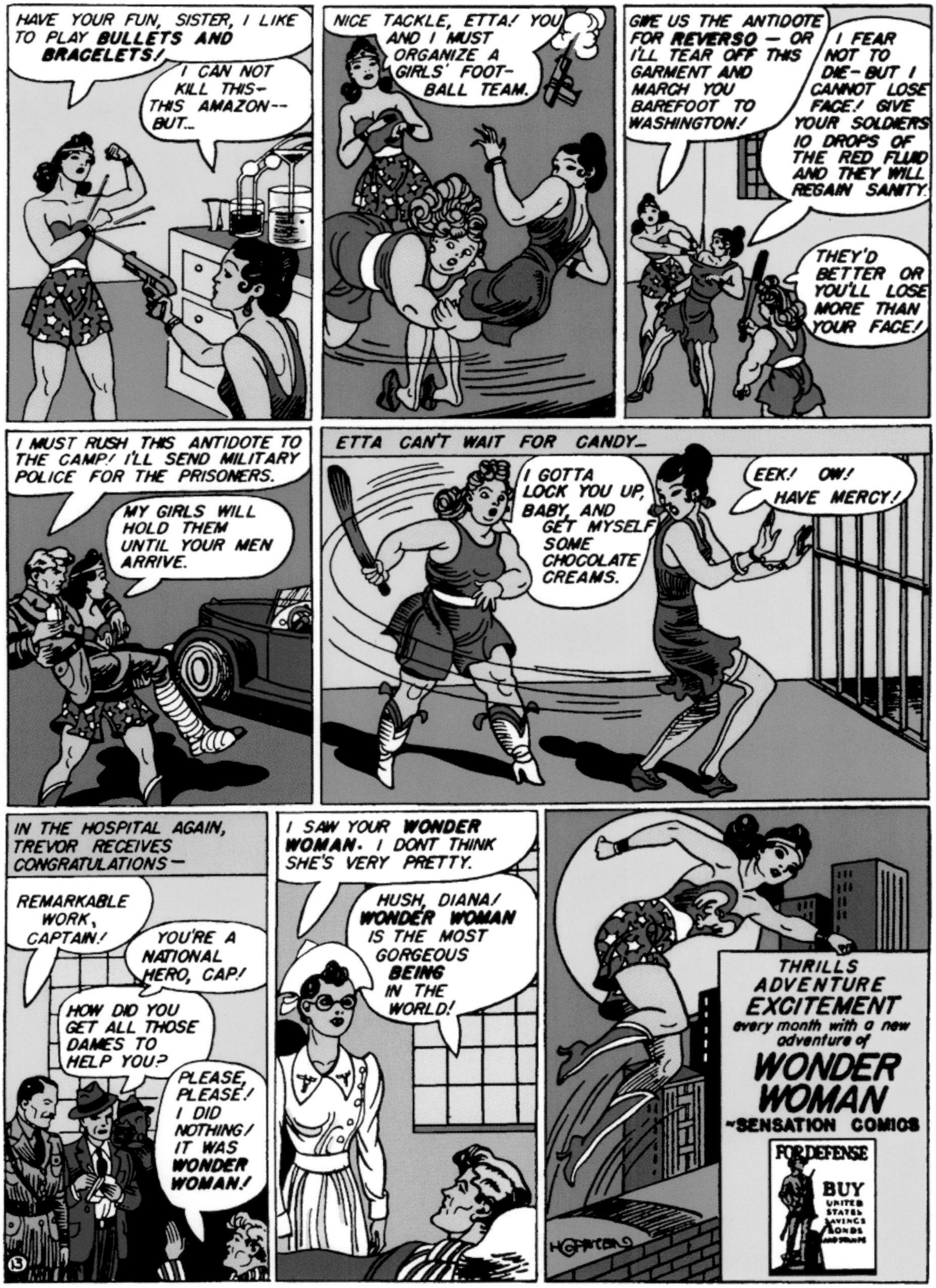
HAVE YOUR FUN, SISTER, I LIKE TO PLAY BULLETS AND BRACELETS!
I CAN NOT KILL THIS- THIS AMAZON-- BUT...
NICE TACKLE, ETTA! YOU AND I MUST ORGANIZE A GIRLS' FOOT-BALL TEAM.
GIVE US THE ANTIDOTE FOR REVERSO — OR I'LL TEAR OFF THIS GARMENT AND MARCH YOU BAREFOOT TO WASHINGTON!
I FEAR NOT TO DIE- BUT I CANNOT LOSE FACE! GIVE YOUR SOLDIERS 10 DROPS OF THE RED FLUID AND THEY WILL REGAIN SANITY.
THEY'D BETTER OR YOU'LL LOSE MORE THAN YOUR FACE!
I MUST RUSH THIS ANTIDOTE TO THE CAMP! I'LL SEND MILITARY POLICE FOR THE PRISONERS.
MY GIRLS WILL HOLD THEM UNTIL YOUR MEN ARRIVE.
ETTA CAN'T WAIT FOR CANDY–
I GOTTA LOCK YOU UP, BABY, AND GET MYSELF SOME CHOCOLATE CREAMS.
EEK! OW! HAVE MERCY!
IN THE HOSPITAL AGAIN, TREVOR RECEIVES CONGRATULATIONS—
REMARKABLE WORK, CAPTAIN!
YOU'RE A NATIONAL HERO, CAP!
HOW DID YOU GET ALL THOSE DAMES TO HELP YOU?
PLEASE, PLEASE! I DID NOTHING! IT WAS WONDER WOMAN!
13
I SAW YOUR WONDER WOMAN. I DONT THINK SHE'S VERY PRETTY.
HUSH, DIANA! WONDER WOMAN IS THE MOST GORGEOUS BEING IN THE WORLD!
THRILLS ADVENTURE EXCITEMENT
every month with a new adventure of
WONDER WOMAN
in SENSATION COMICS
FOR DEFENSE
BUY UNITED STATES SAVINGS BONDS AND STAMPS
H G PETER

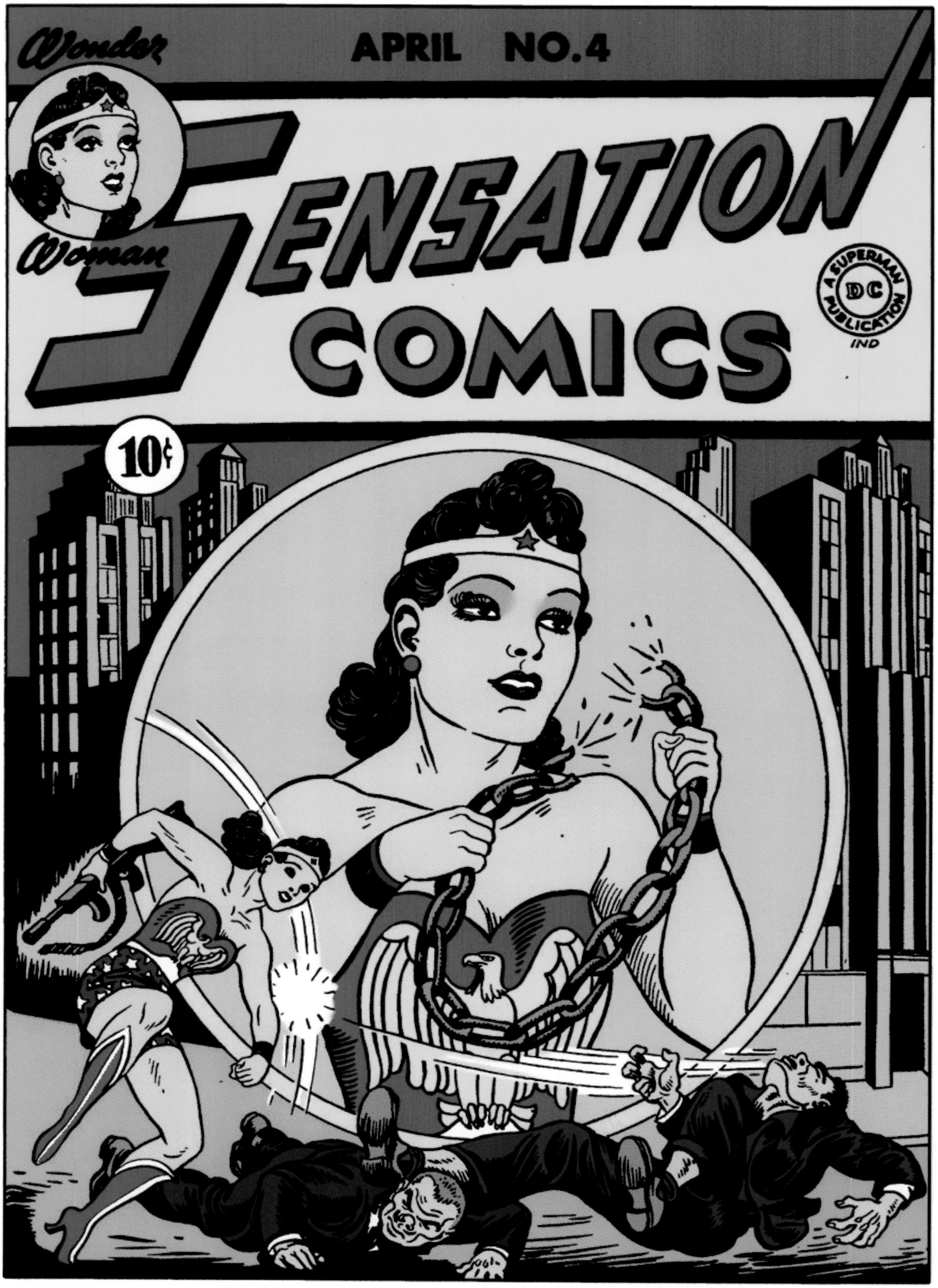
Wonder Woman
APRIL NO.4
SENSATION COMICS
A SUPERMAN DC PUBLICATION
IND
10¢

Sensation Comics #4 (April 1942) - art: H.G. Peter

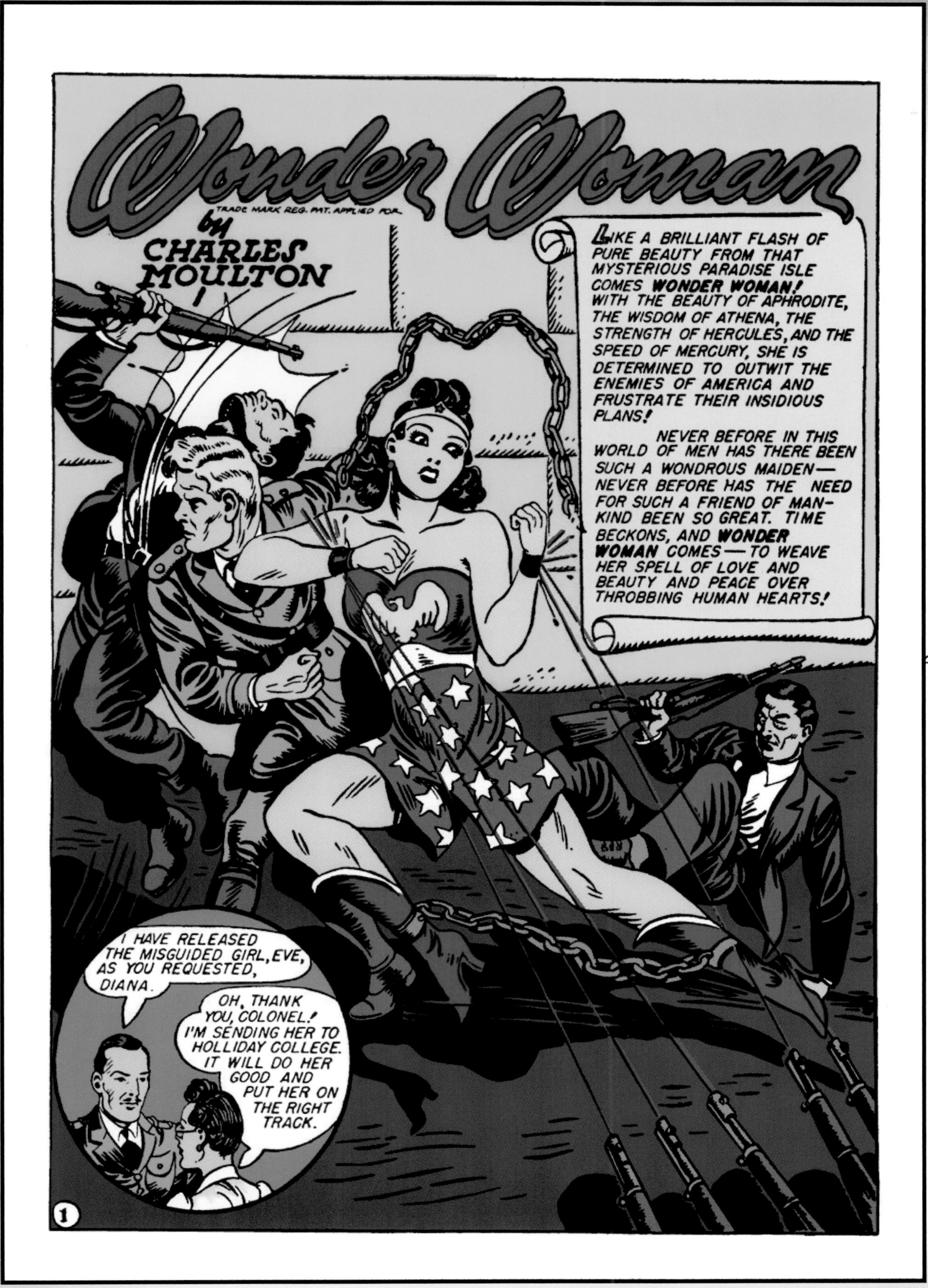
Wonder Woman
TRADE MARK REG. PAT. APPLIED FOR
by CHARLES MOULTON
LIKE A BRILLIANT FLASH OF PURE BEAUTY FROM THAT MYSTERIOUS PARADISE ISLE COMES WONDER WOMAN! WITH THE BEAUTY OF APHRODITE, THE WISDOM OF ATHENA, THE STRENGTH OF HERCULES, AND THE SPEED OF MERCURY, SHE IS DETERMINED TO OUTWIT THE ENEMIES OF AMERICA AND FRUSTRATE THEIR INSIDIOUS PLANS! NEVER BEFORE IN THIS WORLD OF MEN HAS THERE BEEN SUCH A WONDROUS MAIDEN— NEVER BEFORE HAS THE NEED FOR SUCH A FRIEND OF MAN-KIND BEEN SO GREAT. TIME BECKONS, AND WONDER WOMAN COMES—TO WEAVE HER SPELL OF LOVE AND BEAUTY AND PEACE OVER THROBBING HUMAN HEARTS!
I HAVE RELEASED THE MISGUIDED GIRL, EVE, AS YOU REQUESTED, DIANA.
OH, THANK YOU, COLONEL! I'M SENDING HER TO HOLLIDAY COLLEGE. IT WILL DO HER GOOD AND PUT HER ON THE RIGHT TRACK.
1

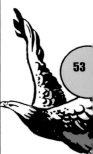

Sensation Comics #4 (April 1942) - script: William Moulton Marston - art: H.G. Peter

I'M SO GLAD THE COLONEL SEES EVE MY WAY—I THINK HE LIKES ME! WOULDN'T IT BE FUN TO MAKE STEVE TREVOR JEALOUS!

NEXT DAY CAPTAIN TREVOR STOPS AT DIANA'S DESK—

SO THE COLONEL RELEASED THAT GIRL, EVE, JUST BECAUSE YOU ASKED HIM TO!

YES, WASN'T THAT SWEET OF HIM?

STEVE IS JEALOUS—HOW PRICELESS!

THAT "SWEET" COLONEL PUT YOU IN CHARGE OF GIRLS' WELFARE, DIDN'T HE? YOU'D BETTER WARN THE GIRLS THERE'S A MANIAC LOOSE. READ THIS!

WHAT? ENID MURDERED! I CAN'T BELIEVE IT!

The Daily Blade

ANOTHER GOV'T GIRL FOUND M POLICE SEEKING ESCAPED FROM

The Daily Blade

ANOTHER GOVERNMENT GIRL FOUND MURDERED ★★★ POLICE SEEKING MANIAC REC ESCAPED FROM INSANE ASYL

THE BODY OF PRETTY ENID HARPER WAS FOUND TODAY NEAR GEORGE-TOWN BRIDGE BRUTALLY MUR-DERED. MISS HARPER WAS A VALUED EM-PLOYEE OF THE ARMY TELLIGENCE ICE.

I DON'T BELIEVE ENID WAS KILLED BY A MANIAC! I'LL BET SHE HAD AN IM-PORTANT MESSAGE THAT ENEMY AGENTS WANTED!

POSITIVELY NOT! ENID HAD NO SECRET DOCUMENTS—SHE'S BEEN OUT SICK FOR A WEEK!

"SICK" FOR A WEEK AND THEN MURDERED---THAT'S QUEER! CAPTAIN TREVOR—STEVE, WON'T YOU PLEASE INVESTIGATE ENID'S MURDER?

SORRY, DIANA. CAN'T DO IT—IT'S FOR THE DISTRICT POLICE AND I CAN'T BUTT IN.

DIANA ISN'T AFRAID OF HURTING THE POLICE DEPARTMENT'S FEELINGS; SHE DETERMINES TO INVESTIGATE.

BRING ME THE ATTENDANCE RECORDS FOR EVERY GIRL IN THIS SERVICE FOR THE LAST MONTH!

YES, MISS PRINCE.

AHA! CARLA SWANSON—SECRETARY TO OUR CHIEF ESPIONAGE OFFICER—REPORTED "SICK" THIS MORNING! MAY BE NOTHING TO IT, BUT I'M GOING TO INVESTIGATE!

②

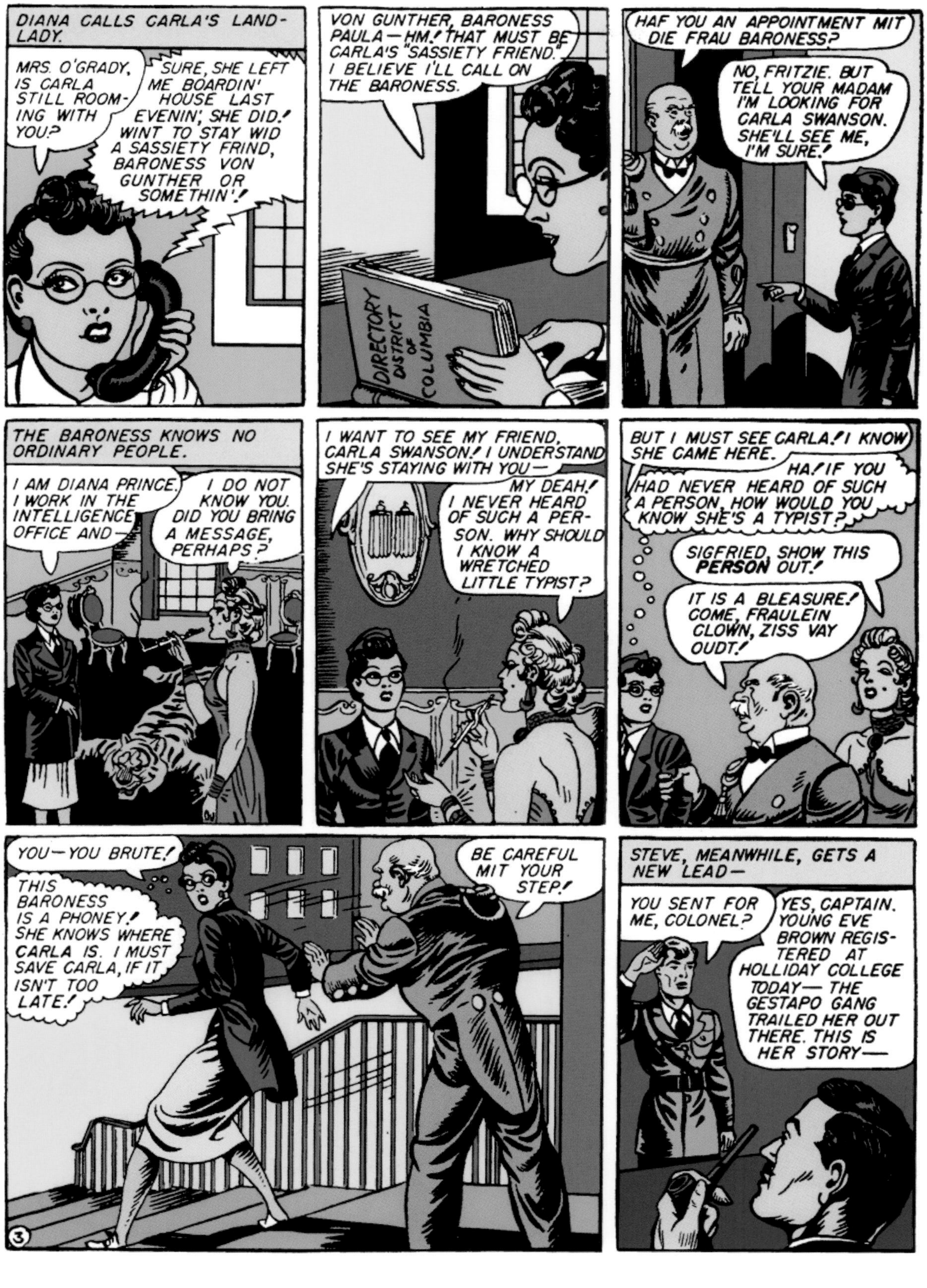
DIANA CALLS CARLA'S LAND-LADY.
MRS. O'GRADY, IS CARLA STILL ROOMING WITH YOU?
SURE, SHE LEFT ME BOARDIN' HOUSE LAST EVENIN', SHE DID! WINT TO STAY WID A SASSIETY FRIND, BARONESS VON GUNTHER OR SOMETHIN'!
VON GUNTHER, BARONESS PAULA—HM! THAT MUST BE CARLA'S "SASSIETY FRIEND." I BELIEVE I'LL CALL ON THE BARONESS.
DIRECTORY DISTRICT OF COLUMBIA
HAF YOU AN APPOINTMENT MIT DIE FRAU BARONESS?
NO, FRITZIE. BUT TELL YOUR MADAM I'M LOOKING FOR CARLA SWANSON. SHE'LL SEE ME, I'M SURE!
THE BARONESS KNOWS NO ORDINARY PEOPLE.
I AM DIANA PRINCE. I WORK IN THE INTELLIGENCE OFFICE AND—
I DO NOT KNOW YOU. DID YOU BRING A MESSAGE, PERHAPS?
I WANT TO SEE MY FRIEND, CARLA SWANSON! I UNDERSTAND SHE'S STAYING WITH YOU—
MY DEAH! I NEVER HEARD OF SUCH A PERSON. WHY SHOULD I KNOW A WRETCHED LITTLE TYPIST?
BUT I MUST SEE CARLA! I KNOW SHE CAME HERE.
HA! IF YOU HAD NEVER HEARD OF SUCH A PERSON, HOW WOULD YOU KNOW SHE'S A TYPIST?
SIGFRIED, SHOW THIS PERSON OUT!
IT IS A BLEASURE! COME, FRAULEIN CLOWN, ZISS VAY OUDT!
YOU—YOU BRUTE!
THIS BARONESS IS A PHONEY! SHE KNOWS WHERE CARLA IS. I MUST SAVE CARLA, IF IT ISN'T TOO LATE!
BE CAREFUL MIT YOUR STEP!
3
STEVE, MEANWHILE, GETS A NEW LEAD—
YOU SENT FOR ME, COLONEL?
YES, CAPTAIN. YOUNG EVE BROWN REGISTERED AT HOLLIDAY COLLEGE TODAY— THE GESTAPO GANG TRAILED HER OUT THERE. THIS IS HER STORY—

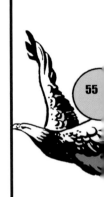

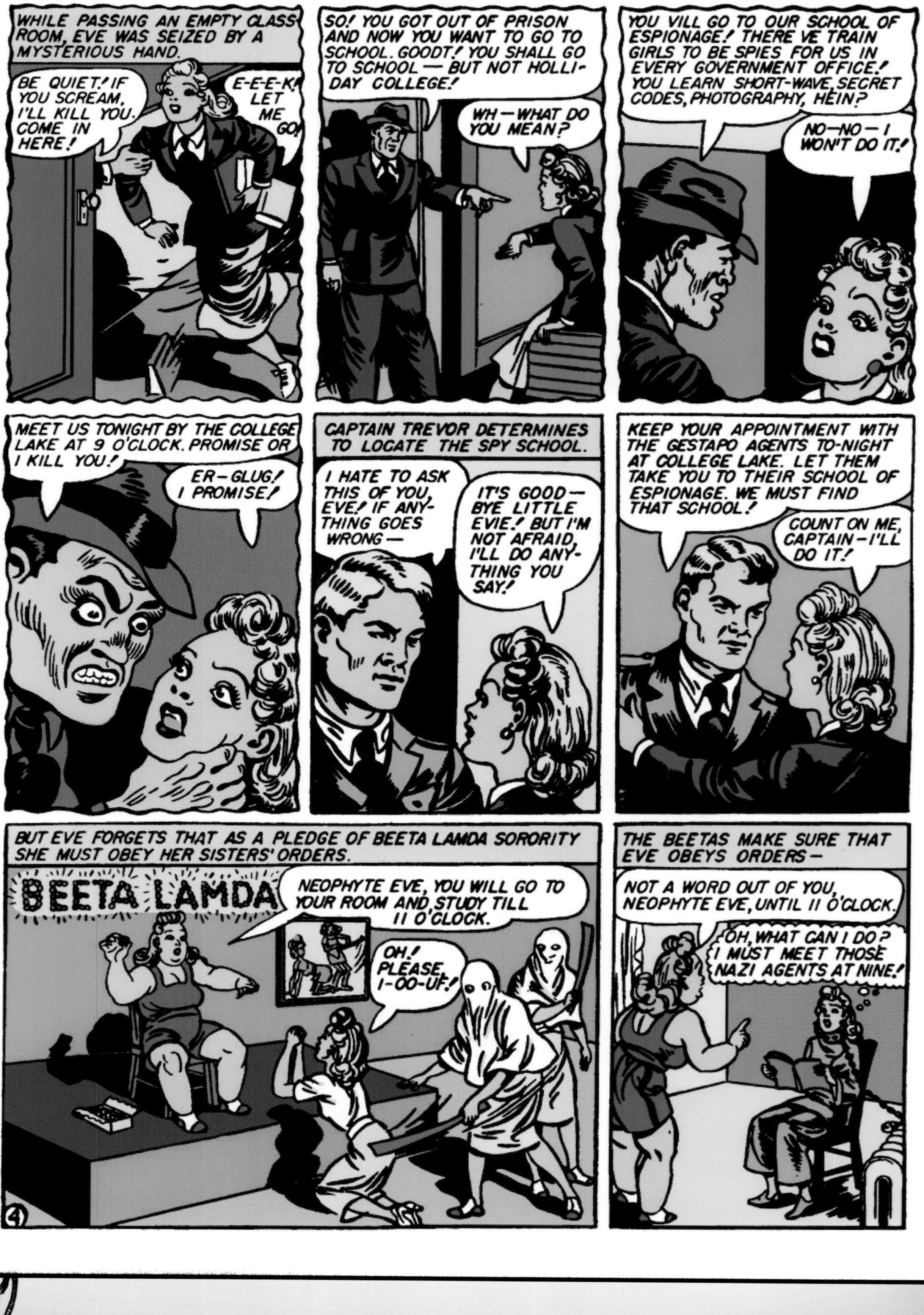
WHILE PASSING AN EMPTY CLASS-ROOM, EVE WAS SEIZED BY A MYSTERIOUS HAND.
BE QUIET! IF YOU SCREAM, I'LL KILL YOU. COME IN HERE!
E-E-E-K! LET ME GO!
SO! YOU GOT OUT OF PRISON AND NOW YOU WANT TO GO TO SCHOOL. GOODT! YOU SHALL GO TO SCHOOL — BUT NOT HOLLI-DAY COLLEGE!
WH—WHAT DO YOU MEAN?
YOU VILL GO TO OUR SCHOOL OF ESPIONAGE! THERE VE TRAIN GIRLS TO BE SPIES FOR US IN EVERY GOVERNMENT OFFICE! YOU LEARN SHORT-WAVE, SECRET CODES, PHOTOGRAPHY, HEIN?
NO—NO—I WON'T DO IT!
MEET US TONIGHT BY THE COLLEGE LAKE AT 9 O'CLOCK. PROMISE OR I KILL YOU!
ER—GLUG! I PROMISE!
CAPTAIN TREVOR DETERMINES TO LOCATE THE SPY SCHOOL.
I HATE TO ASK THIS OF YOU, EVE! IF ANY-THING GOES WRONG —
IT'S GOOD-BYE LITTLE EVIE! BUT I'M NOT AFRAID, I'LL DO ANY-THING YOU SAY!
KEEP YOUR APPOINTMENT WITH THE GESTAPO AGENTS TO-NIGHT AT COLLEGE LAKE. LET THEM TAKE YOU TO THEIR SCHOOL OF ESPIONAGE. WE MUST FIND THAT SCHOOL!
COUNT ON ME, CAPTAIN—I'LL DO IT!
BUT EVE FORGETS THAT AS A PLEDGE OF BEETA LAMDA SORORITY SHE MUST OBEY HER SISTERS' ORDERS.
BEETA LAMDA
NEOPHYTE EVE, YOU WILL GO TO YOUR ROOM AND STUDY TILL 11 O'CLOCK.
OH! PLEASE, I-OO-UF!
4
THE BEETAS MAKE SURE THAT EVE OBEYS ORDERS—
NOT A WORD OUT OF YOU, NEOPHYTE EVE, UNTIL 11 O'CLOCK.
OH, WHAT CAN I DO? I MUST MEET THOSE NAZI AGENTS AT NINE!

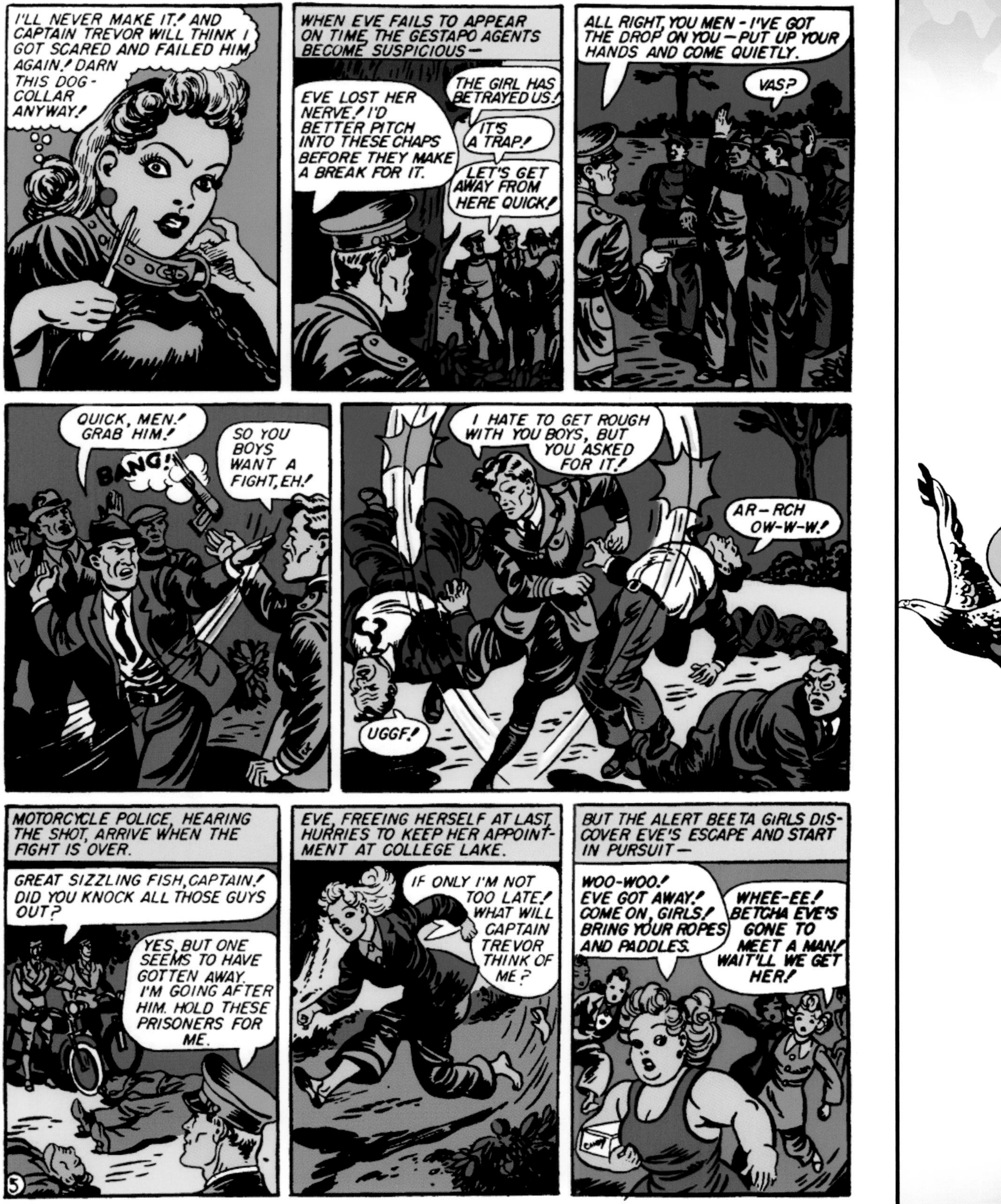

I'LL NEVER MAKE IT! AND CAPTAIN TREVOR WILL THINK I GOT SCARED AND FAILED HIM AGAIN! DARN THIS DOG-COLLAR ANYWAY!
WHEN EVE FAILS TO APPEAR ON TIME, THE GESTAPO AGENTS BECOME SUSPICIOUS—
EVE LOST HER NERVE! I'D BETTER PITCH INTO THESE CHAPS BEFORE THEY MAKE A BREAK FOR IT.
THE GIRL HAS BETRAYED US!
IT'S A TRAP!
LET'S GET AWAY FROM HERE QUICK!
ALL RIGHT, YOU MEN - I'VE GOT THE DROP ON YOU—PUT UP YOUR HANDS AND COME QUIETLY.
VAS?
QUICK, MEN! GRAB HIM!
BANG!
SO YOU BOYS WANT A FIGHT, EH!
I HATE TO GET ROUGH WITH YOU BOYS, BUT YOU ASKED FOR IT!
AR—RCH OW-W-W!
UGGF!
MOTORCYCLE POLICE, HEARING THE SHOT, ARRIVE WHEN THE FIGHT IS OVER.
GREAT SIZZLING FISH, CAPTAIN! DID YOU KNOCK ALL THOSE GUYS OUT?
YES, BUT ONE SEEMS TO HAVE GOTTEN AWAY. I'M GOING AFTER HIM. HOLD THESE PRISONERS FOR ME.
5
EVE, FREEING HERSELF AT LAST, HURRIES TO KEEP HER APPOINTMENT AT COLLEGE LAKE.
IF ONLY I'M NOT TOO LATE! WHAT WILL CAPTAIN TREVOR THINK OF ME?
BUT THE ALERT BEETA GIRLS DISCOVER EVE'S ESCAPE AND START IN PURSUIT—
WOO-WOO! EVE GOT AWAY! COME ON, GIRLS! BRING YOUR ROPES AND PADDLES.
WHEE-EE! BETCHA EVE'S GONE TO MEET A MAN! WAIT'LL WE GET HER!

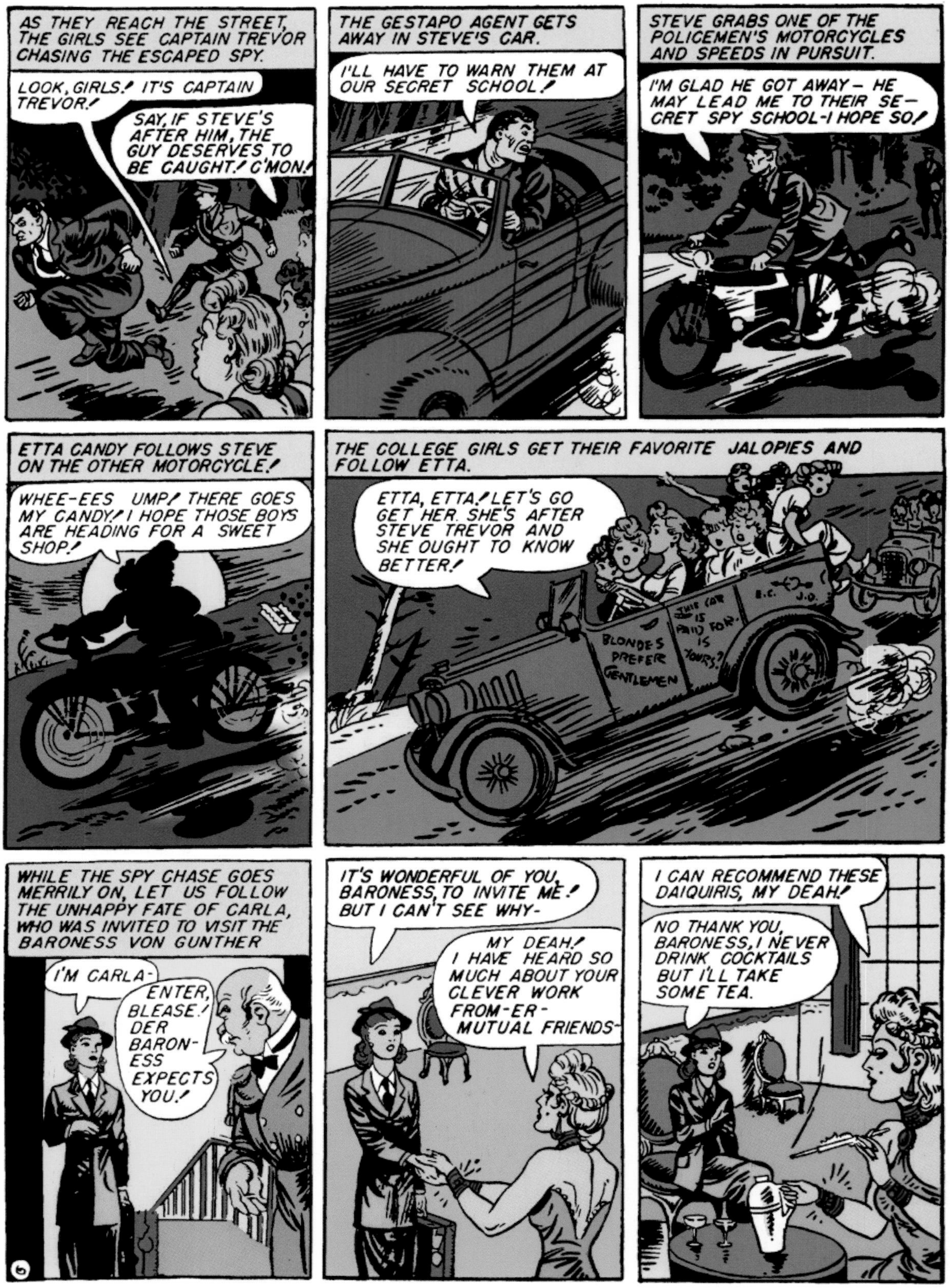
AS THEY REACH THE STREET, THE GIRLS SEE CAPTAIN TREVOR CHASING THE ESCAPED SPY.
LOOK, GIRLS! IT'S CAPTAIN TREVOR!
SAY, IF STEVE'S AFTER HIM, THE GUY DESERVES TO BE CAUGHT! C'MON!
THE GESTAPO AGENT GETS AWAY IN STEVE'S CAR.
I'LL HAVE TO WARN THEM AT OUR SECRET SCHOOL!
STEVE GRABS ONE OF THE POLICEMEN'S MOTORCYCLES AND SPEEDS IN PURSUIT.
I'M GLAD HE GOT AWAY— HE MAY LEAD ME TO THEIR SECRET SPY SCHOOL-I HOPE SO!
ETTA CANDY FOLLOWS STEVE ON THE OTHER MOTORCYCLE!
WHEE-EES UMP! THERE GOES MY CANDY! I HOPE THOSE BOYS ARE HEADING FOR A SWEET SHOP!
THE COLLEGE GIRLS GET THEIR FAVORITE JALOPIES AND FOLLOW ETTA.
ETTA, ETTA! LET'S GO GET HER. SHE'S AFTER STEVE TREVOR AND SHE OUGHT TO KNOW BETTER!
BLONDES PREFER GENTLEMEN
THIS CAR IS PAID FOR- IS YOURS?
WHILE THE SPY CHASE GOES MERRILY ON, LET US FOLLOW THE UNHAPPY FATE OF CARLA, WHO WAS INVITED TO VISIT THE BARONESS VON GUNTHER
I'M CARLA-
ENTER, BLEASE! DER BARONESS EXPECTS YOU!
IT'S WONDERFUL OF YOU, BARONESS, TO INVITE ME! BUT I CAN'T SEE WHY-
MY DEAH! I HAVE HEARD SO MUCH ABOUT YOUR CLEVER WORK FROM-ER-MUTUAL FRIENDS-
I CAN RECOMMEND THESE DAIQUIRIS, MY DEAH!
NO THANK YOU, BARONESS, I NEVER DRINK COCKTAILS BUT I'LL TAKE SOME TEA.

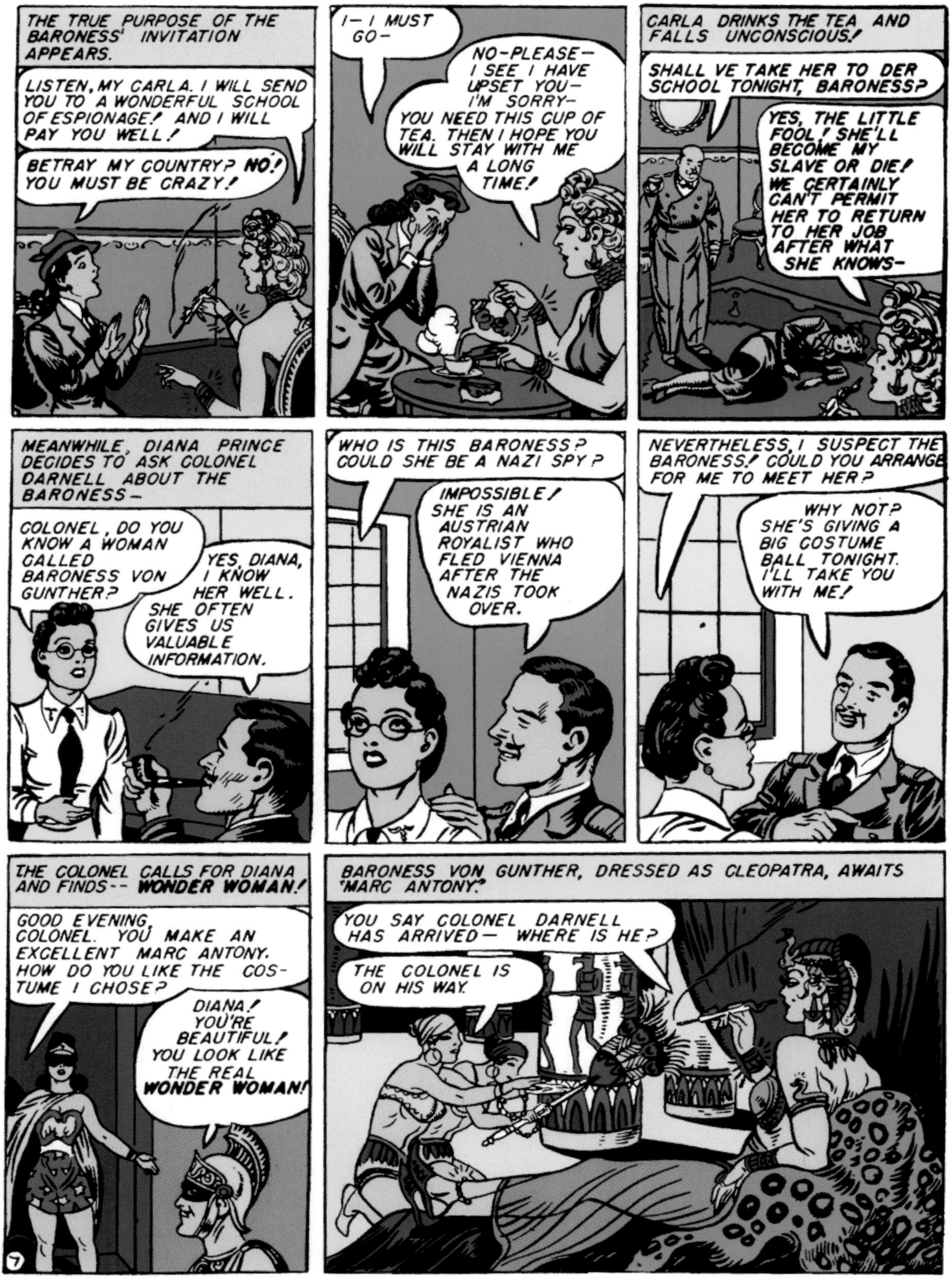
THE TRUE PURPOSE OF THE BARONESS' INVITATION APPEARS.
LISTEN, MY CARLA. I WILL SEND YOU TO A WONDERFUL SCHOOL OF ESPIONAGE! AND I WILL PAY YOU WELL!
BETRAY MY COUNTRY? NO! YOU MUST BE CRAZY!
I-I MUST GO-
NO-PLEASE- I SEE I HAVE UPSET YOU- I'M SORRY- YOU NEED THIS CUP OF TEA. THEN I HOPE YOU WILL STAY WITH ME A LONG TIME!
CARLA DRINKS THE TEA AND FALLS UNCONSCIOUS!
SHALL VE TAKE HER TO DER SCHOOL TONIGHT, BARONESS?
YES, THE LITTLE FOOL! SHE'LL BECOME MY SLAVE OR DIE! WE CERTAINLY CAN'T PERMIT HER TO RETURN TO HER JOB AFTER WHAT SHE KNOWS-
MEANWHILE, DIANA PRINCE DECIDES TO ASK COLONEL DARNELL ABOUT THE BARONESS-
COLONEL, DO YOU KNOW A WOMAN CALLED BARONESS VON GUNTHER?
YES, DIANA, I KNOW HER WELL. SHE OFTEN GIVES US VALUABLE INFORMATION.
WHO IS THIS BARONESS? COULD SHE BE A NAZI SPY?
IMPOSSIBLE! SHE IS AN AUSTRIAN ROYALIST WHO FLED VIENNA AFTER THE NAZIS TOOK OVER.
NEVERTHELESS, I SUSPECT THE BARONESS! COULD YOU ARRANGE FOR ME TO MEET HER?
WHY NOT? SHE'S GIVING A BIG COSTUME BALL TONIGHT. I'LL TAKE YOU WITH ME!
THE COLONEL CALLS FOR DIANA AND FINDS-- WONDER WOMAN!
GOOD EVENING, COLONEL. YOU MAKE AN EXCELLENT MARC ANTONY. HOW DO YOU LIKE THE COSTUME I CHOSE?
DIANA! YOU'RE BEAUTIFUL! YOU LOOK LIKE THE REAL WONDER WOMAN!
7
BARONESS VON GUNTHER, DRESSED AS CLEOPATRA, AWAITS "MARC ANTONY."
YOU SAY COLONEL DARNELL HAS ARRIVED- WHERE IS HE?
THE COLONEL IS ON HIS WAY.

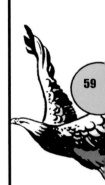

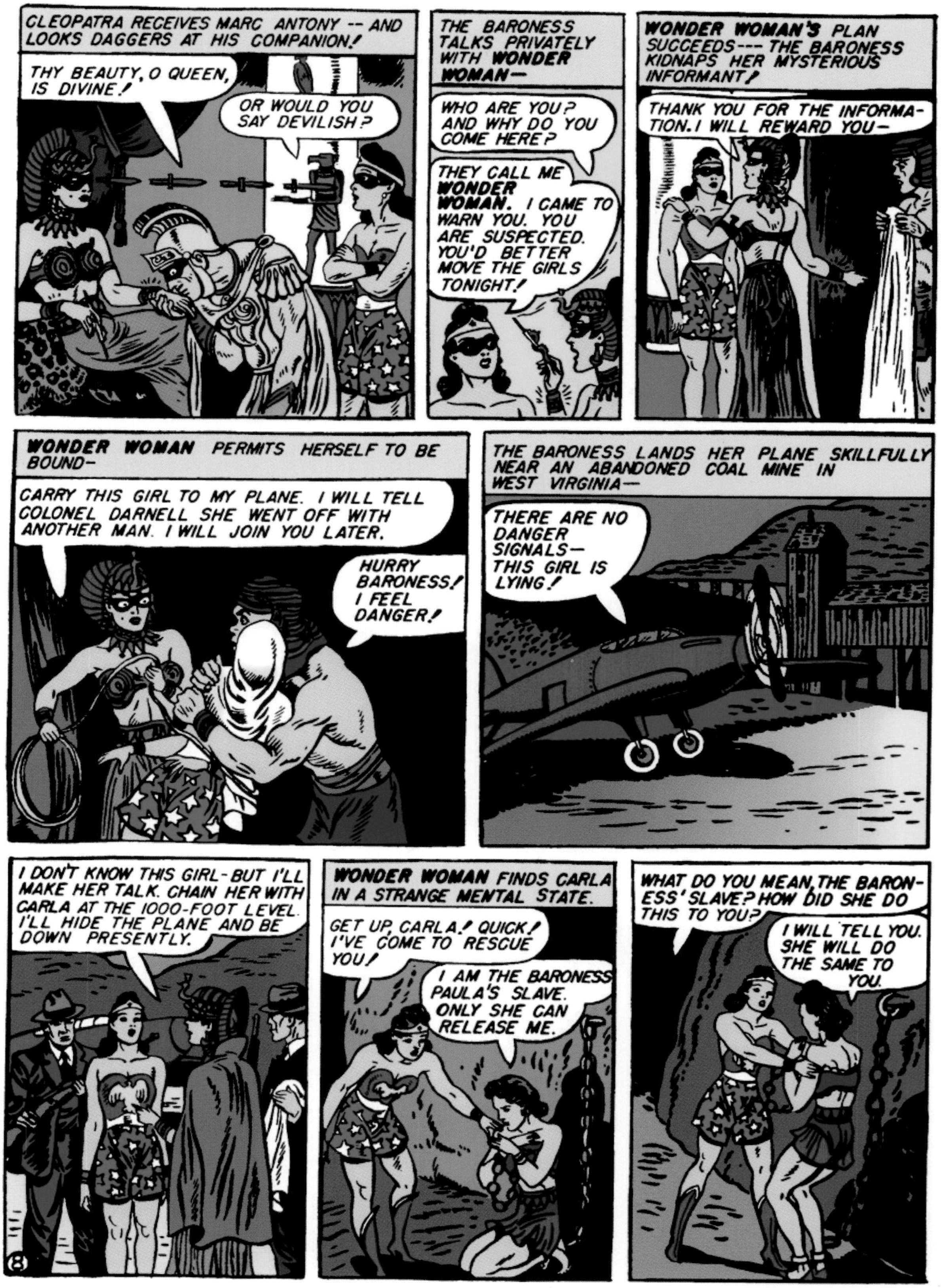
CLEOPATRA RECEIVES MARC ANTONY -- AND LOOKS DAGGERS AT HIS COMPANION!
THY BEAUTY, O QUEEN, IS DIVINE!
OR WOULD YOU SAY DEVILISH?
THE BARONESS TALKS PRIVATELY WITH WONDER WOMAN—
WHO ARE YOU? AND WHY DO YOU COME HERE?
THEY CALL ME WONDER WOMAN. I CAME TO WARN YOU. YOU ARE SUSPECTED. YOU'D BETTER MOVE THE GIRLS TONIGHT!
WONDER WOMAN'S PLAN SUCCEEDS--- THE BARONESS KIDNAPS HER MYSTERIOUS INFORMANT!
THANK YOU FOR THE INFORMATION. I WILL REWARD YOU—
WONDER WOMAN PERMITS HERSELF TO BE BOUND—
CARRY THIS GIRL TO MY PLANE. I WILL TELL COLONEL DARNELL SHE WENT OFF WITH ANOTHER MAN. I WILL JOIN YOU LATER.
HURRY BARONESS! I FEEL DANGER!
THE BARONESS LANDS HER PLANE SKILLFULLY NEAR AN ABANDONED COAL MINE IN WEST VIRGINIA—
THERE ARE NO DANGER SIGNALS— THIS GIRL IS LYING!
I DON'T KNOW THIS GIRL- BUT I'LL MAKE HER TALK. CHAIN HER WITH CARLA AT THE 1000-FOOT LEVEL. I'LL HIDE THE PLANE AND BE DOWN PRESENTLY.
8
WONDER WOMAN FINDS CARLA IN A STRANGE MENTAL STATE.
GET UP, CARLA! QUICK! I'VE COME TO RESCUE YOU!
I AM THE BARONESS PAULA'S SLAVE. ONLY SHE CAN RELEASE ME.
WHAT DO YOU MEAN, THE BARONESS' SLAVE? HOW DID SHE DO THIS TO YOU?
I WILL TELL YOU. SHE WILL DO THE SAME TO YOU.

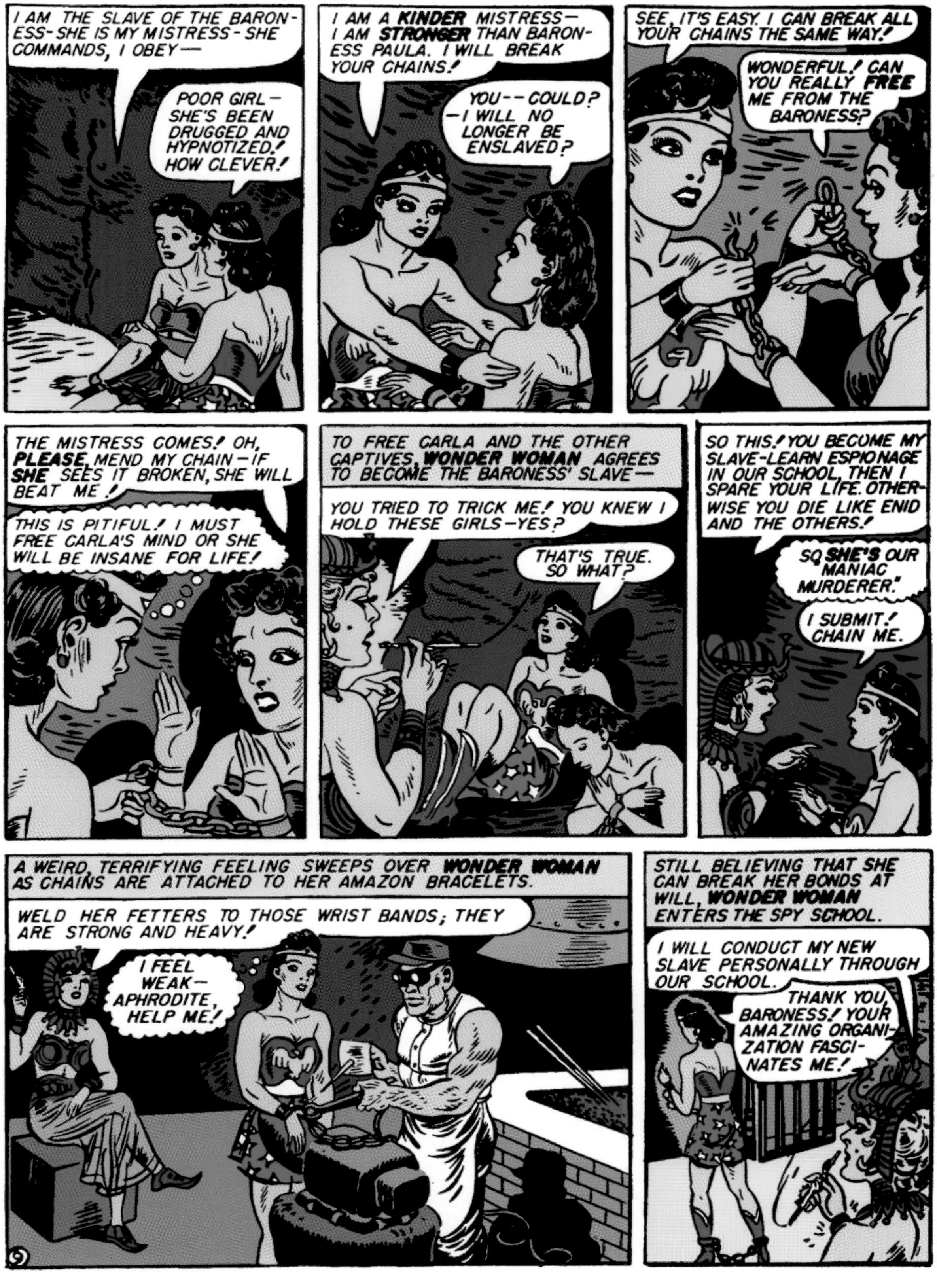
I AM THE SLAVE OF THE BARONESS-SHE IS MY MISTRESS - SHE COMMANDS, I OBEY—
POOR GIRL—SHE'S BEEN DRUGGED AND HYPNOTIZED! HOW CLEVER!
I AM A KINDER MISTRESS—I AM STRONGER THAN BARONESS PAULA. I WILL BREAK YOUR CHAINS!
YOU--COULD? -I WILL NO LONGER BE ENSLAVED?
SEE, IT'S EASY. I CAN BREAK ALL YOUR CHAINS THE SAME WAY!
WONDERFUL! CAN YOU REALLY FREE ME FROM THE BARONESS?
THE MISTRESS COMES! OH, PLEASE, MEND MY CHAIN—IF SHE SEES IT BROKEN, SHE WILL BEAT ME!
THIS IS PITIFUL! I MUST FREE CARLA'S MIND OR SHE WILL BE INSANE FOR LIFE!
TO FREE CARLA AND THE OTHER CAPTIVES, WONDER WOMAN AGREES TO BECOME THE BARONESS' SLAVE—
YOU TRIED TO TRICK ME! YOU KNEW I HOLD THESE GIRLS—YES?
THAT'S TRUE. SO WHAT?
SO THIS! YOU BECOME MY SLAVE-LEARN ESPIONAGE IN OUR SCHOOL, THEN I SPARE YOUR LIFE. OTHERWISE YOU DIE LIKE ENID AND THE OTHERS!
SO SHE'S OUR MANIAC MURDERER!
I SUBMIT! CHAIN ME.
A WEIRD, TERRIFYING FEELING SWEEPS OVER WONDER WOMAN AS CHAINS ARE ATTACHED TO HER AMAZON BRACELETS.
WELD HER FETTERS TO THOSE WRIST BANDS; THEY ARE STRONG AND HEAVY!
I FEEL WEAK—APHRODITE, HELP ME!
9
STILL BELIEVING THAT SHE CAN BREAK HER BONDS AT WILL, WONDER WOMAN ENTERS THE SPY SCHOOL.
I WILL CONDUCT MY NEW SLAVE PERSONALLY THROUGH OUR SCHOOL.
THANK YOU, BARONESS! YOUR AMAZING ORGANIZATION FASCINATES ME!

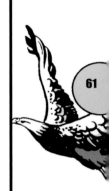

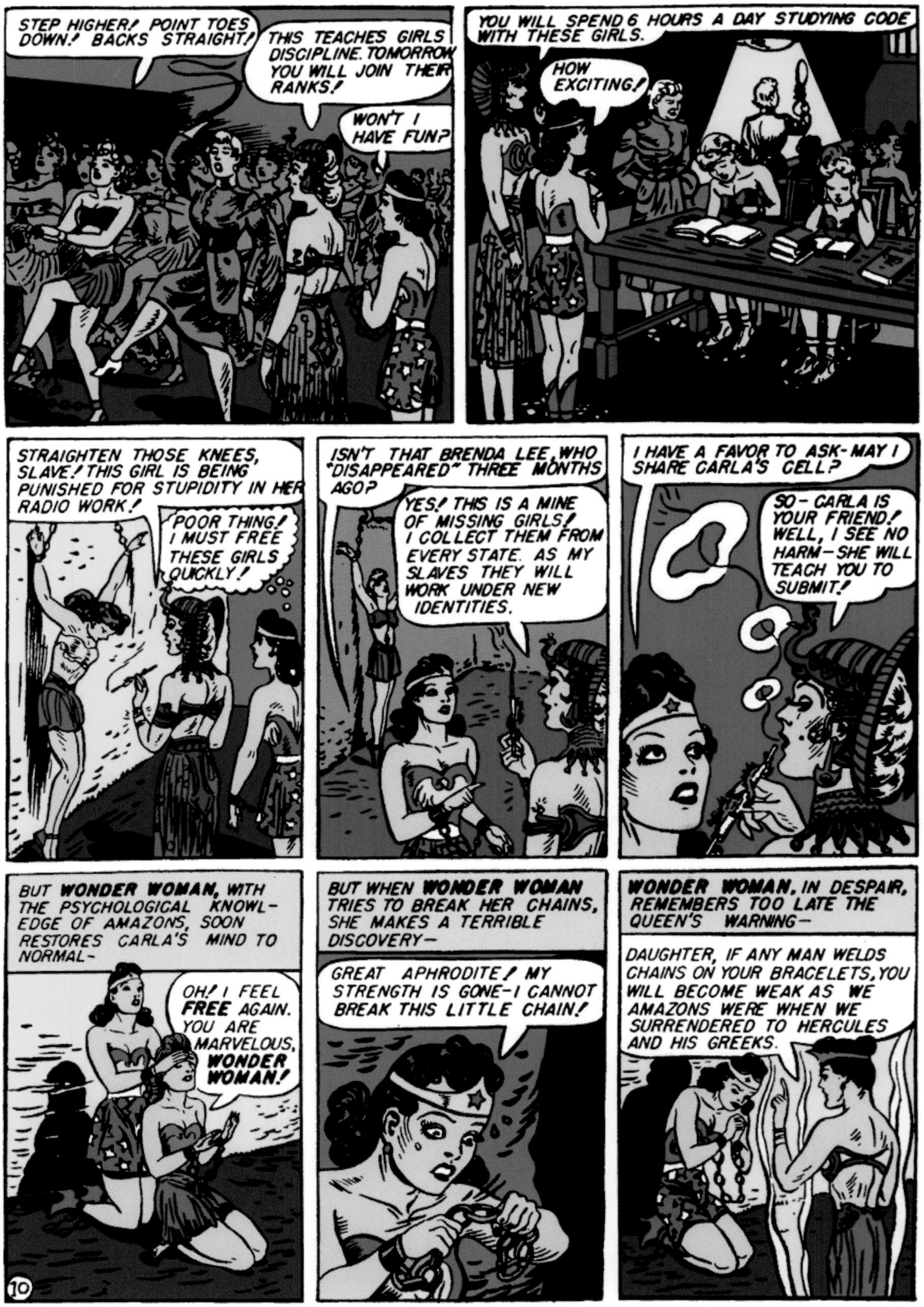
STEP HIGHER! POINT TOES DOWN! BACKS STRAIGHT!
THIS TEACHES GIRLS DISCIPLINE. TOMORROW YOU WILL JOIN THEIR RANKS!
WON'T I HAVE FUN?
YOU WILL SPEND 6 HOURS A DAY STUDYING CODE WITH THESE GIRLS.
HOW EXCITING!
STRAIGHTEN THOSE KNEES, SLAVE! THIS GIRL IS BEING PUNISHED FOR STUPIDITY IN HER RADIO WORK!
POOR THING! I MUST FREE THESE GIRLS QUICKLY!
ISN'T THAT BRENDA LEE, WHO "DISAPPEARED" THREE MONTHS AGO?
YES! THIS IS A MINE OF MISSING GIRLS! I COLLECT THEM FROM EVERY STATE. AS MY SLAVES THEY WILL WORK UNDER NEW IDENTITIES.
I HAVE A FAVOR TO ASK-MAY I SHARE CARLA'S CELL?
SO-CARLA IS YOUR FRIEND! WELL, I SEE NO HARM-SHE WILL TEACH YOU TO SUBMIT!
BUT WONDER WOMAN, WITH THE PSYCHOLOGICAL KNOWLEDGE OF AMAZONS, SOON RESTORES CARLA'S MIND TO NORMAL-
OH! I FEEL FREE AGAIN. YOU ARE MARVELOUS, WONDER WOMAN!
10
BUT WHEN WONDER WOMAN TRIES TO BREAK HER CHAINS, SHE MAKES A TERRIBLE DISCOVERY-
GREAT APHRODITE! MY STRENGTH IS GONE-I CANNOT BREAK THIS LITTLE CHAIN!
WONDER WOMAN, IN DESPAIR, REMEMBERS TOO LATE THE QUEEN'S WARNING-
DAUGHTER, IF ANY MAN WELDS CHAINS ON YOUR BRACELETS, YOU WILL BECOME WEAK AS WE AMAZONS WERE WHEN WE SURRENDERED TO HERCULES AND HIS GREEKS.

DAWN IS BREAKING AS THE GESTAPO AGENT TRAILED BY TREVOR REACHES THE MINE—
WHERE'S THAT DOD-GASTED BOOB GO-ING NOW? LOOKS LIKE A DESERTED MINE.
SUFFERING RABBITS! HE'S GONE DOWN THE MINE SHAFT! WHAT'S DOWN THERE? I'LL HAVE TO SEE!
STEVE WALKS INTO A TRAP—
STICK 'EM UP, SMART BOY! HENKEL TOLD US YOU WERE ON HIS TRAIL!
SO MY PAL'S NAME IS HENKEL, EH? NICE OF YOU TO INTRODUCE US!
KNOWING HENKEL'S NAME WON'T HELP YOU. YOU WON'T LIVE LONG AFTER SEEING THE BARON—
SHUT UP! NO MORE NAMES. GET IN THERE, YOU!
STEVE IS BROUGHT TO THE BARONESS.
AH, MY DEAR BARONESS! THIS IS AN UNEXPECTED PLEASURE!
BUT A SADNESS ALSO, CAPTAIN! SINCE YOU HAVE RECOGNIZED ME, WE MUST PART, I FEAR, FOREVER!
AT LEAST, CAPTAIN, I WILL ESCORT YOU ON YOUR LAST— WHAT YOU SAY— MILE!
THANK YOU, I'D LIKE TO DO THE SAME FOR YOU, BARONESS!
AT DAWN EACH DAY, THE GIRLS ARE DRAWN UP FOR INSPECTION—
11
AS STEVE IS LED PAST THE GIRLS, HE RECOG-NIZES WONDER WOMAN.
WONDER WOMAN! HOW—WHAT—
STEVE! OH, WHAT ARE THEY DOING TO YOU?

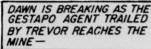

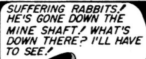

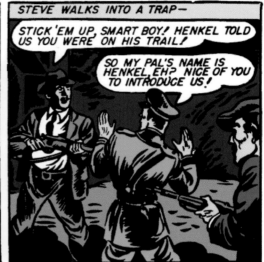

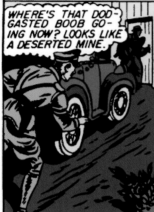

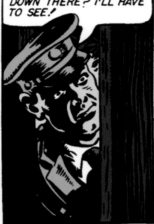

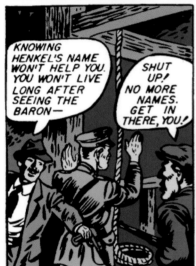

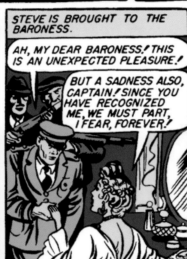

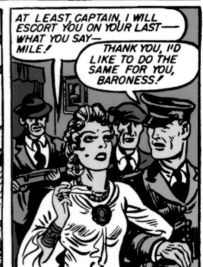

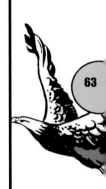

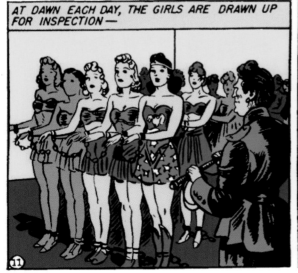

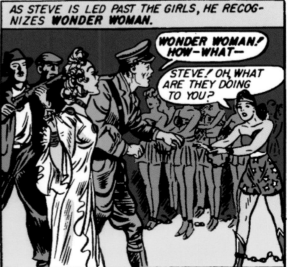

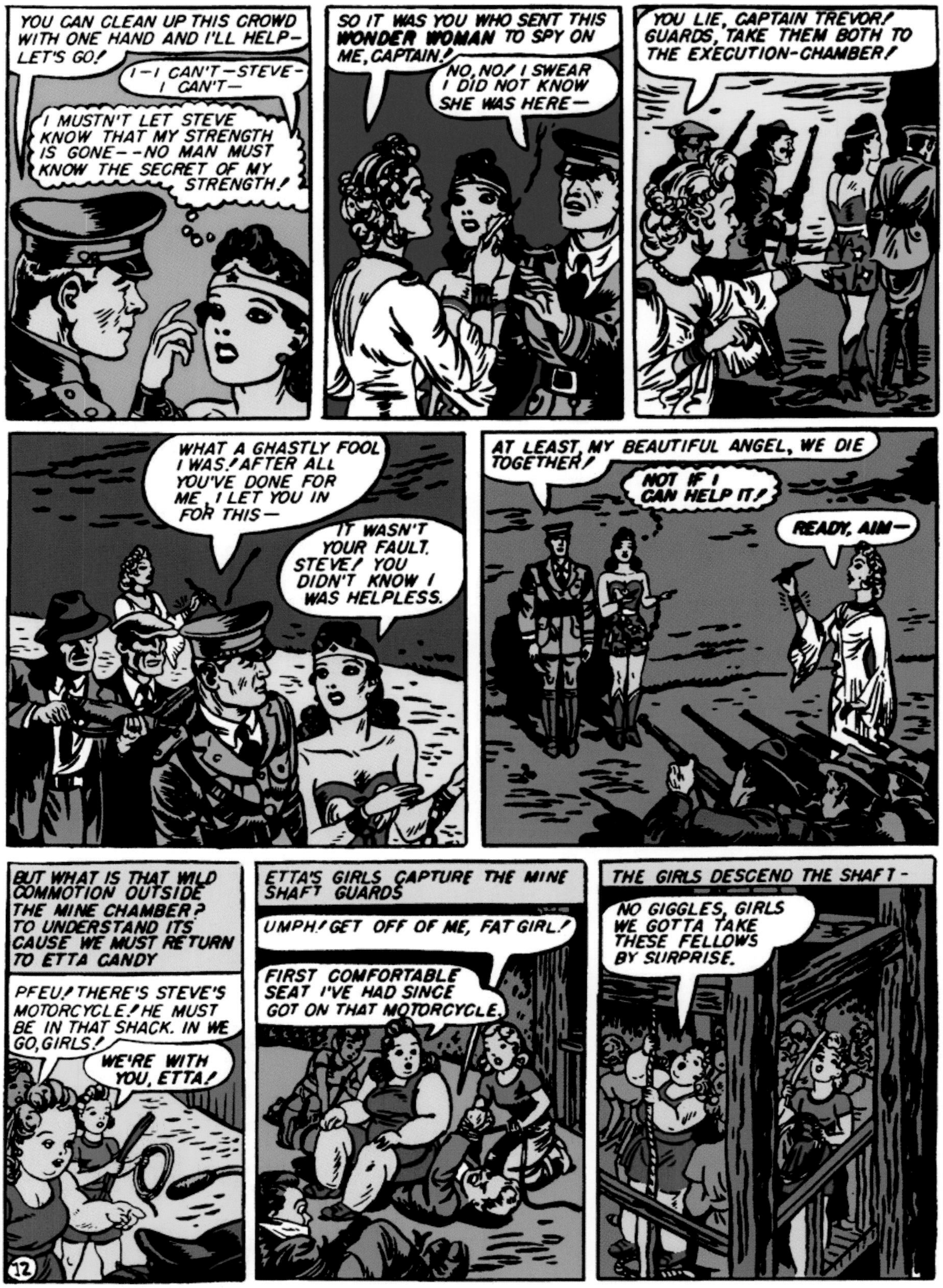

YOU CAN CLEAN UP THIS CROWD WITH ONE HAND AND I'LL HELP-LET'S GO!
I-I CAN'T-STEVE-I CAN'T-
I MUSTN'T LET STEVE KNOW THAT MY STRENGTH IS GONE--NO MAN MUST KNOW THE SECRET OF MY STRENGTH!
SO IT WAS YOU WHO SENT THIS WONDER WOMAN TO SPY ON ME, CAPTAIN!
NO, NO! I SWEAR I DID NOT KNOW SHE WAS HERE-
YOU LIE, CAPTAIN TREVOR! GUARDS, TAKE THEM BOTH TO THE EXECUTION-CHAMBER!
WHAT A GHASTLY FOOL I WAS! AFTER ALL YOU'VE DONE FOR ME, I LET YOU IN FOR THIS-
IT WASN'T YOUR FAULT, STEVE! YOU DIDN'T KNOW I WAS HELPLESS.
AT LEAST, MY BEAUTIFUL ANGEL, WE DIE TOGETHER!
NOT IF I CAN HELP IT!
READY, AIM-
BUT WHAT IS THAT WILD COMMOTION OUTSIDE THE MINE CHAMBER? TO UNDERSTAND ITS CAUSE WE MUST RETURN TO ETTA CANDY
PFEU! THERE'S STEVE'S MOTORCYCLE! HE MUST BE IN THAT SHACK. IN WE GO, GIRLS!
WE'RE WITH YOU, ETTA!
12
ETTA'S GIRLS CAPTURE THE MINE SHAFT GUARDS
UMPH! GET OFF OF ME, FAT GIRL!
FIRST COMFORTABLE SEAT I'VE HAD SINCE GOT ON THAT MOTORCYCLE.
THE GIRLS DESCEND THE SHAFT-
NO GIGGLES, GIRLS WE GOTTA TAKE THESE FELLOWS BY SURPRISE.

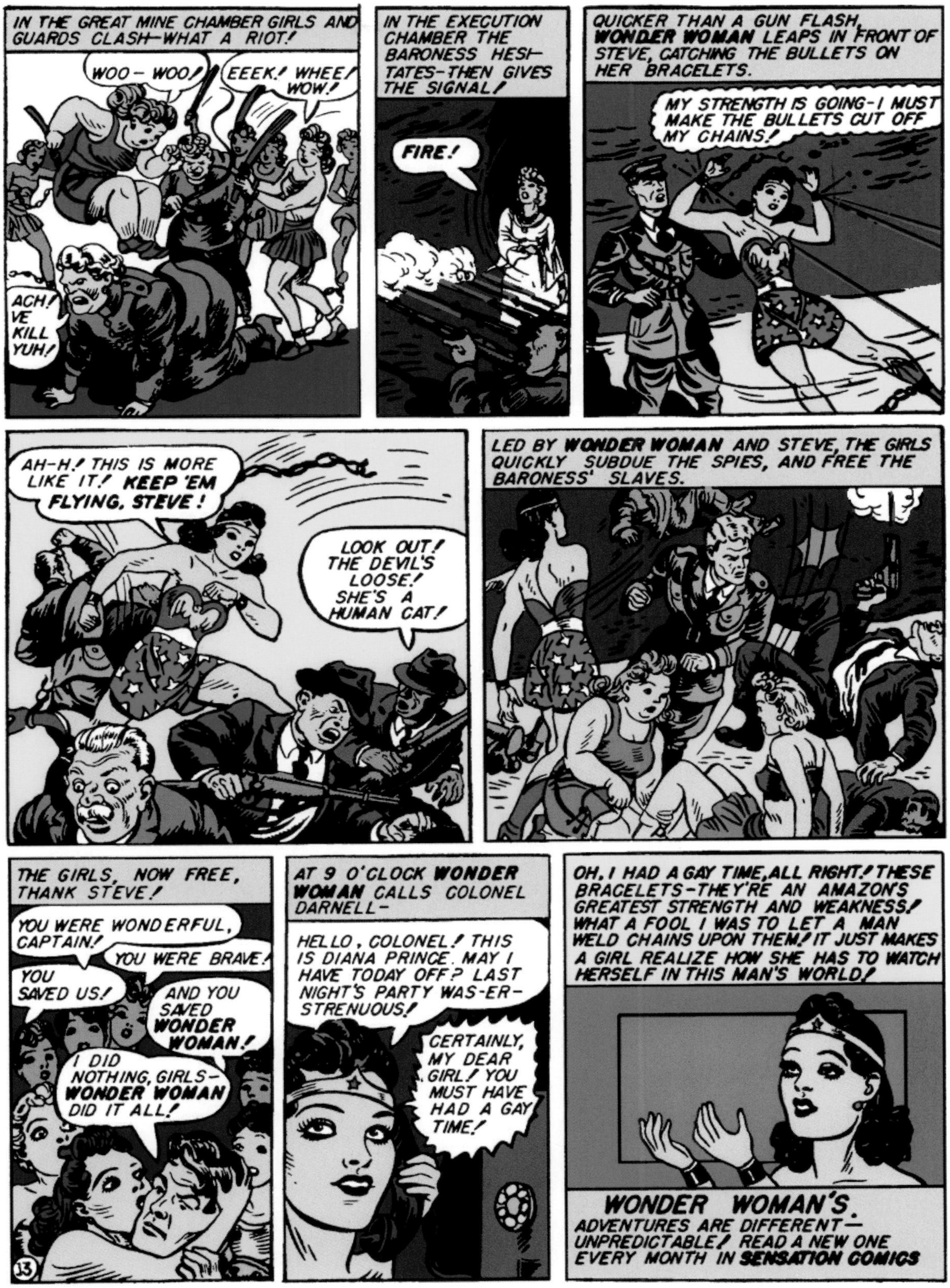
IN THE GREAT MINE CHAMBER GIRLS AND GUARDS CLASH—WHAT A RIOT!
WOO- WOO!
EEEK! WHEE! WOW!
ACH! VE KILL YUH!
IN THE EXECUTION CHAMBER THE BARONESS HESI-TATES-THEN GIVES THE SIGNAL!
FIRE!
QUICKER THAN A GUN FLASH, WONDER WOMAN LEAPS IN FRONT OF STEVE, CATCHING THE BULLETS ON HER BRACELETS.
MY STRENGTH IS GOING-I MUST MAKE THE BULLETS CUT OFF MY CHAINS!
AH-H! THIS IS MORE LIKE IT! KEEP 'EM FLYING, STEVE!
LOOK OUT! THE DEVIL'S LOOSE! SHE'S A HUMAN CAT!
LED BY WONDER WOMAN AND STEVE, THE GIRLS QUICKLY SUBDUE THE SPIES, AND FREE THE BARONESS' SLAVES.
THE GIRLS, NOW FREE, THANK STEVE!
YOU WERE WONDERFUL, CAPTAIN!
YOU WERE BRAVE!
YOU SAVED US!
AND YOU SAVED WONDER WOMAN!
I DID NOTHING, GIRLS- WONDER WOMAN DID IT ALL!
13
AT 9 O'CLOCK WONDER WOMAN CALLS COLONEL DARNELL—
HELLO, COLONEL! THIS IS DIANA PRINCE. MAY I HAVE TODAY OFF? LAST NIGHT'S PARTY WAS-ER-STRENUOUS!
CERTAINLY, MY DEAR GIRL! YOU MUST HAVE HAD A GAY TIME!
OH, I HAD A GAY TIME, ALL RIGHT! THESE BRACELETS-THEY'RE AN AMAZON'S GREATEST STRENGTH AND WEAKNESS! WHAT A FOOL I WAS TO LET A MAN WELD CHAINS UPON THEM! IT JUST MAKES A GIRL REALIZE HOW SHE HAS TO WATCH HERSELF IN THIS MAN'S WORLD!
WONDER WOMAN'S.
ADVENTURES ARE DIFFERENT— UNPREDICTABLE! READ A NEW ONE EVERY MONTH IN SENSATION COMICS

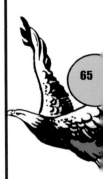

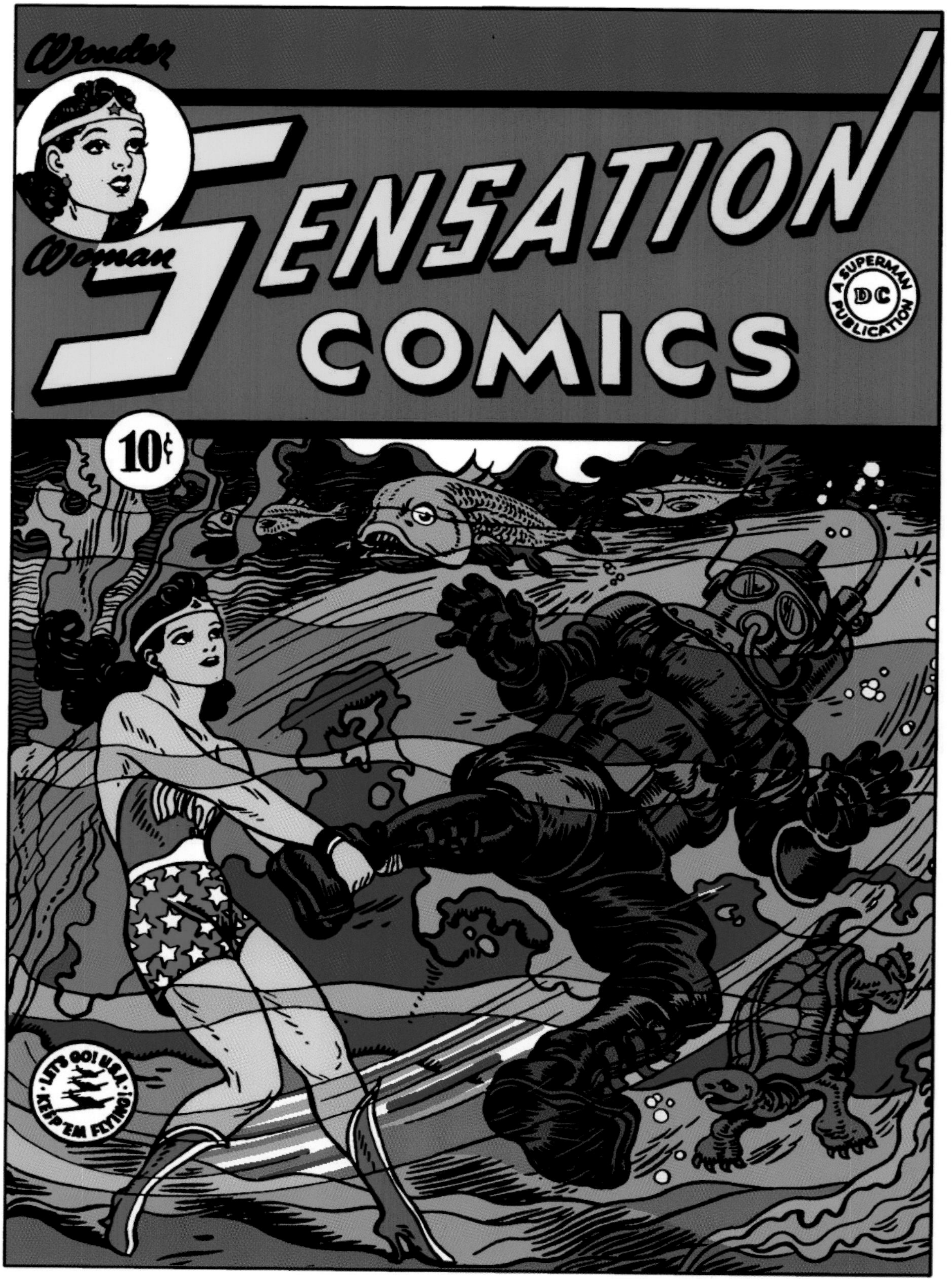

Wonder Woman
SENSATION COMICS
A SUPERMAN DC PUBLICATION
10¢
LET'S GO! U.S.A. KEEP 'EM FLYING!

Sensation Comics #5 (May 1942) - art: H.G. Peter

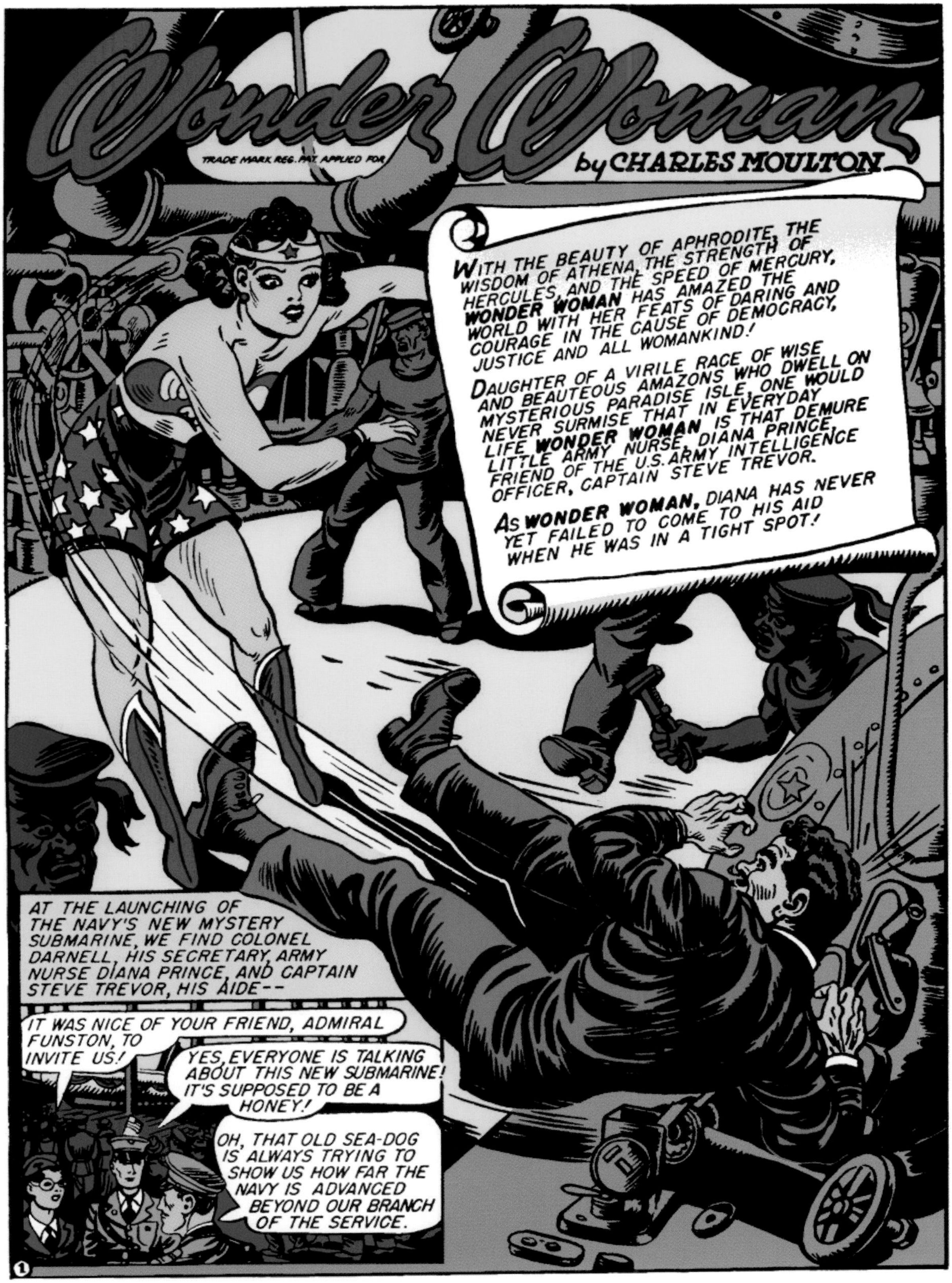

Wonder Woman
TRADE MARK REG. PAT. APPLIED FOR
by CHARLES MOULTON
WITH THE BEAUTY OF APHRODITE, THE WISDOM OF ATHENA, THE STRENGTH OF HERCULES, AND THE SPEED OF MERCURY, WONDER WOMAN HAS AMAZED THE WORLD WITH HER FEATS OF DARING AND COURAGE IN THE CAUSE OF DEMOCRACY, JUSTICE AND ALL WOMANKIND!
DAUGHTER OF A VIRILE RACE OF WISE AND BEAUTEOUS AMAZONS WHO DWELL ON MYSTERIOUS PARADISE ISLE, ONE WOULD NEVER SURMISE THAT IN EVERYDAY LIFE WONDER WOMAN IS THAT DEMURE LITTLE ARMY NURSE, DIANA PRINCE, FRIEND OF THE U.S. ARMY INTELLIGENCE OFFICER, CAPTAIN STEVE TREVOR.
AS WONDER WOMAN, DIANA HAS NEVER YET FAILED TO COME TO HIS AID WHEN HE WAS IN A TIGHT SPOT!
AT THE LAUNCHING OF THE NAVY'S NEW MYSTERY SUBMARINE, WE FIND COLONEL DARNELL, HIS SECRETARY, ARMY NURSE DIANA PRINCE, AND CAPTAIN STEVE TREVOR, HIS AIDE--
IT WAS NICE OF YOUR FRIEND, ADMIRAL FUNSTON, TO INVITE US!
YES, EVERYONE IS TALKING ABOUT THIS NEW SUBMARINE! IT'S SUPPOSED TO BE A HONEY!
OH, THAT OLD SEA-DOG IS ALWAYS TRYING TO SHOW US HOW FAR THE NAVY IS ADVANCED BEYOND OUR BRANCH OF THE SERVICE.
1

Sensation Comics #5 (May 1942) - script: William Moulton Marston - art: H.G. Peter

WHILE NEARBY, THE ADMIRAL SPEAKS TO DR. SANDS, INVENTOR OF THE NEW CRAFT---

MY DREAM HAS COME TRUE!

IF IT DOES ALL YOU PROMISE, IT'LL DOUBLE OUR SEAPOWER.

WIRE FOR YOU, SIR!

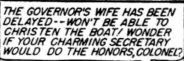

THE GOVERNOR'S WIFE HAS BEEN DELAYED--WON'T BE ABLE TO CHRISTEN THE BOAT! WONDER IF YOUR CHARMING SECRETARY WOULD DO THE HONORS, COLONEL?

HA! WHAT WOULD THE NAVY DO WITHOUT US!

OH! I'VE NEVER CHRISTENED A BOAT.

YOU JUST SAY: I CHRISTEN THEE "THE OCTOPUS"-- AND WHAMO! THAT'S ALL THERE IS TO IT!

THIS IS SO THRILLING!

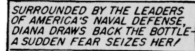

SURROUNDED BY THE LEADERS OF AMERICA'S NAVAL DEFENSE, DIANA DRAWS BACK THE BOTTLE-- A SUDDEN FEAR SEIZES HER!

THIS BOTTLE DOESN'T CONTAIN CHAMPAGNE--IT'S TOO HEAVY! SOMETHING'S WRONG!

GO AHEAD, DIANA! SHOW THEM WHAT AN ARMY WALLOP IS LIKE!

WITH HER MORE THAN NORMAL SENSES, DIANA IS ABLE TO IDENTIFY SUBSTANCES BY THEIR WEIGHT----

WHY, THIS BOTTLE CONTAINS A HIGH EXPLOSIVE! I'LL HAVE TO TRY A FAST RUSE!

WITH A QUICK MOTION OF HER POWERFUL WRISTS, DIANA TEARS THE BOTTLE LOOSE AND HURLS IT FAR INTO THE WATER-----

OH! THE RIBBON BROKE! IT--IT SLIPPED OUT OF MY HAND-- HOW CLUMSY OF ME!

AN ILL OMEN!

②

WITH A DEAFENING ROAR, THE BOTTLE EXPLODES ON A NEARBY SHOAL.

BOOM!

WHEW! IT WOULD HAVE BEEN A WORSE OMEN IF IT HAD EXPLOD-ED HERE!

I THINK I'M GOING TO FAINT!

OR AT LEAST I OUGHT TO MAKE BELIEVE I AM--

POOR CHILD-- SHE'S FAINTING!

TO MAINTAIN HER POSE AS AN ORDINARY HUMAN, DIANA PRETENDS TO FAINT----

EVERYTHING IS ALL RIGHT, DIANA!

THAT EXPLOSION WAS MEANT TO KILL US!

YES! TO DESTROY THE SUBMARINE AND DESTROY THE ONLY ONES WHO FULLY UNDERSTAND HER SECRETS!

MEANWHILE, IN A SEA-GOING TUG OFF SHORE--LOOKING THROUGH GLASSES AS HE TALKS---

WE WILL DRINK REAL CHAMPAGNE WHILE-- HEY, VOT'S HAPPENED?

IT'S NOT THE GOVERNOR'S WIFE AND SHE'S---THROWING THE BOTTLE!

WHAT'S THIS? AN AMERICAN OFFICER PLAYING TRAITOR?

THAT VENT WRONG-- BUT VE GOT ODDER TRICKS YET! VE VILL MAKE THEM THINK THE SUBMARINE IS NO GOOD-- AND THEN--

I GET IT! WE USE IT FOR OURSELVES! MIGHT AS WELL GET RID OF THIS ENSIGN'S UNIFORM! I WON'T NEED IT ANY MORE!

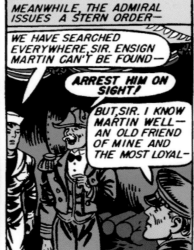

MEANWHILE, THE ADMIRAL ISSUES A STERN ORDER--

WE HAVE SEARCHED EVERYWHERE, SIR. ENSIGN MARTIN CAN'T BE FOUND--

ARREST HIM ON SIGHT!

BUT, SIR. I KNOW MARTIN WELL-- AN OLD FRIEND OF MINE AND THE MOST LOYAL--

HIS DISAPPEARANCE AFTER BRINGING THAT BOTTLE HERE LOOKS MIGHTY BAD. BUT COME, WE MUST GET ON WITH THE LAUNCHING!

BUT, SIR--

69

THE LAUNCHING GOES ON--

DON'T BE AFRAID, MISS PRINCE. THIS BOTTLE HAS BEEN CAREFULLY EXAMINED--

I CHRISTEN THEE OCTOPUS!

I'LL HAVE TO WATCH STEVE--HE MIGHT GET INTO TROUBLE TRYING TO HELP HIS FRIEND.

"THE OCTOPUS" GLIDES GRACEFULLY INTO THE WATER--

SHE'LL STRIKE BACK AT THE ENEMIES OF DEMOCRACY!

SHE CERTAINLY LOOKS GOOD!

THIS WILL BE INTERESTING! THE SUB-COMMANDER IS GOING TO REPORT OVER THAT LOUD SPEAKER--AFTER SUBMERGING--

HOW FASCINATING!

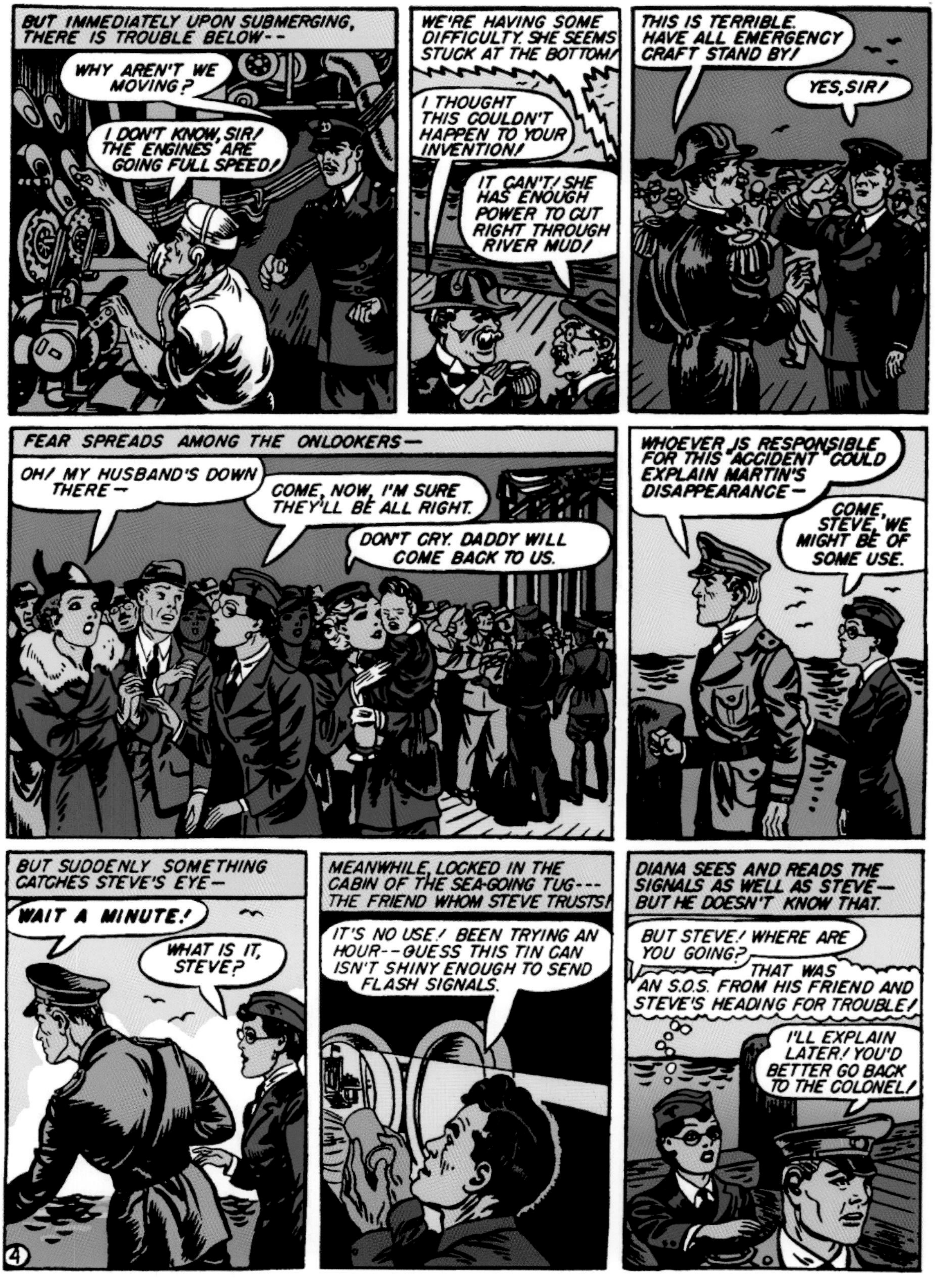

BUT IMMEDIATELY UPON SUBMERGING, THERE IS TROUBLE BELOW--
WHY AREN'T WE MOVING?
I DON'T KNOW, SIR! THE ENGINES ARE GOING FULL SPEED!
WE'RE HAVING SOME DIFFICULTY. SHE SEEMS STUCK AT THE BOTTOM!
I THOUGHT THIS COULDN'T HAPPEN TO YOUR INVENTION!
IT CAN'T! SHE HAS ENOUGH POWER TO CUT RIGHT THROUGH RIVER MUD!
THIS IS TERRIBLE. HAVE ALL EMERGENCY CRAFT STAND BY!
YES, SIR!
FEAR SPREADS AMONG THE ONLOOKERS—
OH! MY HUSBAND'S DOWN THERE—
COME, NOW, I'M SURE THEY'LL BE ALL RIGHT.
DON'T CRY. DADDY WILL COME BACK TO US.
WHOEVER IS RESPONSIBLE FOR THIS "ACCIDENT" COULD EXPLAIN MARTIN'S DISAPPEARANCE—
COME, STEVE, WE MIGHT BE OF SOME USE.
BUT SUDDENLY SOMETHING CATCHES STEVE'S EYE—
WAIT A MINUTE!
WHAT IS IT, STEVE?
4
MEANWHILE, LOCKED IN THE CABIN OF THE SEA-GOING TUG--- THE FRIEND WHOM STEVE TRUSTS!
IT'S NO USE! BEEN TRYING AN HOUR--GUESS THIS TIN CAN ISN'T SHINY ENOUGH TO SEND FLASH SIGNALS.
DIANA SEES AND READS THE SIGNALS AS WELL AS STEVE— BUT HE DOESN'T KNOW THAT.
BUT STEVE! WHERE ARE YOU GOING?
THAT WAS AN S.O.S. FROM HIS FRIEND AND STEVE'S HEADING FOR TROUBLE!
I'LL EXPLAIN LATER! YOU'D BETTER GO BACK TO THE COLONEL!

SPURRED TO ACTION BY STEVE'S IMMINENT DANGER, THE DEMURE LITTLE ARMY NURSE BECOMES ONCE AGAIN THAT GLORIOUS CREATURE OF STRENGTH AND BEAUTY---THE WONDER WOMAN!
IF I KNOW STEVE, HE'LL HEAD RIGHT FOR THAT BOAT! AND SO WILL I - AS THE WONDER WOMAN!
IN MIDSTREAM---
I'LL GET MARTIN OUT OF THIS JAM IF IT'S THE LAST THING I DO! SAY, THAT SPEED BOAT IS HEADED STRAIGHT FOR ME!
I THINK WE'RE GOING TO THE SAME PLACE, SO HOP IN!
WONDER WOMAN!
WHILE ON THE TUG---
VELL, VE GOT THAT SUB IN TROUBLE - AND VE MAKE MORE YET! GIFF AN ORDER TO ATTACK THEIR AIR SUPPLY!
SWELL, CHIEF! THAT WILL MAKE THEM THINK THAT INVENTOR DIDN'T DO SO GOOD!
BUT EVEN AS THE GHASTLY ORDER IS GIVEN-
THOSE RATS! THEY'LL SUFFOCATE THE MEN DOWN THERE! HAVE TO MAKE A DESPERATE EFFORT TO STOP THEM!
YOU WORMS!
PROCEED AS ORDERED - HEY!
THAT ENSIGN! HE'S LOOSE! STOP HIM!
THIS WILL STOP HIM!
ACH! THESE AMERICANS ARE SO STUBBORN THEY DON'T KNOW WHEN THEY'RE BEATEN!
VE HAVE TO GET RID OF HIM. DESE VEIGHTS WILL TAKE HIM DOWN TO DAVY JONES' LOCKER!
YEAH—AND THEY'LL NEVER FIND OUT IT WASN'T HIM WHO SPIKED THAT CHAMPAGNE!
5

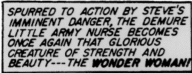

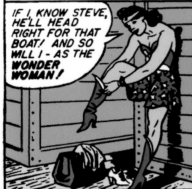

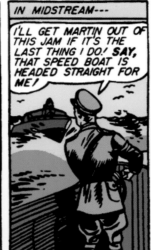

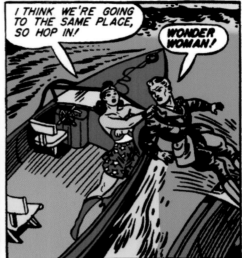

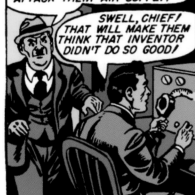

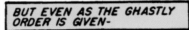

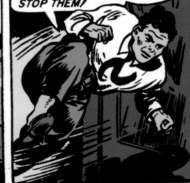

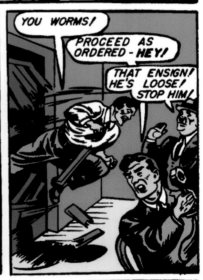

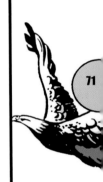

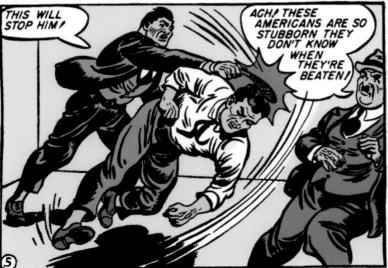

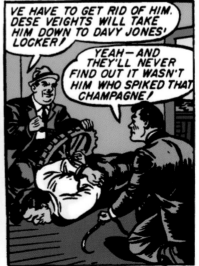

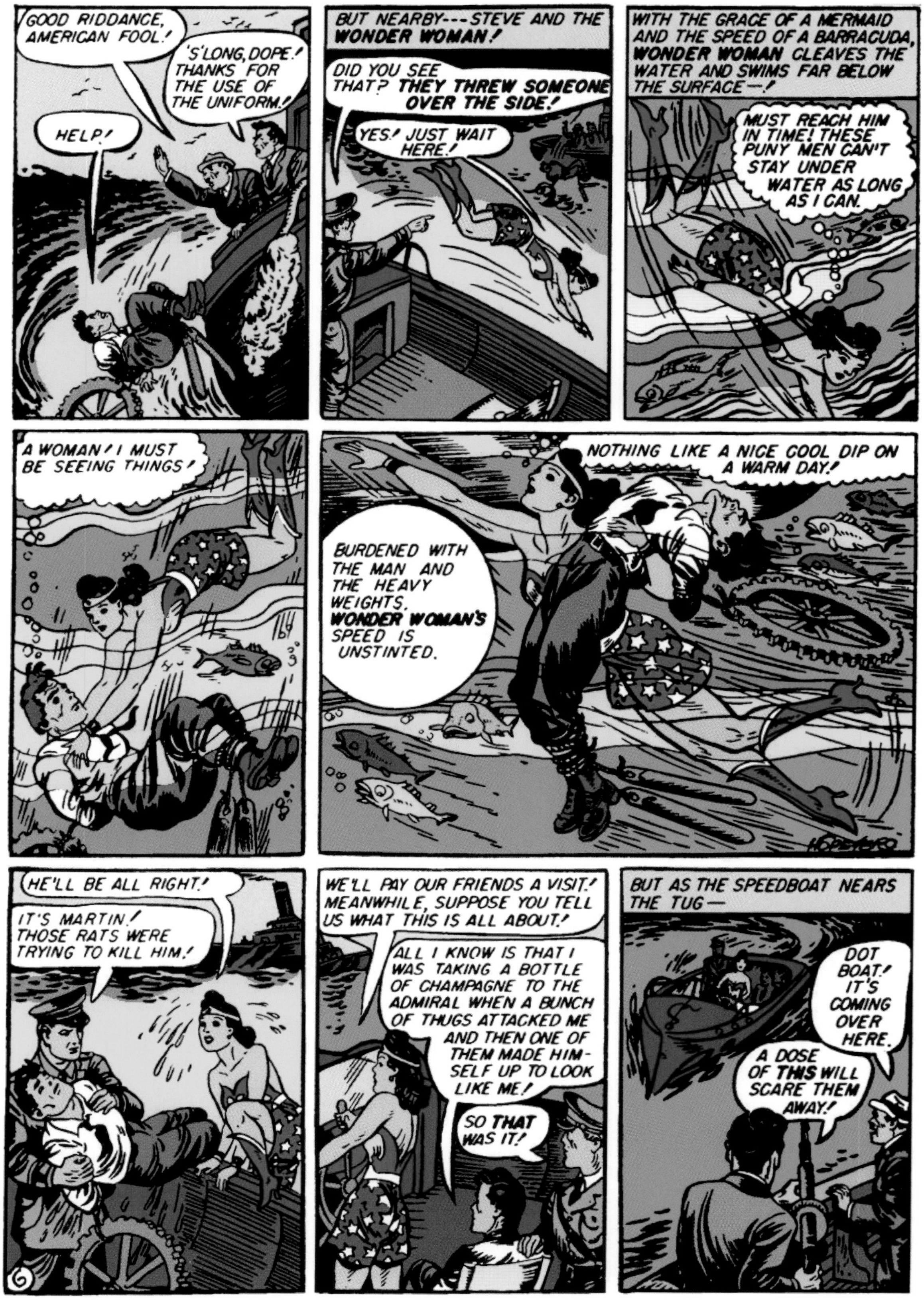
GOOD RIDDANCE, AMERICAN FOOL!
'S'LONG, DOPE! THANKS FOR THE USE OF THE UNIFORM!
HELP!
BUT NEARBY---STEVE AND THE WONDER WOMAN!
DID YOU SEE THAT? THEY THREW SOMEONE OVER THE SIDE!
YES! JUST WAIT HERE!
WITH THE GRACE OF A MERMAID AND THE SPEED OF A BARRACUDA, WONDER WOMAN CLEAVES THE WATER AND SWIMS FAR BELOW THE SURFACE—!
MUST REACH HIM IN TIME! THESE PUNY MEN CAN'T STAY UNDER WATER AS LONG AS I CAN.
A WOMAN! I MUST BE SEEING THINGS!
NOTHING LIKE A NICE COOL DIP ON A WARM DAY!
BURDENED WITH THE MAN AND THE HEAVY WEIGHTS, WONDER WOMAN'S SPEED IS UNSTINTED.
HE'LL BE ALL RIGHT!
IT'S MARTIN! THOSE RATS WERE TRYING TO KILL HIM!
WE'LL PAY OUR FRIENDS A VISIT! MEANWHILE, SUPPOSE YOU TELL US WHAT THIS IS ALL ABOUT!
ALL I KNOW IS THAT I WAS TAKING A BOTTLE OF CHAMPAGNE TO THE ADMIRAL WHEN A BUNCH OF THUGS ATTACKED ME AND THEN ONE OF THEM MADE HIMSELF UP TO LOOK LIKE ME!
SO THAT WAS IT!
BUT AS THE SPEEDBOAT NEARS THE TUG—
DOT BOAT! IT'S COMING OVER HERE.
A DOSE OF THIS WILL SCARE THEM AWAY!

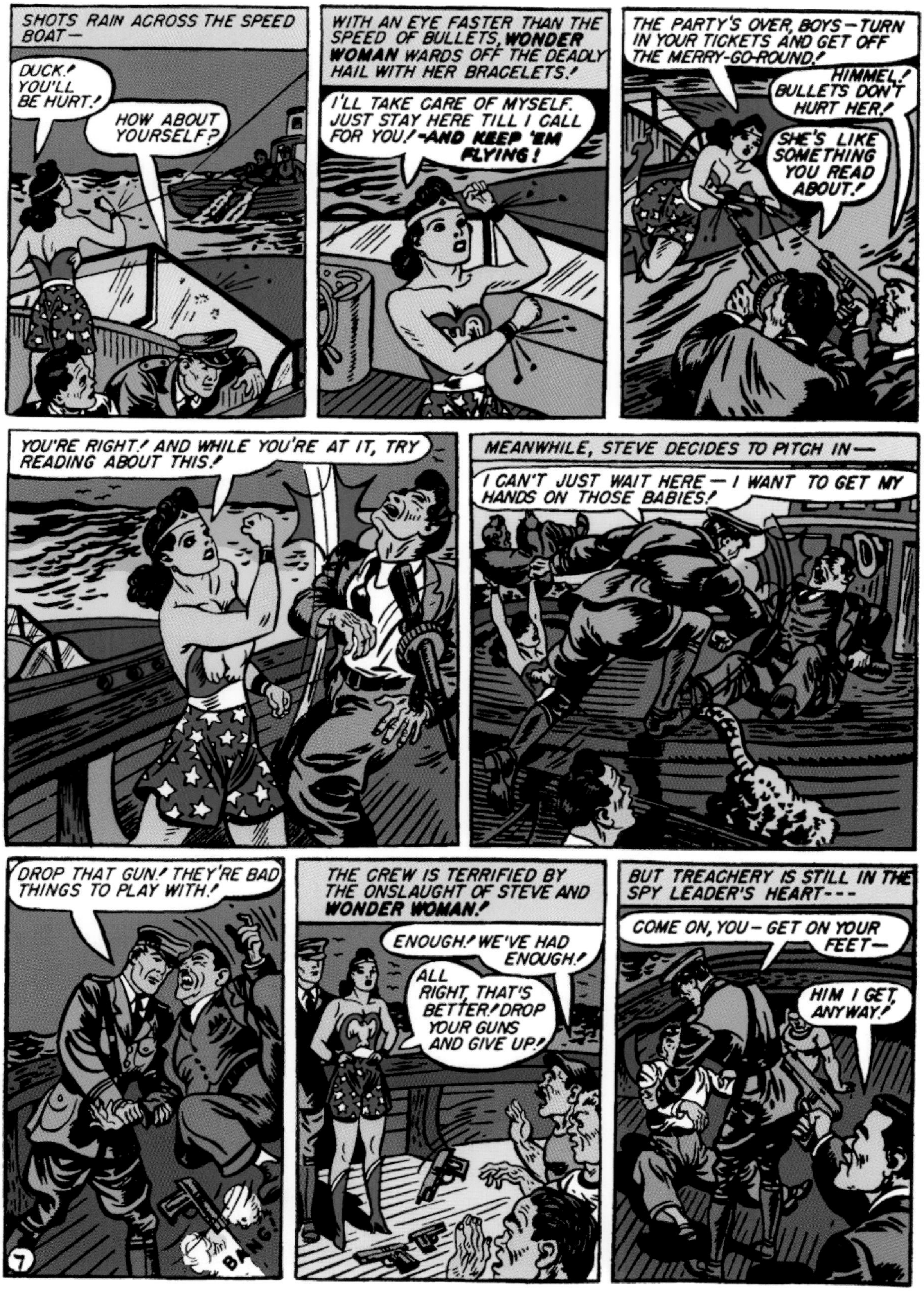

SHOTS RAIN ACROSS THE SPEED BOAT—
DUCK! YOU'LL BE HURT!
HOW ABOUT YOURSELF?
WITH AN EYE FASTER THAN THE SPEED OF BULLETS, WONDER WOMAN WARDS OFF THE DEADLY HAIL WITH HER BRACELETS!
I'LL TAKE CARE OF MYSELF. JUST STAY HERE TILL I CALL FOR YOU! —AND KEEP 'EM FLYING!
THE PARTY'S OVER, BOYS—TURN IN YOUR TICKETS AND GET OFF THE MERRY-GO-ROUND!
HIMMEL! BULLETS DON'T HURT HER!
SHE'S LIKE SOMETHING YOU READ ABOUT!
YOU'RE RIGHT! AND WHILE YOU'RE AT IT, TRY READING ABOUT THIS!
MEANWHILE, STEVE DECIDES TO PITCH IN—
I CAN'T JUST WAIT HERE — I WANT TO GET MY HANDS ON THOSE BABIES!
DROP THAT GUN! THEY'RE BAD THINGS TO PLAY WITH!
BANG!
7
THE CREW IS TERRIFIED BY THE ONSLAUGHT OF STEVE AND WONDER WOMAN!
ENOUGH! WE'VE HAD ENOUGH!
ALL RIGHT, THAT'S BETTER! DROP YOUR GUNS AND GIVE UP!
BUT TREACHERY IS STILL IN THE SPY LEADER'S HEART---
COME ON, YOU – GET ON YOUR FEET—
HIM I GET, ANYWAY!

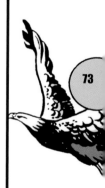

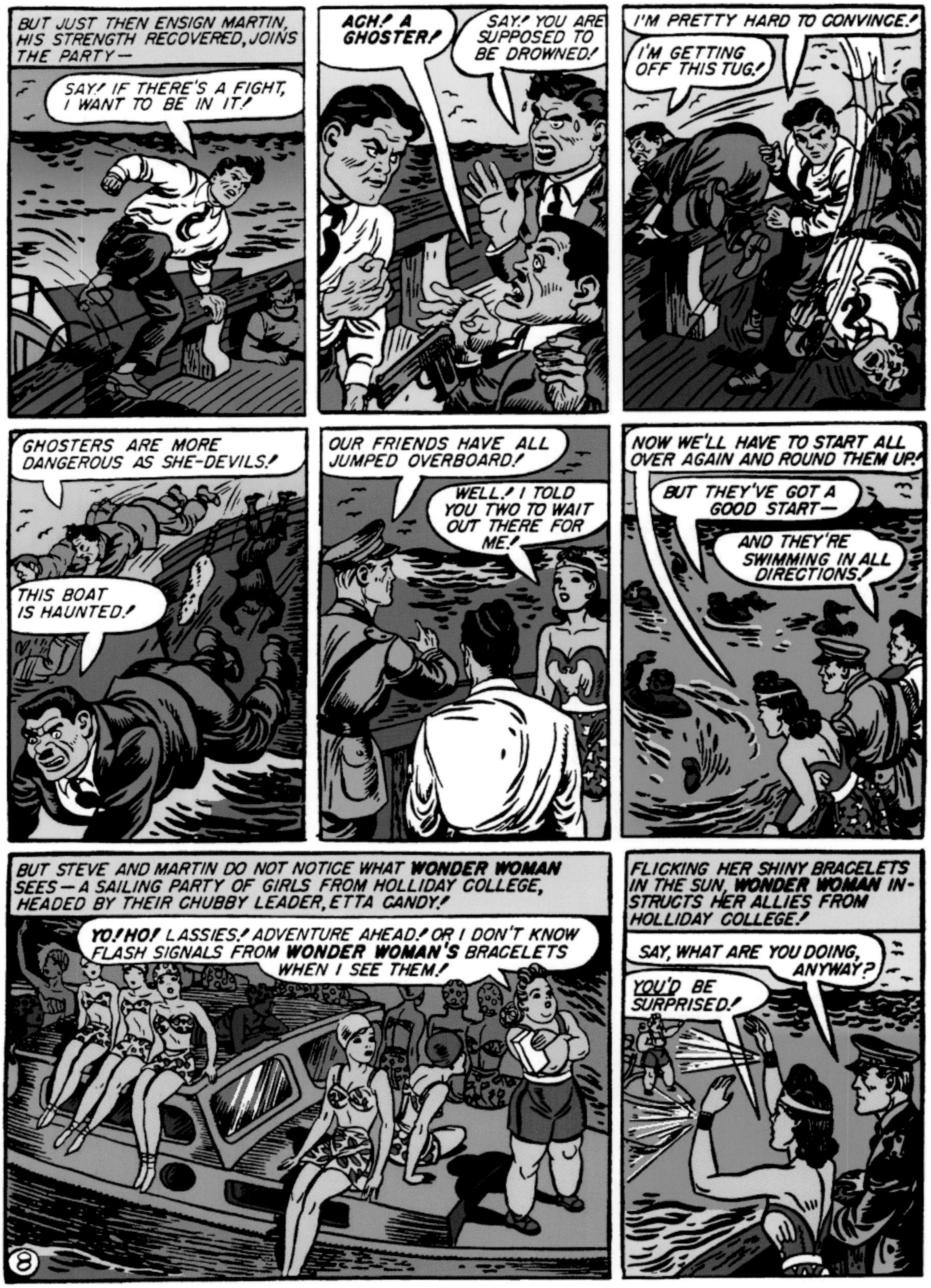
BUT JUST THEN ENSIGN MARTIN, HIS STRENGTH RECOVERED, JOINS THE PARTY—
SAY! IF THERE'S A FIGHT, I WANT TO BE IN IT!
ACH! A GHOSTER!
SAY! YOU ARE SUPPOSED TO BE DROWNED!
I'M PRETTY HARD TO CONVINCE!
I'M GETTING OFF THIS TUG!
GHOSTERS ARE MORE DANGEROUS AS SHE-DEVILS!
THIS BOAT IS HAUNTED!
OUR FRIENDS HAVE ALL JUMPED OVERBOARD!
WELL! I TOLD YOU TWO TO WAIT OUT THERE FOR ME!
NOW WE'LL HAVE TO START ALL OVER AGAIN AND ROUND THEM UP!
BUT THEY'VE GOT A GOOD START—
AND THEY'RE SWIMMING IN ALL DIRECTIONS!
BUT STEVE AND MARTIN DO NOT NOTICE WHAT WONDER WOMAN SEES—A SAILING PARTY OF GIRLS FROM HOLLIDAY COLLEGE, HEADED BY THEIR CHUBBY LEADER, ETTA CANDY!
YO! HO! LASSIES! ADVENTURE AHEAD! OR I DON'T KNOW FLASH SIGNALS FROM WONDER WOMAN'S BRACELETS WHEN I SEE THEM!
8
FLICKING HER SHINY BRACELETS IN THE SUN, WONDER WOMAN INSTRUCTS HER ALLIES FROM HOLLIDAY COLLEGE!
SAY, WHAT ARE YOU DOING, ANYWAY?
YOU'D BE SURPRISED!

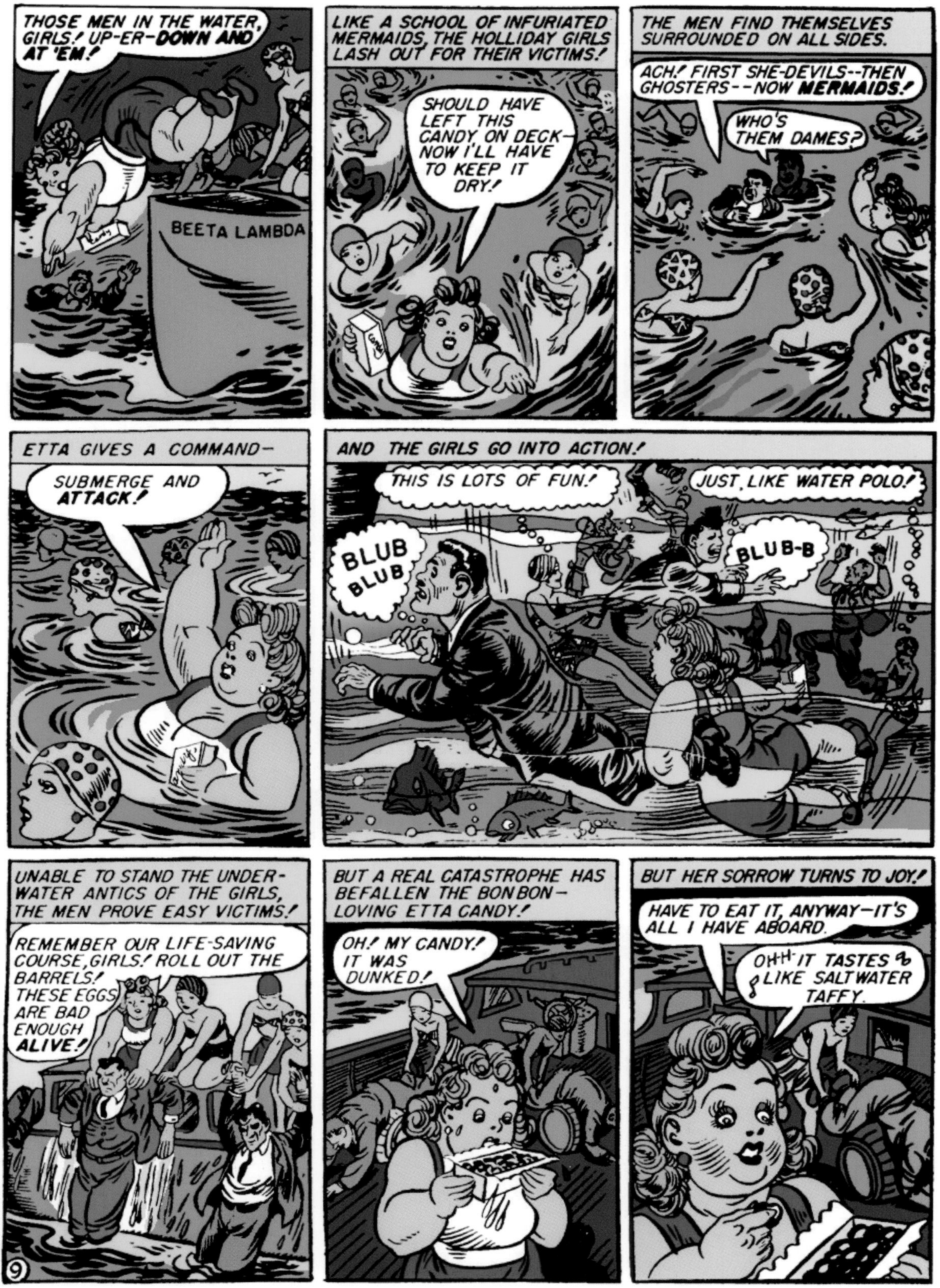
THOSE MEN IN THE WATER, GIRLS! UP-ER-DOWN AND AT 'EM!
BEETA LAMBDA
LIKE A SCHOOL OF INFURIATED MERMAIDS, THE HOLLIDAY GIRLS LASH OUT FOR THEIR VICTIMS!
SHOULD HAVE LEFT THIS CANDY ON DECK-NOW I'LL HAVE TO KEEP IT DRY!
THE MEN FIND THEMSELVES SURROUNDED ON ALL SIDES.
ACH! FIRST SHE-DEVILS--THEN GHOSTERS--NOW MERMAIDS!
WHO'S THEM DAMES?
ETTA GIVES A COMMAND-
SUBMERGE AND ATTACK!
AND THE GIRLS GO INTO ACTION!
THIS IS LOTS OF FUN!
JUST LIKE WATER POLO!
BLUB BLUB
BLUB-B
UNABLE TO STAND THE UNDER-WATER ANTICS OF THE GIRLS, THE MEN PROVE EASY VICTIMS!
REMEMBER OUR LIFE-SAVING COURSE, GIRLS! ROLL OUT THE BARRELS! THESE EGGS ARE BAD ENOUGH ALIVE!
BUT A REAL CATASTROPHE HAS BEFALLEN THE BONBON-LOVING ETTA CANDY!
OH! MY CANDY! IT WAS DUNKED!
BUT HER SORROW TURNS TO JOY!
HAVE TO EAT IT, ANYWAY-IT'S ALL I HAVE ABOARD.
OH-H- IT TASTES LIKE SALTWATER TAFFY.
9

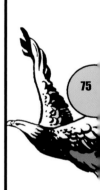

MEANWHILE, BACK ON SHORE, THINGS HAVEN'T BEEN GOING SO WELL—

SAFETY BUOYS JAMMED— SEND HELP QUICK— OXYGEN FAILING

EVERYTHING'S GOING WRONG! SOMETHING'S RESPONSIBLE FOR THIS! YOU MUST DO SOMETHING TO SAVE THE MEN ABOARD THE "OCTOPUS"!

I CAN'T UNDERSTAND IT! THAT SUB WAS FOOLPROOF! PERHAPS WE'D BETTER SEND ANOTHER DIVER. I CAN'T IMAGINE WHAT HAPPENED TO THE OTHER TWO!

WHILE ON THE TUG—

TOO BAD THOSE MEN GOT AWAY!

MAYBE THEY DID NOT—SH-LISTEN TO THAT!

STILL HAVE SUB GROUNDED— UNDER MAGNETIC CONTROL— HAVE PUMPED CARBON DIOXIDE - WILL BOARD AND TAKE OVER WHEN CREW IS UNCONSCIOUS—

YOU WAIT HERE AND DON'T TRY TO BE HEROES! I'LL BE RIGHT BACK!

SAY, WHERE ARE YOU GOING? BLAZES! SHE'S GONE AGAIN!

DEEPER— DEEPER— DEEPER—THE WONDER WOMAN DIVES STRAIGHT TO THE SCENE OF THE DISTRESSED SUBMARINE!

ONE MORE DIVER HAS ATTEMPTED THE DANGEROUS TASK—

THAT DIVER NEEDS MY PROTEC- TION!

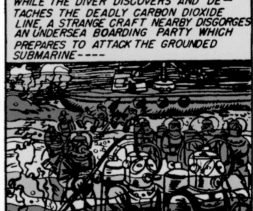

WHILE THE DIVER DISCOVERS AND DE- TACHES THE DEADLY CARBON DIOXIDE LINE, A STRANGE CRAFT NEARBY DISGORGES AN UNDERSEA BOARDING PARTY WHICH PREPARES TO ATTACK THE GROUNDED SUBMARINE----

ADVANCE SCOUTS ATTACK THE LONE DIVER.

THIS CALLS FOR ACTION— HOPE MY BREATH HOLDS OUT!

THEY'VE SEVERED HIS AIR LINE! I'LL HAVE TO GET THIS MAN TO THE SURFACE!

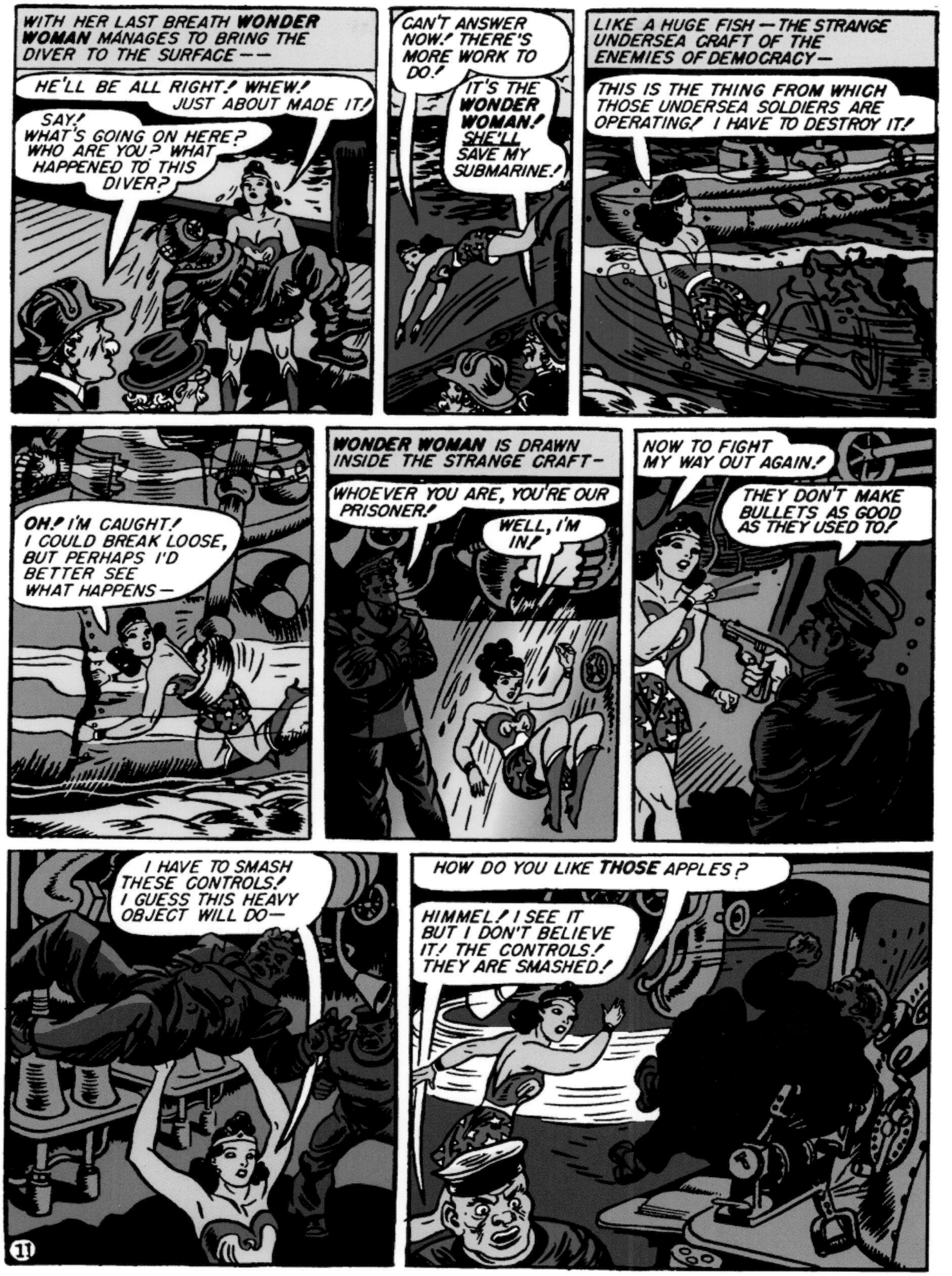

WITH HER LAST BREATH WONDER WOMAN MANAGES TO BRING THE DIVER TO THE SURFACE --
HE'LL BE ALL RIGHT! WHEW! JUST ABOUT MADE IT!
SAY! WHAT'S GOING ON HERE? WHO ARE YOU? WHAT HAPPENED TO THIS DIVER?
CAN'T ANSWER NOW! THERE'S MORE WORK TO DO!
IT'S THE WONDER WOMAN! SHE'LL SAVE MY SUBMARINE!
LIKE A HUGE FISH — THE STRANGE UNDERSEA CRAFT OF THE ENEMIES OF DEMOCRACY —
THIS IS THE THING FROM WHICH THOSE UNDERSEA SOLDIERS ARE OPERATING! I HAVE TO DESTROY IT!
OH! I'M CAUGHT! I COULD BREAK LOOSE, BUT PERHAPS I'D BETTER SEE WHAT HAPPENS —
WONDER WOMAN IS DRAWN INSIDE THE STRANGE CRAFT—
WHOEVER YOU ARE, YOU'RE OUR PRISONER!
WELL, I'M IN!
NOW TO FIGHT MY WAY OUT AGAIN!
THEY DON'T MAKE BULLETS AS GOOD AS THEY USED TO!
I HAVE TO SMASH THESE CONTROLS! I GUESS THIS HEAVY OBJECT WILL DO—
11
HOW DO YOU LIKE THOSE APPLES?
HIMMEL! I SEE IT BUT I DON'T BELIEVE IT! THE CONTROLS! THEY ARE SMASHED!

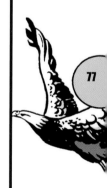

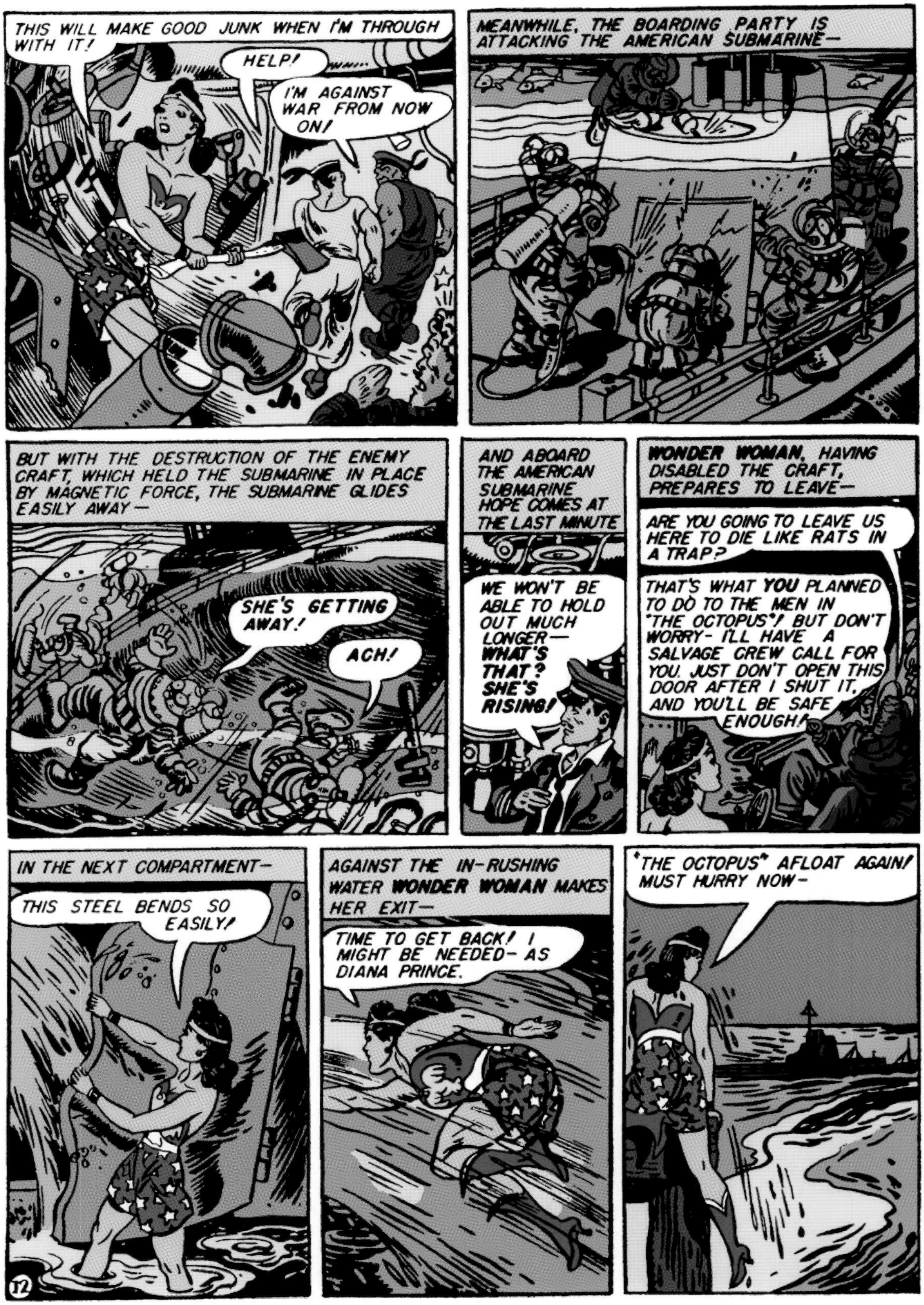
THIS WILL MAKE GOOD JUNK WHEN I'M THROUGH WITH IT!
HELP!
I'M AGAINST WAR FROM NOW ON!
MEANWHILE, THE BOARDING PARTY IS ATTACKING THE AMERICAN SUBMARINE—
BUT WITH THE DESTRUCTION OF THE ENEMY CRAFT, WHICH HELD THE SUBMARINE IN PLACE BY MAGNETIC FORCE, THE SUBMARINE GLIDES EASILY AWAY—
SHE'S GETTING AWAY!
ACH!
AND ABOARD THE AMERICAN SUBMARINE HOPE COMES AT THE LAST MINUTE
WE WON'T BE ABLE TO HOLD OUT MUCH LONGER— WHAT'S THAT? SHE'S RISING!
WONDER WOMAN, HAVING DISABLED THE CRAFT, PREPARES TO LEAVE—
ARE YOU GOING TO LEAVE US HERE TO DIE LIKE RATS IN A TRAP?
THAT'S WHAT YOU PLANNED TO DO TO THE MEN IN "THE OCTOPUS"! BUT DON'T WORRY- I'LL HAVE A SALVAGE CREW CALL FOR YOU. JUST DON'T OPEN THIS DOOR AFTER I SHUT IT, AND YOU'LL BE SAFE ENOUGH!
IN THE NEXT COMPARTMENT—
THIS STEEL BENDS SO EASILY!
12
AGAINST THE IN-RUSHING WATER WONDER WOMAN MAKES HER EXIT—
TIME TO GET BACK! I MIGHT BE NEEDED- AS DIANA PRINCE.
"THE OCTOPUS" AFLOAT AGAIN! MUST HURRY NOW—

WHILE CHANGING TO HER EVERY DAY GUISE, **WONDER WOMAN** MAKES A HURRIED CALL TO THE ADMIRAL—

WHAT! YES, YES, YES, I'LL DO EVERYTHING YOU SAY- BUT **WONDER WOMAN** - **WONDER WOMAN!** SHE'S HUNG UP!

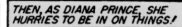

THEN, AS DIANA PRINCE, SHE HURRIES TO BE IN ON THINGS!

YOU'RE A NURSE, MISS PRINCE! GET ON THAT TENDER! CAPTAIN TREVOR AND ENSIGN MARTIN MIGHT NEED SOME FIRST AID!

STEVE DOESN'T KNOW HOW CLOSE HE IS TO THE REAL **WONDER WOMAN!**

STEVE, ARE YOU ALL RIGHT?

YES—THANKS TO THAT WONDERFUL **WONDER WOMAN!**

YES! SHE HELPED TO CLEAR MY NAME!

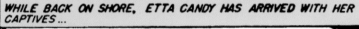

WHILE BACK ON SHORE, ETTA CANDY HAS ARRIVED WITH HER CAPTIVES...

WONDER WOMAN TOLD US TO HAND THEM OVER TO YOU!

THAT WOMAN AGAIN! SAY! WHO'S RUNNING THIS NAVY ANYWAY?

THEN MY SUBMARINE IS A SUCCESS AFTER ALL!

YES! WITH THE AID OF AMERICAN COURAGE, IT WITHSTOOD EVERYTHING THE ENEMIES OF DEMOCRACY COULD OFFER!

AND OUT IN THE BAY A NAVAL SALVAGE CREW DOES SOME STRANGE FISHING...

DOT VONDER WOMAN! ACH!

SAY, WHAT'S THE LOWDOWN ON THIS **WONDER WOMAN?**

DUNNO, BUT I'D SURE LIKE TO HAVE HER RESCUE ME!

WELL, THE LAUNCHING WAS EXCITING, WASN'T IT?

LAUNCHING? OH, YES...

I WONDER IF I'LL SEE HER AGAIN- THAT WONDERFUL, WONDERFUL **WONDER WOMAN**

POOR DIANA DOESN'T RATE WHEN STEVE'S THINKING ABOUT **WONDER WOMAN!** FOLLOW HER AMAZING ADVENTURES EVERY MONTH IN **SENSATION COMICS!**

Part Two

For Wonder Woman, as well as for a number of other DC/AA super-heroes, the Second World War really began in the pages of All-Star Comics #11, cover-dated June–July 1942. That was the first issue of that comic prepared after the attack on Pearl Harbor—and it showed.

The War Comes to America

Despite the Amazon's colorful debut tacked onto *All-Star* #8, there had been no rush to induct her into the all-male Justice Society of America. That ensemble already had eight members—two each from AA's *All-American Comics* and *Flash Comics*, and two each from DC's *More Fun Comics* and *Adventure Comics*—and seemed disinclined to add any more characters. That's understandable, since every issue of *All-Star* contained a solo chapter devoted to the exploits of each member, and the addition of a ninth would either crowd somebody out of his solo spot, or else mean the same page count would have to be divided nine ways instead of eight.

By coincidence, however, America's abrupt entrance into the war coincided with sales figures already indicating that *Sensation* Comics was a runaway hit, and that Wonder Woman was the reason. So M.C. Gaines decided that she should be squeezed into the JSA lineup. And so she was, with the first "post-Pearl" issue of *All-Star Comics*, #11. Her face appears right up there on its cover with those of the other members; on the splash page inside, since she hadn't formally joined yet, she is listed as being a "guest star in a national emergency."

A big deal is made of her in that issue. The JSAers have all joined one branch or another of the armed services right after December 7, and chairman Hawkman and his lady friend Shiera Sanders run into nurse Diana Prince on an armed convoy of U.S. ships. This chance meeting is followed in the comic by a solo chapter starring Wonder Woman.

In it, the Amazon helps American forces secure the Philippines—something that, in real life, the U.S. military was definitely not doing in the dark days of December 1941 when those islands were invaded by Japan. Wonder Woman's chapter is followed by six more, each starring one of the JSA men saving some beleaguered locale in the Pacific war theater. Then, in a two-page epilogue, Wonder Woman and the eight male JSAers are all yanked, by member Johnny Thunder's personal Thunderbolt (don't ask!), into a confab of top American military brass—and all nine of them are immediately inducted into what amounts to a new group created to aid the war effort: the Justice Battalion of America.

Because this volume only reprints the pages from *All-Star* #11 that relate to Wonder Woman, we figured we needed that explanation in the preceding paragraph. Even so, we still haven't revealed precisely *how* she was squeezed into a comic that had room for eight solo-hero chapters surrounded by brief framing sequences. Well, it seems that one of the JSA members—the very powerful Spectre—is a ghost, and thus can't join the Army or Navy like his fellow members, so he sits that adventure out.

By the time Wonder Woman joined the Justice Society, however, she had also proved to be so popular that M.C. Gaines and his partner, Jack Liebowitz (who was also a co-owner of DC Comics), decided to give her her own eponymous title in record time, just six months after her first appearance. And that created a problem, since there was a standing rule that any hero popular

enough to star in his (or presumably her) own title had to become merely an honorary member of the JSA, like Superman, Batman, Flash, and Green Lantern. So, after having her appointed the secretary of the new Justice Battalion in *All-Star Comics* #12 (all secretaries were female, right?) and having her remain behind in Washington, D.C., for that adventure, Gaines decreed she should be given less space in future issues. Thus, though she did play a major part in *All-Star* #13, after that she merely acted as the group's secretary for the next several years, appearing in the opening and finale of most yarns, but never going on solo missions. This was done not because she was "just a girl," but for exactly the opposite reason: she was already so popular that she didn't need the exposure!

Dr. Marston hadn't been very happy with her appearances in *All-Star* anyway, because they were written by Gardner Fox, not himself. In fact, when he was sent the Wonder Woman solo chapter for issue #13, he insisted on rewriting it from top to bottom! He was no doubt delighted when her role in the JSA was subsequently diminished. Reportedly, AA

editor Sheldon Mayer was happy about that, too. He apparently didn't care much for Wonder Woman—or probably for Marston, who could always do an end-run around him to score points with Gaines, who was overly impressed by his academic credentials and media fame.

Diana Prince kept busy in *Sensation* Comics and the brand new *Wonder Woman* mag. In the first issue of the latter, she encountered a Nazi spy ring that was the "fourth ring" of a three-ring circus. The other three stories in that issue retold her origin in great detail, pitted her against German U-boats, and sent her down to Mexico to break up a Japanese spy ring. She was definitely an equal-opportunity freedom fighter!

All the above happened in roughly six months' of Wonder Woman adventures. But the war still had three more years to run—and Wonder Woman, who in the words of cartoonist, Jules Feiffer "got patriotic fast for a country she had never seen," was going to have a big part to play in the four-color version of the Allied victory!

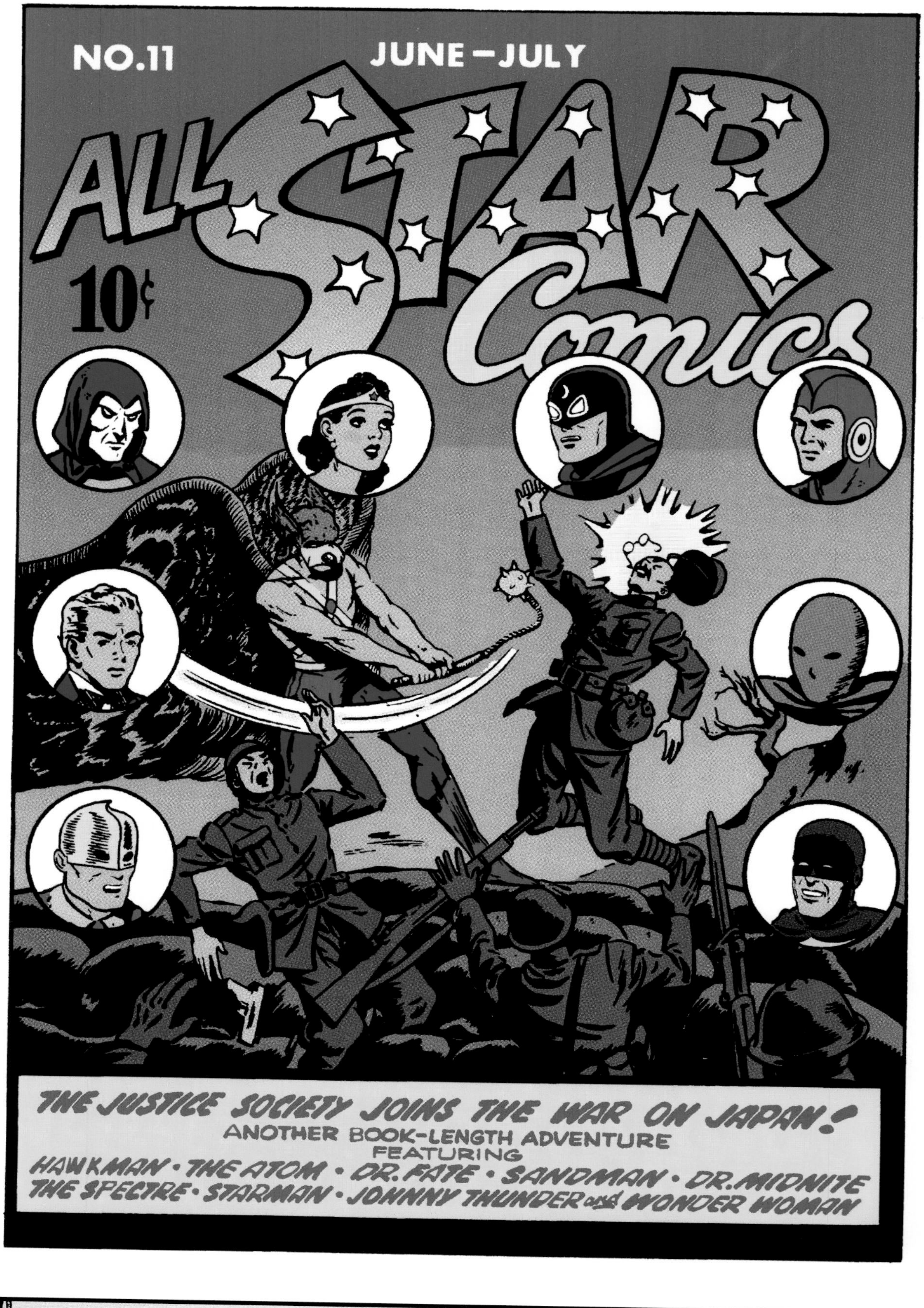

NO.11
JUNE—JULY
ALL STAR Comics
10¢
THE JUSTICE SOCIETY JOINS THE WAR ON JAPAN!
ANOTHER BOOK-LENGTH ADVENTURE
FEATURING
HAWKMAN • THE ATOM • DR. FATE • SANDMAN • DR. MIDNITE
THE SPECTRE • STARMAN • JOHNNY THUNDER and WONDER WOMAN

All-Star Comics #11 (June–July 1942) - art: Sheldon Moldoff, et al.

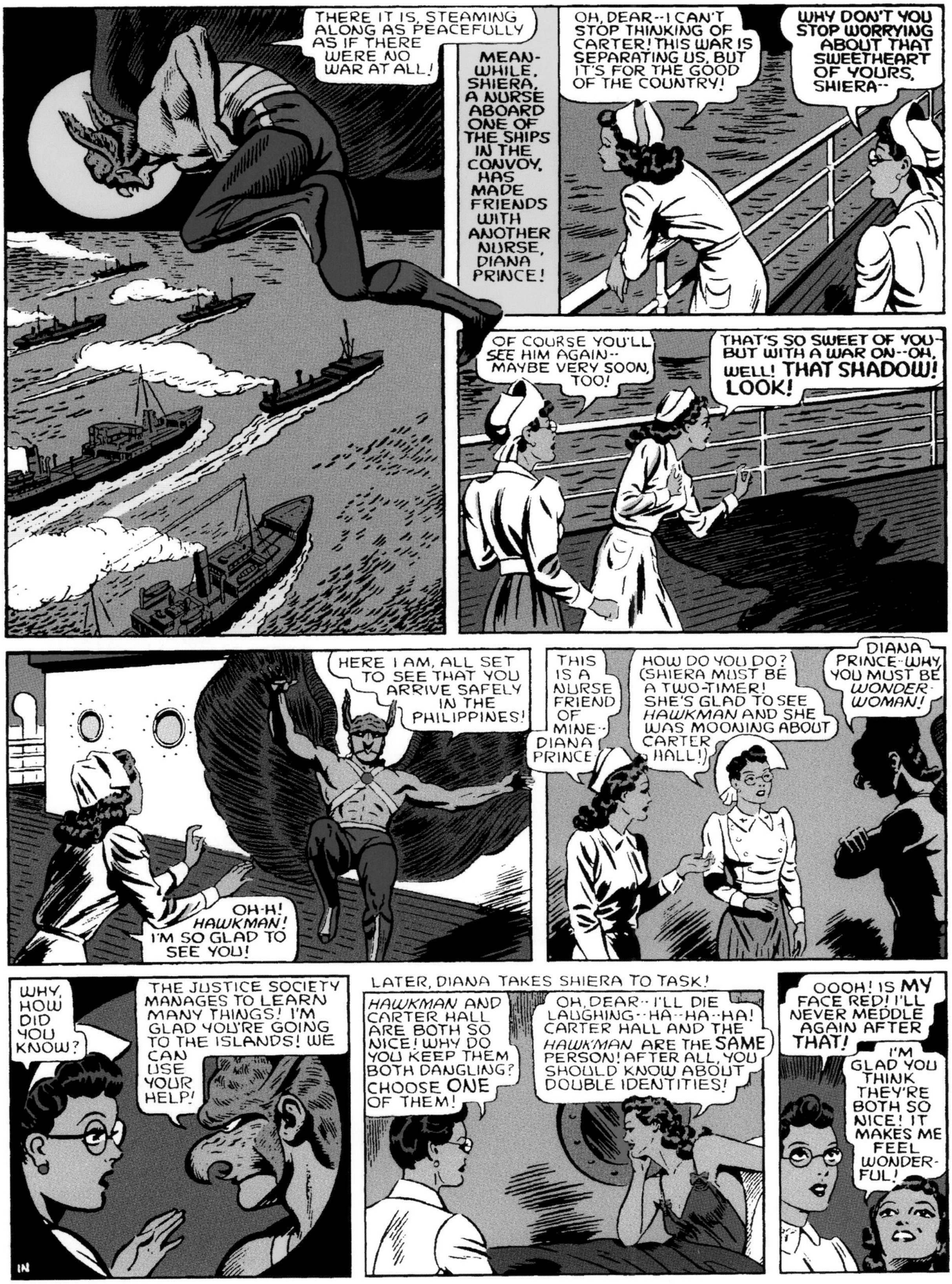
THERE IT IS, STEAMING ALONG AS PEACEFULLY AS IF THERE WERE NO WAR AT ALL!
MEAN-WHILE, SHIERA, A NURSE ABOARD ONE OF THE SHIPS IN THE CONVOY, HAS MADE FRIENDS WITH ANOTHER NURSE, DIANA PRINCE!
OH, DEAR--I CAN'T STOP THINKING OF CARTER! THIS WAR IS SEPARATING US, BUT IT'S FOR THE GOOD OF THE COUNTRY!
WHY DON'T YOU STOP WORRYING ABOUT THAT SWEETHEART OF YOURS, SHIERA--
OF COURSE YOU'LL SEE HIM AGAIN-- MAYBE VERY SOON, TOO!
THAT'S SO SWEET OF YOU-- BUT WITH A WAR ON--OH, WELL! THAT SHADOW! LOOK!
HERE I AM, ALL SET TO SEE THAT YOU ARRIVE SAFELY IN THE PHILIPPINES!
OH-H! HAWKMAN! I'M SO GLAD TO SEE YOU!
THIS IS A NURSE FRIEND OF MINE-- DIANA PRINCE
HOW DO YOU DO? (SHIERA MUST BE A TWO-TIMER! SHE'S GLAD TO SEE HAWKMAN AND SHE WAS MOONING ABOUT CARTER HALL!)
DIANA PRINCE--WHY, YOU MUST BE WONDER-WOMAN!
WHY, HOW DID YOU KNOW?
THE JUSTICE SOCIETY MANAGES TO LEARN MANY THINGS! I'M GLAD YOU'RE GOING TO THE ISLANDS! WE CAN USE YOUR HELP!
LATER, DIANA TAKES SHIERA TO TASK!
HAWKMAN AND CARTER HALL ARE BOTH SO NICE! WHY DO YOU KEEP THEM BOTH DANGLING? CHOOSE ONE OF THEM!
OH, DEAR-- I'LL DIE LAUGHING--HA--HA--HA! CARTER HALL AND THE HAWKMAN ARE THE SAME PERSON! AFTER ALL, YOU SHOULD KNOW ABOUT DOUBLE IDENTITIES!
OOOH! IS MY FACE RED! I'LL NEVER MEDDLE AGAIN AFTER THAT!
I'M GLAD YOU THINK THEY'RE BOTH SO NICE! IT MAKES ME FEEL WONDER-FUL!

All-Star Comics #11 (June–July 1942) - script: Gardner F. Fox - art: Jack Burnley

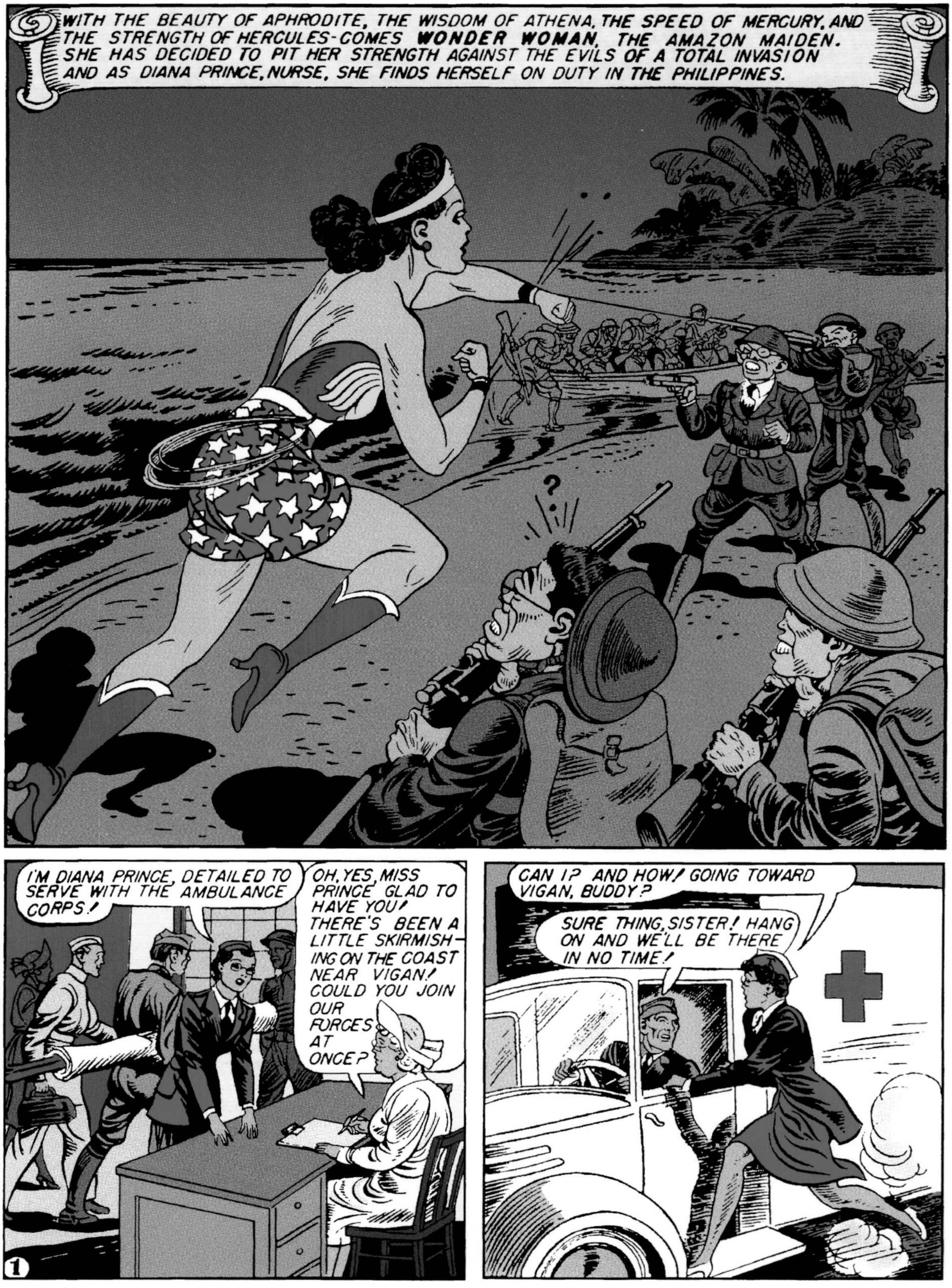
WITH THE BEAUTY OF APHRODITE, THE WISDOM OF ATHENA, THE SPEED OF MERCURY, AND THE STRENGTH OF HERCULES-COMES WONDER WOMAN, THE AMAZON MAIDEN. SHE HAS DECIDED TO PIT HER STRENGTH AGAINST THE EVILS OF A TOTAL INVASION AND AS DIANA PRINCE, NURSE, SHE FINDS HERSELF ON DUTY IN THE PHILIPPINES.
?
I'M DIANA PRINCE, DETAILED TO SERVE WITH THE AMBULANCE CORPS!
OH, YES, MISS PRINCE GLAD TO HAVE YOU! THERE'S BEEN A LITTLE SKIRMISHING ON THE COAST NEAR VIGAN! COULD YOU JOIN OUR FORCES AT ONCE?
1
CAN I? AND HOW! GOING TOWARD VIGAN, BUDDY?
SURE THING, SISTER! HANG ON AND WE'LL BE THERE IN NO TIME!

All-Star Comics #11 (June–July 1942) - script: Gardner F. Fox - art: H.G. Peter

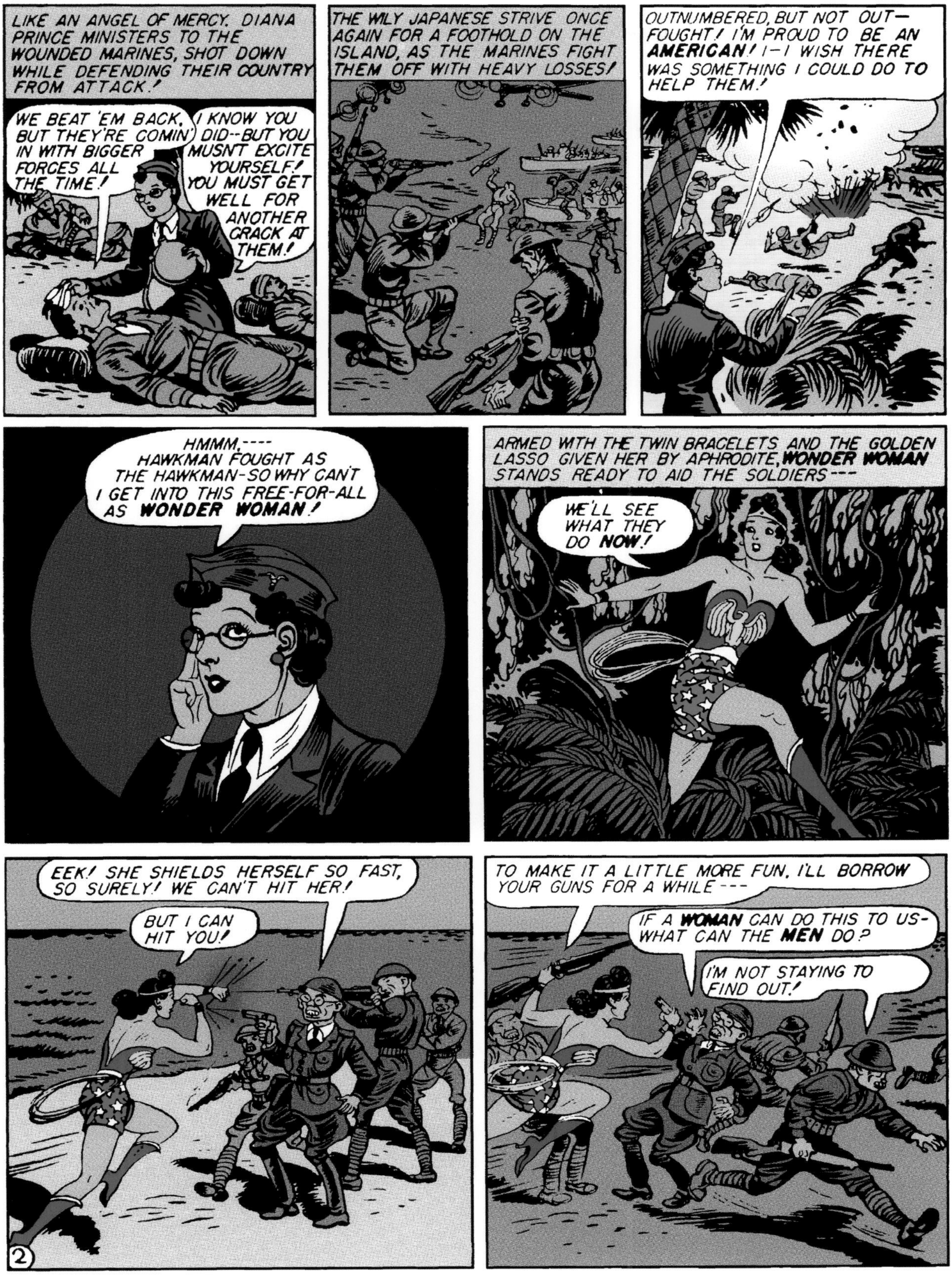
LIKE AN ANGEL OF MERCY, DIANA PRINCE MINISTERS TO THE WOUNDED MARINES, SHOT DOWN WHILE DEFENDING THEIR COUNTRY FROM ATTACK!
WE BEAT 'EM BACK, BUT THEY'RE COMIN' IN WITH BIGGER FORCES ALL THE TIME!
I KNOW YOU DID--BUT YOU MUSN'T EXCITE YOURSELF! YOU MUST GET WELL FOR ANOTHER CRACK AT THEM!
THE WILY JAPANESE STRIVE ONCE AGAIN FOR A FOOTHOLD ON THE ISLAND, AS THE MARINES FIGHT THEM OFF WITH HEAVY LOSSES!
OUTNUMBERED, BUT NOT OUT-FOUGHT! I'M PROUD TO BE AN AMERICAN! I-I WISH THERE WAS SOMETHING I COULD DO TO HELP THEM!
HMMM,---- HAWKMAN FOUGHT AS THE HAWKMAN-SO WHY CAN'T I GET INTO THIS FREE-FOR-ALL AS WONDER WOMAN!
ARMED WITH THE TWIN BRACELETS AND THE GOLDEN LASSO GIVEN HER BY APHRODITE, WONDER WOMAN STANDS READY TO AID THE SOLDIERS---
WE'LL SEE WHAT THEY DO NOW!
EEK! SHE SHIELDS HERSELF SO FAST, SO SURELY! WE CAN'T HIT HER!
BUT I CAN HIT YOU!
2
TO MAKE IT A LITTLE MORE FUN, I'LL BORROW YOUR GUNS FOR A WHILE---
IF A WOMAN CAN DO THIS TO US-WHAT CAN THE MEN DO?
I'M NOT STAYING TO FIND OUT!

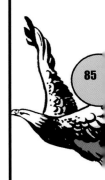

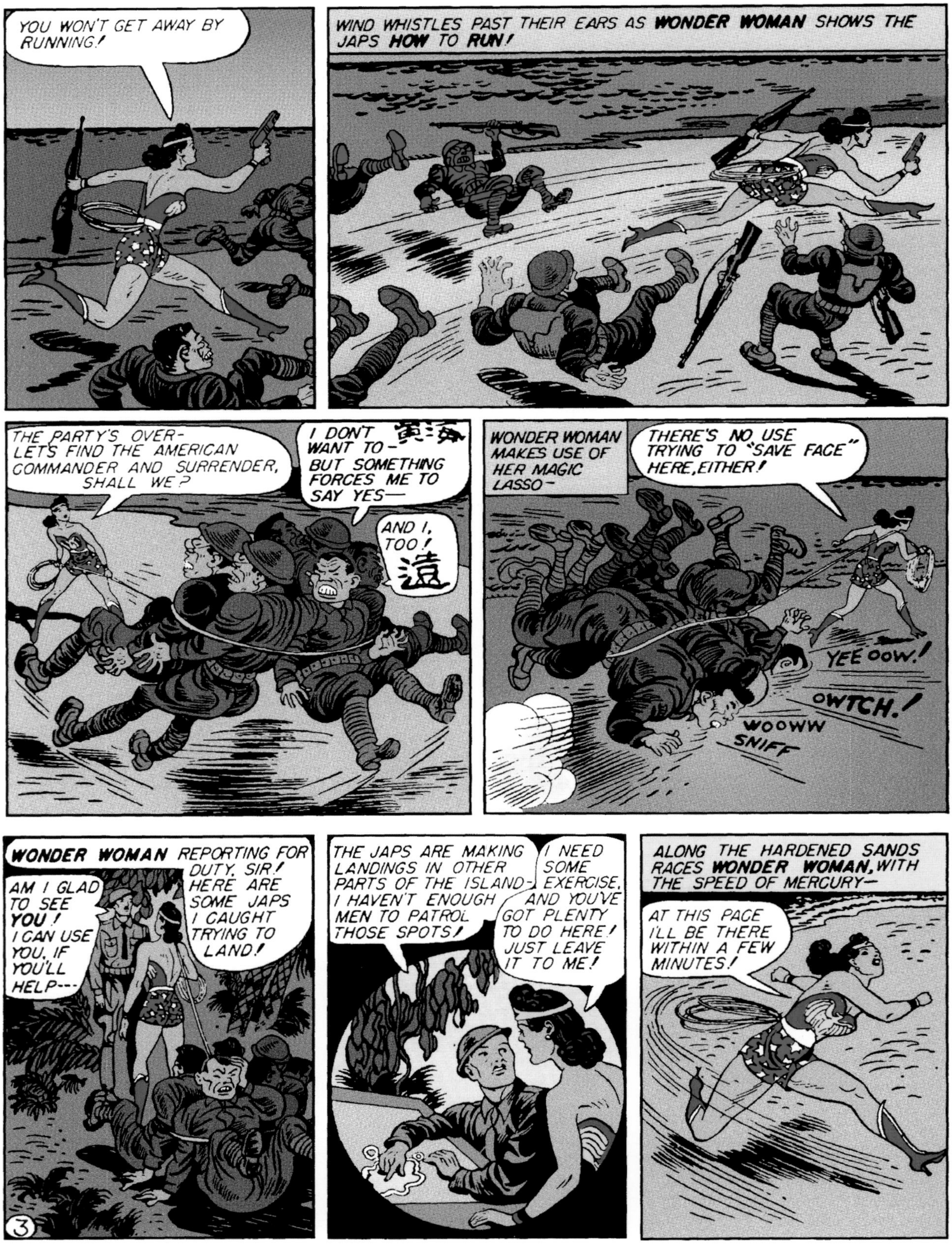
YOU WON'T GET AWAY BY RUNNING!
WIND WHISTLES PAST THEIR EARS AS WONDER WOMAN SHOWS THE JAPS HOW TO RUN!
THE PARTY'S OVER- LET'S FIND THE AMERICAN COMMANDER AND SURRENDER, SHALL WE?
I DON'T WANT TO- BUT SOMETHING FORCES ME TO SAY YES—
AND I, TOO!
WONDER WOMAN MAKES USE OF HER MAGIC LASSO-
THERE'S NO USE TRYING TO "SAVE FACE" HERE, EITHER!
YEE OOW!
OWTCH!
WOOWW
SNIFF
WONDER WOMAN REPORTING FOR DUTY, SIR! HERE ARE SOME JAPS I CAUGHT TRYING TO LAND!
AM I GLAD TO SEE YOU! I CAN USE YOU, IF YOU'LL HELP---
THE JAPS ARE MAKING LANDINGS IN OTHER PARTS OF THE ISLAND- I HAVEN'T ENOUGH MEN TO PATROL THOSE SPOTS!
I NEED SOME EXERCISE, AND YOU'VE GOT PLENTY TO DO HERE! JUST LEAVE IT TO ME!
ALONG THE HARDENED SANDS RACES WONDER WOMAN, WITH THE SPEED OF MERCURY—
AT THIS PACE I'LL BE THERE WITHIN A FEW MINUTES!
3

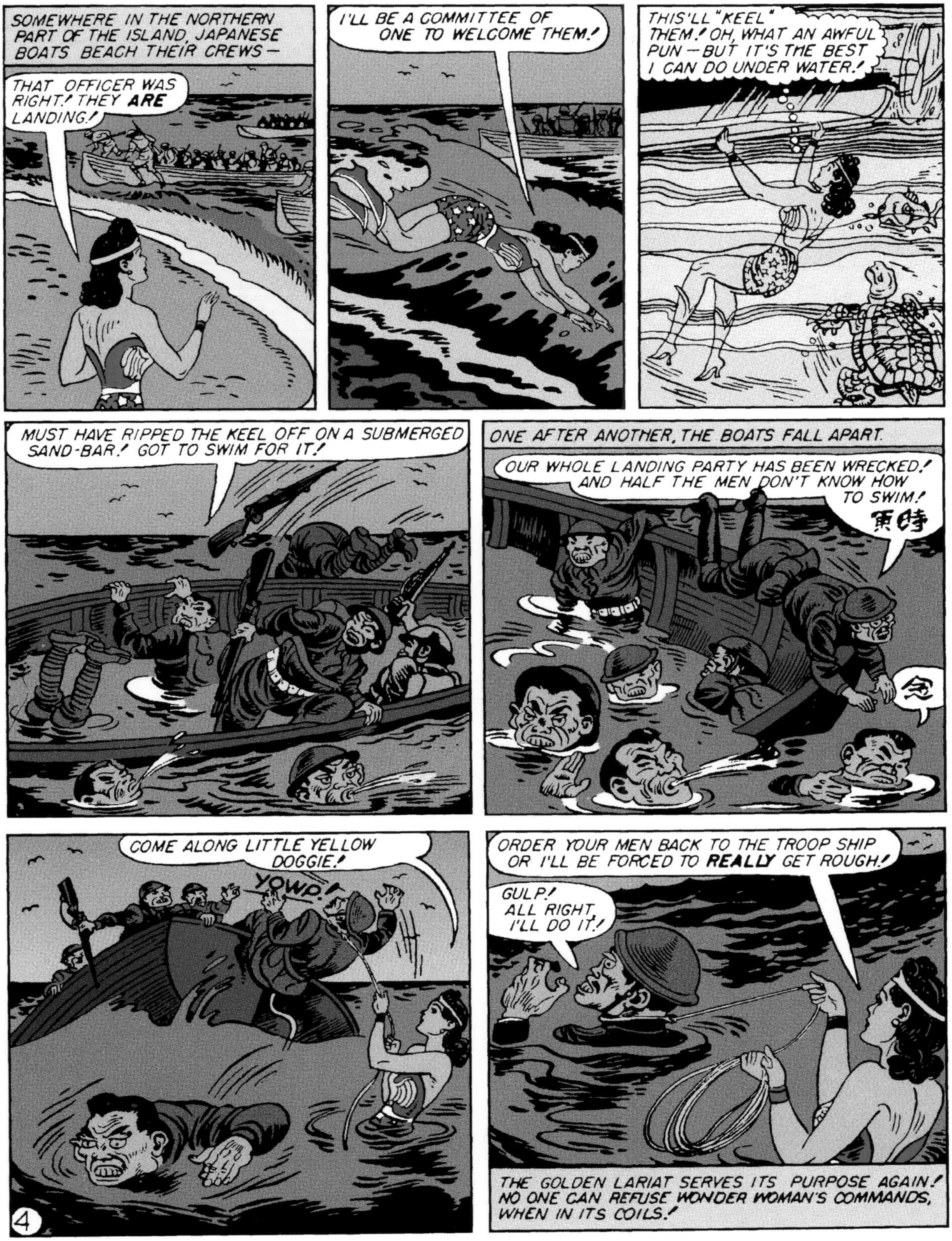
SOMEWHERE IN THE NORTHERN PART OF THE ISLAND, JAPANESE BOATS BEACH THEIR CREWS—
THAT OFFICER WAS RIGHT! THEY ARE LANDING!
I'LL BE A COMMITTEE OF ONE TO WELCOME THEM!
THIS'LL "KEEL" THEM! OH, WHAT AN AWFUL PUN—BUT IT'S THE BEST I CAN DO UNDER WATER!
MUST HAVE RIPPED THE KEEL OFF ON A SUBMERGED SAND-BAR! GOT TO SWIM FOR IT!
ONE AFTER ANOTHER, THE BOATS FALL APART.
OUR WHOLE LANDING PARTY HAS BEEN WRECKED! AND HALF THE MEN DON'T KNOW HOW TO SWIM!
COME ALONG LITTLE YELLOW DOGGIE!
YOWP!
ORDER YOUR MEN BACK TO THE TROOP SHIP OR I'LL BE FORCED TO REALLY GET ROUGH!
GULP! ALL RIGHT, I'LL DO IT!
THE GOLDEN LARIAT SERVES ITS PURPOSE AGAIN! NO ONE CAN REFUSE WONDER WOMAN'S COMMANDS, WHEN IN ITS COILS!
4

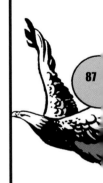

THEY'RE LEAVING FASTER THAN THEY CAME! THE THING TO DO IS **KEEP** 'EM AWAY!
NOW FOR SOME OF THE OTHER ISLANDS! HMMM, THERE MUST BE A QUICKER WAY OF COVERING THEM THAN SWIMMING!
A JAP PLANE! I'LL LET **HIM** SERVE THE PURPOSE!
WITH AN ACCURATE TOSS OF THE LARIAT, **WONDER WOMAN** IS LIFTED HIGH ABOVE THE TREE-TOPS AND CARRIED ALONG!
YOU'RE AWAY OFF YOUR BEAM, BUDDY! HEAD SOUTH—I'LL LET YOU KNOW WHERE TO LET ME OFF—
EEK! IT'S THAT FEMALE DRAGON WE HEARD ABOUT!
I'M EVEN STRONGER WHEN I GET ANGRY! SO DON'T MAKE ME LOSE MY TEMPER!
I—I WOULDN'T **THINK** OF IT!
MAP
5
YOU CAN LET ME OFF HERE! I SEE TROUBLE AHEAD AND I'M GOING TO MEET IT HALF-WAY!

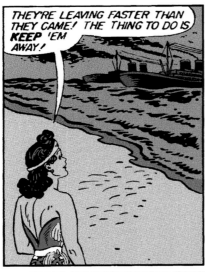

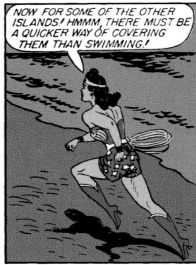

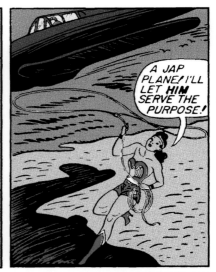

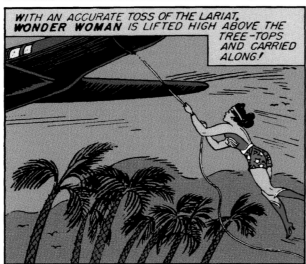

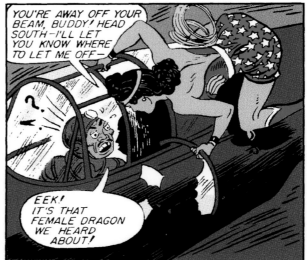

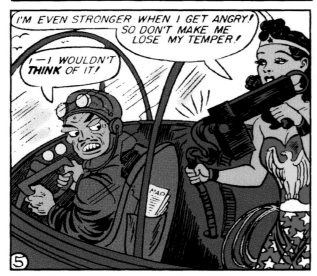

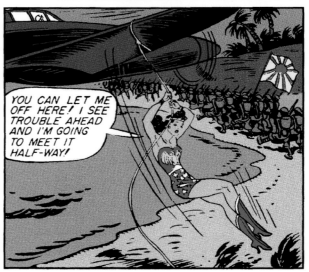

Wonder Woman appears every month in SENSATION COMICS!

A MEETING OF COMMANDERS OF HIGH RANK IN THE AMERICAN ARMY FINDS ONE SUBJECT ESPECIALLY POPULAR
--AND AFTER SMASHING ALL THOSE INVASION ATTEMPTS, HAWKMAN FLEW OUT TO ESCORT A HOSPITAL CONVOY TO THE PHILIPPINES!
I KNOW! WONDER-WOMAN WAS ON THAT SHIP! YOU SHOULD HAVE SEEN HER IN ACTION!
I STILL CONTEND STARMAN'S FEAT IN CAPTURING THE NAVAL BASE OF FORMOSA PRACTICALLY SINGLE HANDED, IS THE FINEST PERFORMANCE OF THE WAR SO FAR!
ARE YOU FORGETTING WHAT I TOLD YOU ABOUT THE SANDMAN! HUH, YOU HAVEN'T SEEN ACTION UNTIL YOU'VE SEEN HIM!
YOU'VE BEEN MY LIFELONG FRIEND, BUT WHEN YOU SAY THE ATOM IS THE BETTER MAN THAN DR. FATE, I FIGHT!
THEN FIGHT, DON'T TALK! THAT LITTLE ATOM IS MORE DESTRUCTIVE THAN A TEN TON DEMOLITION BOMB!
GENTLEMEN, PLEASE!
I'LL TELL YOU WHO DID THE MOST-- DOCTOR MIDNITE!
MEN OF THE ARMY, I PRESENT THE NAVY'S PROUD BOAST--JOHNNY THUNDER!
WE'LL BRING OUR MEN HERE, TOO! THEN WE'LL KNOW WHO IS THE BEST AMONG THEM!
LET'S DO IT!
RADIO OUR STAFF HEAD-QUARTERS FOR THE VARIOUS MEMBERS OF THE JUSTICE SOCIETY TO JOIN US--
SAY, YOU DON'T HAVE TO GO TO ALL THAT BOTHER! MY THUNDER-BOLT WILL FETCH THEM HERE-- I'LL BE GLAD TO SEE 'EM ALL AGAIN, MYSELF! WE'D GO SWELL AS A WHOLE BATTALION, WOULDN'T WE?
WHAT IS THIS, A JAP PLOT TO KIDNAP US? OH, IT'S YOU, IS IT?
JOHNNY, DON'T YOU REALIZE WE'RE AT WAR?
WE HAVE TO BE BACK ON THE JOB--
IT'S ALL RIGHT, FELLOWS! THE DIVISION COMMANDERS WANTED US TO GET TOGETHER, THAT'S ALL, AND WE HAVE A SURPRISE FOR YOU!

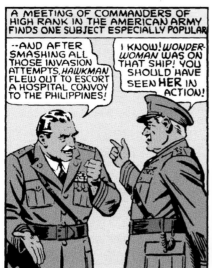

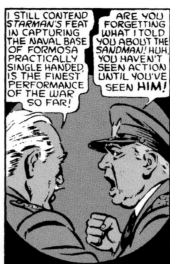

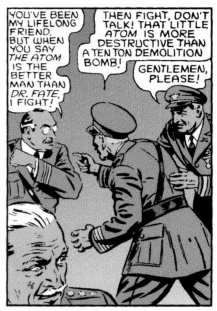

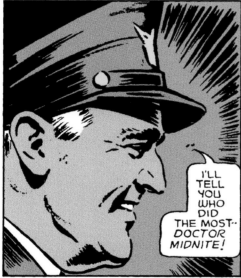

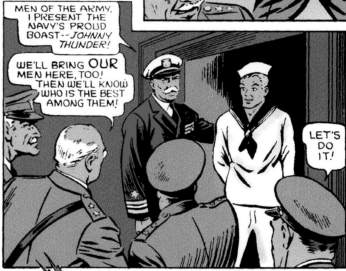

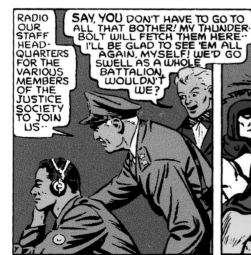

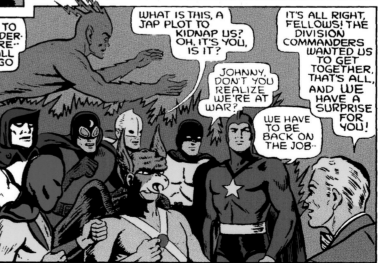

All-Star Comics #11 (June–July 1942) script: Gardner F. Fox - art: Jack Burnley

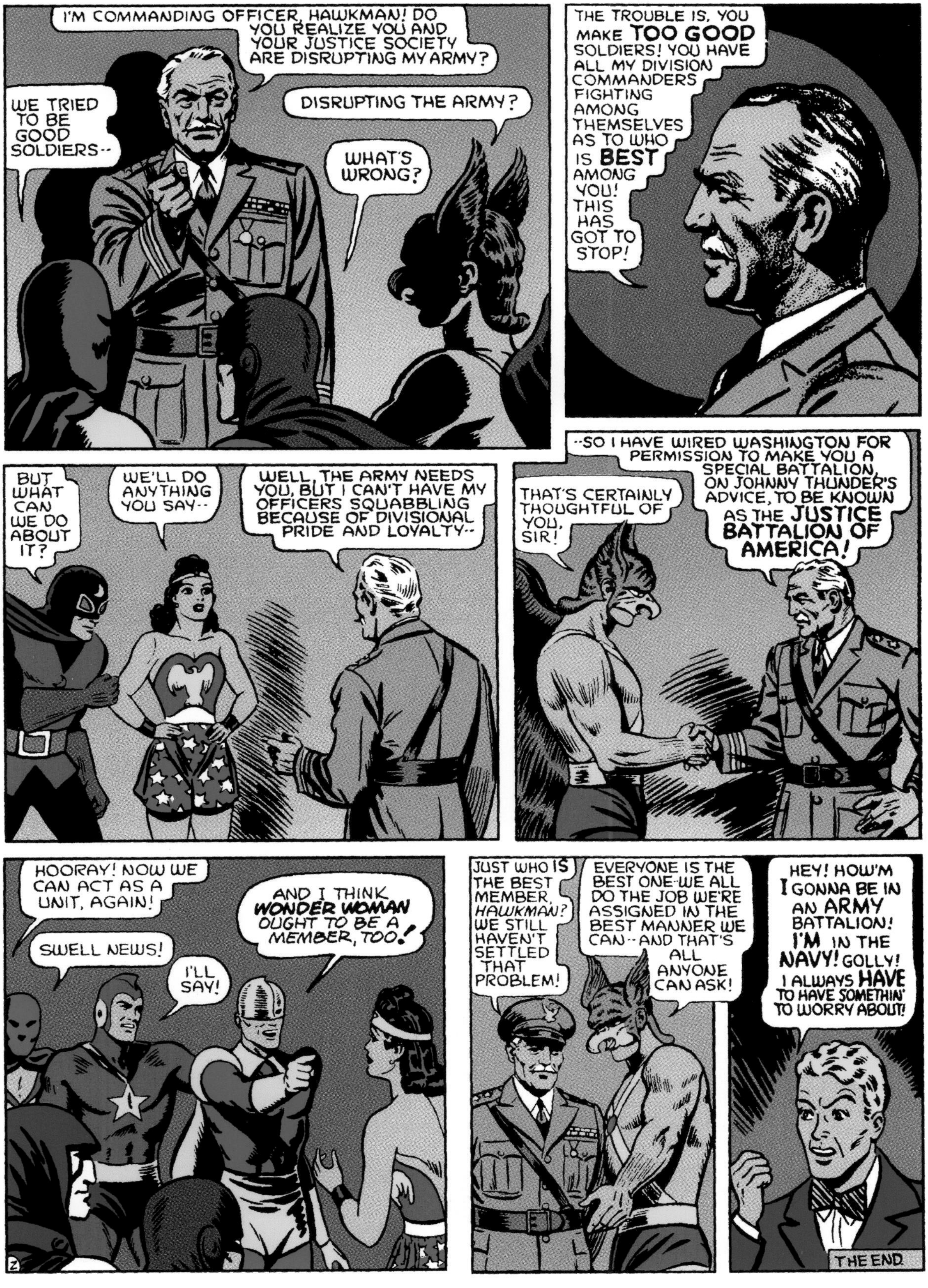
I'M COMMANDING OFFICER, HAWKMAN! DO YOU REALIZE YOU AND YOUR JUSTICE SOCIETY ARE DISRUPTING MY ARMY?
WE TRIED TO BE GOOD SOLDIERS--
DISRUPTING THE ARMY?
WHAT'S WRONG?
THE TROUBLE IS, YOU MAKE TOO GOOD SOLDIERS! YOU HAVE ALL MY DIVISION COMMANDERS FIGHTING AMONG THEMSELVES AS TO WHO IS BEST AMONG YOU! THIS HAS GOT TO STOP!
BUT WHAT CAN WE DO ABOUT IT?
WE'LL DO ANYTHING YOU SAY--
WELL, THE ARMY NEEDS YOU, BUT I CAN'T HAVE MY OFFICERS SQUABBLING BECAUSE OF DIVISIONAL PRIDE AND LOYALTY--
--SO I HAVE WIRED WASHINGTON FOR PERMISSION TO MAKE YOU A SPECIAL BATTALION, ON JOHNNY THUNDER'S ADVICE, TO BE KNOWN AS THE JUSTICE BATTALION OF AMERICA!
THAT'S CERTAINLY THOUGHTFUL OF YOU, SIR!
HOORAY! NOW WE CAN ACT AS A UNIT, AGAIN!
SWELL NEWS!
I'LL SAY!
AND I THINK WONDER WOMAN OUGHT TO BE A MEMBER, TOO!
2
JUST WHO IS THE BEST MEMBER, HAWKMAN? WE STILL HAVEN'T SETTLED THAT PROBLEM!
EVERYONE IS THE BEST ONE-WE ALL DO THE JOB WE'RE ASSIGNED IN THE BEST MANNER WE CAN--AND THAT'S ALL ANYONE CAN ASK!
HEY! HOW'M I GONNA BE IN AN ARMY BATTALION! I'M IN THE NAVY! GOLLY! I ALWAYS HAVE TO HAVE SOMETHIN' TO WORRY ABOUT!
THE END.

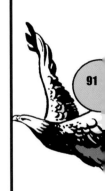

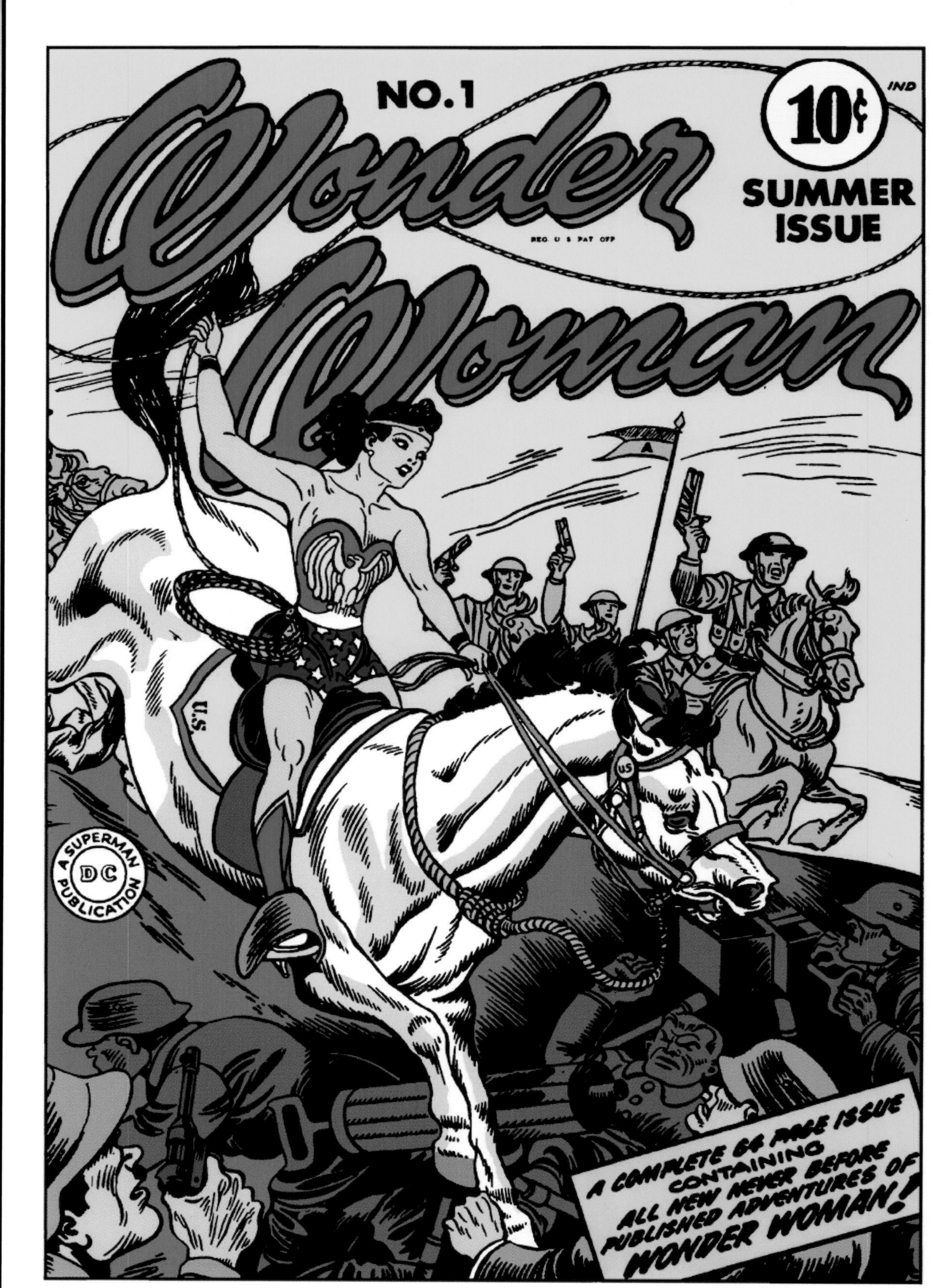
NO.1
Wonder Woman
10¢
IND
SUMMER ISSUE
REG. U.S. PAT. OFF.
A SUPERMAN DC PUBLICATION
A COMPLETE 64 PAGE ISSUE CONTAINING ALL NEW NEVER BEFORE PUBLISHED ADVENTURES OF WONDER WOMAN!

Wonder Woman #1 (Summer 1942) - Art: H.G. Peter

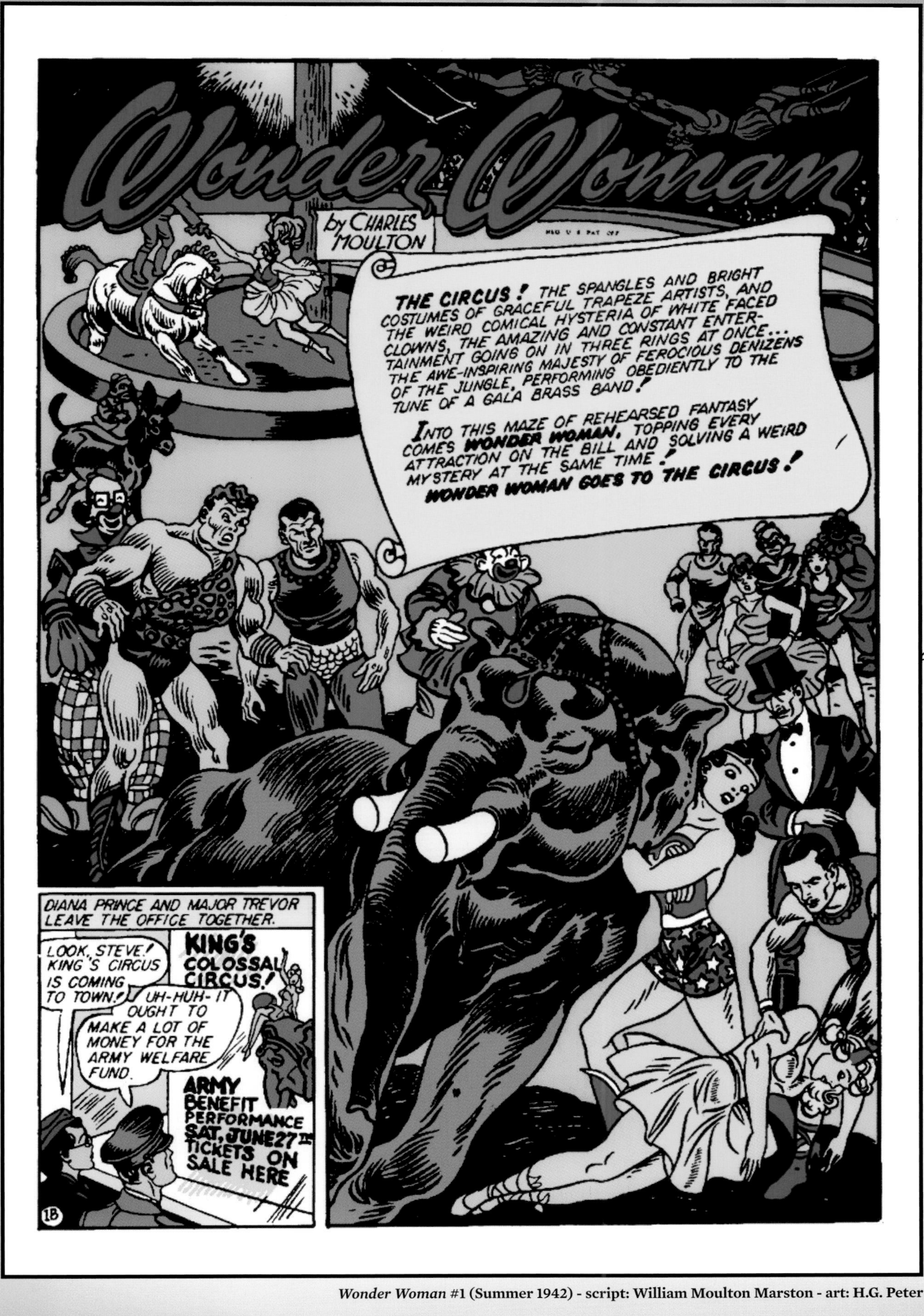

Wonder Woman
by CHARLES MOULTON
THE CIRCUS! THE SPANGLES AND BRIGHT COSTUMES OF GRACEFUL TRAPEZE ARTISTS, AND THE WEIRD COMICAL HYSTERIA OF WHITE FACED CLOWNS, THE AMAZING AND CONSTANT ENTERTAINMENT GOING ON IN THREE RINGS AT ONCE... THE AWE-INSPIRING MAJESTY OF FEROCIOUS DENIZENS OF THE JUNGLE, PERFORMING OBEDIENTLY TO THE TUNE OF A GALA BRASS BAND!
INTO THIS MAZE OF REHEARSED FANTASY COMES WONDER WOMAN, TOPPING EVERY ATTRACTION ON THE BILL AND SOLVING A WEIRD MYSTERY AT THE SAME TIME!
WONDER WOMAN GOES TO THE CIRCUS!
DIANA PRINCE AND MAJOR TREVOR LEAVE THE OFFICE TOGETHER.
LOOK, STEVE! KING'S CIRCUS IS COMING TO TOWN!
UH-HUH- IT OUGHT TO MAKE A LOT OF MONEY FOR THE ARMY WELFARE FUND.
KING'S COLOSSAL CIRCUS!
ARMY BENEFIT PERFORMANCE SAT, JUNE 27TH TICKETS ON SALE HERE
18

Wonder Woman #1 (Summer 1942) - script: William Moulton Marston - art: H.G. Peter

DRUGS

COME ON— I'M GOING TO BUY TICKETS AND TAKE THOSE SETTLEMENT KIDS TO THE CIRCUS. YOU'RE GOING TO HELP ME!

HUH? WHY PICK ON ME? WELL— ALL RIGHT. YOU'D BETTER BRING ETTA CANDY— KIDS CAN BE TOUGH TO HANDLE SOMETIMES.

AT THE CIRCUS ON SATURDAY THE CHILDREN VISIT THE ANIMAL CAGES.

CHILDREN, WHAT ANIMALS DO YOU WANT TO SEE FIRST?

THE ELEPHANTS! WE LIKE THE ELEPHANTS BEST!

DIANA TALKS WITH ELVA KING, THE CIRCUS OWNER'S NIECE, WHO TRAINS THE ELEPHANTS.

WHAT WONDERFUL ELEPHANTS!

YES, THESE ANIMALS COME FROM BURMA WHERE ELEPHANTS ARE WORSHIPPED. THEY ARE VERY VALUABLE.

THIS IS SAN YAN, OUR HEAD ELEPHANT MAN. THESE BURMESE CAME OVER WITH THE ELEPHANTS— DIDN'T YOU, SAN?

OH, SURE! ELEPHANT OUR FATHER - MOTHER! HONORABLE ANCESTORS SOULS IN ELEPHANTS— WE GUARD WITH OUR LIVES.

DAMLEE, MOTHER OF A BABY ELEPHANT, SUDDENLY COLLAPSES, TRUMPETING THE DEATH CRY!

EE-YEA-EEN!

得罪了诗鬼

POOR DAMLEE! SHE IS THE SEVENTH ELEPHANT THAT DIED THIS WEEK. IT WILL RUIN UNCLE ED'S CIRCUS. WHAT CAN BE KILLING THEM?

IT LOOKS LIKE POISON— SOMEONE SHOULD INVESTIGATE!

28

DARING DOM CARNEY, FLYING TRAPEZE PERFORMER, IS IN LOVE WITH ELVA—

OH DOM, ANOTHER ELEPHANT GONE! THIS WILL RUIN UNCLE ED—

SERVES HIM RIGHT! HE THREATENED TO FIRE ME FOR ASKING TO MARRY YOU. I'M AFRAID I CAN'T SYMPATHIZE WITH HIM—

DON'T FEED PAM. HER ACT GOES ON FIRST AND FEEDING NOW IS BAD FOR HER!

DO NOT FEED THE ANIMALS

WHAT DO I CARE IF ALL KING'S ELEPHANTS DIE. YOU'LL HAVE NO JOB. THEN YOU'LL MARRY ME!

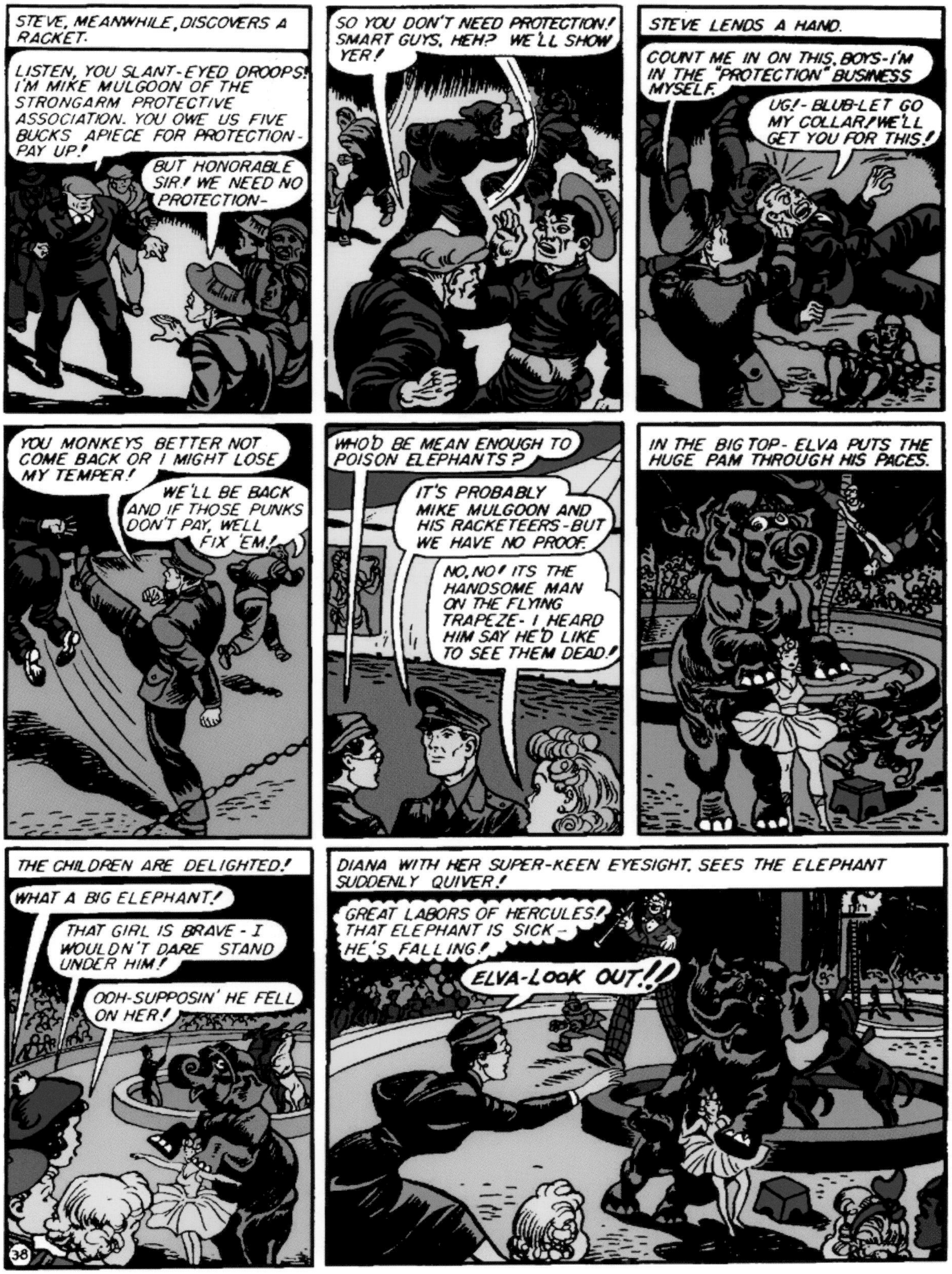
STEVE, MEANWHILE, DISCOVERS A RACKET.
LISTEN, YOU SLANT-EYED DROOPS! I'M MIKE MULGOON OF THE STRONGARM PROTECTIVE ASSOCIATION. YOU OWE US FIVE BUCKS APIECE FOR PROTECTION - PAY UP!
BUT HONORABLE SIR! WE NEED NO PROTECTION-
SO YOU DON'T NEED PROTECTION! SMART GUYS, HEH? WE'LL SHOW YER!
STEVE LENDS A HAND.
COUNT ME IN ON THIS, BOYS-I'M IN THE "PROTECTION" BUSINESS MYSELF.
UG!- BLUB-LET GO MY COLLAR! WE'LL GET YOU FOR THIS!
YOU MONKEYS BETTER NOT COME BACK OR I MIGHT LOSE MY TEMPER!
WE'LL BE BACK AND IF THOSE PUNKS DON'T PAY, WELL FIX 'EM!
WHO'D BE MEAN ENOUGH TO POISON ELEPHANTS?
IT'S PROBABLY MIKE MULGOON AND HIS RACKETEERS-BUT WE HAVE NO PROOF.
NO, NO! ITS THE HANDSOME MAN ON THE FLYING TRAPEZE- I HEARD HIM SAY HE'D LIKE TO SEE THEM DEAD!
IN THE BIG TOP- ELVA PUTS THE HUGE PAM THROUGH HIS PACES.
THE CHILDREN ARE DELIGHTED!
WHAT A BIG ELEPHANT!
THAT GIRL IS BRAVE - I WOULDN'T DARE STAND UNDER HIM!
OOH-SUPPOSIN' HE FELL ON HER!
38
DIANA WITH HER SUPER-KEEN EYESIGHT, SEES THE ELEPHANT SUDDENLY QUIVER!
GREAT LABORS OF HERCULES! THAT ELEPHANT IS SICK- HE'S FALLING!
ELVA-LOOK OUT!!

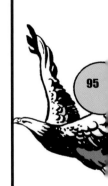

BUT DIANA'S WARNING COMES TOO LATE! THE GREAT PACHYDERM CRASHES TO THE GROUND, PINNING ELVA HELPLESSLY BENEATH HIM!

EE-YEA EEH!

HELP!

THE ELEPHANT IS DEAD - POISONED!

ELVA'S KILLED TOO!

STAND BACK, EVERYBODY! THE GIRL MAY BE ALIVE — GIVE HER AIR!

LUCKILY AN ELEPHANT STAND SUPPORTS PART OF THE ANIMAL'S WEIGHT - ELVA IS UNCONSCIOUS BUT STILL BREATHING!

SHE'S ALIVE - WE'VE GOT TO LIFT THE ELEPHANT OFF HER LEGS!

OKAY - I'LL GET OUR STRONGMAN AND ROUSTABOUTS!

BUT ALL THE COMBINED STRENGTH OF THE STRONGEST MEN IN THE CIRCUS FAILS TO LIFT THE TREMENDOUS WEIGHT OF THE DEAD ELEPHANT.

NO USE — PUFF - CAN'T BUDGE IT!

WHEW! THIS CONSARNED ELEPHANT WEIGHS FORTY TONS!

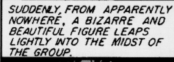

SUDDENLY, FROM APPARENTLY NOWHERE, A BIZARRE AND BEAUTIFUL FIGURE LEAPS LIGHTLY INTO THE MIDST OF THE GROUP.

HOLY HANNAH! IT'S WONDER WOMAN!

BOY! OH BOY! SHE MUSTA DROPPED FROM HEAVEN!

GIVE ME ROOM, BOYS - THERE'S NOT A MINUTE TO LOSE! WHEN I LIFT THE ELEPHANT, YOU PULL THE GIRL CLEAR!

HO! HO! YOU LIFT THAT ELEPHANT? WHAT A LAUGH!

YEAH, YOU AND HOW MANY DERRICKS?

AW, LET HER DO IT -- C'MON WONDER WOMAN!

48

GRASPING THE ELEPHANT'S HARNESS, WONDER WOMAN QUICKLY RAISES ITS VAST WEIGHT FROM THE GROUND.

THIS IS EASY - WHAT MADE YOU FELLOWS THINK THIS ELEPHANT IS HEAVY?

GEE WHILLIKERS! WHAT A WOMAN!

SHE'S SUPERB! MAGNIFICENT!

THE CROWD SHOUTS FOR **WONDER WOMAN**.

YIPEE! **WONDER WOMAN!** GIVE US **WONDER! WOMAN!**

WE WANT WONDER WOMAN!

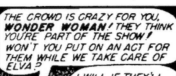

THE CROWD IS CRAZY FOR YOU, **WONDER WOMAN!** THEY THINK YOU'RE PART OF THE SHOW! WON'T YOU PUT ON AN ACT FOR THEM WHILE WE TAKE CARE OF ELVA?

I WILL IF THEY'LL GIVE A SPECIAL COLLECTION FOR THE SOLDIERS!

WONDER WOMAN JUMPS ON A CIRCUS HORSE AND GOES INTO HER ACT.

YEAH! **WONDER WOMAN!**

THEN SHE GIVES THE HORSE A RIDE!

YEA! **WONDER WOMAN!**

?

WONDER WOMAN DASHES TO A CAGE AND WRESTLES WITH A FEROCIOUS LION—

WHEE!

BRAVO WONDER WOMAN!

THEN TOSSES THE KING OF BEASTS INTO HIS CAGE AGAIN!

I HOPE I WASN'T TOO ROUGH WITH PUSSY- I DON'T WANT TO HURT HIM!

97

LAD-EES AND GENTLEMEN! **WONDAH WOMAN** WILL NOW ATTEMPT THE LONGEST DIVE EVER MADE BY MAN OR WOMAN! SHE WILL HURL HERSELF THE ENTIRE LENGTH OF THE BIG TOP, LANDING SAFELY-WE PRAY- ON YONDER TRAPEZE!

SB

A TENSE SILENCE GRIPS THE SPECTATORS -THE CROWD HOLDS ITS BREATH AS **WONDER WOMAN** HURTLES THROUGH THE AIR IN HER DEATH-DEFYING LEAP--

I CAN MAKE IT IF THE TRAPEZE HOLDS STEADY!

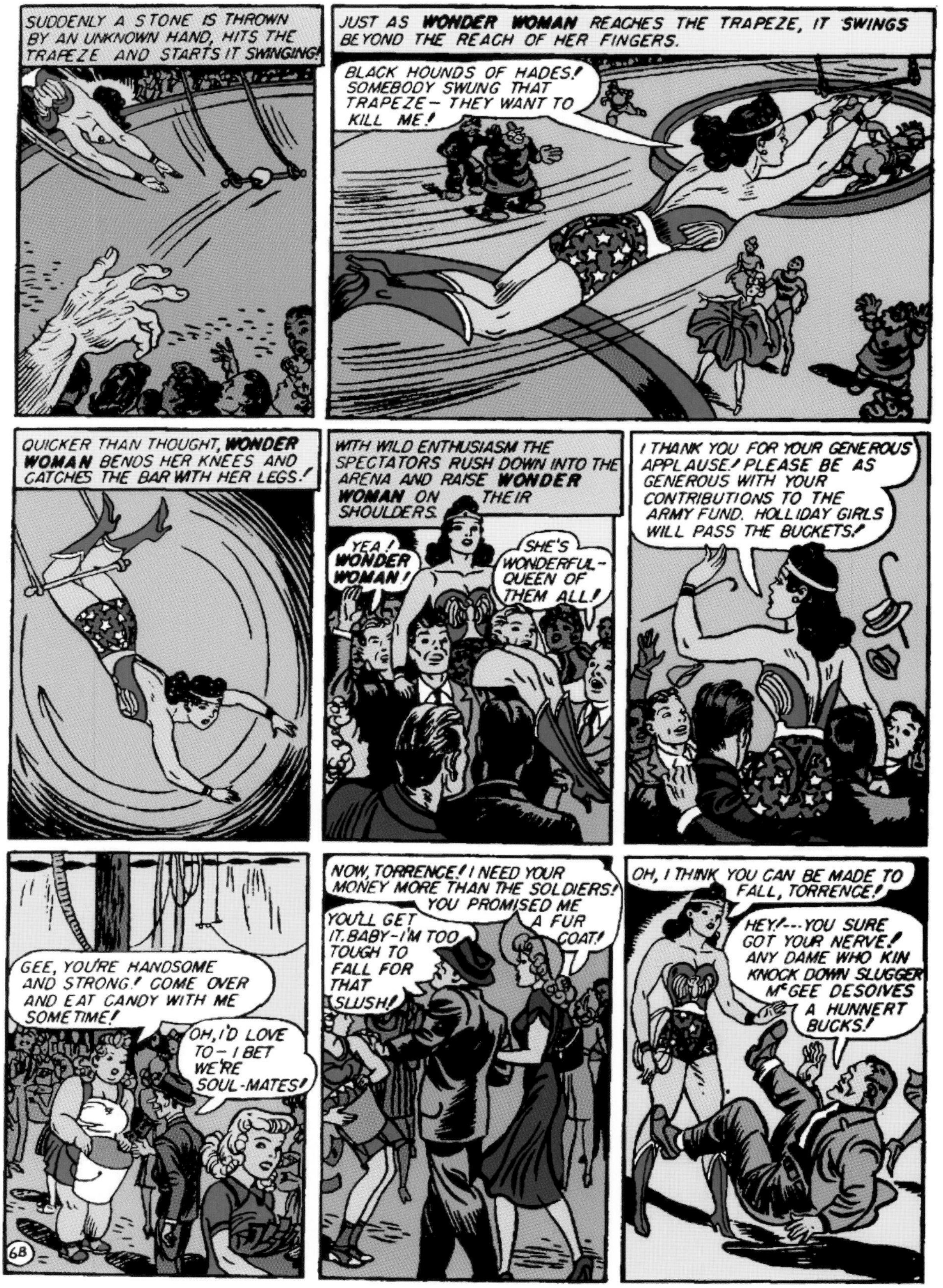

SUDDENLY A STONE IS THROWN BY AN UNKNOWN HAND, HITS THE TRAPEZE AND STARTS IT SWINGING!
JUST AS WONDER WOMAN REACHES THE TRAPEZE, IT SWINGS BEYOND THE REACH OF HER FINGERS.
BLACK HOUNDS OF HADES! SOMEBODY SWUNG THAT TRAPEZE– THEY WANT TO KILL ME!
QUICKER THAN THOUGHT, WONDER WOMAN BENDS HER KNEES AND CATCHES THE BAR WITH HER LEGS!
WITH WILD ENTHUSIASM THE SPECTATORS RUSH DOWN INTO THE ARENA AND RAISE WONDER WOMAN ON THEIR SHOULDERS.
YEA! WONDER WOMAN!
SHE'S WONDERFUL– QUEEN OF THEM ALL!
I THANK YOU FOR YOUR GENEROUS APPLAUSE! PLEASE BE AS GENEROUS WITH YOUR CONTRIBUTIONS TO THE ARMY FUND. HOLLIDAY GIRLS WILL PASS THE BUCKETS!
GEE, YOU'RE HANDSOME AND STRONG! COME OVER AND EAT CANDY WITH ME SOMETIME!
OH, I'D LOVE TO– I BET WE'RE SOUL-MATES!
68
NOW, TORRENCE! I NEED YOUR MONEY MORE THAN THE SOLDIERS! YOU PROMISED ME A FUR COAT!
YOU'LL GET IT. BABY–I'M TOO TOUGH TO FALL FOR THAT SLUSH!
OH, I THINK YOU CAN BE MADE TO FALL, TORRENCE!
HEY!---YOU SURE GOT YOUR NERVE! ANY DAME WHO KIN KNOCK DOWN SLUGGER McGEE DESOIVES A HUNNERT BUCKS!

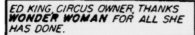

ED KING, CIRCUS OWNER, THANKS **WONDER WOMAN** FOR ALL SHE HAS DONE.

I CAN'T THANK YOU ENOUGH, **WONDER WOMAN**! BUT MY CIRCUS WILL BE RUINED UNLESS I CAN STOP THESE ELEPHANT KILLINGS!

KING'S COLOSSAL STUPENDOUS SHOWS.

IT'S CLEAR WHO THE KILLERS ARE—MULGOON AND HIS RACKETEERS!

YOU'RE WRONG, MAJOR—IT'S THAT SCOUNDREL DOM CARNEY!

THE ELEPHANT MURDERER TRIED TO KILL ME, TOO, ON THE TRAPEZE! I HAVE A PLAN—

WONDER WOMAN BORROWS A STUFFED BABY ELEPHANT FROM THE CIRCUS MUSEUM.

I'VE NEVER DISGUISED MYSELF AS AN ELEPHANT BEFORE — I HOPE THIS IDEA WORKS!

MUSEUM

WONDER WOMAN AND ETTA CANDY TAKE THE PLACE OF THE ELEPHANT'S STUFFING AND THE HOLLIDAY GIRLS SEW THEM UP.

I DON'T MIND BEING A BABY ELEPHANT, BUT I'D RATHER BE THE MOUTH THAN THE HIND LEGS!

DOWN ETTA! STEADY **WONDER WOMAN**! I'LL HAVE TO GIVE THIS ELEPHANT LOTS OF TRAINING.

WITH KING'S HELP, THE HUMAN ELEPHANT SECRETLY REPLACES THE CIRCUS BABY PACHYDERM.

ISN'T THAT BABY ELEPHANT CUTE! IT LOVES CANDY!

THROW THE PEANUTS BACK! MAKE 'EM FEED US MORE CANDY.

WHEN THE LAST VISITOR LEAVES, AND DARKNESS ENVELOPS THE ANIMAL TENT, MYSTERIOUS LIGHTS MOVE SLOWLY TOWARD THE ELEPHANTS

HEY LET'S LIE DOWN— MY FEET ACHE!

SHH! SOMEBODY'S COMING!

WONDER WOMAN WATCHES A WEIRD CEREMONY—

小人未會罷見

99

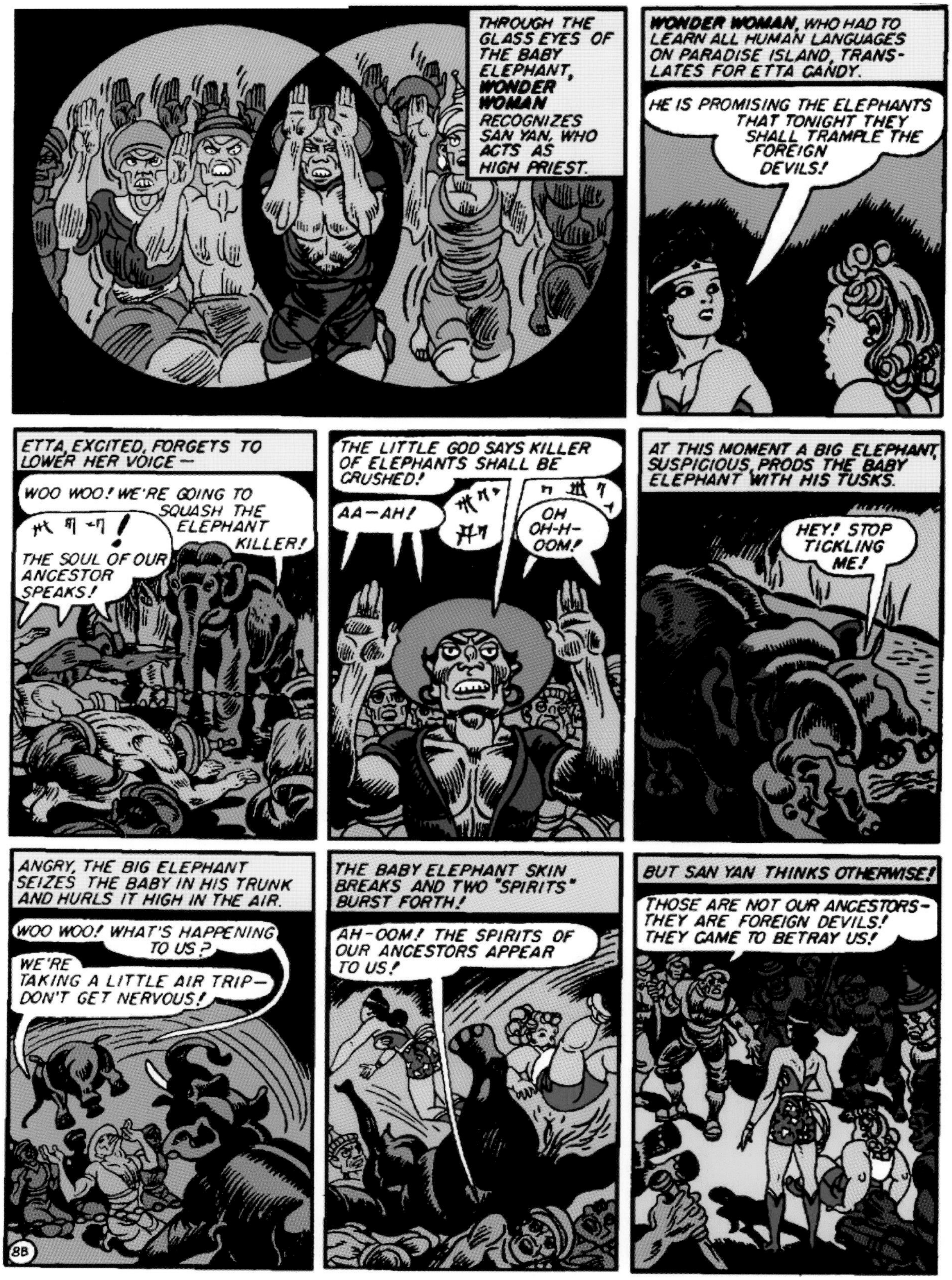
THROUGH THE GLASS EYES OF THE BABY ELEPHANT, WONDER WOMAN RECOGNIZES SAN YAN, WHO ACTS AS HIGH PRIEST.
WONDER WOMAN, WHO HAD TO LEARN ALL HUMAN LANGUAGES ON PARADISE ISLAND, TRANSLATES FOR ETTA CANDY.
HE IS PROMISING THE ELEPHANTS THAT TONIGHT THEY SHALL TRAMPLE THE FOREIGN DEVILS!
ETTA, EXCITED, FORGETS TO LOWER HER VOICE—
WOO WOO! WE'RE GOING TO SQUASH THE ELEPHANT KILLER!
THE SOUL OF OUR ANCESTOR SPEAKS!
THE LITTLE GOD SAYS KILLER OF ELEPHANTS SHALL BE CRUSHED!
AA—AH!
OH OH-H-OOM!
AT THIS MOMENT A BIG ELEPHANT, SUSPICIOUS, PRODS THE BABY ELEPHANT WITH HIS TUSKS.
HEY! STOP TICKLING ME!
ANGRY, THE BIG ELEPHANT SEIZES THE BABY IN HIS TRUNK AND HURLS IT HIGH IN THE AIR.
WOO WOO! WHAT'S HAPPENING TO US?
WE'RE TAKING A LITTLE AIR TRIP— DON'T GET NERVOUS!
8B
THE BABY ELEPHANT SKIN BREAKS AND TWO "SPIRITS" BURST FORTH!
AH-OOM! THE SPIRITS OF OUR ANCESTORS APPEAR TO US!
BUT SAN YAN THINKS OTHERWISE!
THOSE ARE NOT OUR ANCESTORS— THEY ARE FOREIGN DEVILS! THEY CAME TO BETRAY US!

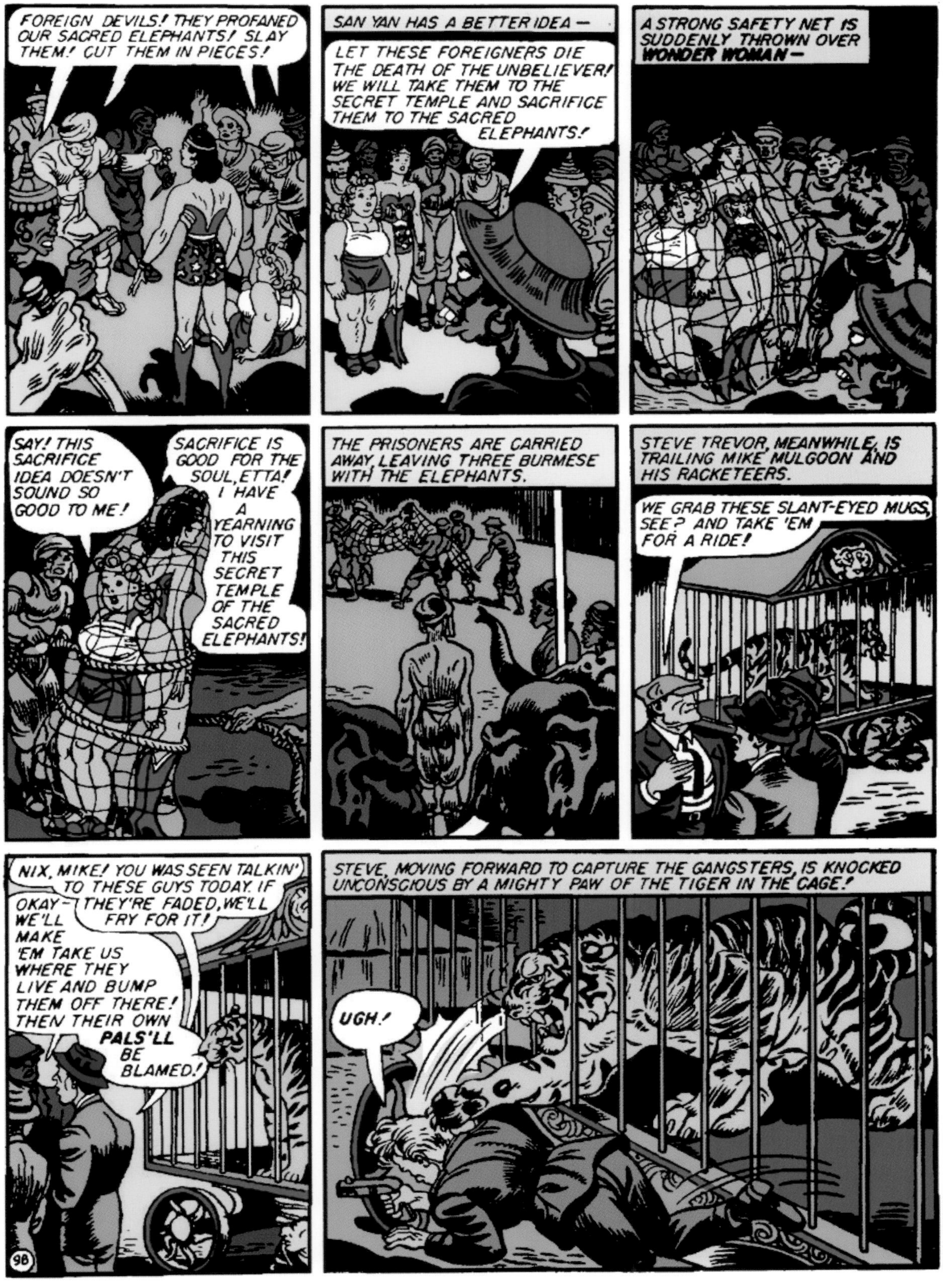
FOREIGN DEVILS! THEY PROFANED OUR SACRED ELEPHANTS! SLAY THEM! CUT THEM IN PIECES!
SAN YAN HAS A BETTER IDEA—
LET THESE FOREIGNERS DIE THE DEATH OF THE UNBELIEVER! WE WILL TAKE THEM TO THE SECRET TEMPLE AND SACRIFICE THEM TO THE SACRED ELEPHANTS!
A STRONG SAFETY NET IS SUDDENLY THROWN OVER WONDER WOMAN—
SAY! THIS SACRIFICE IDEA DOESN'T SOUND SO GOOD TO ME!
SACRIFICE IS GOOD FOR THE SOUL, ETTA! I HAVE A YEARNING TO VISIT THIS SECRET TEMPLE OF THE SACRED ELEPHANTS!
THE PRISONERS ARE CARRIED AWAY, LEAVING THREE BURMESE WITH THE ELEPHANTS.
STEVE TREVOR, MEANWHILE, IS TRAILING MIKE MULGOON AND HIS RACKETEERS.
WE GRAB THESE SLANT-EYED MUGS, SEE? AND TAKE 'EM FOR A RIDE!
NIX, MIKE! YOU WAS SEEN TALKIN' TO THESE GUYS TODAY. IF THEY'RE FADED, WE'LL FRY FOR IT!
OKAY— WE'LL MAKE 'EM TAKE US WHERE THEY LIVE AND BUMP THEM OFF THERE! THEN THEIR OWN PALS'LL BE BLAMED!
98
STEVE, MOVING FORWARD TO CAPTURE THE GANGSTERS, IS KNOCKED UNCONSCIOUS BY A MIGHTY PAW OF THE TIGER IN THE CAGE!
UGH!

REACH FOR THE RAFTERS, CHUMS! IS THIS ALL THERE IS OF YOU?

SURE! TWO MANS TEND ELEPHANTS IS ALL!

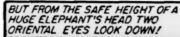

BUT FROM THE SAFE HEIGHT OF A HUGE ELEPHANT'S HEAD TWO ORIENTAL EYES LOOK DOWN!

STEVE TREVOR SITS UP, STILL DAZED, AS THE RACKETEERS PUSH THEIR VICTIMS INTO MULGOON'S CAR.

W-WHERE AM I? TOTTERING TOM CATS! THOSE RACKETEERS ARE KIDNAPPING THE ELEPHANT MEN—THERE THEY GO NOW!

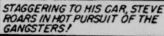

STAGGERING TO HIS CAR, STEVE ROARS IN HOT PURSUIT OF THE GANGSTERS!

I'VE GOT TO CATCH UP WITH THOSE FELLOWS BEFORE THEY KILL THE BURMESE!

DOM CARNEY STEALS QUIETLY INTO THE ELEPHANT TENT WHERE ELVA, RECOVERED FROM HER ACCIDENT, HAS PROMISED TO MEET HIM.

NOBODY HERE! THIS WOULD BE A GOOD TIME TO—OH-OH! ELVA'S COMING!

DARLING! I SHOULDN'T HAVE LET YOU LEAVE YOUR BED AFTER THAT TERRIBLE ACCIDENT!

OH, I'M ALL RIGHT, DOM—I JUST HAD TO SEE YOU!

BUT ELVA'S UNCLE ALSO SEES DOM!

YOU YOUNG JACKANAPES, SNEAKING AROUND WITH ELVA BEHIND MY BACK! YOU'RE FIRED FROM THE CIRCUS! GET OUT!

PLEASE, UNCLE ED! IT WAS MY FAULT—

SUDDENLY A POWERFUL TRUNK WRAPS ITSELF AROUND ELVA'S WAIST, SNATCHING HER HIGH INTO THE AIR!

DELTA! BAD ELEPHANT— PUT ME DOWN!

BUT THE ELEPHANT OBEYS ANOTHER VOICE SPEAKING IN HIS EAR. WITH A POWERFUL LUNGE HE BREAKS HIS LEG CHAIN!

日本ボケ

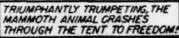
TRIUMPHANTLY TRUMPETING, THE MAMMOTH ANIMAL CRASHES THROUGH THE TENT TO FREEDOM!

EE-EK! SAVE ME, DOM!

COME ON — THESE HORSES CAN OUTRUN AN ELEPHANT! WE'VE GOT TO SAVE ELVA!

CROSSING AN OPEN FIELD THE RESCUERS BEGIN TO GAIN—

FASTER! FASTER!

BUT UNFORTUNATELY THE CIRCUS HORSES ARE TRICK ANIMALS—AT THE COMMAND "FASTER", THEY ARE TRAINED TO LIE DOWN!

FASTER, YOU GOAT! FASTER!

DOM'S HORSE HAS LEARNED TO IMITATE HIS RING LEADER—

UP-UP! STAND UP YOU FOOL!

GIDDAP! ON YOUR FEET!

BY CHANCE, DOM GIVES THE RIGHT COMMAND TO MAKE HIS HORSE GET UP.

WELL, LIE DOWN THEN, YOU MULE!

WHY DIDN'T I THINK! THESE HORSES ARE TRAINED TO WORK WITH CLOWNS!

THE ELEPHANT HAS A BIG START ON US NOW!

BUT WE MUST CATCH HIM — ELVA'S LIFE DEPENDS ON IT!

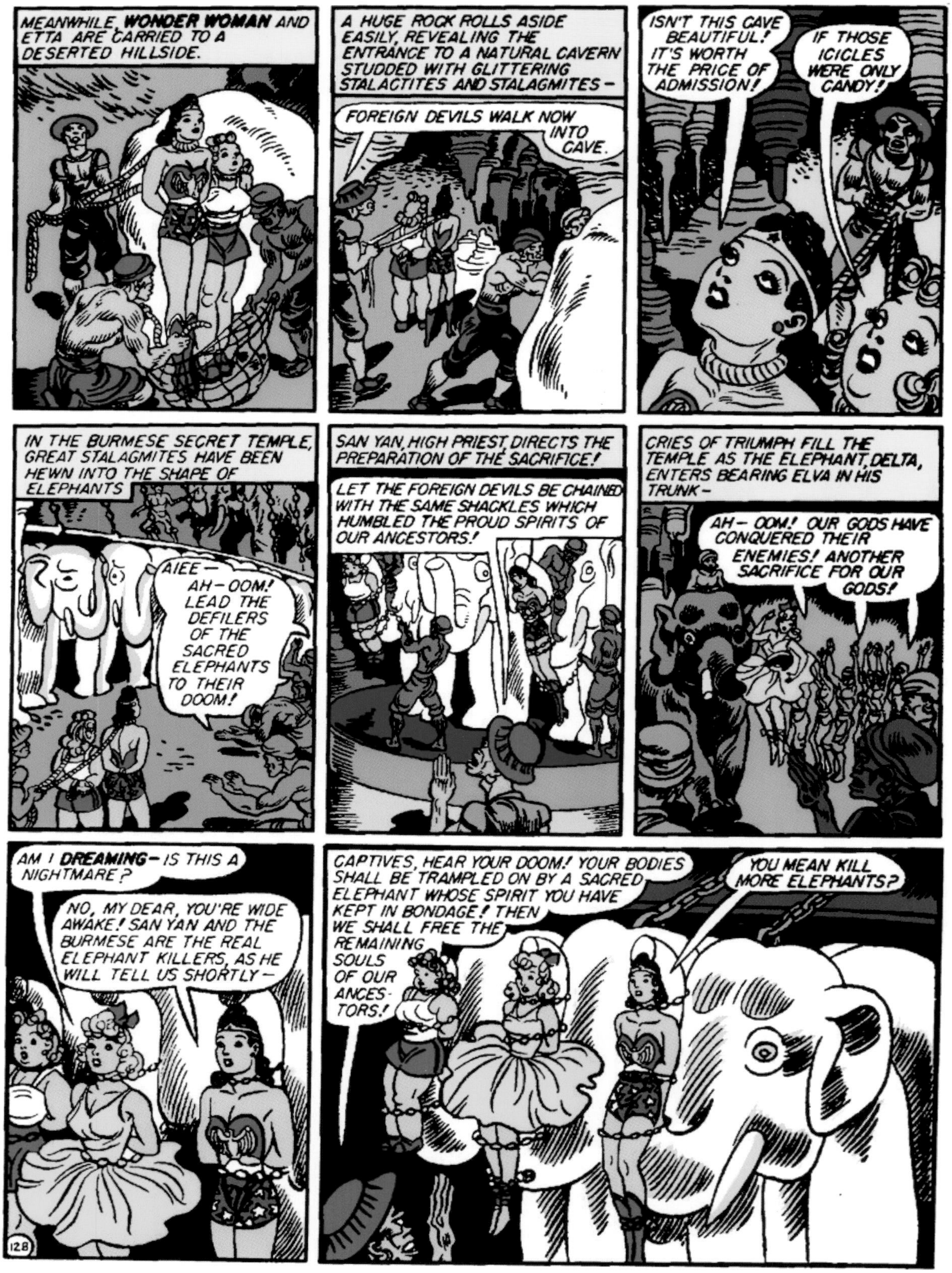
MEANWHILE, WONDER WOMAN AND ETTA ARE CARRIED TO A DESERTED HILLSIDE.
A HUGE ROCK ROLLS ASIDE EASILY, REVEALING THE ENTRANCE TO A NATURAL CAVERN STUDDED WITH GLITTERING STALACTITES AND STALAGMITES –
FOREIGN DEVILS WALK NOW INTO CAVE.
ISN'T THIS CAVE BEAUTIFUL! IT'S WORTH THE PRICE OF ADMISSION!
IF THOSE ICICLES WERE ONLY CANDY!
IN THE BURMESE SECRET TEMPLE, GREAT STALAGMITES HAVE BEEN HEWN INTO THE SHAPE OF ELEPHANTS
AIEE – AH – OOM! LEAD THE DEFILERS OF THE SACRED ELEPHANTS TO THEIR DOOM!
SAN YAN, HIGH PRIEST, DIRECTS THE PREPARATION OF THE SACRIFICE!
LET THE FOREIGN DEVILS BE CHAINED WITH THE SAME SHACKLES WHICH HUMBLED THE PROUD SPIRITS OF OUR ANCESTORS!
CRIES OF TRIUMPH FILL THE TEMPLE AS THE ELEPHANT, DELTA, ENTERS BEARING ELVA IN HIS TRUNK –
AH – OOM! OUR GODS HAVE CONQUERED THEIR ENEMIES! ANOTHER SACRIFICE FOR OUR GODS!
AM I DREAMING – IS THIS A NIGHTMARE?
NO, MY DEAR, YOU'RE WIDE AWAKE! SAN YAN AND THE BURMESE ARE THE REAL ELEPHANT KILLERS, AS HE WILL TELL US SHORTLY –
12B
CAPTIVES, HEAR YOUR DOOM! YOUR BODIES SHALL BE TRAMPLED ON BY A SACRED ELEPHANT WHOSE SPIRIT YOU HAVE KEPT IN BONDAGE! THEN WE SHALL FREE THE REMAINING SOULS OF OUR ANCESTORS!
YOU MEAN KILL MORE ELEPHANTS?

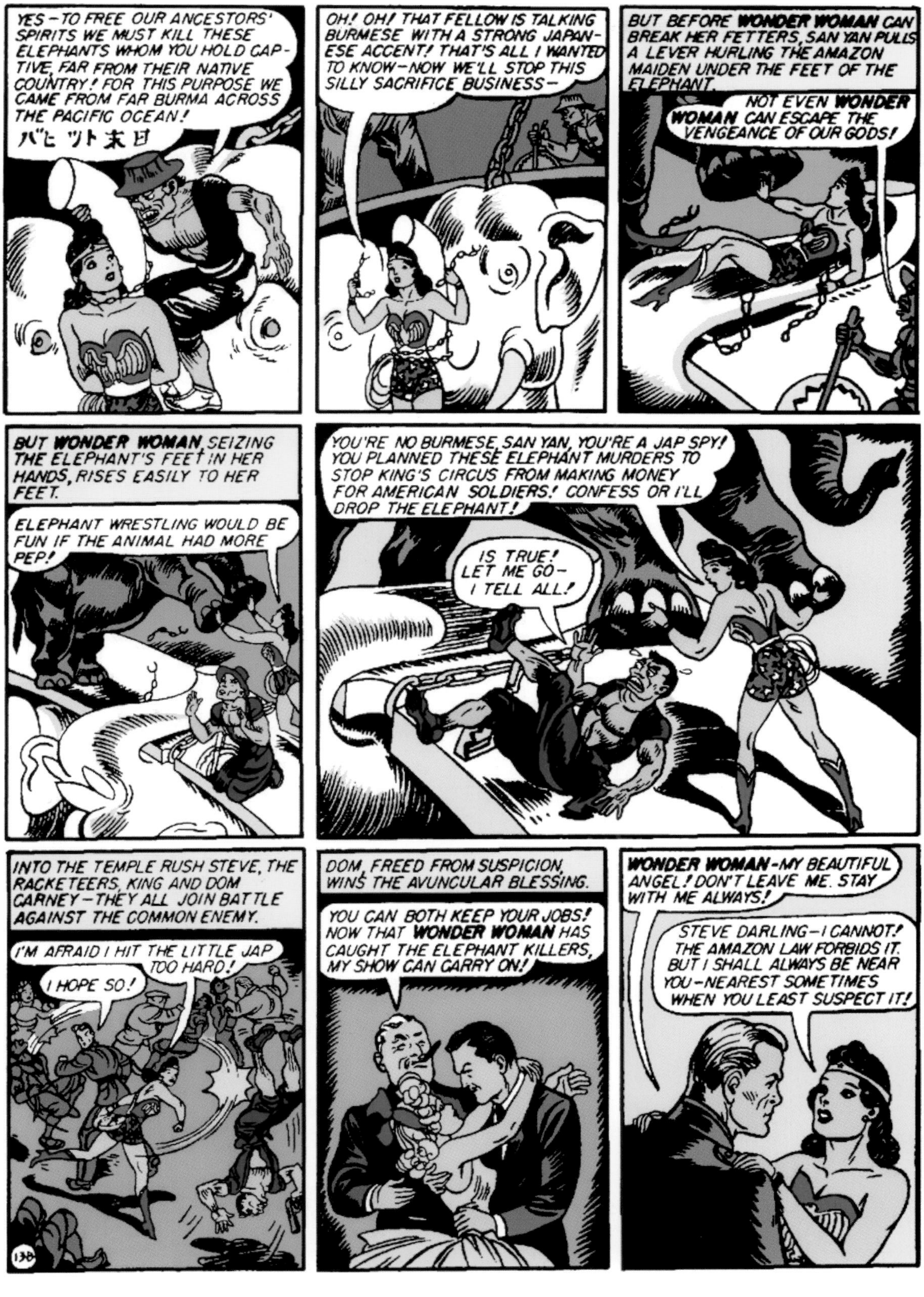
YES—TO FREE OUR ANCESTORS' SPIRITS WE MUST KILL THESE ELEPHANTS WHOM YOU HOLD CAPTIVE, FAR FROM THEIR NATIVE COUNTRY! FOR THIS PURPOSE WE CAME FROM FAR BURMA ACROSS THE PACIFIC OCEAN!
OH! OH! THAT FELLOW IS TALKING BURMESE WITH A STRONG JAPANESE ACCENT! THAT'S ALL I WANTED TO KNOW—NOW WE'LL STOP THIS SILLY SACRIFICE BUSINESS—
BUT BEFORE WONDER WOMAN CAN BREAK HER FETTERS, SAN YAN PULLS A LEVER HURLING THE AMAZON MAIDEN UNDER THE FEET OF THE ELEPHANT.
NOT EVEN WONDER WOMAN CAN ESCAPE THE VENGEANCE OF OUR GODS!
BUT WONDER WOMAN, SEIZING THE ELEPHANT'S FEET IN HER HANDS, RISES EASILY TO HER FEET.
ELEPHANT WRESTLING WOULD BE FUN IF THE ANIMAL HAD MORE PEP!
YOU'RE NO BURMESE, SAN YAN, YOU'RE A JAP SPY! YOU PLANNED THESE ELEPHANT MURDERS TO STOP KING'S CIRCUS FROM MAKING MONEY FOR AMERICAN SOLDIERS! CONFESS OR I'LL DROP THE ELEPHANT!
IS TRUE! LET ME GO—I TELL ALL!
INTO THE TEMPLE RUSH STEVE, THE RACKETEERS, KING AND DOM CARNEY—THEY ALL JOIN BATTLE AGAINST THE COMMON ENEMY.
I'M AFRAID I HIT THE LITTLE JAP TOO HARD!
I HOPE SO!
DOM, FREED FROM SUSPICION, WINS THE AVUNCULAR BLESSING.
YOU CAN BOTH KEEP YOUR JOBS! NOW THAT WONDER WOMAN HAS CAUGHT THE ELEPHANT KILLERS, MY SHOW CAN CARRY ON!
WONDER WOMAN—MY BEAUTIFUL ANGEL! DON'T LEAVE ME. STAY WITH ME ALWAYS!
STEVE DARLING—I CANNOT! THE AMAZON LAW FORBIDS IT. BUT I SHALL ALWAYS BE NEAR YOU—NEAREST SOMETIMES WHEN YOU LEAST SUSPECT IT!
138

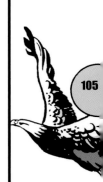

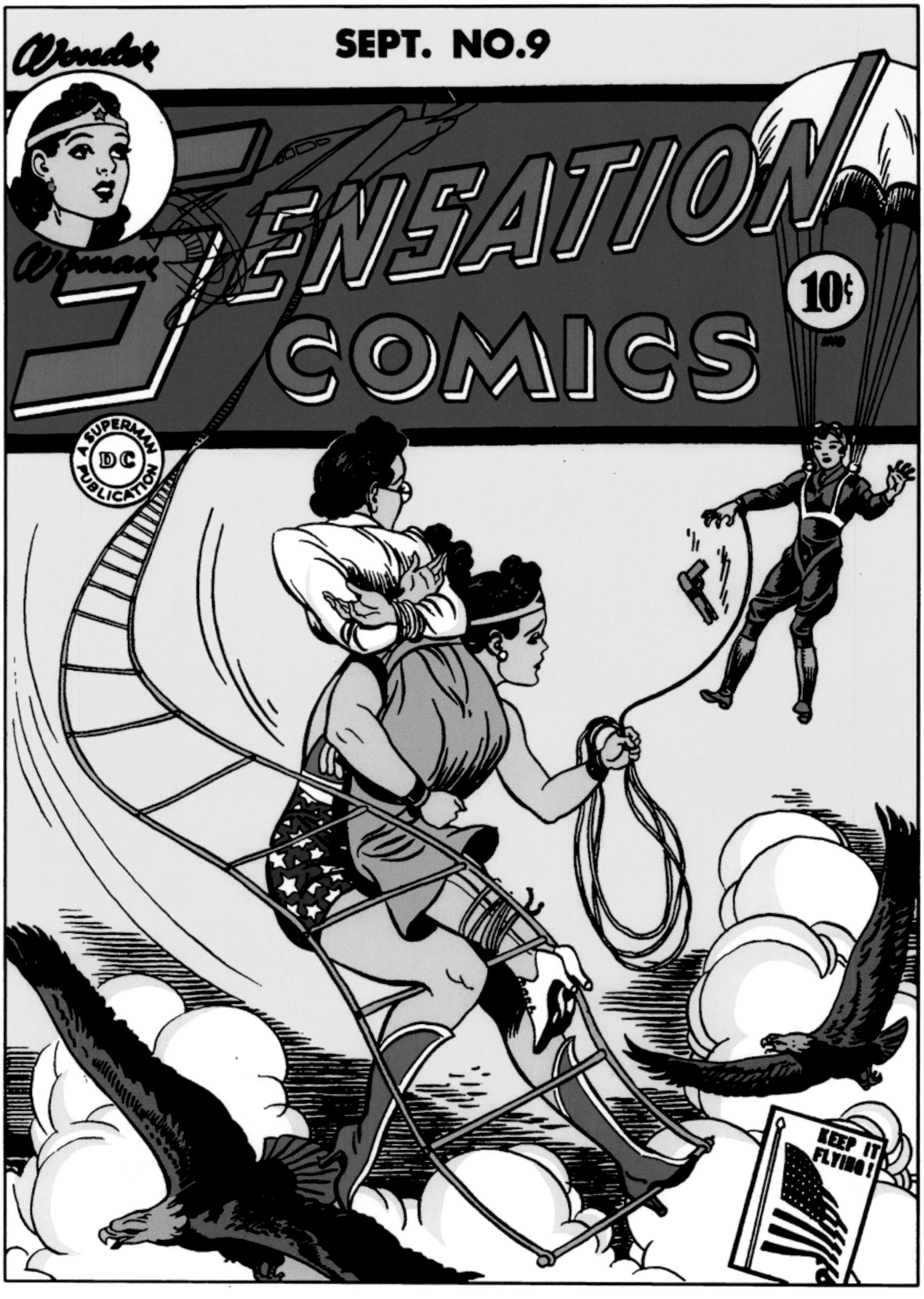
SEPT. NO.9
Wonder Woman
SENSATION COMICS
10¢
A SUPERMAN DC PUBLICATION
KEEP IT FLYING!

Sensation Comics #9 (Sept. 1942) - Art: H.G. Peter

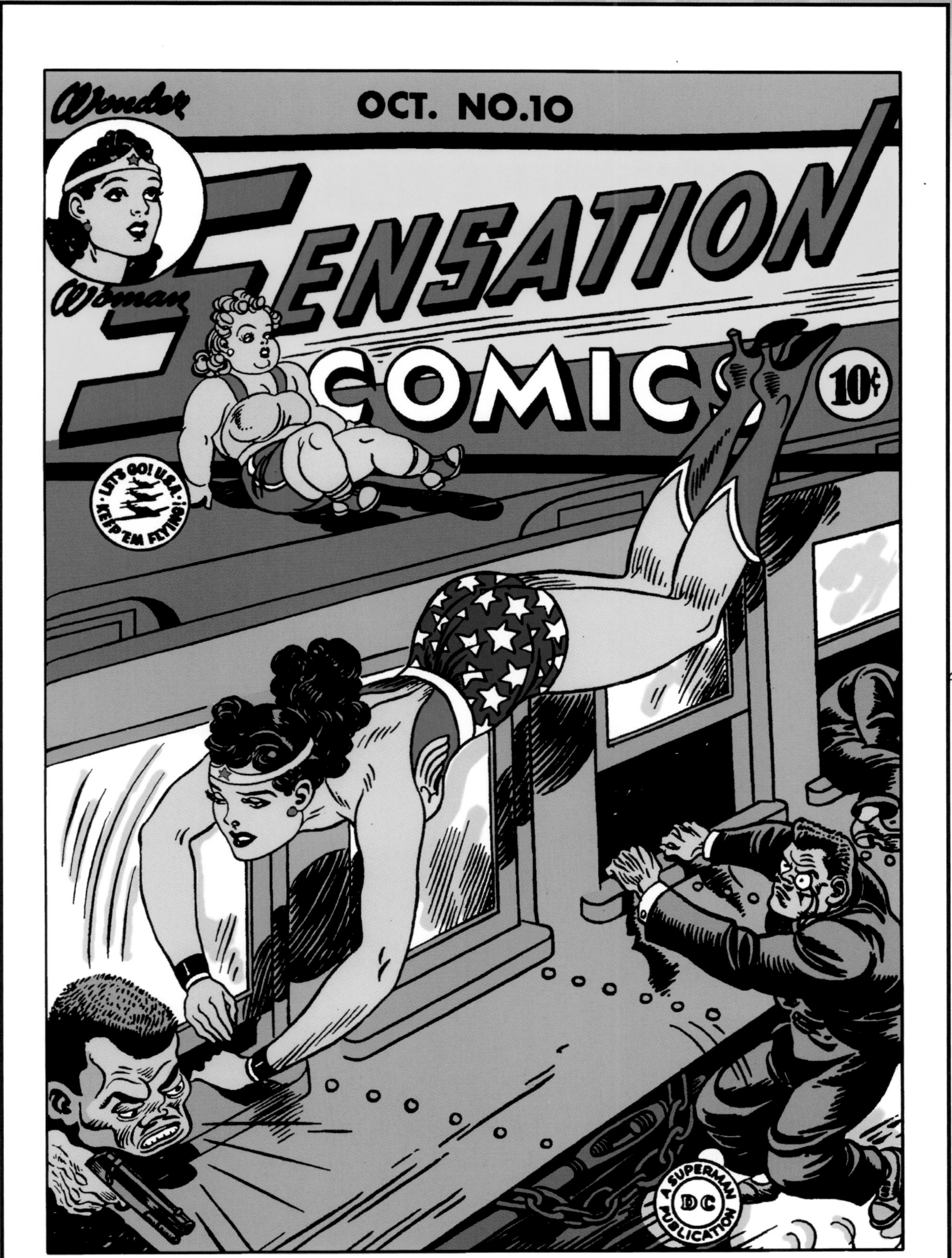
Wonder Woman
OCT. NO.10
SENSATION COMICS
10¢
LET'S GO! U.S.A. KEEP 'EM FLYING!
A SUPERMAN DC PUBLICATION

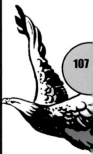

Sensation Comics #10 (Oct. 1942) - art: H.G. Peter

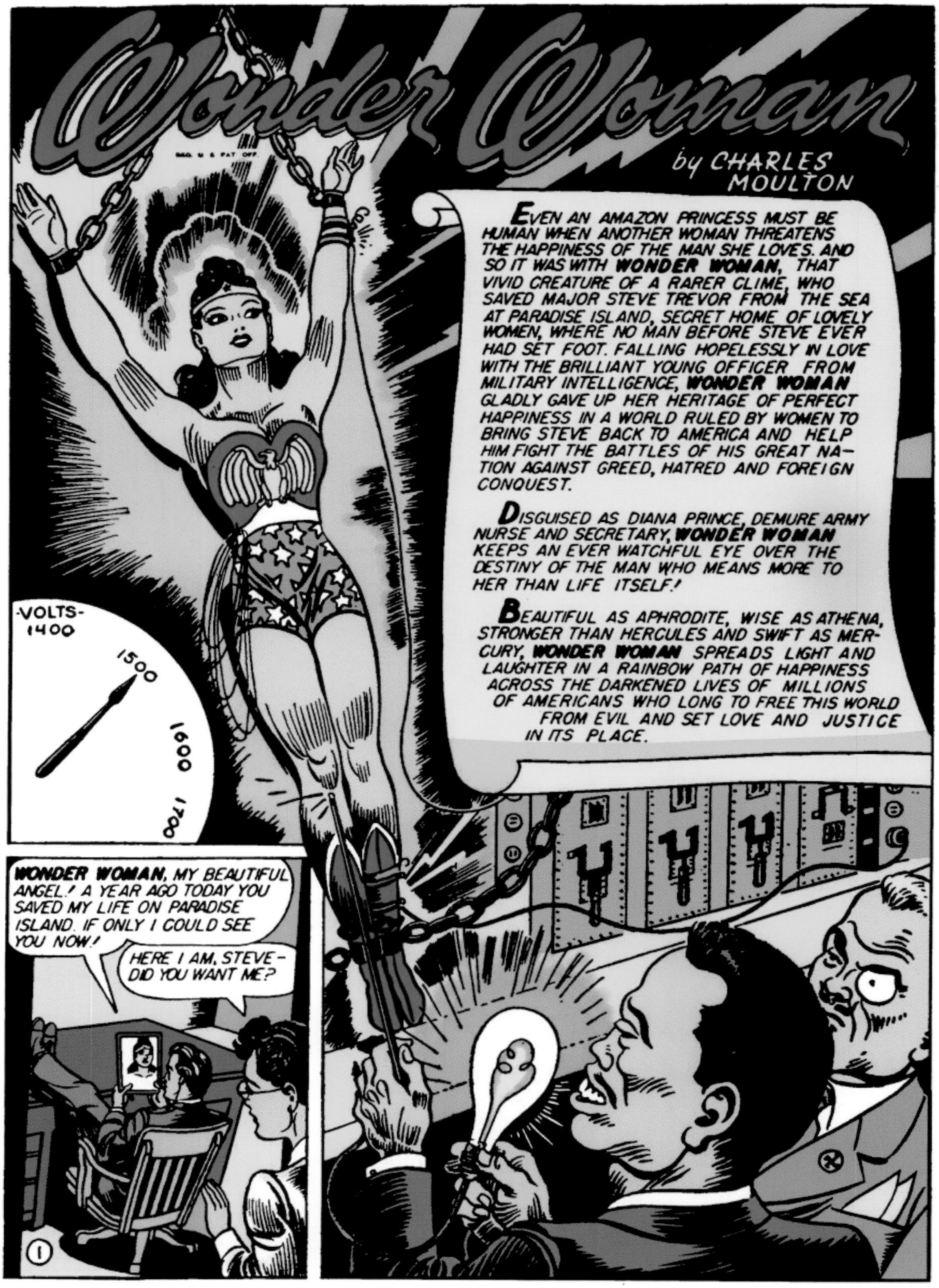
Wonder Woman
REG. U. S. PAT. OFF.
by CHARLES MOULTON
EVEN AN AMAZON PRINCESS MUST BE HUMAN WHEN ANOTHER WOMAN THREATENS THE HAPPINESS OF THE MAN SHE LOVES. AND SO IT WAS WITH WONDER WOMAN, THAT VIVID CREATURE OF A RARER CLIME, WHO SAVED MAJOR STEVE TREVOR FROM THE SEA AT PARADISE ISLAND, SECRET HOME OF LOVELY WOMEN, WHERE NO MAN BEFORE STEVE EVER HAD SET FOOT. FALLING HOPELESSLY IN LOVE WITH THE BRILLIANT YOUNG OFFICER FROM MILITARY INTELLIGENCE, WONDER WOMAN GLADLY GAVE UP HER HERITAGE OF PERFECT HAPPINESS IN A WORLD RULED BY WOMEN TO BRING STEVE BACK TO AMERICA AND HELP HIM FIGHT THE BATTLES OF HIS GREAT NATION AGAINST GREED, HATRED AND FOREIGN CONQUEST.
DISGUISED AS DIANA PRINCE, DEMURE ARMY NURSE AND SECRETARY, WONDER WOMAN KEEPS AN EVER WATCHFUL EYE OVER THE DESTINY OF THE MAN WHO MEANS MORE TO HER THAN LIFE ITSELF!
BEAUTIFUL AS APHRODITE, WISE AS ATHENA, STRONGER THAN HERCULES AND SWIFT AS MERCURY, WONDER WOMAN SPREADS LIGHT AND LAUGHTER IN A RAINBOW PATH OF HAPPINESS ACROSS THE DARKENED LIVES OF MILLIONS OF AMERICANS WHO LONG TO FREE THIS WORLD FROM EVIL AND SET LOVE AND JUSTICE IN ITS PLACE.
-VOLTS-
1400
1500
1600
1700
WONDER WOMAN, MY BEAUTIFUL ANGEL! A YEAR AGO TODAY YOU SAVED MY LIFE ON PARADISE ISLAND. IF ONLY I COULD SEE YOU NOW!
HERE I AM, STEVE - DID YOU WANT ME?
1

Sensation Comics #10 (Oct. 1942) - script: William Moulton Marston - art: H.G. Peter

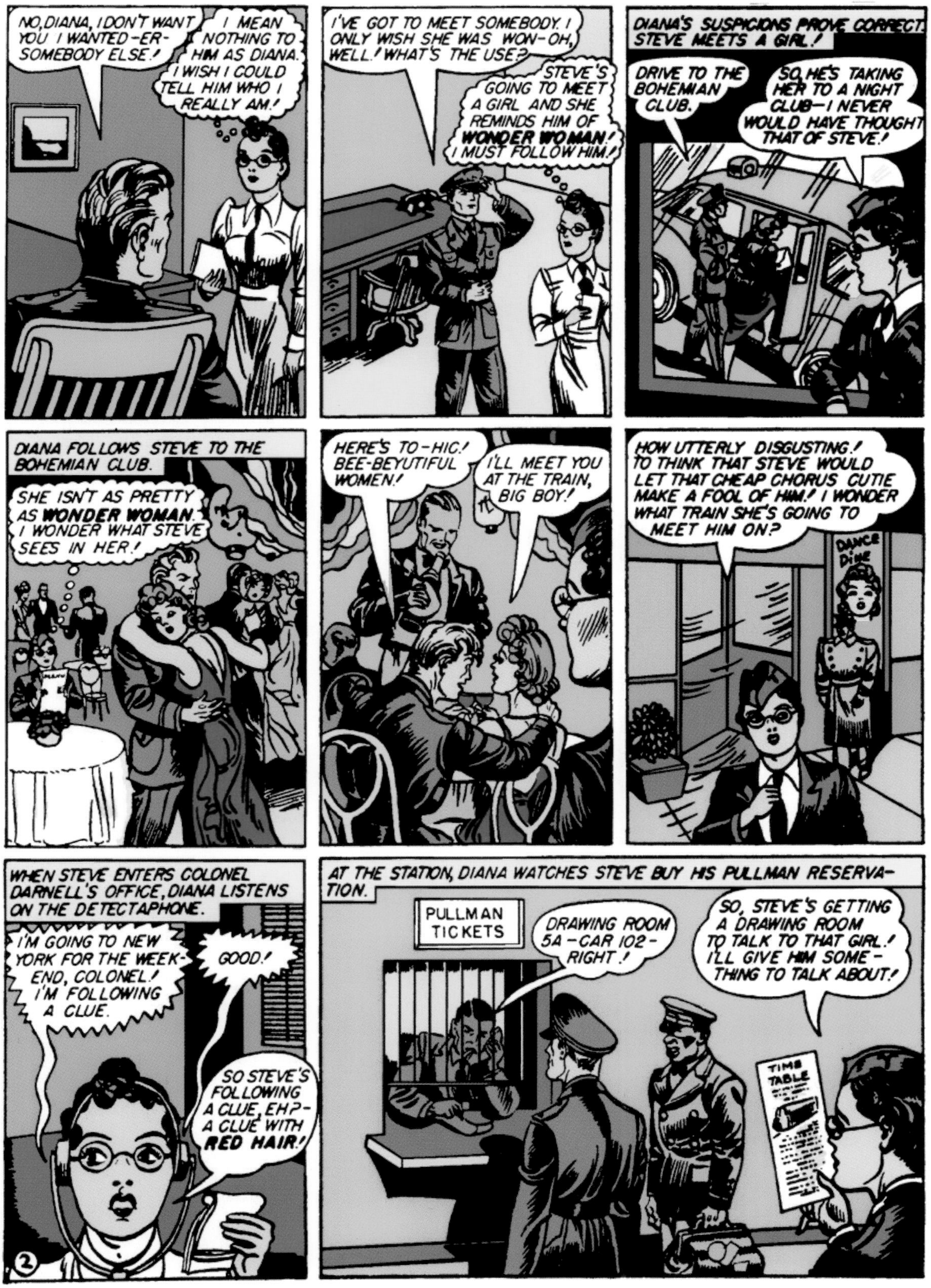
NO, DIANA, I DON'T WANT YOU I WANTED-ER-SOMEBODY ELSE.!
I MEAN NOTHING TO HIM AS DIANA. I WISH I COULD TELL HIM WHO I REALLY AM.!
I'VE GOT TO MEET SOMEBODY. I ONLY WISH SHE WAS WON-OH, WELL.! WHAT'S THE USE?
STEVE'S GOING TO MEET A GIRL AND SHE REMINDS HIM OF WONDER WOMAN! I MUST FOLLOW HIM!
DIANA'S SUSPICIONS PROVE CORRECT! STEVE MEETS A GIRL.!
DRIVE TO THE BOHEMIAN CLUB.
SO HE'S TAKING HER TO A NIGHT CLUB—I NEVER WOULD HAVE THOUGHT THAT OF STEVE.!
DIANA FOLLOWS STEVE TO THE BOHEMIAN CLUB.
SHE ISN'T AS PRETTY AS WONDER WOMAN. I WONDER WHAT STEVE SEES IN HER.!
HERE'S TO-HIC! BEE-BEYUTIFUL WOMEN.!
I'LL MEET YOU AT THE TRAIN, BIG BOY.!
HOW UTTERLY DISGUSTING.! TO THINK THAT STEVE WOULD LET THAT CHEAP CHORUS CUTIE MAKE A FOOL OF HIM.! I WONDER WHAT TRAIN SHE'S GOING TO MEET HIM ON?
DANCE DINE
WHEN STEVE ENTERS COLONEL DARNELL'S OFFICE, DIANA LISTENS ON THE DETECTAPHONE.
I'M GOING TO NEW YORK FOR THE WEEK-END, COLONEL.! I'M FOLLOWING A CLUE.
GOOD.!
SO STEVE'S FOLLOWING A CLUE, EH?- A CLUE WITH RED HAIR!
2
AT THE STATION, DIANA WATCHES STEVE BUY HIS PULLMAN RESERVATION.
PULLMAN TICKETS
DRAWING ROOM 5A-CAR 102-RIGHT.!
SO, STEVE'S GETTING A DRAWING ROOM TO TALK TO THAT GIRL.! I'LL GIVE HIM SOME-THING TO TALK ABOUT.!
TIME TABLE

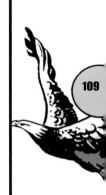

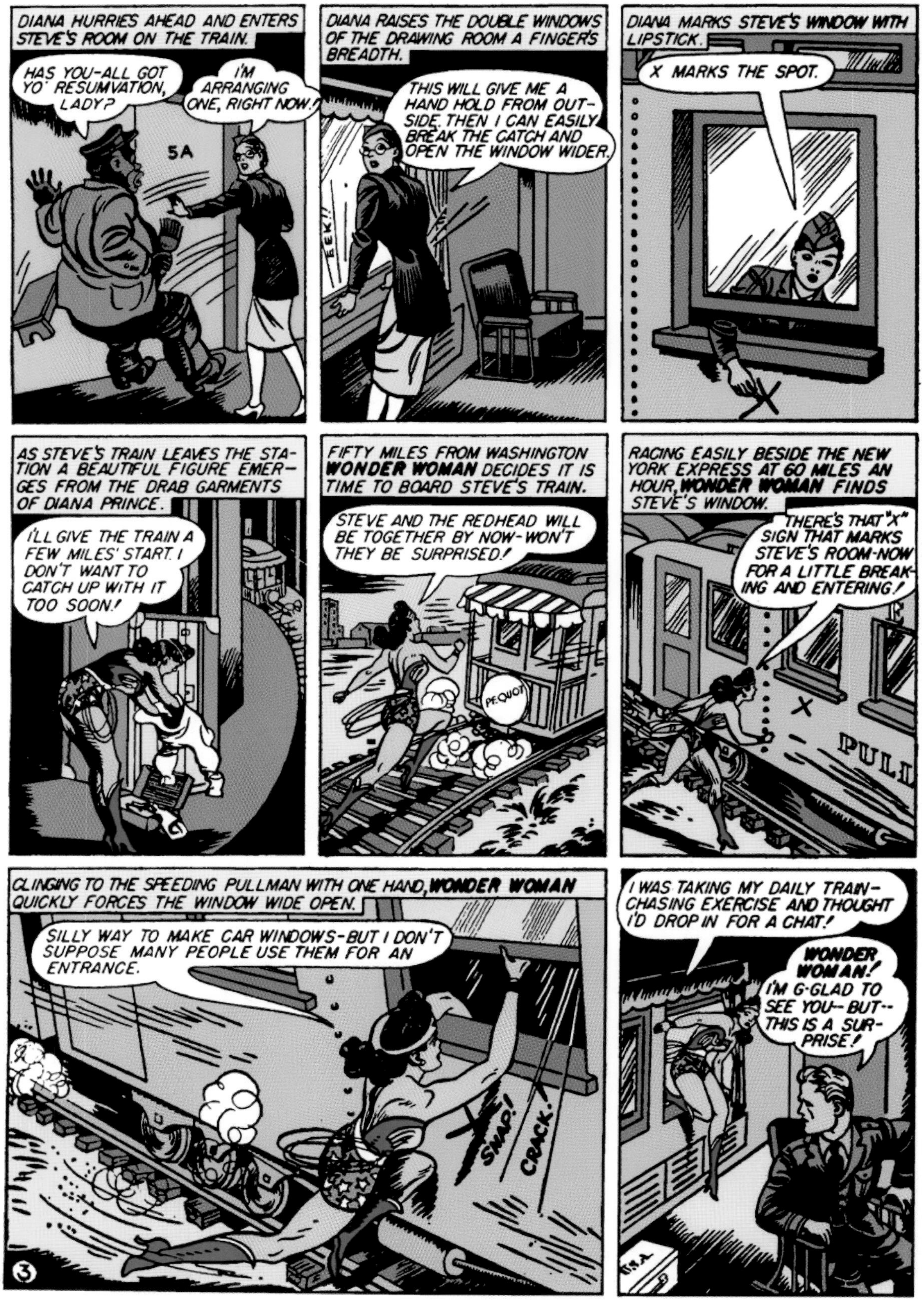
DIANA HURRIES AHEAD AND ENTERS STEVE'S ROOM ON THE TRAIN.
HAS YOU-ALL GOT YO' RESUMVATION, LADY?
I'M ARRANGING ONE, RIGHT NOW!
5A
DIANA RAISES THE DOUBLE WINDOWS OF THE DRAWING ROOM A FINGER'S BREADTH.
THIS WILL GIVE ME A HAND HOLD FROM OUTSIDE. THEN I CAN EASILY BREAK THE CATCH AND OPEN THE WINDOW WIDER.
EEK!
DIANA MARKS STEVE'S WINDOW WITH LIPSTICK.
X MARKS THE SPOT.
AS STEVE'S TRAIN LEAVES THE STATION A BEAUTIFUL FIGURE EMERGES FROM THE DRAB GARMENTS OF DIANA PRINCE.
I'LL GIVE THE TRAIN A FEW MILES' START. I DON'T WANT TO CATCH UP WITH IT TOO SOON!
FIFTY MILES FROM WASHINGTON WONDER WOMAN DECIDES IT IS TIME TO BOARD STEVE'S TRAIN.
STEVE AND THE REDHEAD WILL BE TOGETHER BY NOW-WON'T THEY BE SURPRISED!
PEQUOT
RACING EASILY BESIDE THE NEW YORK EXPRESS AT 60 MILES AN HOUR, WONDER WOMAN FINDS STEVE'S WINDOW.
THERE'S THAT "X" SIGN THAT MARKS STEVE'S ROOM-NOW FOR A LITTLE BREAKING AND ENTERING!
PULL
CLINGING TO THE SPEEDING PULLMAN WITH ONE HAND, WONDER WOMAN QUICKLY FORCES THE WINDOW WIDE OPEN.
SILLY WAY TO MAKE CAR WINDOWS-BUT I DON'T SUPPOSE MANY PEOPLE USE THEM FOR AN ENTRANCE.
SNAP!
CRACK!
3
I WAS TAKING MY DAILY TRAIN-CHASING EXERCISE AND THOUGHT I'D DROP IN FOR A CHAT!
WONDER WOMAN! I'M G-GLAD TO SEE YOU--BUT--THIS IS A SURPRISE!

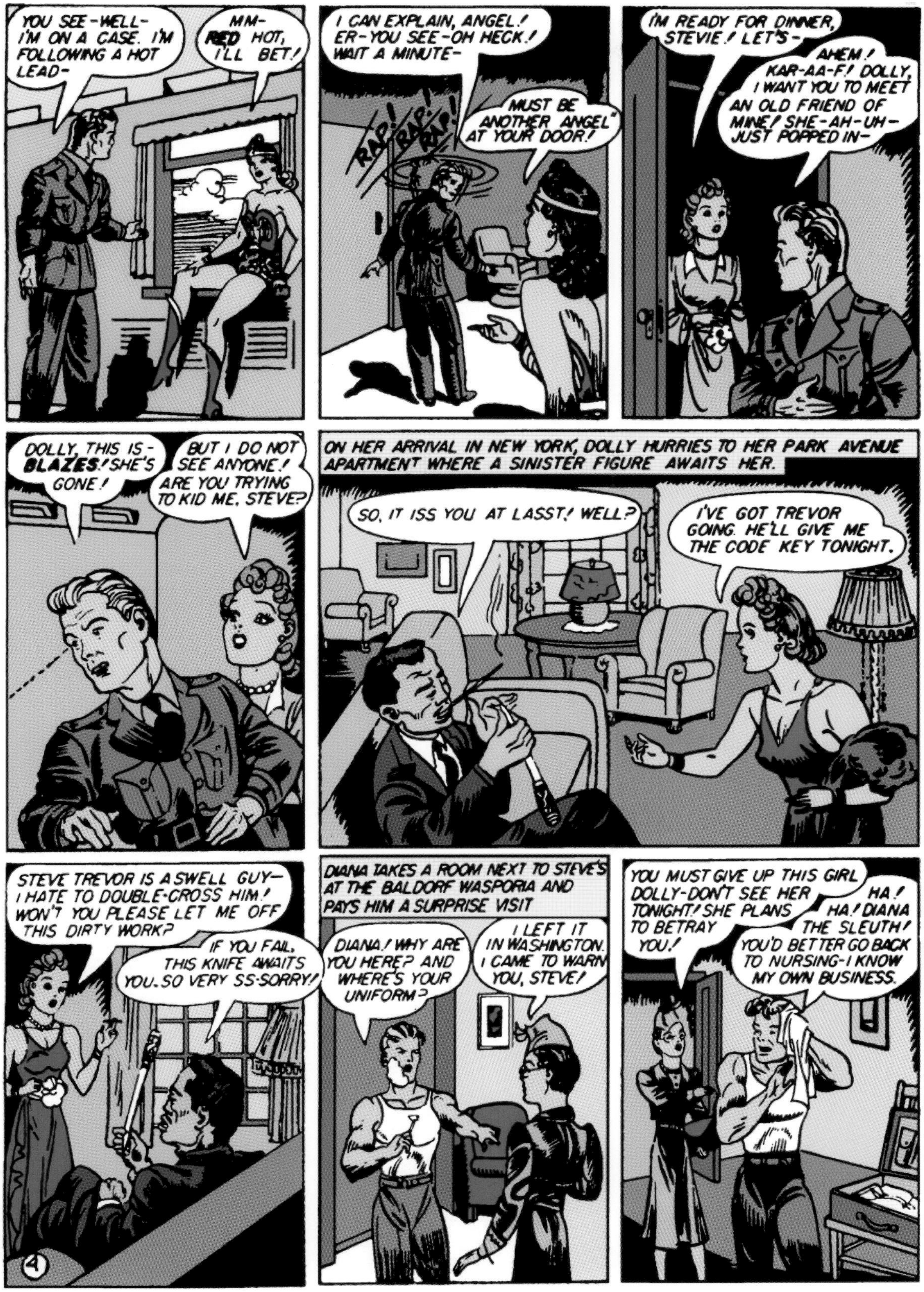
YOU SEE-WELL- I'M ON A CASE. I'M FOLLOWING A HOT LEAD-
MM- RED HOT, I'LL BET!
I CAN EXPLAIN, ANGEL! ER-YOU SEE-OH HECK! WAIT A MINUTE-
RAP! RAP! RAP!
MUST BE ANOTHER ANGEL" AT YOUR DOOR!
I'M READY FOR DINNER, STEVIE! LET'S-
AHEM! KAR-AA-F! DOLLY, I WANT YOU TO MEET AN OLD FRIEND OF MINE! SHE-AH-UH-JUST POPPED IN-
DOLLY, THIS IS- BLAZES! SHE'S GONE!
BUT I DO NOT SEE ANYONE! ARE YOU TRYING TO KID ME, STEVE?
ON HER ARRIVAL IN NEW YORK, DOLLY HURRIES TO HER PARK AVENUE APARTMENT WHERE A SINISTER FIGURE AWAITS HER.
SO, IT ISS YOU AT LASST! WELL?
I'VE GOT TREVOR GOING. HE'LL GIVE ME THE CODE KEY TONIGHT.
STEVE TREVOR IS A SWELL GUY- I HATE TO DOUBLE-CROSS HIM! WON'T YOU PLEASE LET ME OFF THIS DIRTY WORK?
IF YOU FAIL, THIS KNIFE AWAITS YOU. SO VERY SS-SORRY!
4
DIANA TAKES A ROOM NEXT TO STEVE'S AT THE BALDORF WASPORIA AND PAYS HIM A SURPRISE VISIT
DIANA! WHY ARE YOU HERE? AND WHERE'S YOUR UNIFORM?
I LEFT IT IN WASHINGTON. I CAME TO WARN YOU, STEVE!
YOU MUST GIVE UP THIS GIRL DOLLY-DON'T SEE HER TONIGHT! SHE PLANS TO BETRAY YOU!
HA! HA! DIANA THE SLEUTH! YOU'D BETTER GO BACK TO NURSING-I KNOW MY OWN BUSINESS.

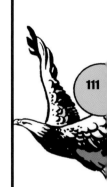

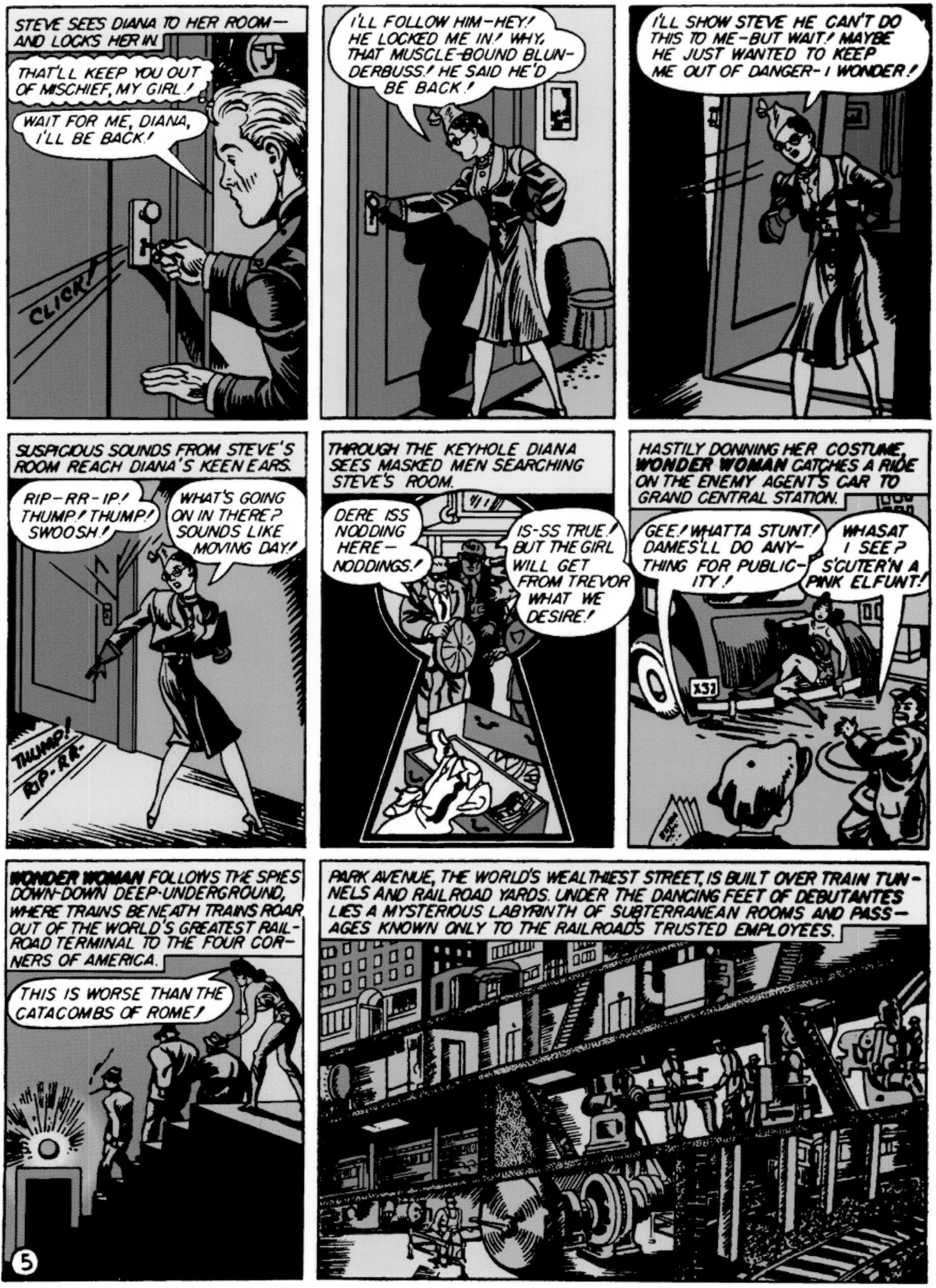
STEVE SEES DIANA TO HER ROOM— AND LOCKS HER IN.
THAT'LL KEEP YOU OUT OF MISCHIEF, MY GIRL!
WAIT FOR ME, DIANA, I'LL BE BACK!
CLICK!
I'LL FOLLOW HIM-HEY! HE LOCKED ME IN! WHY, THAT MUSCLE-BOUND BLUNDERBUSS! HE SAID HE'D BE BACK!
I'LL SHOW STEVE HE CAN'T DO THIS TO ME-BUT WAIT! MAYBE HE JUST WANTED TO KEEP ME OUT OF DANGER- I WONDER!
SUSPICIOUS SOUNDS FROM STEVE'S ROOM REACH DIANA'S KEEN EARS.
RIP-RR-IP! THUMP! THUMP! SWOOSH!
WHAT'S GOING ON IN THERE? SOUNDS LIKE MOVING DAY!
THUMP! RIP-RR-
THROUGH THE KEYHOLE DIANA SEES MASKED MEN SEARCHING STEVE'S ROOM.
DERE ISS NODDING HERE— NODDINGS!
IS-SS TRUE! BUT THE GIRL WILL GET FROM TREVOR WHAT WE DESIRE!
HASTILY DONNING HER COSTUME, WONDER WOMAN CATCHES A RIDE ON THE ENEMY AGENT'S CAR TO GRAND CENTRAL STATION.
GEE! WHATTA STUNT! DAMES'LL DO ANYTHING FOR PUBLICITY!
WHASAT I SEE? S'CUTER'N A PINK ELFUNT!
X37
WONDER WOMAN FOLLOWS THE SPIES DOWN-DOWN DEEP-UNDERGROUND, WHERE TRAINS BENEATH TRAINS ROAR OUT OF THE WORLD'S GREATEST RAILROAD TERMINAL TO THE FOUR CORNERS OF AMERICA.
THIS IS WORSE THAN THE CATACOMBS OF ROME!
5
PARK AVENUE, THE WORLD'S WEALTHIEST STREET, IS BUILT OVER TRAIN TUNNELS AND RAILROAD YARDS. UNDER THE DANCING FEET OF DEBUTANTES LIES A MYSTERIOUS LABYRINTH OF SUBTERRANEAN ROOMS AND PASSAGES KNOWN ONLY TO THE RAILROAD'S TRUSTED EMPLOYEES.

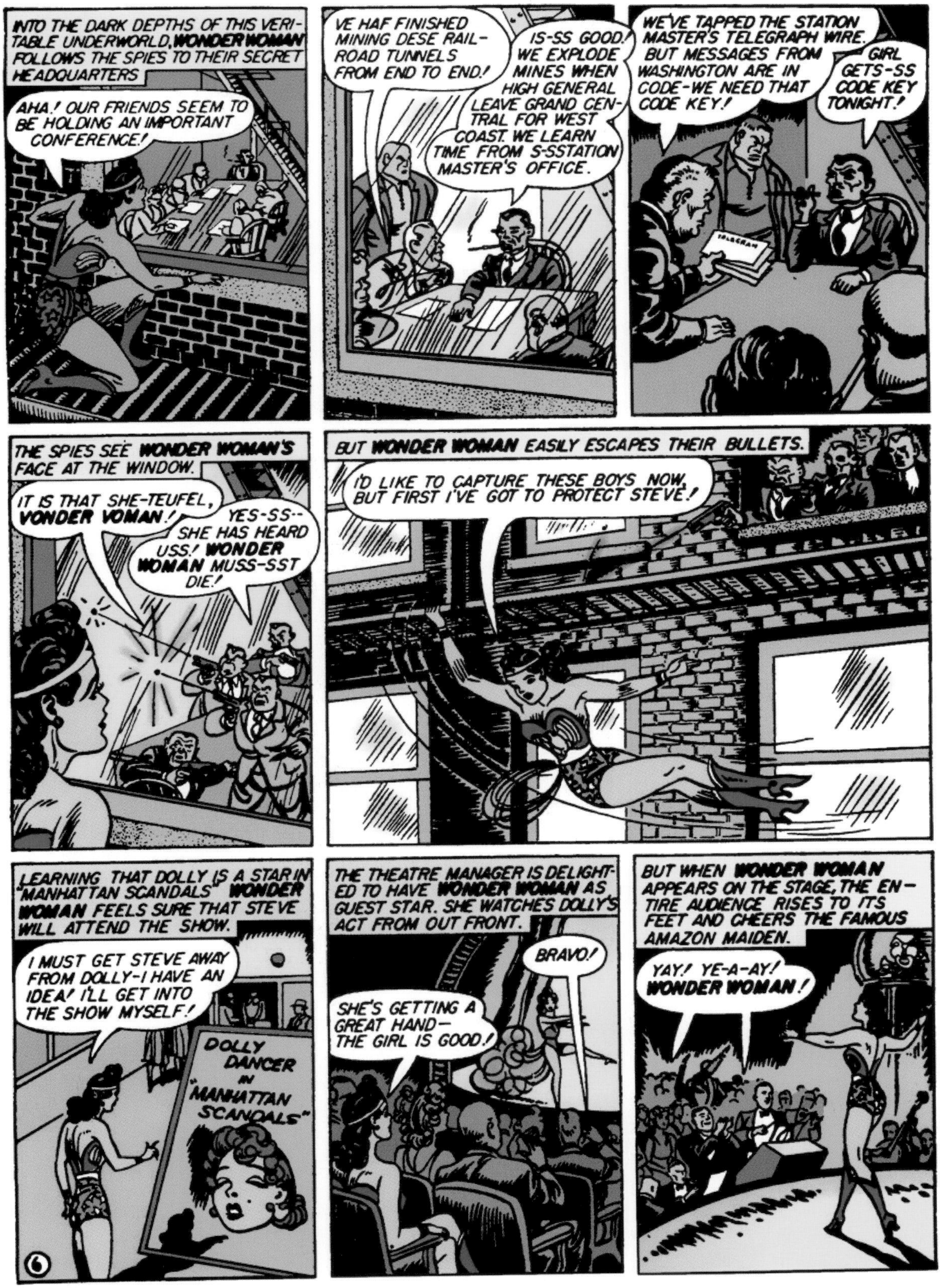
INTO THE DARK DEPTHS OF THIS VERITABLE UNDERWORLD, WONDER WOMAN FOLLOWS THE SPIES TO THEIR SECRET HEADQUARTERS
AHA! OUR FRIENDS SEEM TO BE HOLDING AN IMPORTANT CONFERENCE!
VE HAF FINISHED MINING DESE RAILROAD TUNNELS FROM END TO END!
IS-SS GOOD! WE EXPLODE MINES WHEN HIGH GENERAL LEAVE GRAND CENTRAL FOR WEST COAST. WE LEARN TIME FROM S-SSTATION MASTER'S OFFICE.
WE'VE TAPPED THE STATION MASTER'S TELEGRAPH WIRE. BUT MESSAGES FROM WASHINGTON ARE IN CODE-WE NEED THAT CODE KEY!
GIRL GETS-SS CODE KEY TONIGHT!
TELEGRAM
THE SPIES SEE WONDER WOMAN'S FACE AT THE WINDOW.
IT IS THAT SHE-TEUFEL, WONDER WOMAN!
YES-SS-- SHE HAS HEARD USS! WONDER WOMAN MUSS-SST DIE!
BUT WONDER WOMAN EASILY ESCAPES THEIR BULLETS.
I'D LIKE TO CAPTURE THESE BOYS NOW, BUT FIRST I'VE GOT TO PROTECT STEVE!
LEARNING THAT DOLLY IS A STAR IN "MANHATTAN SCANDALS" WONDER WOMAN FEELS SURE THAT STEVE WILL ATTEND THE SHOW.
I MUST GET STEVE AWAY FROM DOLLY-I HAVE AN IDEA! I'LL GET INTO THE SHOW MYSELF!
DOLLY DANCER IN "MANHATTAN SCANDALS"
6
THE THEATRE MANAGER IS DELIGHTED TO HAVE WONDER WOMAN AS GUEST STAR. SHE WATCHES DOLLY'S ACT FROM OUT FRONT.
BRAVO!
SHE'S GETTING A GREAT HAND— THE GIRL IS GOOD!
BUT WHEN WONDER WOMAN APPEARS ON THE STAGE, THE ENTIRE AUDIENCE RISES TO ITS FEET AND CHEERS THE FAMOUS AMAZON MAIDEN.
YAY! YE-A-AY! WONDER WOMAN!

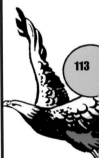

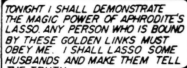

TONIGHT I SHALL DEMONSTRATE THE MAGIC POWER OF APHRODITE'S LASSO. ANY PERSON WHO IS BOUND BY THESE GOLDEN LINKS MUST OBEY ME. I SHALL LASSO SOME HUSBANDS AND MAKE THEM TELL THE TRUTH.

HA! HA! THIS IS GOOD.

WONDER WOMAN LASSOES A BALD-HEADED MAN IN THE FRONT ROW.

COME UP HERE, MY FRIEND, AND SAY HELLO TO THE AUDIENCE.

HELLO! HELLO! HELLO!

TELL ME THE TRUTH— WERE YOU OUT LAST NIGHT WITH A BLONDE?

N-NO! SHE WAS A BRUNETTE!

HA! HA! HO! HA! ASK HIM WHAT HE TOLD HIS WIFE!

WONDER WOMAN LASSOES A HAND-SOME YOUNG SOCIETY MAN.

TELL ME, WHO, IN YOUR OPINION, IS THE GREATEST MAN IN THE WORLD?

WELL—ER—I AM!

HA! HA! HA!

SPOTTING STEVE IN THE AUDIENCE, WONDER WOMAN WHIRLS HER LASSO AT HIM SUDDENLY.

BUT STEVE IS TOO QUICK— HE DODGES HER LASSO AND FLEES UP THE AISLE, FOLLOWED BY ROARS OF LAUGHTER FROM THE AUDIENCE.

HO! HO! HE CAN'T TAKE IT! HE'S AFRAID TO TELL THE TRUTH!

⑦

HASTILY CLOSING HER ACT AMID THUNDEROUS APPLAUSE, WONDER WOMAN HURRIES FROM THE STAGE.

HURRAY! WONDER WOMAN! ENCORE. COME BACK-LASSO SOME WIVES AND MAKE THEM CONFESS!

WONDER WOMAN FOLLOWS DOLLY TO HER APARTMENT ON PARK AVE-NUE WHERE STEVE IS WAITING.

I'LL GO IN AND WATCH DOLLY'S VAMPING METHODS— MAYBE SHE KNOWS SOME NEW TRICKS!

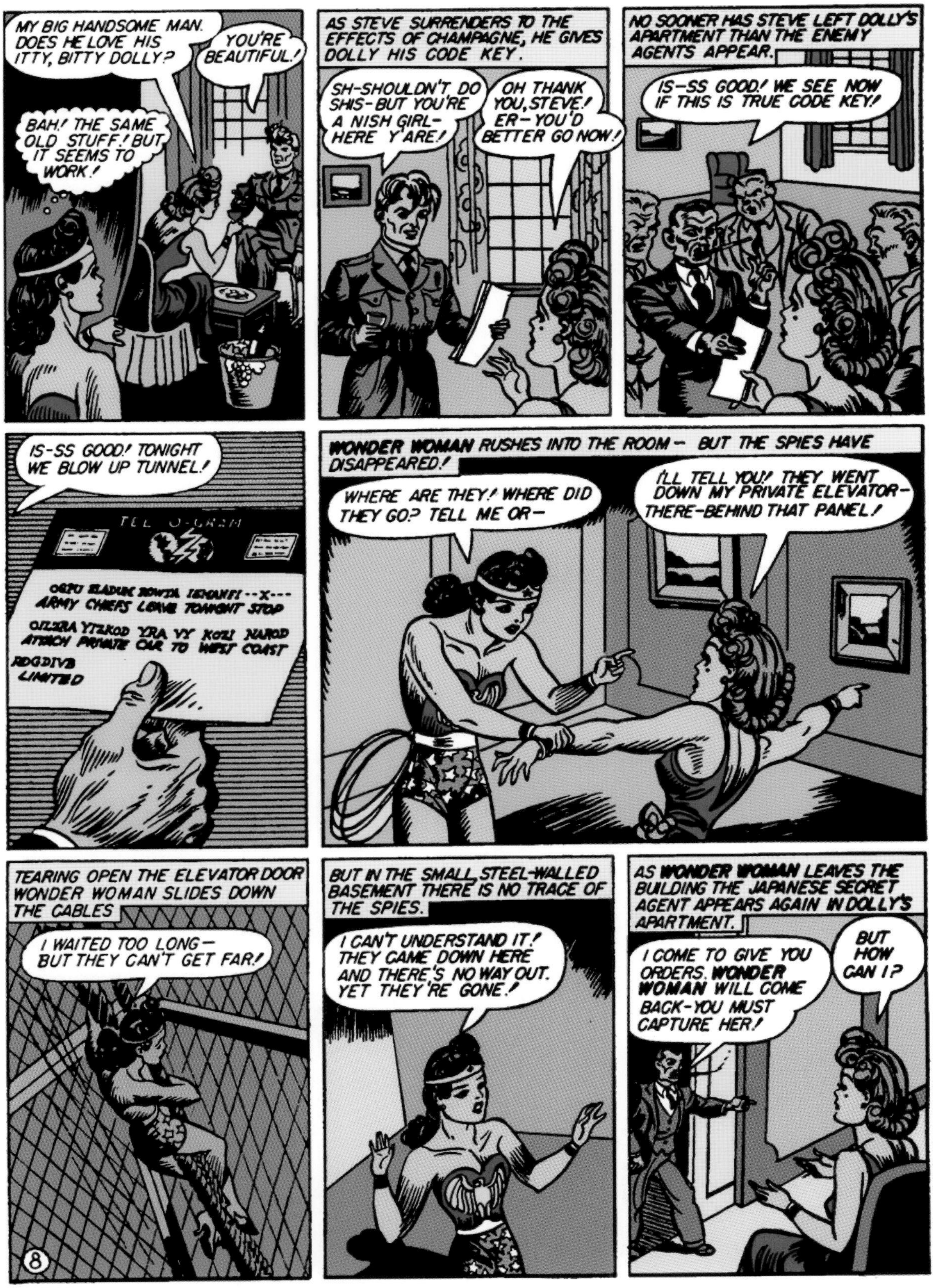
MY BIG HANDSOME MAN. DOES HE LOVE HIS ITTY, BITTY DOLLY?
YOU'RE BEAUTIFUL!
BAH! THE SAME OLD STUFF! BUT IT SEEMS TO WORK!
AS STEVE SURRENDERS TO THE EFFECTS OF CHAMPAGNE, HE GIVES DOLLY HIS CODE KEY.
SH-SHOULDN'T DO SHIS-BUT YOU'RE A NISH GIRL-HERE Y'ARE!
OH THANK YOU, STEVE! ER-YOU'D BETTER GO NOW!
NO SOONER HAS STEVE LEFT DOLLY'S APARTMENT THAN THE ENEMY AGENTS APPEAR.
IS-SS GOOD! WE SEE NOW IF THIS IS TRUE CODE KEY!
IS-SS GOOD! TONIGHT WE BLOW UP TUNNEL!
ARMY CHIEFS LEAVE TONIGHT STOP
ATTACH PRIVATE CAR TO WEST COAST
LIMITED
WONDER WOMAN RUSHES INTO THE ROOM - BUT THE SPIES HAVE DISAPPEARED!
WHERE ARE THEY! WHERE DID THEY GO? TELL ME OR-
I'LL TELL YOU! THEY WENT DOWN MY PRIVATE ELEVATOR-THERE-BEHIND THAT PANEL!
TEARING OPEN THE ELEVATOR DOOR WONDER WOMAN SLIDES DOWN THE CABLES
I WAITED TOO LONG-BUT THEY CAN'T GET FAR!
8
BUT IN THE SMALL, STEEL-WALLED BASEMENT THERE IS NO TRACE OF THE SPIES.
I CAN'T UNDERSTAND IT! THEY CAME DOWN HERE AND THERE'S NO WAY OUT. YET THEY'RE GONE!
AS WONDER WOMAN LEAVES THE BUILDING THE JAPANESE SECRET AGENT APPEARS AGAIN IN DOLLY'S APARTMENT.
I COME TO GIVE YOU ORDERS. WONDER WOMAN WILL COME BACK-YOU MUST CAPTURE HER!
BUT HOW CAN I?

WITH THIS-SS YOU SHALL CONQUER WONDER WOMAN! ATTEND, PLEASE, AND I WILL EXPLAIN-----
ETTA CANDY AND THE HOLLIDAY COLLEGE GIRLS, MEANWHILE, ARRIVE FROM WASHINGTON AND WONDER WOMAN LEADS THEM TO DOLLY'S APARTMENT HOUSE.
LOOK! THOSE MEN ARE SPIES!
WOO! WOO! LET'S CATCH 'EM!
THEY HAVE A CLEVER HIDEAWAY HERE. YOU GIRLS SURROUND THIS BUILDING-WATCH EVERY EXIT! I'M GOING IN. IF I'M NOT BACK IN HALF AN HOUR, RUSH THE BASEMENT AND SEARCH IT THOROUGHLY!
LET'S GO! WOO! WOO!
WONDER WOMAN, CLIMBING THE FIRE-ESCAPE, ENTERS DOLLY'S BEDROOM.
I'VE COME BACK, DOLLY, TO FIND YOUR PLAYMATES.
YOU, AGAIN! CAN'T YOU LEAVE ME ALONE?
I WANT TO KNOW SEVERAL THINGS BUT FIRST YOU WILL TELL ME WHERE YOU KEEP YOUR JAPS AND NAZIS!
I'LL TELL YOU ONE THING--
THIS PERFUME IS A KNOCKOUT!
WONDER WOMAN CAUGHT UNAWARE, BREATHES DEEPLY OF THE ANAESTHETIC AND FALLS UNCONSCIOUS, WHILE DOLLY PRESSES A SECRET SIGNAL BUTTON.
IT TAKES A WOMAN TO OUTSMART A WOMAN, AFTER ALL!
IS-SS NO USE TO BIND WONDER WOMAN WITH ROPES! TAKE HER BELOW- I SSHOW YOU HOW TO MAKE HER HELPLESS!
9

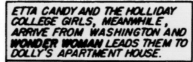

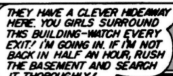

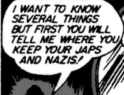

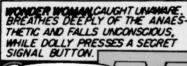

THEY CARRY WONDER WOMAN TO THE BASEMENT.
QVICK, ISHTI! OPEN DER TRAP DOOR! I HEAR FOOT-STEPS ON DER STAIRS!
FAR DOWN BENEATH THE TRAIN TUNNELS WONDER WOMAN IS CARRIED TO AN ELECTRIC REPAIR SHOP.
VE "BORROWED" DER SHOP FROM DER RAILROAD— IT VAS EASY!
WERE THERE NO WORKERS? THEY WILL SOUND ALARMS!
DOSE VORKERS VILL NEFER GIF ALARMS! VE SHOOT THEM ALL EXCEPT DIS VELDER. HE WILL PUT DER CHAINS ON WONDER WOMAN.
ISS GOOD! PROCEED.
WELD CHAINS TO THESE BRACELETS! BARONESS VON GUNTHER TELL ME WHEN SSSO CHAINED, WONDER WOMAN BECOME HELPLESSSS!
IS-SS ANTIDOTE FOR PERFUME GAS. WHEN WONDER WOMAN WAKE, WE MAKE HER TALK!
OH-H-H! AH—UNH!
WHO PUT THESE CHAINS ON MY BRACELETS?
I HAVE PLEASURE TO DIRECT YOUNG MAN WHO CHAIN YOU, WONDER WOMAN!
YOU SSO SSTRONG, WONDER WOMAN, YOU BREAK THESE LITTLE CHAINS VERY EASY!
GREAT APHRODITE! IF A MAN WELDED THESE CHAINS ON MY BRACELETS I AM HELPLESS!
WHY BREAK THEM? I THINK THEY'RE CUTE!
10
HO! YOU CANNOT ESCAPE! COME, WE TRY INTERESTING EX-PERIMENT. I MAKE YOU TELL USSS ALL YOU KNOW!
I'LL TELL YOU NOTHING!
THIS WON'T BE PLEASANT! BUT I'LL SHOW THEM HOW AN AM-AZON CAN TAKE IT!

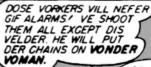

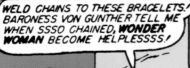

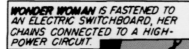

WONDER WOMAN IS FASTENED TO AN ELECTRIC SWITCHBOARD, HER CHAINS CONNECTED TO A HIGH-POWER CIRCUIT.

YOU'D BETTER TALK, BABY! WE'RE HITCHING YOU UP TO 1500 VOLTS!

HOW SHOCKING!

TURNING HER HEAD, WONDER WOMAN STUDIES THE ELECTRIC CIRCUIT.

BY THE SPEAR OF ATHENA! IF I CAN THROW THAT SWITCH TO "DIRECT CURRENT" I'LL BE ABLE TO TAKE 1500 VOLTS AND NEVER FEEL IT!

TAKING THE SWITCH HANDLE IN HER STRONG TEETH, WONDER WOMAN THROWS IT TO "DIRECT CURRENT"--- THIS CURRENT HAS NO DAMAGING EFFECT ON THE HUMAN BODY---

SLOWLY, WITH MALICIOUS GLEE, ISHTI INCREASES THE CURRENT COURSING THROUGH WONDER WOMAN'S BODY.

800 VOLTS, HOW DO YOU LIKE IT? YOU READY TO TELL ME WHAT INTELLIGENCE SERVICE KNOW ABOUT OUR PLANS?

CERTAINLY NOT! I LOVE ELECTRICITY — GIVE ME MORE VOLTS!

SEE! WONDER WOMAN LIKE DYNAMO-SSSHE LIGHTS ELECTRIC LIGHT!

ENJOY YOURSELF, JAPPY, BUT DON'T BURN YOUR FINGERS!

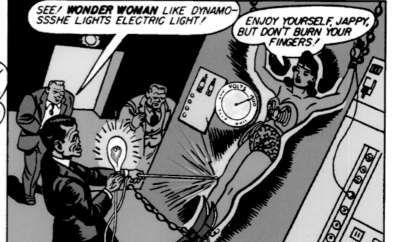

MEANWHILE, A GROUP OF MILITARY FIGURES SLIP QUIETLY ABOARD THE ARMY CHIEF'S PRIVATE CAR AT GRAND CENTRAL.

INSIDE THE CAR BRIGHT LIGHTS REVEAL-NOT GENERAL STAFF OFFICERS BUT MAJOR TREVOR AND HIS G-2 BOYS FROM MILITARY INTELLIGENCE!

I PRETENDED TO FALL FOR DOLLY DANCER AND GAVE HER A PHONY CODE-KEY!

WE GO OUT ON THE UPPER LEVEL! SOMEWHERE IN THE TUNNEL ENEMY SPIES WILL TRY TO BOARD THIS CAR OR DESTROY IT. SHOOT FIRST AND TALK AFTERWARD! WE'RE MOVING!

RIGHT!

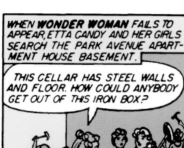

WHEN *WONDER WOMAN* FAILS TO APPEAR, ETTA CANDY AND HER GIRLS SEARCH THE PARK AVENUE APARTMENT HOUSE BASEMENT.

THIS CELLAR HAS STEEL WALLS AND FLOOR. HOW COULD ANYBODY GET OUT OF THIS IRON BOX?

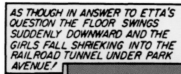

AS THOUGH IN ANSWER TO ETTA'S QUESTION THE FLOOR SWINGS SUDDENLY DOWNWARD AND THE GIRLS FALL SHRIEKING INTO THE RAILROAD TUNNEL UNDER PARK AVENUE!

YEE-EEK! WOW-OW! THIS WAY OUT-EEK! THIS IS THE BUM'S RUSH—BUT GOOD!

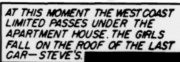

AT THIS MOMENT THE WEST COAST LIMITED PASSES UNDER THE APARTMENT HOUSE. THE GIRLS FALL ON THE ROOF OF THE LAST CAR—STEVE'S.

EEK! WE HIT SOMETHING! HANG ON, WE'RE GOING PLACES!

HEARING THUDS ON THE ROOF, STEVE'S MEN THINK THE ENEMY ATTACK HAS BEGUN.

HOLD YOUR FIRE, BOYS—I'M GOING TO RECONNOITRE!

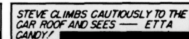

STEVE CLIMBS CAUTIOUSLY TO THE CAR ROOF AND SEES —— ETTA CANDY!

WHY, STEVE, WHAT A SMALL WORLD! HAVE A BON-BON?

YE GODS AND LITTLE FISHBALLS! CLIMB DOWN HERE QUICK—WE MAY BE ATTACKED ANY MINUTE!

IN THE REPAIR SHOP, TWO LEVELS BELOW, ISHTI ADMITS DEFEAT.

IS-SS VERY STRANGE WE CANNOT MAKE YOU TALK. NO MATTER. IN THREE MINUTES TRAIN OF AMERICAN GENERALS MAKE CONTACT. WE FIX, BANG! TUNNEL BLOW UP!

APHRODITE HELP ME!

119

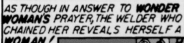

AS THOUGH IN ANSWER TO *WONDER WOMAN'S* PRAYER, THE WELDER WHO CHAINED HER REVEALS HERSELF A *WOMAN!*

HOW HORRIBLE! THERE ARE GIRLS WORKING IN THE TUNNEL SHOPS NOW IN MEN'S PLACES. THEY'LL ALL BE KILLED.

12

WONDER WOMAN IS HERSELF AGAIN!

I HAVE NOT LOST MY POWER—A *GIRL* CHAINED ME!

PARDON ME, BOYS— I'M THE CHATTANOOGA CHOO-CHOO!

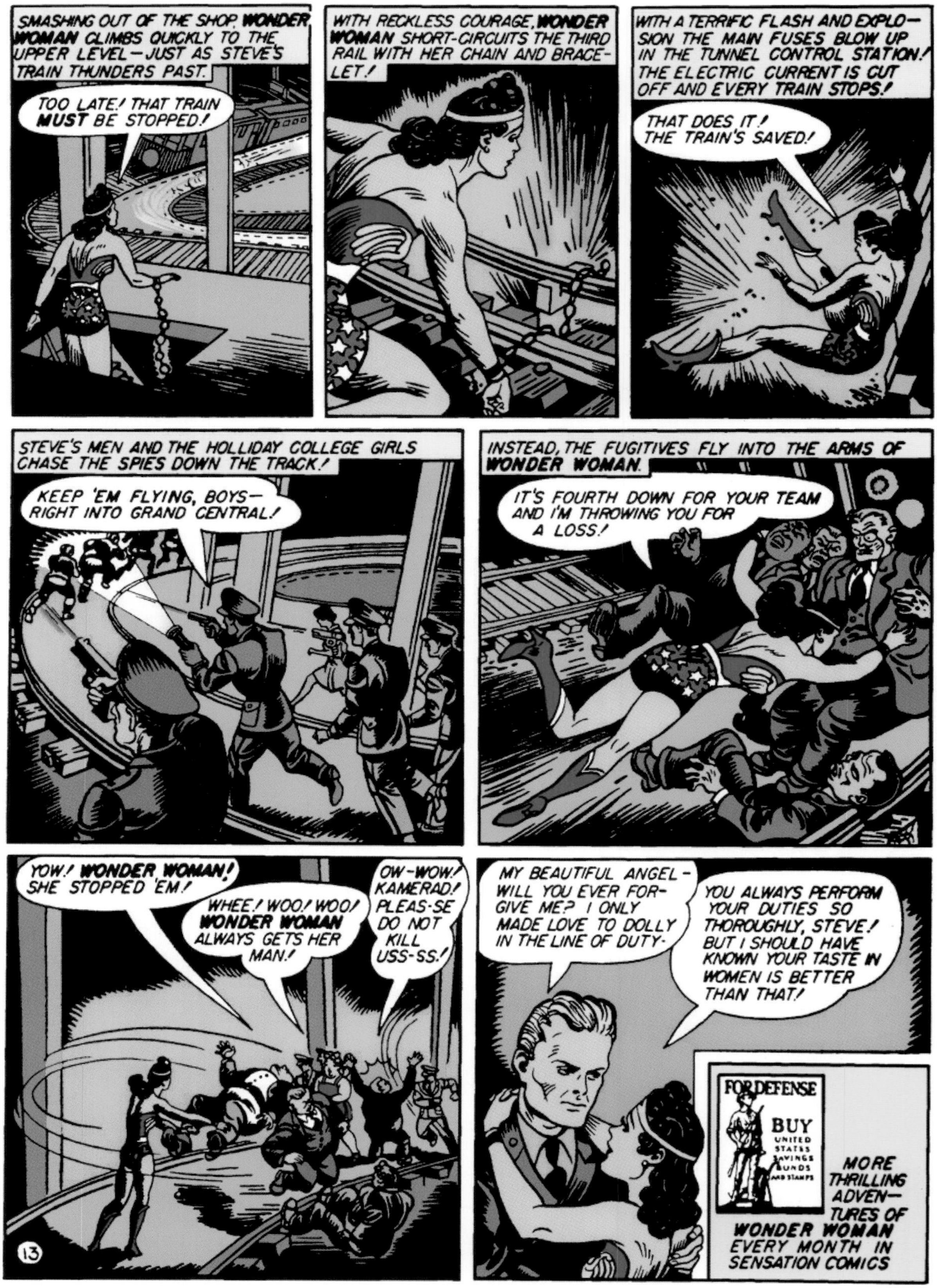
SMASHING OUT OF THE SHOP, WONDER WOMAN CLIMBS QUICKLY TO THE UPPER LEVEL—JUST AS STEVE'S TRAIN THUNDERS PAST.
TOO LATE! THAT TRAIN MUST BE STOPPED!
WITH RECKLESS COURAGE, WONDER WOMAN SHORT-CIRCUITS THE THIRD RAIL WITH HER CHAIN AND BRACELET!
WITH A TERRIFIC FLASH AND EXPLOSION THE MAIN FUSES BLOW UP IN THE TUNNEL CONTROL STATION! THE ELECTRIC CURRENT IS CUT OFF AND EVERY TRAIN STOPS!
THAT DOES IT! THE TRAIN'S SAVED!
STEVE'S MEN AND THE HOLLIDAY COLLEGE GIRLS CHASE THE SPIES DOWN THE TRACK!
KEEP 'EM FLYING, BOYS—RIGHT INTO GRAND CENTRAL!
INSTEAD, THE FUGITIVES FLY INTO THE ARMS OF WONDER WOMAN.
IT'S FOURTH DOWN FOR YOUR TEAM AND I'M THROWING YOU FOR A LOSS!
YOW! WONDER WOMAN! SHE STOPPED 'EM!
WHEE! WOO! WOO! WONDER WOMAN ALWAYS GETS HER MAN!
OW-WOW! KAMERAD! PLEAS-SE DO NOT KILL USS-SS!
13
MY BEAUTIFUL ANGEL—WILL YOU EVER FORGIVE ME? I ONLY MADE LOVE TO DOLLY IN THE LINE OF DUTY—
YOU ALWAYS PERFORM YOUR DUTIES SO THOROUGHLY, STEVE! BUT I SHOULD HAVE KNOWN YOUR TASTE IN WOMEN IS BETTER THAN THAT!
FOR DEFENSE BUY UNITED STATES SAVINGS BONDS AND STAMPS
MORE THRILLING ADVENTURES OF WONDER WOMAN EVERY MONTH IN SENSATION COMICS

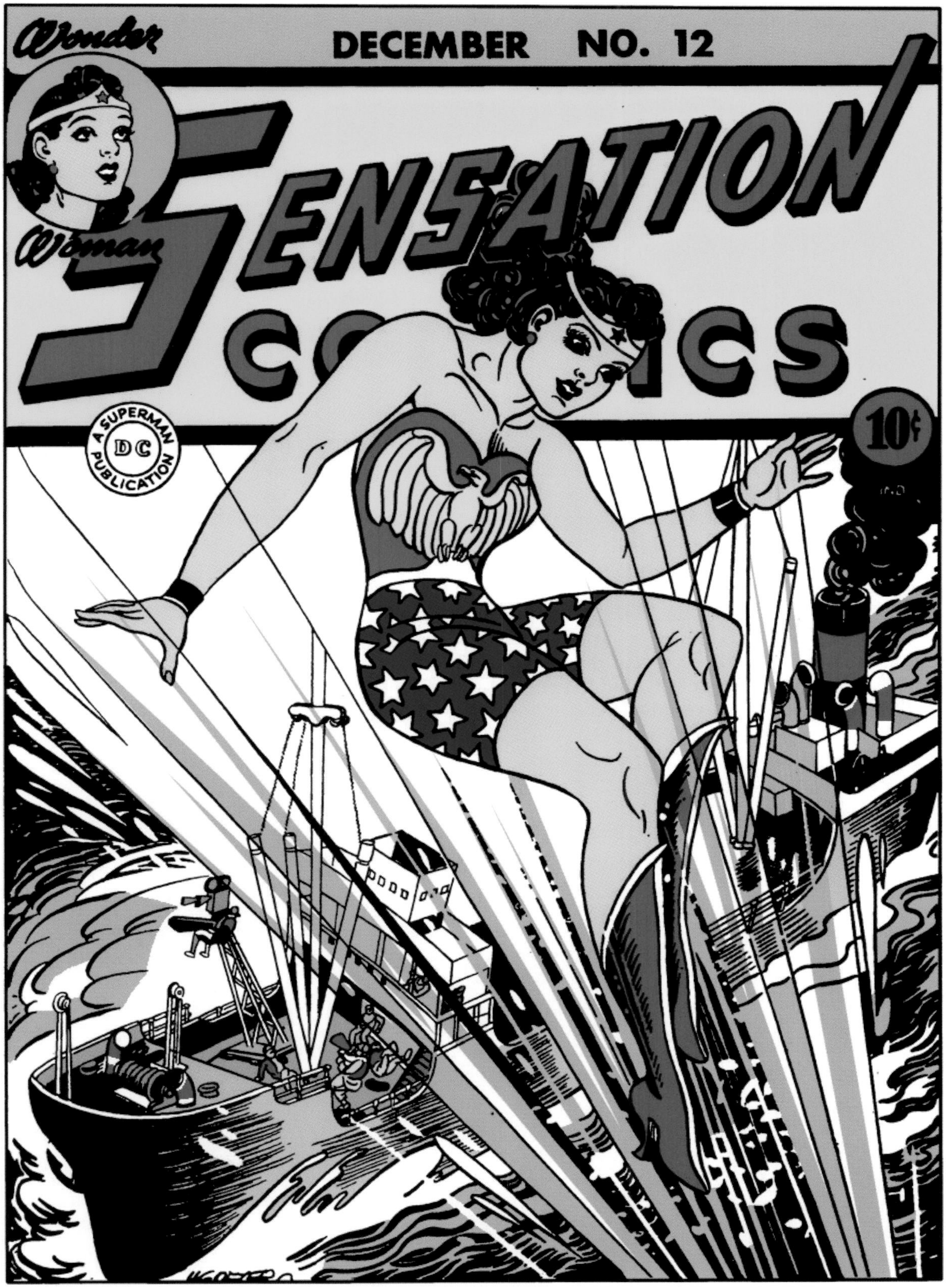
Wonder Woman
DECEMBER NO. 12
SENSATION COMICS
A SUPERMAN DC PUBLICATION
10¢

Sensation Comics #12 (Dec. 1942) - art: H.G. Peter

Part Three

1942 was the high point of World War II as "entertainment," at least in the United States. Which is weirdly ironic, because for most Americans it was also the worst year of the war.

Against the Axis

In the first half of 1942, the Philippines fell to the Japanese, several months after the invasion that began on the preceding December 8th, one day after the Pearl Harbor assault; Burma, Malaya, the Dutch East Indies, Singapore, and other territories also fell to Japan. German offensives in North Africa commanded by General Irwin Rommel ("The Desert Fox") drove the British and Commonwealth forces back, eventually forcing them to retreat deep into Egypt. Everywhere, the Axis—as the loose union of Nazi Germany, Fascist Italy, and Imperial Japan termed themselves—was on the offensive.

Some of the only good war news Americans had during this period occurred in April, when a handful of B25 bombers, led by Lt. Col. Jimmy Doolittle, took off from an aircraft carrier in the western Pacific and managed to damage morale on the U.S. Home Front.

Not until the naval-and-air Battle of Midway in June did the Americans finally win a decisive victory over the Japanese, largely because they had broken the enemy's secret naval codes only a few weeks before. This was followed in August by a landing in force of U.S. Marines on the strategic island of Guadalcanal, with a fierce battle following. That same month, the British and their Commonwealth allies finally repelled a long-standing German attack in North Africa, at an outpost called El Alamein. The Americans first joined face-to-face combat against the Nazis that November, on the western coast of North Africa.

On the U.S. Home Front, though, spirits were kept up by any number of Hollywood movies playing up American (and sometimes English) heroism

and triumphs both at home and abroad, such as *A Yank on the Burma Road, Mrs. Miniver, Nazi Agent, Wake Island, Across the Pacific,* and of course, late in the year, the inimitable *Casablanca.* Radio, too, in those pre-television days, did its part with many a scripted melodrama—as did comic books and comic strips.

And probably no costumed hero at DC saw more war-related action than Wonder Woman.

Superman? He was so powerful that his editors and writers had to come up with specious reasons for why he couldn't go into combat.

Batman? Not being bulletproof, he would've been just one more guy for the enemy to shoot at—and he didn't even use a gun!

Green Lantern and the Justice Society of America took part in several war-related stories early on . . . less so the Flash, Hawkman, and so on.

But Princess Diana covered all the bases. *Wonder Woman #2* (Fall 1942) was a landmark issue. In a special two-page feature therein, she promoted war bonds—and the issue's main four-part, 52-page story was so war-centered from first to last that this volume reprints it in its entirety.

The tale's chief villain is Mars, the grotesque Roman god of war, who was a special enemy of Marston's peace-loving Amazons. He's treated as a bit of a buffoon in the story, but the ancient Greeks (who called him Ares) had never particularly respected him, either. In Greco-Roman myth, he was often

122

made sport of, as when Hephaestus/Vulcan, the husband of Aphrodite/Venus, the goddess of love and beauty, caught him in a net during an illicit tryst between Ares and his wife. In *The Iliad*, Homer's epic poem dealing with the Trojan War, he is wounded by a mortal's spear and runs off the battlefield howling. If anything, the comic book figure is taken more seriously than the mythical one ever was. One of Mars's chief minions, who would make many appearances in Wonder Woman yarns over the years, was the Duke of Deception.

Even Adolf Hitler, Germany's Führer, and Benito Mussolini, Italy's Duce, made token appearances in the tale. So did top Nazis Joseph Goebbels, who was in charge of propaganda and Hermann Göring, who was head of the Nazi's Luftwaffe, who would have been instantly recognizable to many people in 1942 when he appears on page 3 of the third chapter in *Wonder Woman #2*. Even Japan's Emperor Hirohito plays a part in that chapter; in reality, it's always been hotly debated whether the emperor was a merely a puppet in the hands of the ascendant military or an active participant in the war . . . but Marston didn't let such ambiguities slow him down.

By this time, incidentally, Wonder Woman's alter ego, Diana Prince, was no longer a nurse. Eager to

be near Steve Trevor, with whom he had fallen in love, she'd managed to land herself a job at Military Intelligence as secretary to his superior officer. Apparently wartime security standards were a bit lax in that office, since Col. Darnell was in essence hiring an alien national—an Amazon!—who was in the United States illegally.

Also during 1942, Gaines and Mayer had another brainstorm. Their DC sister company had added to the visibility of Superman and Batman by having them share space in a 15¢ (as opposed to 10¢) comic book titled *World's Finest Comics*. The AA equivalent, debuting with a December 1942–January 1943 cover date, was the extra-size *Comic Cavalcade*, whose big guns were Wonder Woman, the Flash, and Green Lantern. Wonder Woman's adventure in that magazine was always the one that led off an issue, as befitted her status as being more popular than her two male colleagues.

Next, we present the cover of *Sensation Comics #13*, in which Wonder Woman goes bowling—with the heads of Hitler, Mussolini, and either Hirohito or General Tojo (it's hard to tell which of the two was meant, sometimes, since Hirohito was often depicted in military garb) serving as the bowling pins for the Amazon's perfect strike!

123

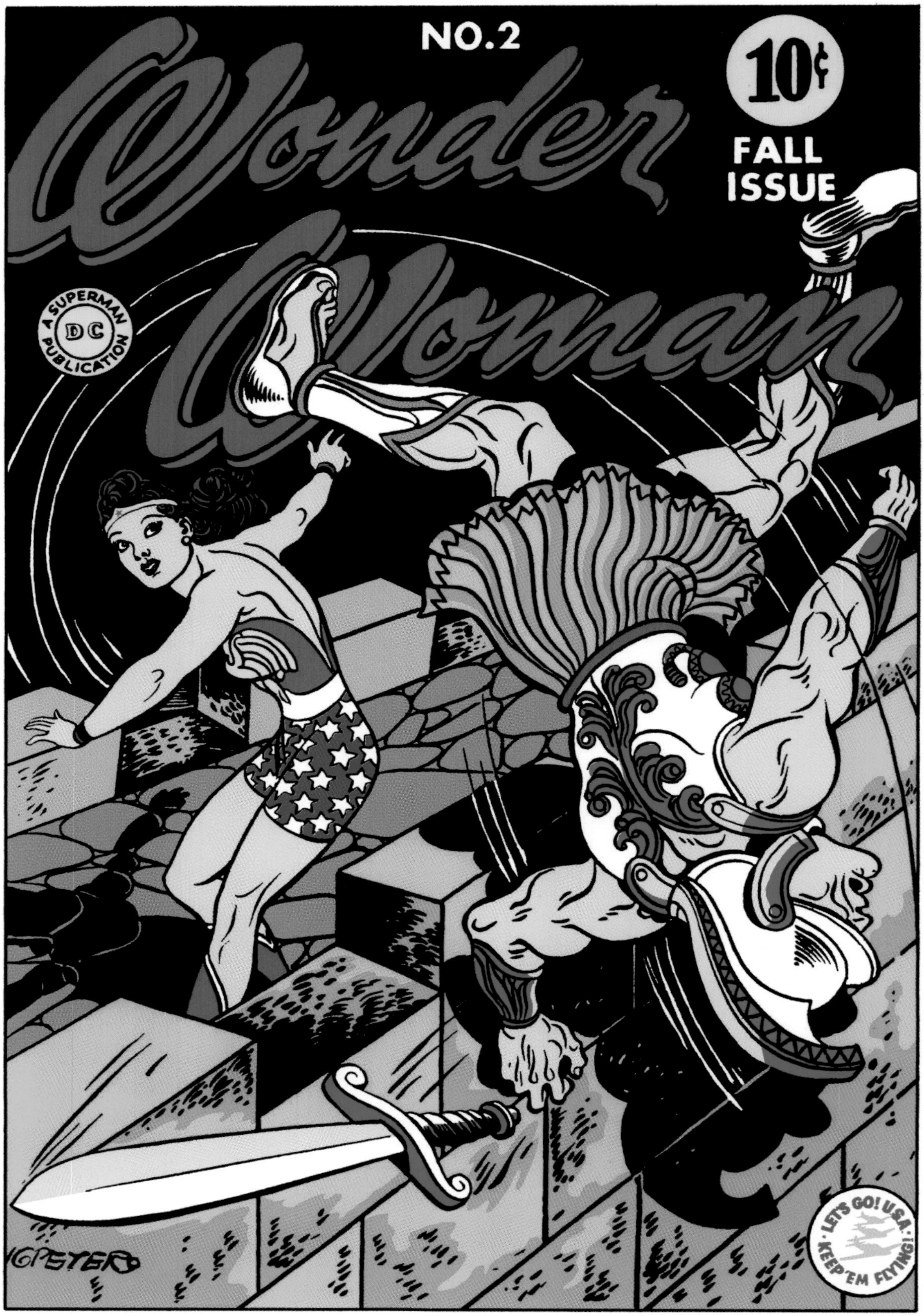
NO.2
Wonder Woman
10¢
FALL ISSUE
A SUPERMAN DC PUBLICATION
H.G. PETER
LET'S GO! U.S.A. KEEP 'EM FLYING!

Wonder Woman #2 (Fall 1942) - art: H.G. Peter

FLASH COMICS
STORIES BIBLE
MUTT JEFF
Wonder Woman

Boys and Girls! Here Are the Men Behind "WONDER WOMAN"

FROM left to right they are: — (1) DR. WM. MOULTON MARSTON, well known psychologist and inventor of the lie detector, who conceived "Wonder Woman" and writes it under the pen name of Charles Moulton ! (2) H. G. PETER, well-known cartoonist, who directs a staff of four assistants who turn out all the "Wonder Woman" drawings ! (3) SHELDON MAYER, creator of "Scribbly" and editor of all the magazines in the All-American Comic Group of the Superman D. C. Publications ! (4) M. C. GAINES, originator of the comic magazine, former school principal and Army officer, now president and general manager of All-American Comics Inc., licensors and publishers of "Flash," "All-American" and "Sensation Comics," "All-Star Comics," "All-Flash," "Green Lantern," "Mutt And Jeff," "Wonder Woman" and "Picture Stories from the Bible" !

Here they are in Mr. Gaines' office discussing this second issue of "Wonder Woman" on a warm day in August. But I almost had to get "Wonder Woman" and her magic lasso to get them to pose, for, being all gallant gentlemen, they insisted that I be in the picture, until I explained I wanted to take the picture myself, and couldn't very well be in it, too.

And so they agreed to let me publish it here, on condition that I tell you that they want you to enjoy reading "Wonder Woman" as much as they enjoy writing, drawing and editing it ! But I know you do, for the first issue was a complete sell-out and we all want to thank you for giving "Wonder Woman" such a swell reception !

Alice Marble
(Associate Editor)

Wonder Woman #2 (Fall 1942) - script attributed to Alice Marble – photographer: unknown

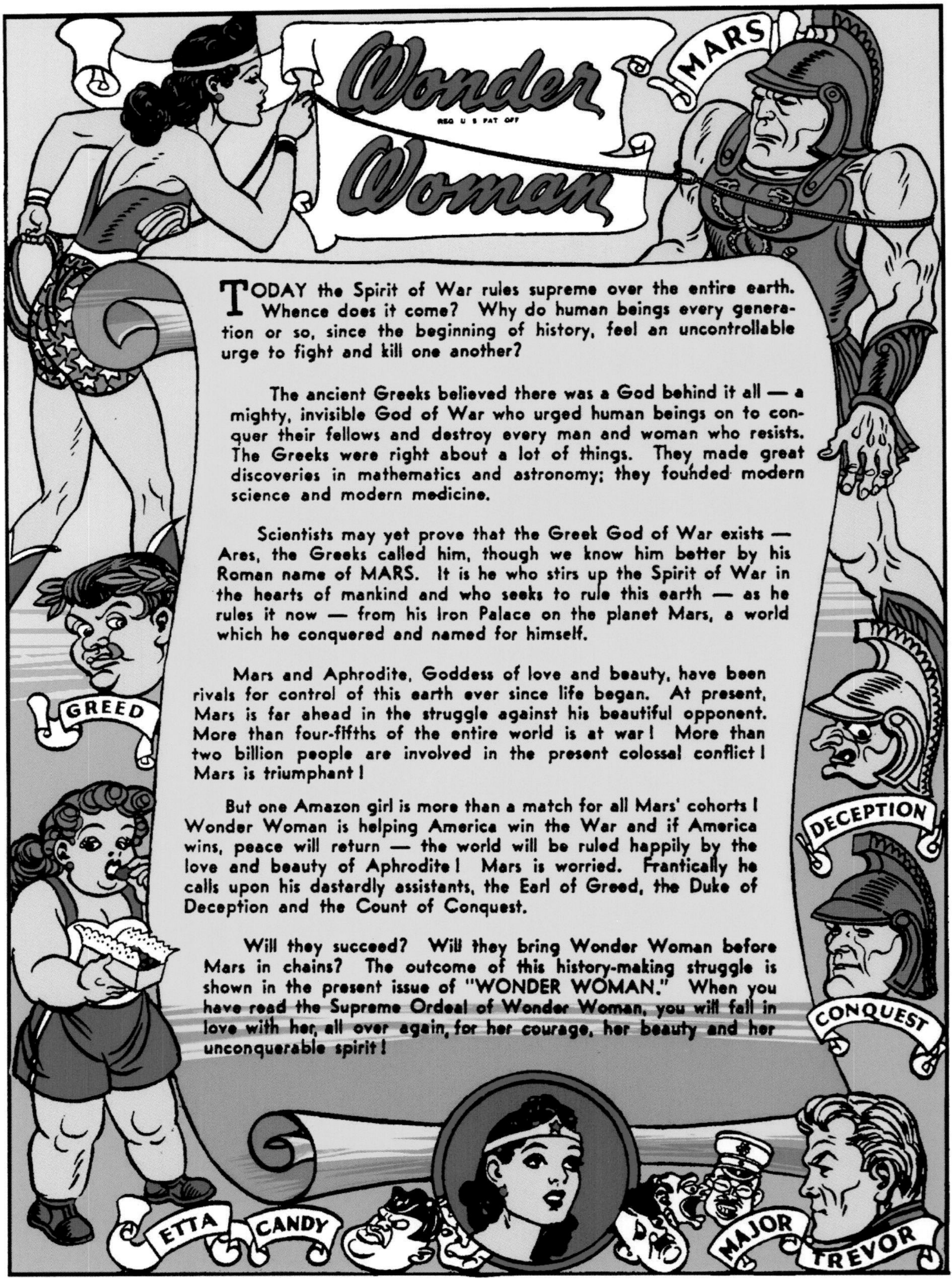
Wonder Woman
REG U S PAT OFF
MARS
TODAY the Spirit of War rules supreme over the entire earth. Whence does it come? Why do human beings every generation or so, since the beginning of history, feel an uncontrollable urge to fight and kill one another?
The ancient Greeks believed there was a God behind it all — a mighty, invisible God of War who urged human beings on to conquer their fellows and destroy every man and woman who resists. The Greeks were right about a lot of things. They made great discoveries in mathematics and astronomy; they founded modern science and modern medicine.
Scientists may yet prove that the Greek God of War exists — Ares, the Greeks called him, though we know him better by his Roman name of MARS. It is he who stirs up the Spirit of War in the hearts of mankind and who seeks to rule this earth — as he rules it now — from his Iron Palace on the planet Mars, a world which he conquered and named for himself.
Mars and Aphrodite, Goddess of love and beauty, have been rivals for control of this earth ever since life began. At present, Mars is far ahead in the struggle against his beautiful opponent. More than four-fifths of the entire world is at war! More than two billion people are involved in the present colossal conflict! Mars is triumphant!
But one Amazon girl is more than a match for all Mars' cohorts! Wonder Woman is helping America win the War and if America wins, peace will return — the world will be ruled happily by the love and beauty of Aphrodite! Mars is worried. Frantically he calls upon his dastardly assistants, the Earl of Greed, the Duke of Deception and the Count of Conquest.
Will they succeed? Will they bring Wonder Woman before Mars in chains? The outcome of this history-making struggle is shown in the present issue of "WONDER WOMAN." When you have read the Supreme Ordeal of Wonder Woman, you will fall in love with her, all over again, for her courage, her beauty and her unconquerable spirit!
GREED
DECEPTION
CONQUEST
ETTA
CANDY
MAJOR
TREVOR

Wonder Woman #2 (Fall 1942) - script: William Moulton Marston - art: H.G. Peter

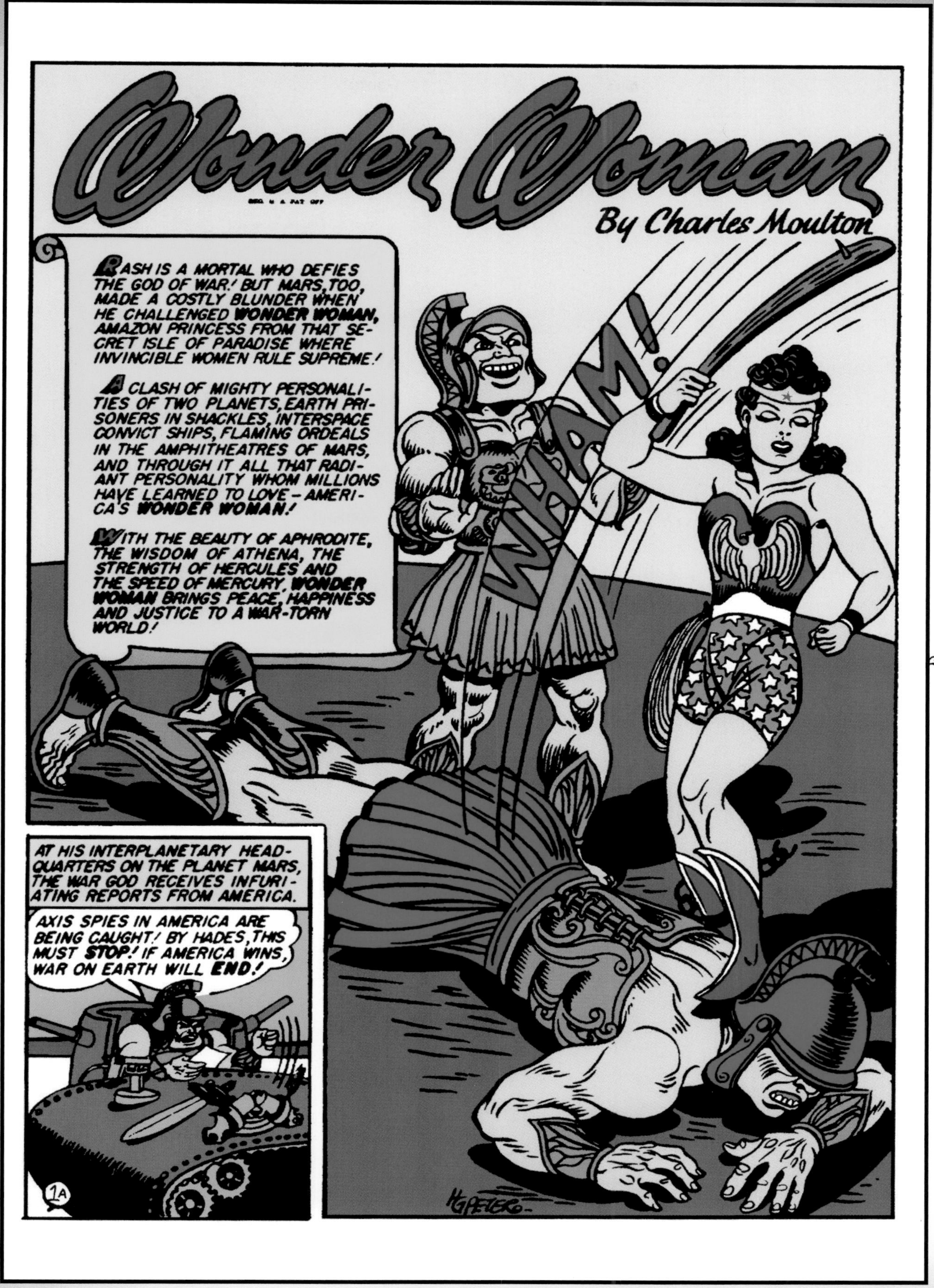
Wonder Woman
By Charles Moulton
RASH IS A MORTAL WHO DEFIES THE GOD OF WAR! BUT MARS, TOO, MADE A COSTLY BLUNDER WHEN HE CHALLENGED WONDER WOMAN, AMAZON PRINCESS FROM THAT SECRET ISLE OF PARADISE WHERE INVINCIBLE WOMEN RULE SUPREME!
A CLASH OF MIGHTY PERSONALITIES OF TWO PLANETS, EARTH PRISONERS IN SHACKLES, INTERSPACE CONVICT SHIPS, FLAMING ORDEALS IN THE AMPHITHEATRES OF MARS, AND THROUGH IT ALL THAT RADIANT PERSONALITY WHOM MILLIONS HAVE LEARNED TO LOVE – AMERICA'S WONDER WOMAN!
WITH THE BEAUTY OF APHRODITE, THE WISDOM OF ATHENA, THE STRENGTH OF HERCULES AND THE SPEED OF MERCURY, WONDER WOMAN BRINGS PEACE, HAPPINESS AND JUSTICE TO A WAR-TORN WORLD!
WHAM!
AT HIS INTERPLANETARY HEADQUARTERS ON THE PLANET MARS, THE WAR GOD RECEIVES INFURIATING REPORTS FROM AMERICA.
AXIS SPIES IN AMERICA ARE BEING CAUGHT! BY HADES, THIS MUST STOP! IF AMERICA WINS, WAR ON EARTH WILL END!
1A
HG PETER

Wonder Woman #2 (Fall 1942) - script: William Moulton Marston - art: H.G. Peter

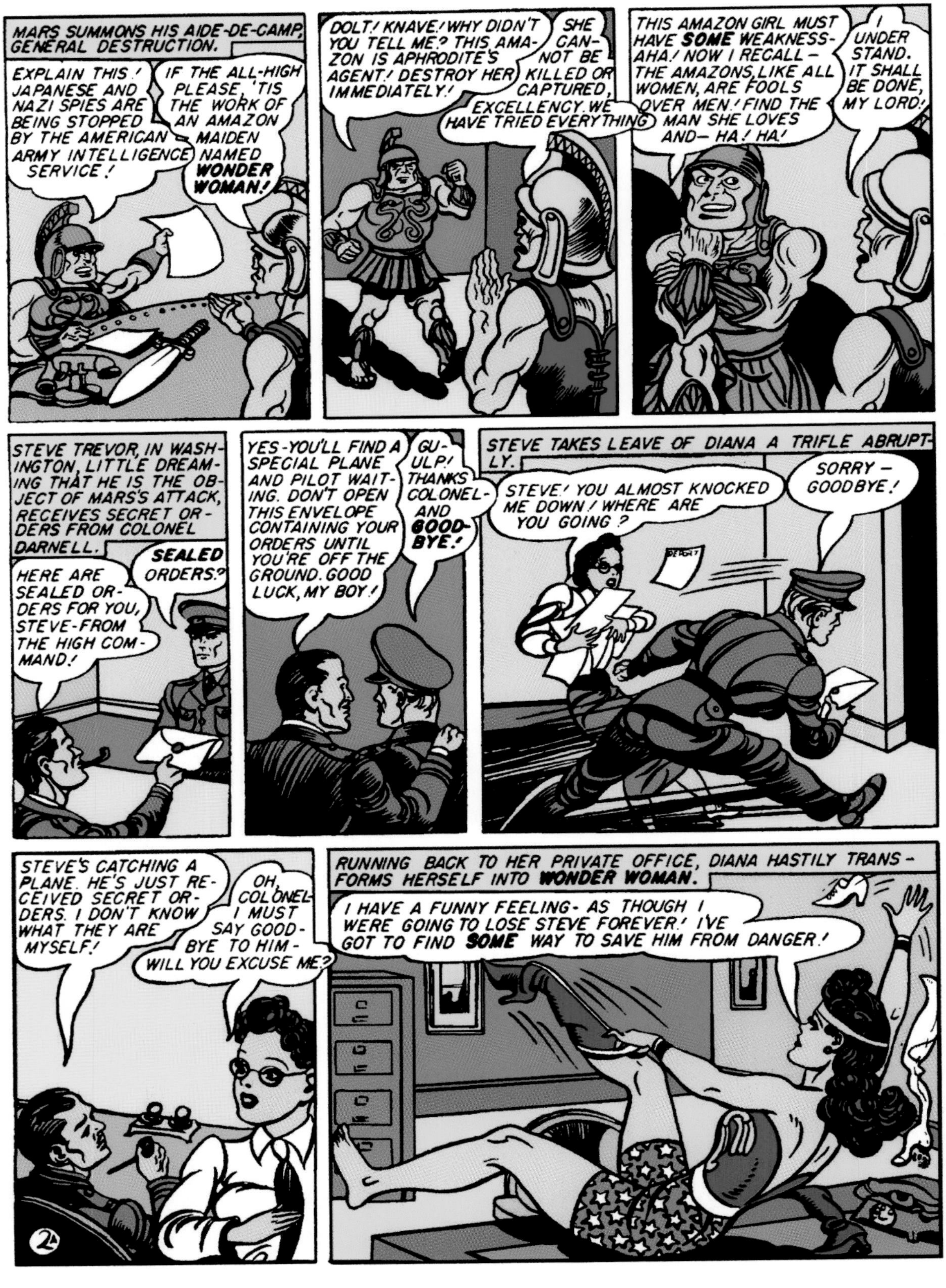

MARS SUMMONS HIS AIDE-DE-CAMP, GENERAL DESTRUCTION.
EXPLAIN THIS! JAPANESE AND NAZI SPIES ARE BEING STOPPED BY THE AMERICAN ARMY INTELLIGENCE SERVICE!
IF THE ALL-HIGH PLEASE, 'TIS THE WORK OF AN AMAZON MAIDEN NAMED WONDER WOMAN!
DOLT! KNAVE! WHY DIDN'T YOU TELL ME? THIS AMAZON IS APHRODITE'S AGENT! DESTROY HER IMMEDIATELY!
SHE CANNOT BE KILLED OR CAPTURED, EXCELLENCY. WE HAVE TRIED EVERYTHING.
THIS AMAZON GIRL MUST HAVE SOME WEAKNESS-AHA! NOW I RECALL - THE AMAZONS, LIKE ALL WOMEN, ARE FOOLS OVER MEN! FIND THE MAN SHE LOVES AND- HA! HA!
I UNDERSTAND. IT SHALL BE DONE, MY LORD!
STEVE TREVOR, IN WASHINGTON, LITTLE DREAMING THAT HE IS THE OBJECT OF MARS'S ATTACK, RECEIVES SECRET ORDERS FROM COLONEL DARNELL.
HERE ARE SEALED ORDERS FOR YOU, STEVE-FROM THE HIGH COMMAND!
SEALED ORDERS?
YES-YOU'LL FIND A SPECIAL PLANE AND PILOT WAITING. DON'T OPEN THIS ENVELOPE CONTAINING YOUR ORDERS UNTIL YOU'RE OFF THE GROUND. GOOD LUCK, MY BOY!
GU-ULP! THANKS COLONEL-AND GOODBYE!
STEVE TAKES LEAVE OF DIANA A TRIFLE ABRUPTLY.
STEVE! YOU ALMOST KNOCKED ME DOWN! WHERE ARE YOU GOING?
SORRY - GOODBYE!
STEVE'S CATCHING A PLANE. HE'S JUST RECEIVED SECRET ORDERS. I DON'T KNOW WHAT THEY ARE MYSELF!
OH, COLONEL-I MUST SAY GOODBYE TO HIM-WILL YOU EXCUSE ME?
RUNNING BACK TO HER PRIVATE OFFICE, DIANA HASTILY TRANSFORMS HERSELF INTO WONDER WOMAN.
I HAVE A FUNNY FEELING- AS THOUGH I WERE GOING TO LOSE STEVE FOREVER! I'VE GOT TO FIND SOME WAY TO SAVE HIM FROM DANGER!
2

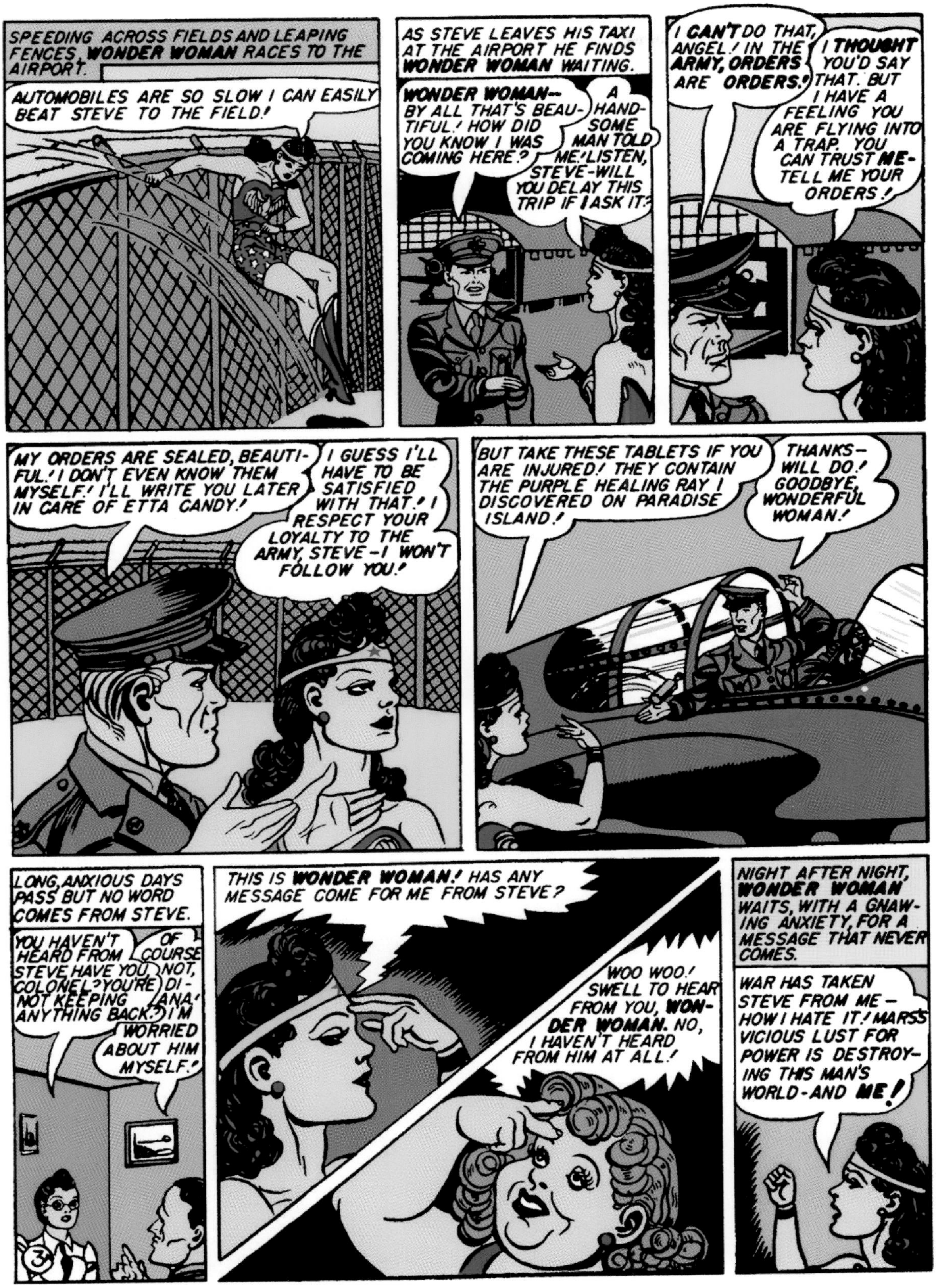
SPEEDING ACROSS FIELDS AND LEAPING FENCES, WONDER WOMAN RACES TO THE AIRPORT.
AUTOMOBILES ARE SO SLOW I CAN EASILY BEAT STEVE TO THE FIELD!
AS STEVE LEAVES HIS TAXI AT THE AIRPORT HE FINDS WONDER WOMAN WAITING.
WONDER WOMAN-- BY ALL THAT'S BEAUTIFUL! HOW DID YOU KNOW I WAS COMING HERE?
A HANDSOME MAN TOLD ME! LISTEN, STEVE-WILL YOU DELAY THIS TRIP IF I ASK IT?
I CAN'T DO THAT, ANGEL! IN THE ARMY, ORDERS ARE ORDERS!
I THOUGHT YOU'D SAY THAT. BUT I HAVE A FEELING YOU ARE FLYING INTO A TRAP. YOU CAN TRUST ME- TELL ME YOUR ORDERS!
MY ORDERS ARE SEALED, BEAUTIFUL! I DON'T EVEN KNOW THEM MYSELF! I'LL WRITE YOU LATER IN CARE OF ETTA CANDY!
I GUESS I'LL HAVE TO BE SATISFIED WITH THAT! I RESPECT YOUR LOYALTY TO THE ARMY, STEVE-I WON'T FOLLOW YOU!
BUT TAKE THESE TABLETS IF YOU ARE INJURED! THEY CONTAIN THE PURPLE HEALING RAY I DISCOVERED ON PARADISE ISLAND!
THANKS- WILL DO! GOODBYE, WONDERFUL WOMAN!
LONG, ANXIOUS DAYS PASS BUT NO WORD COMES FROM STEVE.
YOU HAVEN'T HEARD FROM STEVE HAVE YOU, COLONEL? YOU'RE NOT KEEPING ANYTHING BACK?
OF COURSE NOT, DIANA! I'M WORRIED ABOUT HIM MYSELF!
THIS IS WONDER WOMAN! HAS ANY MESSAGE COME FOR ME FROM STEVE?
WOO WOO! SWELL TO HEAR FROM YOU, WONDER WOMAN. NO, I HAVEN'T HEARD FROM HIM AT ALL!
NIGHT AFTER NIGHT, WONDER WOMAN WAITS, WITH A GNAWING ANXIETY, FOR A MESSAGE THAT NEVER COMES.
WAR HAS TAKEN STEVE FROM ME — HOW I HATE IT! MARS'S VICIOUS LUST FOR POWER IS DESTROYING THIS MAN'S WORLD-AND ME!

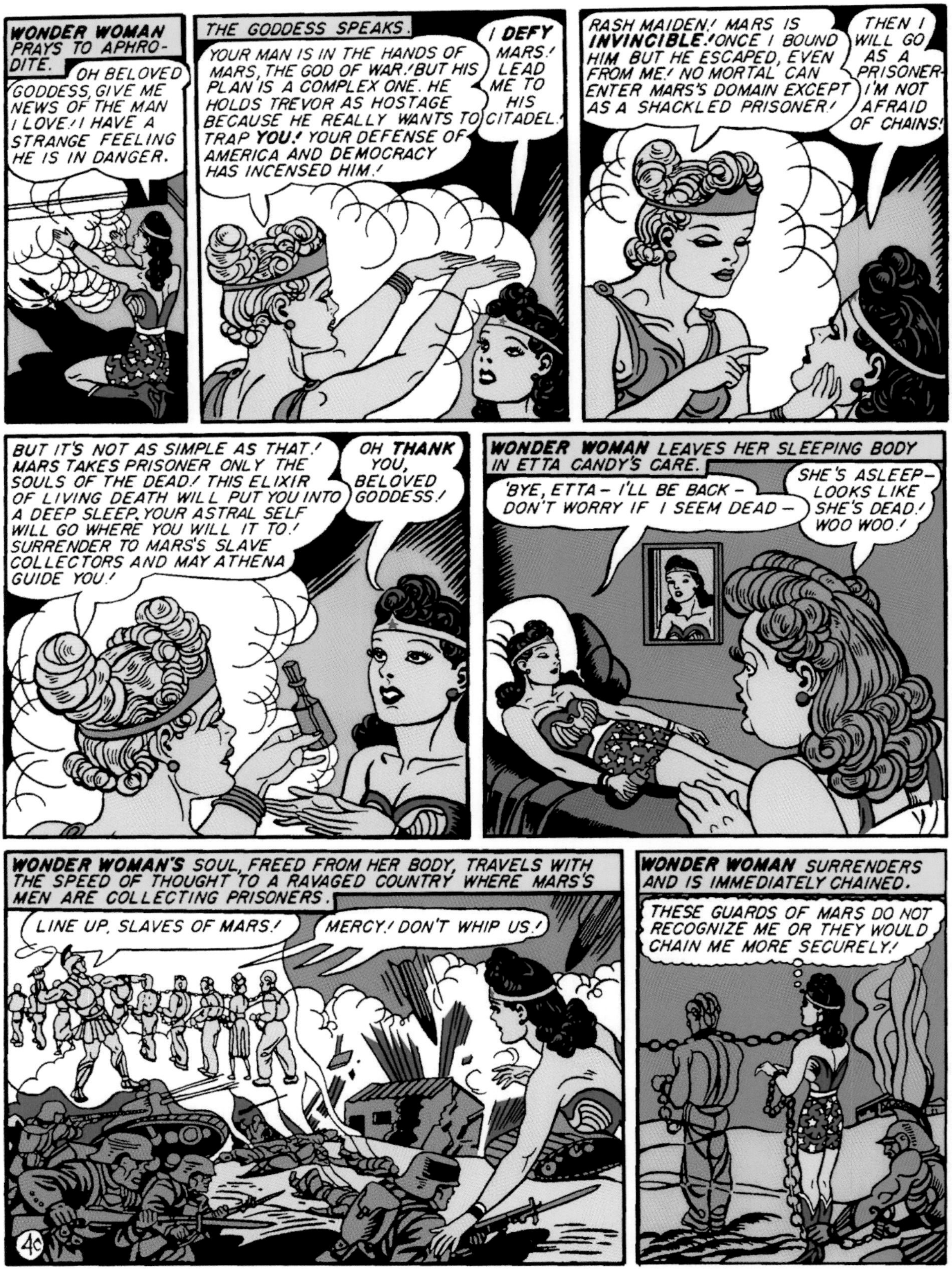
WONDER WOMAN PRAYS TO APHRODITE.
OH BELOVED GODDESS, GIVE ME NEWS OF THE MAN I LOVE! I HAVE A STRANGE FEELING HE IS IN DANGER.
THE GODDESS SPEAKS.
YOUR MAN IS IN THE HANDS OF MARS, THE GOD OF WAR! BUT HIS PLAN IS A COMPLEX ONE. HE HOLDS TREVOR AS HOSTAGE BECAUSE HE REALLY WANTS TO TRAP YOU! YOUR DEFENSE OF AMERICA AND DEMOCRACY HAS INCENSED HIM!
I DEFY MARS! LEAD ME TO HIS CITADEL!
RASH MAIDEN! MARS IS INVINCIBLE! ONCE I BOUND HIM BUT HE ESCAPED, EVEN FROM ME! NO MORTAL CAN ENTER MARS'S DOMAIN EXCEPT AS A SHACKLED PRISONER!
THEN I WILL GO AS A PRISONER- I'M NOT AFRAID OF CHAINS!
BUT IT'S NOT AS SIMPLE AS THAT! MARS TAKES PRISONER ONLY THE SOULS OF THE DEAD! THIS ELIXIR OF LIVING DEATH WILL PUT YOU INTO A DEEP SLEEP. YOUR ASTRAL SELF WILL GO WHERE YOU WILL IT TO! SURRENDER TO MARS'S SLAVE COLLECTORS AND MAY ATHENA GUIDE YOU!
OH THANK YOU, BELOVED GODDESS!
WONDER WOMAN LEAVES HER SLEEPING BODY IN ETTA CANDY'S CARE.
'BYE, ETTA – I'LL BE BACK – DON'T WORRY IF I SEEM DEAD –
SHE'S ASLEEP– LOOKS LIKE SHE'S DEAD! WOO WOO!
WONDER WOMAN'S SOUL, FREED FROM HER BODY, TRAVELS WITH THE SPEED OF THOUGHT TO A RAVAGED COUNTRY WHERE MARS'S MEN ARE COLLECTING PRISONERS.
LINE UP, SLAVES OF MARS!
MERCY! DON'T WHIP US!
4c
WONDER WOMAN SURRENDERS AND IS IMMEDIATELY CHAINED.
THESE GUARDS OF MARS DO NOT RECOGNIZE ME OR THEY WOULD CHAIN ME MORE SECURELY!

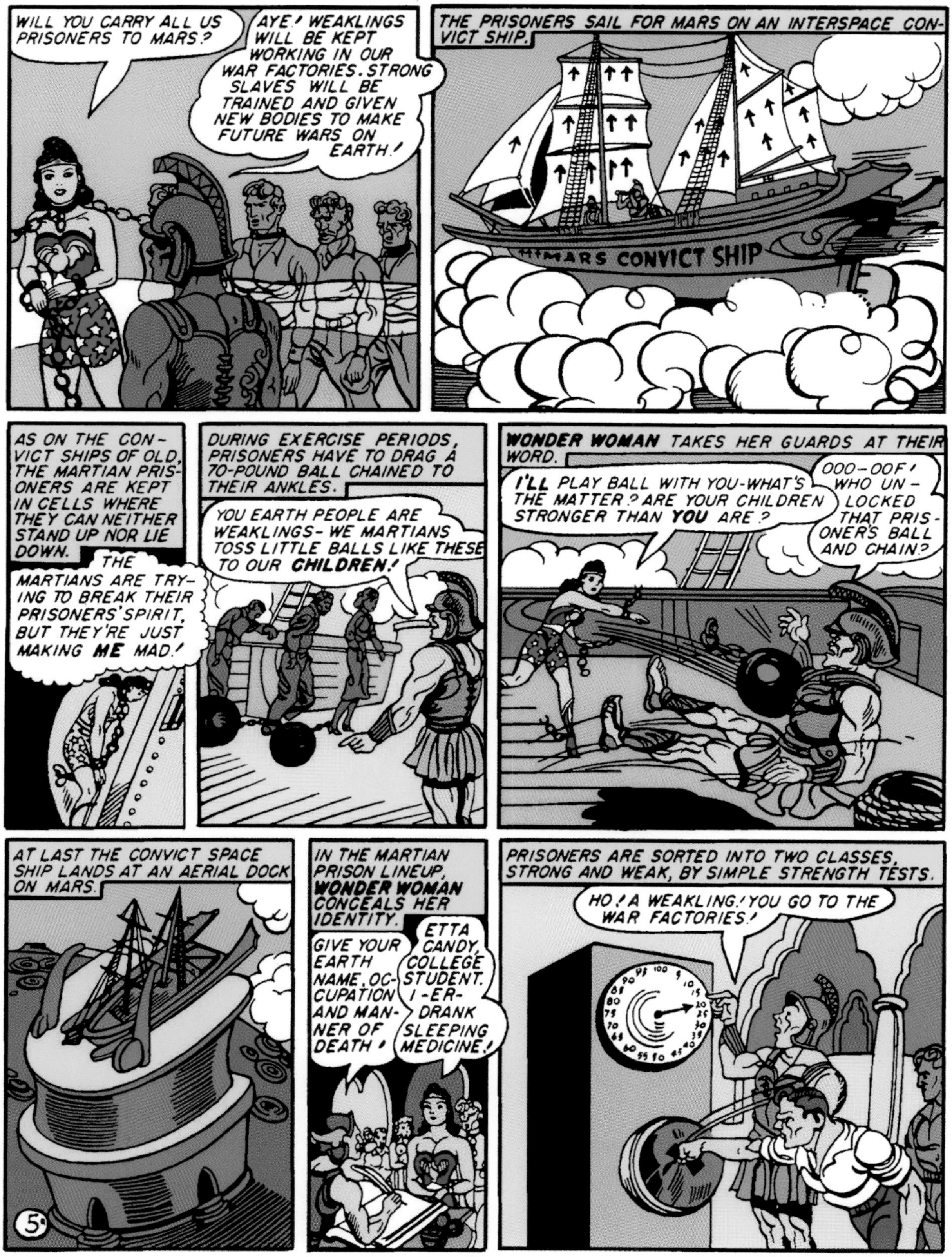

WILL YOU CARRY ALL US PRISONERS TO MARS?
AYE! WEAKLINGS WILL BE KEPT WORKING IN OUR WAR FACTORIES. STRONG SLAVES WILL BE TRAINED AND GIVEN NEW BODIES TO MAKE FUTURE WARS ON EARTH!
THE PRISONERS SAIL FOR MARS ON AN INTERSPACE CONVICT SHIP.
MARS CONVICT SHIP
AS ON THE CONVICT SHIPS OF OLD, THE MARTIAN PRISONERS ARE KEPT IN CELLS WHERE THEY CAN NEITHER STAND UP NOR LIE DOWN.
THE MARTIANS ARE TRYING TO BREAK THEIR PRISONERS' SPIRIT, BUT THEY'RE JUST MAKING ME MAD!
DURING EXERCISE PERIODS, PRISONERS HAVE TO DRAG A 70-POUND BALL CHAINED TO THEIR ANKLES.
YOU EARTH PEOPLE ARE WEAKLINGS- WE MARTIANS TOSS LITTLE BALLS LIKE THESE TO OUR CHILDREN!
WONDER WOMAN TAKES HER GUARDS AT THEIR WORD.
I'LL PLAY BALL WITH YOU-WHAT'S THE MATTER? ARE YOUR CHILDREN STRONGER THAN YOU ARE?
OOO-OOF! WHO UNLOCKED THAT PRISONER'S BALL AND CHAIN?
AT LAST THE CONVICT SPACE SHIP LANDS AT AN AERIAL DOCK ON MARS.
IN THE MARTIAN PRISON LINEUP, WONDER WOMAN CONCEALS HER IDENTITY.
GIVE YOUR EARTH NAME, OCCUPATION AND MANNER OF DEATH!
ETTA CANDY, COLLEGE STUDENT. I-ER-DRANK SLEEPING MEDICINE!
PRISONERS ARE SORTED INTO TWO CLASSES, STRONG AND WEAK, BY SIMPLE STRENGTH TESTS.
HO! A WEAKLING! YOU GO TO THE WAR FACTORIES!
5

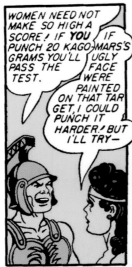

WOMEN NEED NOT MAKE SO HIGH A SCORE! IF **YOU** PUNCH 20 KAGO-GRAMS YOU'LL PASS THE TEST.

MARS'S UGLY FACE WERE PAINTED ON THAT TARGET, I COULD PUNCH IT HARDER! BUT I'LL TRY—

WONDER WOMAN HITS THE TARGET WITH SUCH FORCE THAT SHE SMASHES THE MACHINE.

GREAT GUNS OF WAR! THIS WOMAN HITS LIKE HERCULES!

PRISONERS ARE REQUIRED TO PULL A MARTIAN WARRIOR IN HIS IRON CHARIOT UPHILL FOR ONE MILE.

FASTER, SLAVE! YOU CAN'T TAKE ALL DAY FOR THIS TEST!

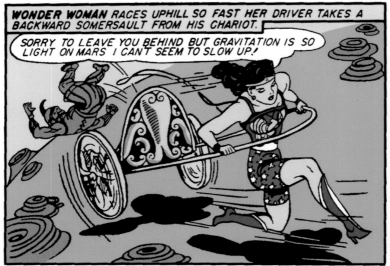

WONDER WOMAN RACES UPHILL SO FAST HER DRIVER TAKES A BACKWARD SOMERSAULT FROM HIS CHARIOT.

SORRY TO LEAVE YOU BEHIND BUT GRAVITATION IS SO LIGHT ON MARS I CAN'T SEEM TO SLOW UP!

104 PRISONERS FROM 18 PLANETS PASS THE TESTS. THESE ARE RETURNED TO THE DUNGEONS TO AWAIT THE NEXT DAY'S TOURNAMENT.

WONDER WOMAN'S CELL MATE IS A MARTIAN GIRL, IMPRISONED FOR SHOWING MERCY TO SLAVES.

TELL ME YOUR STORY, TIVA!

A GANG OF EARTH PRISONERS ARRIVED LAST WEEK. I GAVE THEM WATER. THE GUARDS WERE FURIOUS AND I WAS PUT IN CHAINS.

STEVE MUST HAVE BEEN AMONG THE PRISONERS SHE HELPED!

WHAT WAS DONE WITH THOSE CAPTIVES— WHERE ARE THEY CONFINED?

I DO NOT KNOW—I'VE BEEN IN PRISON EVER SINCE MYSELF!

HOW CAN I FIND STEVE'S PRISON? HM! IF I WIN THIS TOURNAMENT, MARS WILL SUMMON ME TO HIS PALACE AND I'LL FIND SOMEONE THERE WHO KNOWS ABOUT STEVE.

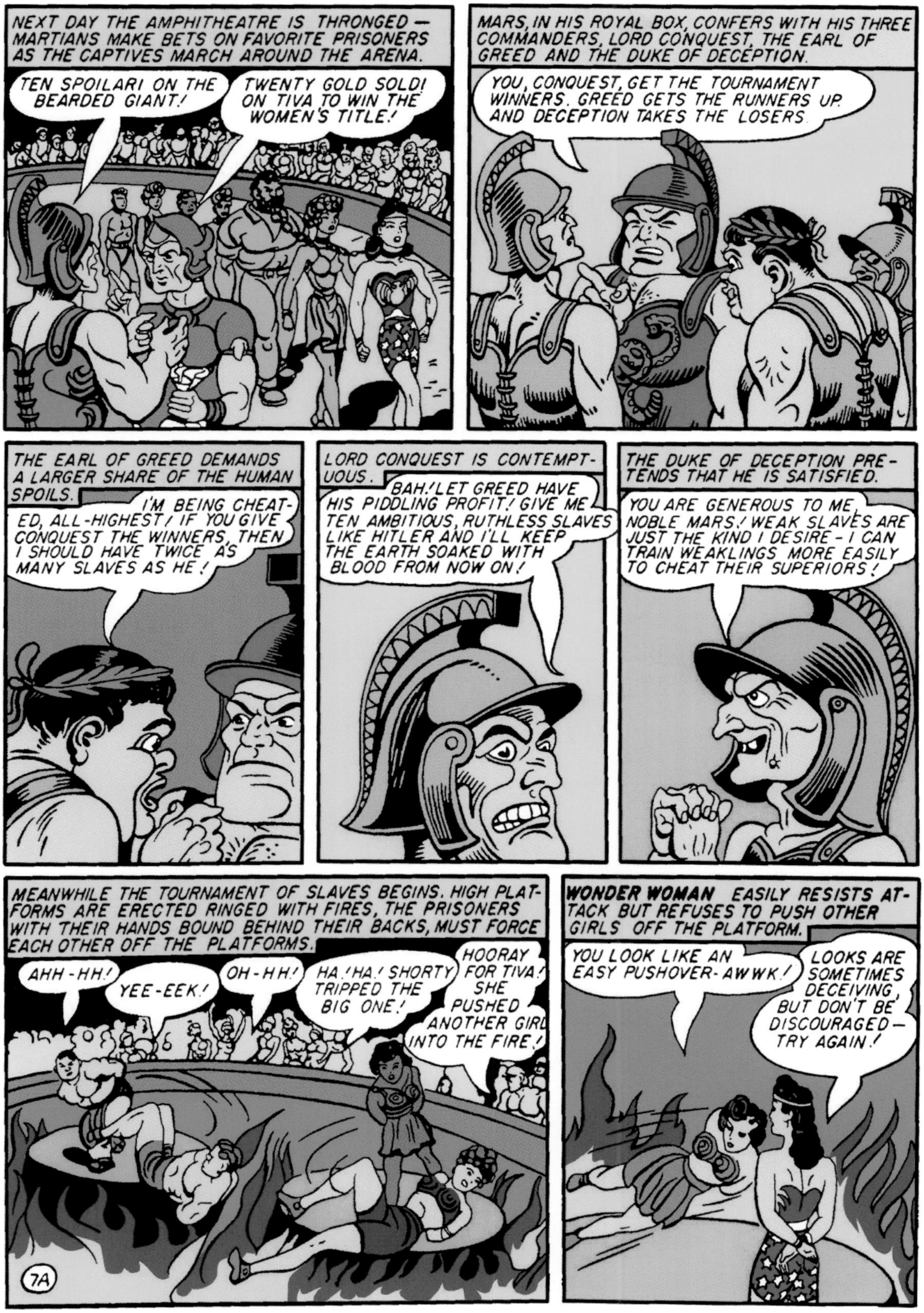
NEXT DAY THE AMPHITHEATRE IS THRONGED — MARTIANS MAKE BETS ON FAVORITE PRISONERS AS THE CAPTIVES MARCH AROUND THE ARENA.
TEN SPOILARI ON THE BEARDED GIANT!
TWENTY GOLD SOLDI ON TIVA TO WIN THE WOMEN'S TITLE!
MARS, IN HIS ROYAL BOX, CONFERS WITH HIS THREE COMMANDERS, LORD CONQUEST, THE EARL OF GREED AND THE DUKE OF DECEPTION.
YOU, CONQUEST, GET THE TOURNAMENT WINNERS. GREED GETS THE RUNNERS UP AND DECEPTION TAKES THE LOSERS.
THE EARL OF GREED DEMANDS A LARGER SHARE OF THE HUMAN SPOILS.
I'M BEING CHEATED, ALL-HIGHEST! IF YOU GIVE CONQUEST THE WINNERS, THEN I SHOULD HAVE TWICE AS MANY SLAVES AS HE!
LORD CONQUEST IS CONTEMPTUOUS.
BAH! LET GREED HAVE HIS PIDDLING PROFIT! GIVE ME TEN AMBITIOUS, RUTHLESS SLAVES LIKE HITLER AND I'LL KEEP THE EARTH SOAKED WITH BLOOD FROM NOW ON!
THE DUKE OF DECEPTION PRETENDS THAT HE IS SATISFIED.
YOU ARE GENEROUS TO ME, NOBLE MARS! WEAK SLAVES ARE JUST THE KIND I DESIRE - I CAN TRAIN WEAKLINGS MORE EASILY TO CHEAT THEIR SUPERIORS!
MEANWHILE THE TOURNAMENT OF SLAVES BEGINS. HIGH PLATFORMS ARE ERECTED RINGED WITH FIRES, THE PRISONERS WITH THEIR HANDS BOUND BEHIND THEIR BACKS, MUST FORCE EACH OTHER OFF THE PLATFORMS.
AHH-HH!
YEE-EEK!
OH-HH!
HA! HA! SHORTY TRIPPED THE BIG ONE!
HOORAY FOR TIVA! SHE PUSHED ANOTHER GIRL INTO THE FIRE!
7A
WONDER WOMAN EASILY RESISTS ATTACK BUT REFUSES TO PUSH OTHER GIRLS OFF THE PLATFORM.
YOU LOOK LIKE AN EASY PUSHOVER-AWWK!
LOOKS ARE SOMETIMES DECEIVING, BUT DON'T BE DISCOURAGED — TRY AGAIN!

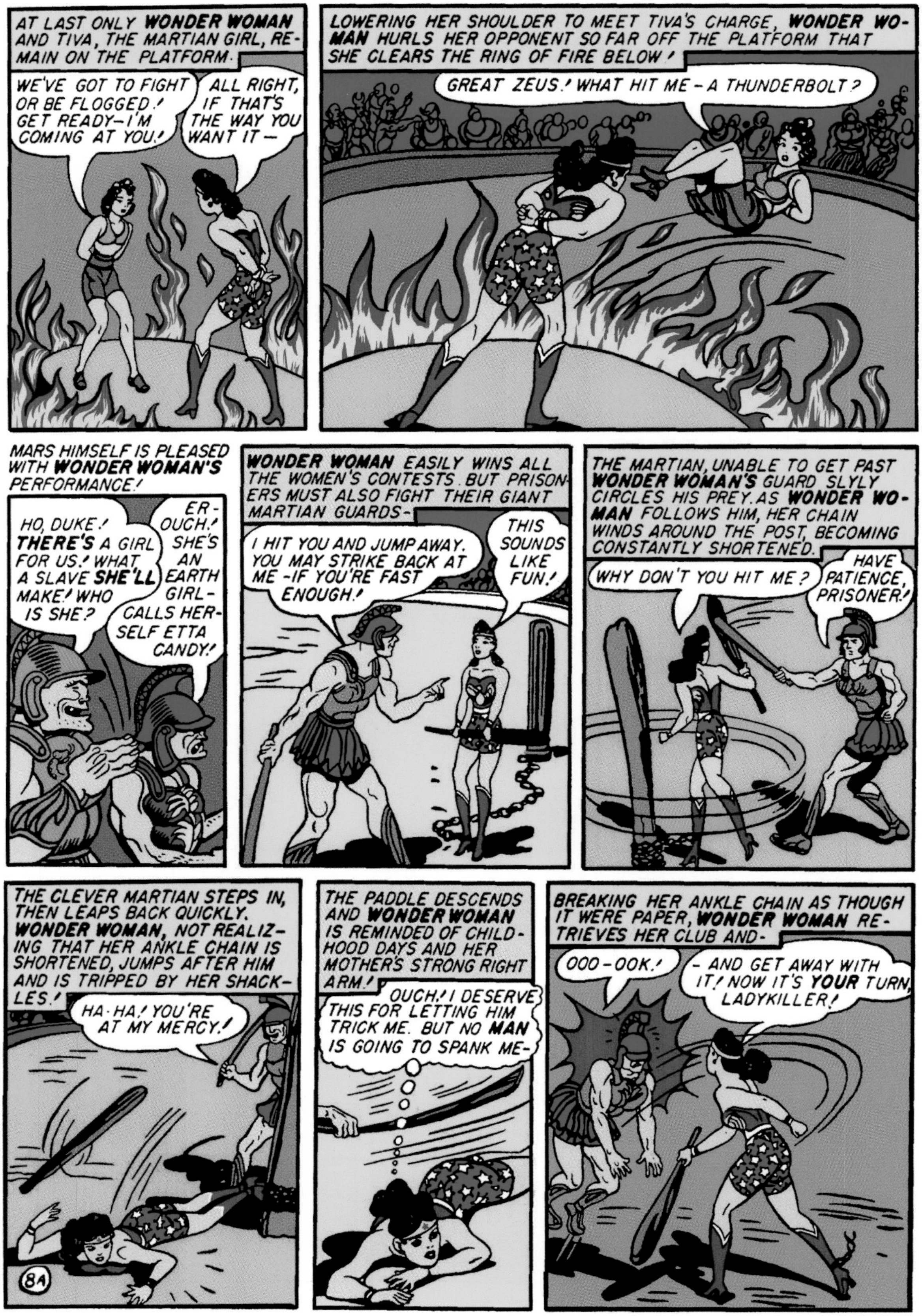
AT LAST ONLY WONDER WOMAN AND TIVA, THE MARTIAN GIRL, REMAIN ON THE PLATFORM.
WE'VE GOT TO FIGHT OR BE FLOGGED! GET READY—I'M COMING AT YOU!
ALL RIGHT, IF THAT'S THE WAY YOU WANT IT—
LOWERING HER SHOULDER TO MEET TIVA'S CHARGE, WONDER WOMAN HURLS HER OPPONENT SO FAR OFF THE PLATFORM THAT SHE CLEARS THE RING OF FIRE BELOW!
GREAT ZEUS! WHAT HIT ME—A THUNDERBOLT?
MARS HIMSELF IS PLEASED WITH WONDER WOMAN'S PERFORMANCE!
HO, DUKE! THERE'S A GIRL FOR US! WHAT A SLAVE SHE'LL MAKE! WHO IS SHE?
ER-OUCH! SHE'S AN EARTH GIRL—CALLS HERSELF ETTA CANDY!
WONDER WOMAN EASILY WINS ALL THE WOMEN'S CONTESTS. BUT PRISONERS MUST ALSO FIGHT THEIR GIANT MARTIAN GUARDS-
I HIT YOU AND JUMP AWAY. YOU MAY STRIKE BACK AT ME—IF YOU'RE FAST ENOUGH!
THIS SOUNDS LIKE FUN!
THE MARTIAN, UNABLE TO GET PAST WONDER WOMAN'S GUARD SLYLY CIRCLES HIS PREY. AS WONDER WOMAN FOLLOWS HIM, HER CHAIN WINDS AROUND THE POST, BECOMING CONSTANTLY SHORTENED.
WHY DON'T YOU HIT ME?
HAVE PATIENCE, PRISONER!
THE CLEVER MARTIAN STEPS IN, THEN LEAPS BACK QUICKLY. WONDER WOMAN, NOT REALIZING THAT HER ANKLE CHAIN IS SHORTENED, JUMPS AFTER HIM AND IS TRIPPED BY HER SHACKLES!
HA-HA! YOU'RE AT MY MERCY!
8A
THE PADDLE DESCENDS AND WONDER WOMAN IS REMINDED OF CHILDHOOD DAYS AND HER MOTHER'S STRONG RIGHT ARM!
OUCH! I DESERVE THIS FOR LETTING HIM TRICK ME. BUT NO MAN IS GOING TO SPANK ME-
BREAKING HER ANKLE CHAIN AS THOUGH IT WERE PAPER, WONDER WOMAN RETRIEVES HER CLUB AND-
OOO-OOK!
—AND GET AWAY WITH IT! NOW IT'S YOUR TURN, LADYKILLER!

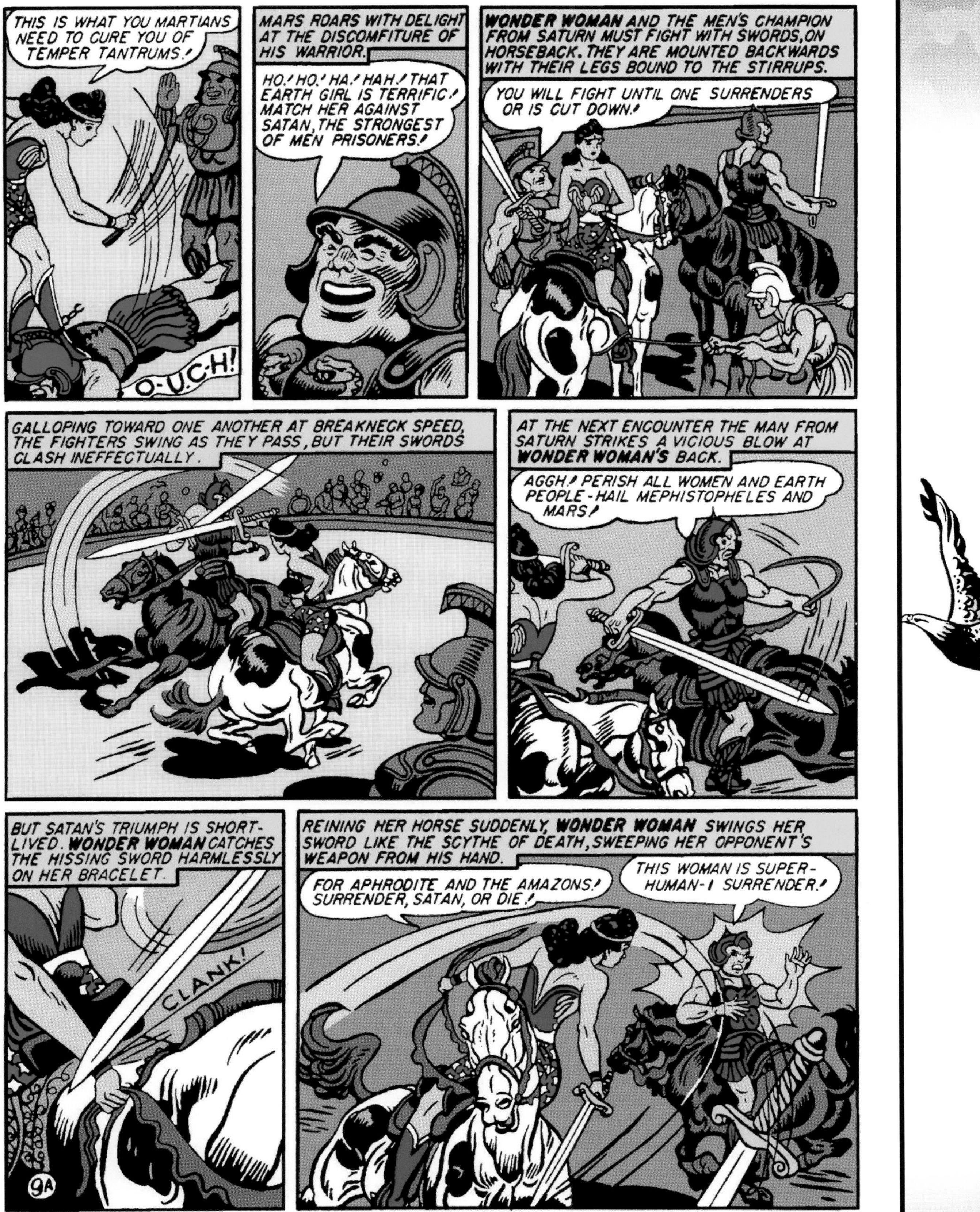
THIS IS WHAT YOU MARTIANS NEED TO CURE YOU OF TEMPER TANTRUMS!
O-U-C-H!
MARS ROARS WITH DELIGHT AT THE DISCOMFITURE OF HIS WARRIOR.
HO! HO! HA! HAH! THAT EARTH GIRL IS TERRIFIC! MATCH HER AGAINST SATAN, THE STRONGEST OF MEN PRISONERS!
WONDER WOMAN AND THE MEN'S CHAMPION FROM SATURN MUST FIGHT WITH SWORDS, ON HORSEBACK. THEY ARE MOUNTED BACKWARDS WITH THEIR LEGS BOUND TO THE STIRRUPS.
YOU WILL FIGHT UNTIL ONE SURRENDERS OR IS CUT DOWN!
GALLOPING TOWARD ONE ANOTHER AT BREAKNECK SPEED, THE FIGHTERS SWING AS THEY PASS, BUT THEIR SWORDS CLASH INEFFECTUALLY.
AT THE NEXT ENCOUNTER THE MAN FROM SATURN STRIKES A VICIOUS BLOW AT WONDER WOMAN'S BACK.
AGGH! PERISH ALL WOMEN AND EARTH PEOPLE - HAIL MEPHISTOPHELES AND MARS!
BUT SATAN'S TRIUMPH IS SHORT-LIVED. WONDER WOMAN CATCHES THE HISSING SWORD HARMLESSLY ON HER BRACELET.
CLANK!
9A
REINING HER HORSE SUDDENLY, WONDER WOMAN SWINGS HER SWORD LIKE THE SCYTHE OF DEATH, SWEEPING HER OPPONENT'S WEAPON FROM HIS HAND.
FOR APHRODITE AND THE AMAZONS! SURRENDER, SATAN, OR DIE!
THIS WOMAN IS SUPER-HUMAN - I SURRENDER!

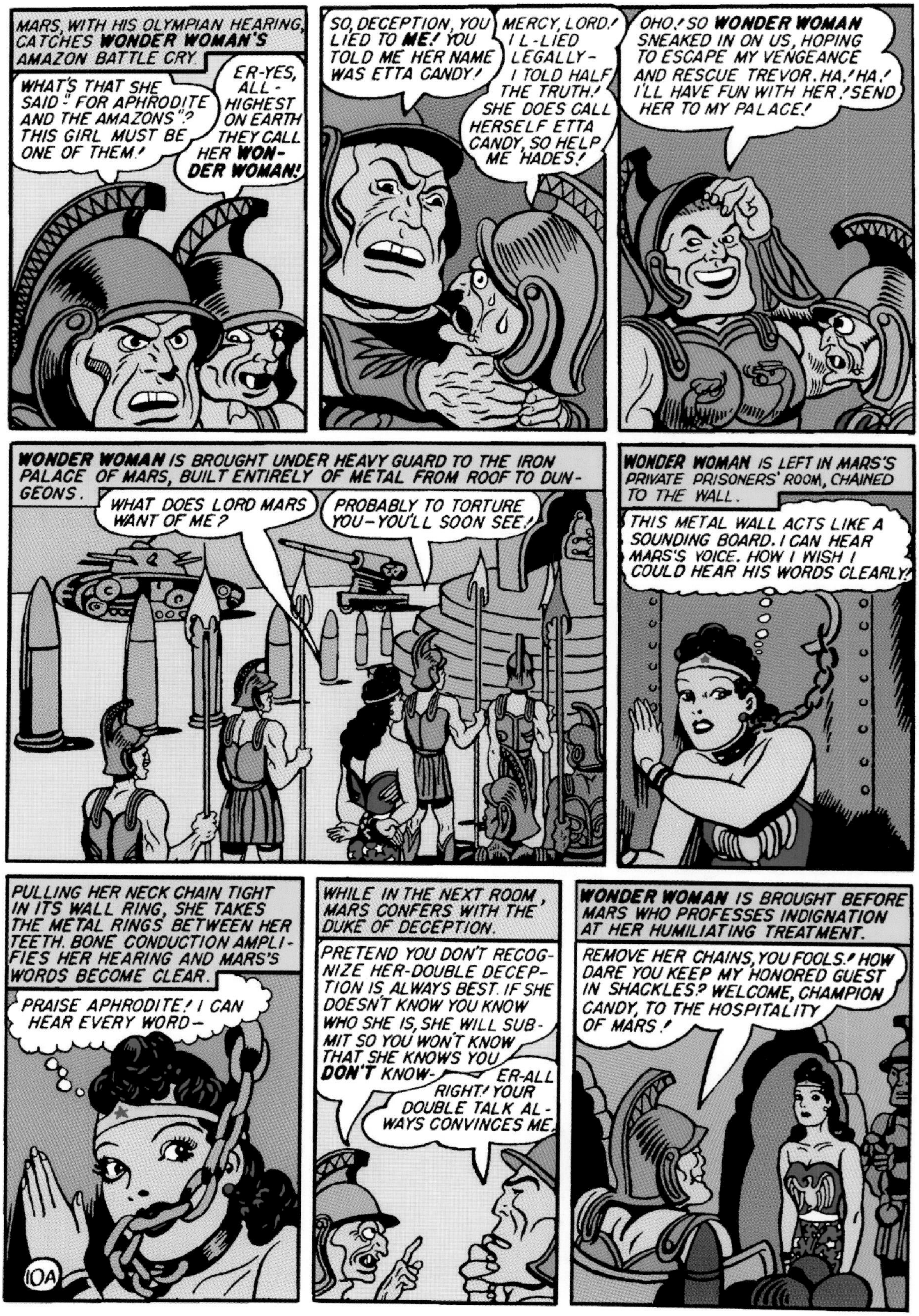

MARS, WITH HIS OLYMPIAN HEARING, CATCHES WONDER WOMAN'S AMAZON BATTLE CRY.
WHAT'S THAT SHE SAID: "FOR APHRODITE AND THE AMAZONS"? THIS GIRL MUST BE ONE OF THEM!
ER-YES, ALL-HIGHEST ON EARTH THEY CALL HER WONDER WOMAN!
SO, DECEPTION, YOU LIED TO ME! YOU TOLD ME HER NAME WAS ETTA CANDY!
MERCY, LORD! I L-LIED LEGALLY - I TOLD HALF THE TRUTH! SHE DOES CALL HERSELF ETTA CANDY, SO HELP ME HADES!
OHO! SO WONDER WOMAN SNEAKED IN ON US, HOPING TO ESCAPE MY VENGEANCE AND RESCUE TREVOR. HA! HA! I'LL HAVE FUN WITH HER! SEND HER TO MY PALACE!
WONDER WOMAN IS BROUGHT UNDER HEAVY GUARD TO THE IRON PALACE OF MARS, BUILT ENTIRELY OF METAL FROM ROOF TO DUNGEONS.
WHAT DOES LORD MARS WANT OF ME?
PROBABLY TO TORTURE YOU-YOU'LL SOON SEE!
WONDER WOMAN IS LEFT IN MARS'S PRIVATE PRISONERS' ROOM, CHAINED TO THE WALL.
THIS METAL WALL ACTS LIKE A SOUNDING BOARD. I CAN HEAR MARS'S VOICE. HOW I WISH I COULD HEAR HIS WORDS CLEARLY!
PULLING HER NECK CHAIN TIGHT IN ITS WALL RING, SHE TAKES THE METAL RINGS BETWEEN HER TEETH. BONE CONDUCTION AMPLIFIES HER HEARING AND MARS'S WORDS BECOME CLEAR.
PRAISE APHRODITE! I CAN HEAR EVERY WORD-
10A
WHILE IN THE NEXT ROOM, MARS CONFERS WITH THE DUKE OF DECEPTION.
PRETEND YOU DON'T RECOGNIZE HER-DOUBLE DECEPTION IS ALWAYS BEST. IF SHE DOESN'T KNOW YOU KNOW WHO SHE IS, SHE WILL SUBMIT SO YOU WON'T KNOW THAT SHE KNOWS YOU DON'T KNOW-
ER-ALL RIGHT! YOUR DOUBLE TALK ALWAYS CONVINCES ME.
WONDER WOMAN IS BROUGHT BEFORE MARS WHO PROFESSES INDIGNATION AT HER HUMILIATING TREATMENT.
REMOVE HER CHAINS, YOU FOOLS! HOW DARE YOU KEEP MY HONORED GUEST IN SHACKLES? WELCOME, CHAMPION CANDY, TO THE HOSPITALITY OF MARS!

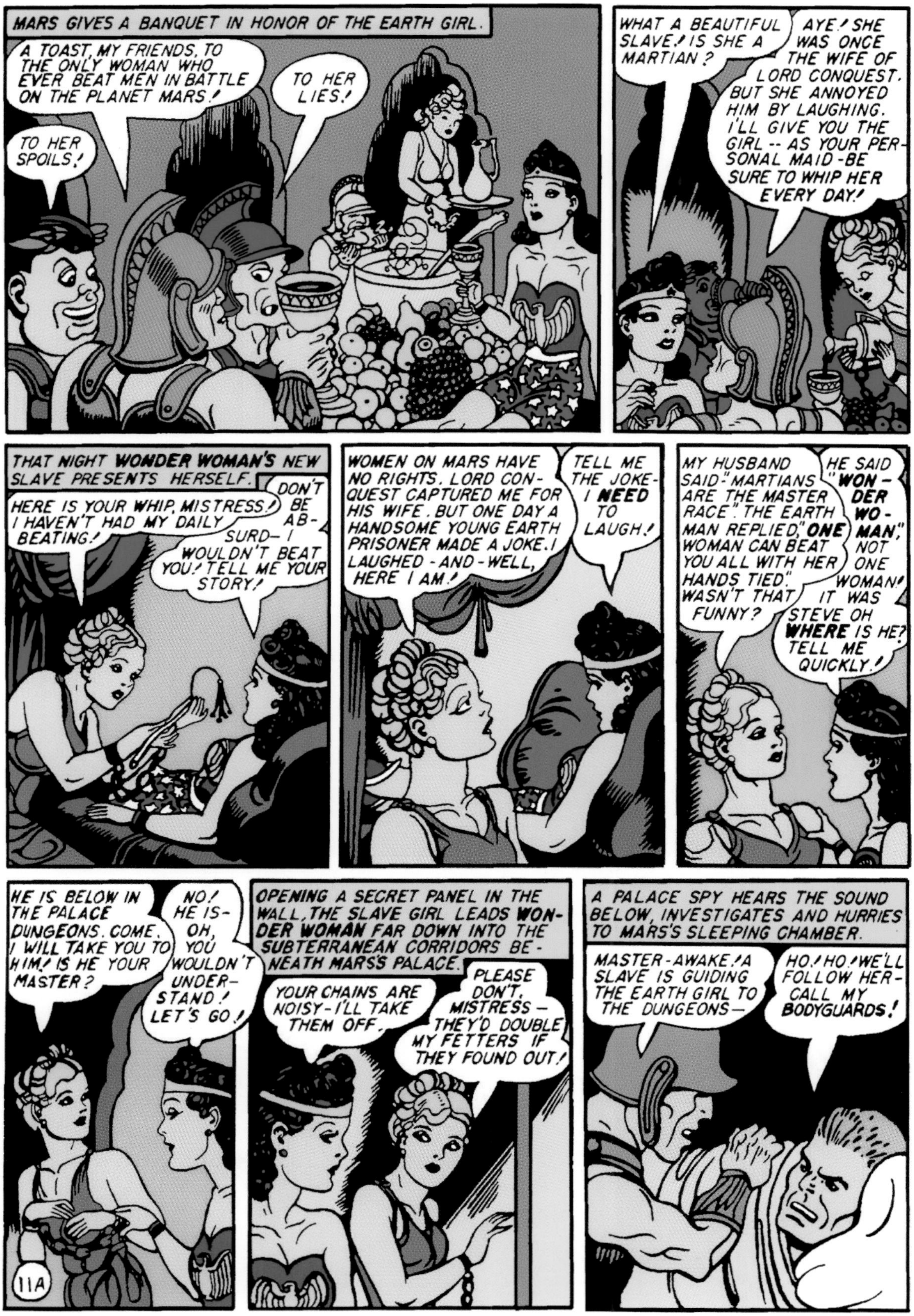
MARS GIVES A BANQUET IN HONOR OF THE EARTH GIRL.
A TOAST, MY FRIENDS, TO THE ONLY WOMAN WHO EVER BEAT MEN IN BATTLE ON THE PLANET MARS!
TO HER LIES!
TO HER SPOILS!
WHAT A BEAUTIFUL SLAVE! IS SHE A MARTIAN?
AYE! SHE WAS ONCE THE WIFE OF LORD CONQUEST. BUT SHE ANNOYED HIM BY LAUGHING. I'LL GIVE YOU THE GIRL -- AS YOUR PERSONAL MAID - BE SURE TO WHIP HER EVERY DAY!
THAT NIGHT WONDER WOMAN'S NEW SLAVE PRESENTS HERSELF.
HERE IS YOUR WHIP, MISTRESS! I HAVEN'T HAD MY DAILY BEATING!
DON'T BE ABSURD - I WOULDN'T BEAT YOU! TELL ME YOUR STORY!
WOMEN ON MARS HAVE NO RIGHTS. LORD CONQUEST CAPTURED ME FOR HIS WIFE. BUT ONE DAY A HANDSOME YOUNG EARTH PRISONER MADE A JOKE. I LAUGHED - AND - WELL, HERE I AM!
TELL ME THE JOKE - I NEED TO LAUGH!
MY HUSBAND SAID: "MARTIANS ARE THE MASTER RACE." THE EARTH MAN REPLIED, "ONE WOMAN CAN BEAT YOU ALL WITH HER HANDS TIED." WASN'T THAT FUNNY?
HE SAID "WONDER WOMAN," NOT ONE WOMAN! IT WAS STEVE OH WHERE IS HE? TELL ME QUICKLY!
HE IS BELOW IN THE PALACE DUNGEONS. COME, I WILL TAKE YOU TO HIM! IS HE YOUR MASTER?
NO! HE IS - OH, YOU WOULDN'T UNDERSTAND! LET'S GO!
11A
OPENING A SECRET PANEL IN THE WALL, THE SLAVE GIRL LEADS WONDER WOMAN FAR DOWN INTO THE SUBTERRANEAN CORRIDORS BENEATH MARS'S PALACE.
YOUR CHAINS ARE NOISY - I'LL TAKE THEM OFF.
PLEASE DON'T, MISTRESS — THEY'D DOUBLE MY FETTERS IF THEY FOUND OUT!
A PALACE SPY HEARS THE SOUND BELOW, INVESTIGATES AND HURRIES TO MARS'S SLEEPING CHAMBER.
MASTER - AWAKE! A SLAVE IS GUIDING THE EARTH GIRL TO THE DUNGEONS—
HO! HO! WE'LL FOLLOW HER - CALL MY BODYGUARDS!

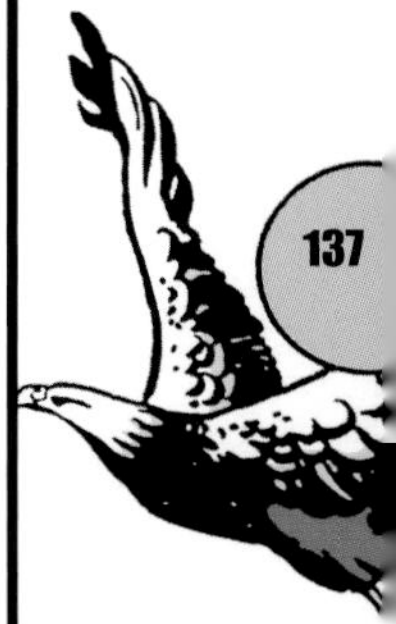

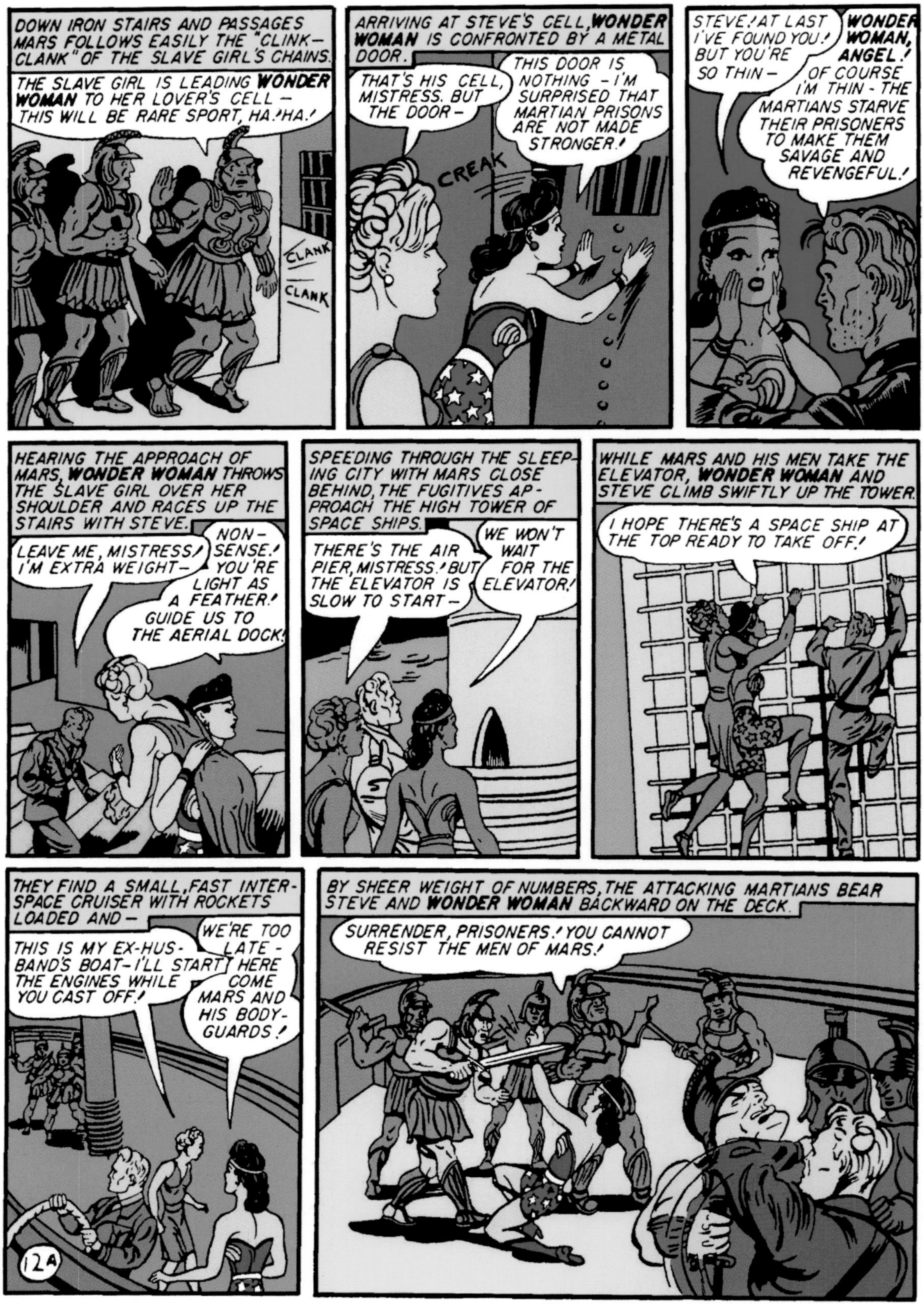

DOWN IRON STAIRS AND PASSAGES MARS FOLLOWS EASILY THE "CLINK-CLANK" OF THE SLAVE GIRL'S CHAINS.
THE SLAVE GIRL IS LEADING WONDER WOMAN TO HER LOVER'S CELL — THIS WILL BE RARE SPORT, HA! HA!
CLANK
CLANK
ARRIVING AT STEVE'S CELL, WONDER WOMAN IS CONFRONTED BY A METAL DOOR.
THAT'S HIS CELL, MISTRESS. BUT THE DOOR—
THIS DOOR IS NOTHING — I'M SURPRISED THAT MARTIAN PRISONS ARE NOT MADE STRONGER!
CREAK
STEVE! AT LAST I'VE FOUND YOU! BUT YOU'RE SO THIN—
WONDER WOMAN, ANGEL! OF COURSE I'M THIN - THE MARTIANS STARVE THEIR PRISONERS TO MAKE THEM SAVAGE AND REVENGEFUL!
HEARING THE APPROACH OF MARS, WONDER WOMAN THROWS THE SLAVE GIRL OVER HER SHOULDER AND RACES UP THE STAIRS WITH STEVE.
LEAVE ME, MISTRESS! I'M EXTRA WEIGHT—
NON-SENSE! YOU'RE LIGHT AS A FEATHER! GUIDE US TO THE AERIAL DOCK!
SPEEDING THROUGH THE SLEEPING CITY WITH MARS CLOSE BEHIND, THE FUGITIVES APPROACH THE HIGH TOWER OF SPACE SHIPS.
THERE'S THE AIR PIER, MISTRESS! BUT THE ELEVATOR IS SLOW TO START—
WE WON'T WAIT FOR THE ELEVATOR!
WHILE MARS AND HIS MEN TAKE THE ELEVATOR, WONDER WOMAN AND STEVE CLIMB SWIFTLY UP THE TOWER.
I HOPE THERE'S A SPACE SHIP AT THE TOP READY TO TAKE OFF!
THEY FIND A SMALL, FAST INTER-SPACE CRUISER WITH ROCKETS LOADED AND—
THIS IS MY EX-HUSBAND'S BOAT- I'LL START THE ENGINES WHILE YOU CAST OFF!
WE'RE TOO LATE - HERE COME MARS AND HIS BODY-GUARDS!
12A
BY SHEER WEIGHT OF NUMBERS, THE ATTACKING MARTIANS BEAR STEVE AND WONDER WOMAN BACKWARD ON THE DECK.
SURRENDER, PRISONERS! YOU CANNOT RESIST THE MEN OF MARS!

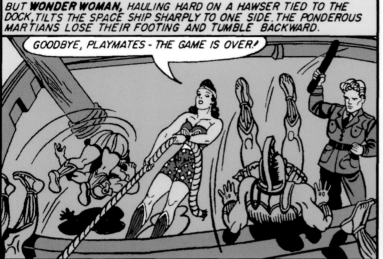

BUT **WONDER WOMAN**, HAULING HARD ON A HAWSER TIED TO THE DOCK, TILTS THE SPACE SHIP SHARPLY TO ONE SIDE. THE PONDEROUS MARTIANS LOSE THEIR FOOTING AND TUMBLE BACKWARD.

GOODBYE, PLAYMATES - THE GAME IS OVER!

MARS IS FURIOUS-NEVER BEFORE HAS HE SUFFERED DEFEAT BY MORTAL MAN OR WOMAN!

CURSE YOU, **WONDER WOMAN!** I'LL SEND CONQUEST, GREED AND DECEPTION TO EARTH- THEY'LL BRING YOU BACK, AND THEN — !!

139

ON THE SPACE CRUISER STEVE EXPLAINS.

THE PILOT OF MY PLANE WAS A JAP SPY. WITHOUT WARNING HE SHOT ME AND TOSSED ME OUT. I SWALLOWED THE TABLETS YOU GAVE ME—

THEN YOUR EARTH BODY IS STILL ALIVE-WE'LL FIND IT!

STEVE'S WOUNDED BODY HAD BEEN FOUND AND CARRIED TO A HOSPITAL WHERE IT LAY IN A COMA. HIS RETURNING SOUL SUDDENLY REANIMATES HIS BODY—

GREAT HEAVENS! MAJOR TREVOR'S COME TO! WAIT-STAY IN BED—

OUT OF MY WAY, NURSE! I'VE GOT TO GET DRESSED AND FIND **WONDER WOMAN!**

WHILE IN ETTA CANDY'S ROOM—

WOO! WOO! YOU'RE BACK! WE THOUGHT SURE YOU WERE DEAD- NO PULSE- NO BREATHING—

NONSENSE, ETTA! I TOLD YOU NOT TO WORRY. STEVE AND I HAD A LITTLE ARGUMENT WITH MARS—

LATER, AT HOLLIDAY COLLEGE—

BUT WHAT BECAME OF THE PRETTY SLAVE GIRL?

YOU **WOULD** THINK OF HER. THE SILLY THING WENT BACK TO HER HUSBAND. SHE SAID LORD CONQUEST WOULD BE INTERESTED IN CONQUERING HER AGAIN BECAUSE SHE HAD ESCAPED!

13A

I'VE GOT YOU NOW, STEVE-LISTEN! MARS WILL SEND GREED, DECEPTION AND CONQUEST TO RECAPTURE US. SO PROMISE ME THIS-WHENEVER YOU GO INTO DANGER, **TAKE ME WITH YOU!**

ER-AH—SOMETHING COMPELS ME- I PROMISE.

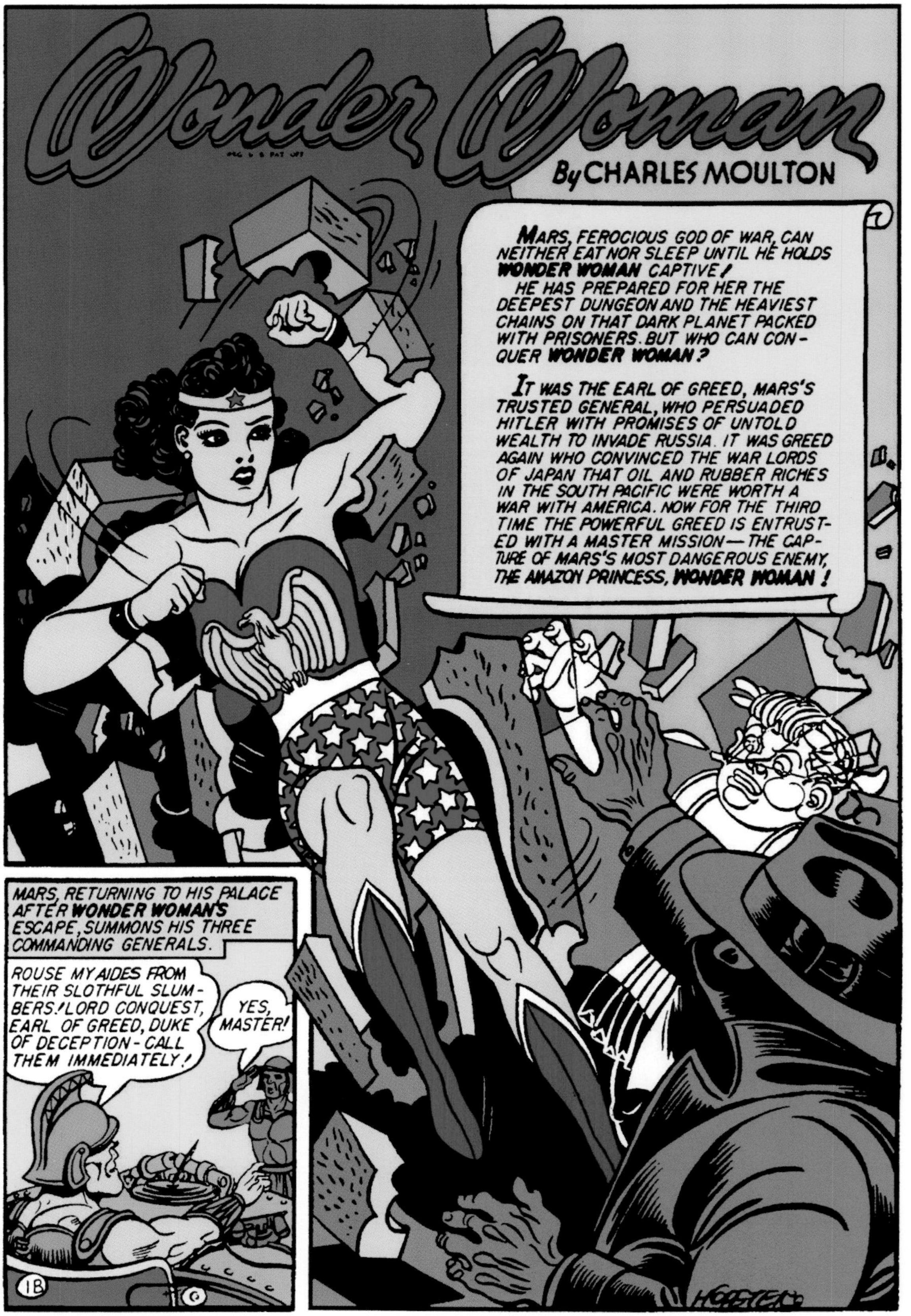
Wonder Woman
By CHARLES MOULTON
MARS, FEROCIOUS GOD OF WAR, CAN NEITHER EAT NOR SLEEP UNTIL HE HOLDS WONDER WOMAN CAPTIVE! HE HAS PREPARED FOR HER THE DEEPEST DUNGEON AND THE HEAVIEST CHAINS ON THAT DARK PLANET PACKED WITH PRISONERS. BUT WHO CAN CONQUER WONDER WOMAN?
IT WAS THE EARL OF GREED, MARS'S TRUSTED GENERAL, WHO PERSUADED HITLER WITH PROMISES OF UNTOLD WEALTH TO INVADE RUSSIA. IT WAS GREED AGAIN WHO CONVINCED THE WAR LORDS OF JAPAN THAT OIL AND RUBBER RICHES IN THE SOUTH PACIFIC WERE WORTH A WAR WITH AMERICA. NOW FOR THE THIRD TIME THE POWERFUL GREED IS ENTRUSTED WITH A MASTER MISSION—THE CAPTURE OF MARS'S MOST DANGEROUS ENEMY, THE AMAZON PRINCESS, WONDER WOMAN!
MARS, RETURNING TO HIS PALACE AFTER WONDER WOMAN'S ESCAPE, SUMMONS HIS THREE COMMANDING GENERALS.
ROUSE MY AIDES FROM THEIR SLOTHFUL SLUMBERS! LORD CONQUEST, EARL OF GREED, DUKE OF DECEPTION - CALL THEM IMMEDIATELY!
YES, MASTER!
1B
HOGSTER

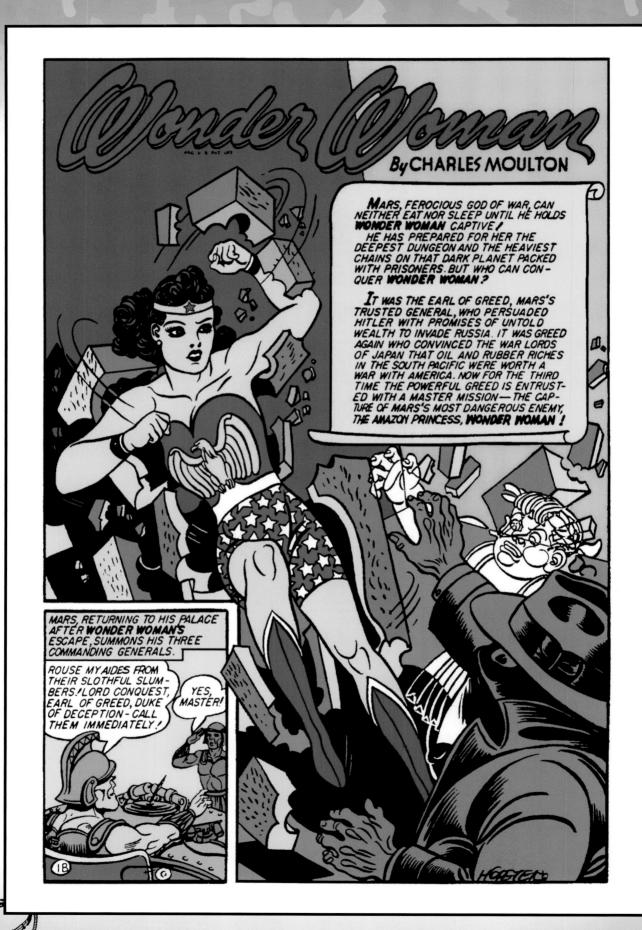

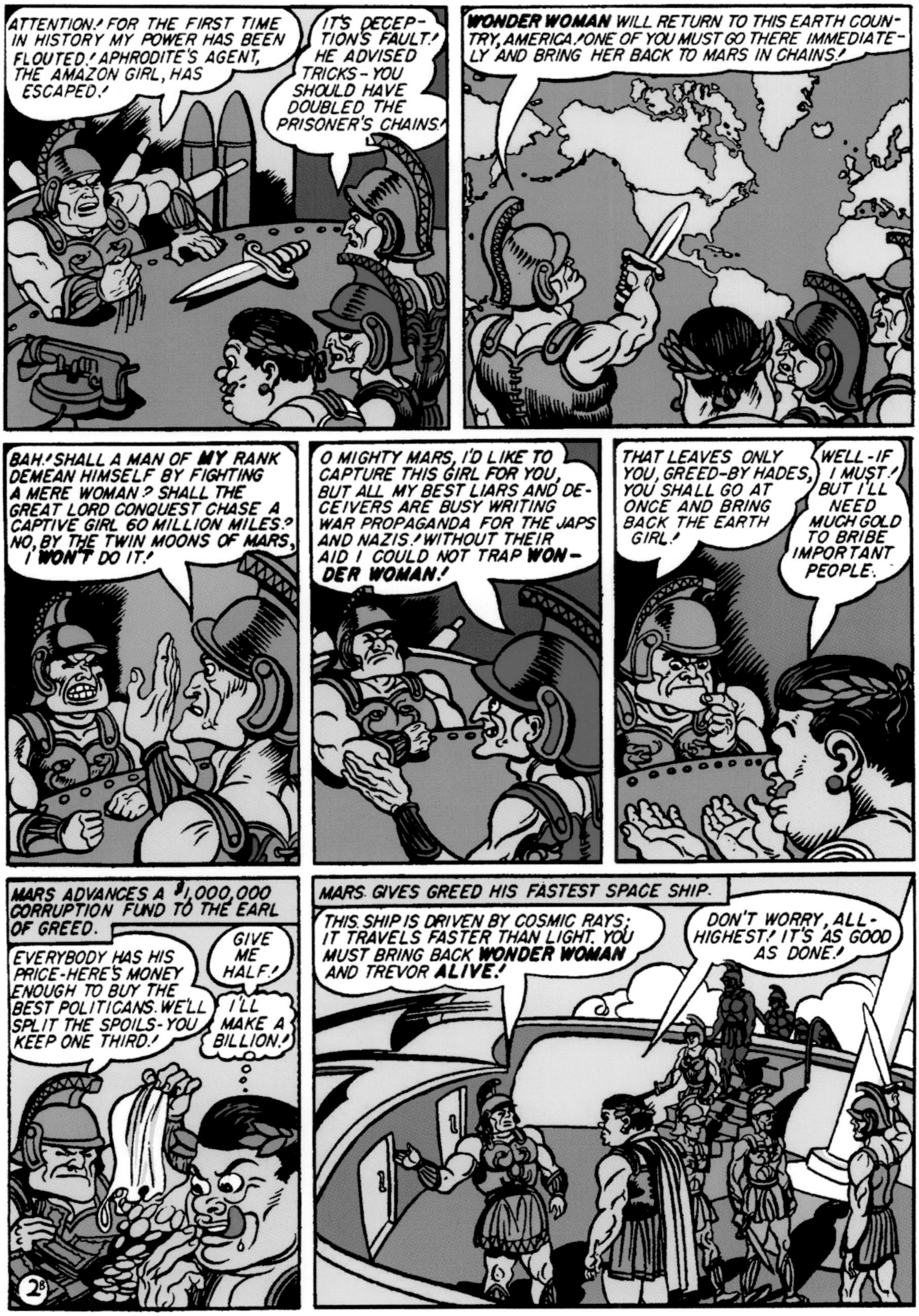
ATTENTION! FOR THE FIRST TIME IN HISTORY MY POWER HAS BEEN FLOUTED! APHRODITE'S AGENT, THE AMAZON GIRL, HAS ESCAPED!
IT'S DECEPTION'S FAULT! HE ADVISED TRICKS - YOU SHOULD HAVE DOUBLED THE PRISONER'S CHAINS!
WONDER WOMAN WILL RETURN TO THIS EARTH COUNTRY, AMERICA! ONE OF YOU MUST GO THERE IMMEDIATELY AND BRING HER BACK TO MARS IN CHAINS!
BAH! SHALL A MAN OF MY RANK DEMEAN HIMSELF BY FIGHTING A MERE WOMAN? SHALL THE GREAT LORD CONQUEST CHASE A CAPTIVE GIRL 60 MILLION MILES? NO, BY THE TWIN MOONS OF MARS, I WON'T DO IT!
O MIGHTY MARS, I'D LIKE TO CAPTURE THIS GIRL FOR YOU, BUT ALL MY BEST LIARS AND DECEIVERS ARE BUSY WRITING WAR PROPAGANDA FOR THE JAPS AND NAZIS! WITHOUT THEIR AID I COULD NOT TRAP WONDER WOMAN!
THAT LEAVES ONLY YOU, GREED-BY HADES, YOU SHALL GO AT ONCE AND BRING BACK THE EARTH GIRL!
WELL-IF I MUST! BUT I'LL NEED MUCH GOLD TO BRIBE IMPORTANT PEOPLE.
MARS ADVANCES A $1,000,000 CORRUPTION FUND TO THE EARL OF GREED.
EVERYBODY HAS HIS PRICE-HERE'S MONEY ENOUGH TO BUY THE BEST POLITICANS. WE'LL SPLIT THE SPOILS-YOU KEEP ONE THIRD!
GIVE ME HALF!
I'LL MAKE A BILLION!
2B
MARS GIVES GREED HIS FASTEST SPACE SHIP.
THIS SHIP IS DRIVEN BY COSMIC RAYS; IT TRAVELS FASTER THAN LIGHT. YOU MUST BRING BACK WONDER WOMAN AND TREVOR ALIVE!
DON'T WORRY, ALL-HIGHEST! IT'S AS GOOD AS DONE!

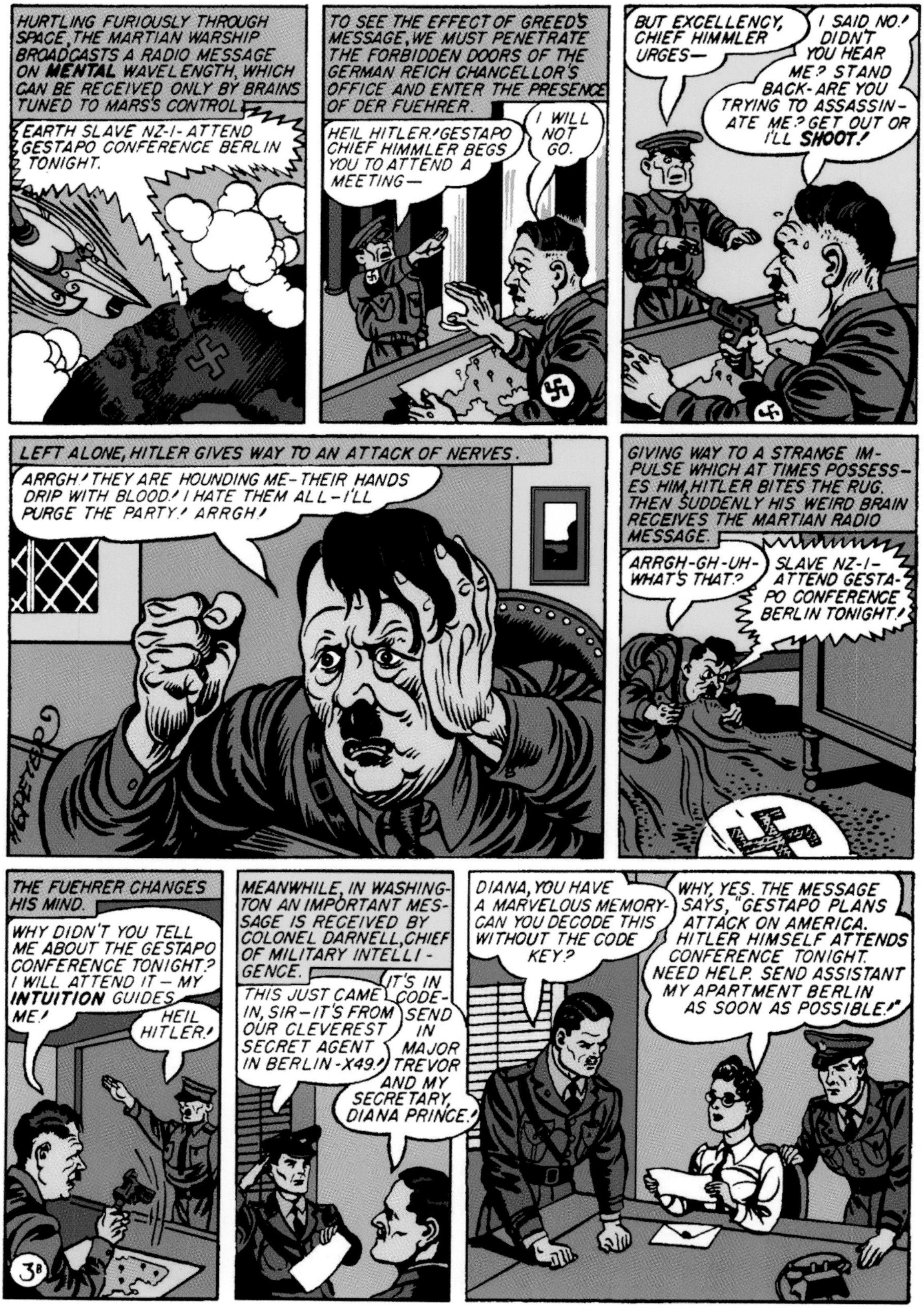

HURTLING FURIOUSLY THROUGH SPACE, THE MARTIAN WARSHIP BROADCASTS A RADIO MESSAGE ON MENTAL WAVELENGTH, WHICH CAN BE RECEIVED ONLY BY BRAINS TUNED TO MARS'S CONTROL.
EARTH SLAVE NZ-1- ATTEND GESTAPO CONFERENCE BERLIN TONIGHT.
TO SEE THE EFFECT OF GREED'S MESSAGE, WE MUST PENETRATE THE FORBIDDEN DOORS OF THE GERMAN REICH CHANCELLOR'S OFFICE AND ENTER THE PRESENCE OF DER FUEHRER.
HEIL HITLER! GESTAPO CHIEF HIMMLER BEGS YOU TO ATTEND A MEETING—
I WILL NOT GO.
BUT EXCELLENCY, CHIEF HIMMLER URGES—
I SAID NO! DIDN'T YOU HEAR ME? STAND BACK- ARE YOU TRYING TO ASSASSIN-ATE ME? GET OUT OR I'LL SHOOT!
LEFT ALONE, HITLER GIVES WAY TO AN ATTACK OF NERVES.
ARRGH! THEY ARE HOUNDING ME- THEIR HANDS DRIP WITH BLOOD! I HATE THEM ALL - I'LL PURGE THE PARTY! ARRGH!
GIVING WAY TO A STRANGE IM-PULSE WHICH AT TIMES POSSESS-ES HIM, HITLER BITES THE RUG. THEN SUDDENLY HIS WEIRD BRAIN RECEIVES THE MARTIAN RADIO MESSAGE.
ARRGH-GH-UH- WHAT'S THAT?
SLAVE NZ-1- ATTEND GESTA-PO CONFERENCE BERLIN TONIGHT!
THE FUEHRER CHANGES HIS MIND.
WHY DIDN'T YOU TELL ME ABOUT THE GESTAPO CONFERENCE TONIGHT? I WILL ATTEND IT — MY INTUITION GUIDES ME!
HEIL HITLER!
MEANWHILE, IN WASHING-TON AN IMPORTANT MES-SAGE IS RECEIVED BY COLONEL DARNELL, CHIEF OF MILITARY INTELLI-GENCE.
THIS JUST CAME IN, SIR — IT'S FROM OUR CLEVEREST SECRET AGENT IN BERLIN - X49!
IT'S IN CODE- SEND IN MAJOR TREVOR AND MY SECRETARY, DIANA PRINCE!
DIANA, YOU HAVE A MARVELOUS MEMORY- CAN YOU DECODE THIS WITHOUT THE CODE KEY?
WHY, YES. THE MESSAGE SAYS, "GESTAPO PLANS ATTACK ON AMERICA. HITLER HIMSELF ATTENDS CONFERENCE TONIGHT. NEED HELP. SEND ASSISTANT MY APARTMENT BERLIN AS SOON AS POSSIBLE!"

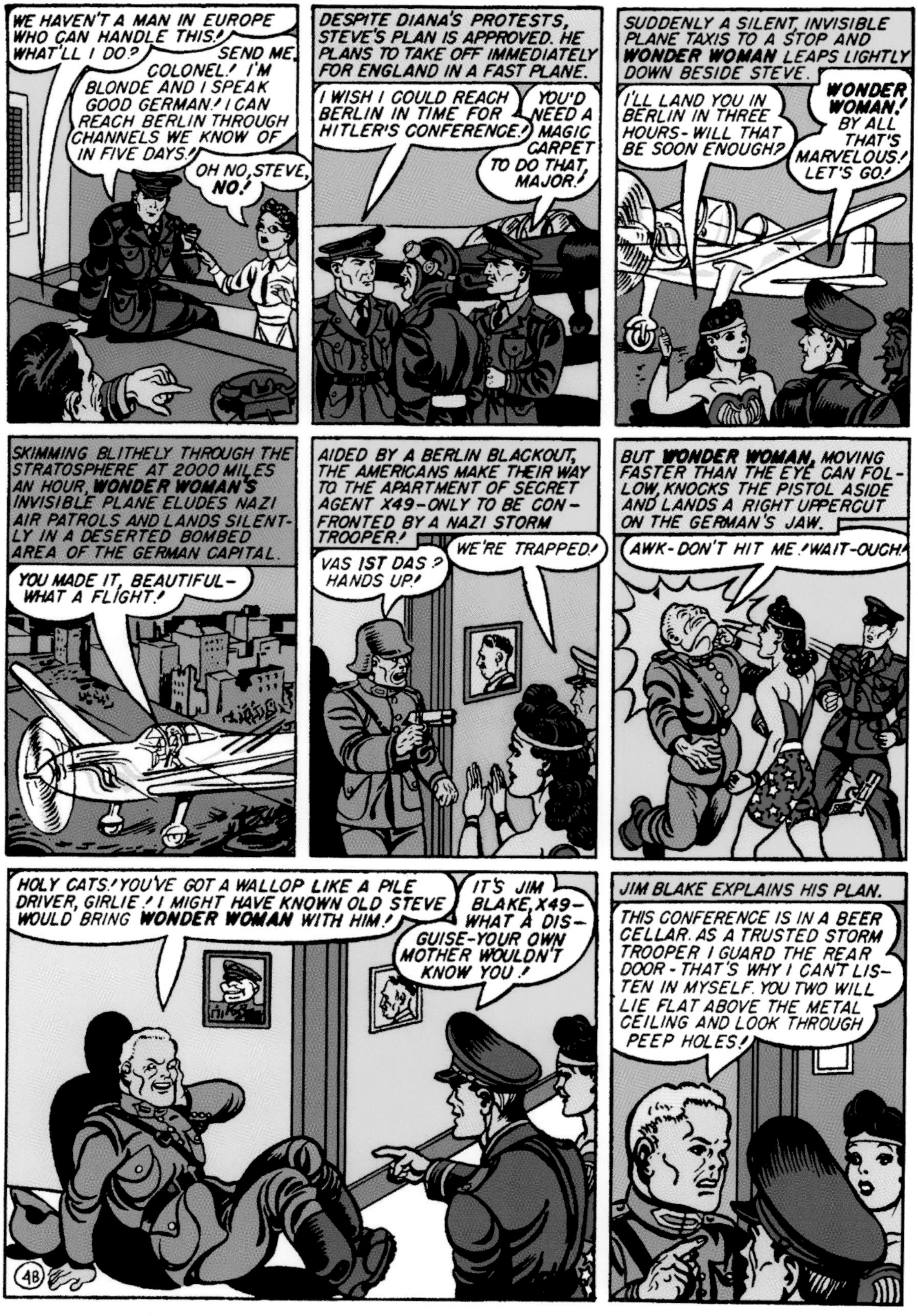
WE HAVEN'T A MAN IN EUROPE WHO CAN HANDLE THIS! WHAT'LL I DO?
SEND ME, COLONEL! I'M BLONDE AND I SPEAK GOOD GERMAN! I CAN REACH BERLIN THROUGH CHANNELS WE KNOW OF IN FIVE DAYS!
OH NO, STEVE, NO!
DESPITE DIANA'S PROTESTS, STEVE'S PLAN IS APPROVED. HE PLANS TO TAKE OFF IMMEDIATELY FOR ENGLAND IN A FAST PLANE.
I WISH I COULD REACH BERLIN IN TIME FOR HITLER'S CONFERENCE!
YOU'D NEED A MAGIC CARPET TO DO THAT, MAJOR!
SUDDENLY A SILENT, INVISIBLE PLANE TAXIS TO A STOP AND WONDER WOMAN LEAPS LIGHTLY DOWN BESIDE STEVE.
I'LL LAND YOU IN BERLIN IN THREE HOURS - WILL THAT BE SOON ENOUGH?
WONDER WOMAN! BY ALL THAT'S MARVELOUS! LET'S GO!
SKIMMING BLITHELY THROUGH THE STRATOSPHERE AT 2000 MILES AN HOUR, WONDER WOMAN'S INVISIBLE PLANE ELUDES NAZI AIR PATROLS AND LANDS SILENTLY IN A DESERTED BOMBED AREA OF THE GERMAN CAPITAL.
YOU MADE IT, BEAUTIFUL - WHAT A FLIGHT!
AIDED BY A BERLIN BLACKOUT, THE AMERICANS MAKE THEIR WAY TO THE APARTMENT OF SECRET AGENT X49 - ONLY TO BE CONFRONTED BY A NAZI STORM TROOPER!
VAS IST DAS? HANDS UP!
WE'RE TRAPPED!
BUT WONDER WOMAN, MOVING FASTER THAN THE EYE CAN FOLLOW, KNOCKS THE PISTOL ASIDE AND LANDS A RIGHT UPPERCUT ON THE GERMAN'S JAW.
AWK - DON'T HIT ME! WAIT - OUCH!
HOLY CATS! YOU'VE GOT A WALLOP LIKE A PILE DRIVER, GIRLIE! I MIGHT HAVE KNOWN OLD STEVE WOULD BRING WONDER WOMAN WITH HIM!
IT'S JIM BLAKE, X49 - WHAT A DISGUISE - YOUR OWN MOTHER WOULDN'T KNOW YOU!
4B
JIM BLAKE EXPLAINS HIS PLAN.
THIS CONFERENCE IS IN A BEER CELLAR. AS A TRUSTED STORM TROOPER I GUARD THE REAR DOOR - THAT'S WHY I CAN'T LISTEN IN MYSELF. YOU TWO WILL LIE FLAT ABOVE THE METAL CEILING AND LOOK THROUGH PEEP HOLES!

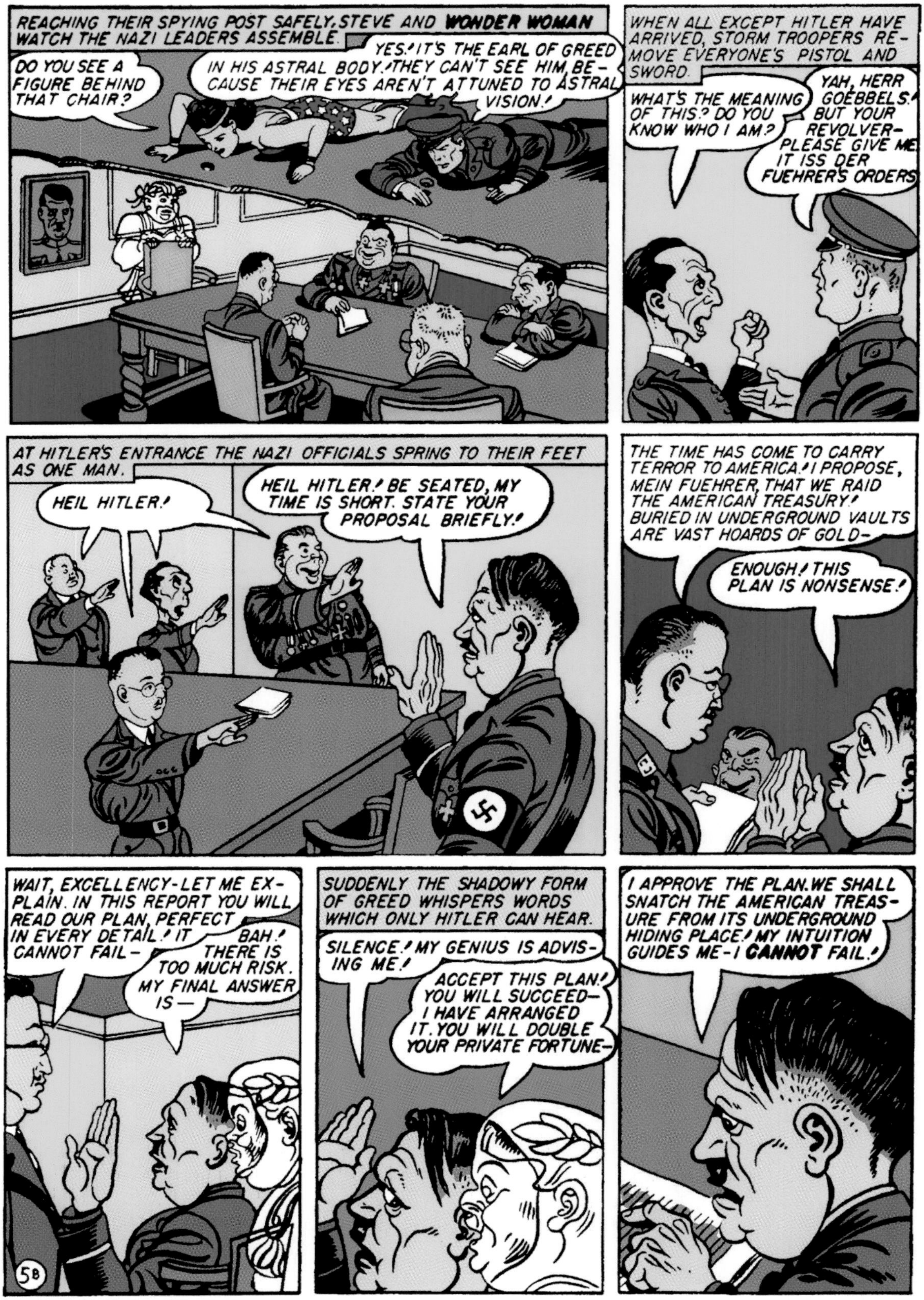
REACHING THEIR SPYING POST SAFELY, STEVE AND **WONDER WOMAN** WATCH THE NAZI LEADERS ASSEMBLE.
DO YOU SEE A FIGURE BEHIND THAT CHAIR?
YES! IT'S THE EARL OF GREED IN HIS ASTRAL BODY! THEY CAN'T SEE HIM, BECAUSE THEIR EYES AREN'T ATTUNED TO ASTRAL VISION!
WHEN ALL EXCEPT HITLER HAVE ARRIVED, STORM TROOPERS REMOVE EVERYONE'S PISTOL AND SWORD.
WHAT'S THE MEANING OF THIS? DO YOU KNOW WHO I AM?
YAH, HERR GOEBBELS! BUT YOUR REVOLVER-PLEASE GIVE ME! IT ISS DER FUEHRER'S ORDERS
AT HITLER'S ENTRANCE THE NAZI OFFICIALS SPRING TO THEIR FEET AS ONE MAN.
HEIL HITLER!
HEIL HITLER! BE SEATED, MY TIME IS SHORT. STATE YOUR PROPOSAL BRIEFLY!
THE TIME HAS COME TO CARRY TERROR TO AMERICA! I PROPOSE, MEIN FUEHRER, THAT WE RAID THE AMERICAN TREASURY! BURIED IN UNDERGROUND VAULTS ARE VAST HOARDS OF GOLD-
ENOUGH! THIS PLAN IS NONSENSE!
WAIT, EXCELLENCY-LET ME EXPLAIN. IN THIS REPORT YOU WILL READ OUR PLAN, PERFECT IN EVERY DETAIL! IT CANNOT FAIL-
BAH! THERE IS TOO MUCH RISK. MY FINAL ANSWER IS—
5B
SUDDENLY THE SHADOWY FORM OF GREED WHISPERS WORDS WHICH ONLY HITLER CAN HEAR.
SILENCE! MY GENIUS IS ADVISING ME!
ACCEPT THIS PLAN! YOU WILL SUCCEED—I HAVE ARRANGED IT. YOU WILL DOUBLE YOUR PRIVATE FORTUNE-
I APPROVE THE PLAN. WE SHALL SNATCH THE AMERICAN TREASURE FROM ITS UNDERGROUND HIDING PLACE! MY INTUITION GUIDES ME-I **CANNOT** FAIL!

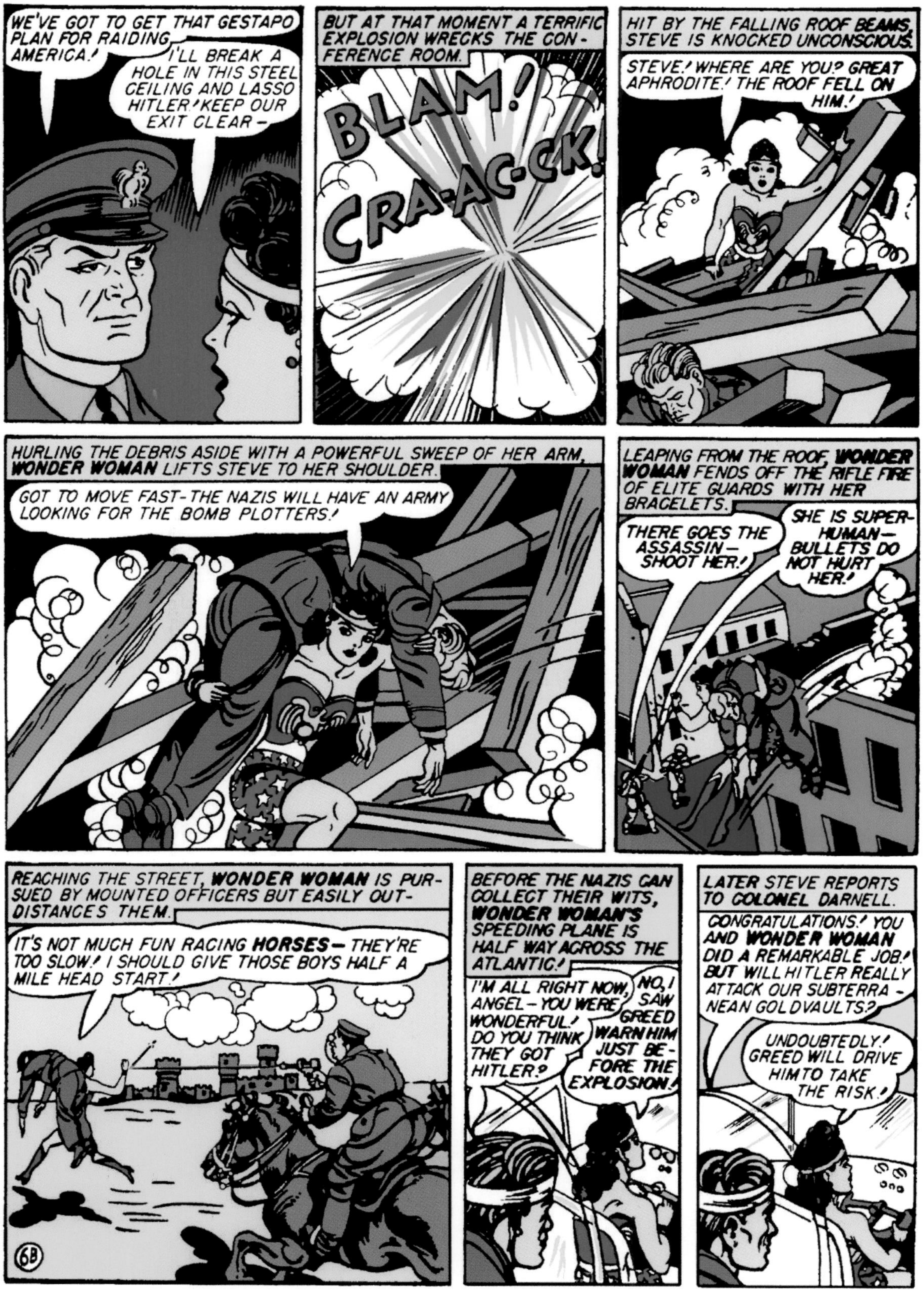
WE'VE GOT TO GET THAT GESTAPO PLAN FOR RAIDING AMERICA!
I'LL BREAK A HOLE IN THIS STEEL CEILING AND LASSO HITLER! KEEP OUR EXIT CLEAR –
BUT AT THAT MOMENT A TERRIFIC EXPLOSION WRECKS THE CON-FERENCE ROOM.
BLAM! CRA-AC-CK!
HIT BY THE FALLING ROOF BEAMS, STEVE IS KNOCKED UNCONSCIOUS.
STEVE! WHERE ARE YOU? GREAT APHRODITE! THE ROOF FELL ON HIM!
HURLING THE DEBRIS ASIDE WITH A POWERFUL SWEEP OF HER ARM, WONDER WOMAN LIFTS STEVE TO HER SHOULDER.
GOT TO MOVE FAST-THE NAZIS WILL HAVE AN ARMY LOOKING FOR THE BOMB PLOTTERS!
LEAPING FROM THE ROOF, WONDER WOMAN FENDS OFF THE RIFLE FIRE OF ELITE GUARDS WITH HER BRACELETS.
THERE GOES THE ASSASSIN– SHOOT HER!
SHE IS SUPER-HUMAN– BULLETS DO NOT HURT HER!
REACHING THE STREET, WONDER WOMAN IS PUR-SUED BY MOUNTED OFFICERS BUT EASILY OUT-DISTANCES THEM.
IT'S NOT MUCH FUN RACING HORSES– THEY'RE TOO SLOW! I SHOULD GIVE THOSE BOYS HALF A MILE HEAD START!
6B
BEFORE THE NAZIS CAN COLLECT THEIR WITS, WONDER WOMAN'S SPEEDING PLANE IS HALF WAY ACROSS THE ATLANTIC!
I'M ALL RIGHT NOW, ANGEL– YOU WERE WONDERFUL! DO YOU THINK THEY GOT HITLER?
NO, I SAW GREED WARN HIM JUST BE-FORE THE EXPLOSION!
LATER STEVE REPORTS TO COLONEL DARNELL.
CONGRATULATIONS! YOU AND WONDER WOMAN DID A REMARKABLE JOB! BUT WILL HITLER REALLY ATTACK OUR SUBTERRA-NEAN GOLDVAULTS?
UNDOUBTEDLY! GREED WILL DRIVE HIM TO TAKE THE RISK!

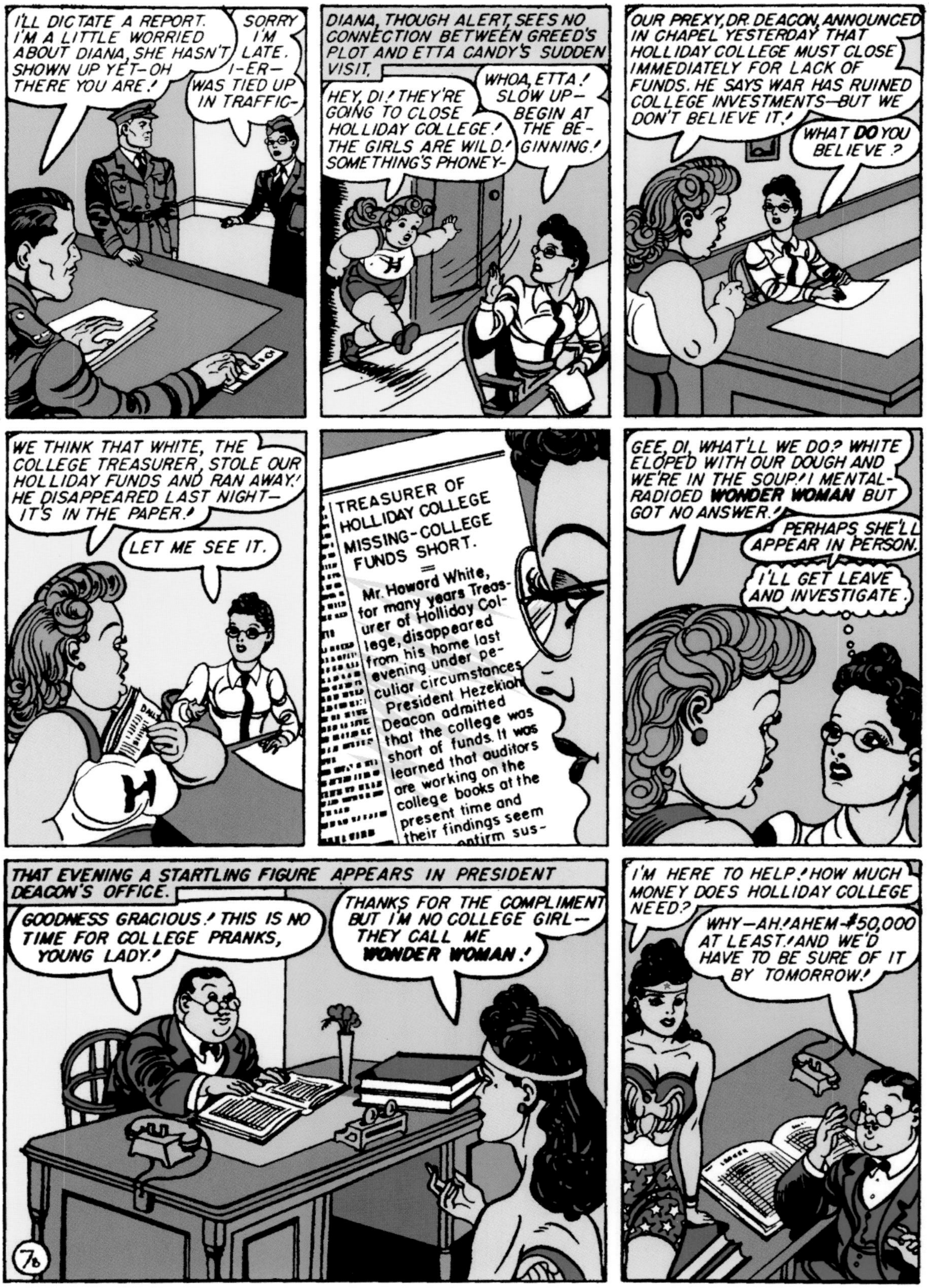

I'LL DICTATE A REPORT. I'M A LITTLE WORRIED ABOUT DIANA, SHE HASN'T SHOWN UP YET—OH THERE YOU ARE.!
SORRY I'M LATE. I-ER—WAS TIED UP IN TRAFFIC-
DIANA, THOUGH ALERT, SEES NO CONNECTION BETWEEN GREED'S PLOT AND ETTA CANDY'S SUDDEN VISIT.
HEY, DI! THEY'RE GOING TO CLOSE HOLLIDAY COLLEGE! THE GIRLS ARE WILD! SOMETHING'S PHONEY-
WHOA, ETTA! SLOW UP—BEGIN AT THE BE-GINNING!
OUR PREXY, DR. DEACON, ANNOUNCED IN CHAPEL YESTERDAY THAT HOLLIDAY COLLEGE MUST CLOSE IMMEDIATELY FOR LACK OF FUNDS. HE SAYS WAR HAS RUINED COLLEGE INVESTMENTS—BUT WE DON'T BELIEVE IT!
WHAT DO YOU BELIEVE?
WE THINK THAT WHITE, THE COLLEGE TREASURER, STOLE OUR HOLLIDAY FUNDS AND RAN AWAY! HE DISAPPEARED LAST NIGHT—IT'S IN THE PAPER!
LET ME SEE IT.
TREASURER OF HOLLIDAY COLLEGE MISSING-COLLEGE FUNDS SHORT.
Mr. Howard White, for many years Treasurer of Holliday College, disappeared from his home last evening under peculiar circumstances. President Hezekiah Deacon admitted that the college was short of funds. It was learned that auditors are working on the college books at the present time and their findings seem
GEE, DI, WHAT'LL WE DO? WHITE ELOPED WITH OUR DOUGH AND WE'RE IN THE SOUP! I MENTAL-RADIOED WONDER WOMAN BUT GOT NO ANSWER.
PERHAPS SHE'LL APPEAR IN PERSON.
I'LL GET LEAVE AND INVESTIGATE.
THAT EVENING A STARTLING FIGURE APPEARS IN PRESIDENT DEACON'S OFFICE.
GOODNESS GRACIOUS! THIS IS NO TIME FOR COLLEGE PRANKS, YOUNG LADY!
THANKS FOR THE COMPLIMENT BUT I'M NO COLLEGE GIRL—THEY CALL ME WONDER WOMAN!
7B
I'M HERE TO HELP! HOW MUCH MONEY DOES HOLLIDAY COLLEGE NEED?
WHY—AH! AHEM—$50,000 AT LEAST! AND WE'D HAVE TO BE SURE OF IT BY TOMORROW!

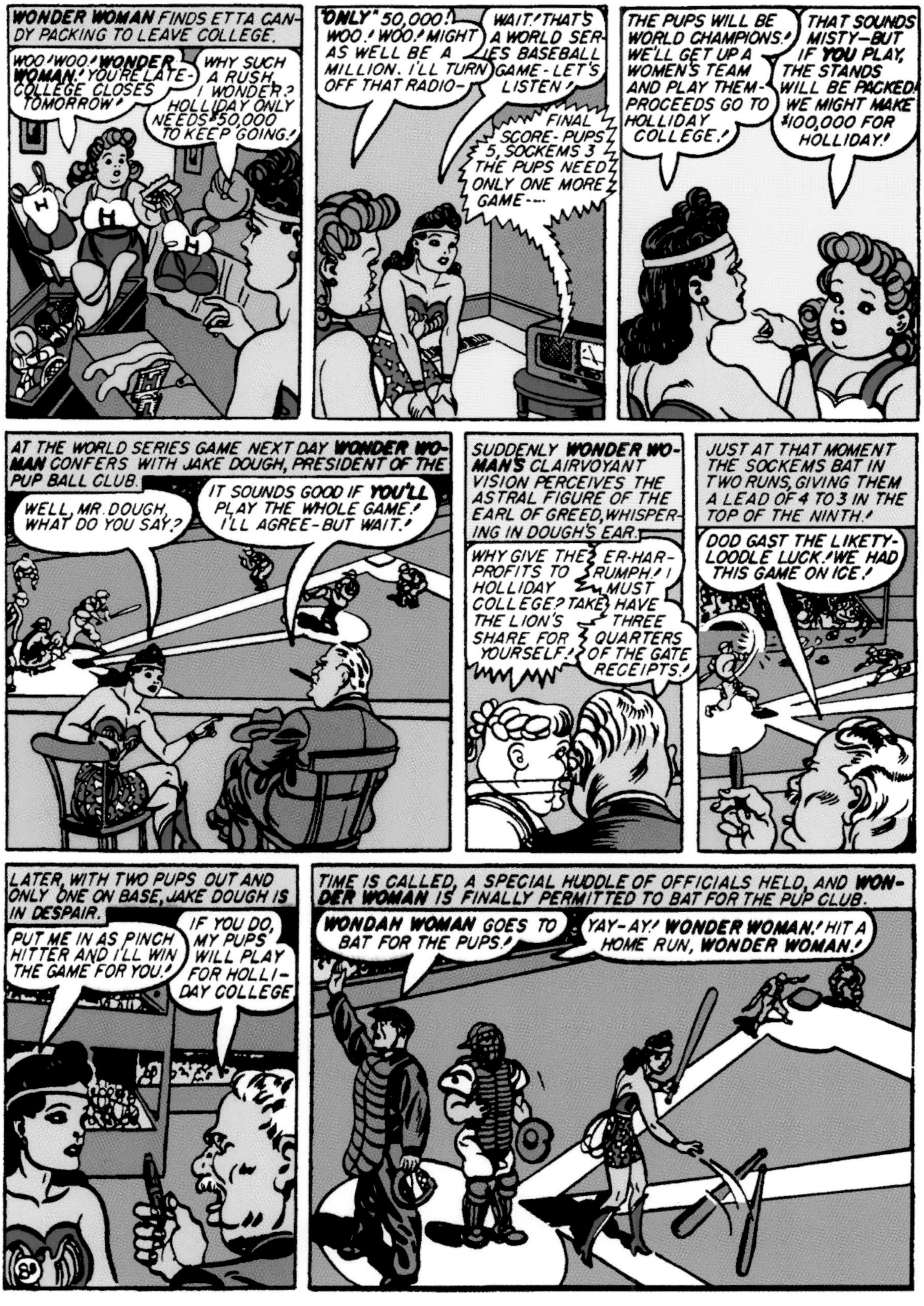
WONDER WOMAN FINDS ETTA CANDY PACKING TO LEAVE COLLEGE.
WOO! WOO! WONDER WOMAN! YOU'RE LATE-COLLEGE CLOSES TOMORROW!
WHY SUCH A RUSH, I WONDER? HOLLIDAY ONLY NEEDS $50,000 TO KEEP GOING!
"ONLY" 50,000! WOO! WOO! MIGHT AS WELL BE A MILLION. I'LL TURN OFF THAT RADIO-
WAIT! THAT'S A WORLD SERIES BASEBALL GAME-LET'S LISTEN!
FINAL SCORE-PUPS 5, SOCKEMS 3 THE PUPS NEED ONLY ONE MORE GAME---
THE PUPS WILL BE WORLD CHAMPIONS! WE'LL GET UP A WOMEN'S TEAM AND PLAY THEM-PROCEEDS GO TO HOLLIDAY COLLEGE!
THAT SOUNDS MISTY-BUT IF YOU PLAY, THE STANDS WILL BE PACKED! WE MIGHT MAKE $100,000 FOR HOLLIDAY!
AT THE WORLD SERIES GAME NEXT DAY WONDER WOMAN CONFERS WITH JAKE DOUGH, PRESIDENT OF THE PUP BALL CLUB.
WELL, MR. DOUGH, WHAT DO YOU SAY?
IT SOUNDS GOOD IF YOU'LL PLAY THE WHOLE GAME! I'LL AGREE-BUT WAIT!
SUDDENLY WONDER WOMAN'S CLAIRVOYANT VISION PERCEIVES THE ASTRAL FIGURE OF THE EARL OF GREED, WHISPERING IN DOUGH'S EAR.
WHY GIVE THE PROFITS TO HOLLIDAY COLLEGE? TAKE THE LION'S SHARE FOR YOURSELF!
ER-HARRUMPH! I MUST HAVE THREE QUARTERS OF THE GATE RECEIPTS!
JUST AT THAT MOMENT THE SOCKEMS BAT IN TWO RUNS, GIVING THEM A LEAD OF 4 TO 3 IN THE TOP OF THE NINTH!
DOD GAST THE LIKETY-LOODLE LUCK! WE HAD THIS GAME ON ICE!
LATER, WITH TWO PUPS OUT AND ONLY ONE ON BASE, JAKE DOUGH IS IN DESPAIR.
PUT ME IN AS PINCH HITTER AND I'LL WIN THE GAME FOR YOU!
IF YOU DO, MY PUPS WILL PLAY FOR HOLLIDAY COLLEGE
TIME IS CALLED, A SPECIAL HUDDLE OF OFFICIALS HELD, AND WONDER WOMAN IS FINALLY PERMITTED TO BAT FOR THE PUP CLUB.
WONDAH WOMAN GOES TO BAT FOR THE PUPS!
YAY-AY! WONDER WOMAN! HIT A HOME RUN, WONDER WOMAN!

THE SOCKEM PITCHER, DECIDEDLY NERVOUS, THROWS THREE WIDE ONES.

BA-WL THREE!

BOO-OO! BUM! YELLOW LEG! YA DASN'T GIVE WONDER WOMAN A GOOD ONE!

THE NEXT PITCH IS A SLOW FLOATER! WONDER WOMAN, FOOLED BY THE CHANGE OF PACE, SWINGS HARD — AND MISSES!

STR-RR-IKE ONE!

OO--AH! HIT IT WONDER WOMAN!

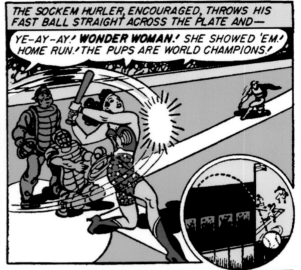

THE SOCKEM HURLER, ENCOURAGED, THROWS HIS FAST BALL STRAIGHT ACROSS THE PLATE AND—

YE—AY—AY! WONDER WOMAN! SHE SHOWED 'EM! HOME RUN! THE PUPS ARE WORLD CHAMPIONS!

JAKE DOUGH, OVERJOYED AT WONDER WOMAN'S PERFORMANCE, PROMISES A HOLLIDAY BENEFIT GAME DESPITE GREED'S WHISPERS.

YOU WERE SWELL WONDER WOMAN, I'LL DO ANYTHING YOU ASK!

YOU'RE A FOOL, DOUGH··· THIS IS GOING TO COST YOU MONEY.

THANKS!

WHILE THE GAME IS BEING AR-RANGED, GREED APPEARS TO THE TERRIFIED HOLLIDAY COL-LEGE EMBEZZLER.

YOU HAVE FAILED ME! I SHOWED YOU HOW TO STEAL MILLIONS AND STILL THE COLLEGE IS NOT CLOSED!

I C-CAN'T HELP IT! WONDER WOMAN—

AH–HR! WONDER WOMAN! SHE IS THE ENEMY I MUST DE-STROY! YOU WILL FOLLOW MY IN-STRUCTIONS OR I WILL REVEAL YOUR CRIMES!

D-DON'T DO THAT. IT'LL MEAN MY D-DEATH! I WILL OBEY YOU!

BEFORE 70,000 CHEERING SPECTATORS IN THE HOLLIDAY BOWL, THE PUPS AND ALL-WOMAN TEAMS SALUTE EACH OTHER.

YAY—AY! ALL WOMEN!

YAY FOR THE PUPS!

HOORAY FOR WONDER WOMAN!

"BABE" WILLIAMS, FAMOUS GIRL ATHLETE, PITCHES FOR THE ALL-WOMAN TEAM.

SWISH

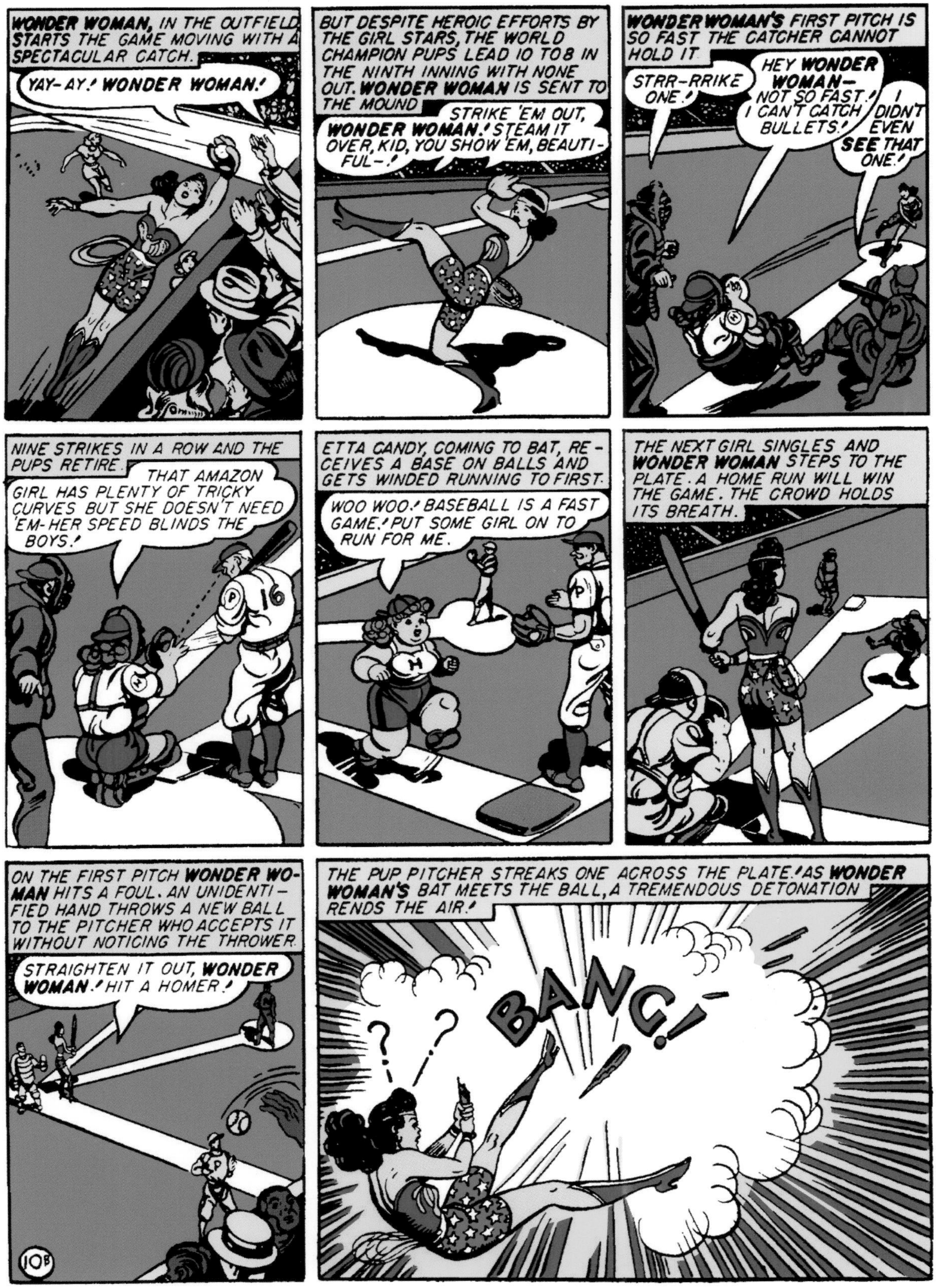
WONDER WOMAN, IN THE OUTFIELD, STARTS THE GAME MOVING WITH A SPECTACULAR CATCH.
YAY-AY! WONDER WOMAN!
BUT DESPITE HEROIC EFFORTS BY THE GIRL STARS, THE WORLD CHAMPION PUPS LEAD 10 TO 8 IN THE NINTH INNING WITH NONE OUT. WONDER WOMAN IS SENT TO THE MOUND
STRIKE 'EM OUT, WONDER WOMAN! STEAM IT OVER, KID, YOU SHOW 'EM, BEAUTI-FUL-!
WONDER WOMAN'S FIRST PITCH IS SO FAST THE CATCHER CANNOT HOLD IT.
STRR-RRIKE ONE!
HEY WONDER WOMAN— NOT SO FAST! I CAN'T CATCH BULLETS!
I DIDN'T EVEN SEE THAT ONE!
NINE STRIKES IN A ROW AND THE PUPS RETIRE.
THAT AMAZON GIRL HAS PLENTY OF TRICKY CURVES BUT SHE DOESN'T NEED 'EM-HER SPEED BLINDS THE BOYS!
ETTA CANDY, COMING TO BAT, RE-CEIVES A BASE ON BALLS AND GETS WINDED RUNNING TO FIRST.
WOO WOO! BASEBALL IS A FAST GAME! PUT SOME GIRL ON TO RUN FOR ME.
THE NEXT GIRL SINGLES AND WONDER WOMAN STEPS TO THE PLATE. A HOME RUN WILL WIN THE GAME. THE CROWD HOLDS ITS BREATH.
ON THE FIRST PITCH WONDER WO-MAN HITS A FOUL. AN UNIDENTI-FIED HAND THROWS A NEW BALL TO THE PITCHER WHO ACCEPTS IT WITHOUT NOTICING THE THROWER.
STRAIGHTEN IT OUT, WONDER WOMAN! HIT A HOMER!
10B
THE PUP PITCHER STREAKS ONE ACROSS THE PLATE! AS WONDER WOMAN'S BAT MEETS THE BALL, A TREMENDOUS DETONATION RENDS THE AIR!
? ?
BANG!

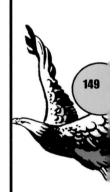

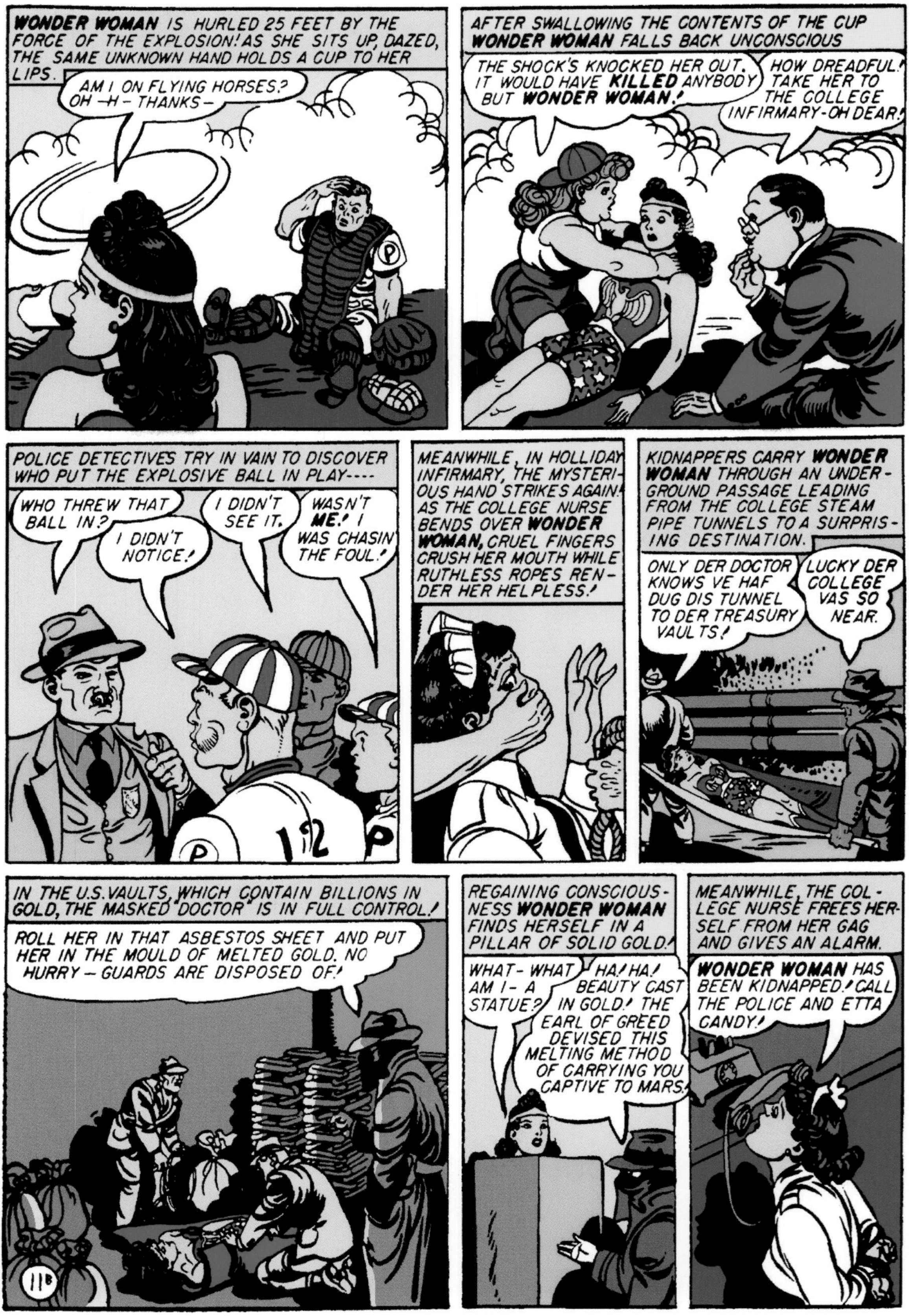
WONDER WOMAN IS HURLED 25 FEET BY THE FORCE OF THE EXPLOSION! AS SHE SITS UP, DAZED, THE SAME UNKNOWN HAND HOLDS A CUP TO HER LIPS.
AM I ON FLYING HORSES? OH —H — THANKS—
AFTER SWALLOWING THE CONTENTS OF THE CUP WONDER WOMAN FALLS BACK UNCONSCIOUS
THE SHOCK'S KNOCKED HER OUT. IT WOULD HAVE KILLED ANYBODY BUT WONDER WOMAN!
HOW DREADFUL! TAKE HER TO THE COLLEGE INFIRMARY-OH DEAR!
POLICE DETECTIVES TRY IN VAIN TO DISCOVER WHO PUT THE EXPLOSIVE BALL IN PLAY----
WHO THREW THAT BALL IN?
I DIDN'T NOTICE!
I DIDN'T SEE IT.
WASN'T ME! I WAS CHASIN' THE FOUL!
MEANWHILE, IN HOLLIDAY INFIRMARY, THE MYSTERIOUS HAND STRIKES AGAIN! AS THE COLLEGE NURSE BENDS OVER WONDER WOMAN, CRUEL FINGERS CRUSH HER MOUTH WHILE RUTHLESS ROPES RENDER HER HELPLESS!
KIDNAPPERS CARRY WONDER WOMAN THROUGH AN UNDERGROUND PASSAGE LEADING FROM THE COLLEGE STEAM PIPE TUNNELS TO A SURPRISING DESTINATION.
ONLY DER DOCTOR KNOWS VE HAF DUG DIS TUNNEL TO DER TREASURY VAULTS!
LUCKY DER COLLEGE VAS SO NEAR.
IN THE U.S. VAULTS, WHICH CONTAIN BILLIONS IN GOLD, THE MASKED "DOCTOR" IS IN FULL CONTROL!
ROLL HER IN THAT ASBESTOS SHEET AND PUT HER IN THE MOULD OF MELTED GOLD. NO HURRY — GUARDS ARE DISPOSED OF!
11C
REGAINING CONSCIOUSNESS WONDER WOMAN FINDS HERSELF IN A PILLAR OF SOLID GOLD!
WHAT- WHAT AM I- A STATUE?
HA! HA! BEAUTY CAST IN GOLD! THE EARL OF GREED DEVISED THIS MELTING METHOD OF CARRYING YOU CAPTIVE TO MARS.
MEANWHILE, THE COLLEGE NURSE FREES HERSELF FROM HER GAG AND GIVES AN ALARM.
WONDER WOMAN HAS BEEN KIDNAPPED! CALL THE POLICE AND ETTA CANDY!

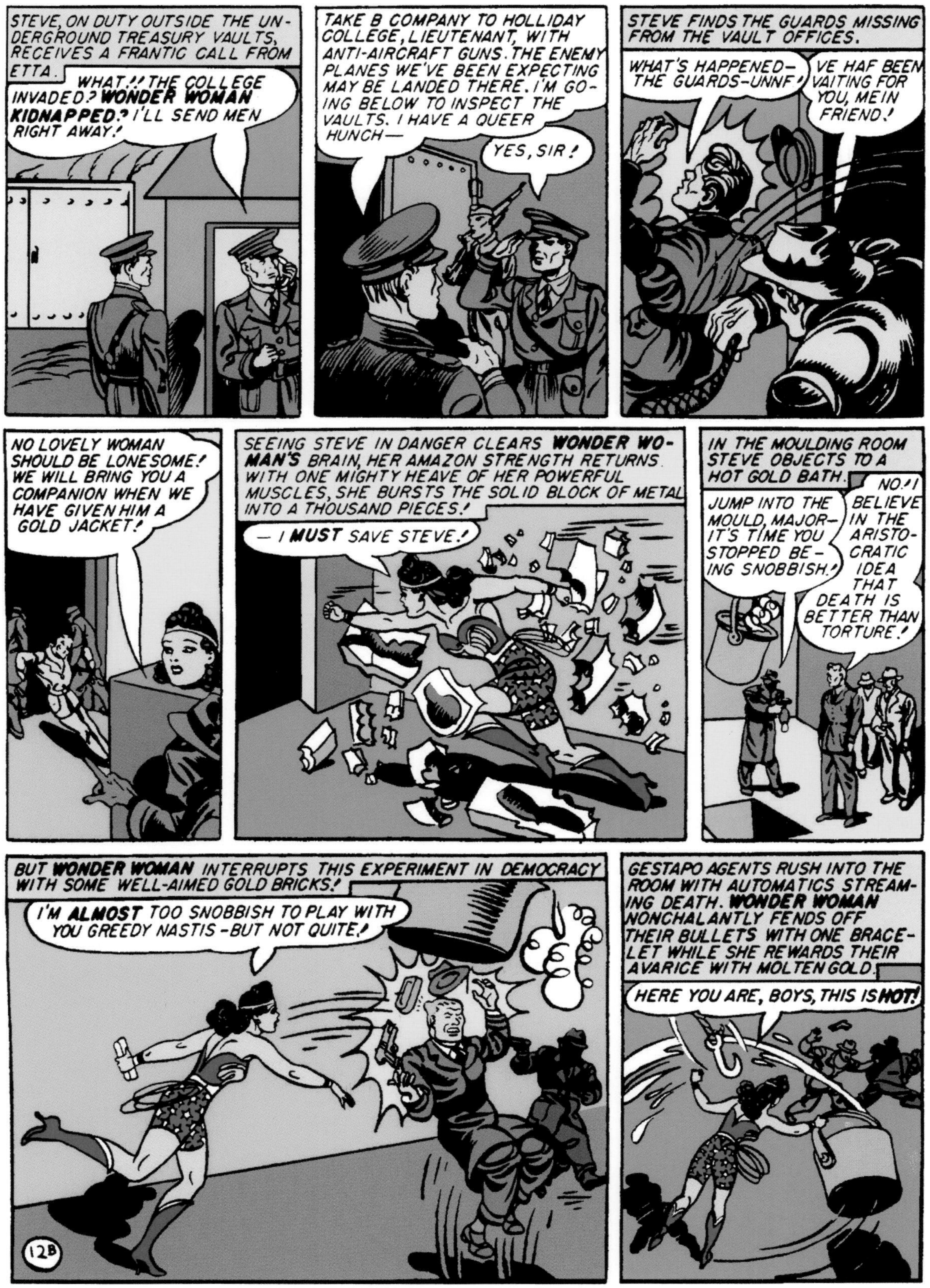
STEVE, ON DUTY OUTSIDE THE UNDERGROUND TREASURY VAULTS, RECEIVES A FRANTIC CALL FROM ETTA.
WHAT!! THE COLLEGE INVADED? WONDER WOMAN KIDNAPPED? I'LL SEND MEN RIGHT AWAY!
TAKE B COMPANY TO HOLLIDAY COLLEGE, LIEUTENANT, WITH ANTI-AIRCRAFT GUNS. THE ENEMY PLANES WE'VE BEEN EXPECTING MAY BE LANDED THERE. I'M GOING BELOW TO INSPECT THE VAULTS. I HAVE A QUEER HUNCH—
YES, SIR!
STEVE FINDS THE GUARDS MISSING FROM THE VAULT OFFICES.
WHAT'S HAPPENED—THE GUARDS—UNNF!
VE HAF BEEN VAITING FOR YOU, MEIN FRIEND!
NO LOVELY WOMAN SHOULD BE LONESOME! WE WILL BRING YOU A COMPANION WHEN WE HAVE GIVEN HIM A GOLD JACKET!
SEEING STEVE IN DANGER CLEARS WONDER WOMAN'S BRAIN, HER AMAZON STRENGTH RETURNS. WITH ONE MIGHTY HEAVE OF HER POWERFUL MUSCLES, SHE BURSTS THE SOLID BLOCK OF METAL INTO A THOUSAND PIECES!
— I MUST SAVE STEVE!
IN THE MOULDING ROOM STEVE OBJECTS TO A HOT GOLD BATH.
JUMP INTO THE MOULD, MAJOR—IT'S TIME YOU STOPPED BEING SNOBBISH!
NO! I BELIEVE IN THE ARISTOCRATIC IDEA THAT DEATH IS BETTER THAN TORTURE!
BUT WONDER WOMAN INTERRUPTS THIS EXPERIMENT IN DEMOCRACY WITH SOME WELL-AIMED GOLD BRICKS!
I'M ALMOST TOO SNOBBISH TO PLAY WITH YOU GREEDY NASTIS—BUT NOT QUITE!
12B
GESTAPO AGENTS RUSH INTO THE ROOM WITH AUTOMATICS STREAMING DEATH. WONDER WOMAN NONCHALANTLY FENDS OFF THEIR BULLETS WITH ONE BRACELET WHILE SHE REWARDS THEIR AVARICE WITH MOLTEN GOLD.
HERE YOU ARE, BOYS, THIS IS HOT!

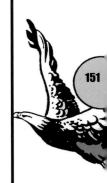

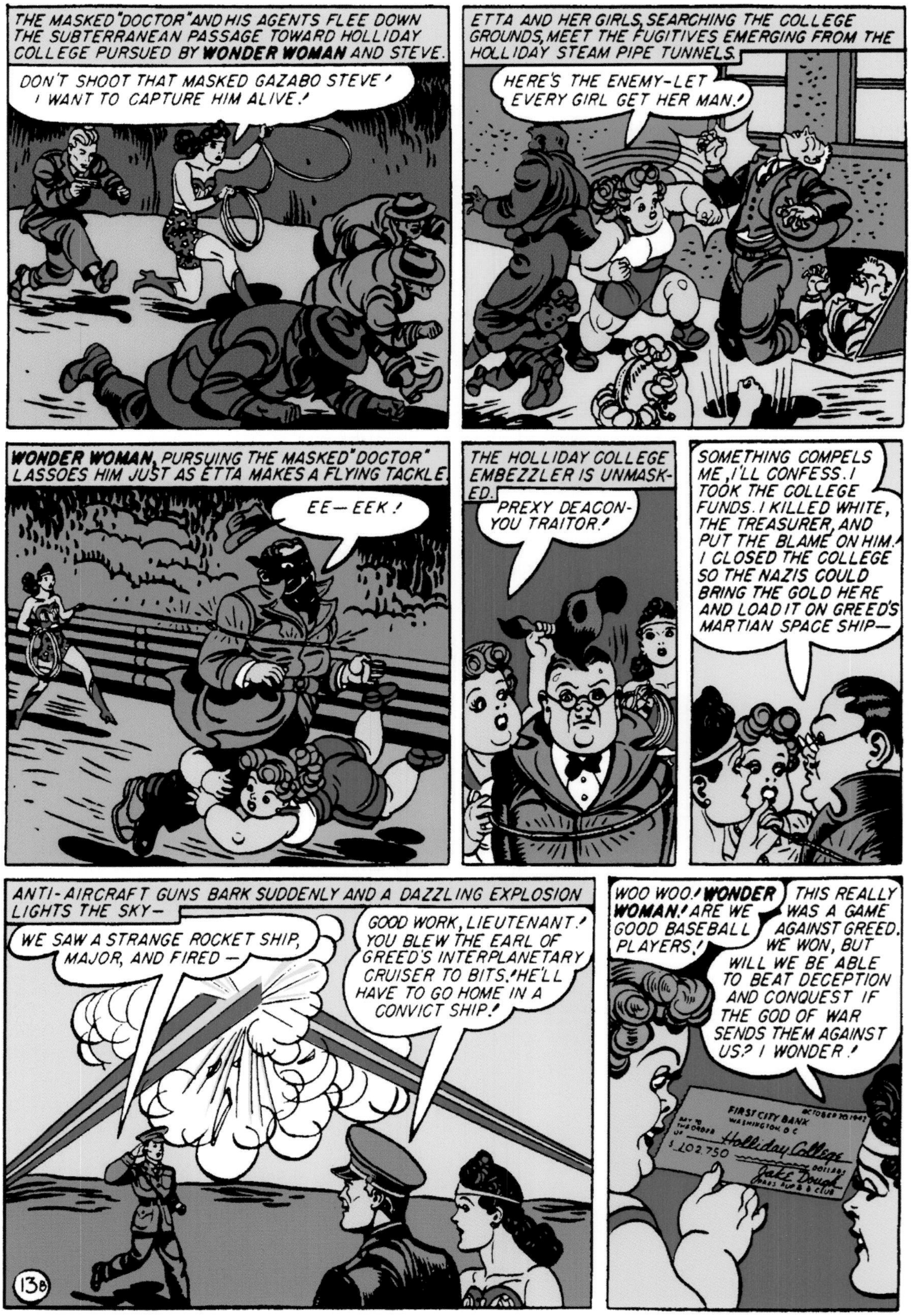
THE MASKED "DOCTOR" AND HIS AGENTS FLEE DOWN THE SUBTERRANEAN PASSAGE TOWARD HOLLIDAY COLLEGE PURSUED BY WONDER WOMAN AND STEVE.
DON'T SHOOT THAT MASKED GAZABO STEVE! I WANT TO CAPTURE HIM ALIVE!
ETTA AND HER GIRLS, SEARCHING THE COLLEGE GROUNDS, MEET THE FUGITIVES EMERGING FROM THE HOLLIDAY STEAM PIPE TUNNELS.
HERE'S THE ENEMY—LET EVERY GIRL GET HER MAN!
WONDER WOMAN, PURSUING THE MASKED "DOCTOR" LASSOES HIM JUST AS ETTA MAKES A FLYING TACKLE.
EE—EEK!
THE HOLLIDAY COLLEGE EMBEZZLER IS UNMASKED.
PREXY DEACON—YOU TRAITOR!
SOMETHING COMPELS ME, I'LL CONFESS. I TOOK THE COLLEGE FUNDS. I KILLED WHITE, THE TREASURER, AND PUT THE BLAME ON HIM! I CLOSED THE COLLEGE SO THE NAZIS COULD BRING THE GOLD HERE AND LOAD IT ON GREED'S MARTIAN SPACE SHIP—
ANTI-AIRCRAFT GUNS BARK SUDDENLY AND A DAZZLING EXPLOSION LIGHTS THE SKY—
WE SAW A STRANGE ROCKET SHIP, MAJOR, AND FIRED—
GOOD WORK, LIEUTENANT! YOU BLEW THE EARL OF GREED'S INTERPLANETARY CRUISER TO BITS! HE'LL HAVE TO GO HOME IN A CONVICT SHIP!
13B
WOO WOO! WONDER WOMAN! ARE WE GOOD BASEBALL PLAYERS!
THIS REALLY WAS A GAME AGAINST GREED. WE WON, BUT WILL WE BE ABLE TO BEAT DECEPTION AND CONQUEST IF THE GOD OF WAR SENDS THEM AGAINST US? I WONDER!
FIRST CITY BANK
WASHINGTON, D.C.
OCTOBER 20, 1942
Holliday College
$ 102,750
Jake Dough

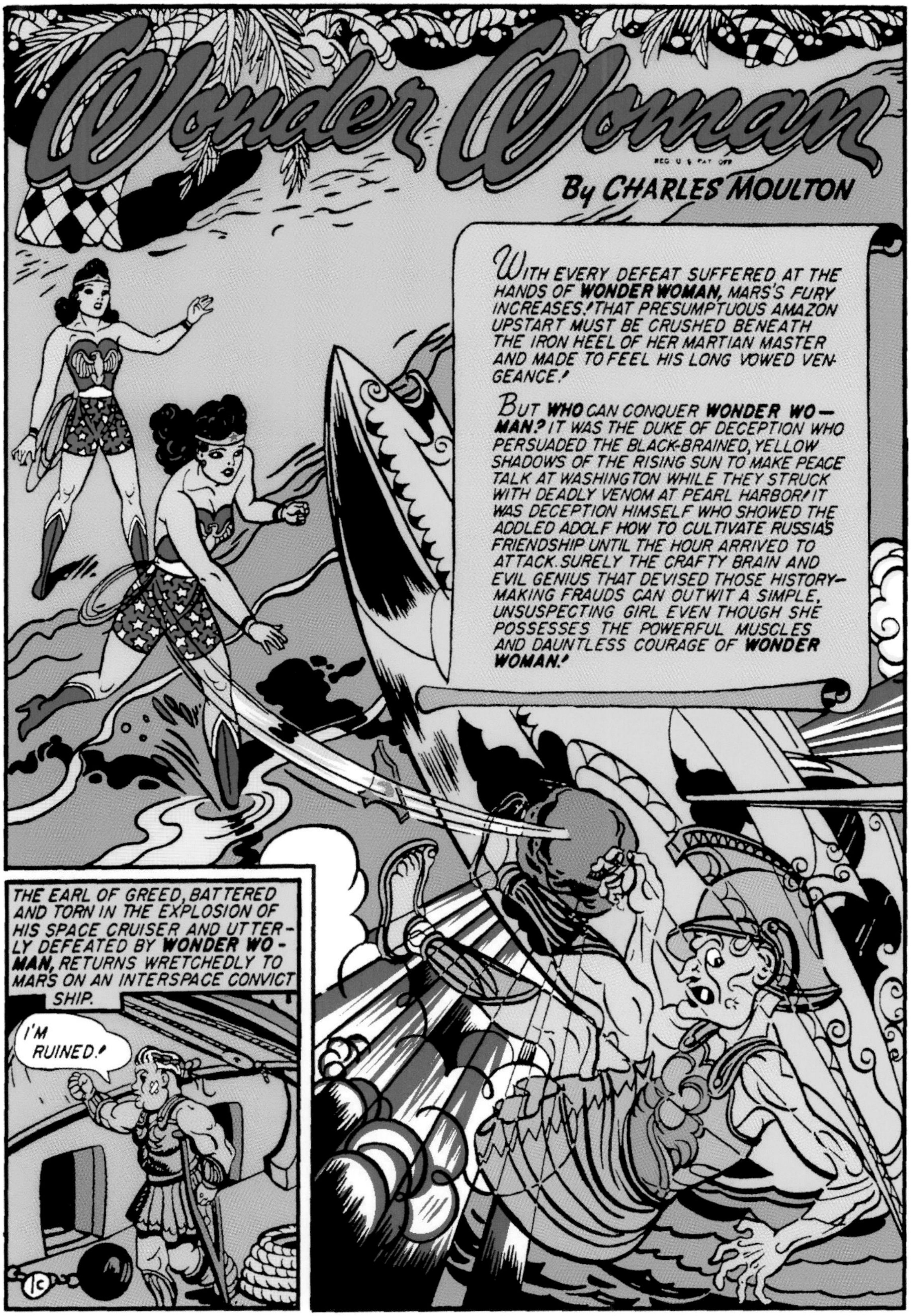
Wonder Woman
REG. U.S. PAT. OFF.
By CHARLES MOULTON
WITH EVERY DEFEAT SUFFERED AT THE HANDS OF WONDER WOMAN, MARS'S FURY INCREASES! THAT PRESUMPTUOUS AMAZON UPSTART MUST BE CRUSHED BENEATH THE IRON HEEL OF HER MARTIAN MASTER AND MADE TO FEEL HIS LONG VOWED VENGEANCE!
BUT WHO CAN CONQUER WONDER WOMAN? IT WAS THE DUKE OF DECEPTION WHO PERSUADED THE BLACK-BRAINED, YELLOW SHADOWS OF THE RISING SUN TO MAKE PEACE TALK AT WASHINGTON WHILE THEY STRUCK WITH DEADLY VENOM AT PEARL HARBOR! IT WAS DECEPTION HIMSELF WHO SHOWED THE ADDLED ADOLF HOW TO CULTIVATE RUSSIA'S FRIENDSHIP UNTIL THE HOUR ARRIVED TO ATTACK. SURELY THE CRAFTY BRAIN AND EVIL GENIUS THAT DEVISED THOSE HISTORY-MAKING FRAUDS CAN OUTWIT A SIMPLE, UNSUSPECTING GIRL EVEN THOUGH SHE POSSESSES THE POWERFUL MUSCLES AND DAUNTLESS COURAGE OF WONDER WOMAN!
THE EARL OF GREED, BATTERED AND TORN IN THE EXPLOSION OF HIS SPACE CRUISER AND UTTERLY DEFEATED BY WONDER WOMAN, RETURNS WRETCHEDLY TO MARS ON AN INTERSPACE CONVICT SHIP.
I'M RUINED!
1c

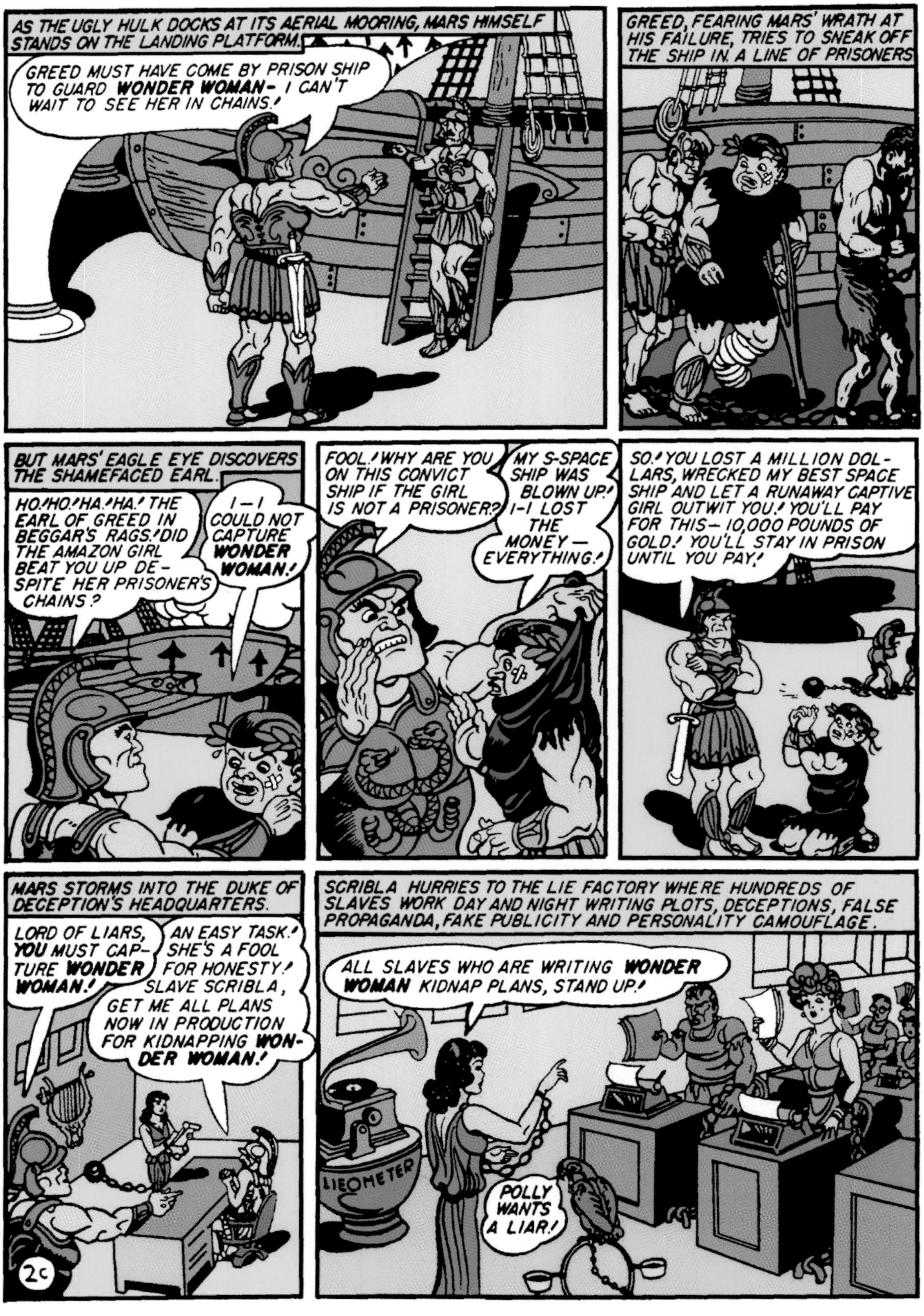

AS THE UGLY HULK DOCKS AT ITS AERIAL MOORING, MARS HIMSELF STANDS ON THE LANDING PLATFORM.
GREED MUST HAVE COME BY PRISON SHIP TO GUARD WONDER WOMAN- I CAN'T WAIT TO SEE HER IN CHAINS!
GREED, FEARING MARS' WRATH AT HIS FAILURE, TRIES TO SNEAK OFF THE SHIP IN A LINE OF PRISONERS
BUT MARS' EAGLE EYE DISCOVERS THE SHAMEFACED EARL.
HO! HO! HA! HA! THE EARL OF GREED IN BEGGAR'S RAGS! DID THE AMAZON GIRL BEAT YOU UP DESPITE HER PRISONER'S CHAINS?
I-I COULD NOT CAPTURE WONDER WOMAN!
FOOL! WHY ARE YOU ON THIS CONVICT SHIP IF THE GIRL IS NOT A PRISONER?
MY S-SPACE SHIP WAS BLOWN UP! I-I LOST THE MONEY — EVERYTHING!
SO! YOU LOST A MILLION DOLLARS, WRECKED MY BEST SPACE SHIP AND LET A RUNAWAY CAPTIVE GIRL OUTWIT YOU! YOU'LL PAY FOR THIS- 10,000 POUNDS OF GOLD! YOU'LL STAY IN PRISON UNTIL YOU PAY!
MARS STORMS INTO THE DUKE OF DECEPTION'S HEADQUARTERS.
LORD OF LIARS, YOU MUST CAPTURE WONDER WOMAN!
AN EASY TASK! SHE'S A FOOL FOR HONESTY! SLAVE SCRIBLA, GET ME ALL PLANS NOW IN PRODUCTION FOR KIDNAPPING WONDER WOMAN!
2c
SCRIBLA HURRIES TO THE LIE FACTORY WHERE HUNDREDS OF SLAVES WORK DAY AND NIGHT WRITING PLOTS, DECEPTIONS, FALSE PROPAGANDA, FAKE PUBLICITY AND PERSONALITY CAMOUFLAGE.
ALL SLAVES WHO ARE WRITING WONDER WOMAN KIDNAP PLANS, STAND UP!
LIEOMETER
POLLY WANTS A LIAR!

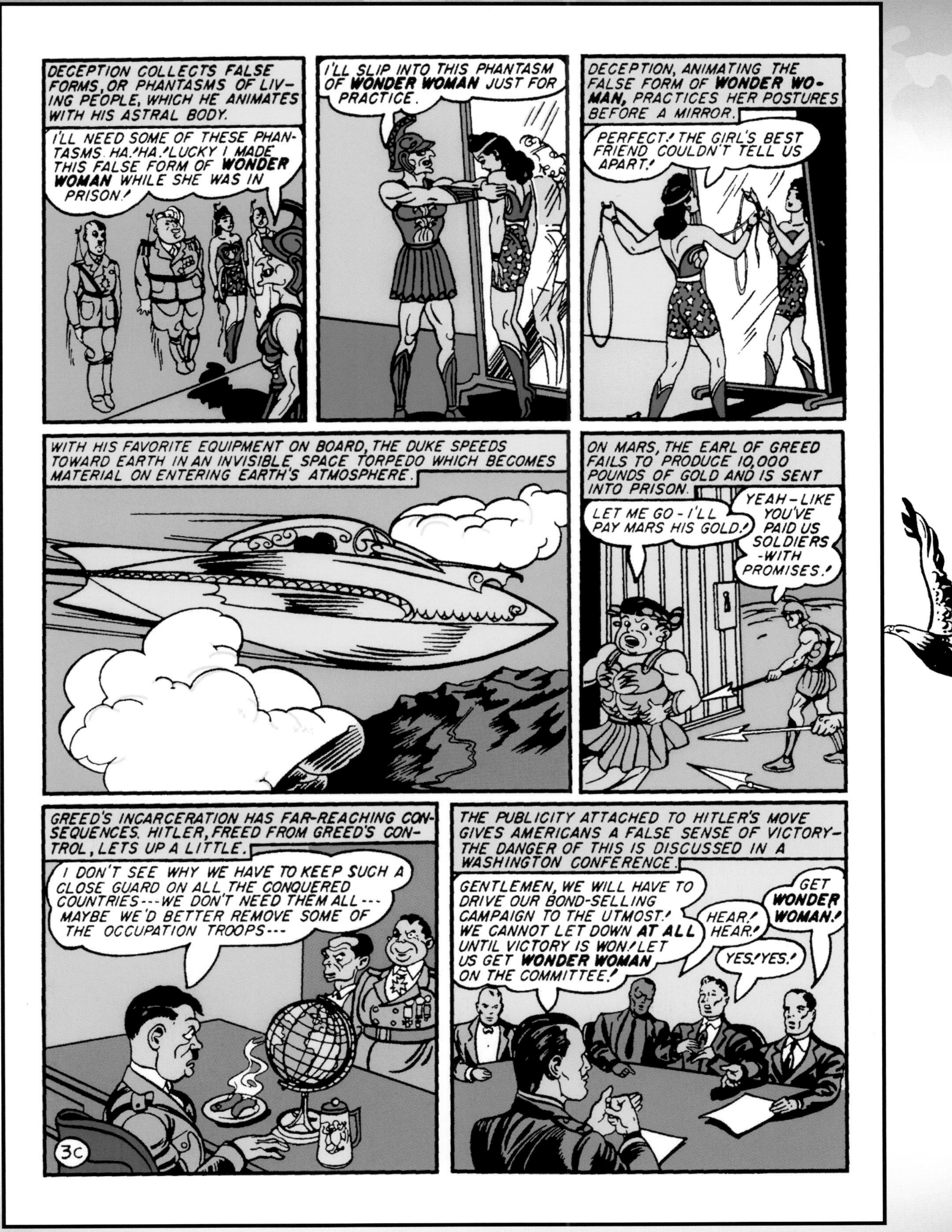
DECEPTION COLLECTS FALSE FORMS, OR PHANTASMS OF LIVING PEOPLE, WHICH HE ANIMATES WITH HIS ASTRAL BODY.
I'LL NEED SOME OF THESE PHANTASMS. HA! HA! LUCKY I MADE THIS FALSE FORM OF WONDER WOMAN WHILE SHE WAS IN PRISON!
I'LL SLIP INTO THIS PHANTASM OF WONDER WOMAN JUST FOR PRACTICE.
DECEPTION, ANIMATING THE FALSE FORM OF WONDER WOMAN, PRACTICES HER POSTURES BEFORE A MIRROR.
PERFECT! THE GIRL'S BEST FRIEND COULDN'T TELL US APART!
WITH HIS FAVORITE EQUIPMENT ON BOARD, THE DUKE SPEEDS TOWARD EARTH IN AN INVISIBLE SPACE TORPEDO WHICH BECOMES MATERIAL ON ENTERING EARTH'S ATMOSPHERE.
ON MARS, THE EARL OF GREED FAILS TO PRODUCE 10,000 POUNDS OF GOLD AND IS SENT INTO PRISON.
LET ME GO - I'LL PAY MARS HIS GOLD!
YEAH - LIKE YOU'VE PAID US SOLDIERS -WITH PROMISES!
GREED'S INCARCERATION HAS FAR-REACHING CONSEQUENCES. HITLER, FREED FROM GREED'S CONTROL, LETS UP A LITTLE.
I DON'T SEE WHY WE HAVE TO KEEP SUCH A CLOSE GUARD ON ALL THE CONQUERED COUNTRIES---WE DON'T NEED THEM ALL--- MAYBE WE'D BETTER REMOVE SOME OF THE OCCUPATION TROOPS---
3C
THE PUBLICITY ATTACHED TO HITLER'S MOVE GIVES AMERICANS A FALSE SENSE OF VICTORY- THE DANGER OF THIS IS DISCUSSED IN A WASHINGTON CONFERENCE.
GENTLEMEN, WE WILL HAVE TO DRIVE OUR BOND-SELLING CAMPAIGN TO THE UTMOST! WE CANNOT LET DOWN AT ALL UNTIL VICTORY IS WON! LET US GET WONDER WOMAN ON THE COMMITTEE!
HEAR! HEAR!
YES! YES!
GET WONDER WOMAN!

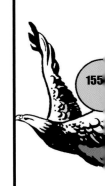

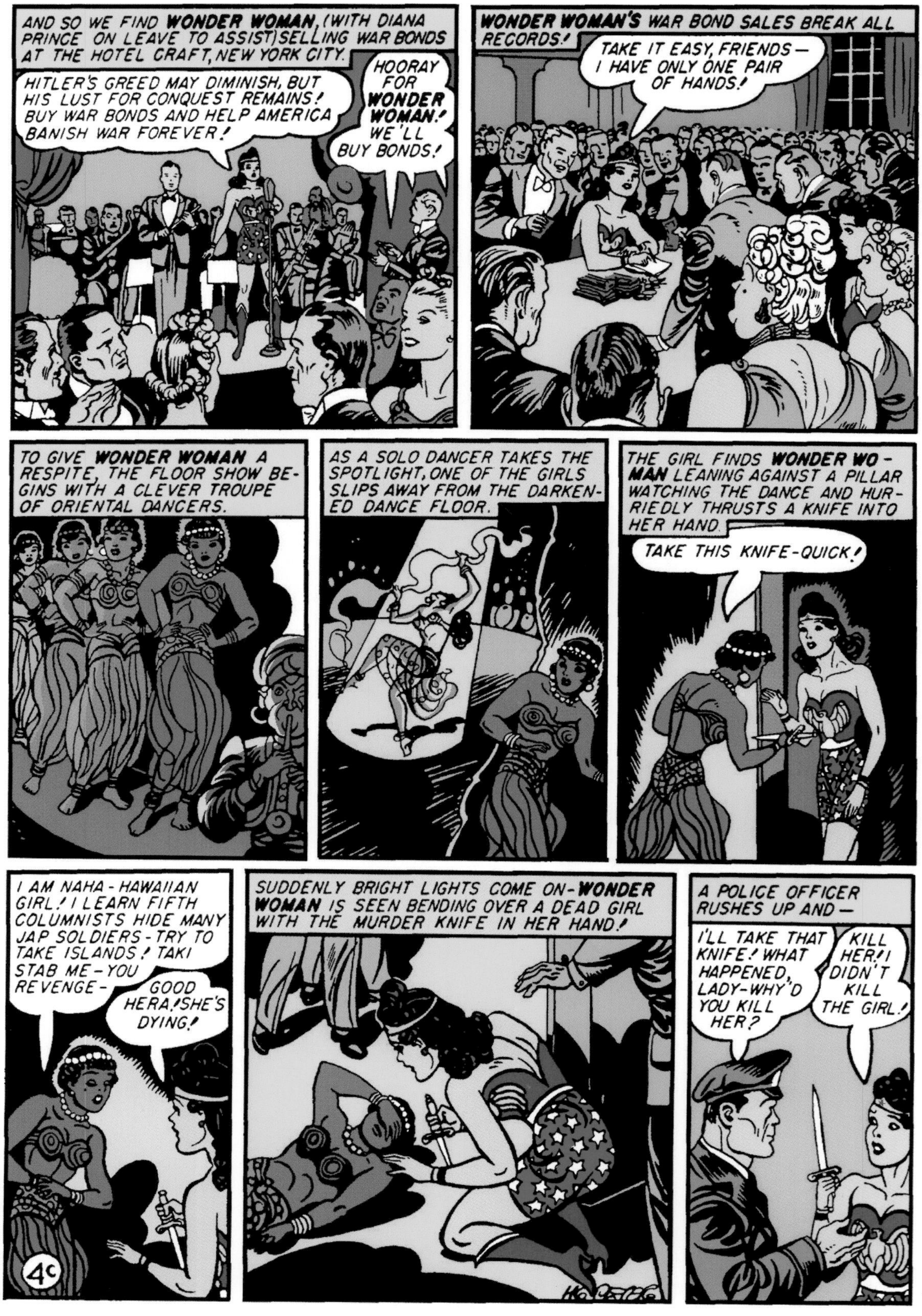
AND SO WE FIND WONDER WOMAN, (WITH DIANA PRINCE ON LEAVE TO ASSIST) SELLING WAR BONDS AT THE HOTEL CRAFT, NEW YORK CITY.
HITLER'S GREED MAY DIMINISH, BUT HIS LUST FOR CONQUEST REMAINS! BUY WAR BONDS AND HELP AMERICA BANISH WAR FOREVER!
HOORAY FOR WONDER WOMAN! WE'LL BUY BONDS!
WONDER WOMAN'S WAR BOND SALES BREAK ALL RECORDS!
TAKE IT EASY, FRIENDS— I HAVE ONLY ONE PAIR OF HANDS!
TO GIVE WONDER WOMAN A RESPITE, THE FLOOR SHOW BEGINS WITH A CLEVER TROUPE OF ORIENTAL DANCERS.
AS A SOLO DANCER TAKES THE SPOTLIGHT, ONE OF THE GIRLS SLIPS AWAY FROM THE DARKENED DANCE FLOOR.
THE GIRL FINDS WONDER WOMAN LEANING AGAINST A PILLAR WATCHING THE DANCE AND HURRIEDLY THRUSTS A KNIFE INTO HER HAND.
TAKE THIS KNIFE-QUICK!
I AM NAHA-HAWAIIAN GIRL! I LEARN FIFTH COLUMNISTS HIDE MANY JAP SOLDIERS-TRY TO TAKE ISLANDS! TAKI STAB ME-YOU REVENGE-
GOOD HERA! SHE'S DYING!
4c
SUDDENLY BRIGHT LIGHTS COME ON-WONDER WOMAN IS SEEN BENDING OVER A DEAD GIRL WITH THE MURDER KNIFE IN HER HAND!
A POLICE OFFICER RUSHES UP AND—
I'LL TAKE THAT KNIFE! WHAT HAPPENED, LADY-WHY'D YOU KILL HER?
KILL HER! I DIDN'T KILL THE GIRL!

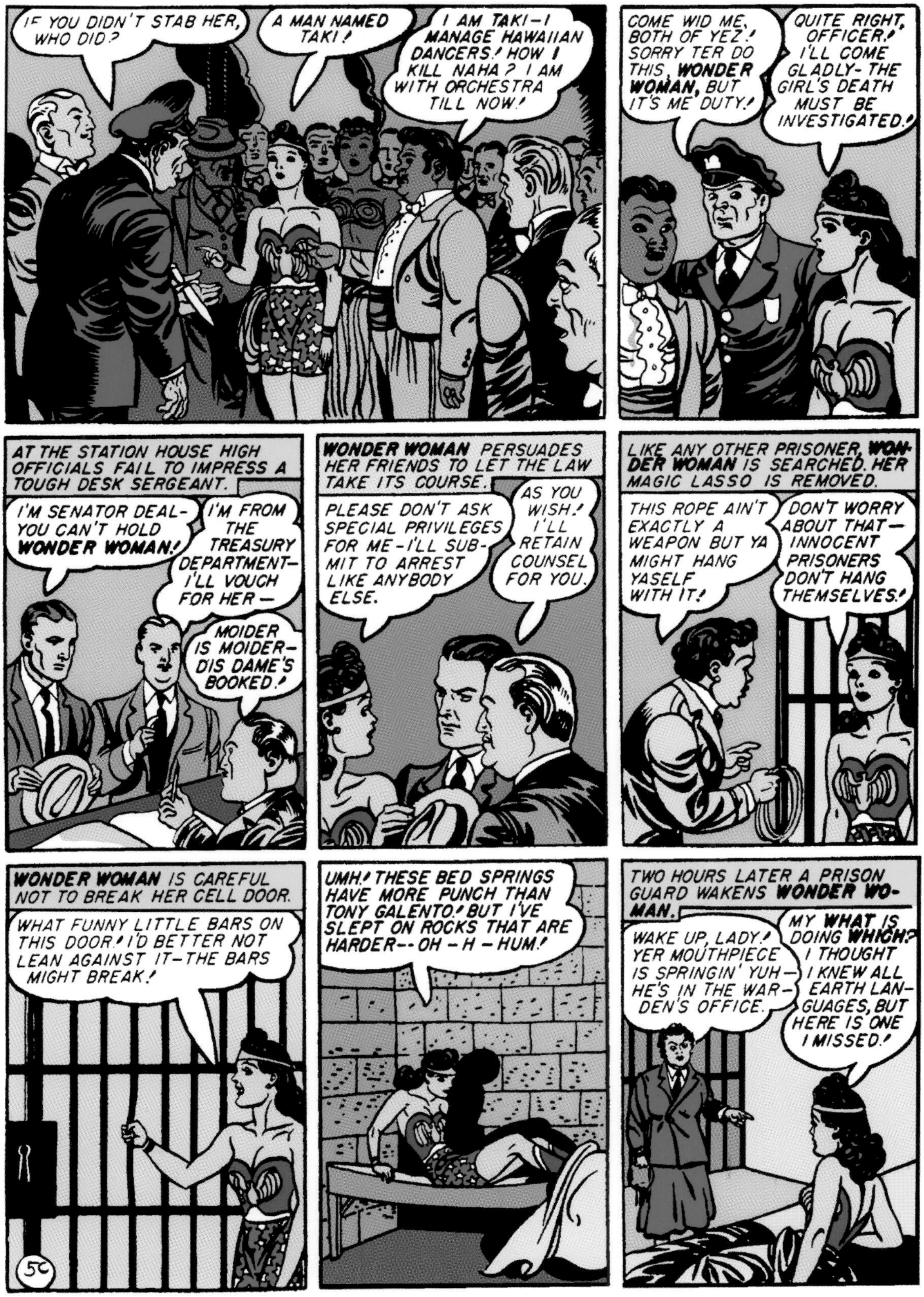
IF YOU DIDN'T STAB HER, WHO DID?
A MAN NAMED TAKI!
I AM TAKI—I MANAGE HAWAIIAN DANCERS! HOW I KILL NAHA? I AM WITH ORCHESTRA TILL NOW!
COME WID ME, BOTH OF YEZ! SORRY TER DO THIS, WONDER WOMAN, BUT IT'S ME DUTY!
QUITE RIGHT, OFFICER! I'LL COME GLADLY- THE GIRL'S DEATH MUST BE INVESTIGATED!
AT THE STATION HOUSE HIGH OFFICIALS FAIL TO IMPRESS A TOUGH DESK SERGEANT.
I'M SENATOR DEAL- YOU CAN'T HOLD WONDER WOMAN!
I'M FROM THE TREASURY DEPARTMENT- I'LL VOUCH FOR HER—
MOIDER IS MOIDER- DIS DAME'S BOOKED!
WONDER WOMAN PERSUADES HER FRIENDS TO LET THE LAW TAKE ITS COURSE.
PLEASE DON'T ASK SPECIAL PRIVILEGES FOR ME - I'LL SUB- MIT TO ARREST LIKE ANYBODY ELSE.
AS YOU WISH! I'LL RETAIN COUNSEL FOR YOU.
LIKE ANY OTHER PRISONER, WON- DER WOMAN IS SEARCHED. HER MAGIC LASSO IS REMOVED.
THIS ROPE AIN'T EXACTLY A WEAPON BUT YA MIGHT HANG YASELF WITH IT!
DON'T WORRY ABOUT THAT— INNOCENT PRISONERS DON'T HANG THEMSELVES!
WONDER WOMAN IS CAREFUL NOT TO BREAK HER CELL DOOR.
WHAT FUNNY LITTLE BARS ON THIS DOOR! I'D BETTER NOT LEAN AGAINST IT—THE BARS MIGHT BREAK!
5C
UMH! THESE BED SPRINGS HAVE MORE PUNCH THAN TONY GALENTO! BUT I'VE SLEPT ON ROCKS THAT ARE HARDER-- OH - H - HUM!
TWO HOURS LATER A PRISON GUARD WAKENS WONDER WO- MAN.
WAKE UP, LADY! YER MOUTHPIECE IS SPRINGIN' YUH— HE'S IN THE WAR- DEN'S OFFICE.
MY WHAT IS DOING WHICH? I THOUGHT I KNEW ALL EARTH LAN- GUAGES, BUT HERE IS ONE I MISSED!

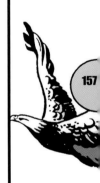

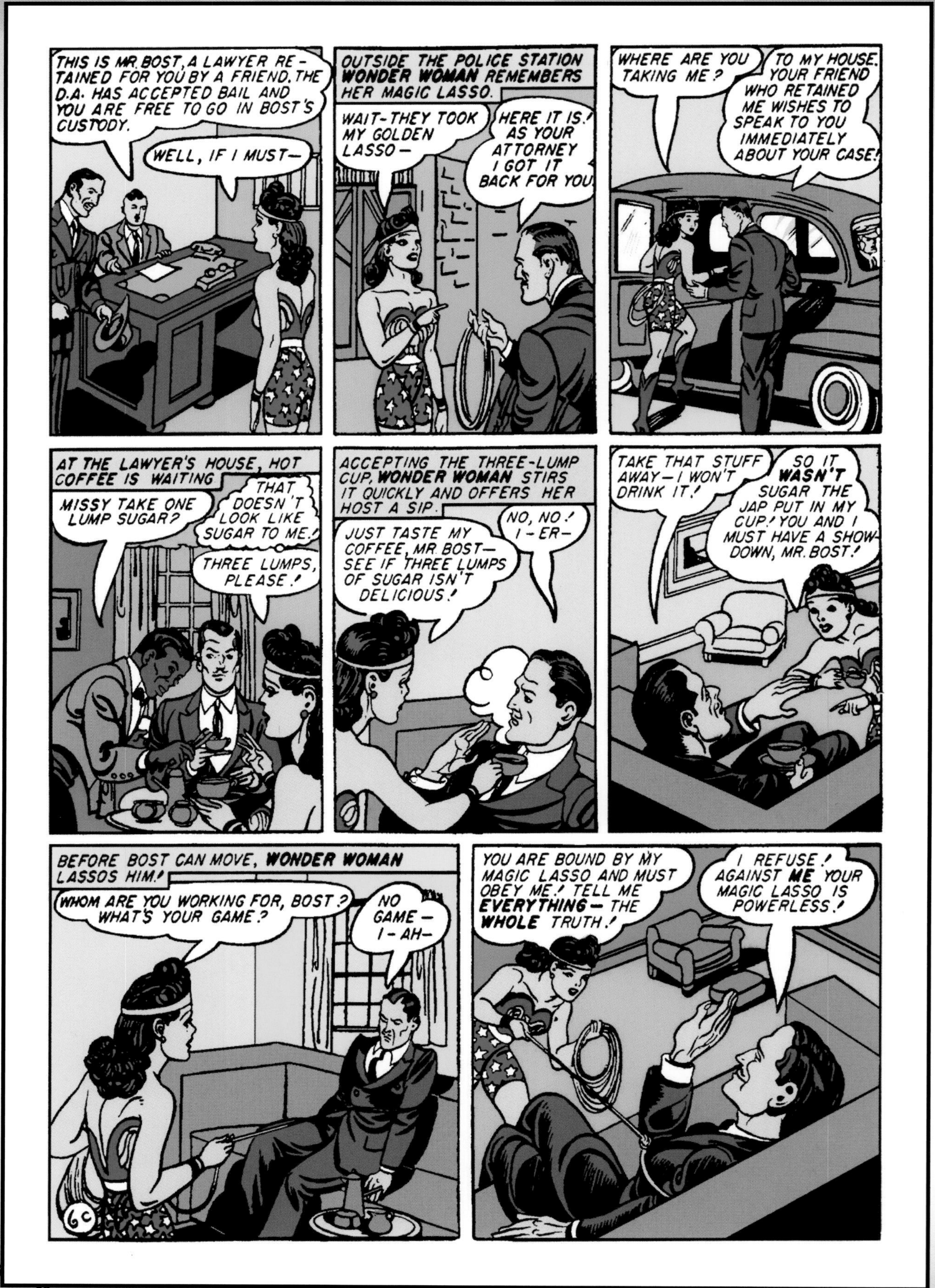
THIS IS MR. BOST, A LAWYER RETAINED FOR YOU BY A FRIEND. THE D.A. HAS ACCEPTED BAIL AND YOU ARE FREE TO GO IN BOST'S CUSTODY.
WELL, IF I MUST—
OUTSIDE THE POLICE STATION WONDER WOMAN REMEMBERS HER MAGIC LASSO.
WAIT-THEY TOOK MY GOLDEN LASSO—
HERE IT IS! AS YOUR ATTORNEY I GOT IT BACK FOR YOU
WHERE ARE YOU TAKING ME?
TO MY HOUSE. YOUR FRIEND WHO RETAINED ME WISHES TO SPEAK TO YOU IMMEDIATELY ABOUT YOUR CASE!
AT THE LAWYER'S HOUSE, HOT COFFEE IS WAITING
MISSY TAKE ONE LUMP SUGAR?
THAT DOESN'T LOOK LIKE SUGAR TO ME!
THREE LUMPS, PLEASE!
ACCEPTING THE THREE-LUMP CUP, WONDER WOMAN STIRS IT QUICKLY AND OFFERS HER HOST A SIP.
JUST TASTE MY COFFEE, MR. BOST— SEE IF THREE LUMPS OF SUGAR ISN'T DELICIOUS!
NO, NO! I-ER-
TAKE THAT STUFF AWAY—I WON'T DRINK IT!
SO IT WASN'T SUGAR THE JAP PUT IN MY CUP! YOU AND I MUST HAVE A SHOW-DOWN, MR. BOST!
BEFORE BOST CAN MOVE, WONDER WOMAN LASSOS HIM!
WHOM ARE YOU WORKING FOR, BOST? WHAT'S YOUR GAME?
NO GAME— I-AH-
6C
YOU ARE BOUND BY MY MAGIC LASSO AND MUST OBEY ME! TELL ME EVERYTHING— THE WHOLE TRUTH!
I REFUSE! AGAINST ME YOUR MAGIC LASSO IS POWERLESS!

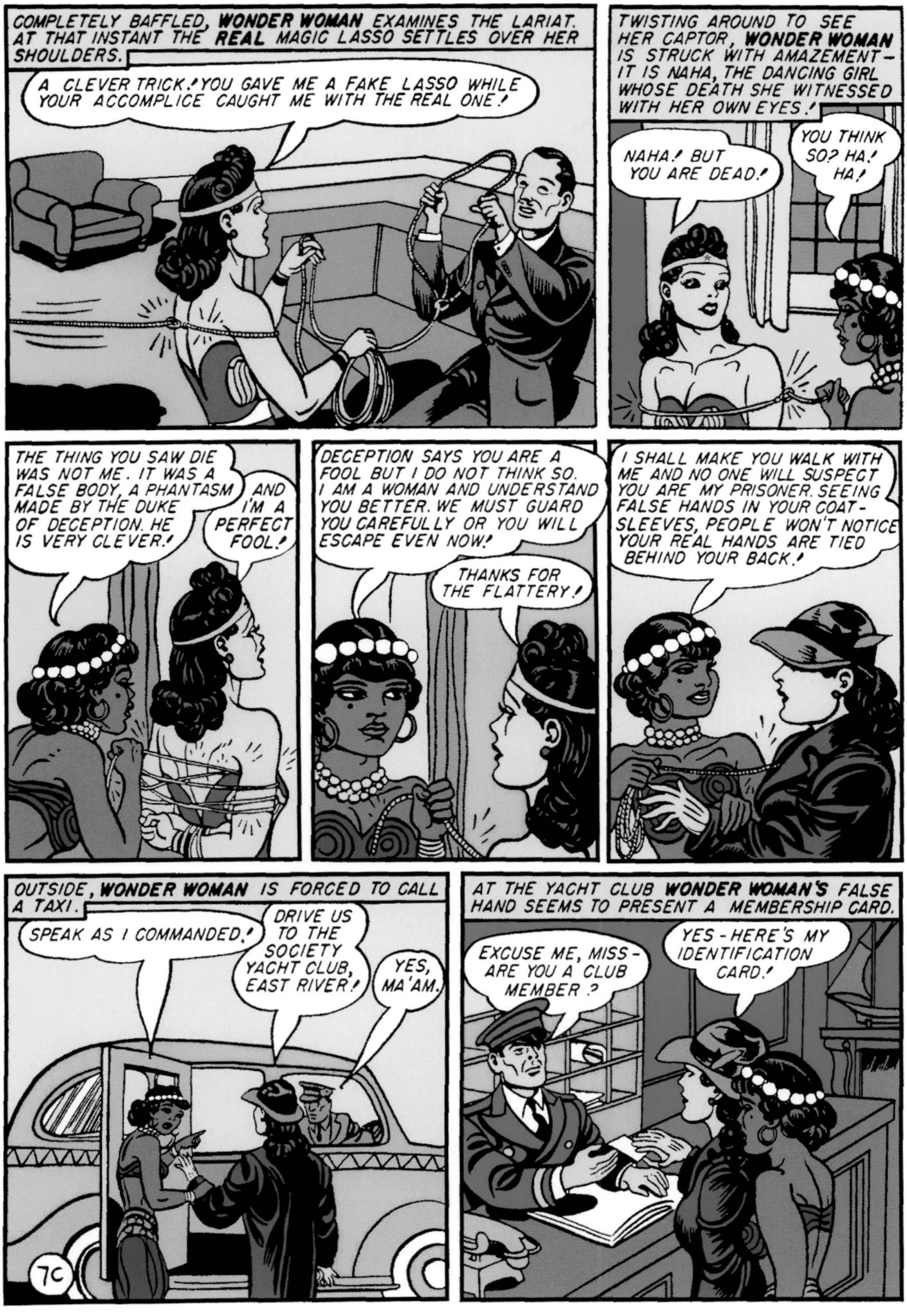
COMPLETELY BAFFLED, WONDER WOMAN EXAMINES THE LARIAT. AT THAT INSTANT THE REAL MAGIC LASSO SETTLES OVER HER SHOULDERS.
A CLEVER TRICK! YOU GAVE ME A FAKE LASSO WHILE YOUR ACCOMPLICE CAUGHT ME WITH THE REAL ONE!
TWISTING AROUND TO SEE HER CAPTOR, WONDER WOMAN IS STRUCK WITH AMAZEMENT— IT IS NAHA, THE DANCING GIRL WHOSE DEATH SHE WITNESSED WITH HER OWN EYES!
NAHA! BUT YOU ARE DEAD!
YOU THINK SO? HA! HA!
THE THING YOU SAW DIE WAS NOT ME. IT WAS A FALSE BODY, A PHANTASM MADE BY THE DUKE OF DECEPTION. HE IS VERY CLEVER!
AND I'M A PERFECT FOOL!
DECEPTION SAYS YOU ARE A FOOL BUT I DO NOT THINK SO. I AM A WOMAN AND UNDERSTAND YOU BETTER. WE MUST GUARD YOU CAREFULLY OR YOU WILL ESCAPE EVEN NOW!
THANKS FOR THE FLATTERY!
I SHALL MAKE YOU WALK WITH ME AND NO ONE WILL SUSPECT YOU ARE MY PRISONER. SEEING FALSE HANDS IN YOUR COAT-SLEEVES, PEOPLE WON'T NOTICE YOUR REAL HANDS ARE TIED BEHIND YOUR BACK!
OUTSIDE, WONDER WOMAN IS FORCED TO CALL A TAXI.
SPEAK AS I COMMANDED!
DRIVE US TO THE SOCIETY YACHT CLUB, EAST RIVER!
YES, MA'AM.
7C
AT THE YACHT CLUB WONDER WOMAN'S FALSE HAND SEEMS TO PRESENT A MEMBERSHIP CARD.
EXCUSE ME, MISS- ARE YOU A CLUB MEMBER ?
YES - HERE'S MY IDENTIFICATION CARD!

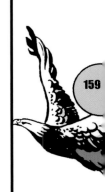

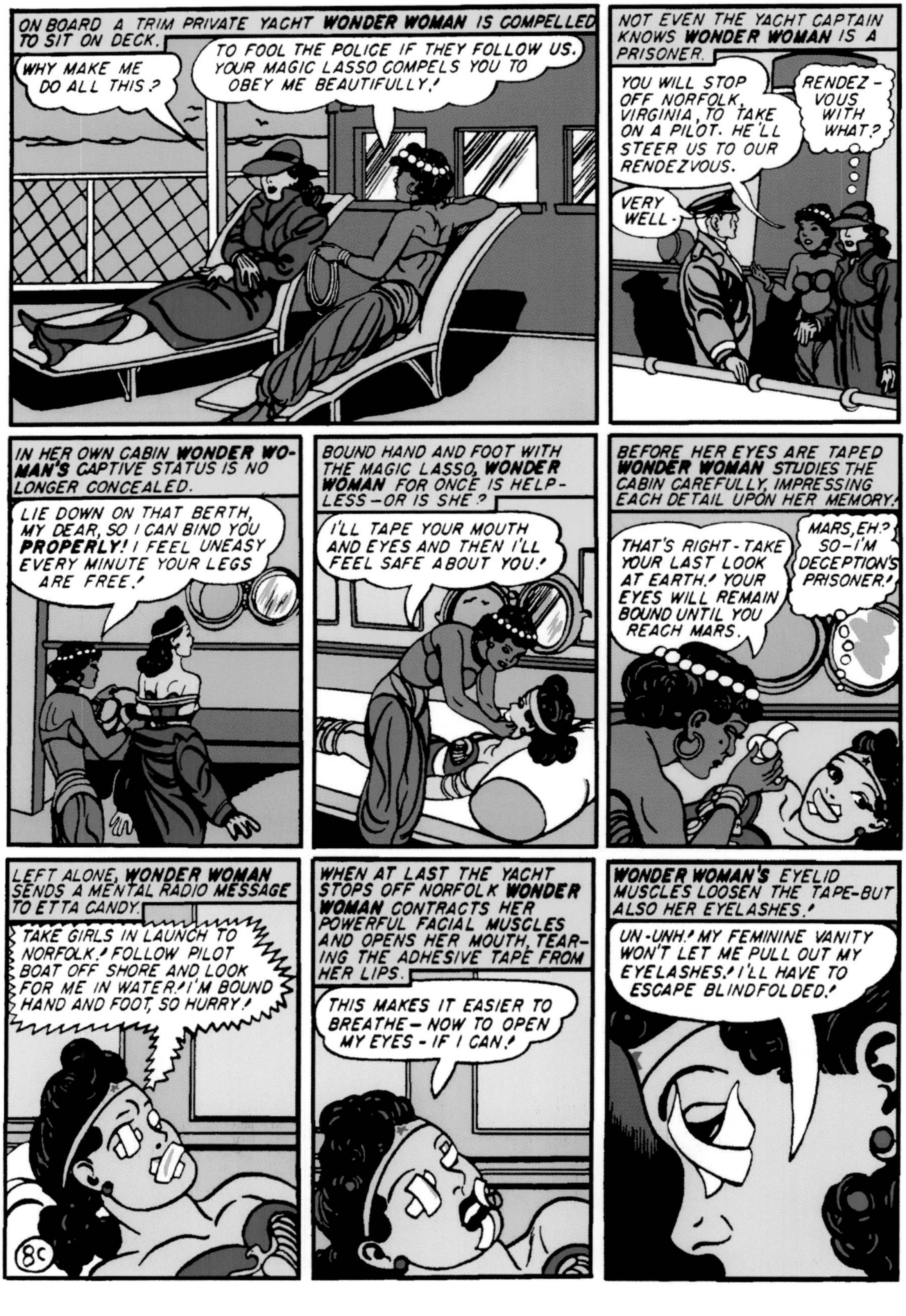
ON BOARD A TRIM PRIVATE YACHT WONDER WOMAN IS COMPELLED TO SIT ON DECK.
WHY MAKE ME DO ALL THIS?
TO FOOL THE POLICE IF THEY FOLLOW US. YOUR MAGIC LASSO COMPELS YOU TO OBEY ME BEAUTIFULLY!
NOT EVEN THE YACHT CAPTAIN KNOWS WONDER WOMAN IS A PRISONER.
YOU WILL STOP OFF NORFOLK, VIRGINIA, TO TAKE ON A PILOT. HE'LL STEER US TO OUR RENDEZVOUS.
RENDEZ-VOUS WITH WHAT?
VERY WELL-
IN HER OWN CABIN WONDER WOMAN'S CAPTIVE STATUS IS NO LONGER CONCEALED.
LIE DOWN ON THAT BERTH, MY DEAR, SO I CAN BIND YOU PROPERLY! I FEEL UNEASY EVERY MINUTE YOUR LEGS ARE FREE!
BOUND HAND AND FOOT WITH THE MAGIC LASSO, WONDER WOMAN FOR ONCE IS HELPLESS—OR IS SHE?
I'LL TAPE YOUR MOUTH AND EYES AND THEN I'LL FEEL SAFE ABOUT YOU!
BEFORE HER EYES ARE TAPED WONDER WOMAN STUDIES THE CABIN CAREFULLY, IMPRESSING EACH DETAIL UPON HER MEMORY!
THAT'S RIGHT-TAKE YOUR LAST LOOK AT EARTH! YOUR EYES WILL REMAIN BOUND UNTIL YOU REACH MARS.
MARS, EH? SO-I'M DECEPTION'S PRISONER!
LEFT ALONE, WONDER WOMAN SENDS A MENTAL RADIO MESSAGE TO ETTA CANDY.
TAKE GIRLS IN LAUNCH TO NORFOLK! FOLLOW PILOT BOAT OFF SHORE AND LOOK FOR ME IN WATER! I'M BOUND HAND AND FOOT, SO HURRY!
8C
WHEN AT LAST THE YACHT STOPS OFF NORFOLK WONDER WOMAN CONTRACTS HER POWERFUL FACIAL MUSCLES AND OPENS HER MOUTH, TEARING THE ADHESIVE TAPE FROM HER LIPS.
THIS MAKES IT EASIER TO BREATHE—NOW TO OPEN MY EYES-IF I CAN!
WONDER WOMAN'S EYELID MUSCLES LOOSEN THE TAPE-BUT ALSO HER EYELASHES!
UN-UNH! MY FEMININE VANITY WON'T LET ME PULL OUT MY EYELASHES! I'LL HAVE TO ESCAPE BLINDFOLDED!

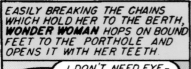

EASILY BREAKING THE CHAINS WHICH HOLD HER TO THE BERTH, **WONDER WOMAN** HOPS ON BOUND FEET TO THE PORTHOLE AND OPENS IT WITH HER TEETH.

I DON'T NEED EYE-SIGHT HERE—I REMEMBER THIS PORTHOLE LATCH PERFECTLY.

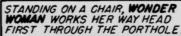

STANDING ON A CHAIR, **WONDER WOMAN** WORKS HER WAY HEAD FIRST THROUGH THE PORTHOLE.

BUT NAHA, LEANING OVER THE DECK RAIL ABOVE, SEES **WONDER WOMAN** PLUNGE INTO THE SEA. UNHESITATINGLY THE HAWAIIAN GIRL DIVES AFTER HER.!

WONDER WOMAN IS MARVEL-OUS! I'D LOVE TO LET HER ESCAPE BUT DECEPTION WOULD KILL ME!

HANDICAPPED AS SHE IS BY HER BONDS, **WONDER WOMAN** STILL OUTRACES NAHA, WHO WAS A CHAMPION SWIMMER IN HAWAII.

UNABLE TO SEE, HOWEVER, **WONDER WOMAN** SWIMS IN A CIRCLE AND NAHA, CUTTING ACROSS, OVERTAKES THE ESCAPING PRISONER.

SURRENDER,— **WONDER WOMAN**— I'VE CAUGHT YOU AGAIN!

NO! YOU'VE NOT CAUGHT ME UNTIL YOU HOLD THE MAGIC LASSO THAT BINDS ME!

TURNING ON HER BACK, **WONDER WOMAN** THRUSTS HER BOUND FEET AGAINST NAHA'S BODY AND PUSHES WITH ALL HER MIGHT.

OW-W-W! YOU'RE KILLING ME!

NO—JUST **KICKING** YOU!

9c

AT THIS MOMENT ETTA CANDY AND HER GIRLS DASH UP IN THEIR SPEED LAUNCH. NAHA, LIFTED CLEAR OF THE WATER BY **WONDER WOMAN'S** POWER-FUL KICK, LANDS IN THE BOAT!

WEH—EE-E-OW!

NICE KICKING, **WONDER WOMAN**, OLD GIRL!

WONDER WOMAN, FREED OF HER BONDS, ADMINISTERS SOME BAD-LY NEEDED CHASTISEMENT.

YOU'RE A SILLY GIRL, NAHA, TO LET DE-CEPTION RULE YOU! I'M GOING TO CURE YOU OF THIS FOOL-ISHNESS!

OW—OW! I'M CURED! I'LL OBEY YOU!

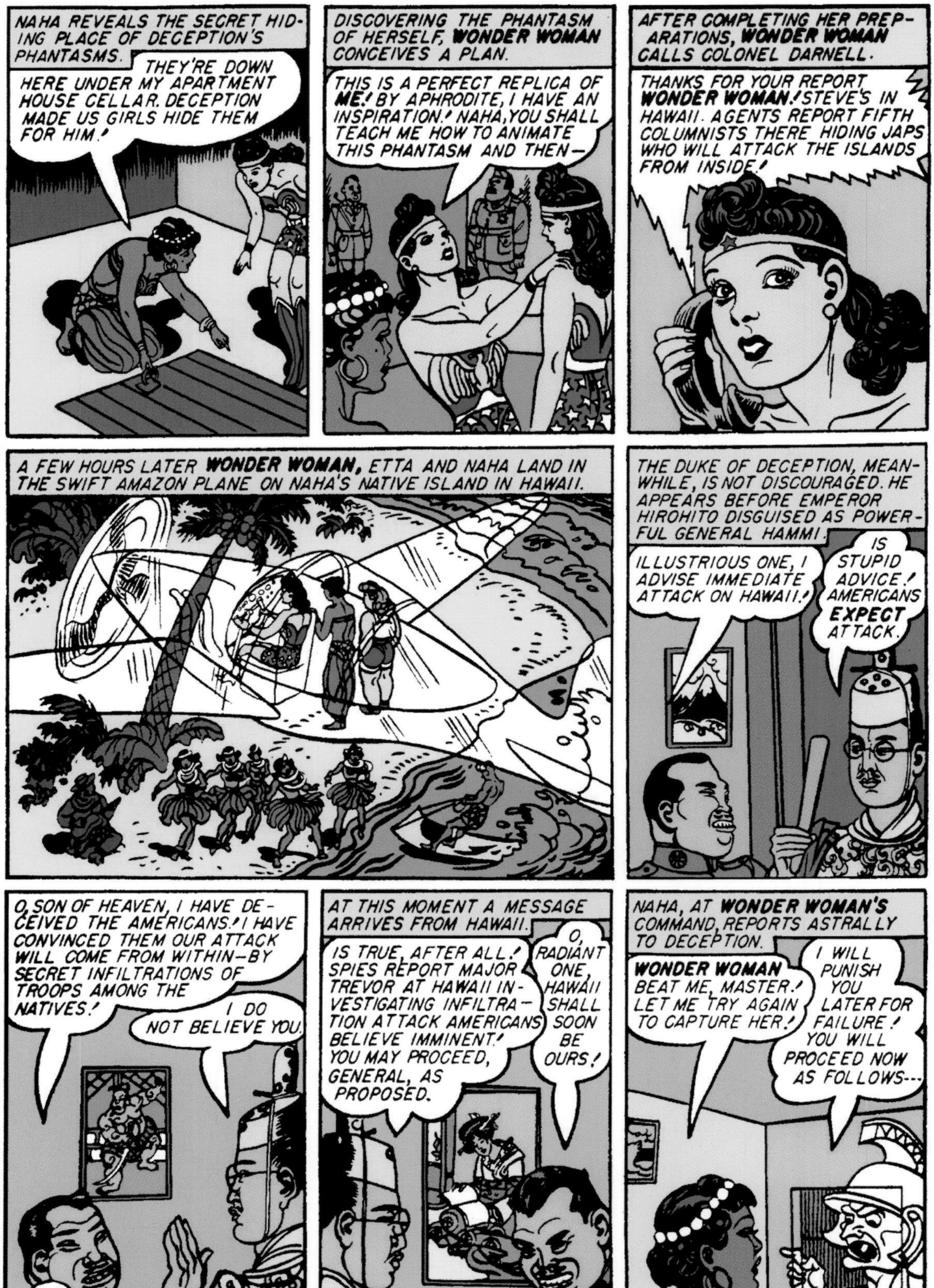
NAHA REVEALS THE SECRET HIDING PLACE OF DECEPTION'S PHANTASMS.
THEY'RE DOWN HERE UNDER MY APARTMENT HOUSE CELLAR. DECEPTION MADE US GIRLS HIDE THEM FOR HIM!
DISCOVERING THE PHANTASM OF HERSELF, WONDER WOMAN CONCEIVES A PLAN.
THIS IS A PERFECT REPLICA OF ME! BY APHRODITE, I HAVE AN INSPIRATION! NAHA, YOU SHALL TEACH ME HOW TO ANIMATE THIS PHANTASM AND THEN—
AFTER COMPLETING HER PREPARATIONS, WONDER WOMAN CALLS COLONEL DARNELL.
THANKS FOR YOUR REPORT WONDER WOMAN! STEVE'S IN HAWAII. AGENTS REPORT FIFTH COLUMNISTS THERE HIDING JAPS WHO WILL ATTACK THE ISLANDS FROM INSIDE!
A FEW HOURS LATER WONDER WOMAN, ETTA AND NAHA LAND IN THE SWIFT AMAZON PLANE ON NAHA'S NATIVE ISLAND IN HAWAII.
THE DUKE OF DECEPTION, MEANWHILE, IS NOT DISCOURAGED. HE APPEARS BEFORE EMPEROR HIROHITO DISGUISED AS POWERFUL GENERAL HAMMI.
ILLUSTRIOUS ONE, I ADVISE IMMEDIATE ATTACK ON HAWAII!
IS STUPID ADVICE! AMERICANS EXPECT ATTACK.
O, SON OF HEAVEN, I HAVE DECEIVED THE AMERICANS! I HAVE CONVINCED THEM OUR ATTACK WILL COME FROM WITHIN—BY SECRET INFILTRATIONS OF TROOPS AMONG THE NATIVES!
I DO NOT BELIEVE YOU.
10¢
AT THIS MOMENT A MESSAGE ARRIVES FROM HAWAII.
IS TRUE, AFTER ALL! SPIES REPORT MAJOR TREVOR AT HAWAII INVESTIGATING INFILTRATION ATTACK AMERICANS BELIEVE IMMINENT! YOU MAY PROCEED, GENERAL, AS PROPOSED.
O, RADIANT ONE, HAWAII SHALL SOON BE OURS!
NAHA, AT WONDER WOMAN'S COMMAND, REPORTS ASTRALLY TO DECEPTION.
WONDER WOMAN BEAT ME, MASTER! LET ME TRY AGAIN TO CAPTURE HER!
I WILL PUNISH YOU LATER FOR FAILURE! YOU WILL PROCEED NOW AS FOLLOWS---

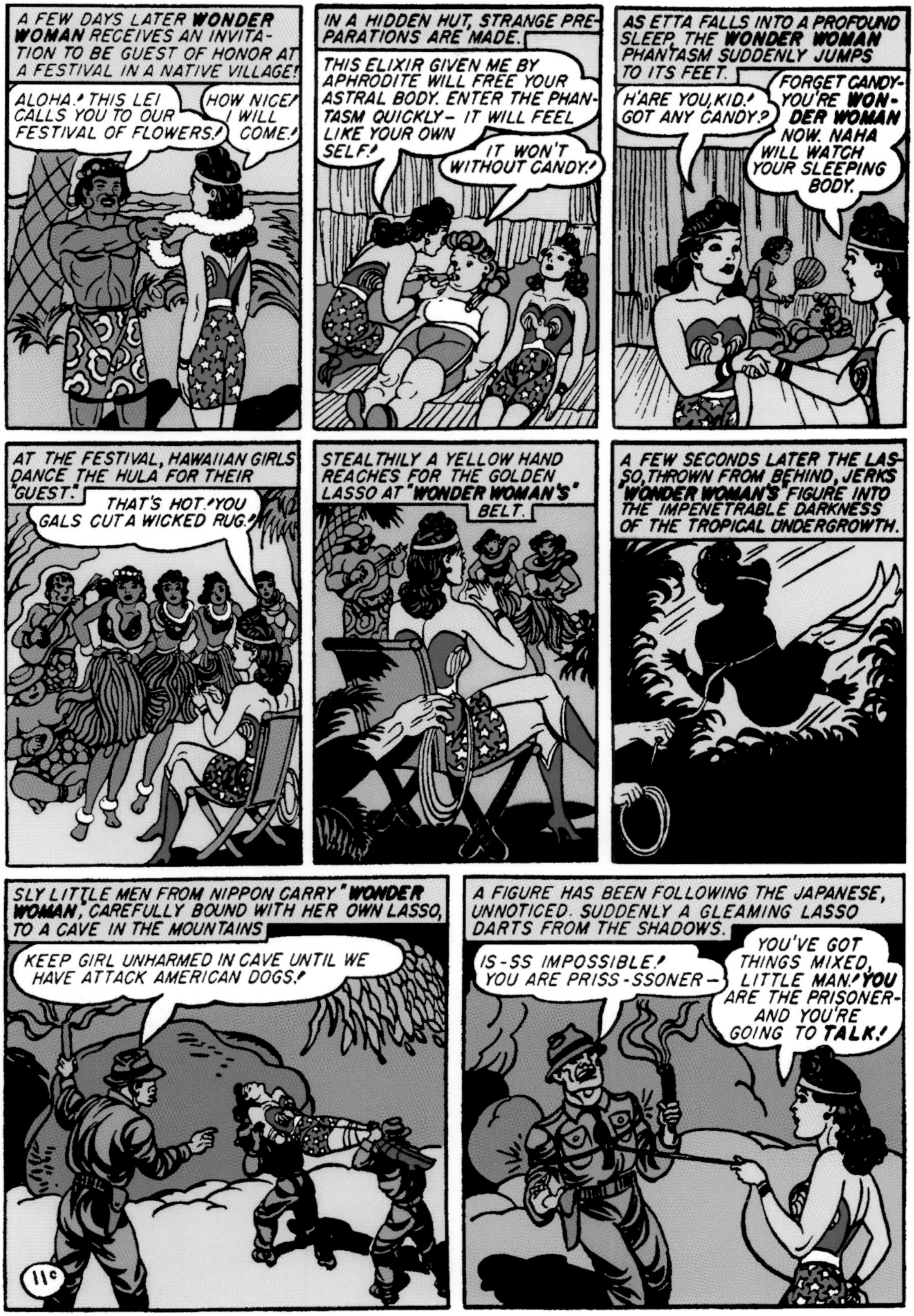
A FEW DAYS LATER WONDER WOMAN RECEIVES AN INVITATION TO BE GUEST OF HONOR AT A FESTIVAL IN A NATIVE VILLAGE!
ALOHA! THIS LEI CALLS YOU TO OUR FESTIVAL OF FLOWERS!
HOW NICE! I WILL COME!
IN A HIDDEN HUT, STRANGE PREPARATIONS ARE MADE.
THIS ELIXIR GIVEN ME BY APHRODITE WILL FREE YOUR ASTRAL BODY. ENTER THE PHANTASM QUICKLY– IT WILL FEEL LIKE YOUR OWN SELF!
IT WON'T WITHOUT CANDY!
AS ETTA FALLS INTO A PROFOUND SLEEP, THE WONDER WOMAN PHANTASM SUDDENLY JUMPS TO ITS FEET.
H'ARE YOU, KID! GOT ANY CANDY?
FORGET CANDY–YOU'RE WONDER WOMAN NOW. NAHA WILL WATCH YOUR SLEEPING BODY.
AT THE FESTIVAL, HAWAIIAN GIRLS DANCE THE HULA FOR THEIR "GUEST."
THAT'S HOT! YOU GALS CUT A WICKED RUG!
STEALTHILY A YELLOW HAND REACHES FOR THE GOLDEN LASSO AT "WONDER WOMAN'S" BELT.
A FEW SECONDS LATER THE LASSO, THROWN FROM BEHIND, JERKS "WONDER WOMAN'S" FIGURE INTO THE IMPENETRABLE DARKNESS OF THE TROPICAL UNDERGROWTH.
SLY LITTLE MEN FROM NIPPON CARRY "WONDER WOMAN", CAREFULLY BOUND WITH HER OWN LASSO, TO A CAVE IN THE MOUNTAINS
KEEP GIRL UNHARMED IN CAVE UNTIL WE HAVE ATTACK AMERICAN DOGS!
11c
A FIGURE HAS BEEN FOLLOWING THE JAPANESE, UNNOTICED. SUDDENLY A GLEAMING LASSO DARTS FROM THE SHADOWS.
IS-SS IMPOSSIBLE! YOU ARE PRISS-SSONER–
YOU'VE GOT THINGS MIXED, LITTLE MAN! YOU ARE THE PRISONER–AND YOU'RE GOING TO TALK!

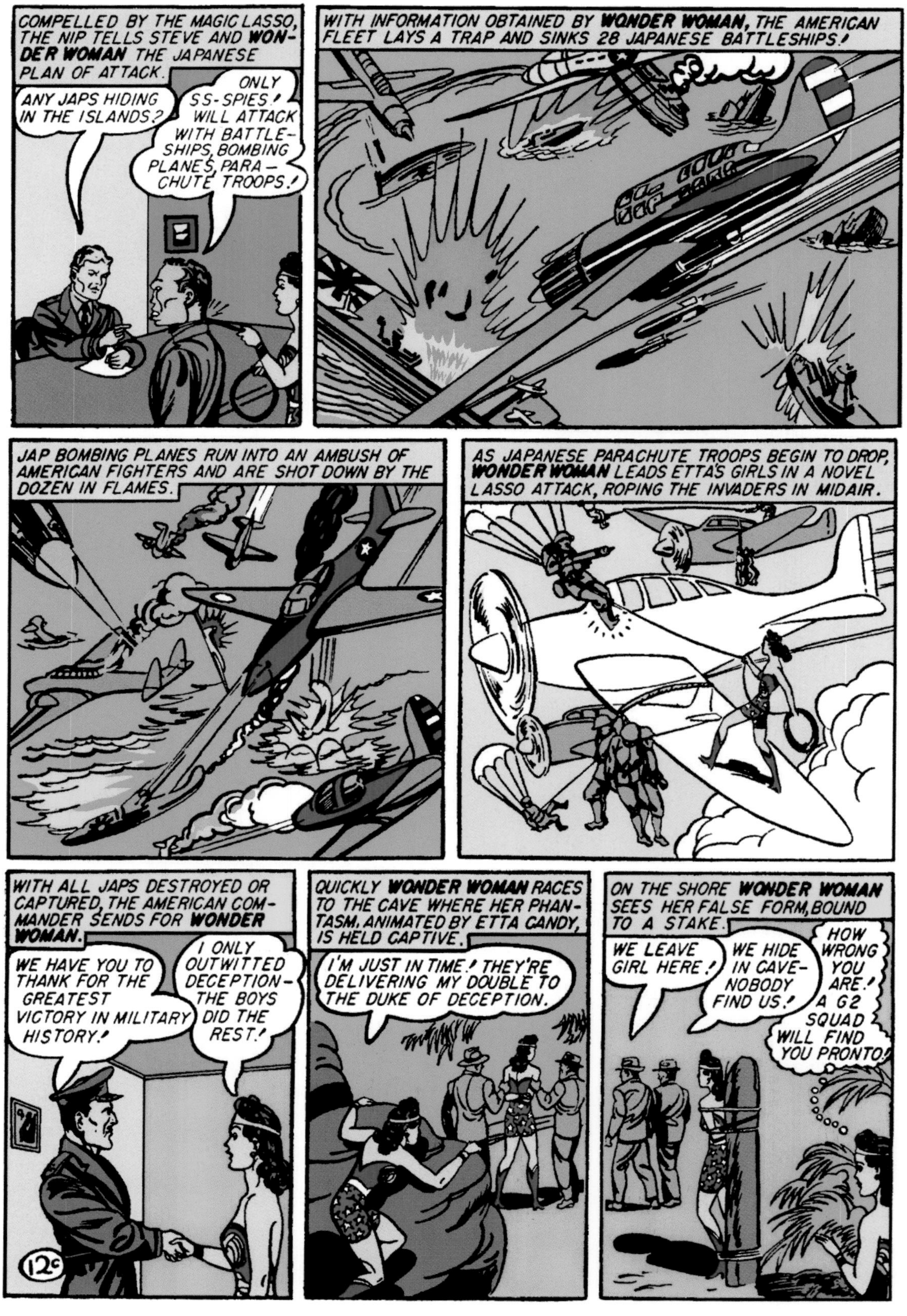
COMPELLED BY THE MAGIC LASSO, THE NIP TELLS STEVE AND WONDER WOMAN THE JAPANESE PLAN OF ATTACK.
ANY JAPS HIDING IN THE ISLANDS?
ONLY SS-SPIES! WILL ATTACK WITH BATTLESHIPS, BOMBING PLANES, PARACHUTE TROOPS!
WITH INFORMATION OBTAINED BY WONDER WOMAN, THE AMERICAN FLEET LAYS A TRAP AND SINKS 28 JAPANESE BATTLESHIPS!
JAP BOMBING PLANES RUN INTO AN AMBUSH OF AMERICAN FIGHTERS AND ARE SHOT DOWN BY THE DOZEN IN FLAMES.
AS JAPANESE PARACHUTE TROOPS BEGIN TO DROP, WONDER WOMAN LEADS ETTA'S GIRLS IN A NOVEL LASSO ATTACK, ROPING THE INVADERS IN MIDAIR.
WITH ALL JAPS DESTROYED OR CAPTURED, THE AMERICAN COMMANDER SENDS FOR WONDER WOMAN.
WE HAVE YOU TO THANK FOR THE GREATEST VICTORY IN MILITARY HISTORY!
I ONLY OUTWITTED DECEPTION-THE BOYS DID THE REST!
12c
QUICKLY WONDER WOMAN RACES TO THE CAVE WHERE HER PHANTASM, ANIMATED BY ETTA CANDY, IS HELD CAPTIVE.
I'M JUST IN TIME! THEY'RE DELIVERING MY DOUBLE TO THE DUKE OF DECEPTION.
ON THE SHORE WONDER WOMAN SEES HER FALSE FORM, BOUND TO A STAKE.
WE LEAVE GIRL HERE!
WE HIDE IN CAVE-NOBODY FIND US!
HOW WRONG YOU ARE! A G2 SQUAD WILL FIND YOU PRONTO!

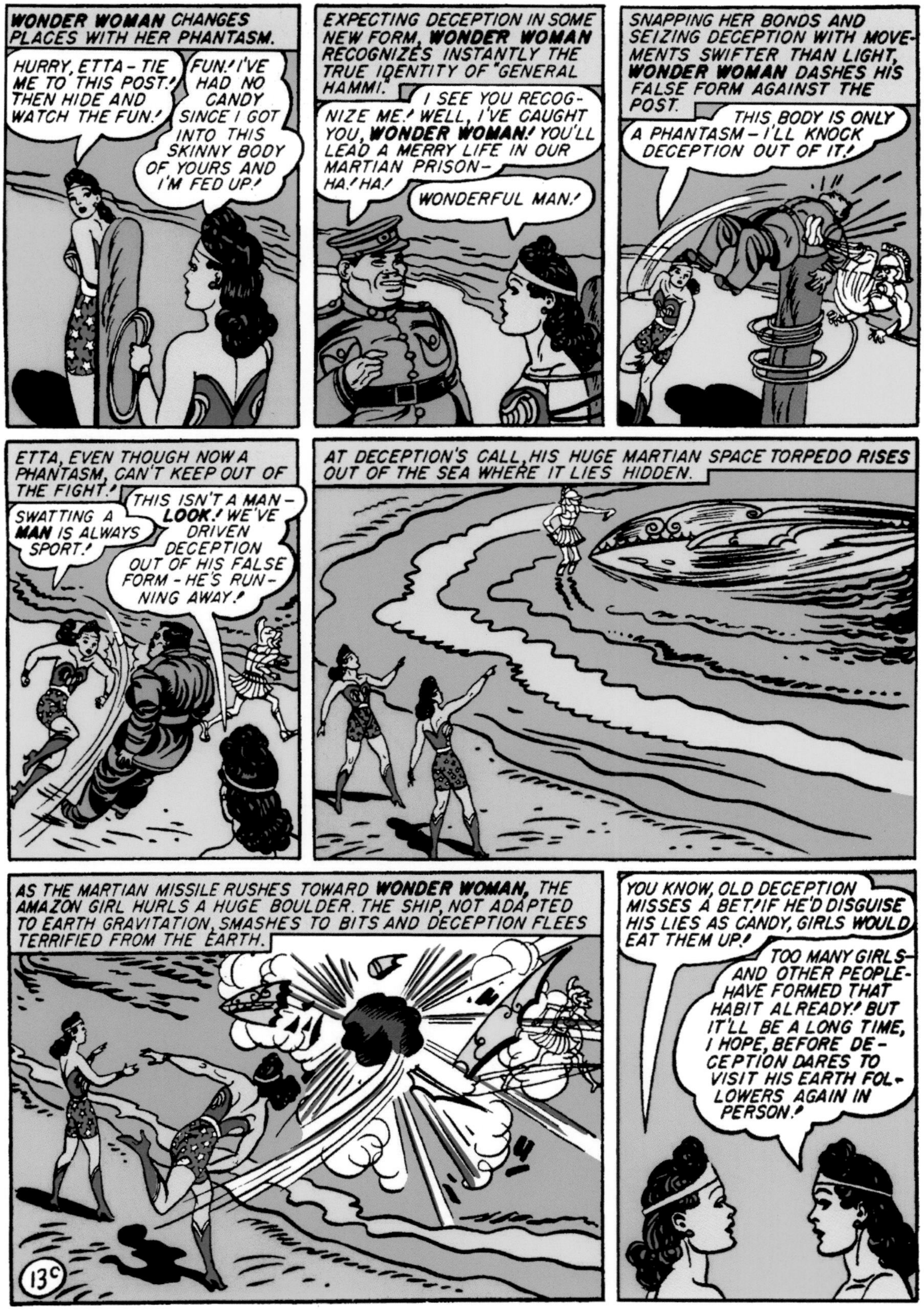
WONDER WOMAN CHANGES PLACES WITH HER PHANTASM.
HURRY, ETTA–TIE ME TO THIS POST! THEN HIDE AND WATCH THE FUN!
FUN! I'VE HAD NO CANDY SINCE I GOT INTO THIS SKINNY BODY OF YOURS AND I'M FED UP!
EXPECTING DECEPTION IN SOME NEW FORM, WONDER WOMAN RECOGNIZES INSTANTLY THE TRUE IDENTITY OF "GENERAL HAMMI."
I SEE YOU RECOGNIZE ME! WELL, I'VE CAUGHT YOU, WONDER WOMAN! YOU'LL LEAD A MERRY LIFE IN OUR MARTIAN PRISON–HA! HA!
WONDERFUL MAN!
SNAPPING HER BONDS AND SEIZING DECEPTION WITH MOVEMENTS SWIFTER THAN LIGHT, WONDER WOMAN DASHES HIS FALSE FORM AGAINST THE POST.
THIS BODY IS ONLY A PHANTASM–I'LL KNOCK DECEPTION OUT OF IT!
ETTA, EVEN THOUGH NOW A PHANTASM, CAN'T KEEP OUT OF THE FIGHT!
SWATTING A MAN IS ALWAYS SPORT!
THIS ISN'T A MAN–LOOK! WE'VE DRIVEN DECEPTION OUT OF HIS FALSE FORM–HE'S RUNNING AWAY!
AT DECEPTION'S CALL, HIS HUGE MARTIAN SPACE TORPEDO RISES OUT OF THE SEA WHERE IT LIES HIDDEN.
AS THE MARTIAN MISSILE RUSHES TOWARD WONDER WOMAN, THE AMAZON GIRL HURLS A HUGE BOULDER. THE SHIP, NOT ADAPTED TO EARTH GRAVITATION, SMASHES TO BITS AND DECEPTION FLEES TERRIFIED FROM THE EARTH.
13C
YOU KNOW, OLD DECEPTION MISSES A BET! IF HE'D DISGUISE HIS LIES AS CANDY, GIRLS WOULD EAT THEM UP!
TOO MANY GIRLS–AND OTHER PEOPLE–HAVE FORMED THAT HABIT ALREADY! BUT IT'LL BE A LONG TIME, I HOPE, BEFORE DECEPTION DARES TO VISIT HIS EARTH FOLLOWERS AGAIN IN PERSON!

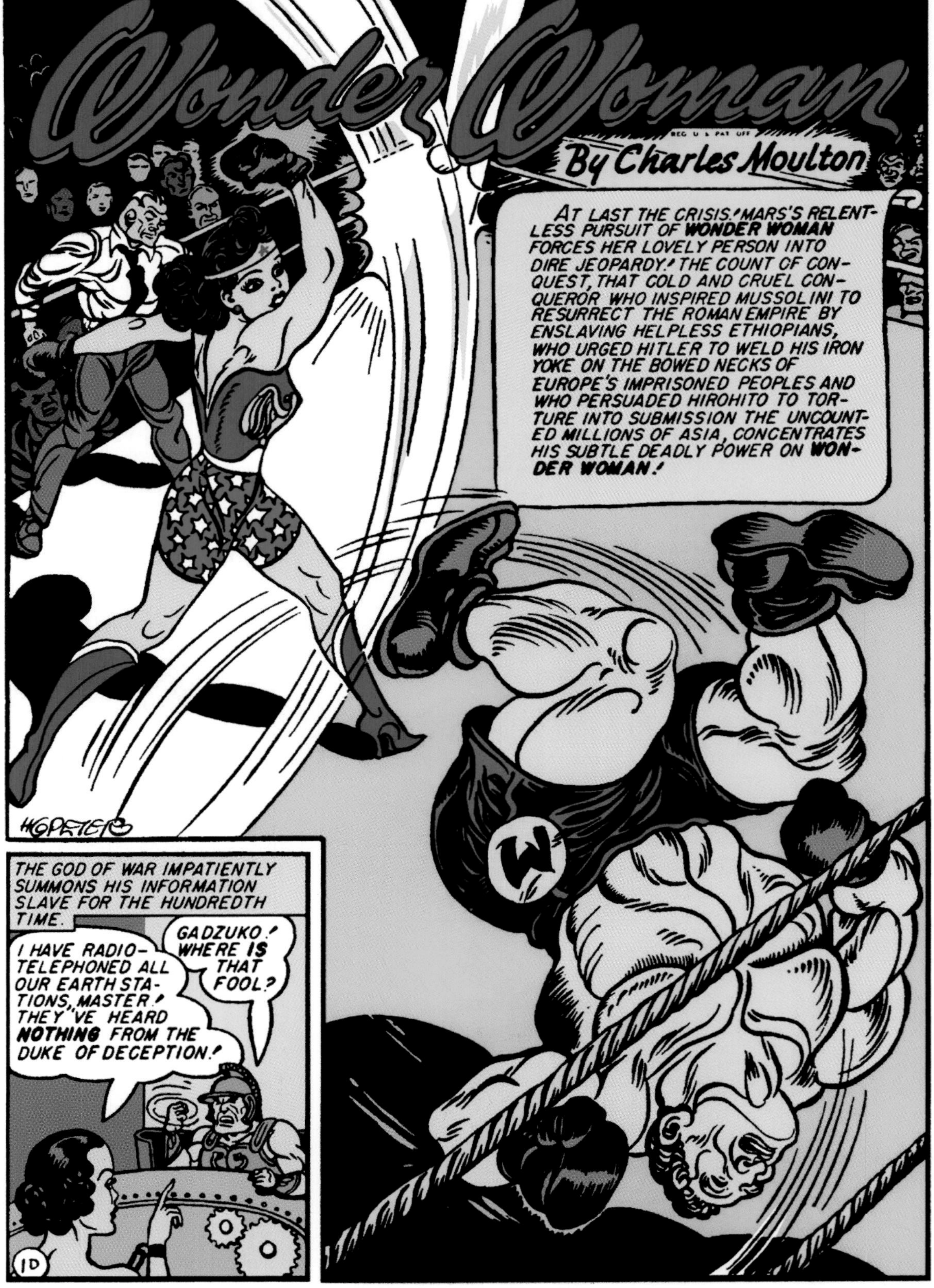
Wonder Woman
REG. U.S. PAT. OFF.
By Charles Moulton
AT LAST THE CRISIS! MARS'S RELENTLESS PURSUIT OF WONDER WOMAN FORCES HER LOVELY PERSON INTO DIRE JEOPARDY! THE COUNT OF CONQUEST, THAT COLD AND CRUEL CONQUEROR WHO INSPIRED MUSSOLINI TO RESURRECT THE ROMAN EMPIRE BY ENSLAVING HELPLESS ETHIOPIANS, WHO URGED HITLER TO WELD HIS IRON YOKE ON THE BOWED NECKS OF EUROPE'S IMPRISONED PEOPLES AND WHO PERSUADED HIROHITO TO TORTURE INTO SUBMISSION THE UNCOUNTED MILLIONS OF ASIA, CONCENTRATES HIS SUBTLE DEADLY POWER ON WONDER WOMAN!
HGPETER
THE GOD OF WAR IMPATIENTLY SUMMONS HIS INFORMATION SLAVE FOR THE HUNDREDTH TIME.
GADZUKO! WHERE IS THAT FOOL?
I HAVE RADIO-TELEPHONED ALL OUR EARTH STATIONS, MASTER! THEY'VE HEARD NOTHING FROM THE DUKE OF DECEPTION!
1D

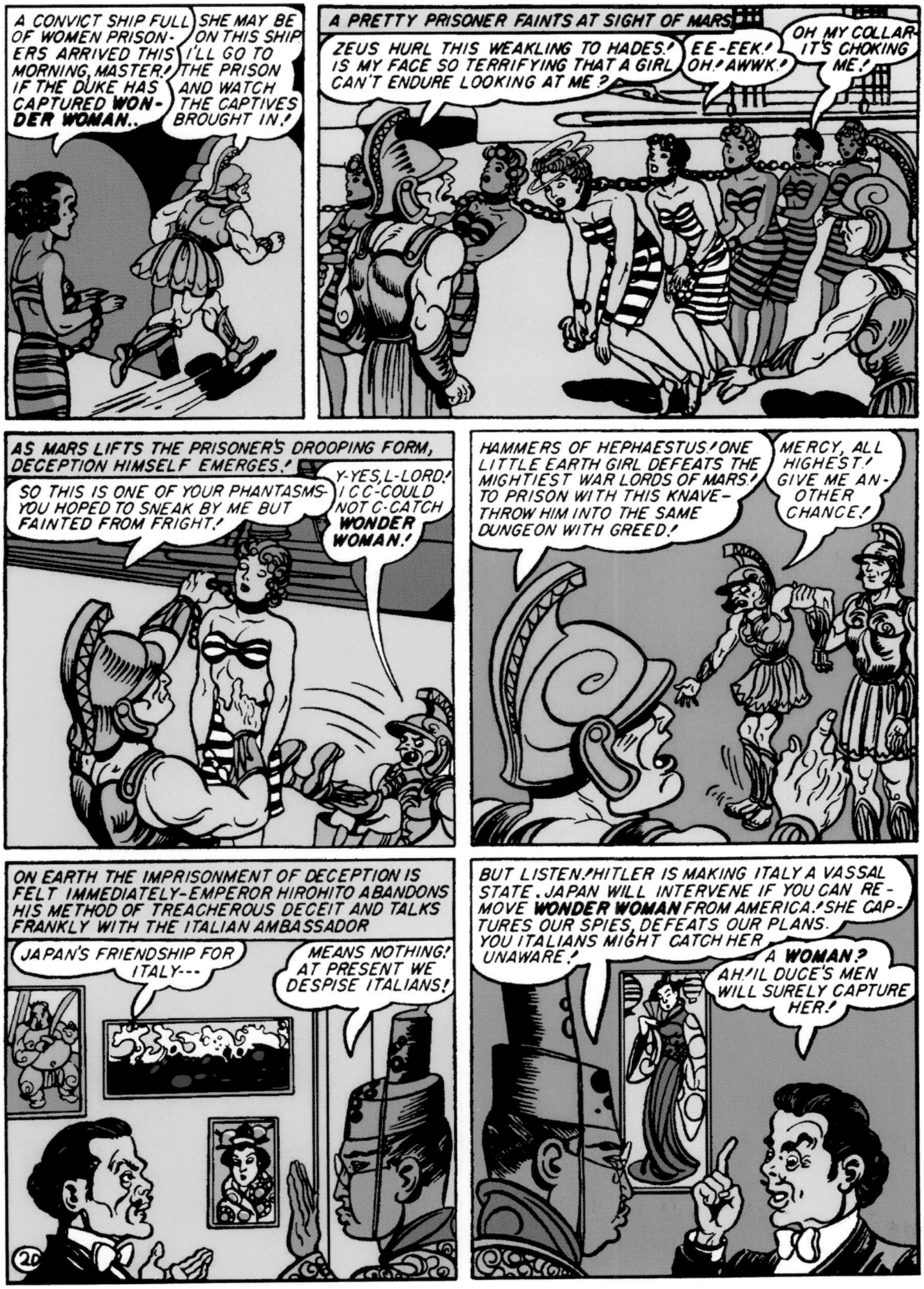
A CONVICT SHIP FULL OF WOMEN PRISONERS ARRIVED THIS MORNING, MASTER! IF THE DUKE HAS CAPTURED WONDER WOMAN..
SHE MAY BE ON THIS SHIP I'LL GO TO THE PRISON AND WATCH THE CAPTIVES BROUGHT IN!
A PRETTY PRISONER FAINTS AT SIGHT OF MARS
ZEUS HURL THIS WEAKLING TO HADES! IS MY FACE SO TERRIFYING THAT A GIRL CAN'T ENDURE LOOKING AT ME?
EE-EEK! OH! AWWK!
OH MY COLLAR IT'S CHOKING ME!
AS MARS LIFTS THE PRISONER'S DROOPING FORM, DECEPTION HIMSELF EMERGES!
SO THIS IS ONE OF YOUR PHANTASMS-YOU HOPED TO SNEAK BY ME BUT FAINTED FROM FRIGHT!
Y-YES, L-LORD! I C-C-COULD NOT C-CATCH WONDER WOMAN!
HAMMERS OF HEPHAESTUS! ONE LITTLE EARTH GIRL DEFEATS THE MIGHTIEST WAR LORDS OF MARS! TO PRISON WITH THIS KNAVE-THROW HIM INTO THE SAME DUNGEON WITH GREED!
MERCY, ALL HIGHEST! GIVE ME ANOTHER CHANCE!
ON EARTH THE IMPRISONMENT OF DECEPTION IS FELT IMMEDIATELY-EMPEROR HIROHITO ABANDONS HIS METHOD OF TREACHEROUS DECEIT AND TALKS FRANKLY WITH THE ITALIAN AMBASSADOR
JAPAN'S FRIENDSHIP FOR ITALY---
MEANS NOTHING! AT PRESENT WE DESPISE ITALIANS!
20
BUT LISTEN! HITLER IS MAKING ITALY A VASSAL STATE. JAPAN WILL INTERVENE IF YOU CAN REMOVE WONDER WOMAN FROM AMERICA! SHE CAPTURES OUR SPIES, DEFEATS OUR PLANS. YOU ITALIANS MIGHT CATCH HER UNAWARE!
A WOMAN? AH! IL DUCE'S MEN WILL SURELY CAPTURE HER!

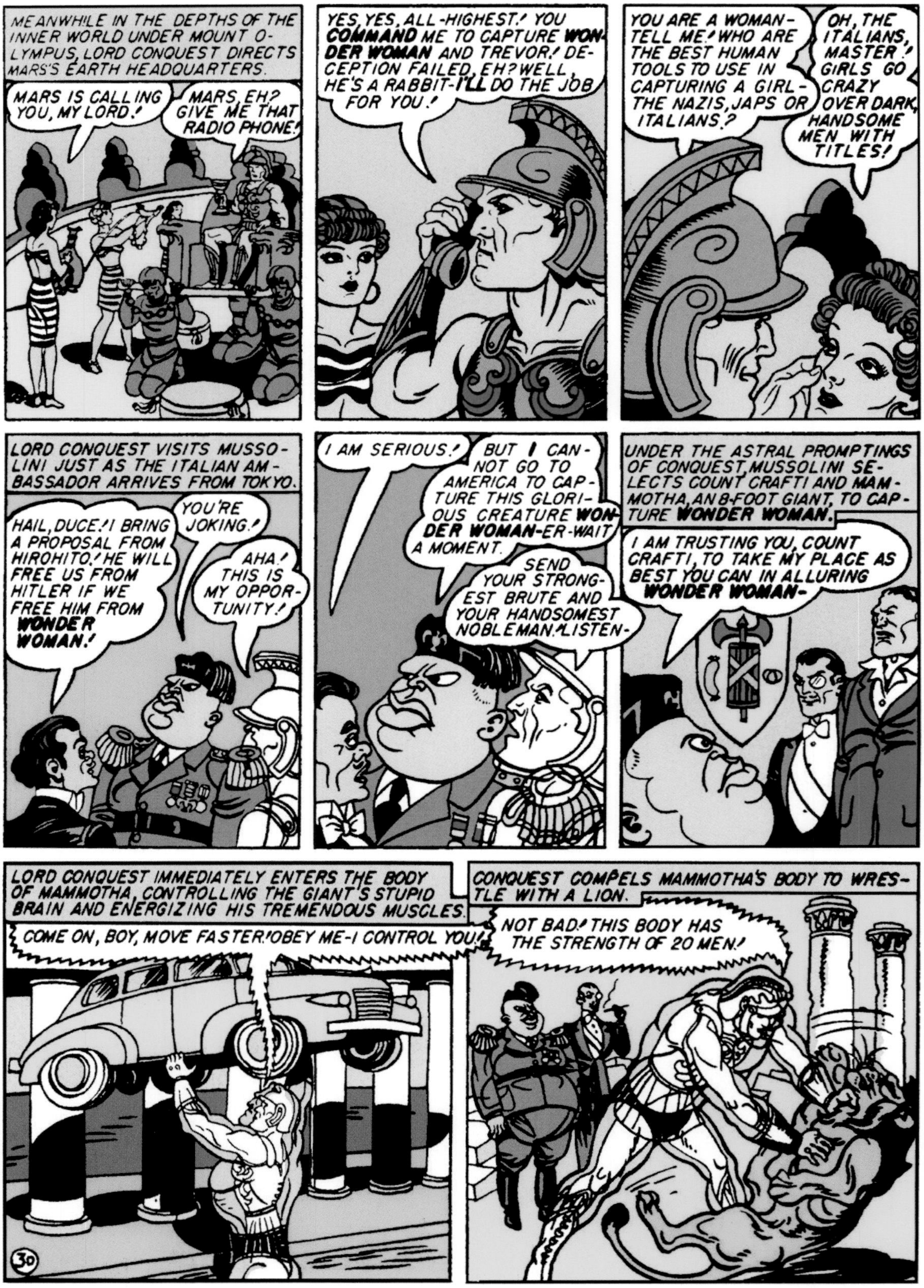

MEANWHILE IN THE DEPTHS OF THE INNER WORLD UNDER MOUNT O-LYMPUS, LORD CONQUEST DIRECTS MARS'S EARTH HEADQUARTERS.
MARS IS CALLING YOU, MY LORD!
MARS, EH? GIVE ME THAT RADIO PHONE!
YES, YES, ALL-HIGHEST! YOU COMMAND ME TO CAPTURE WONDER WOMAN AND TREVOR! DECEPTION FAILED, EH? WELL, HE'S A RABBIT-I'LL DO THE JOB FOR YOU!
YOU ARE A WOMAN-TELL ME! WHO ARE THE BEST HUMAN TOOLS TO USE IN CAPTURING A GIRL-THE NAZIS, JAPS OR ITALIANS?
OH, THE ITALIANS, MASTER! GIRLS GO CRAZY OVER DARK, HANDSOME MEN WITH TITLES!
LORD CONQUEST VISITS MUSSOLINI JUST AS THE ITALIAN AMBASSADOR ARRIVES FROM TOKYO.
HAIL, DUCE! I BRING A PROPOSAL FROM HIROHITO! HE WILL FREE US FROM HITLER IF WE FREE HIM FROM WONDER WOMAN!
YOU'RE JOKING!
AHA! THIS IS MY OPPORTUNITY!
I AM SERIOUS!
BUT I CANNOT GO TO AMERICA TO CAPTURE THIS GLORIOUS CREATURE WONDER WOMAN-ER-WAIT A MOMENT.
SEND YOUR STRONGEST BRUTE AND YOUR HANDSOMEST NOBLEMAN! LISTEN-
UNDER THE ASTRAL PROMPTINGS OF CONQUEST, MUSSOLINI SELECTS COUNT CRAFTI AND MAMMOTHA, AN 8-FOOT GIANT, TO CAPTURE WONDER WOMAN.
I AM TRUSTING YOU, COUNT CRAFTI, TO TAKE MY PLACE AS BEST YOU CAN IN ALLURING WONDER WOMAN-
LORD CONQUEST IMMEDIATELY ENTERS THE BODY OF MAMMOTHA, CONTROLLING THE GIANT'S STUPID BRAIN AND ENERGIZING HIS TREMENDOUS MUSCLES.
COME ON, BOY, MOVE FASTER! OBEY ME-I CONTROL YOU!
30
CONQUEST COMPELS MAMMOTHA'S BODY TO WRESTLE WITH A LION.
NOT BAD! THIS BODY HAS THE STRENGTH OF 20 MEN!

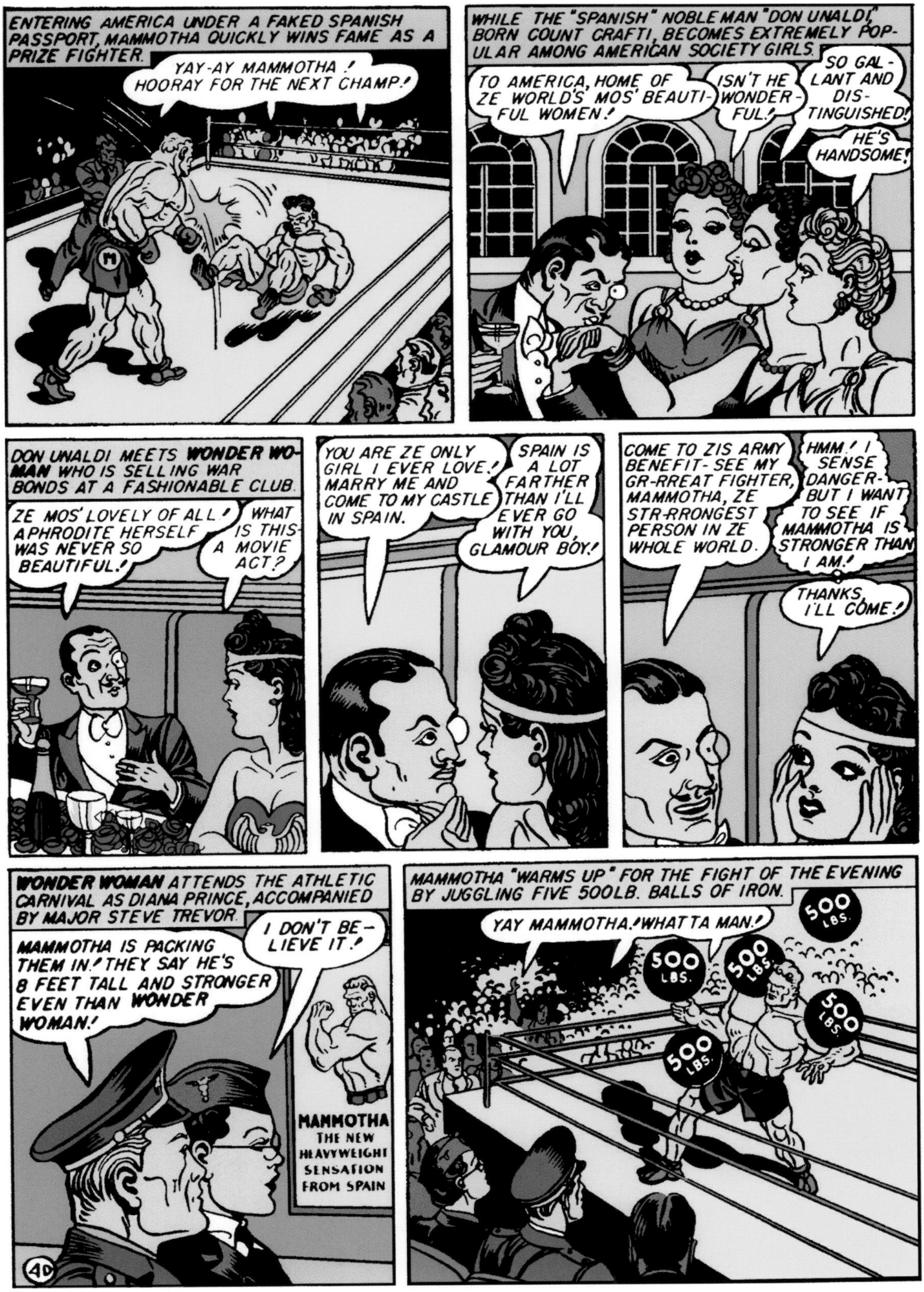
ENTERING AMERICA UNDER A FAKED SPANISH PASSPORT, MAMMOTHA QUICKLY WINS FAME AS A PRIZE FIGHTER.
YAY-AY MAMMOTHA! HOORAY FOR THE NEXT CHAMP!
WHILE THE "SPANISH" NOBLEMAN "DON UNALDI," BORN COUNT CRAFTI, BECOMES EXTREMELY POPULAR AMONG AMERICAN SOCIETY GIRLS.
TO AMERICA, HOME OF ZE WORLD'S MOS' BEAUTIFUL WOMEN!
ISN'T HE WONDERFUL!
SO GALLANT AND DISTINGUISHED!
HE'S HANDSOME!
DON UNALDI MEETS WONDER WOMAN WHO IS SELLING WAR BONDS AT A FASHIONABLE CLUB.
ZE MOS' LOVELY OF ALL! APHRODITE HERSELF WAS NEVER SO BEAUTIFUL!
WHAT IS THIS-A MOVIE ACT?
YOU ARE ZE ONLY GIRL I EVER LOVE! MARRY ME AND COME TO MY CASTLE IN SPAIN.
SPAIN IS A LOT FARTHER THAN I'LL EVER GO WITH YOU, GLAMOUR BOY!
COME TO ZIS ARMY BENEFIT- SEE MY GR-RREAT FIGHTER, MAMMOTHA, ZE STR-RRONGEST PERSON IN ZE WHOLE WORLD.
HMM! I SENSE DANGER- BUT I WANT TO SEE IF MAMMOTHA IS STRONGER THAN I AM!
THANKS, I'LL COME!
WONDER WOMAN ATTENDS THE ATHLETIC CARNIVAL AS DIANA PRINCE, ACCOMPANIED BY MAJOR STEVE TREVOR.
MAMMOTHA IS PACKING THEM IN! THEY SAY HE'S 8 FEET TALL AND STRONGER EVEN THAN WONDER WOMAN!
I DON'T BELIEVE IT!
MAMMOTHA THE NEW HEAVYWEIGHT SENSATION FROM SPAIN
MAMMOTHA "WARMS UP" FOR THE FIGHT OF THE EVENING BY JUGGLING FIVE 500LB. BALLS OF IRON.
YAY MAMMOTHA! WHATTA MAN!
500 LBS.
500 LBS.
500 LBS.
500 LBS.
500 LBS.

THE GIANT "LIMBERS HIS MUSCLES" BY HAVING A TUG O'WAR WITH AN ELEPHANT.

LOOK AT THAT! MAMMOTHA IS PULLING THE ELEPHANT!

POOH! THAT'S NOTHING - I CAN - I MEAN **WONDER WOMAN** CAN DO THAT WITH ONE HAND!

THE FIGHT IS ANNOUNCED.

LA-DEES AND GENTLEMEN! TONIGHT MAMMOTHA WILL FIGHT SAILOR MAHAN, CHAMPE-EEN OF THE NAVY AND LEADING CONTENDER FOR THE WORLD'S CHAMPEEN-SHIP!

SAILOR MAHAN OUTBOXES HIS GIANT OPPONENT, POUNDING HIM WITH RIGHTS AND LEFTS BUT MAMMOTHA ONLY LAUGHS.

HO! HO! LITTLE MAN, I CAN-NOT FEEL ZOSE LOVE TAPS!

THE FIRST BLOW MAMMOTHA LANDS BLASTS THE SAILOR CLEAR OUT OF THE RING.

YAY - AY! WOW! WHATTA SOCK! YAY - AY MAMMOTHA! THE COMING CHAMP!

MAMMOTHA WINS BY A KNOCKOUT IN 1 MINUTE, 20 SECONDS OF THE FIRST ROUND! HE OFFERS $5000 TO ANY FIGHTER WHO CAN STAY WITH HIM A FULL ROUND!

MAMMOTHA AND DON UNALDI EXPECT **WONDER WOMAN** TO APPEAR.

WONDER WOMAN CANNOT RE-SIST MY CHALLENGE - SHE LONGS TO CONQUER EVERY-ONE AT GAMES!

SHE PROMISED TO BE HERE - BUT THE TICKET TAKERS HAVEN'T SEEN HER!

50

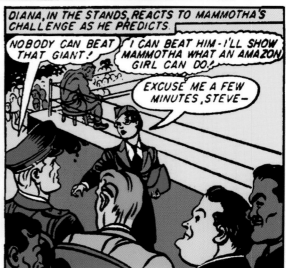

DIANA, IN THE STANDS, REACTS TO MAMMOTHA'S CHALLENGE AS HE PREDICTS.

NOBODY CAN BEAT THAT GIANT!

I CAN BEAT HIM - I'LL SHOW MAMMOTHA WHAT AN AMAZON GIRL CAN DO!

EXCUSE ME A FEW MINUTES, STEVE -

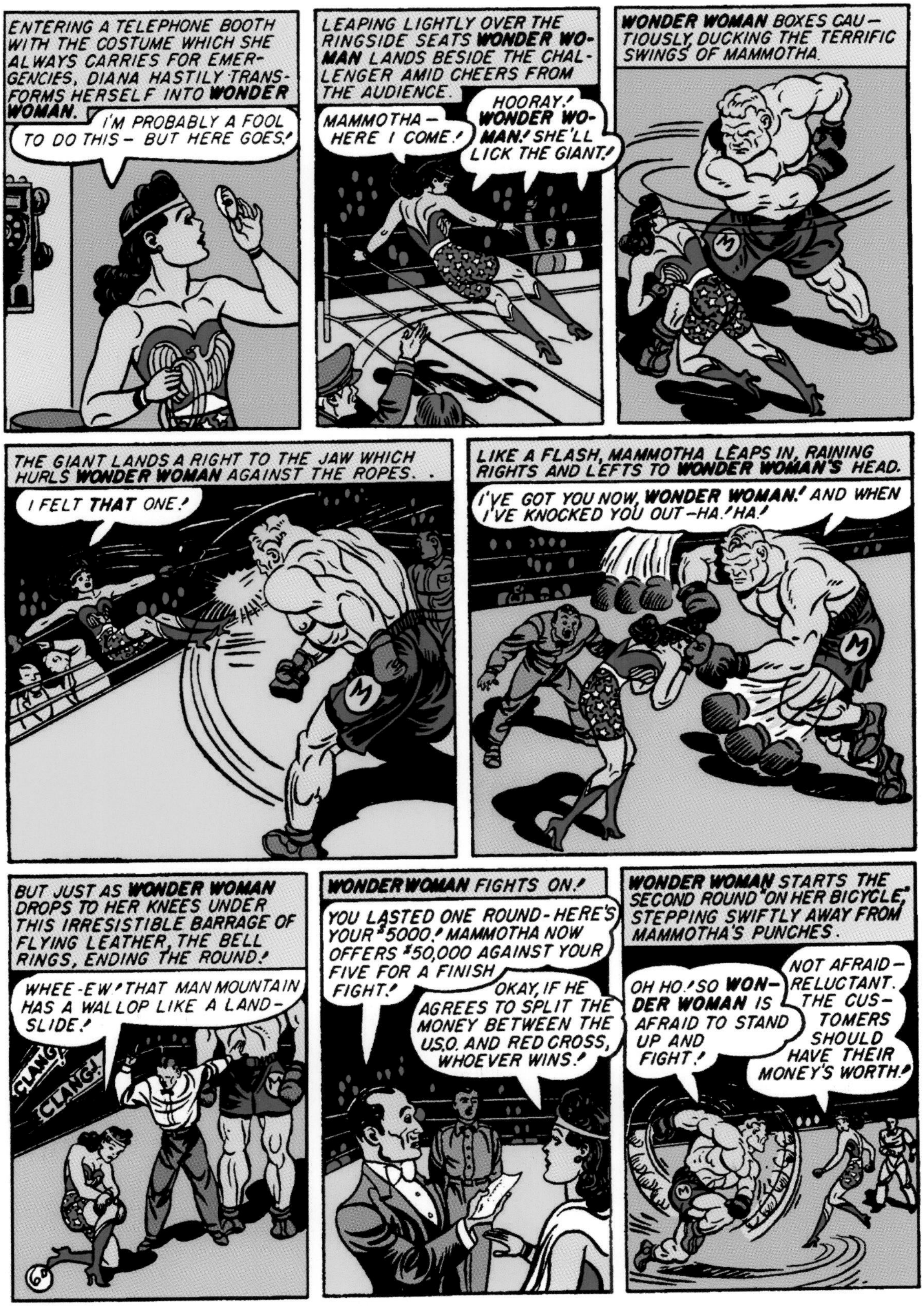
ENTERING A TELEPHONE BOOTH WITH THE COSTUME WHICH SHE ALWAYS CARRIES FOR EMERGENCIES, DIANA HASTILY TRANSFORMS HERSELF INTO WONDER WOMAN.
I'M PROBABLY A FOOL TO DO THIS – BUT HERE GOES!
LEAPING LIGHTLY OVER THE RINGSIDE SEATS WONDER WOMAN LANDS BESIDE THE CHALLENGER AMID CHEERS FROM THE AUDIENCE.
MAMMOTHA – HERE I COME!
HOORAY! WONDER WOMAN! SHE'LL LICK THE GIANT!
WONDER WOMAN BOXES CAUTIOUSLY, DUCKING THE TERRIFIC SWINGS OF MAMMOTHA.
THE GIANT LANDS A RIGHT TO THE JAW WHICH HURLS WONDER WOMAN AGAINST THE ROPES. .
I FELT THAT ONE!
LIKE A FLASH, MAMMOTHA LEAPS IN, RAINING RIGHTS AND LEFTS TO WONDER WOMAN'S HEAD.
I'VE GOT YOU NOW, WONDER WOMAN! AND WHEN I'VE KNOCKED YOU OUT—HA! HA!
BUT JUST AS WONDER WOMAN DROPS TO HER KNEES UNDER THIS IRRESISTIBLE BARRAGE OF FLYING LEATHER, THE BELL RINGS, ENDING THE ROUND!
WHEE-EW! THAT MAN MOUNTAIN HAS A WALLOP LIKE A LANDSLIDE!
CLANG!
CLANG!
WONDER WOMAN FIGHTS ON!
YOU LASTED ONE ROUND - HERE'S YOUR $5000! MAMMOTHA NOW OFFERS $50,000 AGAINST YOUR FIVE FOR A FINISH FIGHT!
OKAY, IF HE AGREES TO SPLIT THE MONEY BETWEEN THE U.S.O. AND RED CROSS, WHOEVER WINS!
WONDER WOMAN STARTS THE SECOND ROUND "ON HER BICYCLE," STEPPING SWIFTLY AWAY FROM MAMMOTHA'S PUNCHES.
OH HO! SO WONDER WOMAN IS AFRAID TO STAND UP AND FIGHT!
NOT AFRAID – RELUCTANT. THE CUSTOMERS SHOULD HAVE THEIR MONEY'S WORTH!
6

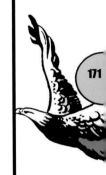

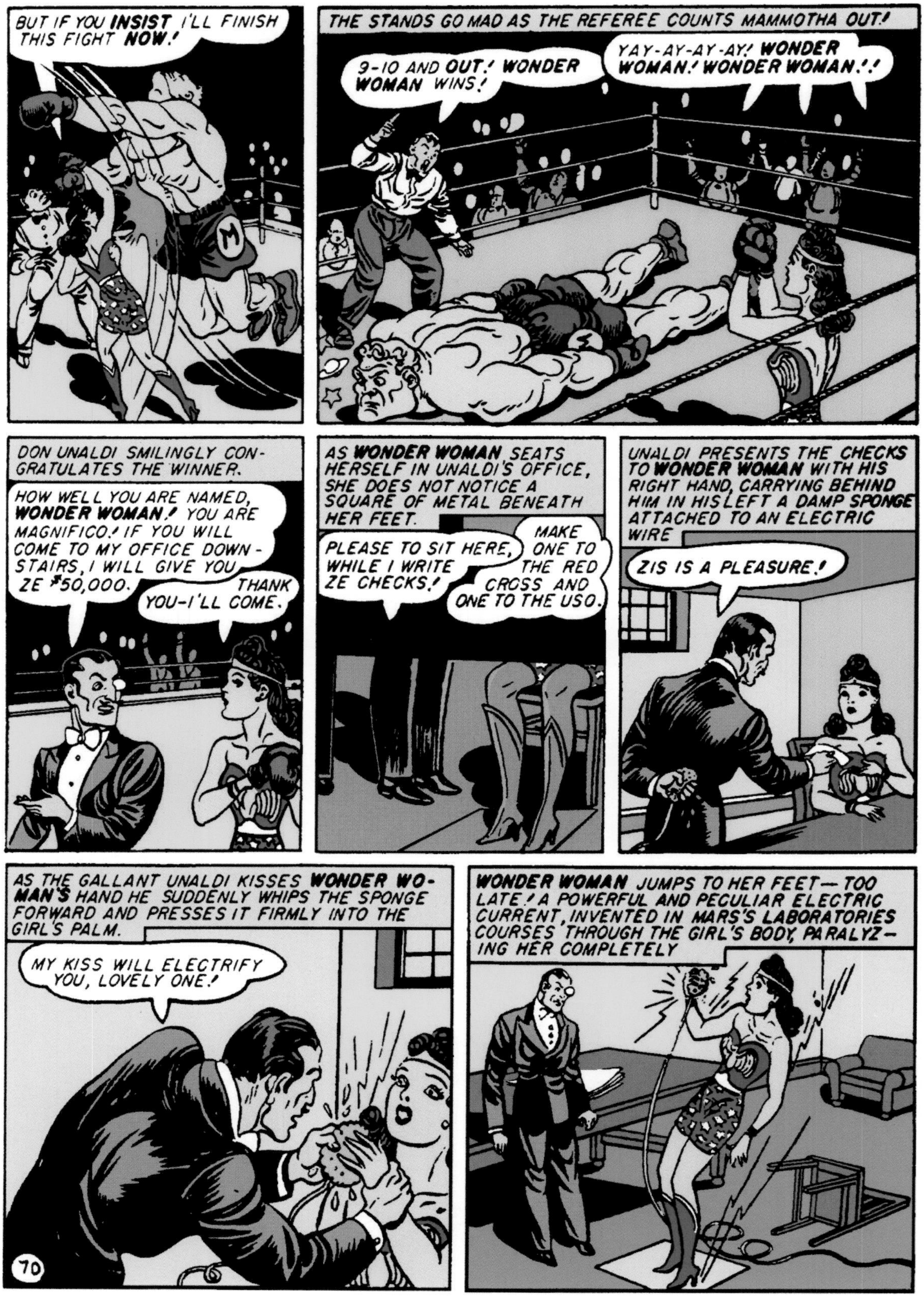
BUT IF YOU INSIST I'LL FINISH THIS FIGHT NOW!
THE STANDS GO MAD AS THE REFEREE COUNTS MAMMOTHA OUT!
9-10 AND OUT! WONDER WOMAN WINS!
YAY-AY-AY-AY! WONDER WOMAN! WONDER WOMAN!!
DON UNALDI SMILINGLY CONGRATULATES THE WINNER.
HOW WELL YOU ARE NAMED, WONDER WOMAN! YOU ARE MAGNIFICO! IF YOU WILL COME TO MY OFFICE DOWNSTAIRS, I WILL GIVE YOU ZE $50,000.
THANK YOU-I'LL COME.
AS WONDER WOMAN SEATS HERSELF IN UNALDI'S OFFICE, SHE DOES NOT NOTICE A SQUARE OF METAL BENEATH HER FEET.
PLEASE TO SIT HERE, WHILE I WRITE ZE CHECKS!
MAKE ONE TO THE RED CROSS AND ONE TO THE USO.
UNALDI PRESENTS THE CHECKS TO WONDER WOMAN WITH HIS RIGHT HAND, CARRYING BEHIND HIM IN HIS LEFT A DAMP SPONGE ATTACHED TO AN ELECTRIC WIRE
ZIS IS A PLEASURE!
AS THE GALLANT UNALDI KISSES WONDER WOMAN'S HAND HE SUDDENLY WHIPS THE SPONGE FORWARD AND PRESSES IT FIRMLY INTO THE GIRL'S PALM.
MY KISS WILL ELECTRIFY YOU, LOVELY ONE!
70
WONDER WOMAN JUMPS TO HER FEET—TOO LATE! A POWERFUL AND PECULIAR ELECTRIC CURRENT, INVENTED IN MARS'S LABORATORIES COURSES THROUGH THE GIRL'S BODY, PARALYZING HER COMPLETELY

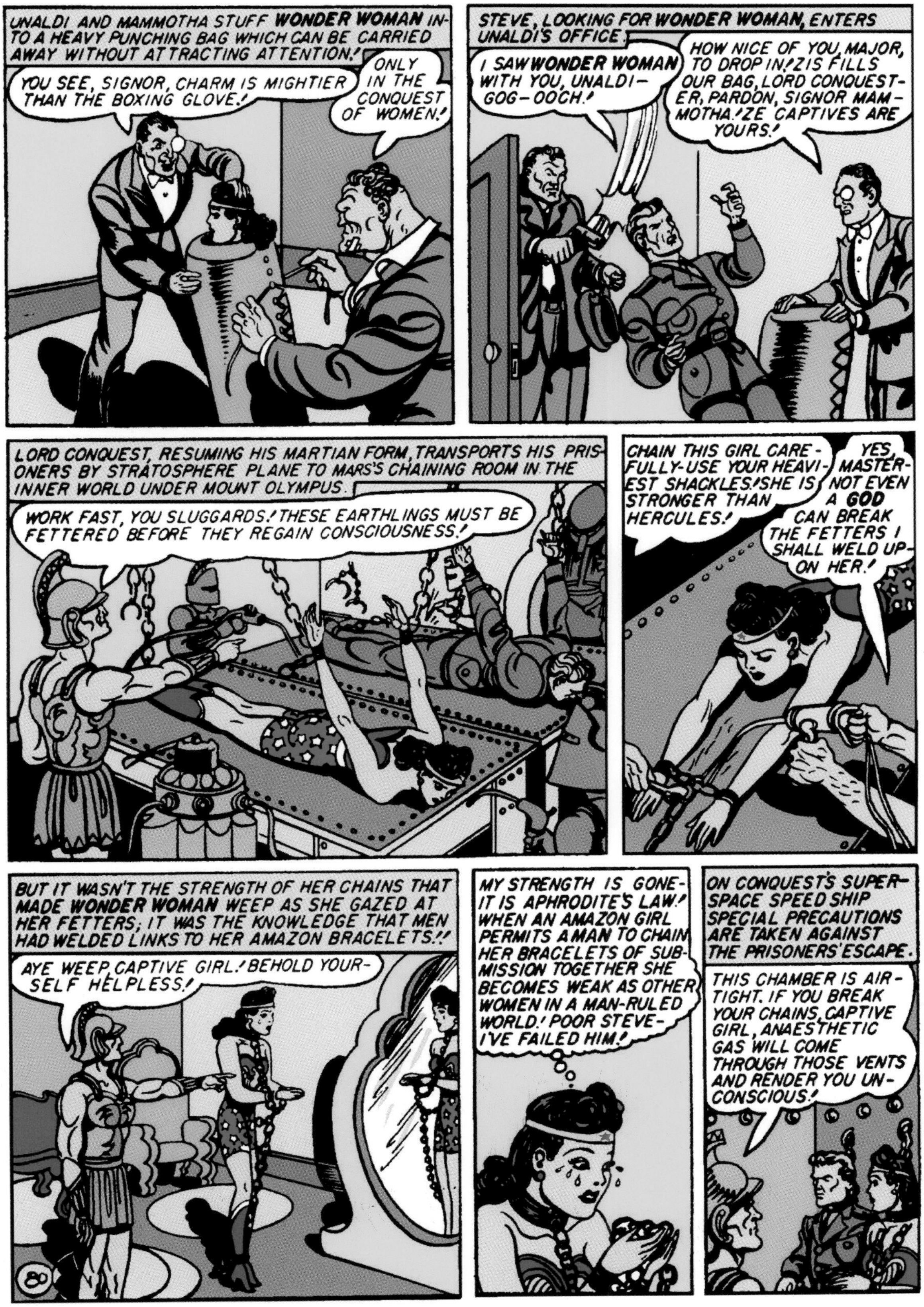
UNALDI AND MAMMOTHA STUFF WONDER WOMAN INTO A HEAVY PUNCHING BAG WHICH CAN BE CARRIED AWAY WITHOUT ATTRACTING ATTENTION!
YOU SEE, SIGNOR, CHARM IS MIGHTIER THAN THE BOXING GLOVE!
ONLY IN THE CONQUEST OF WOMEN!
STEVE, LOOKING FOR WONDER WOMAN, ENTERS UNALDI'S OFFICE.
I SAW WONDER WOMAN WITH YOU, UNALDI— GOG—OOCH!
HOW NICE OF YOU, MAJOR, TO DROP IN! ZIS FILLS OUR BAG, LORD CONQUESTER, PARDON, SIGNOR MAMMOTHA! ZE CAPTIVES ARE YOURS!
LORD CONQUEST, RESUMING HIS MARTIAN FORM, TRANSPORTS HIS PRISONERS BY STRATOSPHERE PLANE TO MARS'S CHAINING ROOM IN THE INNER WORLD UNDER MOUNT OLYMPUS.
WORK FAST, YOU SLUGGARDS! THESE EARTHLINGS MUST BE FETTERED BEFORE THEY REGAIN CONSCIOUSNESS!
CHAIN THIS GIRL CAREFULLY-USE YOUR HEAVIEST SHACKLES! SHE IS STRONGER THAN HERCULES!
YES, MASTER— NOT EVEN A GOD CAN BREAK THE FETTERS I SHALL WELD UPON HER!
BUT IT WASN'T THE STRENGTH OF HER CHAINS THAT MADE WONDER WOMAN WEEP AS SHE GAZED AT HER FETTERS; IT WAS THE KNOWLEDGE THAT MEN HAD WELDED LINKS TO HER AMAZON BRACELETS!!
AYE WEEP, CAPTIVE GIRL! BEHOLD YOURSELF HELPLESS!
80
MY STRENGTH IS GONE— IT IS APHRODITE'S LAW! WHEN AN AMAZON GIRL PERMITS A MAN TO CHAIN HER BRACELETS OF SUBMISSION TOGETHER SHE BECOMES WEAK AS OTHER WOMEN IN A MAN-RULED WORLD! POOR STEVE— I'VE FAILED HIM!
ON CONQUEST'S SUPER-SPACE SPEED SHIP SPECIAL PRECAUTIONS ARE TAKEN AGAINST THE PRISONERS' ESCAPE.
THIS CHAMBER IS AIRTIGHT. IF YOU BREAK YOUR CHAINS, CAPTIVE GIRL, ANAESTHETIC GAS WILL COME THROUGH THOSE VENTS AND RENDER YOU UNCONSCIOUS!

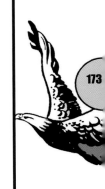

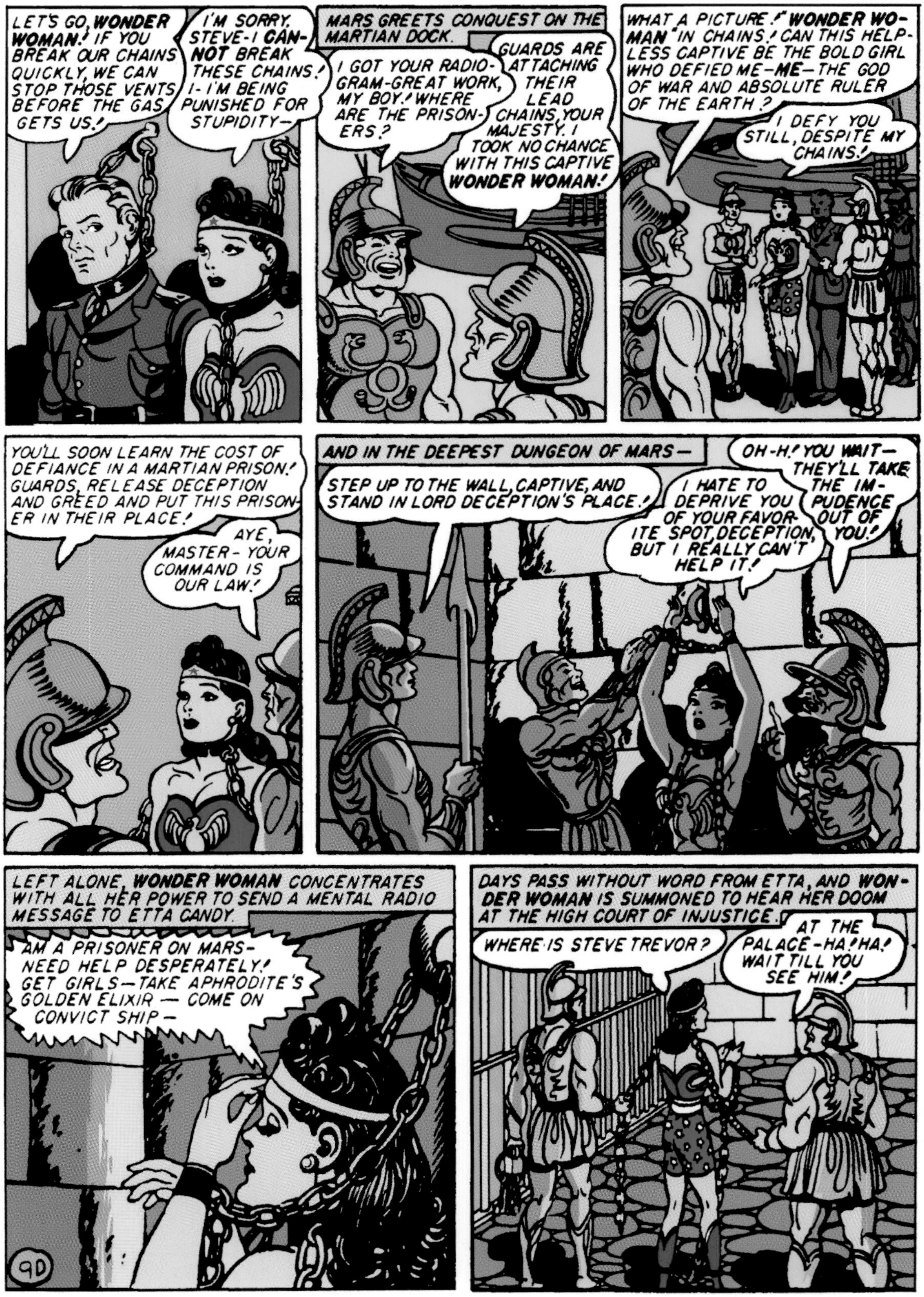

LET'S GO, WONDER WOMAN! IF YOU BREAK OUR CHAINS QUICKLY, WE CAN STOP THOSE VENTS BEFORE THE GAS GETS US!
I'M SORRY, STEVE-I CAN-NOT BREAK THESE CHAINS! I- I'M BEING PUNISHED FOR STUPIDITY—
MARS GREETS CONQUEST ON THE MARTIAN DOCK.
I GOT YOUR RADIO-GRAM-GREAT WORK, MY BOY! WHERE ARE THE PRISON-ERS?
GUARDS ARE ATTACHING THEIR LEAD CHAINS, YOUR MAJESTY. I TOOK NO CHANCE WITH THIS CAPTIVE WONDER WOMAN!
WHAT A PICTURE! "WONDER WO-MAN" IN CHAINS! CAN THIS HELP-LESS CAPTIVE BE THE BOLD GIRL WHO DEFIED ME—ME—THE GOD OF WAR AND ABSOLUTE RULER OF THE EARTH?
I DEFY YOU STILL, DESPITE MY CHAINS!
YOU'LL SOON LEARN THE COST OF DEFIANCE IN A MARTIAN PRISON! GUARDS, RELEASE DECEPTION AND GREED AND PUT THIS PRISON-ER IN THEIR PLACE!
AYE, MASTER- YOUR COMMAND IS OUR LAW!
AND IN THE DEEPEST DUNGEON OF MARS—
STEP UP TO THE WALL, CAPTIVE, AND STAND IN LORD DECEPTION'S PLACE!
I HATE TO DEPRIVE YOU OF YOUR FAVOR-ITE SPOT, DECEPTION, BUT I REALLY CAN'T HELP IT!
OH-H! YOU WAIT—THEY'LL TAKE THE IM-PUDENCE OUT OF YOU!
LEFT ALONE, WONDER WOMAN CONCENTRATES WITH ALL HER POWER TO SEND A MENTAL RADIO MESSAGE TO ETTA CANDY.
AM A PRISONER ON MARS-NEED HELP DESPERATELY! GET GIRLS—TAKE APHRODITE'S GOLDEN ELIXIR — COME ON CONVICT SHIP—
9D
DAYS PASS WITHOUT WORD FROM ETTA, AND WON-DER WOMAN IS SUMMONED TO HEAR HER DOOM AT THE HIGH COURT OF INJUSTICE.
WHERE IS STEVE TREVOR?
AT THE PALACE-HA! HA! WAIT TILL YOU SEE HIM!

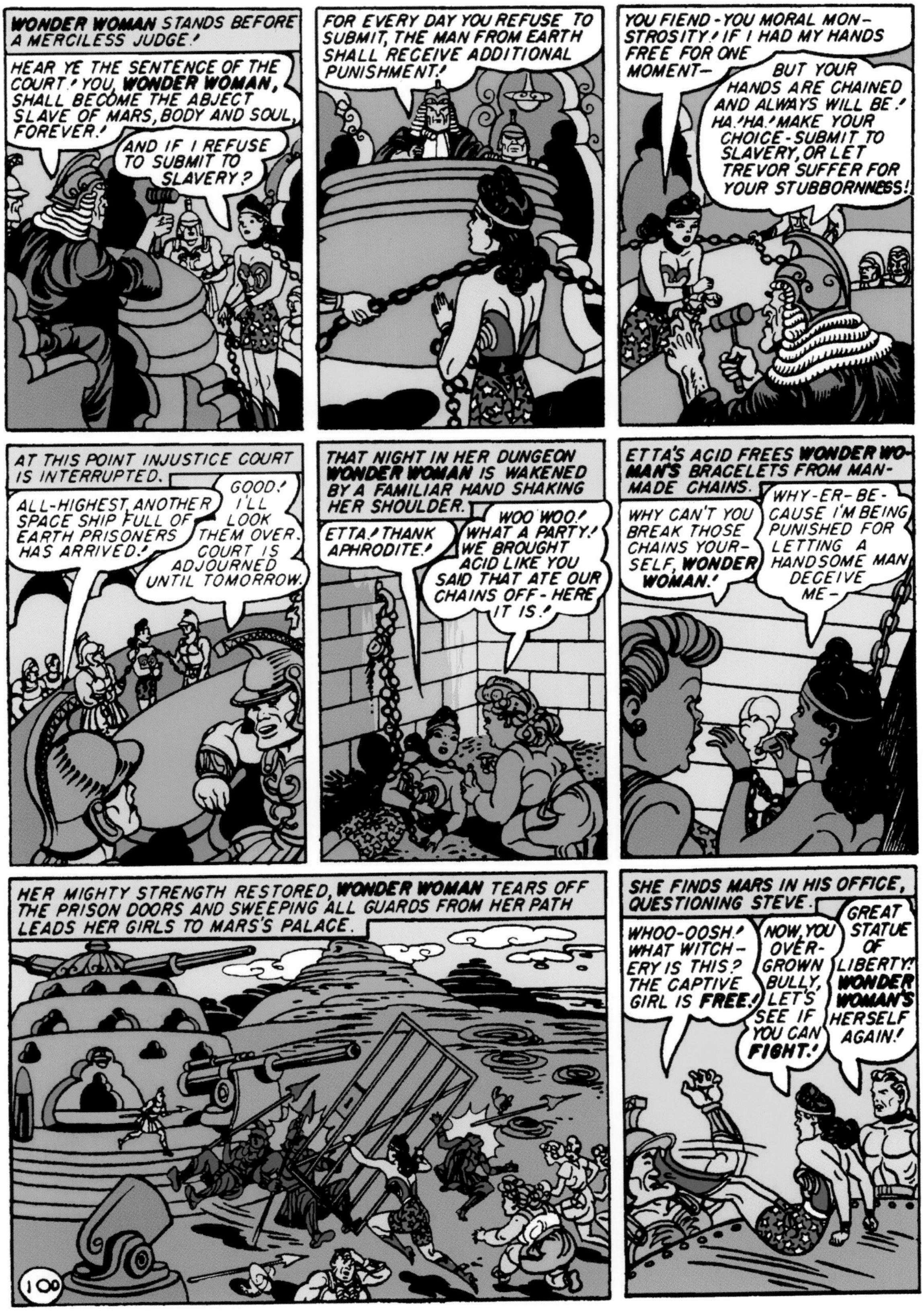
WONDER WOMAN STANDS BEFORE A MERCILESS JUDGE!
HEAR YE THE SENTENCE OF THE COURT! YOU, WONDER WOMAN, SHALL BECOME THE ABJECT SLAVE OF MARS, BODY AND SOUL, FOREVER!
AND IF I REFUSE TO SUBMIT TO SLAVERY?
FOR EVERY DAY YOU REFUSE TO SUBMIT, THE MAN FROM EARTH SHALL RECEIVE ADDITIONAL PUNISHMENT!
YOU FIEND - YOU MORAL MONSTROSITY! IF I HAD MY HANDS FREE FOR ONE MOMENT—
BUT YOUR HANDS ARE CHAINED AND ALWAYS WILL BE! HA! HA! MAKE YOUR CHOICE - SUBMIT TO SLAVERY, OR LET TREVOR SUFFER FOR YOUR STUBBORNNESS!
AT THIS POINT INJUSTICE COURT IS INTERRUPTED.
ALL-HIGHEST, ANOTHER SPACE SHIP FULL OF EARTH PRISONERS HAS ARRIVED!
GOOD! I'LL LOOK THEM OVER. COURT IS ADJOURNED UNTIL TOMORROW.
THAT NIGHT IN HER DUNGEON WONDER WOMAN IS WAKENED BY A FAMILIAR HAND SHAKING HER SHOULDER.
ETTA! THANK APHRODITE!
WOO WOO! WHAT A PARTY! WE BROUGHT ACID LIKE YOU SAID THAT ATE OUR CHAINS OFF - HERE IT IS!
ETTA'S ACID FREES WONDER WOMAN'S BRACELETS FROM MAN-MADE CHAINS.
WHY CAN'T YOU BREAK THOSE CHAINS YOURSELF, WONDER WOMAN!
WHY-ER-BE-CAUSE I'M BEING PUNISHED FOR LETTING A HANDSOME MAN DECEIVE ME—
HER MIGHTY STRENGTH RESTORED, WONDER WOMAN TEARS OFF THE PRISON DOORS AND SWEEPING ALL GUARDS FROM HER PATH LEADS HER GIRLS TO MARS'S PALACE.
100
SHE FINDS MARS IN HIS OFFICE, QUESTIONING STEVE.
WHOO-OOSH! WHAT WITCHERY IS THIS? THE CAPTIVE GIRL IS FREE!
NOW, YOU OVERGROWN BULLY, LET'S SEE IF YOU CAN FIGHT!
GREAT STATUE OF LIBERTY! WONDER WOMAN'S HERSELF AGAIN!

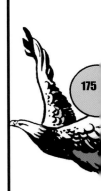

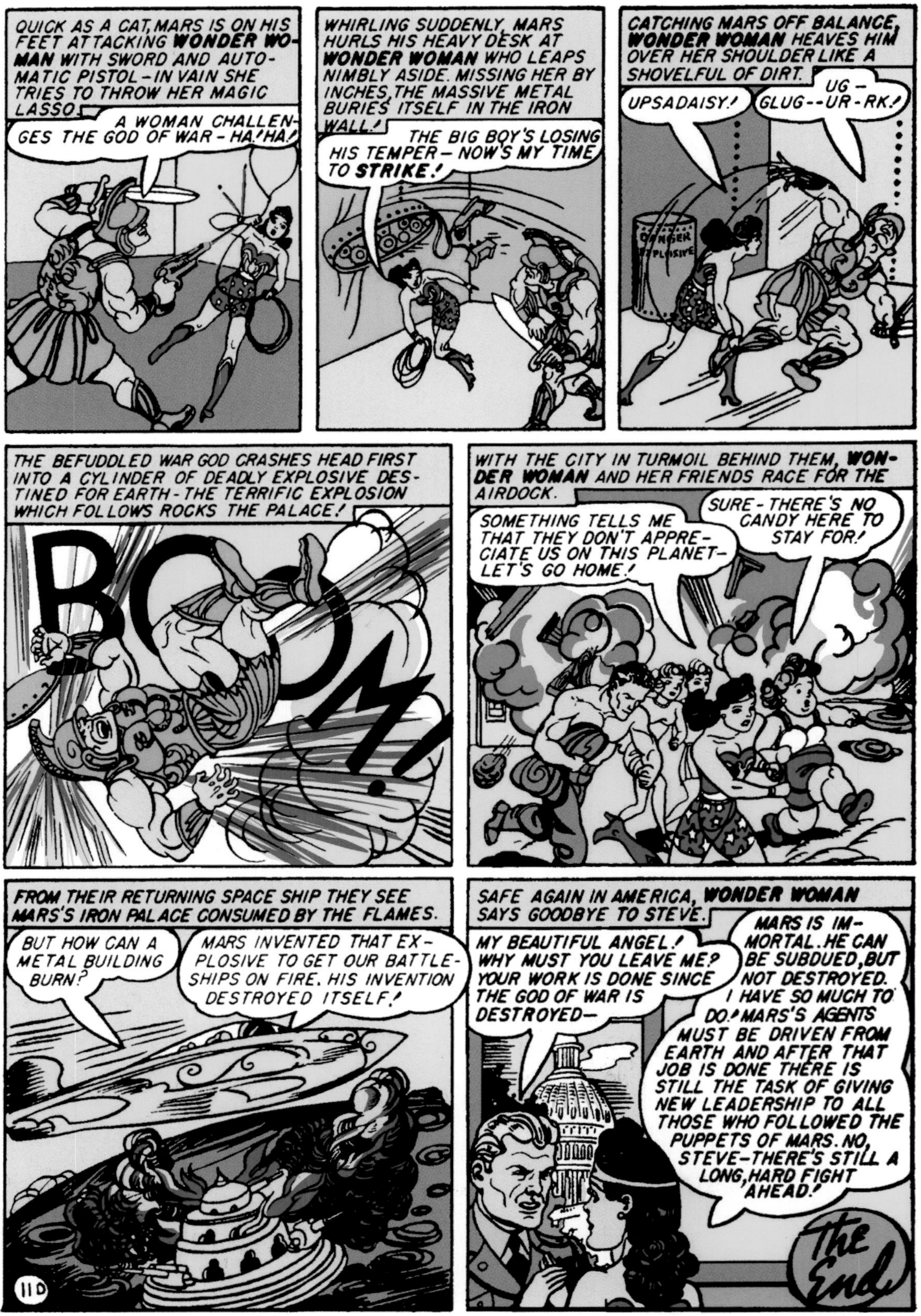
QUICK AS A CAT, MARS IS ON HIS FEET ATTACKING WONDER WOMAN WITH SWORD AND AUTOMATIC PISTOL—IN VAIN SHE TRIES TO THROW HER MAGIC LASSO.
A WOMAN CHALLENGES THE GOD OF WAR—HA! HA!
WHIRLING SUDDENLY, MARS HURLS HIS HEAVY DESK AT WONDER WOMAN WHO LEAPS NIMBLY ASIDE. MISSING HER BY INCHES, THE MASSIVE METAL BURIES ITSELF IN THE IRON WALL!
THE BIG BOY'S LOSING HIS TEMPER—NOW'S MY TIME TO STRIKE!
CATCHING MARS OFF BALANCE, WONDER WOMAN HEAVES HIM OVER HER SHOULDER LIKE A SHOVELFUL OF DIRT.
UPSADAISY!
UG—GLUG--UR-RK!
THE BEFUDDLED WAR GOD CRASHES HEAD FIRST INTO A CYLINDER OF DEADLY EXPLOSIVE DESTINED FOR EARTH—THE TERRIFIC EXPLOSION WHICH FOLLOWS ROCKS THE PALACE!
BOOM!
WITH THE CITY IN TURMOIL BEHIND THEM, WONDER WOMAN AND HER FRIENDS RACE FOR THE AIRDOCK.
SOMETHING TELLS ME THAT THEY DON'T APPRECIATE US ON THIS PLANET—LET'S GO HOME!
SURE—THERE'S NO CANDY HERE TO STAY FOR!
FROM THEIR RETURNING SPACE SHIP THEY SEE MARS'S IRON PALACE CONSUMED BY THE FLAMES.
BUT HOW CAN A METAL BUILDING BURN?
MARS INVENTED THAT EXPLOSIVE TO GET OUR BATTLESHIPS ON FIRE. HIS INVENTION DESTROYED ITSELF!
110
SAFE AGAIN IN AMERICA, WONDER WOMAN SAYS GOODBYE TO STEVE.
MY BEAUTIFUL ANGEL! WHY MUST YOU LEAVE ME? YOUR WORK IS DONE SINCE THE GOD OF WAR IS DESTROYED—
MARS IS IMMORTAL..HE CAN BE SUBDUED, BUT NOT DESTROYED. I HAVE SO MUCH TO DO! MARS'S AGENTS MUST BE DRIVEN FROM EARTH AND AFTER THAT JOB IS DONE THERE IS STILL THE TASK OF GIVING NEW LEADERSHIP TO ALL THOSE WHO FOLLOWED THE PUPPETS OF MARS. NO, STEVE—THERE'S STILL A LONG, HARD FIGHT AHEAD!
The End

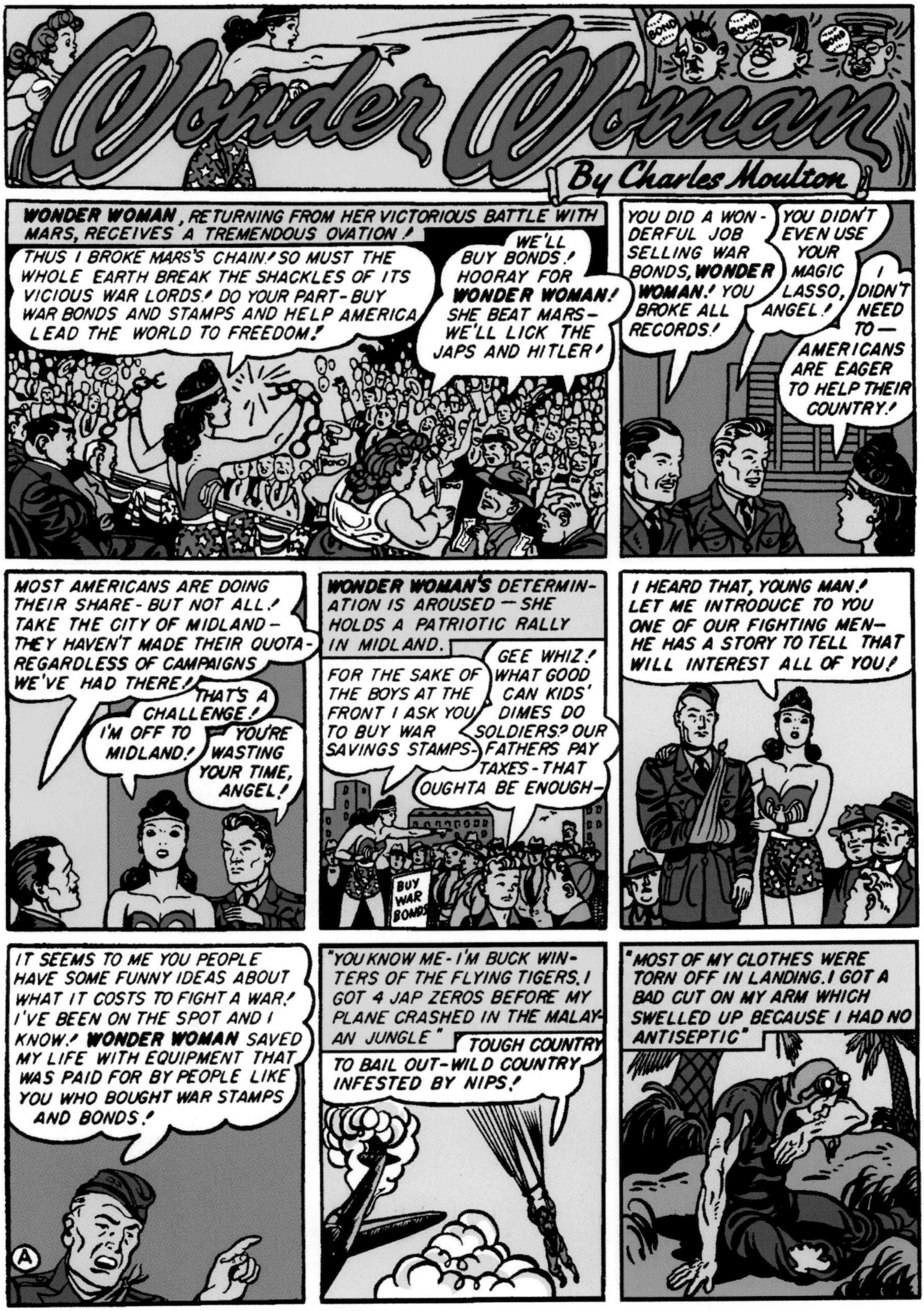

Wonder Woman
By Charles Moulton
BOND
BOND
BOND
WONDER WOMAN, RETURNING FROM HER VICTORIOUS BATTLE WITH MARS, RECEIVES A TREMENDOUS OVATION!
THUS I BROKE MARS'S CHAIN! SO MUST THE WHOLE EARTH BREAK THE SHACKLES OF ITS VICIOUS WAR LORDS! DO YOUR PART-BUY WAR BONDS AND STAMPS AND HELP AMERICA LEAD THE WORLD TO FREEDOM!
WE'LL BUY BONDS! HOORAY FOR WONDER WOMAN! SHE BEAT MARS-WE'LL LICK THE JAPS AND HITLER!
YOU DID A WONDERFUL JOB SELLING WAR BONDS, WONDER WOMAN! YOU BROKE ALL RECORDS!
YOU DIDN'T EVEN USE YOUR MAGIC LASSO, ANGEL!
I DIDN'T NEED TO— AMERICANS ARE EAGER TO HELP THEIR COUNTRY!
MOST AMERICANS ARE DOING THEIR SHARE-BUT NOT ALL! TAKE THE CITY OF MIDLAND-THEY HAVEN'T MADE THEIR QUOTA-REGARDLESS OF CAMPAIGNS WE'VE HAD THERE!
THAT'S A CHALLENGE! I'M OFF TO MIDLAND!
YOU'RE WASTING YOUR TIME, ANGEL!
WONDER WOMAN'S DETERMINATION IS AROUSED — SHE HOLDS A PATRIOTIC RALLY IN MIDLAND.
FOR THE SAKE OF THE BOYS AT THE FRONT I ASK YOU TO BUY WAR SAVINGS STAMPS-
GEE WHIZ! WHAT GOOD CAN KIDS' DIMES DO SOLDIERS? OUR FATHERS PAY TAXES-THAT OUGHTA BE ENOUGH-
BUY WAR BONDS
I HEARD THAT, YOUNG MAN! LET ME INTRODUCE TO YOU ONE OF OUR FIGHTING MEN-HE HAS A STORY TO TELL THAT WILL INTEREST ALL OF YOU!
IT SEEMS TO ME YOU PEOPLE HAVE SOME FUNNY IDEAS ABOUT WHAT IT COSTS TO FIGHT A WAR! I'VE BEEN ON THE SPOT AND I KNOW! WONDER WOMAN SAVED MY LIFE WITH EQUIPMENT THAT WAS PAID FOR BY PEOPLE LIKE YOU WHO BOUGHT WAR STAMPS AND BONDS!
A
"YOU KNOW ME-I'M BUCK WINTERS OF THE FLYING TIGERS. I GOT 4 JAP ZEROS BEFORE MY PLANE CRASHED IN THE MALAYAN JUNGLE"
TOUGH COUNTRY TO BAIL OUT-WILD COUNTRY INFESTED BY NIPS!
"MOST OF MY CLOTHES WERE TORN OFF IN LANDING. I GOT A BAD CUT ON MY ARM WHICH SWELLED UP BECAUSE I HAD NO ANTISEPTIC"

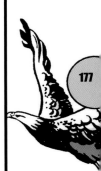

Wonder Woman #2 (Fall 1942) - script: William Moulton Marston - art: H.G. Peter

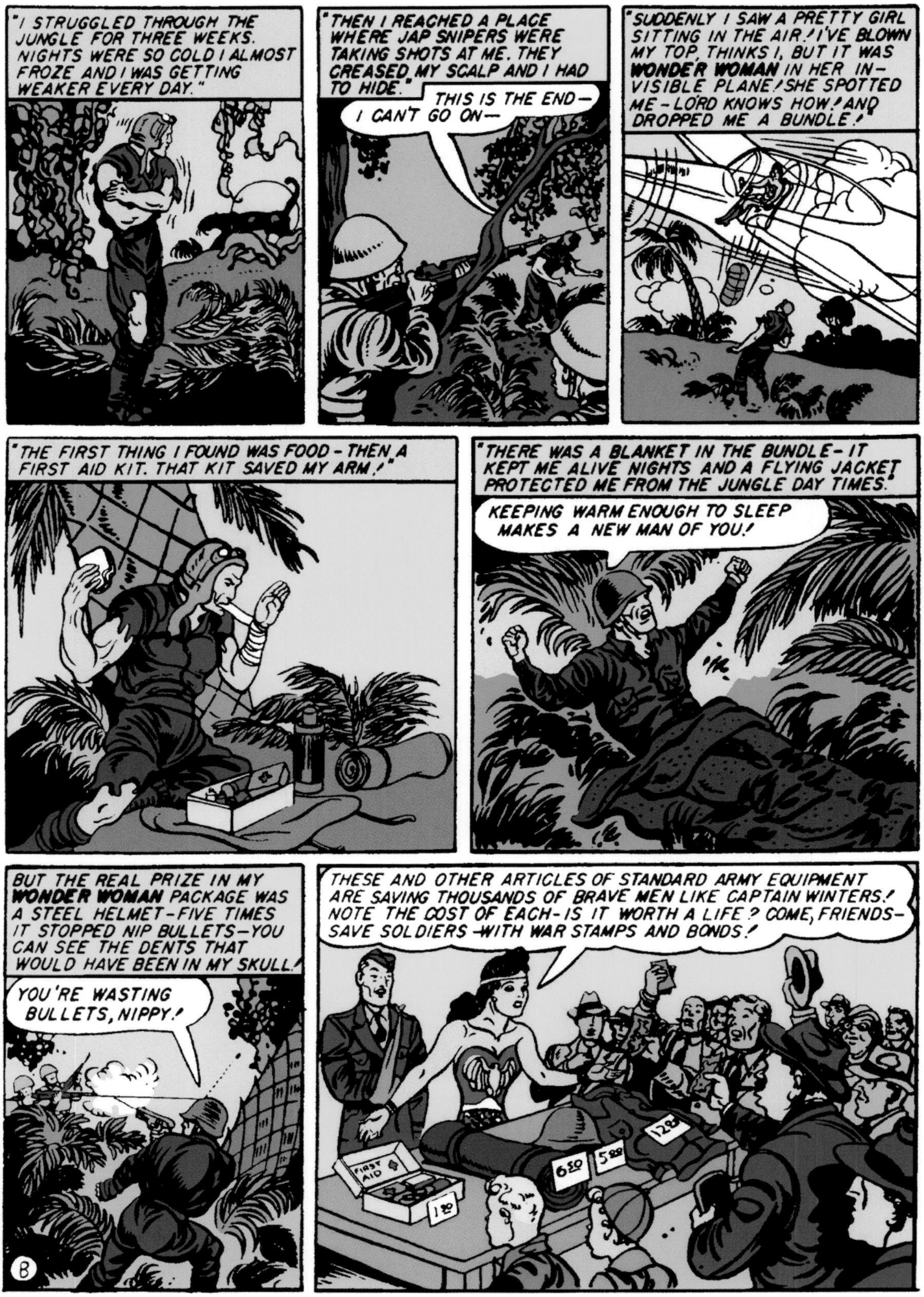
"I STRUGGLED THROUGH THE JUNGLE FOR THREE WEEKS. NIGHTS WERE SO COLD I ALMOST FROZE AND I WAS GETTING WEAKER EVERY DAY."
"THEN I REACHED A PLACE WHERE JAP SNIPERS WERE TAKING SHOTS AT ME. THEY CREASED MY SCALP AND I HAD TO HIDE."
THIS IS THE END— I CAN'T GO ON—
"SUDDENLY I SAW A PRETTY GIRL SITTING IN THE AIR! I'VE BLOWN MY TOP, THINKS I, BUT IT WAS WONDER WOMAN IN HER INVISIBLE PLANE! SHE SPOTTED ME - LORD KNOWS HOW! AND DROPPED ME A BUNDLE!"
"THE FIRST THING I FOUND WAS FOOD - THEN A FIRST AID KIT. THAT KIT SAVED MY ARM!"
"THERE WAS A BLANKET IN THE BUNDLE - IT KEPT ME ALIVE NIGHTS AND A FLYING JACKET PROTECTED ME FROM THE JUNGLE DAY TIMES."
KEEPING WARM ENOUGH TO SLEEP MAKES A NEW MAN OF YOU!
BUT THE REAL PRIZE IN MY WONDER WOMAN PACKAGE WAS A STEEL HELMET - FIVE TIMES IT STOPPED NIP BULLETS—YOU CAN SEE THE DENTS THAT WOULD HAVE BEEN IN MY SKULL!
YOU'RE WASTING BULLETS, NIPPY!
THESE AND OTHER ARTICLES OF STANDARD ARMY EQUIPMENT ARE SAVING THOUSANDS OF BRAVE MEN LIKE CAPTAIN WINTERS! NOTE THE COST OF EACH - IS IT WORTH A LIFE? COME, FRIENDS - SAVE SOLDIERS - WITH WAR STAMPS AND BONDS!
FIRST AID
B

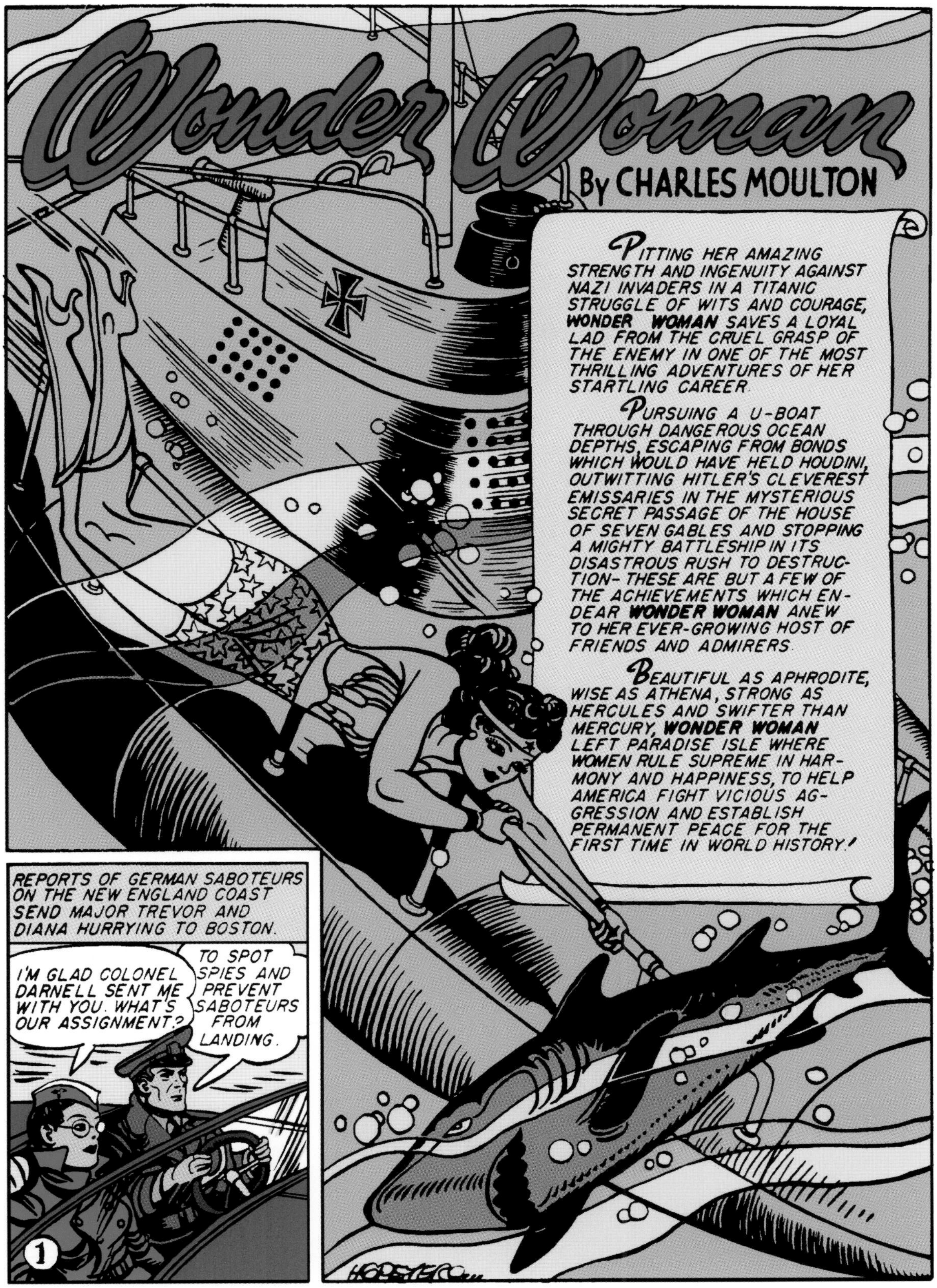
Wonder Woman
By CHARLES MOULTON
PITTING HER AMAZING STRENGTH AND INGENUITY AGAINST NAZI INVADERS IN A TITANIC STRUGGLE OF WITS AND COURAGE, WONDER WOMAN SAVES A LOYAL LAD FROM THE CRUEL GRASP OF THE ENEMY IN ONE OF THE MOST THRILLING ADVENTURES OF HER STARTLING CAREER.
PURSUING A U-BOAT THROUGH DANGEROUS OCEAN DEPTHS, ESCAPING FROM BONDS WHICH WOULD HAVE HELD HOUDINI, OUTWITTING HITLER'S CLEVEREST EMISSARIES IN THE MYSTERIOUS SECRET PASSAGE OF THE HOUSE OF SEVEN GABLES AND STOPPING A MIGHTY BATTLESHIP IN ITS DISASTROUS RUSH TO DESTRUCTION- THESE ARE BUT A FEW OF THE ACHIEVEMENTS WHICH ENDEAR WONDER WOMAN ANEW TO HER EVER-GROWING HOST OF FRIENDS AND ADMIRERS.
BEAUTIFUL AS APHRODITE, WISE AS ATHENA, STRONG AS HERCULES AND SWIFTER THAN MERCURY, WONDER WOMAN LEFT PARADISE ISLE WHERE WOMEN RULE SUPREME IN HARMONY AND HAPPINESS, TO HELP AMERICA FIGHT VICIOUS AGGRESSION AND ESTABLISH PERMANENT PEACE FOR THE FIRST TIME IN WORLD HISTORY!
REPORTS OF GERMAN SABOTEURS ON THE NEW ENGLAND COAST SEND MAJOR TREVOR AND DIANA HURRYING TO BOSTON.
I'M GLAD COLONEL DARNELL SENT ME WITH YOU. WHAT'S OUR ASSIGNMENT?
TO SPOT SPIES AND PREVENT SABOTEURS FROM LANDING.
1

Comic Cavalcade #1 (Dec. 1942–Jan. 1943) - script: William Moulton Marston - art: H.G. Peter

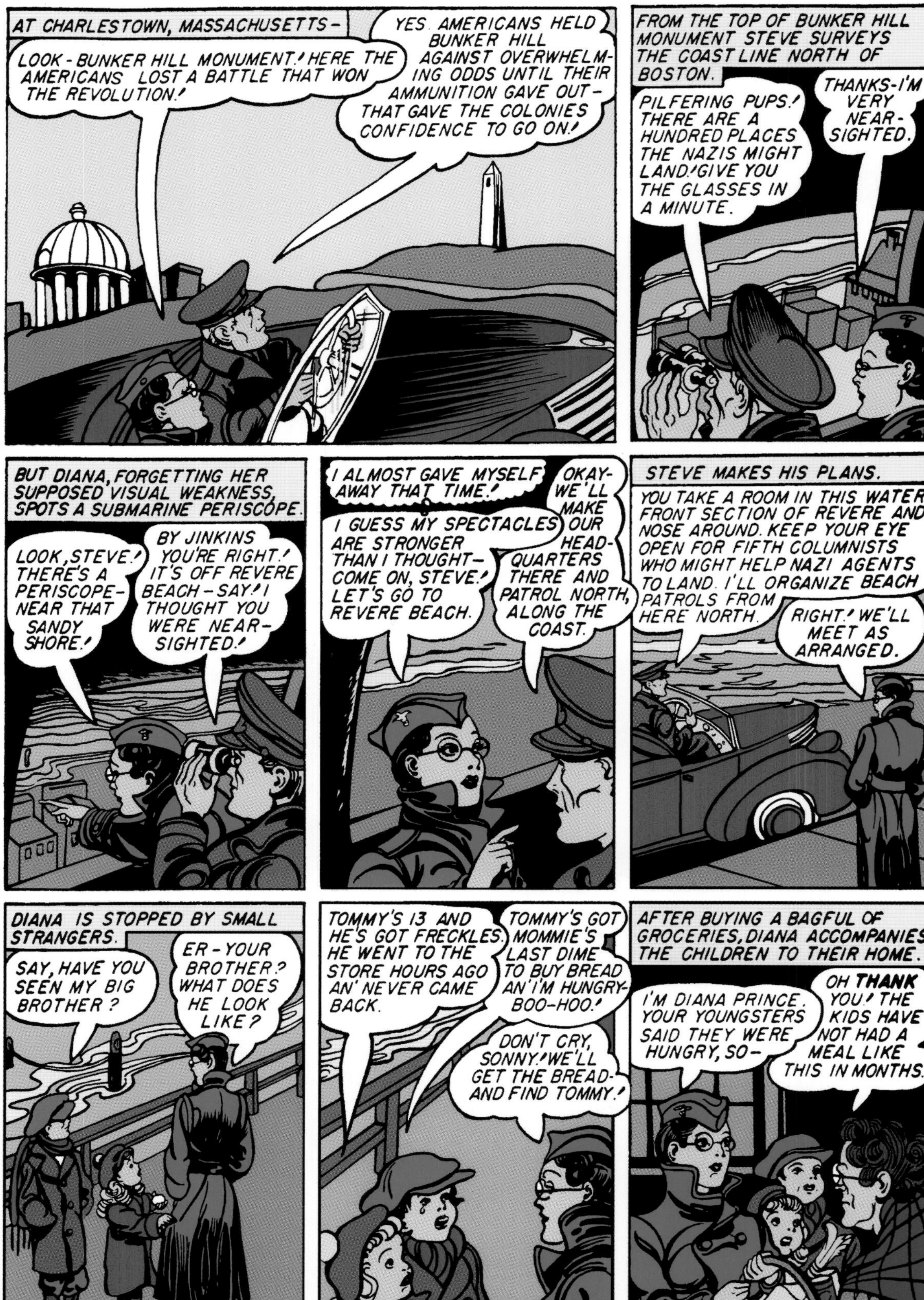
AT CHARLESTOWN, MASSACHUSETTS-
LOOK-BUNKER HILL MONUMENT! HERE THE AMERICANS LOST A BATTLE THAT WON THE REVOLUTION!
YES. AMERICANS HELD BUNKER HILL AGAINST OVERWHELMING ODDS UNTIL THEIR AMMUNITION GAVE OUT-THAT GAVE THE COLONIES CONFIDENCE TO GO ON!
FROM THE TOP OF BUNKER HILL MONUMENT STEVE SURVEYS THE COAST LINE NORTH OF BOSTON.
PILFERING PUPS! THERE ARE A HUNDRED PLACES THE NAZIS MIGHT LAND! GIVE YOU THE GLASSES IN A MINUTE.
THANKS-I'M VERY NEAR-SIGHTED.
BUT DIANA, FORGETTING HER SUPPOSED VISUAL WEAKNESS, SPOTS A SUBMARINE PERISCOPE.
LOOK, STEVE! THERE'S A PERISCOPE-NEAR THAT SANDY SHORE!
BY JINKINS YOU'RE RIGHT! IT'S OFF REVERE BEACH-SAY! I THOUGHT YOU WERE NEAR-SIGHTED!
I ALMOST GAVE MYSELF AWAY THAT TIME!
I GUESS MY SPECTACLES ARE STRONGER THAN I THOUGHT-COME ON, STEVE! LET'S GO TO REVERE BEACH.
OKAY-WE'LL MAKE OUR HEADQUARTERS THERE AND PATROL NORTH, ALONG THE COAST.
STEVE MAKES HIS PLANS.
YOU TAKE A ROOM IN THIS WATER-FRONT SECTION OF REVERE AND NOSE AROUND. KEEP YOUR EYE OPEN FOR FIFTH COLUMNISTS WHO MIGHT HELP NAZI AGENTS TO LAND. I'LL ORGANIZE BEACH PATROLS FROM HERE NORTH.
RIGHT! WE'LL MEET AS ARRANGED.
DIANA IS STOPPED BY SMALL STRANGERS.
SAY, HAVE YOU SEEN MY BIG BROTHER?
ER-YOUR BROTHER? WHAT DOES HE LOOK LIKE?
2
TOMMY'S 13 AND HE'S GOT FRECKLES. HE WENT TO THE STORE HOURS AGO AN' NEVER CAME BACK.
TOMMY'S GOT MOMMIE'S LAST DIME TO BUY BREAD AN' I'M HUNGRY-BOO-HOO!
DON'T CRY, SONNY! WE'LL GET THE BREAD-AND FIND TOMMY!
AFTER BUYING A BAGFUL OF GROCERIES, DIANA ACCOMPANIES THE CHILDREN TO THEIR HOME.
I'M DIANA PRINCE. YOUR YOUNGSTERS SAID THEY WERE HUNGRY, SO-
OH THANK YOU! THE KIDS HAVE NOT HAD A MEAL LIKE THIS IN MONTHS!
BREAD

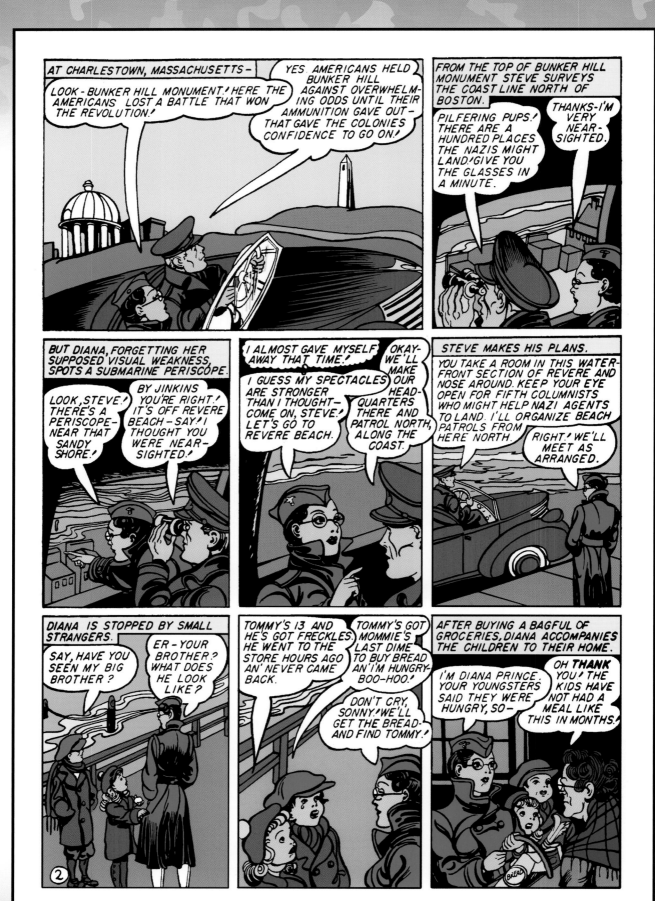

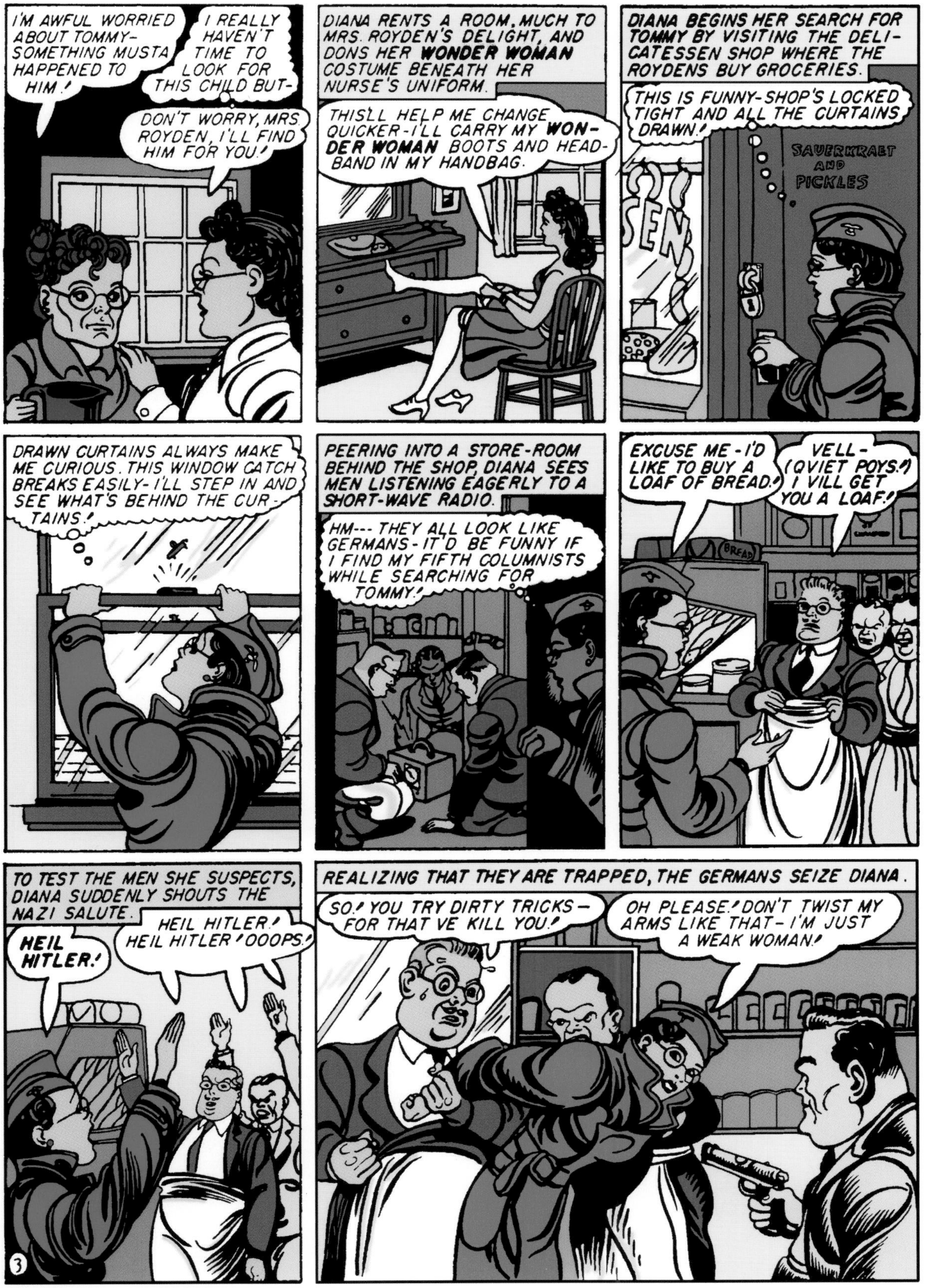
I'M AWFUL WORRIED ABOUT TOMMY- SOMETHING MUSTA HAPPENED TO HIM!
I REALLY HAVEN'T TIME TO LOOK FOR THIS CHILD BUT-
DON'T WORRY, MRS. ROYDEN, I'LL FIND HIM FOR YOU!
DIANA RENTS A ROOM, MUCH TO MRS. ROYDEN'S DELIGHT, AND DONS HER WONDER WOMAN COSTUME BENEATH HER NURSE'S UNIFORM.
THIS'LL HELP ME CHANGE QUICKER-I'LL CARRY MY WONDER WOMAN BOOTS AND HEADBAND IN MY HANDBAG.
DIANA BEGINS HER SEARCH FOR TOMMY BY VISITING THE DELICATESSEN SHOP WHERE THE ROYDENS BUY GROCERIES.
THIS IS FUNNY-SHOP'S LOCKED TIGHT AND ALL THE CURTAINS DRAWN!
SAUERKRAUT AND PICKLES
DRAWN CURTAINS ALWAYS MAKE ME CURIOUS. THIS WINDOW CATCH BREAKS EASILY-I'LL STEP IN AND SEE WHAT'S BEHIND THE CURTAINS!
PEERING INTO A STORE-ROOM BEHIND THE SHOP, DIANA SEES MEN LISTENING EAGERLY TO A SHORT-WAVE RADIO.
HM--- THEY ALL LOOK LIKE GERMANS-IT'D BE FUNNY IF I FIND MY FIFTH COLUMNISTS WHILE SEARCHING FOR TOMMY!
EXCUSE ME-I'D LIKE TO BUY A LOAF OF BREAD!
VELL- (QVIET POYS!) I VILL GET YOU A LOAF!
BREAD
TO TEST THE MEN SHE SUSPECTS, DIANA SUDDENLY SHOUTS THE NAZI SALUTE.
HEIL HITLER!
HEIL HITLER! HEIL HITLER! OOOPS!
3
REALIZING THAT THEY ARE TRAPPED, THE GERMANS SEIZE DIANA.
SO! YOU TRY DIRTY TRICKS- FOR THAT VE KILL YOU!
OH PLEASE! DON'T TWIST MY ARMS LIKE THAT-I'M JUST A WEAK WOMAN!

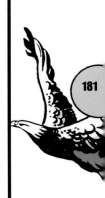

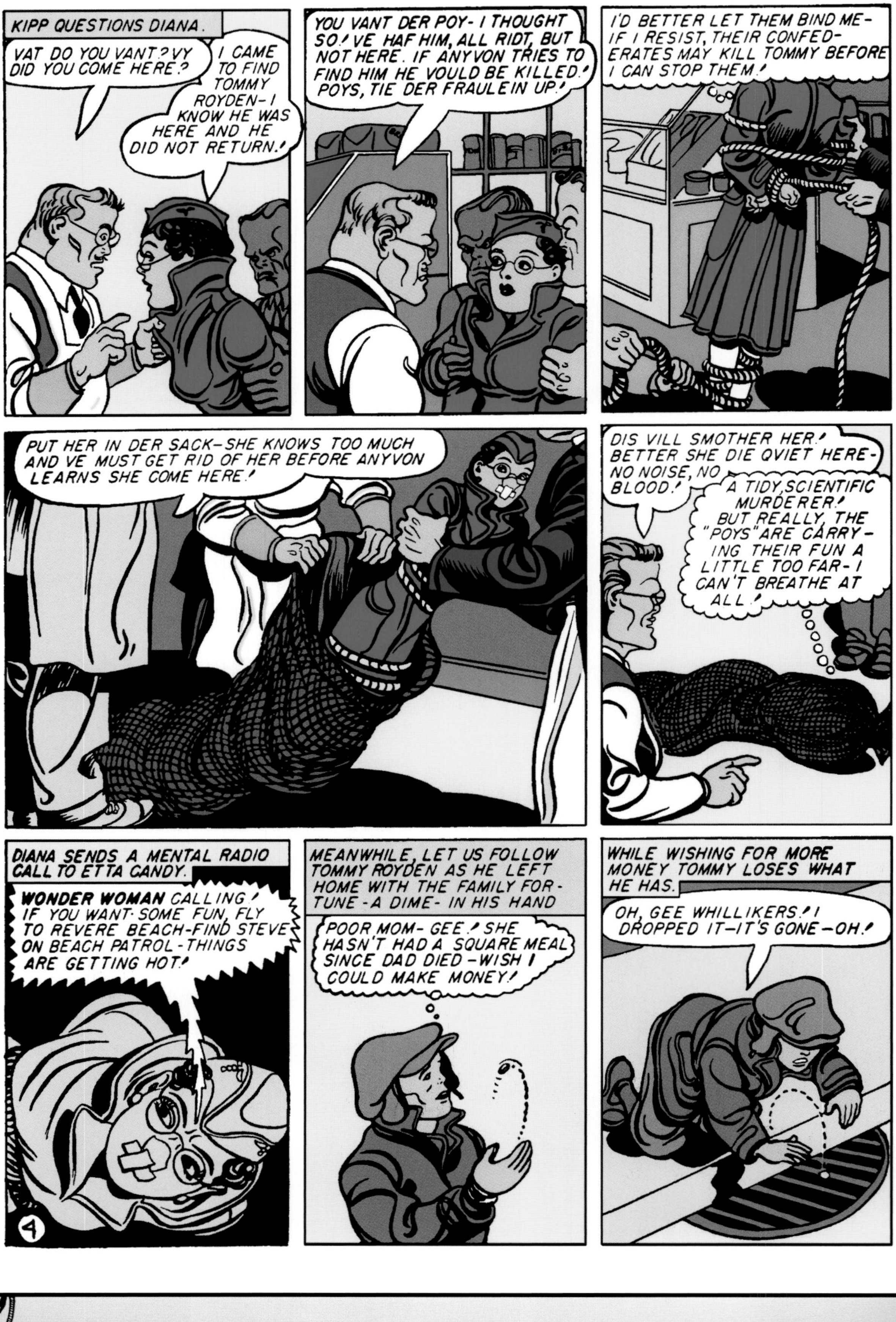

KIPP QUESTIONS DIANA.
VAT DO YOU VANT? VY DID YOU COME HERE?
I CAME TO FIND TOMMY ROYDEN- I KNOW HE WAS HERE AND HE DID NOT RETURN.!
YOU VANT DER POY- I THOUGHT SO.! VE HAF HIM, ALL RIDT, BUT NOT HERE. IF ANYVON TRIES TO FIND HIM HE VOULD BE KILLED.! POYS, TIE DER FRAULEIN UP.!
I'D BETTER LET THEM BIND ME- IF I RESIST, THEIR CONFEDERATES MAY KILL TOMMY BEFORE I CAN STOP THEM.!
PUT HER IN DER SACK-SHE KNOWS TOO MUCH AND VE MUST GET RID OF HER BEFORE ANYVON LEARNS SHE COME HERE.!
DIS VILL SMOTHER HER.! BETTER SHE DIE QVIET HERE-NO NOISE, NO BLOOD.!
A TIDY, SCIENTIFIC MURDERER.! BUT REALLY, THE "POYS" ARE CARRYING THEIR FUN A LITTLE TOO FAR- I CAN'T BREATHE AT ALL.!
DIANA SENDS A MENTAL RADIO CALL TO ETTA CANDY.
WONDER WOMAN CALLING.! IF YOU WANT SOME FUN, FLY TO REVERE BEACH-FIND STEVE ON BEACH PATROL-THINGS ARE GETTING HOT.!
4
MEANWHILE, LET US FOLLOW TOMMY ROYDEN AS HE LEFT HOME WITH THE FAMILY FORTUNE -A DIME- IN HIS HAND
POOR MOM- GEE.! SHE HASN'T HAD A SQUARE MEAL SINCE DAD DIED -WISH I COULD MAKE MONEY.!
WHILE WISHING FOR MORE MONEY TOMMY LOSES WHAT HE HAS.
OH, GEE WHILLIKERS.! I DROPPED IT-IT'S GONE-OH.!

TOMMY IS IN DESPAIR.

NOW I'VE GONE AND DONE IT—OUR SUPPER'S GONE DOWN THE SEWER! WHAT'LL I DO—I **GOTTA** GET BREAD FOR MOM AND THE KIDS!

TOMMY ASKS MR. KIPP FOR CREDIT.

SAY, LISTEN! I LOST THE DIME MOM GAVE ME AND THE KIDS **GOTTA** HAVE BREAD. WILL YOU TRUST ME—JUST THIS ONCE?

I VOULDN'T TRUST ANYBODY—NO CASH, NO BREAD!

MAYBE YOU'D LET ME EARN A LOAF OF BREAD BY TENDING STORE FOR YOU—

VOT! SO DOT'S HIS GAME. HE IS SPYING ON ME! MAYBE HE FIND OUT SOMEDING ALREADY! HE MUST BE ELIMINATED!

CAN YOU ROW A BOAT?

SURE I CAN ROW—AND SAIL, TOO! I USED TO GO OUT WITH DAD. I KNOW THE COAST ALL THE WAY TO SALEM HARBOR!

GOOT! I GIFF YOU A JOB—COME MIT ME!

AT A DESERTED PIER KIPP SHOWS TOMMY A DORY PARTLY FILLED WITH FISH.

YOU ROW DER BOAT TO DER BELL BUOY UND I GIFF YOU A QVARTER!

SWELL! A QUARTER'LL BUY A GRAND SUPPER FOR THE KIDS!

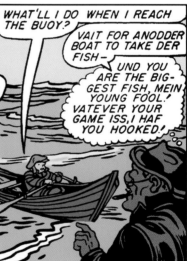

WHAT'LL I DO WHEN I REACH THE BUOY?

VAIT FOR ANODDER BOAT TO TAKE DER FISH—

UND YOU ARE THE BIGGEST FISH, MEIN YOUNG FOOL! VATEVER YOUR GAME ISS, I HAF YOU HOOKED!

183

THE WAVES ARE RUNNING HIGH BUT TOMMY PULLS STURDILY TOWARD HIS DESTINATION.

THE WIND'S AGAINST ME—BUT I'LL MAKE IT.

⑤

TOMMY HOOKS THE BUOY WITH HIS ANCHOR AND MAKES HIS DORY FAST.

THERE ARE NO BOATS IN SIGHT—I MAY HAVE A LONG WAIT!

TOMMY LOOKS IN EVERY DIRECTION BUT THE RIGHT ONE FOR THE BOAT HE IS TO MEET— IT RISES SUDDENLY FROM BENEATH HIM!

MY GOSH! A U-BOAT! IF THEY T-TORPEDO ME I W-WON'T GET MY QUARTER!

HEIL HITLER!

DOWN WITH HITLER! US AMERICANS'LL WHALE THE TAR OUTA THAT CROOKED RAT!

THE NAZI OFFICERS, SPEAKING IN GERMAN, DISCUSS TOMMY'S FATE.

IT IS EVIDENT THE BOY IS AN ENEMY— KIPP MUST HAVE SENT HIM TO US TO DESTROY HIM!

YAH! WHEN WE SUBMERGE WE LEAVE HIM ON DECK.

THE NAZIS HIDE EXPLOSIVES AND SABOTAGE EQUIPMENT IN THE DORY UNDER THE FISH.

IF DER BOAT ISS STOPPED, NO VON VILL LOOK UNTER DER FISH!

ACH, WHO VOULD EVEN BOTHER TO STOP A FISHERMAN'S BOAT?

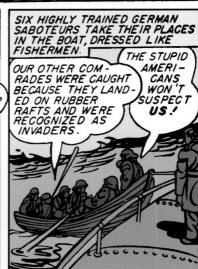

SIX HIGHLY TRAINED GERMAN SABOTEURS TAKE THEIR PLACES IN THE BOAT, DRESSED LIKE FISHERMEN.

OUR OTHER COMRADES WERE CAUGHT BECAUSE THEY LANDED ON RUBBER RAFTS AND WERE RECOGNIZED AS INVADERS.

THE STUPID AMERICANS WON'T SUSPECT US!

A POSSIBLE USE FOR TOMMY OCCURS TO THE SUBMARINE COMMANDER.

MAYBE THIS BOY CAN HELP US MAKE LANDINGS.

SURE—LIKE MY OWN BACK YARD—BUT WHAT'S IT TO YOU?

YOU DID VELL TO FIND DER BUOY—YOU KNOW DER COAST GOOT?

THE COMMANDER ISSUES ORDERS IN GERMAN CONCERNING TOMMY.

TAKE THIS BOY BELOW! WE'LL MAKE HIM PILOT OUR MEN ASHORE AT SALEM AND THEN DISPOSE OF HIM!

MEANWHILE DIANA, IN THE BAG AT KIPP'S STORE DECIDES TO BREAK HER BONDS.

MY GERMAN FRIENDS ARE IN THE OTHER ROOM WAITING FOR ME TO DIE—IT'S TIME TO GET OUT OF HERE!

THE "POYS" AREN'T WATCHING—GOOD! I DON'T WANT THEM TO KNOW I HAVE ESCAPED.

LUCKY I WORE MY **WONDER WO-MAN** CLOTHES UNDERNEATH—THIS HAS TO BE A QUICK CHANGE.

TO MAKE A DUMMY TO TAKE HER PLACE IN THE SACK, **WONDER WOMAN** SPEARS HAMS ON A BROOM HANDLE.

A PERFECT WOMAN'S FIGURE! WHEN MY DUMMY'S IN THE BAG THE NAZIS WON'T KNOW THE DIFFERENCE.

SUGAR CURED HAM

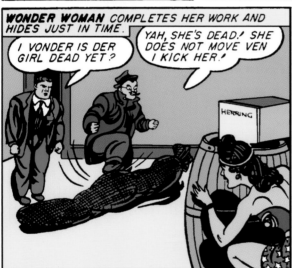

WONDER WOMAN COMPLETES HER WORK AND HIDES JUST IN TIME.

I VONDER IS DER GIRL DEAD YET?

YAH, SHE'S DEAD! SHE DOES NOT MOVE VEN I KICK HER!

HERRING

THE KINDLY GERMANS PLAN A QUICK OCEAN BURIAL FOR THEIR SUPPOSED VICTIM.

DER VOMAN HAS GROWN HEAFIER SINCE SHE DIED!

YAH! UND LOOK HOW STIFF SHE GETS IN FIFTEEN MINUTES!

WEIGHTING THE SACK WITH A HEAVY ANCHOR, THEY THROW IF OFF A DESERTED PIER INTO DEEP WATER.

GOOT VORK! DER VAY ISS NOW CLEAR FOR DER FUEHRER'S AGENTS!

⑦

THE NAZI INVADERS FROM THE SUBMARINE LAND AT THE PIER

HEIL HITLER!

HEIL HITLER!

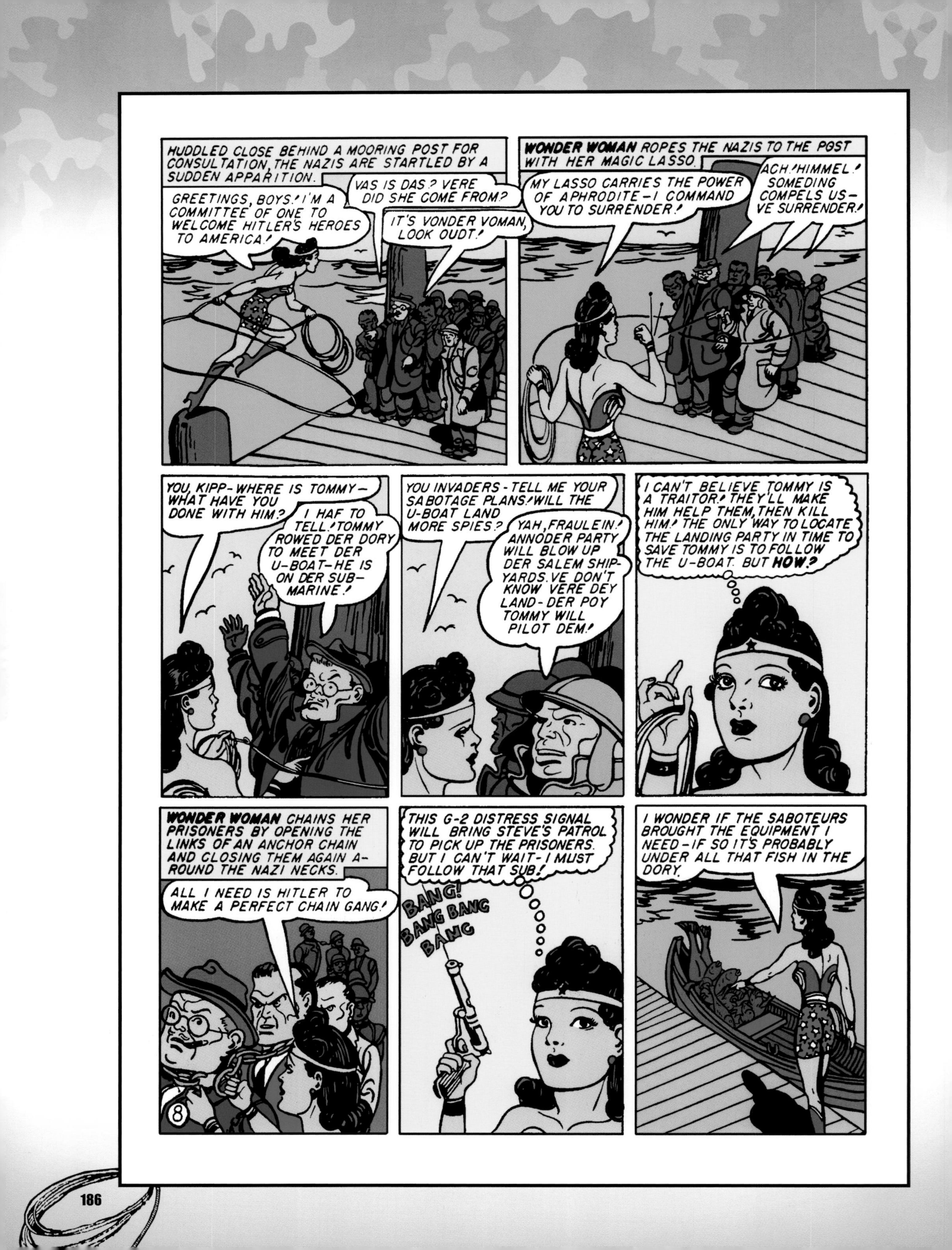

HUDDLED CLOSE BEHIND A MOORING POST FOR CONSULTATION, THE NAZIS ARE STARTLED BY A SUDDEN APPARITION.
GREETINGS, BOYS! I'M A COMMITTEE OF ONE TO WELCOME HITLER'S HEROES TO AMERICA!
VAS IS DAS? VERE DID SHE COME FROM?
IT'S VONDER VOMAN, LOOK OUDT!
WONDER WOMAN ROPES THE NAZIS TO THE POST WITH HER MAGIC LASSO.
MY LASSO CARRIES THE POWER OF APHRODITE—I COMMAND YOU TO SURRENDER!
ACH! HIMMEL! SOMEDING COMPELS US—VE SURRENDER!
YOU, KIPP—WHERE IS TOMMY—WHAT HAVE YOU DONE WITH HIM?
I HAF TO TELL! TOMMY ROWED DER DORY TO MEET DER U-BOAT—HE IS ON DER SUBMARINE!
YOU INVADERS—TELL ME YOUR SABOTAGE PLANS! WILL THE U-BOAT LAND MORE SPIES?
YAH, FRAULEIN! ANNODER PARTY WILL BLOW UP DER SALEM SHIPYARDS. VE DON'T KNOW VERE DEY LAND—DER POY TOMMY WILL PILOT DEM!
I CAN'T BELIEVE TOMMY IS A TRAITOR! THEY'LL MAKE HIM HELP THEM, THEN KILL HIM! THE ONLY WAY TO LOCATE THE LANDING PARTY IN TIME TO SAVE TOMMY IS TO FOLLOW THE U-BOAT. BUT HOW?
WONDER WOMAN CHAINS HER PRISONERS BY OPENING THE LINKS OF AN ANCHOR CHAIN AND CLOSING THEM AGAIN AROUND THE NAZI NECKS.
ALL I NEED IS HITLER TO MAKE A PERFECT CHAIN GANG!
8
THIS G-2 DISTRESS SIGNAL WILL BRING STEVE'S PATROL TO PICK UP THE PRISONERS. BUT I CAN'T WAIT—I MUST FOLLOW THAT SUB!
BANG! BANG BANG BANG
I WONDER IF THE SABOTEURS BROUGHT THE EQUIPMENT I NEED—IF SO IT'S PROBABLY UNDER ALL THAT FISH IN THE DORY.

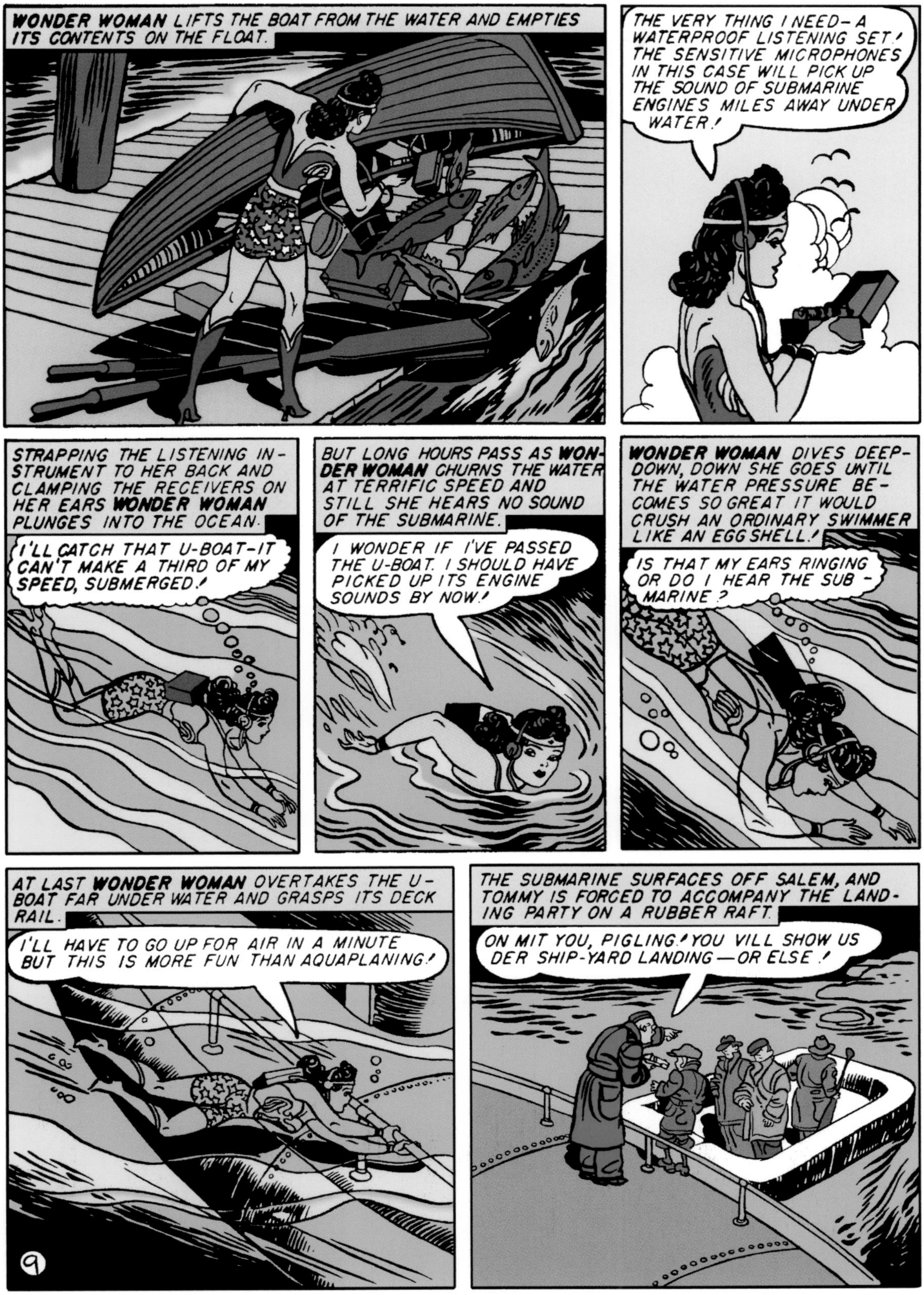
WONDER WOMAN LIFTS THE BOAT FROM THE WATER AND EMPTIES ITS CONTENTS ON THE FLOAT.
THE VERY THING I NEED— A WATERPROOF LISTENING SET! THE SENSITIVE MICROPHONES IN THIS CASE WILL PICK UP THE SOUND OF SUBMARINE ENGINES MILES AWAY UNDER WATER!
STRAPPING THE LISTENING INSTRUMENT TO HER BACK AND CLAMPING THE RECEIVERS ON HER EARS WONDER WOMAN PLUNGES INTO THE OCEAN.
I'LL CATCH THAT U-BOAT-IT CAN'T MAKE A THIRD OF MY SPEED, SUBMERGED!
BUT LONG HOURS PASS AS WONDER WOMAN CHURNS THE WATER AT TERRIFIC SPEED AND STILL SHE HEARS NO SOUND OF THE SUBMARINE.
I WONDER IF I'VE PASSED THE U-BOAT. I SHOULD HAVE PICKED UP ITS ENGINE SOUNDS BY NOW!
WONDER WOMAN DIVES DEEP-DOWN, DOWN SHE GOES UNTIL THE WATER PRESSURE BECOMES SO GREAT IT WOULD CRUSH AN ORDINARY SWIMMER LIKE AN EGG SHELL!
IS THAT MY EARS RINGING OR DO I HEAR THE SUBMARINE?
AT LAST WONDER WOMAN OVERTAKES THE U-BOAT FAR UNDER WATER AND GRASPS ITS DECK RAIL.
I'LL HAVE TO GO UP FOR AIR IN A MINUTE BUT THIS IS MORE FUN THAN AQUAPLANING!
9
THE SUBMARINE SURFACES OFF SALEM, AND TOMMY IS FORCED TO ACCOMPANY THE LANDING PARTY ON A RUBBER RAFT.
ON MIT YOU, PIGLING! YOU VILL SHOW US DER SHIP-YARD LANDING —OR ELSE!

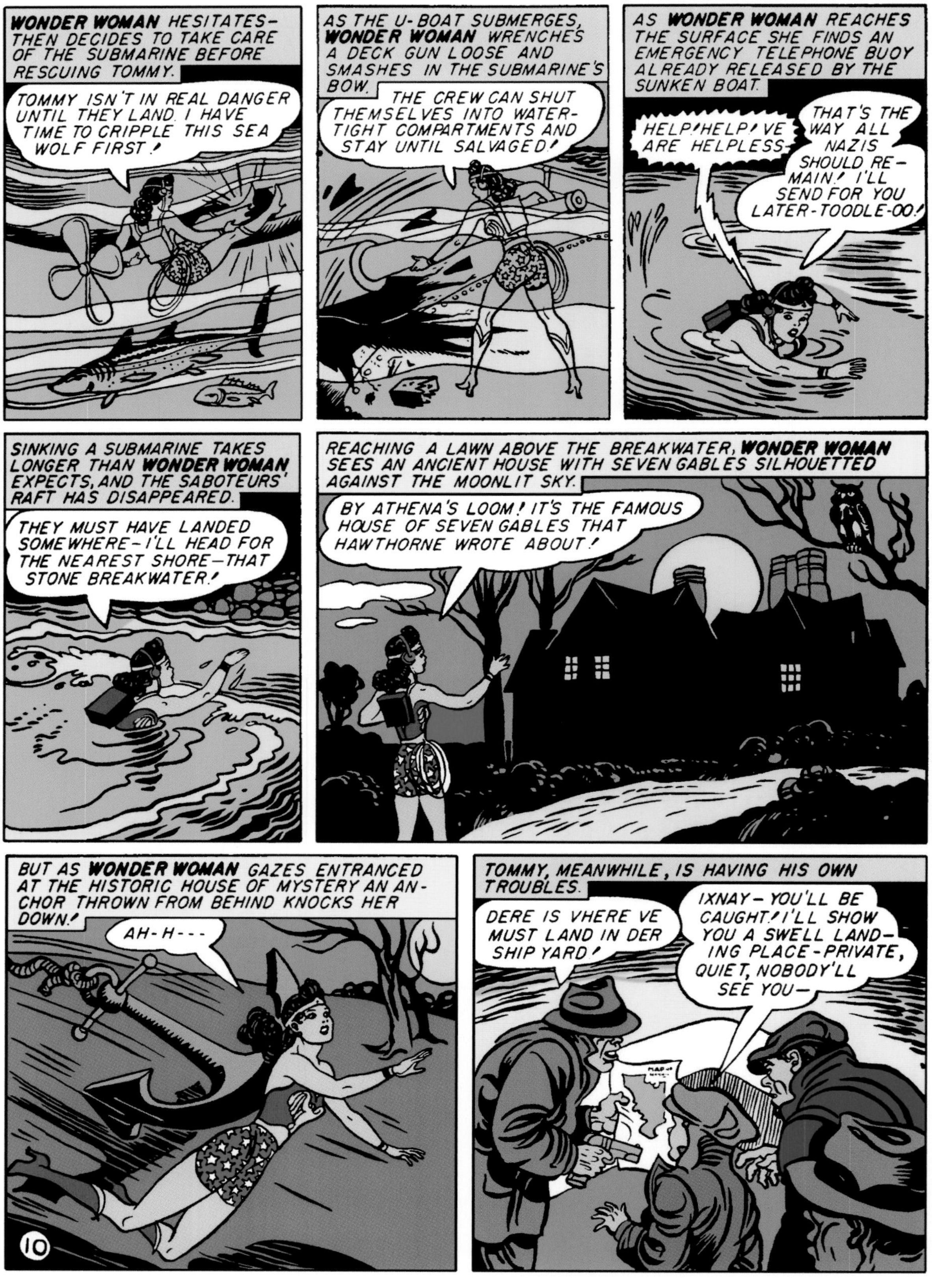
WONDER WOMAN HESITATES– THEN DECIDES TO TAKE CARE OF THE SUBMARINE BEFORE RESCUING TOMMY.
TOMMY ISN'T IN REAL DANGER UNTIL THEY LAND. I HAVE TIME TO CRIPPLE THIS SEA WOLF FIRST!
AS THE U-BOAT SUBMERGES, WONDER WOMAN WRENCHES A DECK GUN LOOSE AND SMASHES IN THE SUBMARINE'S BOW.
THE CREW CAN SHUT THEMSELVES INTO WATER-TIGHT COMPARTMENTS AND STAY UNTIL SALVAGED!
AS WONDER WOMAN REACHES THE SURFACE SHE FINDS AN EMERGENCY TELEPHONE BUOY ALREADY RELEASED BY THE SUNKEN BOAT.
HELP! HELP! VE ARE HELPLESS–
THAT'S THE WAY ALL NAZIS SHOULD RE-MAIN! I'LL SEND FOR YOU LATER-TOODLE-OO!
SINKING A SUBMARINE TAKES LONGER THAN WONDER WOMAN EXPECTS, AND THE SABOTEURS' RAFT HAS DISAPPEARED.
THEY MUST HAVE LANDED SOMEWHERE–I'LL HEAD FOR THE NEAREST SHORE–THAT STONE BREAKWATER!
REACHING A LAWN ABOVE THE BREAKWATER, WONDER WOMAN SEES AN ANCIENT HOUSE WITH SEVEN GABLES SILHOUETTED AGAINST THE MOONLIT SKY.
BY ATHENA'S LOOM! IT'S THE FAMOUS HOUSE OF SEVEN GABLES THAT HAWTHORNE WROTE ABOUT!
BUT AS WONDER WOMAN GAZES ENTRANCED AT THE HISTORIC HOUSE OF MYSTERY AN AN-CHOR THROWN FROM BEHIND KNOCKS HER DOWN!
AH-H---
10
TOMMY, MEANWHILE, IS HAVING HIS OWN TROUBLES.
DERE IS VHERE VE MUST LAND IN DER SHIP YARD!
IXNAY– YOU'LL BE CAUGHT! I'LL SHOW YOU A SWELL LAND-ING PLACE-PRIVATE, QUIET, NOBODY'LL SEE YOU–

TOMMY PERSUADES THE INVADERS TO LAND AT THE HOUSE OF SEVEN GABLES, KNOWING THAT CUSTODIANS WATCH THE PREMISES DAY AND NIGHT.

VAT IS DIS PLACE? QVIET YOU—

HELP! HELP! NAZI SPIES!

TOMMY IS KNOCKED UNCONSCIOUS BUT HIS CRIES AROUSE ONE OF THE HOUSE CUSTODIANS.

WHO GOES THERE? SPEAK OR I'LL CALL THE POLICE!

189

CREEPING STEALTHILY TO THE HOUSE, A NAZI INVADER SEIZES THE GIRL.

OOOG-GLUB-UGH!

KEEP STILL OR I'LL KILL YOU!

THE NAZIS, SEARCHING THE HOUSE, FIND ANOTHER GIRL EMPLOYEE IN AN ATTIC BEDROOM.

QVIET OR I'LL BLOW YOUR HEAD OFF!

OOOH—

THE GIRLS ARE GAGGED AND BOUND TO THE BEDPOSTS.

DO NOT MIND IF DESE ROPES ARE A LITTLE UNCOMFORTABLE—IT VILL NOT BE FOR LONG!

WHEN TOMMY RECOVERS CONSCIOUSNESS HE FINDS HIMSELF BOUND IN A CHAIR FACING THE FAMOUS SEVEN GABLES FIREPLACE, IN THE GROUND FLOOR LIVING ROOM.

DIS VILL BLOW YOU UP AND SET DER HOUSE ON FIRE, LEAVING NO TRACE.

MEANWHILE WONDER WOMAN, CHAINED TO THE ANCHOR THAT KNOCKED HER DOWN, IS ADDED TO THE COLLECTION OF PRISONERS IN THE GIRLS' BEDROOM.

VE HEAR ABOUT VONDER VOMAN UND FIX HER SO SHE CANNOT ESCAPE!

BUT THE MOMENT THE NAZIS LEAVE THE ROOM, WONDER WOMAN BREAKS HER HEAVY CHAINS LIKE COTTON THREAD.

I LET THEM CHAIN ME TO SAVE TIME IN FINDING OTHER PRISONERS—I'LL HAVE YOU GIRLS FREE IN A JIFFY.

AS **WONDER WOMAN** RELEASES THE GIRLS, THEY HEAR HEAVY FOOTSTEPS ASCENDING THE STAIRS.

THOSE TERRIBLE MEN ARE COMING! I'LL OPEN THE SECRET PASSAGE—

QUICK, **WONDER WOMAN!** STEP THROUGH — THEY'LL NEVER FIND THIS HIDDEN DOOR!

THE NAZI INVADER IS COMPLETELY BEWILDERED AT FINDING THE ROOM EMPTY.

THIS BOMB VILL SET FIRE--- HUH? VERE ARE DOSE GIRLS? HOW COULD DEY ESCAPE? I VATCH DER STAIRS- FRITZ VATCH VINDOWS OUTSIDE— DONNERVETTER! ARE DEY GONE OR AM I CRAZY?

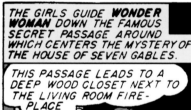

THE GIRLS GUIDE **WONDER WOMAN** DOWN THE FAMOUS SECRET PASSAGE AROUND WHICH CENTERS THE MYSTERY OF THE HOUSE OF SEVEN GABLES.

THIS PASSAGE LEADS TO A DEEP WOOD CLOSET NEXT TO THE LIVING ROOM FIREPLACE

PEERING CAUTIOUSLY FROM THE WOOD CLOSET DOOR, **WONDER WOMAN** SEES TOMMY IN A DANGEROUS SPOT.

IN THREE MINUTES DER POY UND DER HOUSE VILL DISAPPEAR.

YOU'RE WRONG ABOUT WHAT'S GOING TO DISAPPEAR.

REACHING A LONG ARM, **WONDER WOMAN** YANKS THE NAZI INTO THE WOOD CLOSET.

MUSTN'T PLAY WITH MATCHES, LITTLE BOY— MAMA SPANK!

ACH-VOT ISS?

THE OTHER NAZI, WHOSE BACK WAS TURNED, IS PUZZLED BY HIS COMRADE'S DISAPPEARANCE.

HURRY, ANTON- VOT! VERE ARE YOU, ANTON? VERE COULD HE HAF GONE? ISS DISS MAGIC!

IT'S TIME WE STOPPED PLAYING HIDE AND SEEK, MY FRIEND - I LIKE THIS GAME BETTER!

UGH— UMH! A HUMAN BIG BERTHA!

GEE, YOU MUST BE **WONDER WOMAN!** WOW-DID YOU HIT THAT GUY! LISTEN- THIS GANG'S GOT PASSES TO THE SHIPYARDS- THEY'RE GONNA BLOW UP THE NEW AIRCRAFT CARRIER BEING BUILT THERE! WE GOTTA STOP 'EM!

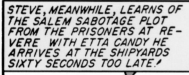

STEVE, MEANWHILE, LEARNS OF THE SALEM SABOTAGE PLOT FROM THE PRISONERS AT REVERE. WITH ETTA CANDY HE ARRIVES AT THE SHIPYARDS SIXTY SECONDS TOO LATE!

THEY'RE BOMBING THE NEW AIRCRAFT CARRIER!

COME ON—BETTER LATE THAN NEVER!

ETTA TACKLES THE BOMB THROWER.

I'M THROWIN' YOU BEFORE YOU MAKE THAT FORWARD PASS!

STEVE STOPS THE INVADERS AT THE POINT OF HIS AUTOMATIC.

HANDS UP! THE GAME'S OVER!

KAMERAD! DON'T SHOOT—VE SURRENDER!

BUT TOMMY, ARRIVING WITH **WONDER WOMAN**, MAKES A STARTLING DISCOVERY.

LOOK, **WONDER WOMAN**, THE AIRCRAFT CARRIER'S SLIDIN' DOWN THE WAYS! THE BOMB MUSTA LAUNCHED HER.

BY HERCULES, YOU'RE RIGHT! HER HULL'S INCOMPLETE—SHE'LL SINK, A TOTAL LOSS!

LEAPING RECKLESSLY IN FRONT OF THE SLOWLY SLIDING MONSTER, **WONDER WOMAN** PITS HER AMAZON STRENGTH AGAINST 35,000 TONS OF GRINDING STEEL!

THIS MAY CRUSH ME! BUT AMERICA **NEEDS** THIS SHIP!

WONDER WOMAN WINS! THE HUGE MASS STOPS ITS FORWARD MOVEMENT, WORKMEN RUSHED BY THE HUNDRED FROM ALL PARTS OF THE YARDS, DRIVE WEDGES AND STAYS WHICH HOLD THE SHIP IN PLACE.

WOO WOO! YOU SHOWED 'EM BABY!

YOU'RE STRONGER'N A BATTLESHIP! BOY, WILL THE REVERE KIDS ENVY ME KNOWIN' YOU!

MY BEAUTIFUL ANGEL! IF I COULD ONLY HOLD YOU LIKE YOU HELD THAT SHIP!

DON'T LET DIANA PRINCE HEAR YOU SAY THAT—I THINK SHE'S GOT A CRUSH ON YOU, STEVE!

MORE ADVENTURES OF **WONDER WOMAN** EVERY MONTH IN SENSATION COMICS !!

FOR VICTORY BUY UNITED STATES SAVINGS BONDS AND STAMPS

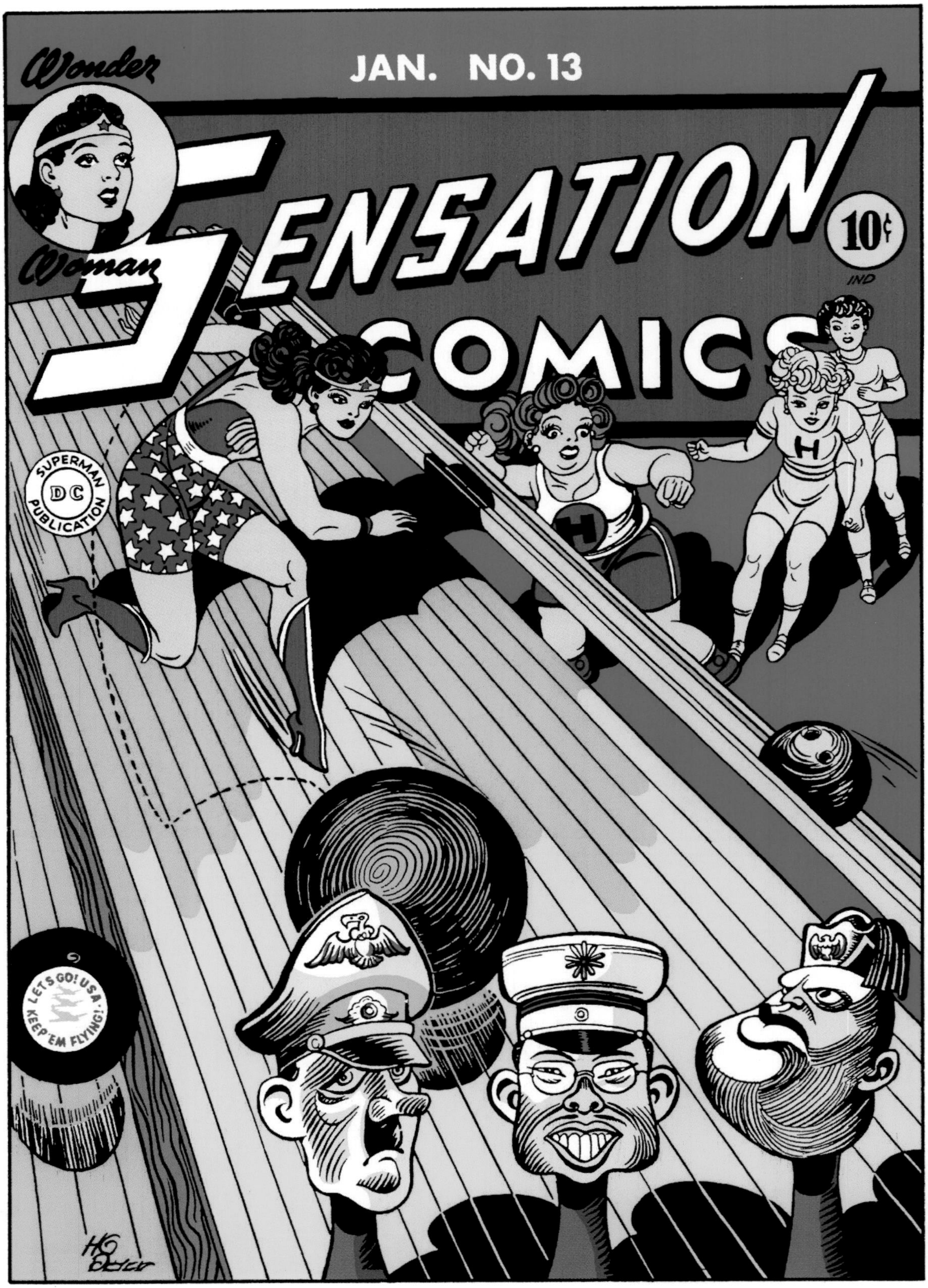
Wonder Woman
JAN. NO. 13
SENSATION COMICS
10¢
IND
SUPERMAN DC PUBLICATION
LETS GO! U.S.A. KEEP 'EM FLYING!
H
H
HG Peter

Sensation Comics #13 (Jan. 1943) - art: H.G. Peter

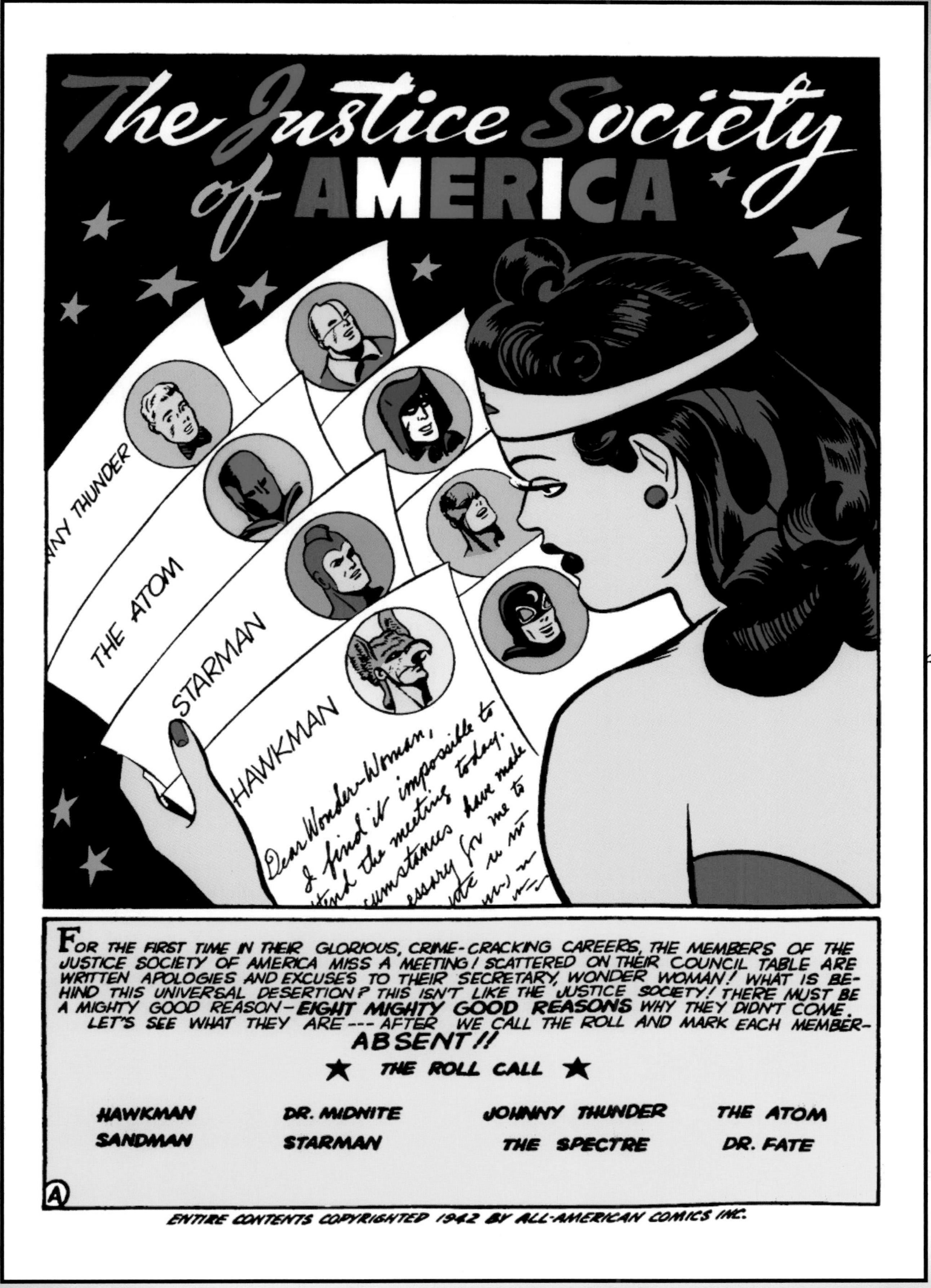
The Justice Society of AMERICA
NNY THUNDER
THE ATOM
STARMAN
HAWKMAN
Dear Wonder-Woman,
FOR THE FIRST TIME IN THEIR GLORIOUS, CRIME-CRACKING CAREERS, THE MEMBERS OF THE JUSTICE SOCIETY OF AMERICA MISS A MEETING! SCATTERED ON THEIR COUNCIL TABLE ARE WRITTEN APOLOGIES AND EXCUSES TO THEIR SECRETARY, WONDER WOMAN! WHAT IS BEHIND THIS UNIVERSAL DESERTION? THIS ISN'T LIKE THE JUSTICE SOCIETY! THERE MUST BE A MIGHTY GOOD REASON—EIGHT MIGHTY GOOD REASONS WHY THEY DIDN'T COME. LET'S SEE WHAT THEY ARE --- AFTER WE CALL THE ROLL AND MARK EACH MEMBER—ABSENT!!
★ THE ROLL CALL ★
HAWKMAN
SANDMAN
DR. MIDNITE
STARMAN
JOHNNY THUNDER
THE SPECTRE
THE ATOM
DR. FATE
ENTIRE CONTENTS COPYRIGHTED 1942 BY ALL-AMERICAN COMICS INC.

All-Star Comics #15 (Feb.–March 1943) - script: unknown - art: various

Part Four

Wonder Woman's stories had more World War II content than either Superman or Batman.

"Don't You Know There's a War On?"

The above phrase was ubiquitous during the Second World War. Anytime one person did anything—anything at all—that another person felt was unhelpful to the war effort, he was pointedly asked that question, as if it's mere repeating would shame the offender into changing his behavior. And once in a while maybe it did.

Well, Wonder Woman and her creators definitely knew there was a war on—especially in her stories inside issues of *Sensation Comics, Wonder Woman,* and *Comic Cavalcade.* Strangely, though, although there are quite a few more Wonder Woman stories with World War II content than there are in which Superman or Batman take part in the war, there weren't as many war-oriented covers showcasing the Amazon princess as you might expect. It's impossible to say precisely why that is so.

Not that there weren't some good war covers featuring Wonder Woman. On that of *Sensation* #15 (March 1943), she's drawn by H.G. Peter twisting Nazi naval artillery into pretzels, much as Superman had done on some earlier *Action Comics* covers. On #20 (Aug. 1943) she steers an Army Jeep—apparently with her tailbone—while several female service-people are bounced around; and a month late, on #21, she uses her Amazonian strength to stop a Japanese plane's propeller.

There was, however, no death of war-oriented stories in her mags. In *Comic Cavalcade* #2 (Spring 1493), she went toe to toe with Fausta, a female Nazi spy—one of an apparently inexhaustible supply of that coed commodity. And this one seems to be super-powered, as well!

The most unique thing about that story, though, is that it's one of a few Wonder Woman stories between 1941 and 1958, when H.G. Peter was abruptly put out to pasture, that is not drawn by the character's originating artist. Although reportedly there were some artists in the Marston "studio" who helped Peter with backgrounds and the like, eventually the mushrooming of the Amazon's appearances meant that he needed to be spelled on occasion. The only artist to do so prior to 1958 was Frank Godwin, an artist then in his fifties who had a highly illustrative style, as evidenced by the Connie comic strip he was drawing at that time. Apparently he found time to churn out a handful of Wonder Woman stories in between doing the strip, and his style was just close enough to the very individualistic style of Harry Peter not to be jarring. Still, after a small number of such stories, Wonder Woman went back to being just the artistic product of "all H.G. Peter all the time."

The story in *Sensation* #15 has the Amazon preventing Nazi battleships from shelling New York City and shipping to and from it. This may seem far-fetched—since, for most of the war, Germany had no surface warships plying the world's oceans, let alone attacking the Big Apple. But there were other dangers posed to Manhattan and its environs by the Nazis. Their U-boats posed a constant threat to Allied shipping, from the moment a vessel sailed from or approached New York, Boston, or some other port. In the early months of the war, when New York's authorities astonishingly refused to impose a blackout (a mandatory dousing of lights at night) because they were afraid of harming the city's lucrative tourist trade, the U-boats could actually use the metropolis' lights as a backdrop behind

Allied ship, lining them up in their sights like tin ducks in a shooting alley. Those enemy submarines could probably have lobbed a few torpedoes at piers or dockside buildings, as well, but the German held them back for the more valuable ships.

And then there was Hitler's infamous concept of a "New York bomber," or "Amerika-Bomber," which pops up in more than one comic book story or other outlandish fantasy of the era. Apparently, Hitler was obsessed for a time with the notion of sending New York City up in flames. As a result, several German airplane manufacturers competed to see which could best design a bomber that could fly the 3600 miles from Germany to the United States and drop its cargo of bombs. Fortunately, after things began to turn against Germany during 1942, with the Russians standing up to them at Stalingrad and so on, the idea was abandoned as impractical—or, at the very least, not worth all the effort. A lone plane of that type could hardly have carried enough bombs to do substantial damage to a major city in that day and age. That had to wait three years—for the atomic bomb.

Wonder Woman #5 (June–July 1943) contains a back-handed version of Marston's feminist philosophy. Dr. Psycho, one of the Amazon's most fiendish (and most disturbed) foes, issues propaganda saying that using women in factories and other capacities will lose the war for the U.S.—quite the opposite of what really happened, of course. But then, hey—his name was Psycho, right?

All in all, there were many other enemy encounters and Axis agents in Wonder Woman's adventures—far more than there were in Superman and Batman stories put together!

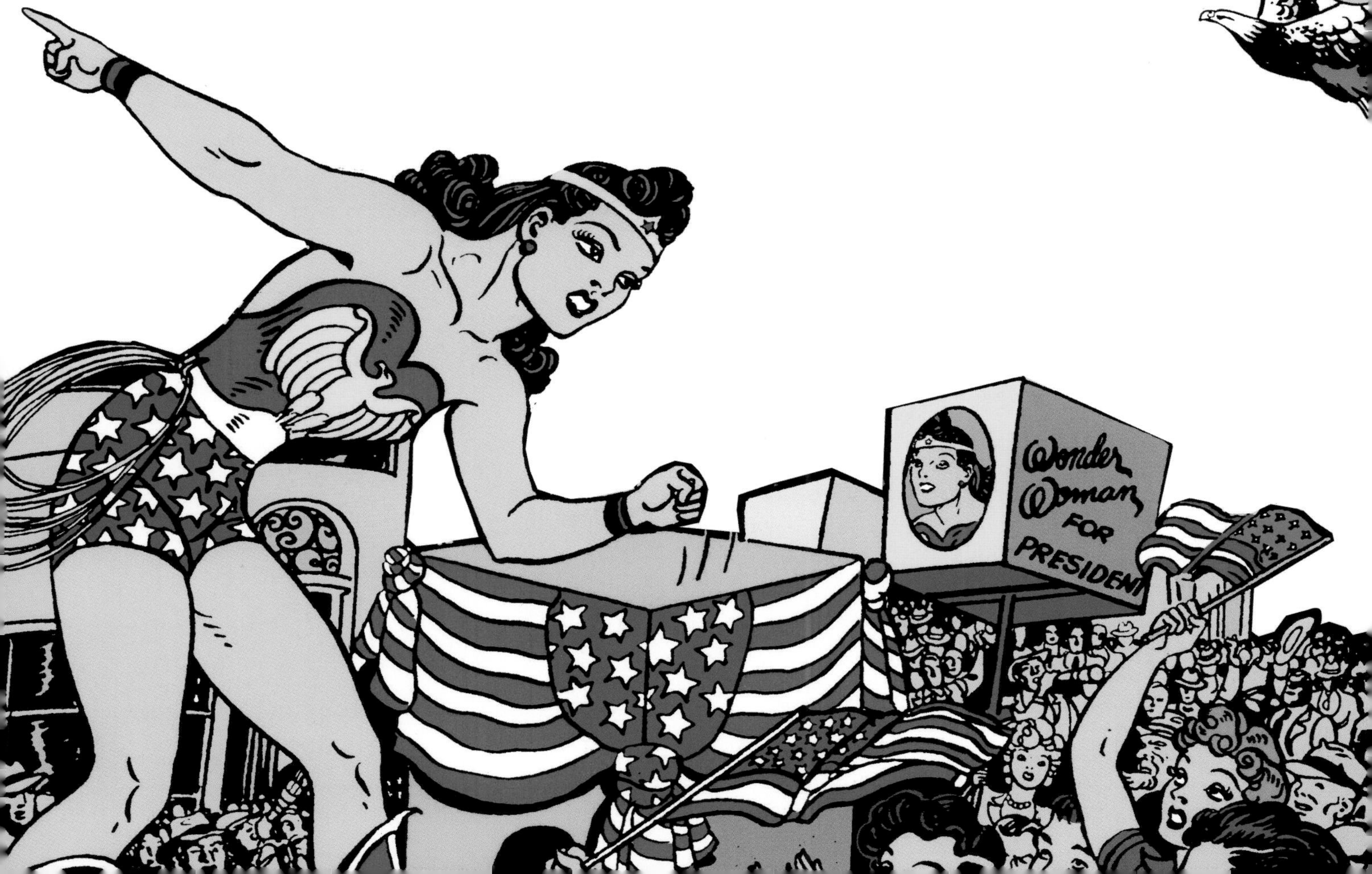
Wonder
Woman
FOR
PRESIDEN

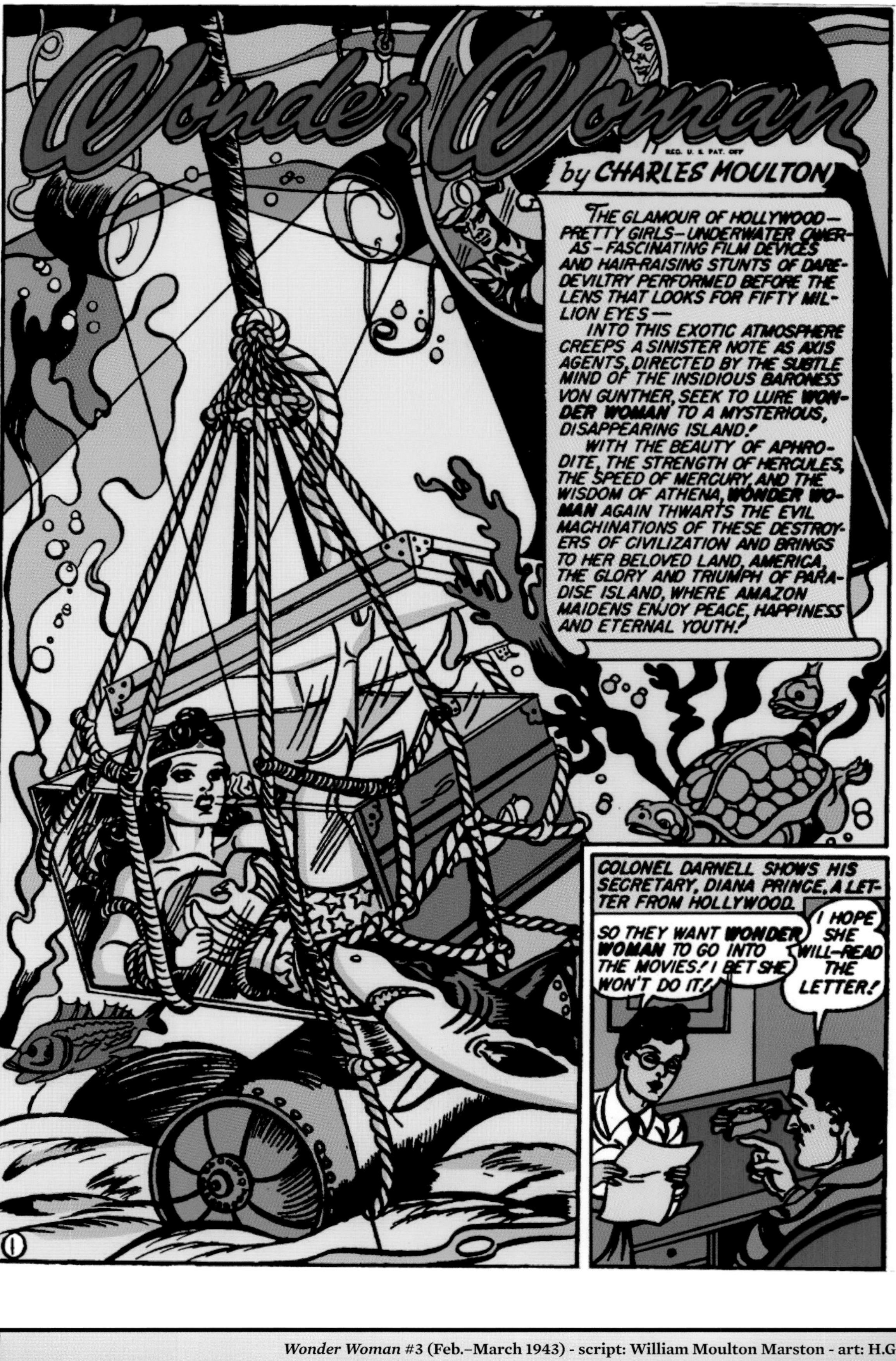
Wonder Woman
REG. U. S. PAT. OFF
by CHARLES MOULTON
THE GLAMOUR OF HOLLYWOOD—PRETTY GIRLS—UNDERWATER CAMERAS—FASCINATING FILM DEVICES AND HAIR-RAISING STUNTS OF DAREDEVILTRY PERFORMED BEFORE THE LENS THAT LOOKS FOR FIFTY MILLION EYES— INTO THIS EXOTIC ATMOSPHERE CREEPS A SINISTER NOTE AS AXIS AGENTS, DIRECTED BY THE SUBTLE MIND OF THE INSIDIOUS BARONESS VON GUNTHER, SEEK TO LURE WONDER WOMAN TO A MYSTERIOUS, DISAPPEARING ISLAND! WITH THE BEAUTY OF APHRODITE, THE STRENGTH OF HERCULES, THE SPEED OF MERCURY, AND THE WISDOM OF ATHENA, WONDER WOMAN AGAIN THWARTS THE EVIL MACHINATIONS OF THESE DESTROYERS OF CIVILIZATION AND BRINGS TO HER BELOVED LAND, AMERICA, THE GLORY AND TRIUMPH OF PARADISE ISLAND, WHERE AMAZON MAIDENS ENJOY PEACE, HAPPINESS AND ETERNAL YOUTH!
1
COLONEL DARNELL SHOWS HIS SECRETARY, DIANA PRINCE, A LETTER FROM HOLLYWOOD.
SO THEY WANT WONDER WOMAN TO GO INTO THE MOVIES! I BET SHE WON'T DO IT!
I HOPE SHE WILL—READ THE LETTER!

Wonder Woman #3 (Feb.–March 1943) - script: William Moulton Marston - art: H.G. Peter

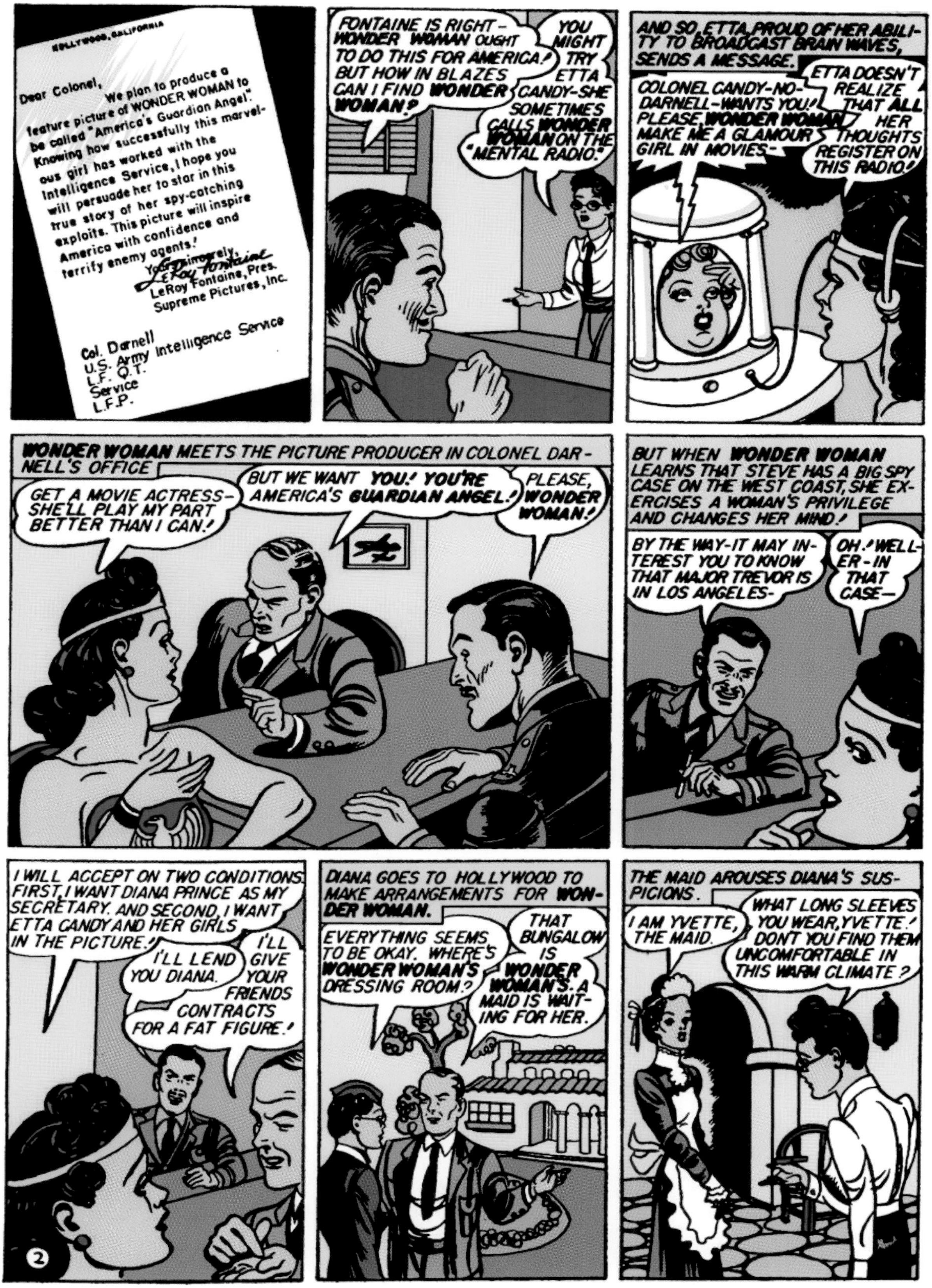
HOLLYWOOD, CALIFORNIA
Dear Colonel,
We plan to produce a feature picture of WONDER WOMAN to be called "America's Guardian Angel". Knowing how successfully this marvelous girl has worked with the Intelligence Service, I hope you will persuade her to star in this true story of her spy-catching exploits. This picture will inspire America with confidence and terrify enemy agents!
Yours sincerely,
LeRoy Fontaine
LeRoy Fontaine, Pres.
Supreme Pictures, Inc.
Col. Darnell
U.S. Army Intelligence Service
L.F. Q.T.
Service
L.F.P.
FONTAINE IS RIGHT – WONDER WOMAN OUGHT TO DO THIS FOR AMERICA! BUT HOW IN BLAZES CAN I FIND WONDER WOMAN?
YOU MIGHT TRY ETTA CANDY-SHE SOMETIMES CALLS WONDER WOMAN ON THE "MENTAL RADIO."
AND SO, ETTA, PROUD OF HER ABILITY TO BROADCAST BRAIN WAVES, SENDS A MESSAGE.
COLONEL CANDY-NO-DARNELL-WANTS YOU! PLEASE, WONDER WOMAN MAKE ME A GLAMOUR GIRL IN MOVIES-
ETTA DOESN'T REALIZE THAT ALL HER THOUGHTS REGISTER ON THIS RADIO!
WONDER WOMAN MEETS THE PICTURE PRODUCER IN COLONEL DARNELL'S OFFICE
GET A MOVIE ACTRESS-SHE'LL PLAY MY PART BETTER THAN I CAN!
BUT WE WANT YOU! YOU'RE AMERICA'S GUARDIAN ANGEL!
PLEASE, WONDER WOMAN!
BUT WHEN WONDER WOMAN LEARNS THAT STEVE HAS A BIG SPY CASE ON THE WEST COAST, SHE EXERCISES A WOMAN'S PRIVILEGE AND CHANGES HER MIND!
BY THE WAY-IT MAY INTEREST YOU TO KNOW THAT MAJOR TREVOR IS IN LOS ANGELES-
OH! WELL-ER-IN THAT CASE-
I WILL ACCEPT ON TWO CONDITIONS: FIRST, I WANT DIANA PRINCE AS MY SECRETARY. AND SECOND, I WANT ETTA CANDY AND HER GIRLS IN THE PICTURE!
I'LL LEND YOU DIANA.
I'LL GIVE YOUR FRIENDS CONTRACTS FOR A FAT FIGURE!
2
DIANA GOES TO HOLLYWOOD TO MAKE ARRANGEMENTS FOR WONDER WOMAN.
EVERYTHING SEEMS TO BE OKAY. WHERE'S WONDER WOMAN'S DRESSING ROOM?
THAT BUNGALOW IS WONDER WOMAN'S. A MAID IS WAITING FOR HER.
THE MAID AROUSES DIANA'S SUSPICIONS.
I AM YVETTE, THE MAID.
WHAT LONG SLEEVES YOU WEAR, YVETTE! DON'T YOU FIND THEM UNCOMFORTABLE IN THIS WARM CLIMATE?

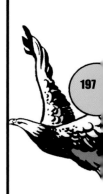

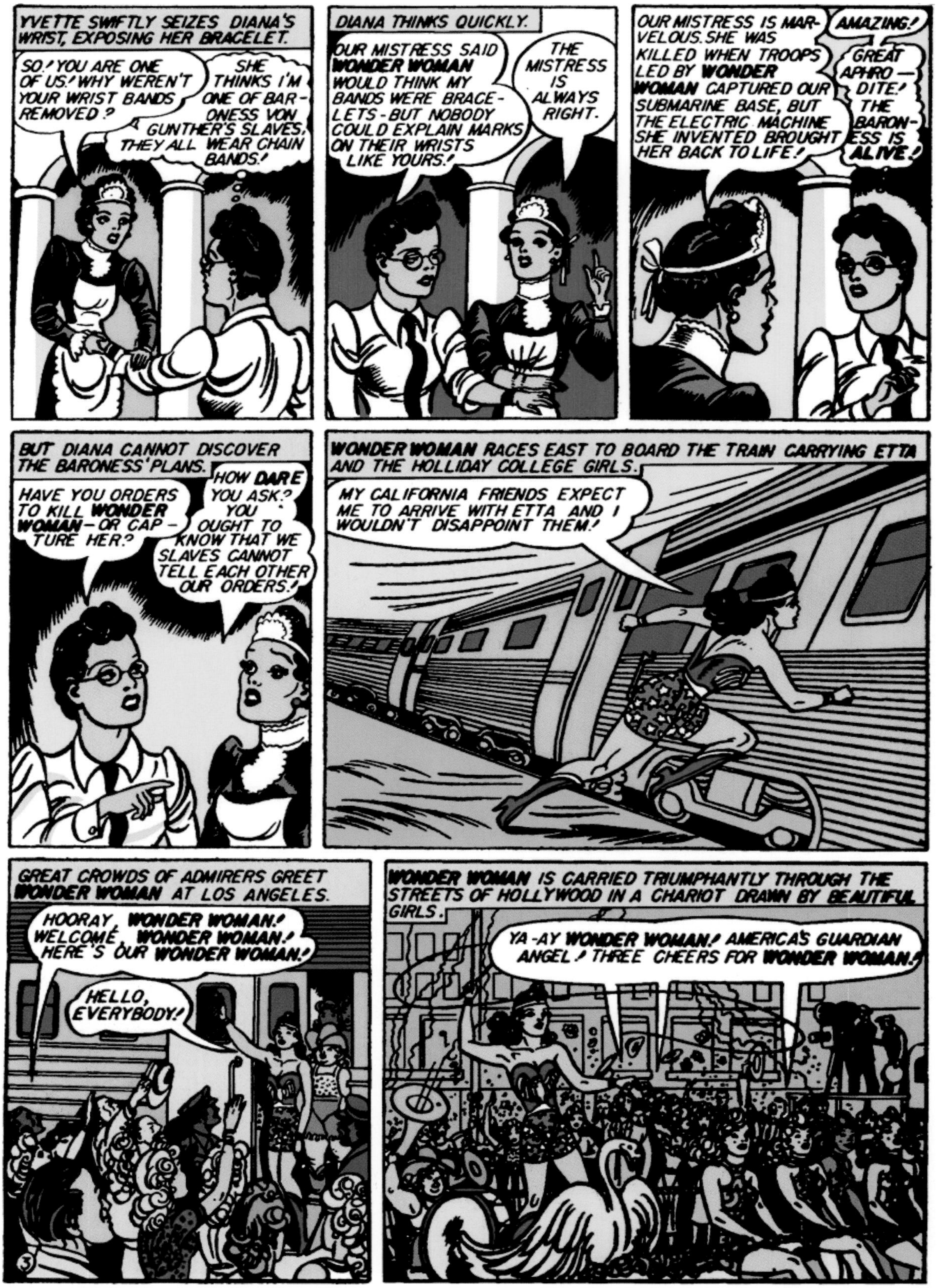
YVETTE SWIFTLY SEIZES DIANA'S WRIST, EXPOSING HER BRACELET.
SO! YOU ARE ONE OF US! WHY WEREN'T YOUR WRIST BANDS REMOVED?
SHE THINKS I'M ONE OF BARONESS VON GUNTHER'S SLAVES. THEY ALL WEAR CHAIN BANDS!
DIANA THINKS QUICKLY.
OUR MISTRESS SAID WONDER WOMAN WOULD THINK MY BANDS WERE BRACELETS - BUT NOBODY COULD EXPLAIN MARKS ON THEIR WRISTS LIKE YOURS!
THE MISTRESS IS ALWAYS RIGHT.
OUR MISTRESS IS MARVELOUS. SHE WAS KILLED WHEN TROOPS LED BY WONDER WOMAN CAPTURED OUR SUBMARINE BASE, BUT THE ELECTRIC MACHINE SHE INVENTED BROUGHT HER BACK TO LIFE!
AMAZING!
GREAT APHRODITE! THE BARONESS IS ALIVE!
BUT DIANA CANNOT DISCOVER THE BARONESS' PLANS.
HAVE YOU ORDERS TO KILL WONDER WOMAN - OR CAPTURE HER?
HOW DARE YOU ASK? YOU OUGHT TO KNOW THAT WE SLAVES CANNOT TELL EACH OTHER OUR ORDERS!
WONDER WOMAN RACES EAST TO BOARD THE TRAIN CARRYING ETTA AND THE HOLLIDAY COLLEGE GIRLS.
MY CALIFORNIA FRIENDS EXPECT ME TO ARRIVE WITH ETTA AND I WOULDN'T DISAPPOINT THEM!
GREAT CROWDS OF ADMIRERS GREET WONDER WOMAN AT LOS ANGELES.
HOORAY, WONDER WOMAN! WELCOME, WONDER WOMAN! HERE'S OUR WONDER WOMAN!
HELLO, EVERYBODY!
3
WONDER WOMAN IS CARRIED TRIUMPHANTLY THROUGH THE STREETS OF HOLLYWOOD IN A CHARIOT DRAWN BY BEAUTIFUL GIRLS.
YA-AY WONDER WOMAN! AMERICA'S GUARDIAN ANGEL! THREE CHEERS FOR WONDER WOMAN!

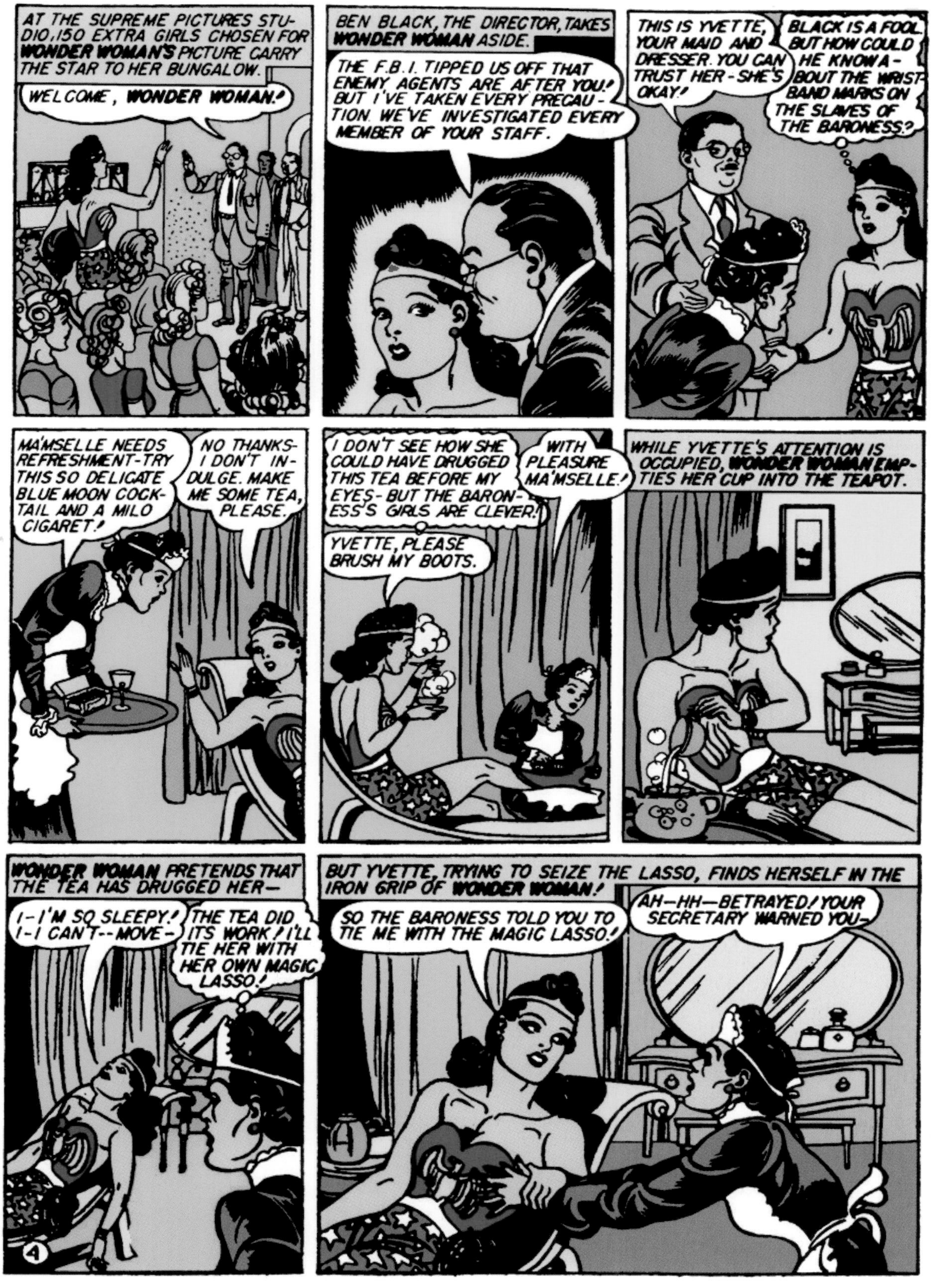
AT THE SUPREME PICTURES STUDIO, 150 EXTRA GIRLS CHOSEN FOR WONDER WOMAN'S PICTURE CARRY THE STAR TO HER BUNGALOW.
WELCOME, WONDER WOMAN!
BEN BLACK, THE DIRECTOR, TAKES WONDER WOMAN ASIDE.
THE F.B.I. TIPPED US OFF THAT ENEMY AGENTS ARE AFTER YOU! BUT I'VE TAKEN EVERY PRECAUTION. WE'VE INVESTIGATED EVERY MEMBER OF YOUR STAFF.
THIS IS YVETTE, YOUR MAID AND DRESSER. YOU CAN TRUST HER - SHE'S OKAY!
BLACK IS A FOOL. BUT HOW COULD HE KNOW ABOUT THE WRIST-BAND MARKS ON THE SLAVES OF THE BARONESS?
MA'MSELLE NEEDS REFRESHMENT-TRY THIS SO DELICATE BLUE MOON COCKTAIL AND A MILO CIGARET!
NO THANKS- I DON'T INDULGE. MAKE ME SOME TEA, PLEASE.
I DON'T SEE HOW SHE COULD HAVE DRUGGED THIS TEA BEFORE MY EYES- BUT THE BARONESS'S GIRLS ARE CLEVER!
WITH PLEASURE MA'MSELLE!
YVETTE, PLEASE BRUSH MY BOOTS.
WHILE YVETTE'S ATTENTION IS OCCUPIED, WONDER WOMAN EMPTIES HER CUP INTO THE TEAPOT.
WONDER WOMAN PRETENDS THAT THE TEA HAS DRUGGED HER—
I-I'M SO SLEEPY! I-I CAN'T--MOVE-
THE TEA DID ITS WORK! I'LL TIE HER WITH HER OWN MAGIC LASSO!
BUT YVETTE, TRYING TO SEIZE THE LASSO, FINDS HERSELF IN THE IRON GRIP OF WONDER WOMAN!
SO THE BARONESS TOLD YOU TO TIE ME WITH THE MAGIC LASSO!
AH-HH—BETRAYED! YOUR SECRETARY WARNED YOU-
4

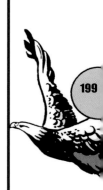

WRENCHING HERSELF LOOSE, YVETTE POINTS HYSTERICALLY AT **WONDER WOMAN'S** BRACELETS

NOW I KNOW YOUR SECRET!YOU-**YOU** ARE DIANA PRINCE!

I SHOULD HAVE KNOWN THIS GIRL WOULD REC-OGNIZE MY BRACELETS-

YOU KNOW MY SECRET BUT SOON I SHALL KNOW YOURS! THIS MAGIC LASSO WILL COMPEL YOU TO BE-TRAY THE FIEND WHO CONTROLS YOU –

NEVER! I WILL DIE RATHER THAN BE-TRAY MY MISTRESS! FAREWELL!

WONDER WOMAN HASTILY SUM-MONS A DOCTOR BUT-

SHE DRANK HYDRO-CYANIC ACID-DEATH WAS INSTANTANEOUS!

I AM SORRY! I NEVER IMAGINED SHE WOULD HARM HERSELF.

MY SECRET IS SAFE AGAIN BUT AT WHAT A PRICE!

WONDER WOMAN SHOWS THE DRUGGED TEA TO DIRECTOR BLACK.

HAVE THAT TEA ANALYZED-YOU'LL FIND IT CONTAINS KNOCK-OUT DROPS. LUCKY I DIDN'T **TRUST** YVETTE AS YOU ADVISED!

I'LL HIRE NEW DETECTIVES-DOUBLE ALL PRECAUTIONS!

DIRECTOR BLACK DECIDES TO START BY SHOOTING THE SCENE OF **WONDER WOMAN'S** FAMOUS ESCAPE FROM "BURIAL AT SEA"

YOU'LL BE BOUND IN THE TRUNK, **WONDER WOMAN**, AND DROPPED OVERBOARD. START STRUGGLING THE MINUTE YOU HIT THE WATER.

ASSISTANT DIRECTOR ABEL SHOWS **WONDER WOMAN** THE WEIGHTED TRUNK.

UNDERWATER CAMERAS PHOTO-GRAPH YOU THROUGH THIS GLASS SIDE OF THE TRUNK-SEE?

I GET IT-I'M A GOLD FISH AND THIS IS MY BOWL!OKAY-LET'S GO!

THIS LOOKS LIKE A MARINE MINE - THE KIND THAT EXPLODES WHEN A SHIP HITS A TRIGGER WIRE STRETCHED ACROSS THE CHANNEL!

I DUNNO WHERE THEY GOT THAT TRUNK WEIGHT-IT MAY BE A DUD MINE FILL-ED WITH CEMENT.

WONDER WOMAN, SUSPICIOUS, EXAMINES THE INSIDE OF THE TRUNK AND MAKES A STARTLING DISCOVERY!

GREAT TRIDENT OF NEPTUNE!THERE'S THE TRIGGER WIRE! IT'S A LIVE MINE AND THEY'RE GOING TO MAKE ME BLOW MYSELF UP!

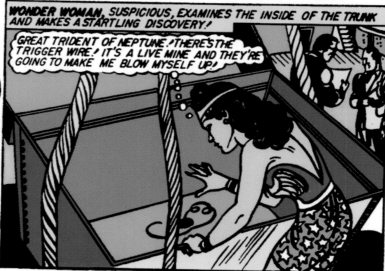

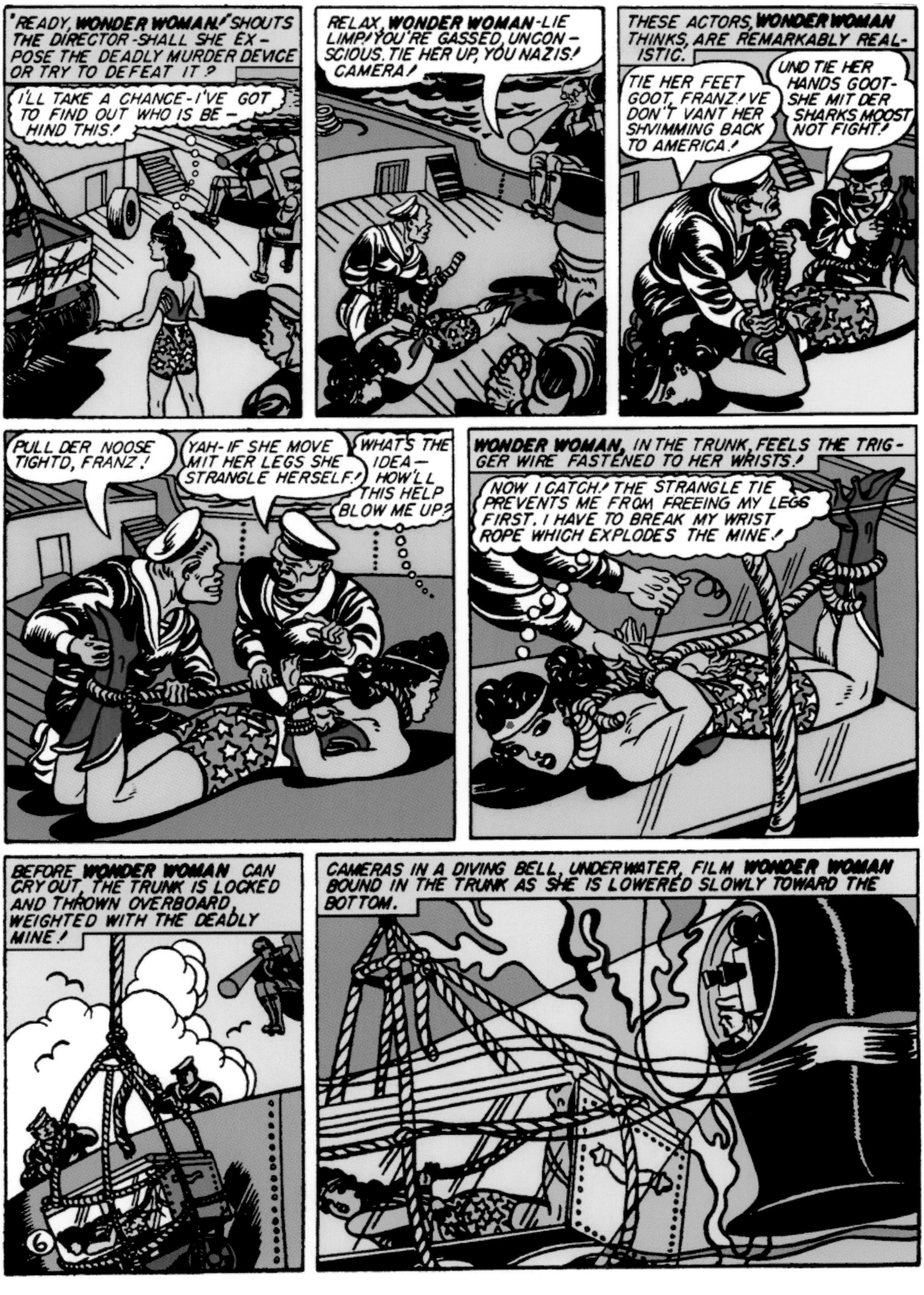
"READY, WONDER WOMAN!" SHOUTS THE DIRECTOR - SHALL SHE EXPOSE THE DEADLY MURDER DEVICE OR TRY TO DEFEAT IT?
I'LL TAKE A CHANCE - I'VE GOT TO FIND OUT WHO IS BEHIND THIS!
RELAX, WONDER WOMAN - LIE LIMP! YOU'RE GASSED, UNCONSCIOUS. TIE HER UP, YOU NAZIS! CAMERA!
THESE ACTORS, WONDER WOMAN THINKS, ARE REMARKABLY REALISTIC.
TIE HER FEET GOOT, FRANZ! VE DON'T VANT HER SHVIMMING BACK TO AMERICA!
UND TIE HER HANDS GOOT - SHE MIT DER SHARKS MOOST NOT FIGHT!
PULL DER NOOSE TIGHTD, FRANZ!
YAH - IF SHE MOVE MIT HER LEGS SHE STRANGLE HERSELF!
WHAT'S THE IDEA — HOW'LL THIS HELP BLOW ME UP?
WONDER WOMAN, IN THE TRUNK, FEELS THE TRIGGER WIRE FASTENED TO HER WRISTS!
NOW I CATCH! THE STRANGLE TIE PREVENTS ME FROM FREEING MY LEGS FIRST. I HAVE TO BREAK MY WRIST ROPE WHICH EXPLODES THE MINE!
BEFORE WONDER WOMAN CAN CRY OUT, THE TRUNK IS LOCKED AND THROWN OVERBOARD, WEIGHTED WITH THE DEADLY MINE!
6
CAMERAS IN A DIVING BELL, UNDERWATER, FILM WONDER WOMAN BOUND IN THE TRUNK AS SHE IS LOWERED SLOWLY TOWARD THE BOTTOM.

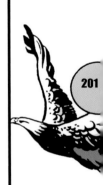

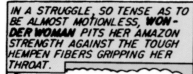

IN A STRUGGLE, SO TENSE AS TO BE ALMOST MOTIONLESS, **WONDER WOMAN** PITS HER AMAZON STRENGTH AGAINST THE TOUGH HEMPEN FIBERS GRIPPING HER THROAT.

I'VE GOT TO STIFFEN MY NECK MUSCLES AND BREAK THIS STRANGLE ROPE WITHOUT JERKING THAT WIRE.

THE ROPE BITES DEEP, THE STRAIN BECOMES TERRIFIC- BUT **WONDER WOMAN'S** COURAGE NEVER FALTERS! AT LONG LAST THE STRONG STRANDS SNAP AND **WONDER WOMAN'S** LEGS ARE FREE!

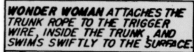

TURNING CAUTIOUSLY ON HER BACK TO PUT SLACK IN THE TRIGGER WIRE, **WONDER WOMAN** EASILY BREAKS HER WRIST ROPES AND KICKS OFF THE TRUNK LID.

JUST IN TIME- I CAN'T HOLD MY BREATH FOREVER!

MEANWHILE, ON THE SHIP, DIRECTOR BLACK BECOMES INCREASINGLY ANXIOUS.

WE'VE GOT TO PULL HER UP— NOBODY CAN STAY UNDER WATER THIS LONG! RAISE THE DIVING BELL FIRST SO IT WON'T FOUL THE TRUNK LINE!

AS **WONDER WOMAN** SWIMS FREE SHE SEES THE DIVING BELL RISING ABOVE HER.

WONDER WHY THEY'RE PULLING THE BELL UP AND LEAVING ME DOWN HERE? I'LL TRY A LITTLE EXPERIMENT!

WONDER WOMAN ATTACHES THE TRUNK ROPE TO THE TRIGGER WIRE, INSIDE THE TRUNK, AND SWIMS SWIFTLY TO THE SURFACE.

SOMETHING TELLS ME I'M RACING DEATH!

THE BELL'S ON BOARD-NOW, FELLOWS, HAUL IN THE TRUNK ROPE!

⑦

AT THE FIRST PULL ON THE ROPE, A TREMENDOUS UNDERWATER EXPLOSION TOSSES THE SHIP ON ITS BEAM ENDS AND SENDS A GREAT GEYSER OF WATER HIGH INTO THE AIR!

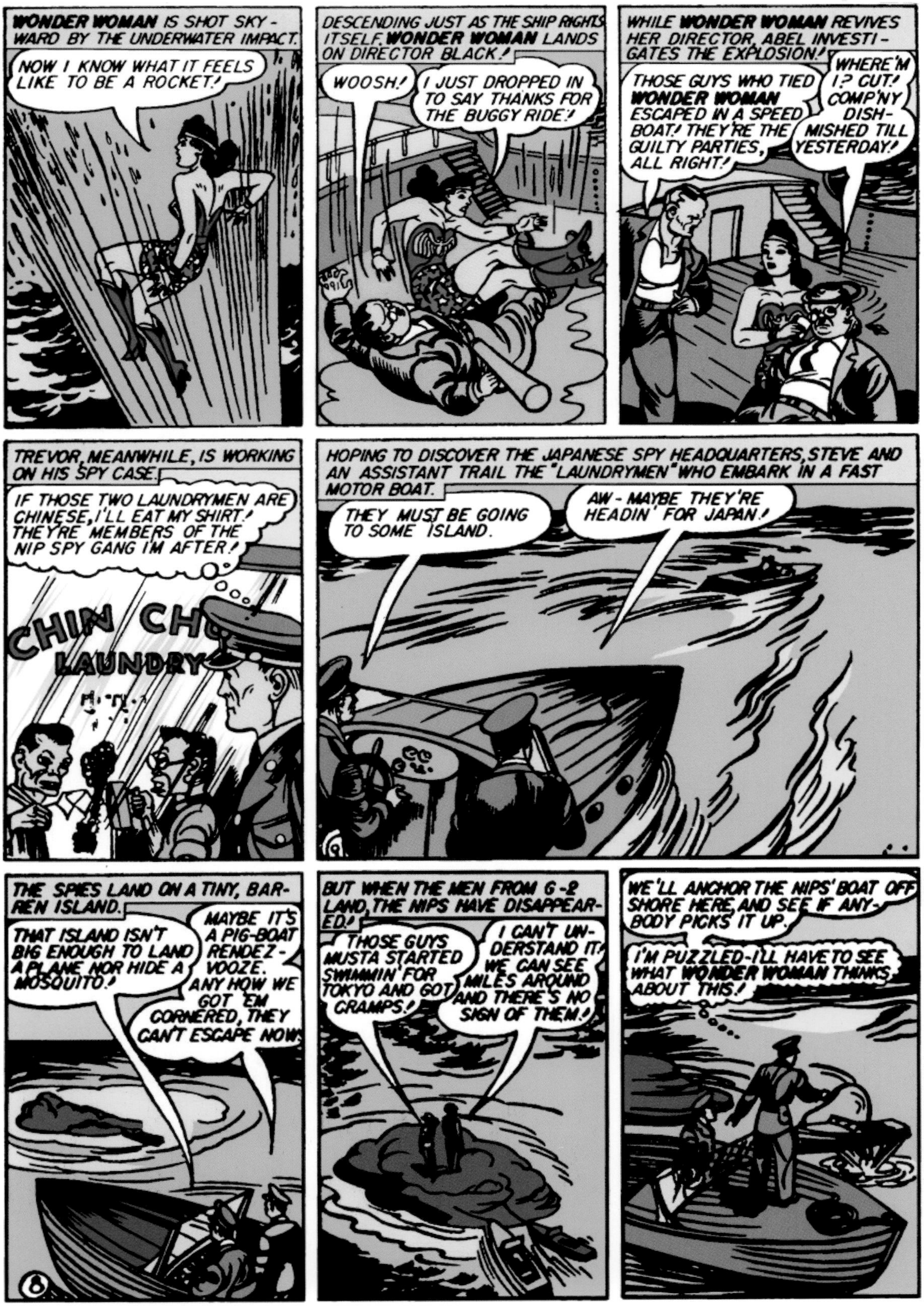
WONDER WOMAN IS SHOT SKY-WARD BY THE UNDERWATER IMPACT.
NOW I KNOW WHAT IT FEELS LIKE TO BE A ROCKET!
DESCENDING JUST AS THE SHIP RIGHTS ITSELF, WONDER WOMAN LANDS ON DIRECTOR BLACK!
WOOSH!
I JUST DROPPED IN TO SAY THANKS FOR THE BUGGY RIDE!
WHILE WONDER WOMAN REVIVES HER DIRECTOR, ABEL INVESTI-GATES THE EXPLOSION!
THOSE GUYS WHO TIED WONDER WOMAN ESCAPED IN A SPEED BOAT! THEY'RE THE GUILTY PARTIES, ALL RIGHT!
WHERE'M I? CUT! COMP'NY DISH-MISHED TILL YESTERDAY!
TREVOR, MEANWHILE, IS WORKING ON HIS SPY CASE.
IF THOSE TWO LAUNDRYMEN ARE CHINESE, I'LL EAT MY SHIRT! THEY'RE MEMBERS OF THE NIP SPY GANG I'M AFTER!
CHIN CH
LAUNDRY
HOPING TO DISCOVER THE JAPANESE SPY HEADQUARTERS, STEVE AND AN ASSISTANT TRAIL THE "LAUNDRYMEN" WHO EMBARK IN A FAST MOTOR BOAT.
THEY MUST BE GOING TO SOME ISLAND.
AW - MAYBE THEY'RE HEADIN' FOR JAPAN!
THE SPIES LAND ON A TINY, BAR-REN ISLAND.
THAT ISLAND ISN'T BIG ENOUGH TO LAND A PLANE NOR HIDE A MOSQUITO!
MAYBE IT'S A PIG-BOAT RENDEZ-VOOZE. ANY HOW WE GOT 'EM CORNERED, THEY CAN'T ESCAPE NOW!
8
BUT WHEN THE MEN FROM G-2 LAND, THE NIPS HAVE DISAPPEAR-ED!
THOSE GUYS MUSTA STARTED SWIMMIN' FOR TOKYO AND GOT CRAMPS!
I CAN'T UN-DERSTAND IT! WE CAN SEE MILES AROUND AND THERE'S NO SIGN OF THEM!
WE'LL ANCHOR THE NIPS' BOAT OFF SHORE HERE AND SEE IF ANY-BODY PICKS IT UP.
I'M PUZZLED-I'LL HAVE TO SEE WHAT WONDER WOMAN THINKS ABOUT THIS!

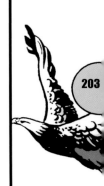

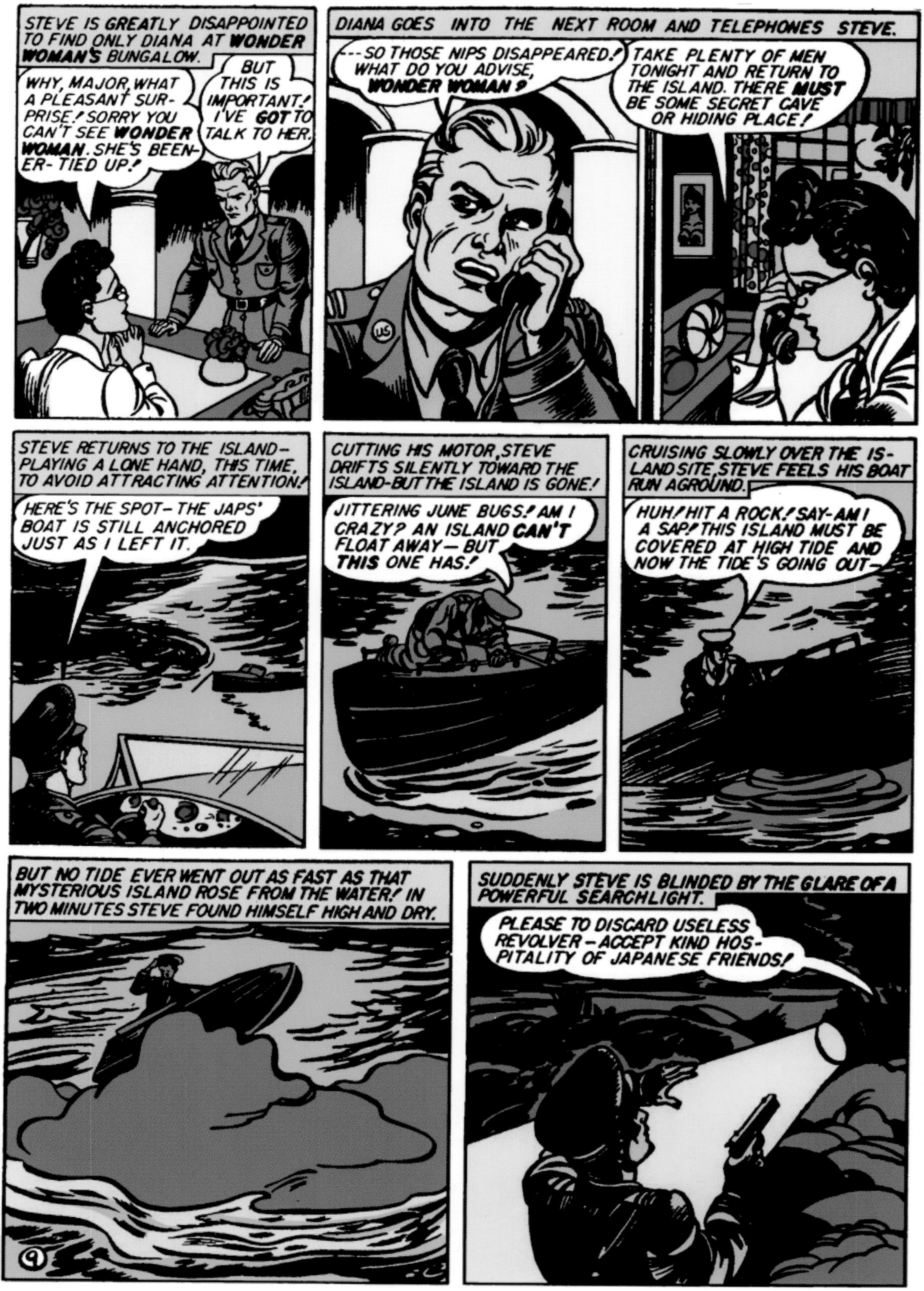

STEVE IS GREATLY DISAPPOINTED TO FIND ONLY DIANA AT WONDER WOMAN'S BUNGALOW.
WHY, MAJOR, WHAT A PLEASANT SURPRISE! SORRY YOU CAN'T SEE WONDER WOMAN. SHE'S BEEN-ER-TIED UP!
BUT THIS IS IMPORTANT! I'VE GOT TO TALK TO HER.
DIANA GOES INTO THE NEXT ROOM AND TELEPHONES STEVE.
---SO THOSE NIPS DISAPPEARED! WHAT DO YOU ADVISE, WONDER WOMAN ?
TAKE PLENTY OF MEN TONIGHT AND RETURN TO THE ISLAND. THERE MUST BE SOME SECRET CAVE OR HIDING PLACE!
STEVE RETURNS TO THE ISLAND- PLAYING A LONE HAND, THIS TIME, TO AVOID ATTRACTING ATTENTION!
HERE'S THE SPOT- THE JAPS' BOAT IS STILL ANCHORED JUST AS I LEFT IT.
CUTTING HIS MOTOR, STEVE DRIFTS SILENTLY TOWARD THE ISLAND-BUT THE ISLAND IS GONE!
JITTERING JUNE BUGS! AM I CRAZY? AN ISLAND CAN'T FLOAT AWAY— BUT THIS ONE HAS!
CRUISING SLOWLY OVER THE ISLAND SITE, STEVE FEELS HIS BOAT RUN AGROUND.
HUH! HIT A ROCK! SAY-AM I A SAP! THIS ISLAND MUST BE COVERED AT HIGH TIDE AND NOW THE TIDE'S GOING OUT-
BUT NO TIDE EVER WENT OUT AS FAST AS THAT MYSTERIOUS ISLAND ROSE FROM THE WATER! IN TWO MINUTES STEVE FOUND HIMSELF HIGH AND DRY.
9
SUDDENLY STEVE IS BLINDED BY THE GLARE OF A POWERFUL SEARCHLIGHT.
PLEASE TO DISCARD USELESS REVOLVER – ACCEPT KIND HOSPITALITY OF JAPANESE FRIENDS!

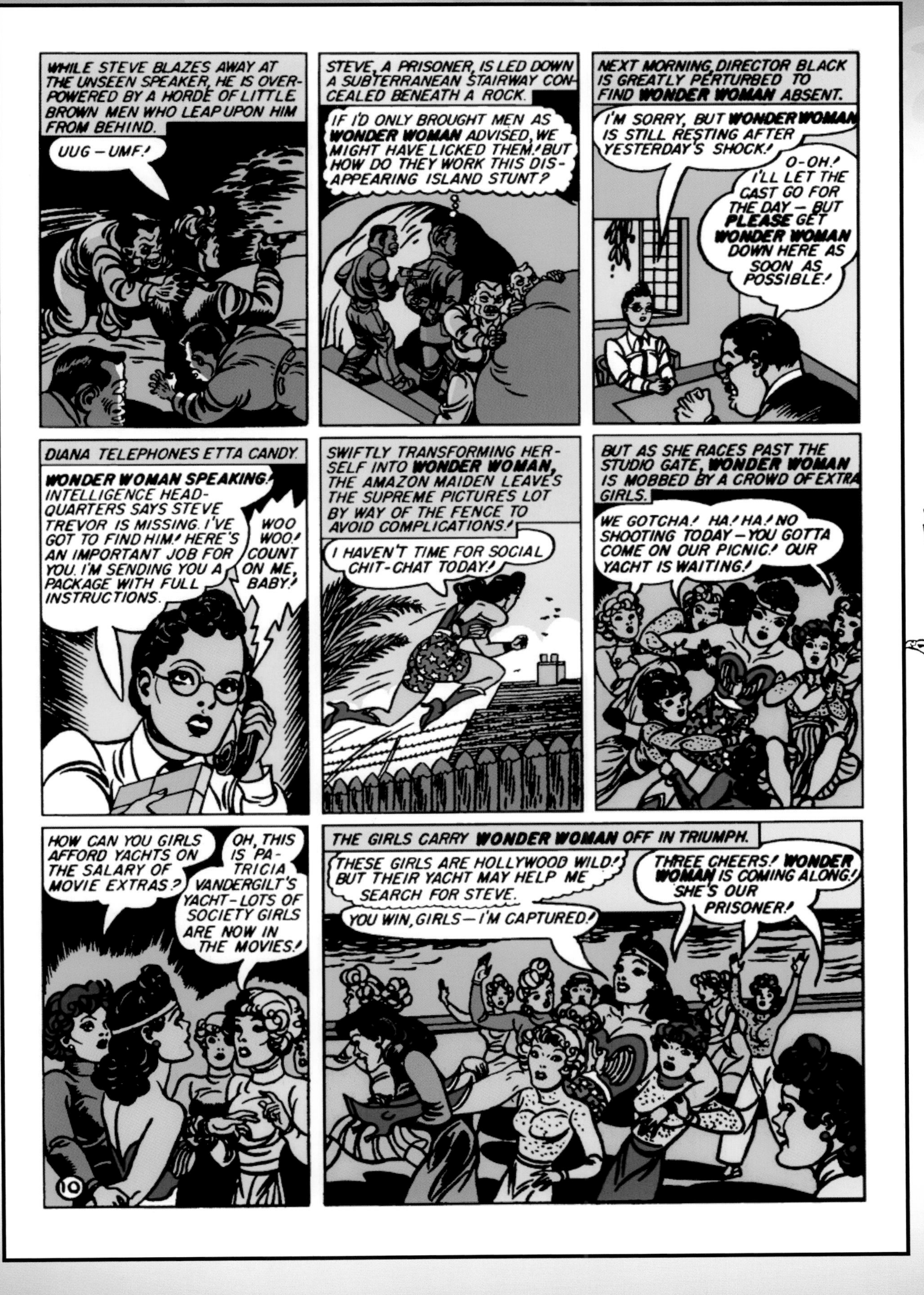
WHILE STEVE BLAZES AWAY AT THE UNSEEN SPEAKER, HE IS OVERPOWERED BY A HORDE OF LITTLE BROWN MEN WHO LEAP UPON HIM FROM BEHIND.
UUG – UMF!
STEVE, A PRISONER, IS LED DOWN A SUBTERRANEAN STAIRWAY CONCEALED BENEATH A ROCK.
IF I'D ONLY BROUGHT MEN AS WONDER WOMAN ADVISED, WE MIGHT HAVE LICKED THEM! BUT HOW DO THEY WORK THIS DISAPPEARING ISLAND STUNT?
NEXT MORNING, DIRECTOR BLACK IS GREATLY PERTURBED TO FIND WONDER WOMAN ABSENT.
I'M SORRY, BUT WONDER WOMAN IS STILL RESTING AFTER YESTERDAY'S SHOCK!
O-OH! I'LL LET THE CAST GO FOR THE DAY – BUT PLEASE GET WONDER WOMAN DOWN HERE AS SOON AS POSSIBLE!
DIANA TELEPHONES ETTA CANDY.
WONDER WOMAN SPEAKING! INTELLIGENCE HEADQUARTERS SAYS STEVE TREVOR IS MISSING. I'VE GOT TO FIND HIM! HERE'S AN IMPORTANT JOB FOR YOU. I'M SENDING YOU A PACKAGE WITH FULL INSTRUCTIONS.
WOO WOO! COUNT ON ME, BABY!
SWIFTLY TRANSFORMING HERSELF INTO WONDER WOMAN, THE AMAZON MAIDEN LEAVES THE SUPREME PICTURES LOT BY WAY OF THE FENCE TO AVOID COMPLICATIONS!
I HAVEN'T TIME FOR SOCIAL CHIT-CHAT TODAY!
BUT AS SHE RACES PAST THE STUDIO GATE, WONDER WOMAN IS MOBBED BY A CROWD OF EXTRA GIRLS.
WE GOTCHA! HA! HA! NO SHOOTING TODAY – YOU GOTTA COME ON OUR PICNIC! OUR YACHT IS WAITING!
HOW CAN YOU GIRLS AFFORD YACHTS ON THE SALARY OF MOVIE EXTRAS?
OH, THIS IS PATRICIA VANDERGILT'S YACHT – LOTS OF SOCIETY GIRLS ARE NOW IN THE MOVIES!
10
THE GIRLS CARRY WONDER WOMAN OFF IN TRIUMPH.
THESE GIRLS ARE HOLLYWOOD WILD! BUT THEIR YACHT MAY HELP ME SEARCH FOR STEVE.
YOU WIN, GIRLS – I'M CAPTURED!
THREE CHEERS! WONDER WOMAN IS COMING ALONG! SHE'S OUR PRISONER!

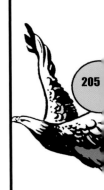

ON THE YACHT'S DECK THE GIRLS BIND **WONDER WOMAN** WITH FLOWERS.

WHAT LOVELY BONDS! THESE FLOWERS ARE SO FRAGRANT—

BUT PRESENTLY THIS FRAGRANCE BECOMES OVERPOWERING. **WONDER WOMAN**, DIZZY, FALLS TO THE DECK. DOES SHE ONLY **IMAGINE** IT'S DIRECTOR BLACK BEHAVING SO QUEERLY—

STUFF HER NOSE AND MOUTH WITH FLOWERS! THE PERFUME IS A POWERFUL ANAESTHETIC—

WHEN **WONDER WOMAN** WAKES, IT STILL SEEMS A DREAM—THAT FACE! IT **CAN'T** BE THE BARONESS!

THE GIRL'S AWAKE— IT IS TIME FOR OUR LITTLE EXPERI- MENT, ICHI!

IS GOOD, BARON- ESS! PRISONER WILL ENJOY SAME!

LET US RETURN, NOW, TO ETTA CANDY AS SHE OPENS THE PACK- AGE FROM **WONDER WOMAN**.

WOO WOO! THE MAGIC LASSO! LET'S SEE WHAT THE LETTER SAYS.

Dear Etta:—

I suspect that Ben Black is directing these plots against me. He wanted me to come to the stu- dio today and probably has some trap prepared.

I am leaving you the magic lasso. You must lasso him and make him talk! Make him tell where Baroness von Gunther is hiding.

Wonder Woman

ETTA AND HER HOLLIDAY GIRLS IN- VADE DIRECTOR BLACK'S OFFICE.

YOU'RE BLACK'S SEC- RETARY, AREN'T YOU? YOU KNOW DARNED WELL WHERE HE IS—COME ACROSS!

ER-AH- WELL— MR. BLACK WENT DOWN TO PIER 17 TO SEE **WONDER WOMAN** OFF ON A YACHT PICNIC!

⑪

THE HOLLIDAY GANG PILE INTO STUDIO CARS.

PIER 17, JAMES, AND DON'T RATION THE GAS! WE GOTTA SAVE **WON- DER WOMAN**! I BETCHA THIS IS THE TRAP SHE SAID BLACK HAD WAITING FOR HER!

BLACK'S CAR, DRIVING FURIOUSLY OFF THE PIER, IS STOPPED BY THE FEARLESS HOLLIDAY GIRLS.

STOP! IF YOU GO AHEAD, IT'S OVER OUR DEAD BODIES!

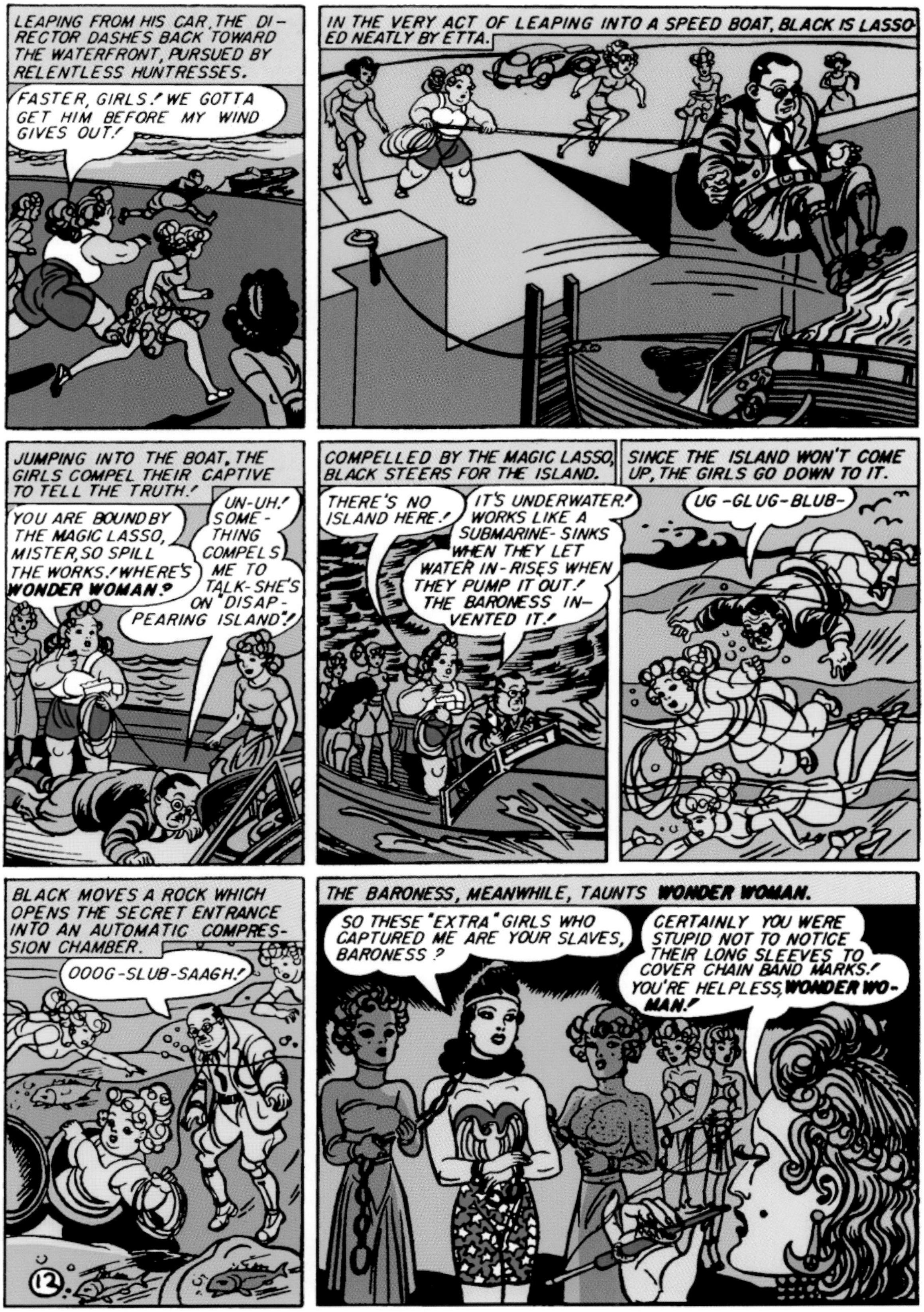
LEAPING FROM HIS CAR, THE DIRECTOR DASHES BACK TOWARD THE WATERFRONT, PURSUED BY RELENTLESS HUNTRESSES.
FASTER, GIRLS! WE GOTTA GET HIM BEFORE MY WIND GIVES OUT!
IN THE VERY ACT OF LEAPING INTO A SPEED BOAT, BLACK IS LASSOED NEATLY BY ETTA.
JUMPING INTO THE BOAT, THE GIRLS COMPEL THEIR CAPTIVE TO TELL THE TRUTH!
YOU ARE BOUND BY THE MAGIC LASSO, MISTER, SO SPILL THE WORKS! WHERE'S WONDER WOMAN?
UN-UH! SOME-THING COMPELS ME TO TALK-SHE'S ON "DISAPPEARING ISLAND"!
COMPELLED BY THE MAGIC LASSO, BLACK STEERS FOR THE ISLAND.
THERE'S NO ISLAND HERE!
IT'S UNDERWATER! WORKS LIKE A SUBMARINE- SINKS WHEN THEY LET WATER IN-RISES WHEN THEY PUMP IT OUT! THE BARONESS INVENTED IT!
SINCE THE ISLAND WON'T COME UP, THE GIRLS GO DOWN TO IT.
UG-GLUG-BLUB-
BLACK MOVES A ROCK WHICH OPENS THE SECRET ENTRANCE INTO AN AUTOMATIC COMPRESSION CHAMBER.
OOOG-SLUB-SAAGH!
12
THE BARONESS, MEANWHILE, TAUNTS WONDER WOMAN.
SO THESE "EXTRA" GIRLS WHO CAPTURED ME ARE YOUR SLAVES, BARONESS?
CERTAINLY YOU WERE STUPID NOT TO NOTICE THEIR LONG SLEEVES TO COVER CHAIN BAND MARKS! YOU'RE HELPLESS, WONDER WOMAN!

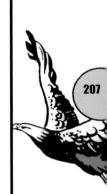

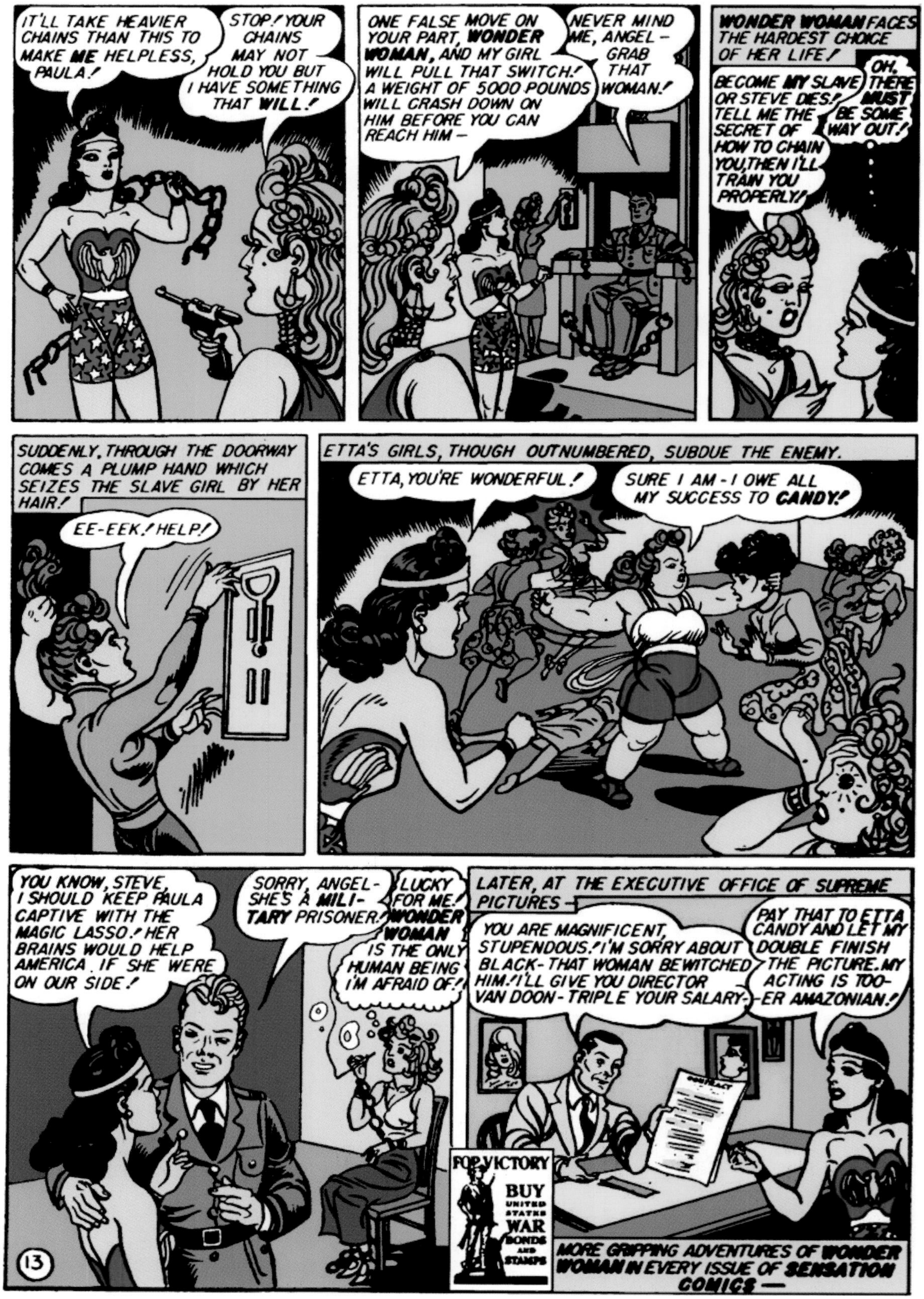

IT'LL TAKE HEAVIER CHAINS THAN THIS TO MAKE ME HELPLESS, PAULA!
STOP! YOUR CHAINS MAY NOT HOLD YOU BUT I HAVE SOMETHING THAT WILL!
ONE FALSE MOVE ON YOUR PART, WONDER WOMAN, AND MY GIRL WILL PULL THAT SWITCH! A WEIGHT OF 5000 POUNDS WILL CRASH DOWN ON HIM BEFORE YOU CAN REACH HIM –
NEVER MIND ME, ANGEL – GRAB THAT WOMAN!
WONDER WOMAN FACES THE HARDEST CHOICE OF HER LIFE!
BECOME MY SLAVE OR STEVE DIES! TELL ME THE SECRET OF HOW TO CHAIN YOU, THEN I'LL TRAIN YOU PROPERLY!
OH, THERE MUST BE SOME WAY OUT!
SUDDENLY, THROUGH THE DOORWAY COMES A PLUMP HAND WHICH SEIZES THE SLAVE GIRL BY HER HAIR!
EE-EEK! HELP!
ETTA'S GIRLS, THOUGH OUTNUMBERED, SUBDUE THE ENEMY.
ETTA, YOU'RE WONDERFUL!
SURE I AM - I OWE ALL MY SUCCESS TO CANDY!
YOU KNOW, STEVE, I SHOULD KEEP PAULA CAPTIVE WITH THE MAGIC LASSO! HER BRAINS WOULD HELP AMERICA IF SHE WERE ON OUR SIDE!
SORRY, ANGEL- SHE'S A MILITARY PRISONER!
LUCKY FOR ME! WONDER WOMAN IS THE ONLY HUMAN BEING I'M AFRAID OF!
13
LATER, AT THE EXECUTIVE OFFICE OF SUPREME PICTURES –
YOU ARE MAGNIFICENT, STUPENDOUS! I'M SORRY ABOUT BLACK-THAT WOMAN BEWITCHED HIM! I'LL GIVE YOU DIRECTOR VAN DOON-TRIPLE YOUR SALARY-
PAY THAT TO ETTA CANDY AND LET MY DOUBLE FINISH THE PICTURE. MY ACTING IS TOO-ER AMAZONIAN!
FOR VICTORY BUY UNITED STATES WAR BONDS AND STAMPS
MORE GRIPPING ADVENTURES OF WONDER WOMAN IN EVERY ISSUE OF SENSATION COMICS —

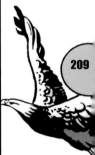

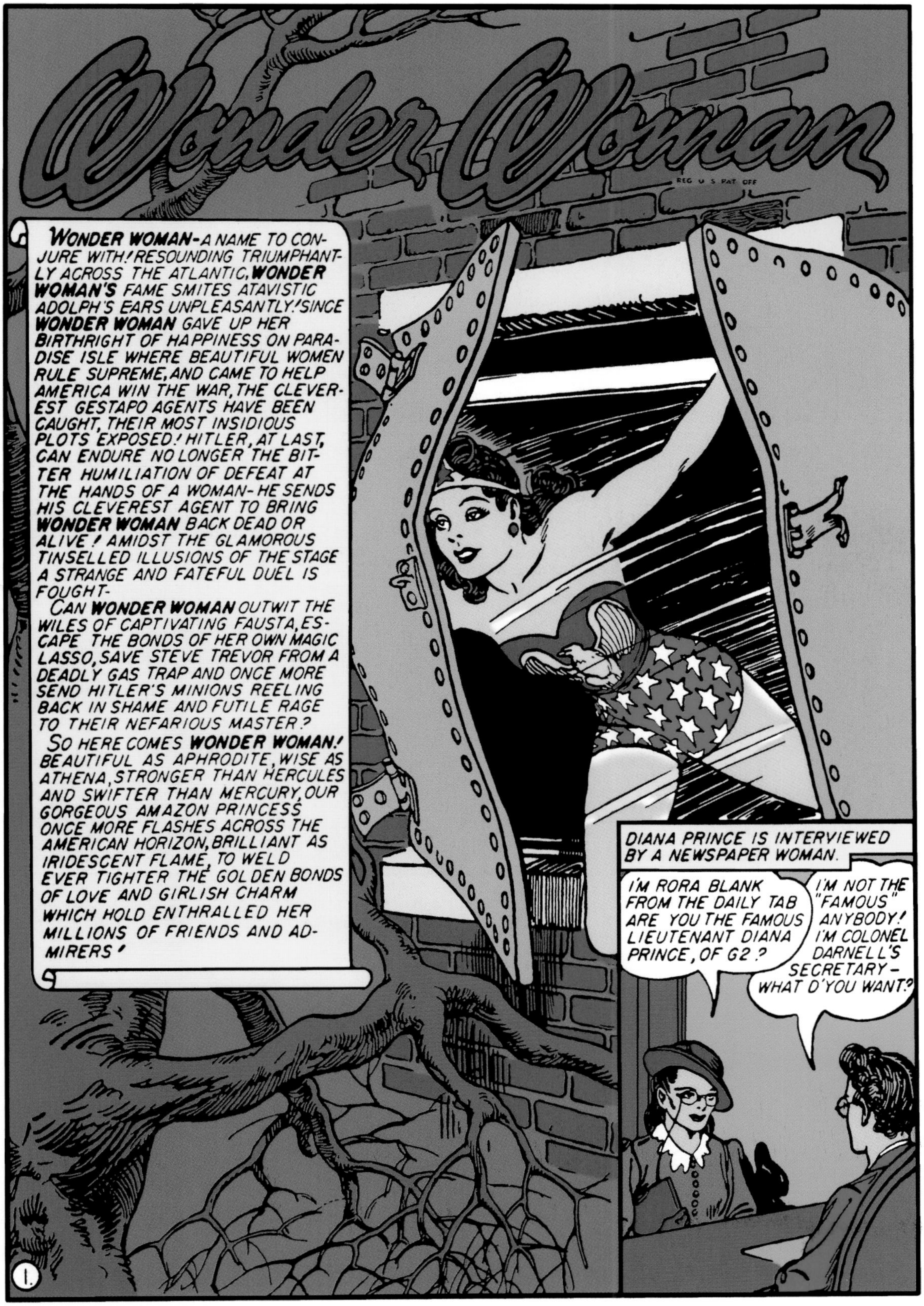
Wonder Woman
REG. U.S. PAT. OFF.
WONDER WOMAN-A NAME TO CONJURE WITH! RESOUNDING TRIUMPHANTLY ACROSS THE ATLANTIC, WONDER WOMAN'S FAME SMITES ATAVISTIC ADOLPH'S EARS UNPLEASANTLY! SINCE WONDER WOMAN GAVE UP HER BIRTHRIGHT OF HAPPINESS ON PARADISE ISLE WHERE BEAUTIFUL WOMEN RULE SUPREME, AND CAME TO HELP AMERICA WIN THE WAR, THE CLEVEREST GESTAPO AGENTS HAVE BEEN CAUGHT, THEIR MOST INSIDIOUS PLOTS EXPOSED! HITLER, AT LAST, CAN ENDURE NO LONGER THE BITTER HUMILIATION OF DEFEAT AT THE HANDS OF A WOMAN- HE SENDS HIS CLEVEREST AGENT TO BRING WONDER WOMAN BACK DEAD OR ALIVE! AMIDST THE GLAMOROUS TINSELLED ILLUSIONS OF THE STAGE A STRANGE AND FATEFUL DUEL IS FOUGHT-
CAN WONDER WOMAN OUTWIT THE WILES OF CAPTIVATING FAUSTA, ESCAPE THE BONDS OF HER OWN MAGIC LASSO, SAVE STEVE TREVOR FROM A DEADLY GAS TRAP AND ONCE MORE SEND HITLER'S MINIONS REELING BACK IN SHAME AND FUTILE RAGE TO THEIR NEFARIOUS MASTER?
SO HERE COMES WONDER WOMAN! BEAUTIFUL AS APHRODITE, WISE AS ATHENA, STRONGER THAN HERCULES AND SWIFTER THAN MERCURY, OUR GORGEOUS AMAZON PRINCESS ONCE MORE FLASHES ACROSS THE AMERICAN HORIZON, BRILLIANT AS IRIDESCENT FLAME, TO WELD EVER TIGHTER THE GOLDEN BONDS OF LOVE AND GIRLISH CHARM WHICH HOLD ENTHRALLED HER MILLIONS OF FRIENDS AND ADMIRERS!
1.
DIANA PRINCE IS INTERVIEWED BY A NEWSPAPER WOMAN.
I'M RORA BLANK FROM THE DAILY TAB ARE YOU THE FAMOUS LIEUTENANT DIANA PRINCE, OF G2?
I'M NOT THE "FAMOUS" ANYBODY! I'M COLONEL DARNELL'S SECRETARY – WHAT D'YOU WANT?

Comic Cavalcade #2 (Spring 1943) - script: William Moulton Marston - art: Frank Godwin

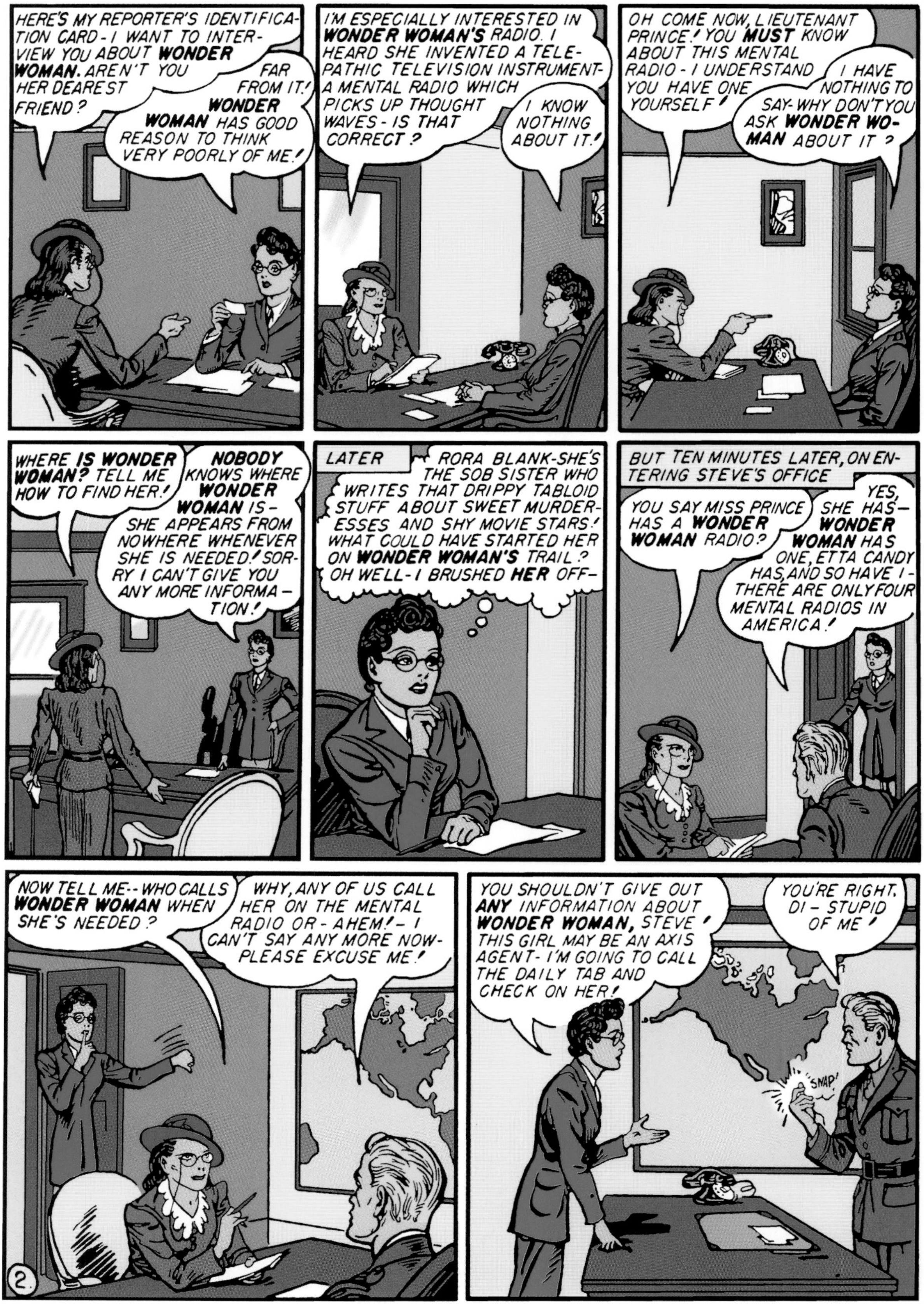

HERE'S MY REPORTER'S IDENTIFICATION CARD - I WANT TO INTERVIEW YOU ABOUT WONDER WOMAN. AREN'T YOU HER DEAREST FRIEND?
FAR FROM IT! WONDER WOMAN HAS GOOD REASON TO THINK VERY POORLY OF ME!
I'M ESPECIALLY INTERESTED IN WONDER WOMAN'S RADIO. I HEARD SHE INVENTED A TELEPATHIC TELEVISION INSTRUMENT- A MENTAL RADIO WHICH PICKS UP THOUGHT WAVES - IS THAT CORRECT?
I KNOW NOTHING ABOUT IT!
OH COME NOW, LIEUTENANT PRINCE! YOU MUST KNOW ABOUT THIS MENTAL RADIO - I UNDERSTAND YOU HAVE ONE YOURSELF!
I HAVE NOTHING TO SAY- WHY DON'T YOU ASK WONDER WOMAN ABOUT IT?
WHERE IS WONDER WOMAN? TELL ME HOW TO FIND HER!
NOBODY KNOWS WHERE WONDER WOMAN IS - SHE APPEARS FROM NOWHERE WHENEVER SHE IS NEEDED! SORRY I CAN'T GIVE YOU ANY MORE INFORMATION!
LATER
RORA BLANK-SHE'S THE SOB SISTER WHO WRITES THAT DRIPPY TABLOID STUFF ABOUT SWEET MURDERESSES AND SHY MOVIE STARS! WHAT COULD HAVE STARTED HER ON WONDER WOMAN'S TRAIL? OH WELL- I BRUSHED HER OFF-
BUT TEN MINUTES LATER, ON ENTERING STEVE'S OFFICE
YOU SAY MISS PRINCE HAS A WONDER WOMAN RADIO?
YES, SHE HAS- WONDER WOMAN HAS ONE, ETTA CANDY HAS, AND SO HAVE I - THERE ARE ONLY FOUR MENTAL RADIOS IN AMERICA!
NOW TELL ME-- WHO CALLS WONDER WOMAN WHEN SHE'S NEEDED?
WHY, ANY OF US CALL HER ON THE MENTAL RADIO OR - AHEM! - I CAN'T SAY ANY MORE NOW- PLEASE EXCUSE ME!
2.
YOU SHOULDN'T GIVE OUT ANY INFORMATION ABOUT WONDER WOMAN, STEVE! THIS GIRL MAY BE AN AXIS AGENT- I'M GOING TO CALL THE DAILY TAB AND CHECK ON HER!
YOU'RE RIGHT, DI - STUPID OF ME!
SNAP!

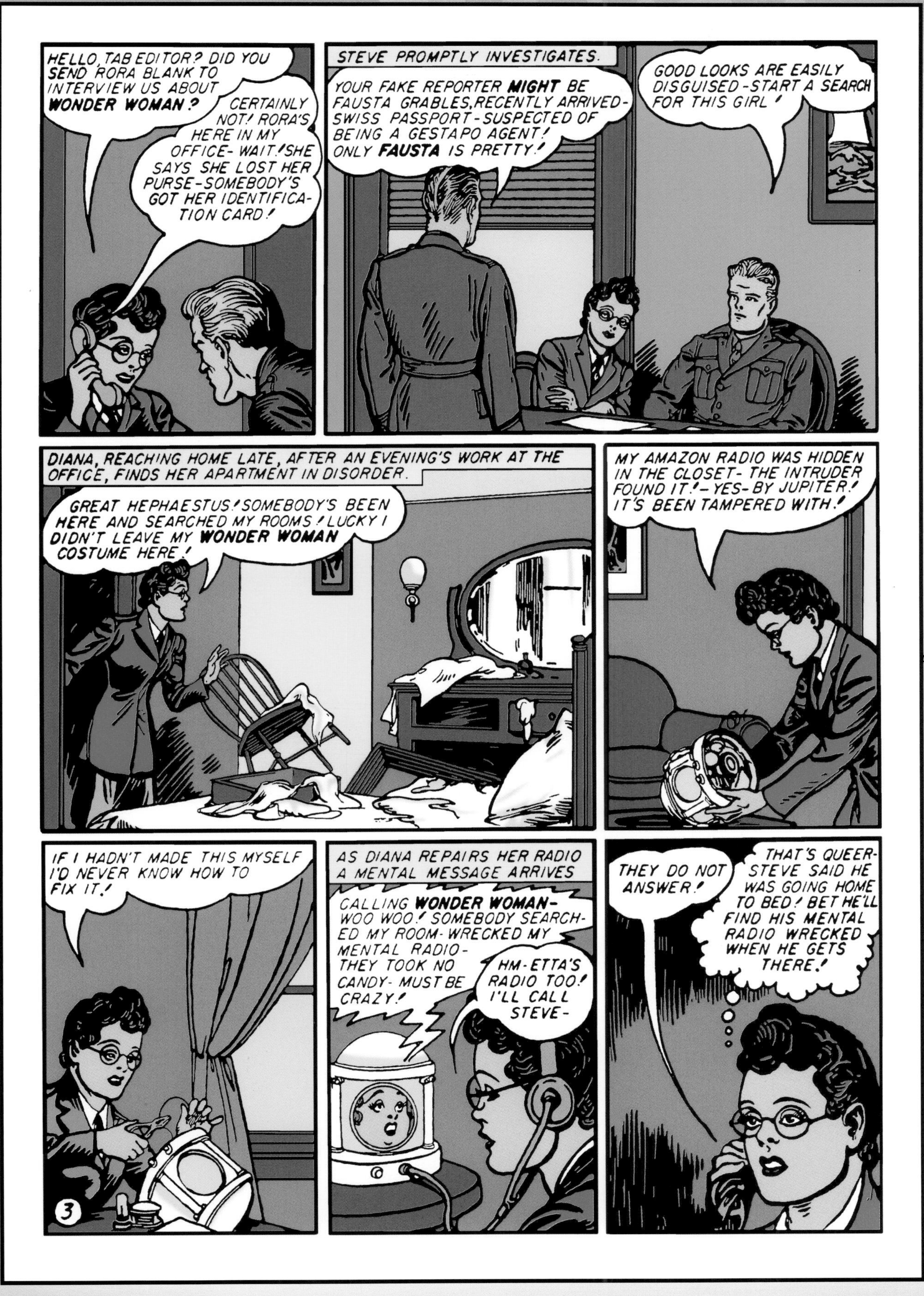
HELLO, TAB EDITOR? DID YOU SEND RORA BLANK TO INTERVIEW US ABOUT WONDER WOMAN?
CERTAINLY NOT! RORA'S HERE IN MY OFFICE- WAIT! SHE SAYS SHE LOST HER PURSE-SOMEBODY'S GOT HER IDENTIFICATION CARD!
STEVE PROMPTLY INVESTIGATES.
YOUR FAKE REPORTER MIGHT BE FAUSTA GRABLES, RECENTLY ARRIVED- SWISS PASSPORT- SUSPECTED OF BEING A GESTAPO AGENT! ONLY FAUSTA IS PRETTY!
GOOD LOOKS ARE EASILY DISGUISED-START A SEARCH FOR THIS GIRL!
DIANA, REACHING HOME LATE, AFTER AN EVENING'S WORK AT THE OFFICE, FINDS HER APARTMENT IN DISORDER.
GREAT HEPHAESTUS! SOMEBODY'S BEEN HERE AND SEARCHED MY ROOMS! LUCKY I DIDN'T LEAVE MY WONDER WOMAN COSTUME HERE!
MY AMAZON RADIO WAS HIDDEN IN THE CLOSET- THE INTRUDER FOUND IT!-YES- BY JUPITER! IT'S BEEN TAMPERED WITH!
IF I HADN'T MADE THIS MYSELF I'D NEVER KNOW HOW TO FIX IT!
3
AS DIANA REPAIRS HER RADIO A MENTAL MESSAGE ARRIVES
CALLING WONDER WOMAN- WOO WOO! SOMEBODY SEARCHED MY ROOM- WRECKED MY MENTAL RADIO- THEY TOOK NO CANDY- MUST BE CRAZY!
HM- ETTA'S RADIO TOO! I'LL CALL STEVE-
THEY DO NOT ANSWER!
THAT'S QUEER- STEVE SAID HE WAS GOING HOME TO BED! BET HE'LL FIND HIS MENTAL RADIO WRECKED WHEN HE GETS THERE!

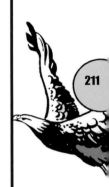

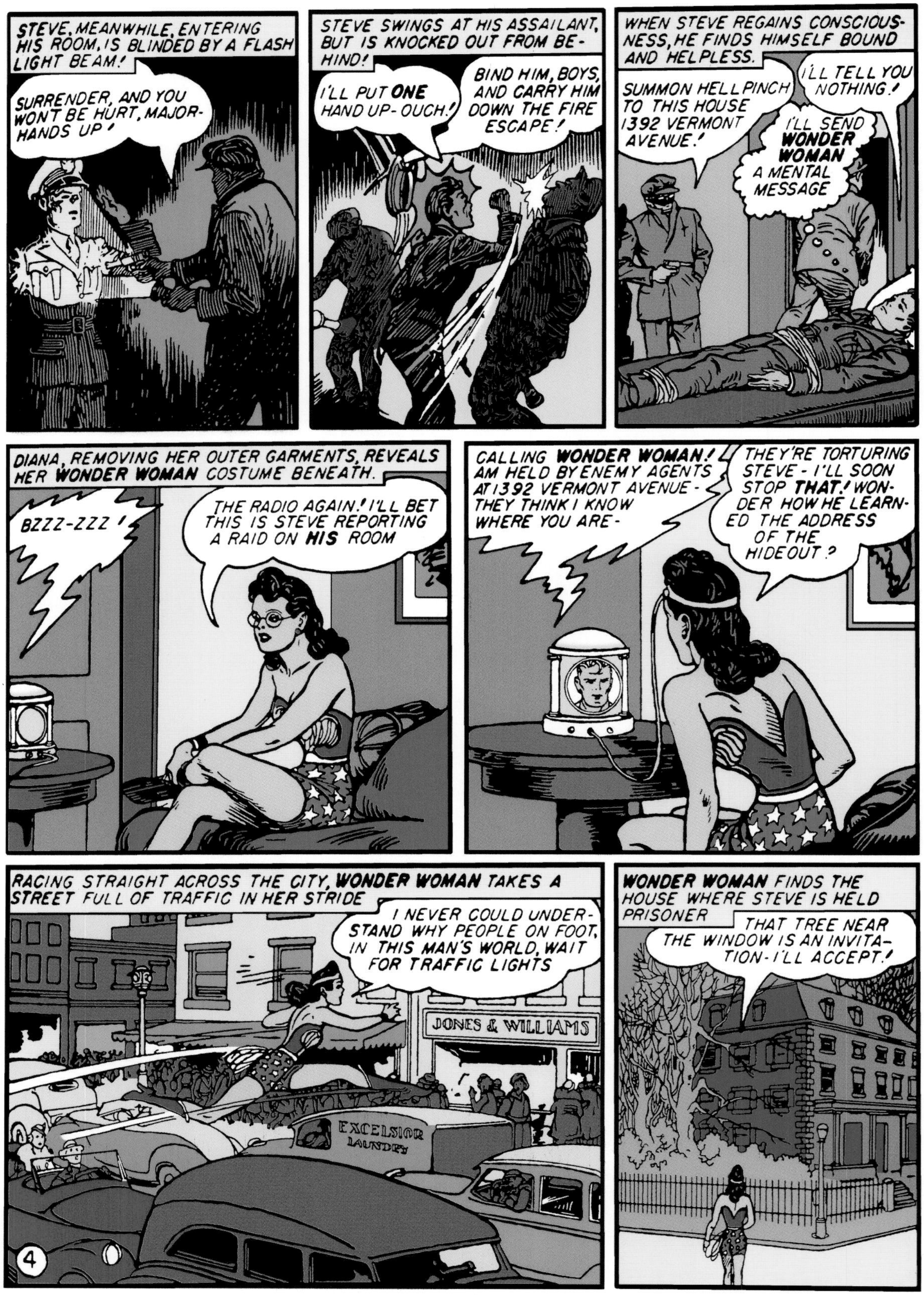
STEVE, MEANWHILE, ENTERING HIS ROOM, IS BLINDED BY A FLASH LIGHT BEAM!
SURRENDER, AND YOU WON'T BE HURT, MAJOR-HANDS UP!
STEVE SWINGS AT HIS ASSAILANT, BUT IS KNOCKED OUT FROM BEHIND!
I'LL PUT ONE HAND UP-OUCH!
BIND HIM, BOYS, AND CARRY HIM DOWN THE FIRE ESCAPE!
WHEN STEVE REGAINS CONSCIOUSNESS, HE FINDS HIMSELF BOUND AND HELPLESS.
SUMMON HELLPINCH TO THIS HOUSE 1392 VERMONT AVENUE!
I'LL TELL YOU NOTHING!
I'LL SEND WONDER WOMAN A MENTAL MESSAGE
DIANA, REMOVING HER OUTER GARMENTS, REVEALS HER WONDER WOMAN COSTUME BENEATH.
BZZZ-ZZZ!
THE RADIO AGAIN! I'LL BET THIS IS STEVE REPORTING A RAID ON HIS ROOM
CALLING WONDER WOMAN! AM HELD BY ENEMY AGENTS AT 1392 VERMONT AVENUE - THEY THINK I KNOW WHERE YOU ARE-
THEY'RE TORTURING STEVE - I'LL SOON STOP THAT! WONDER HOW HE LEARNED THE ADDRESS OF THE HIDEOUT?
RACING STRAIGHT ACROSS THE CITY, WONDER WOMAN TAKES A STREET FULL OF TRAFFIC IN HER STRIDE
I NEVER COULD UNDERSTAND WHY PEOPLE ON FOOT, IN THIS MAN'S WORLD, WAIT FOR TRAFFIC LIGHTS
JONES & WILLIAMS
EXCELSIOR LAUNDRY
4
WONDER WOMAN FINDS THE HOUSE WHERE STEVE IS HELD PRISONER
THAT TREE NEAR THE WINDOW IS AN INVITATION-I'LL ACCEPT!

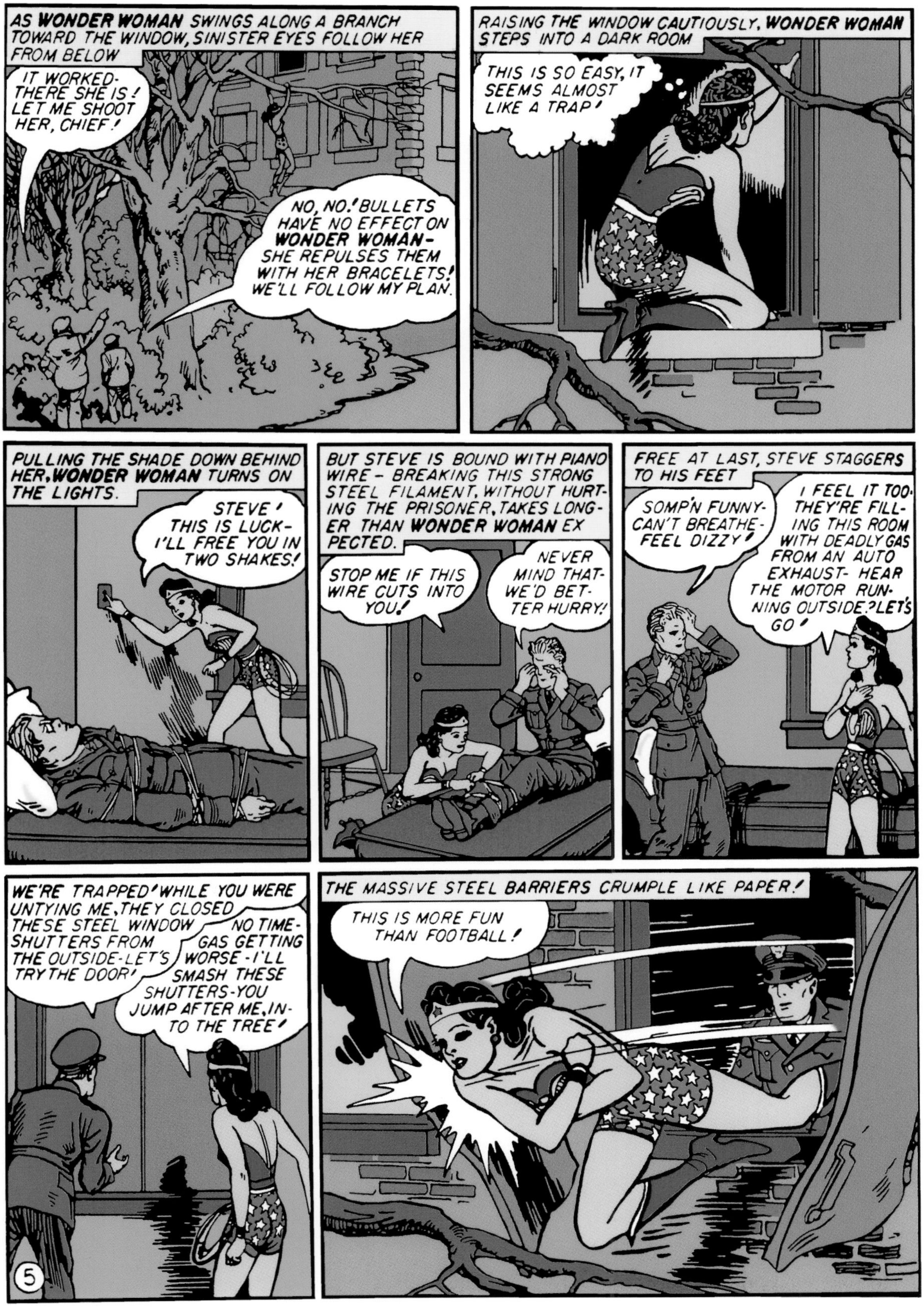
AS WONDER WOMAN SWINGS ALONG A BRANCH TOWARD THE WINDOW, SINISTER EYES FOLLOW HER FROM BELOW
IT WORKED- THERE SHE IS! LET ME SHOOT HER, CHIEF!
NO, NO! BULLETS HAVE NO EFFECT ON WONDER WOMAN- SHE REPULSES THEM WITH HER BRACELETS! WE'LL FOLLOW MY PLAN.
RAISING THE WINDOW CAUTIOUSLY, WONDER WOMAN STEPS INTO A DARK ROOM
THIS IS SO EASY, IT SEEMS ALMOST LIKE A TRAP!
PULLING THE SHADE DOWN BEHIND HER, WONDER WOMAN TURNS ON THE LIGHTS.
STEVE! THIS IS LUCK- I'LL FREE YOU IN TWO SHAKES!
BUT STEVE IS BOUND WITH PIANO WIRE - BREAKING THIS STRONG STEEL FILAMENT, WITHOUT HURTING THE PRISONER, TAKES LONGER THAN WONDER WOMAN EXPECTED.
STOP ME IF THIS WIRE CUTS INTO YOU!
NEVER MIND THAT- WE'D BETTER HURRY!
FREE AT LAST, STEVE STAGGERS TO HIS FEET
SOMP'N FUNNY- CAN'T BREATHE- FEEL DIZZY!
I FEEL IT TOO- THEY'RE FILLING THIS ROOM WITH DEADLY GAS FROM AN AUTO EXHAUST- HEAR THE MOTOR RUNNING OUTSIDE? LET'S GO!
WE'RE TRAPPED! WHILE YOU WERE UNTYING ME, THEY CLOSED THESE STEEL WINDOW SHUTTERS FROM THE OUTSIDE- LET'S TRY THE DOOR!
NO TIME- GAS GETTING WORSE - I'LL SMASH THESE SHUTTERS- YOU JUMP AFTER ME, INTO THE TREE!
5
THE MASSIVE STEEL BARRIERS CRUMPLE LIKE PAPER!
THIS IS MORE FUN THAN FOOTBALL!

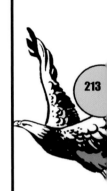

STEVE FOLLOWS **WONDER WOMAN**.

SWING UP ON THE BRANCH, STEVE - I SEE SOME LADS BELOW US WITH SHOOTING IRONS!

MOVING ALONG THE BRANCH, HEAD DOWN, **WONDER WOMAN** COVERS THEIR RETREAT WITH HER BRACELETS.

CROSS-EYED CATFISH! IF I ONLY HAD MY AUTOMATIC!

I'M GLAD YOU HAVEN'T - I NEED PRACTICE PLAYING BULLETS AND BRACELETS

UNABLE TO SHOOT **WONDER WO-MAN**, THE GUNMEN FLEE.

IT'S NO USE-BULLETS WON'T KILL HER! SHE ISS NOT HUMAN!

LOOKS AS IF THE BOYS AREN'T WAITING FOR US! TOO BAD. I WANTED TO TALK WITH THEM!

NEXT DAY, A VICIOUS GROUP ASSEMBLES-THE COUNCIL OF AXIS CHIEFS, AMERICA'S MOST DEADLY ENEMIES!

VELL, FRAULEIN FAUSTA GRABLES, YOU HAF FAILED AGAIN!

WONDER WOMAN'S STRENGTH IS UNBELIEVABLE - THOSE STEEL SHUTTERS WEREN'T STRONG ENOUGH!

DOT ISS NO EXCUSE! DER FUEHRER SENT YOU HERE TO GET **VONDER VOMAN** - YOU KNOW DER PENALTY FOR FAILURE?

I'LL GET HER, HERR SPADER - GIVE ME ANOTHER CHANCE!

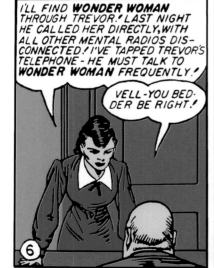

I'LL FIND **WONDER WOMAN** THROUGH TREVOR! LAST NIGHT HE CALLED HER DIRECTLY, WITH ALL OTHER MENTAL RADIOS DISCONNECTED! I'VE TAPPED TREVOR'S TELEPHONE - HE MUST TALK TO **WONDER WOMAN** FREQUENTLY!

VELL-YOU BED-DER BE RIGHT!

THAT NIGHT, BEFORE GOING TO BED, TREVOR CALLS DIANA.

I'M WORRIED-THEY MAY KIDNAP YOU NEXT! HOW ABOUT A GUARD TO WATCH YOUR PLACE?

HEAVENS, NO! **WONDER WOMAN'S** STAYING WITH ME TONIGHT - SHE'LL PROTECT ME!

FAUSTA, LISTENING ON THE TAPPED TELEPHONE, GRINS WITH TRIUMPHANT MALICE!

I **KNEW** TREVOR WOULD LEAD ME TO **WONDER WOMAN** - I MUST ACT QUICKLY!

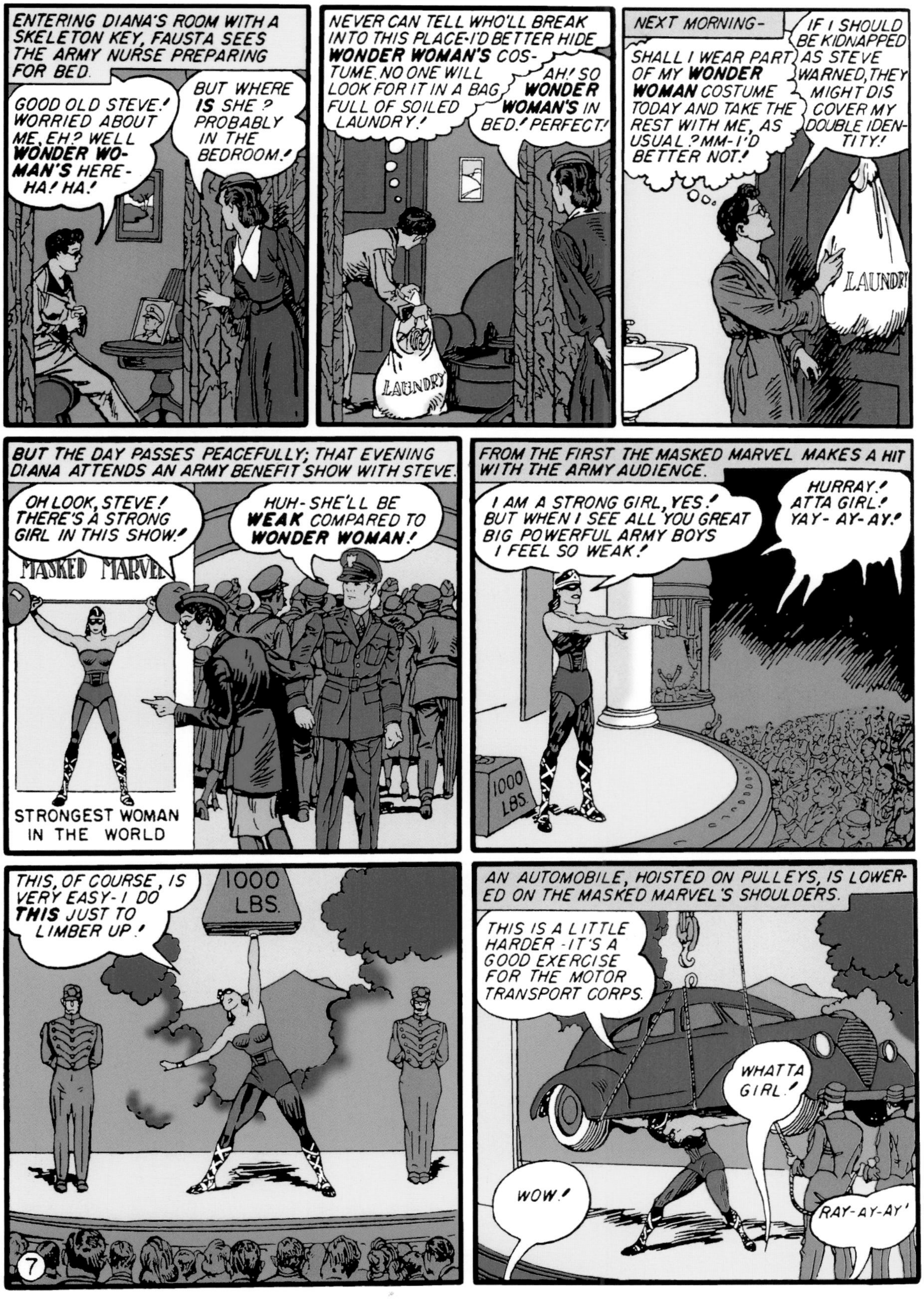
ENTERING DIANA'S ROOM WITH A SKELETON KEY, FAUSTA SEES THE ARMY NURSE PREPARING FOR BED.
GOOD OLD STEVE! WORRIED ABOUT ME, EH? WELL WONDER WOMAN'S HERE - HA! HA!
BUT WHERE IS SHE ? PROBABLY IN THE BEDROOM!
NEVER CAN TELL WHO'LL BREAK INTO THIS PLACE-I'D BETTER HIDE WONDER WOMAN'S COSTUME. NO ONE WILL LOOK FOR IT IN A BAG FULL OF SOILED LAUNDRY!
AH! SO WONDER WOMAN'S IN BED! PERFECT!
LAUNDRY
NEXT MORNING-
SHALL I WEAR PART OF MY WONDER WOMAN COSTUME TODAY AND TAKE THE REST WITH ME, AS USUAL ? MM-I'D BETTER NOT!
IF I SHOULD BE KIDNAPPED AS STEVE WARNED, THEY MIGHT DISCOVER MY DOUBLE IDENTITY!
LAUNDRY
BUT THE DAY PASSES PEACEFULLY; THAT EVENING DIANA ATTENDS AN ARMY BENEFIT SHOW WITH STEVE.
OH LOOK, STEVE! THERE'S A STRONG GIRL IN THIS SHOW!
HUH- SHE'LL BE WEAK COMPARED TO WONDER WOMAN!
MASKED MARVEL
STRONGEST WOMAN IN THE WORLD
FROM THE FIRST THE MASKED MARVEL MAKES A HIT WITH THE ARMY AUDIENCE.
I AM A STRONG GIRL, YES! BUT WHEN I SEE ALL YOU GREAT BIG POWERFUL ARMY BOYS I FEEL SO WEAK!
HURRAY! ATTA GIRL! YAY- AY-AY!
1000 LBS.
THIS, OF COURSE, IS VERY EASY- I DO THIS JUST TO LIMBER UP!
1000 LBS.
AN AUTOMOBILE, HOISTED ON PULLEYS, IS LOWERED ON THE MASKED MARVEL'S SHOULDERS.
THIS IS A LITTLE HARDER -IT'S A GOOD EXERCISE FOR THE MOTOR TRANSPORT CORPS.
WHATTA GIRL!
WOW!
RAY-AY-AY!
7

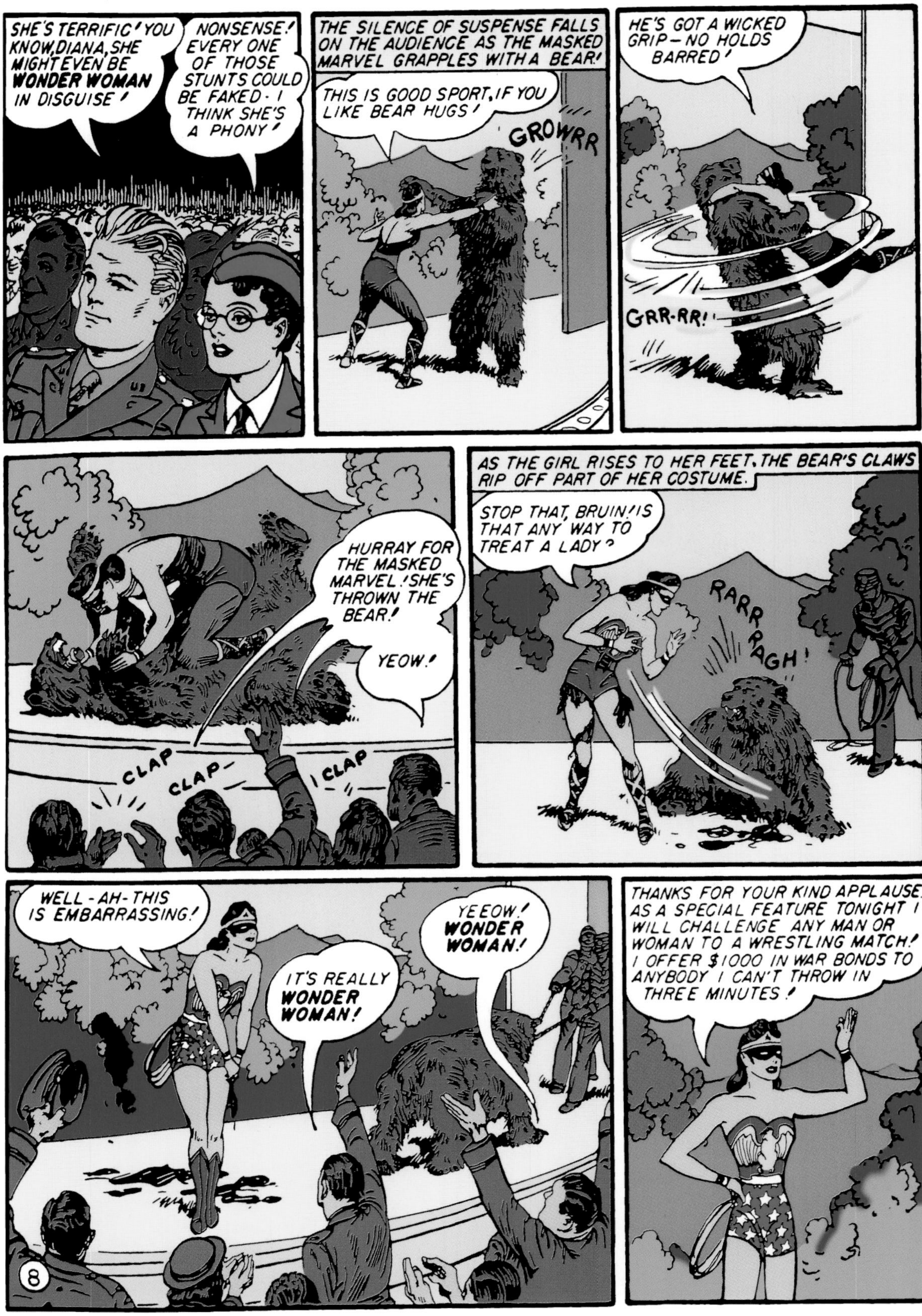

SHE'S TERRIFIC! YOU KNOW, DIANA, SHE MIGHT EVEN BE WONDER WOMAN IN DISGUISE!
NONSENSE! EVERY ONE OF THOSE STUNTS COULD BE FAKED - I THINK SHE'S A PHONY!
THE SILENCE OF SUSPENSE FALLS ON THE AUDIENCE AS THE MASKED MARVEL GRAPPLES WITH A BEAR!
THIS IS GOOD SPORT, IF YOU LIKE BEAR HUGS!
GROWRR
HE'S GOT A WICKED GRIP—NO HOLDS BARRED!
GRR-RR!
HURRAY FOR THE MASKED MARVEL! SHE'S THROWN THE BEAR!
YEOW!
CLAP
CLAP
CLAP
AS THE GIRL RISES TO HER FEET, THE BEAR'S CLAWS RIP OFF PART OF HER COSTUME.
STOP THAT, BRUIN! IS THAT ANY WAY TO TREAT A LADY?
RARRRAGH!
WELL - AH - THIS IS EMBARRASSING!
IT'S REALLY WONDER WOMAN!
YEEOW! WONDER WOMAN!
8
THANKS FOR YOUR KIND APPLAUSE. AS A SPECIAL FEATURE TONIGHT I WILL CHALLENGE ANY MAN OR WOMAN TO A WRESTLING MATCH! I OFFER $1000 IN WAR BONDS TO ANYBODY I CAN'T THROW IN THREE MINUTES!

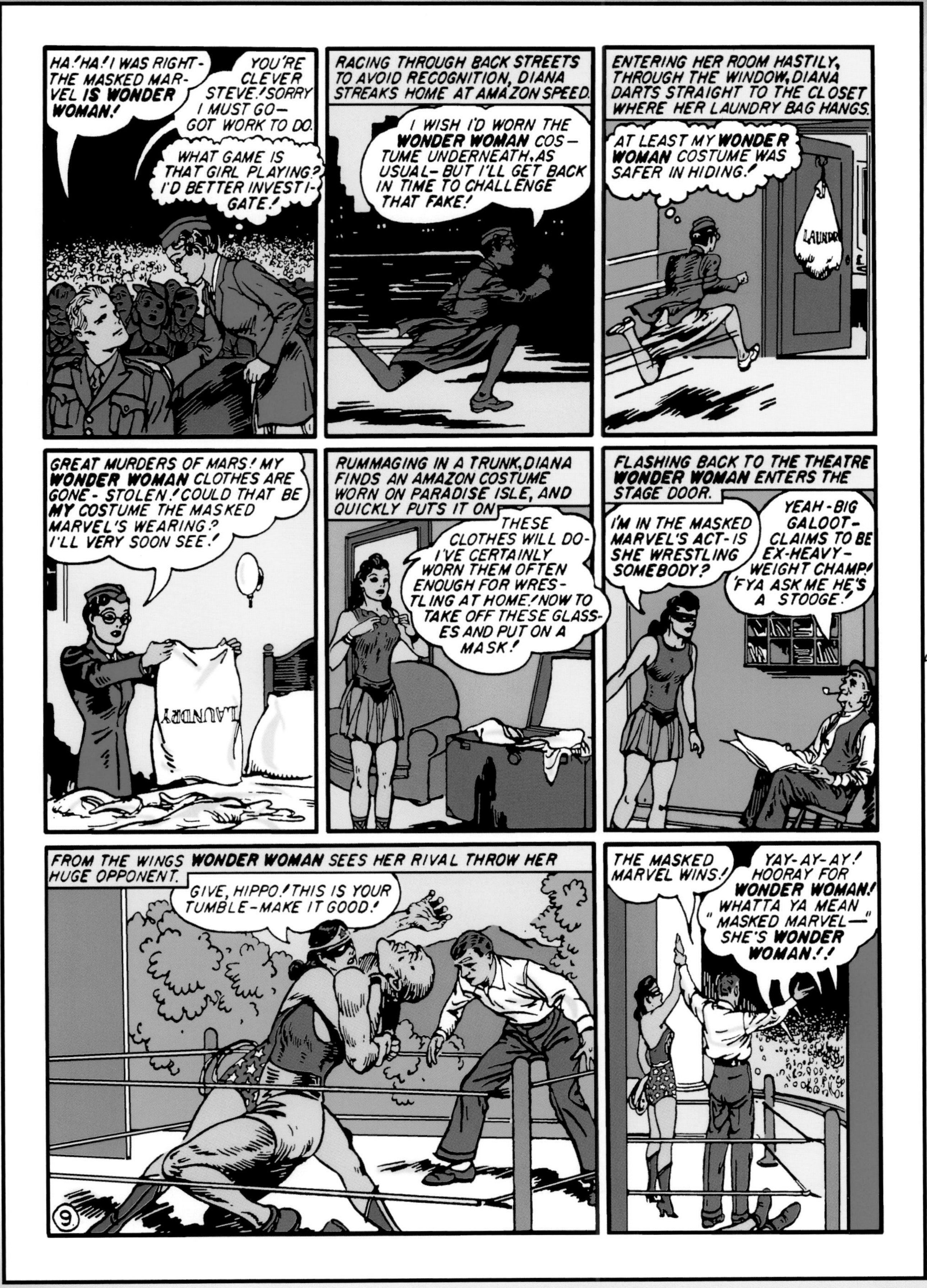

HA! HA! I WAS RIGHT- THE MASKED MARVEL IS WONDER WOMAN!
YOU'RE CLEVER STEVE! SORRY I MUST GO- GOT WORK TO DO.
WHAT GAME IS THAT GIRL PLAYING? I'D BETTER INVESTI-GATE!
RACING THROUGH BACK STREETS TO AVOID RECOGNITION, DIANA STREAKS HOME AT AMAZON SPEED.
I WISH I'D WORN THE WONDER WOMAN COS-TUME UNDERNEATH, AS USUAL- BUT I'LL GET BACK IN TIME TO CHALLENGE THAT FAKE!
ENTERING HER ROOM HASTILY, THROUGH THE WINDOW, DIANA DARTS STRAIGHT TO THE CLOSET WHERE HER LAUNDRY BAG HANGS.
AT LEAST MY WONDER WOMAN COSTUME WAS SAFER IN HIDING!
GREAT MURDERS OF MARS! MY WONDER WOMAN CLOTHES ARE GONE - STOLEN! COULD THAT BE MY COSTUME THE MASKED MARVEL'S WEARING? I'LL VERY SOON SEE!
LAUNDRY
RUMMAGING IN A TRUNK, DIANA FINDS AN AMAZON COSTUME WORN ON PARADISE ISLE, AND QUICKLY PUTS IT ON
THESE CLOTHES WILL DO- I'VE CERTAINLY WORN THEM OFTEN ENOUGH FOR WRES-TLING AT HOME! NOW TO TAKE OFF THESE GLASS-ES AND PUT ON A MASK!
FLASHING BACK TO THE THEATRE WONDER WOMAN ENTERS THE STAGE DOOR.
I'M IN THE MASKED MARVEL'S ACT- IS SHE WRESTLING SOMEBODY?
YEAH - BIG GALOOT- CLAIMS TO BE EX-HEAVY-WEIGHT CHAMP! 'FYA ASK ME HE'S A STOOGE!
FROM THE WINGS WONDER WOMAN SEES HER RIVAL THROW HER HUGE OPPONENT.
GIVE, HIPPO! THIS IS YOUR TUMBLE- MAKE IT GOOD!
9
THE MASKED MARVEL WINS!
YAY-AY-AY! HOORAY FOR WONDER WOMAN! WHATTA YA MEAN "MASKED MARVEL—" SHE'S WONDER WOMAN!!

ANOTHER MASKED WOMAN STEPS SUDDENLY FROM THE WINGS.

I DARE YOU TO WRESTLE **ME!**

YOU? HA!HA! RUN HOME TO MAMA, LITTLE GIRL, BEFORE I HURT YOU!

HA!HA!HA! HO!HO!

THE MASKED MARVEL INSISTS THAT THE MYSTERIOUS STRANGER PROVE HER STRENGTH.

LET'S SEE YOU LIFT THAT WEIGHT!

1000 POUNDS?THAT'S EASY-UNH-HUH? SOMETHING'S QUEER!

1000 LBS.

EXERTING HER STRENGTH, **WONDER WOMAN** WRENCHES THE "WEIGHT" FROM THE FLOOR.

YOU CAN'T LIFT THAT-EEK-EEK-STOP!

ANYBODY COULD LIFT THIS WOODEN BLOCK! YOU SHOULD USE A STRONGER MAGNET TO HOLD ITS METAL BASE TO THE FLOOR!

AHA! THIS IS **WONDER WOMAN!** NO ONE ELSE COULD HAVE PULLED THAT "WEIGHT" LOOSE.

THAT MAGNETIC BLOCK IS A JOKE WE PLAY ON AMATEURS! **NOW** I'LL WRESTLE YOU!

GOOD! I'LL GIVE $1000 TO THE U.S.O. IF I DON'T THROW YOU IN TWO MINUTES!

USING A FLYING TACKLE HOLD, **WONDER WOMAN** HURLS HER OPPONENT TO THE MAT.

NOW IT'S **YOUR** TURN TO TUMBLE-DO IT GRACEFULLY, LIKE YOUR STOOGE!

AS **WONDER WOMAN** KNEELS ABOVE HER FALLEN OPPONENT, THE MASKED MARVEL'S HAND STEALS TO THE GOLDEN LASSO AT HER WAIST.

YOU STOLE MY COSTUME-DID YOU THINK IT WOULD GIVE YOU STRENGTH?

YES — IT HAS!

⑩

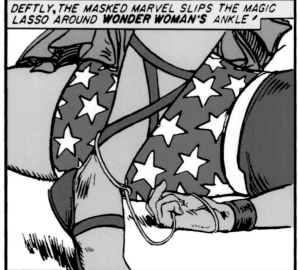

DEFTLY, THE MASKED MARVEL SLIPS THE MAGIC LASSO AROUND **WONDER WOMAN'S** ANKLE!

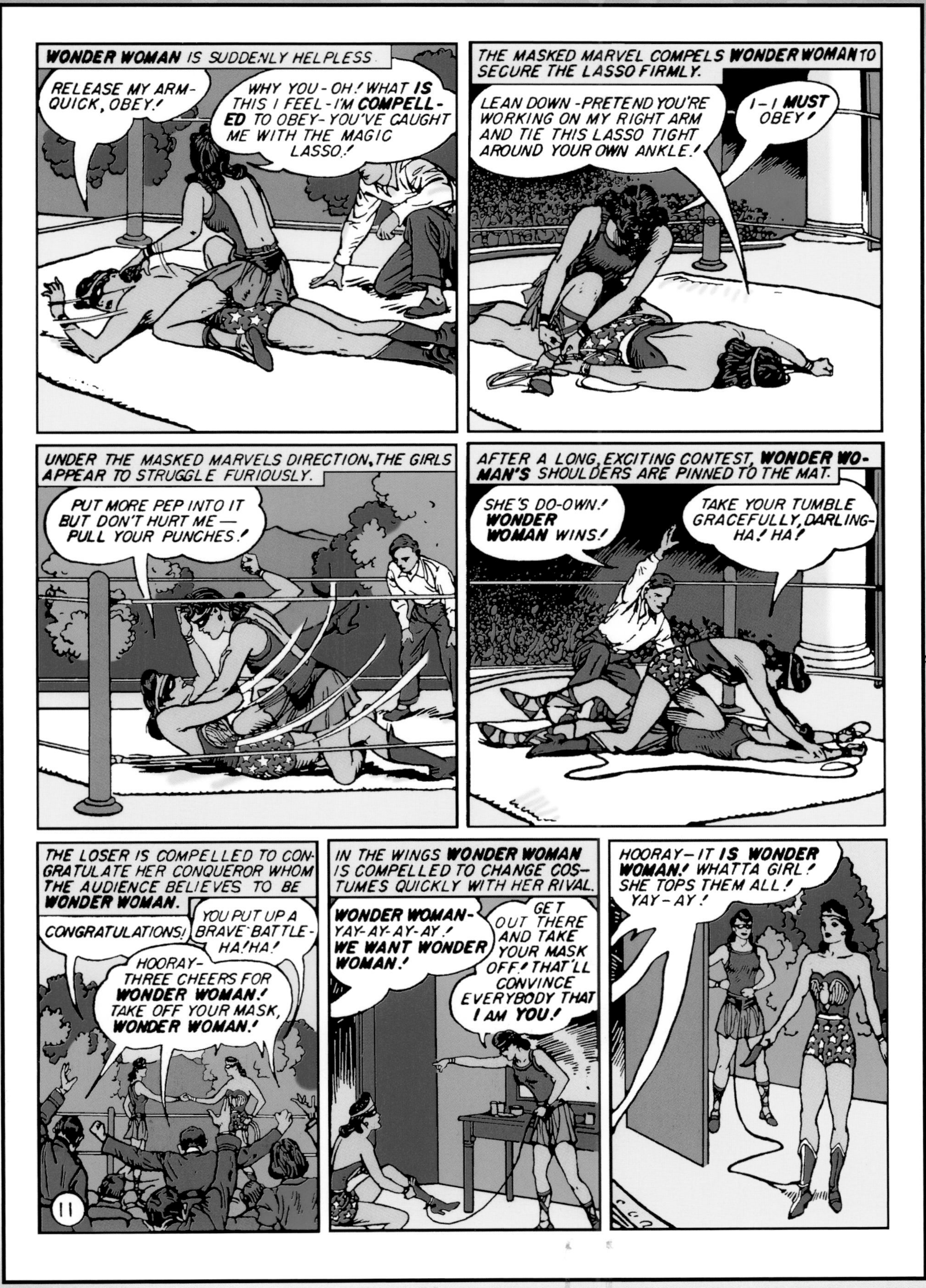
WONDER WOMAN IS SUDDENLY HELPLESS.
RELEASE MY ARM-QUICK, OBEY!
WHY YOU-OH! WHAT IS THIS I FEEL-I'M COMPELLED TO OBEY-YOU'VE CAUGHT ME WITH THE MAGIC LASSO!
THE MASKED MARVEL COMPELS WONDER WOMAN TO SECURE THE LASSO FIRMLY.
LEAN DOWN-PRETEND YOU'RE WORKING ON MY RIGHT ARM AND TIE THIS LASSO TIGHT AROUND YOUR OWN ANKLE!
I-I MUST OBEY!
UNDER THE MASKED MARVELS DIRECTION, THE GIRLS APPEAR TO STRUGGLE FURIOUSLY.
PUT MORE PEP INTO IT BUT DON'T HURT ME — PULL YOUR PUNCHES!
AFTER A LONG, EXCITING CONTEST, WONDER WOMAN'S SHOULDERS ARE PINNED TO THE MAT.
SHE'S DO-OWN! WONDER WOMAN WINS!
TAKE YOUR TUMBLE GRACEFULLY, DARLING-HA! HA!
THE LOSER IS COMPELLED TO CONGRATULATE HER CONQUEROR WHOM THE AUDIENCE BELIEVES TO BE WONDER WOMAN.
CONGRATULATIONS!
YOU PUT UP A BRAVE BATTLE-HA! HA!
HOORAY-THREE CHEERS FOR WONDER WOMAN! TAKE OFF YOUR MASK, WONDER WOMAN!
11
IN THE WINGS WONDER WOMAN IS COMPELLED TO CHANGE COSTUMES QUICKLY WITH HER RIVAL.
WONDER WOMAN-YAY-AY-AY-AY! WE WANT WONDER WOMAN!
GET OUT THERE AND TAKE YOUR MASK OFF! THAT'LL CONVINCE EVERYBODY THAT I AM YOU!
HOORAY-IT IS WONDER WOMAN! WHATTA GIRL! SHE TOPS THEM ALL! YAY-AY!

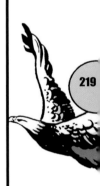

THE MASKED MARVEL TAKES **WON-DER WOMAN** TO HER DRESSING ROOM AND MAKES HER CHANGE COSTUMES AGAIN!

WITH MY CLOAK OVER YOUR SHOULDERS, NOBODY WILL SEE THAT YOUR ARMS ARE BOUND BEHIND YOU!

AS THE GIRLS LEAVE THE THEATRE TOGETHER, THEY MEET STEVE!

MY ANGEL! YOU WERE WONDERFUL TONIGHT! LET'S HAVE SUPPER TOGETHER.

SORRY—I CAN'T. I MUST TAKE CARE OF THIS POOR LITTLE GIRL—SHE FEELS DEPRESSED!

STAGE DOOR

WONDER WOMAN IS FORCED TO LIE ON THE FLOOR OF HER CAPTOR'S CAR.

YOU MAKE A SOFT FOOTREST! DRIVE TO HEADQUARTERS, FRITZY—HERR SPADER EXPECTS US!

WHEN THE CAR FINALLY STOPS, **WONDER WOMAN** SOMERSAULTS, KICKING THE DOOR OFF.

WHAM! CRA-AK!

WONDER WOMAN IS QUICKLY RECAPTURED—BUT HER PURPOSE IS ACCOMPLISHED.

MUCH GOOD THAT NONSENSE DID YOU!

HM—I RECOGNIZE THIS PLACE—IT'S THE FORMER JAP EMBASSY AND SUPPOSED TO BE CLOSED! IF ONLY I CAN INFORM STEVE—

KNOWING THAT STEVE AND ETTA'S RADIOS ARE DISCONNECTED, **WONDER WOMAN** SENDS A MIND MESSAGE TO HER MOTHER, QUEEN HIPPOLYTE, ON PARADISE ISLAND.

MOTHER—PLEASE RADIO STEVE AND ETTA I AM PRISONER AT FORMER JAP EMBASSY—

I'VE CAPTURED **WONDER WOMAN**, HERR SPADER—HERE'S THE PRISONER!

GOOT! YOU HAF DONE WELL, FAUSTA—ACH! SUCH IMPERTINENCE SIDDING ON MY DESK—STAND AT ATTENTION, PRISONER!

WONDER WOMAN, TRUSSED INTO A NEAT BUNDLE WITH THE MAGIC LASSO, IS PLACED IN A TRUNK

DER FUEHRER COMMANDS THIS PRISONER BE BROUGHT TO GERMANY! A PLANE IS WAITING—TAKE DER TRUNK TO OUR SECRET AIR FIELD.

12

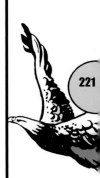

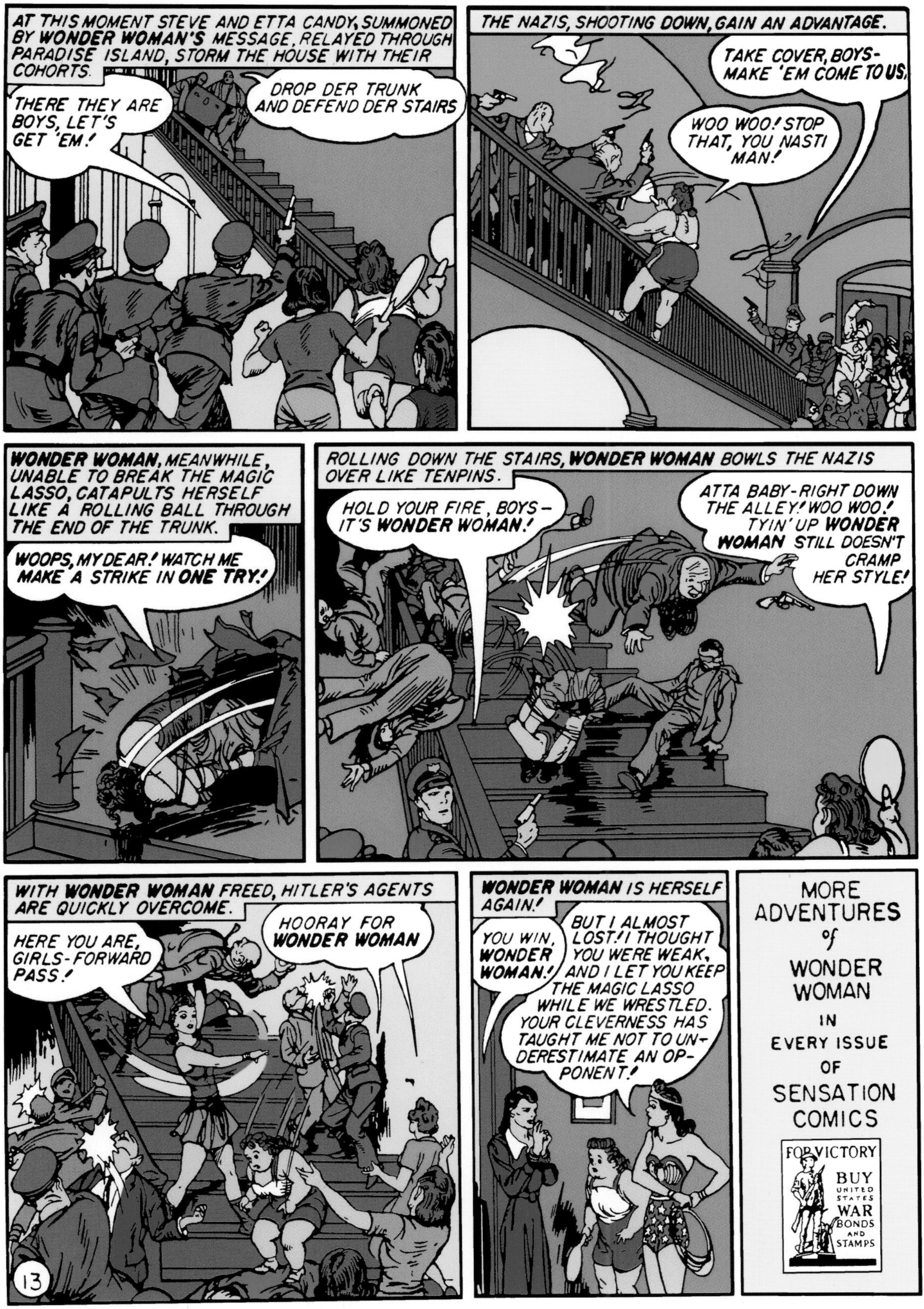
AT THIS MOMENT STEVE AND ETTA CANDY, SUMMONED BY WONDER WOMAN'S MESSAGE, RELAYED THROUGH PARADISE ISLAND, STORM THE HOUSE WITH THEIR COHORTS.
THERE THEY ARE BOYS, LET'S GET 'EM!
DROP DER TRUNK AND DEFEND DER STAIRS
THE NAZIS, SHOOTING DOWN, GAIN AN ADVANTAGE.
TAKE COVER, BOYS- MAKE 'EM COME TO US!
WOO WOO! STOP THAT, YOU NASTI MAN!
WONDER WOMAN, MEANWHILE, UNABLE TO BREAK THE MAGIC LASSO, CATAPULTS HERSELF LIKE A ROLLING BALL THROUGH THE END OF THE TRUNK.
WOOPS, MY DEAR! WATCH ME MAKE A STRIKE IN ONE TRY!
ROLLING DOWN THE STAIRS, WONDER WOMAN BOWLS THE NAZIS OVER LIKE TENPINS.
HOLD YOUR FIRE, BOYS- IT'S WONDER WOMAN!
ATTA BABY-RIGHT DOWN THE ALLEY! WOO WOO! TYIN' UP WONDER WOMAN STILL DOESN'T CRAMP HER STYLE!
WITH WONDER WOMAN FREED, HITLER'S AGENTS ARE QUICKLY OVERCOME.
HERE YOU ARE, GIRLS-FORWARD PASS!
HOORAY FOR WONDER WOMAN
13
WONDER WOMAN IS HERSELF AGAIN!
YOU WIN, WONDER WOMAN!
BUT I ALMOST LOST! I THOUGHT YOU WERE WEAK, AND I LET YOU KEEP THE MAGIC LASSO WHILE WE WRESTLED. YOUR CLEVERNESS HAS TAUGHT ME NOT TO UNDERESTIMATE AN OPPONENT!
MORE ADVENTURES of WONDER WOMAN IN EVERY ISSUE OF SENSATION COMICS
FOR VICTORY BUY UNITED STATES WAR BONDS AND STAMPS

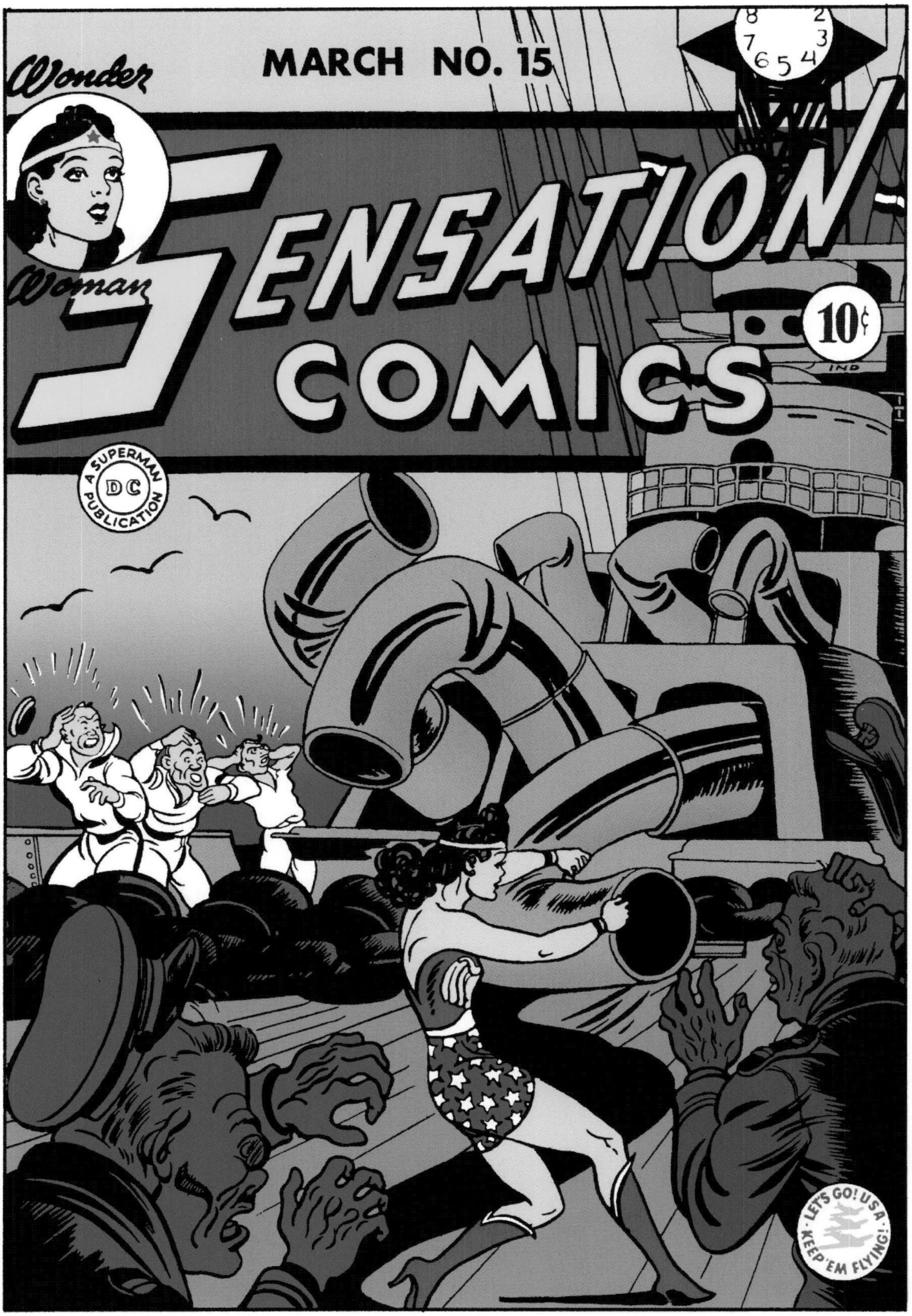
MARCH NO. 15
Wonder Woman
SENSATION COMICS
10¢
A SUPERMAN DC PUBLICATION
LET'S GO! U.S.A. KEEP 'EM FLYING!

Sensation Comics #15 (March 1943) - art: H.G. Peter

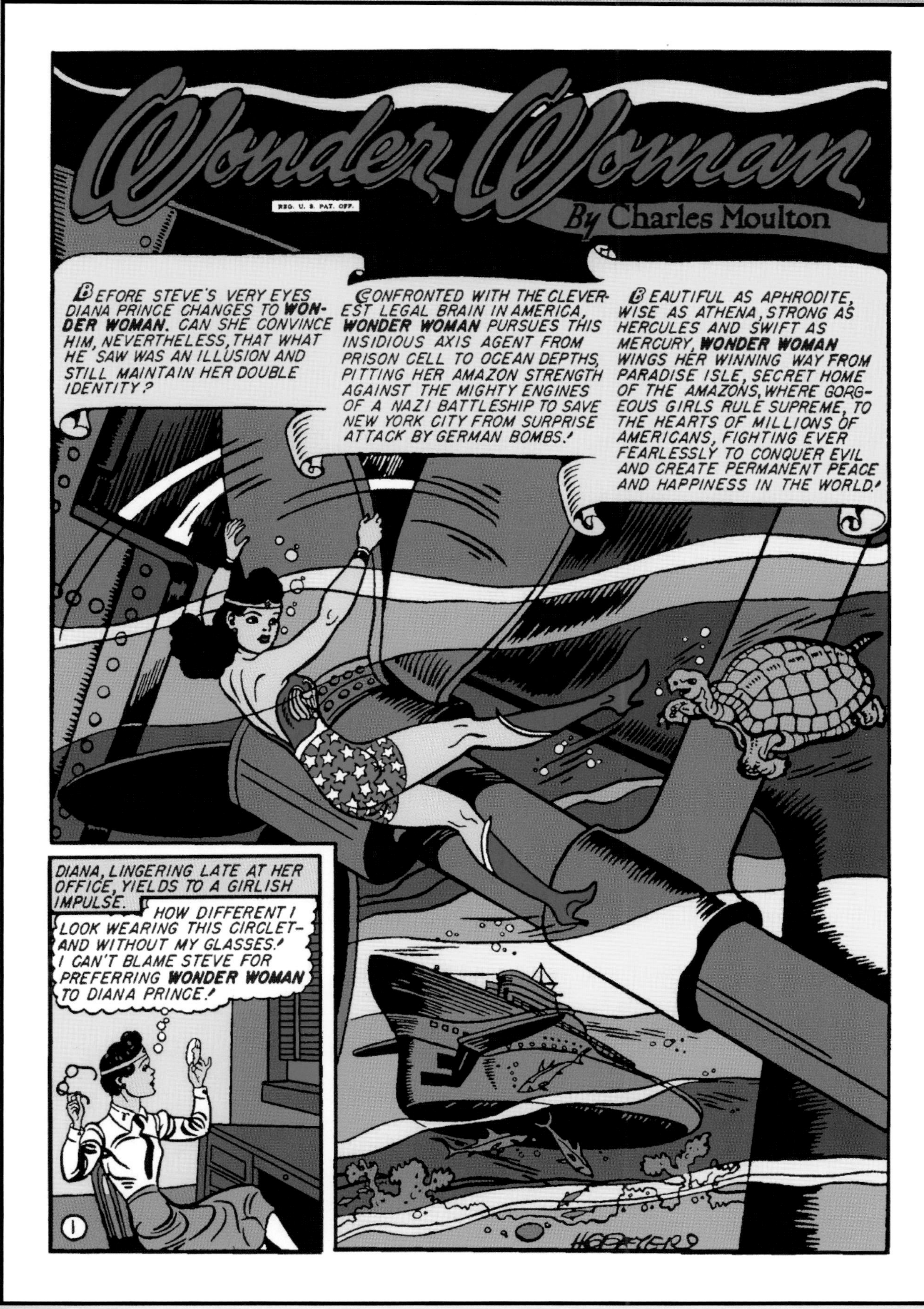
Wonder Woman
REG. U. S. PAT. OFF.
By Charles Moulton
BEFORE STEVE'S VERY EYES DIANA PRINCE CHANGES TO WONDER WOMAN. CAN SHE CONVINCE HIM, NEVERTHELESS, THAT WHAT HE SAW WAS AN ILLUSION AND STILL MAINTAIN HER DOUBLE IDENTITY?
CONFRONTED WITH THE CLEVEREST LEGAL BRAIN IN AMERICA, WONDER WOMAN PURSUES THIS INSIDIOUS AXIS AGENT FROM PRISON CELL TO OCEAN DEPTHS, PITTING HER AMAZON STRENGTH AGAINST THE MIGHTY ENGINES OF A NAZI BATTLESHIP TO SAVE NEW YORK CITY FROM SURPRISE ATTACK BY GERMAN BOMBS!
BEAUTIFUL AS APHRODITE, WISE AS ATHENA, STRONG AS HERCULES AND SWIFT AS MERCURY, WONDER WOMAN WINGS HER WINNING WAY FROM PARADISE ISLE, SECRET HOME OF THE AMAZONS, WHERE GORGEOUS GIRLS RULE SUPREME, TO THE HEARTS OF MILLIONS OF AMERICANS, FIGHTING EVER FEARLESSLY TO CONQUER EVIL AND CREATE PERMANENT PEACE AND HAPPINESS IN THE WORLD!
DIANA, LINGERING LATE AT HER OFFICE, YIELDS TO A GIRLISH IMPULSE.
HOW DIFFERENT I LOOK WEARING THIS CIRCLET—AND WITHOUT MY GLASSES! I CAN'T BLAME STEVE FOR PREFERRING WONDER WOMAN TO DIANA PRINCE!
1

Sensation Comics #15 (March 1943) - script: William Moulton Marston - art: H.G. Peter

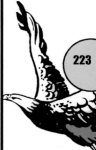

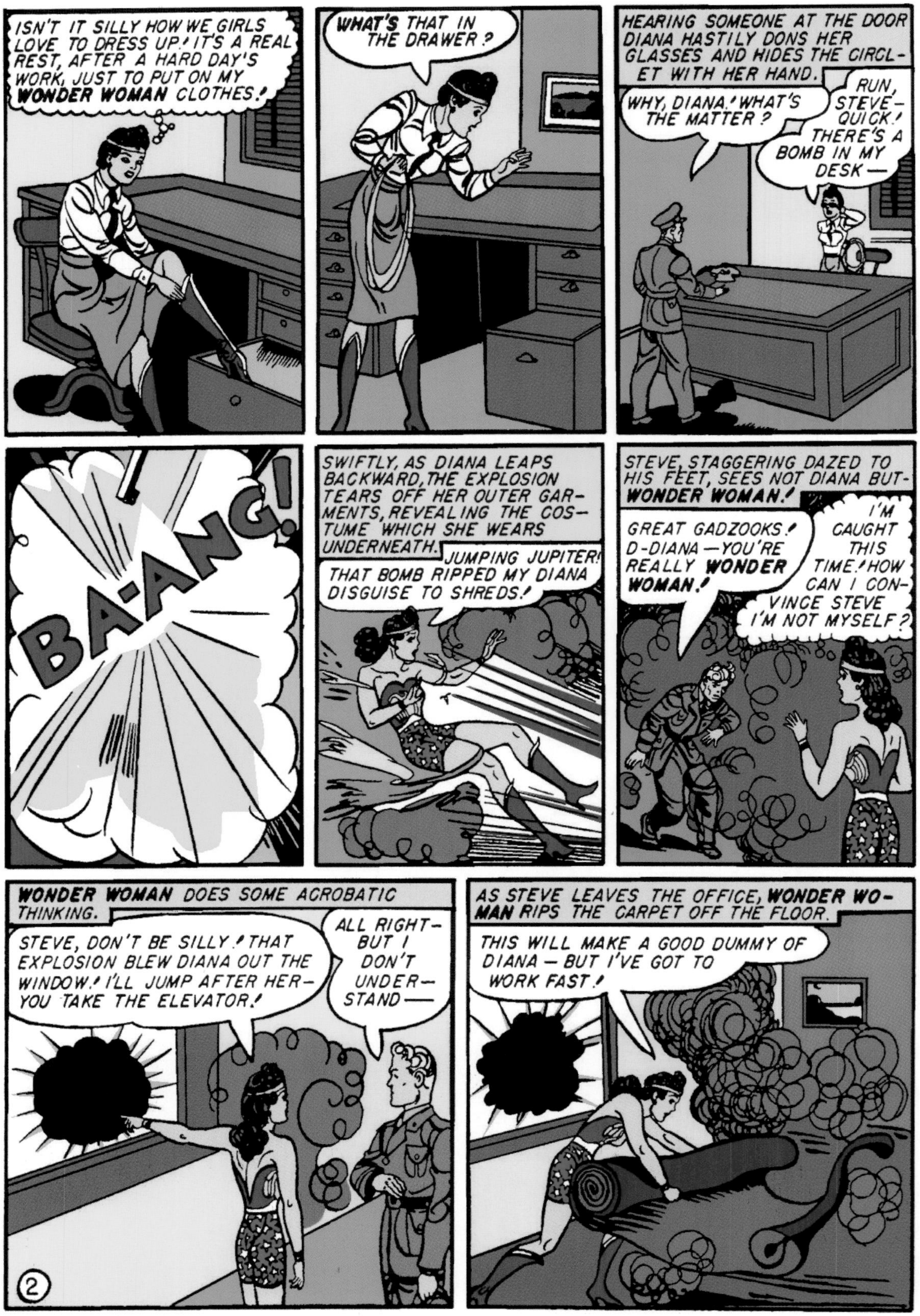
ISN'T IT SILLY HOW WE GIRLS LOVE TO DRESS UP! IT'S A REAL REST, AFTER A HARD DAY'S WORK, JUST TO PUT ON MY WONDER WOMAN CLOTHES!
WHAT'S THAT IN THE DRAWER?
HEARING SOMEONE AT THE DOOR DIANA HASTILY DONS HER GLASSES AND HIDES THE CIRCLET WITH HER HAND.
WHY, DIANA! WHAT'S THE MATTER?
RUN, STEVE-QUICK! THERE'S A BOMB IN MY DESK—
BA-ANG!
SWIFTLY, AS DIANA LEAPS BACKWARD, THE EXPLOSION TEARS OFF HER OUTER GARMENTS, REVEALING THE COSTUME WHICH SHE WEARS UNDERNEATH.
JUMPING JUPITER! THAT BOMB RIPPED MY DIANA DISGUISE TO SHREDS!
STEVE, STAGGERING DAZED TO HIS FEET, SEES NOT DIANA BUT-WONDER WOMAN!
GREAT GADZOOKS! D-DIANA—YOU'RE REALLY WONDER WOMAN!
I'M CAUGHT THIS TIME! HOW CAN I CONVINCE STEVE I'M NOT MYSELF?
WONDER WOMAN DOES SOME ACROBATIC THINKING.
STEVE, DON'T BE SILLY! THAT EXPLOSION BLEW DIANA OUT THE WINDOW! I'LL JUMP AFTER HER-YOU TAKE THE ELEVATOR!
ALL RIGHT-BUT I DON'T UNDERSTAND—
2
AS STEVE LEAVES THE OFFICE, WONDER WOMAN RIPS THE CARPET OFF THE FLOOR.
THIS WILL MAKE A GOOD DUMMY OF DIANA — BUT I'VE GOT TO WORK FAST!

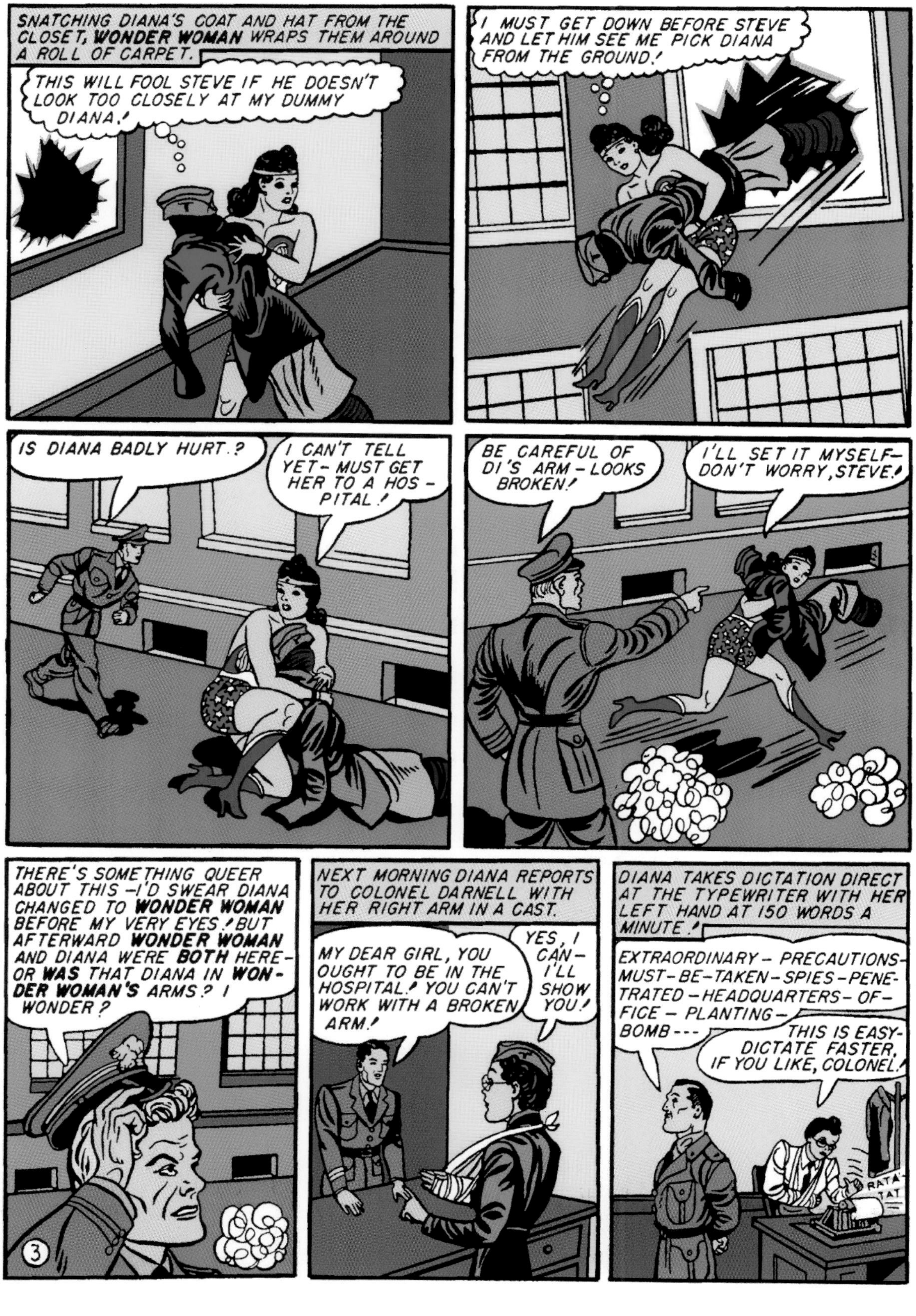
SNATCHING DIANA'S COAT AND HAT FROM THE CLOSET, WONDER WOMAN WRAPS THEM AROUND A ROLL OF CARPET.
THIS WILL FOOL STEVE IF HE DOESN'T LOOK TOO CLOSELY AT MY DUMMY DIANA.!
I MUST GET DOWN BEFORE STEVE AND LET HIM SEE ME PICK DIANA FROM THE GROUND.!
IS DIANA BADLY HURT.?
I CAN'T TELL YET- MUST GET HER TO A HOS-PITAL.!
BE CAREFUL OF DI'S ARM - LOOKS BROKEN.!
I'LL SET IT MYSELF- DON'T WORRY, STEVE.!
THERE'S SOMETHING QUEER ABOUT THIS -I'D SWEAR DIANA CHANGED TO WONDER WOMAN BEFORE MY VERY EYES.! BUT AFTERWARD WONDER WOMAN AND DIANA WERE BOTH HERE- OR WAS THAT DIANA IN WONDER WOMAN'S ARMS? I WONDER?
3
NEXT MORNING DIANA REPORTS TO COLONEL DARNELL WITH HER RIGHT ARM IN A CAST.
MY DEAR GIRL, YOU OUGHT TO BE IN THE HOSPITAL.! YOU CAN'T WORK WITH A BROKEN ARM.!
YES, I CAN - I'LL SHOW YOU.!
DIANA TAKES DICTATION DIRECT AT THE TYPEWRITER WITH HER LEFT HAND AT 150 WORDS A MINUTE.!
EXTRAORDINARY - PRECAUTIONS-MUST-BE-TAKEN-SPIES-PENETRATED-HEADQUARTERS-OFFICE- PLANTING-BOMB---
THIS IS EASY- DICTATE FASTER, IF YOU LIKE, COLONEL.!
RATA-TAT

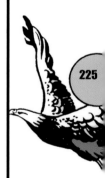

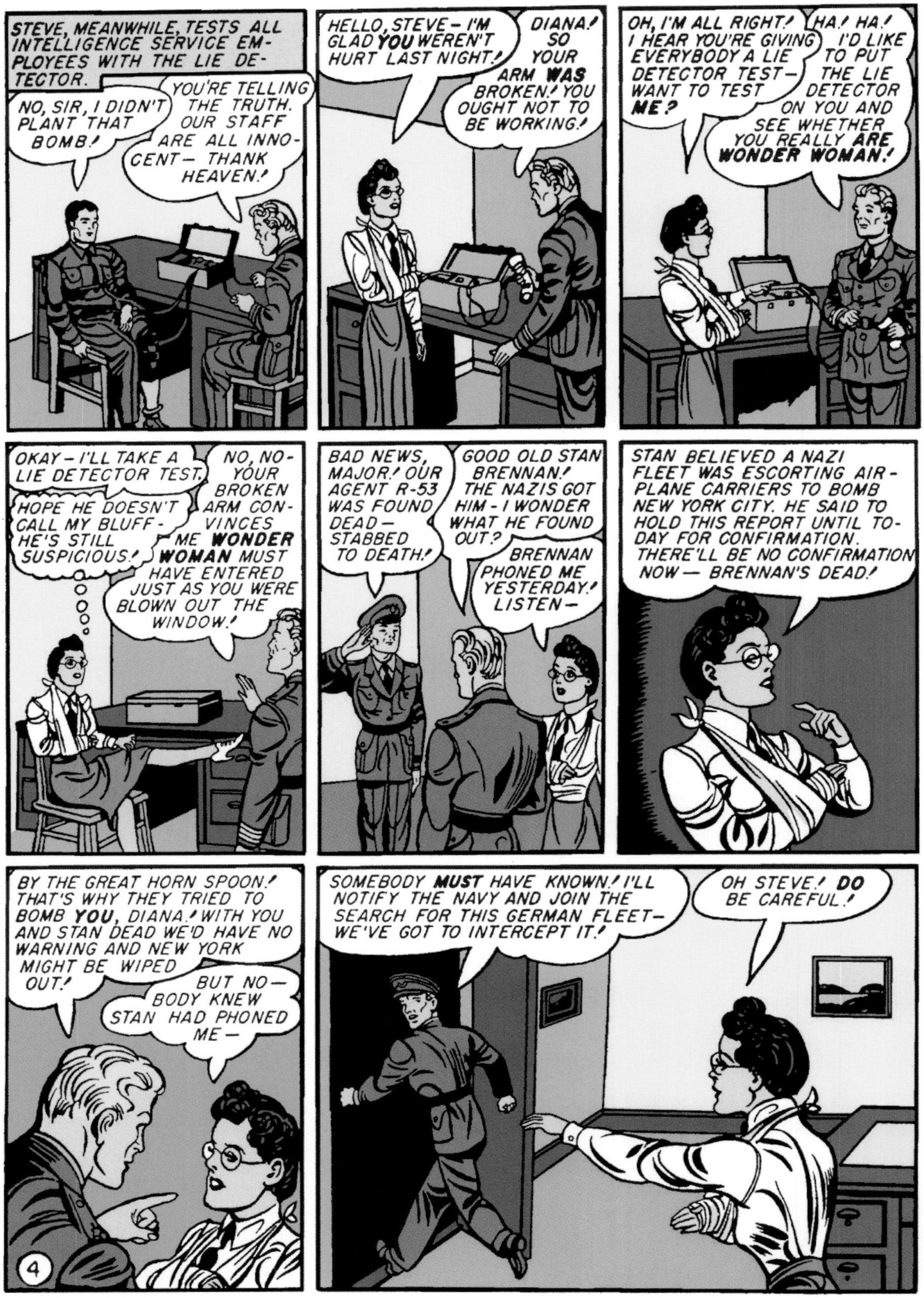

STEVE, MEANWHILE, TESTS ALL INTELLIGENCE SERVICE EMPLOYEES WITH THE LIE DETECTOR.
NO, SIR, I DIDN'T PLANT THAT BOMB!
YOU'RE TELLING THE TRUTH. OUR STAFF ARE ALL INNOCENT — THANK HEAVEN!
HELLO, STEVE — I'M GLAD YOU WEREN'T HURT LAST NIGHT!
DIANA! SO YOUR ARM WAS BROKEN! YOU OUGHT NOT TO BE WORKING!
OH, I'M ALL RIGHT! I HEAR YOU'RE GIVING EVERYBODY A LIE DETECTOR TEST — WANT TO TEST ME?
HA! HA! I'D LIKE TO PUT THE LIE DETECTOR ON YOU AND SEE WHETHER YOU REALLY ARE WONDER WOMAN!
OKAY — I'LL TAKE A LIE DETECTOR TEST.
HOPE HE DOESN'T CALL MY BLUFF - HE'S STILL SUSPICIOUS!
NO, NO - YOUR BROKEN ARM CONVINCES ME WONDER WOMAN MUST HAVE ENTERED JUST AS YOU WERE BLOWN OUT THE WINDOW!
BAD NEWS, MAJOR! OUR AGENT R-53 WAS FOUND DEAD — STABBED TO DEATH!
GOOD OLD STAN BRENNAN! THE NAZIS GOT HIM - I WONDER WHAT HE FOUND OUT?
BRENNAN PHONED ME YESTERDAY! LISTEN —
STAN BELIEVED A NAZI FLEET WAS ESCORTING AIRPLANE CARRIERS TO BOMB NEW YORK CITY. HE SAID TO HOLD THIS REPORT UNTIL TODAY FOR CONFIRMATION. THERE'LL BE NO CONFIRMATION NOW — BRENNAN'S DEAD!
BY THE GREAT HORN SPOON! THAT'S WHY THEY TRIED TO BOMB YOU, DIANA! WITH YOU AND STAN DEAD WE'D HAVE NO WARNING AND NEW YORK MIGHT BE WIPED OUT!
BUT NOBODY KNEW STAN HAD PHONED ME —
4
SOMEBODY MUST HAVE KNOWN! I'LL NOTIFY THE NAVY AND JOIN THE SEARCH FOR THIS GERMAN FLEET — WE'VE GOT TO INTERCEPT IT!
OH STEVE! DO BE CAREFUL!

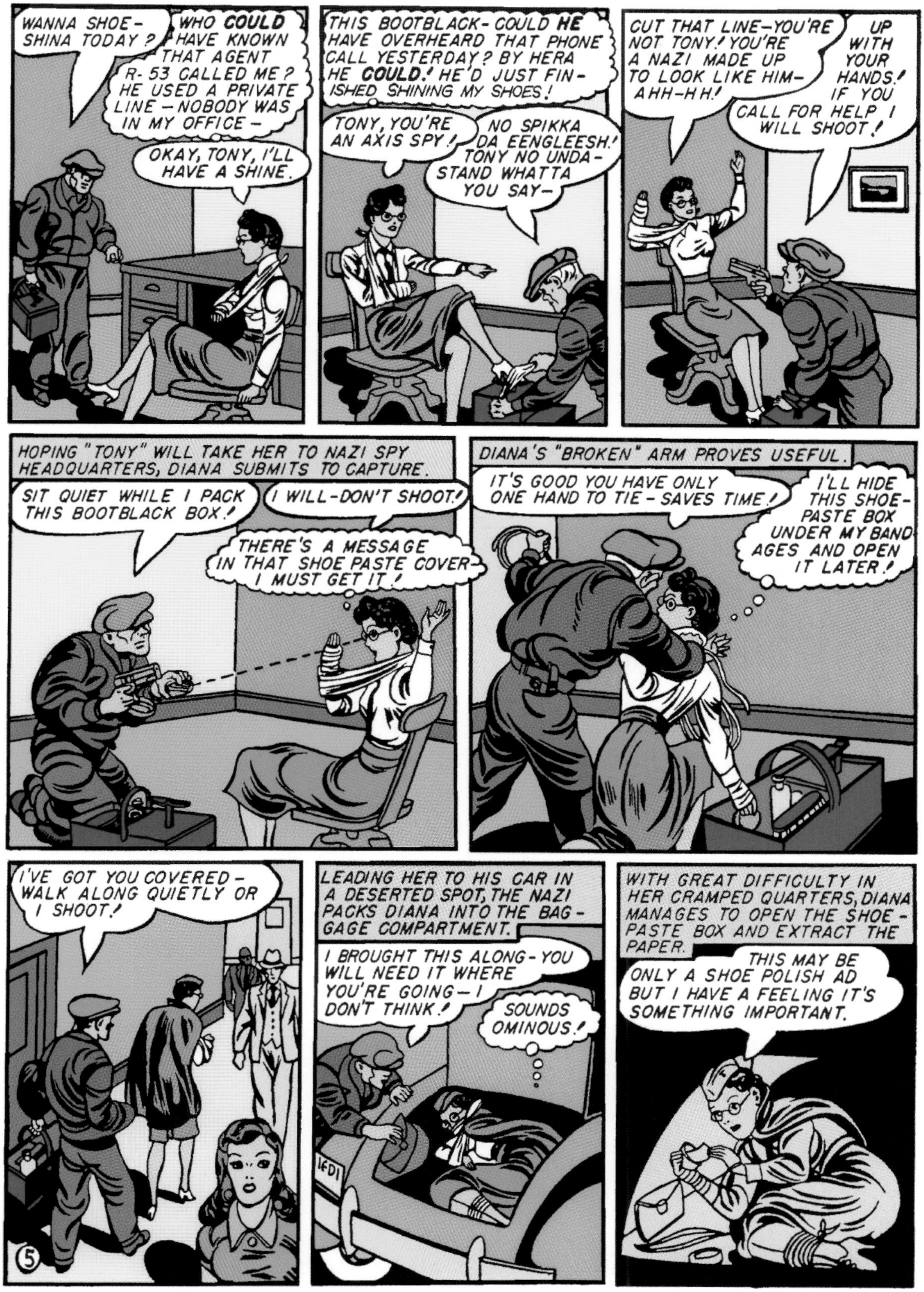
WANNA SHOE-SHINA TODAY?
WHO COULD HAVE KNOWN THAT AGENT R-53 CALLED ME? HE USED A PRIVATE LINE—NOBODY WAS IN MY OFFICE—
OKAY, TONY, I'LL HAVE A SHINE.
THIS BOOTBLACK-COULD HE HAVE OVERHEARD THAT PHONE CALL YESTERDAY? BY HERA HE COULD! HE'D JUST FIN-ISHED SHINING MY SHOES!
TONY, YOU'RE AN AXIS SPY!
NO SPIKKA DA EENGLEESH! TONY NO UNDA-STAND WHATTA YOU SAY—
CUT THAT LINE—YOU'RE NOT TONY! YOU'RE A NAZI MADE UP TO LOOK LIKE HIM—AHH-HH!
UP WITH YOUR HANDS! IF YOU CALL FOR HELP I WILL SHOOT!
HOPING "TONY" WILL TAKE HER TO NAZI SPY HEADQUARTERS, DIANA SUBMITS TO CAPTURE.
SIT QUIET WHILE I PACK THIS BOOTBLACK BOX!
I WILL-DON'T SHOOT!
THERE'S A MESSAGE IN THAT SHOE PASTE COVER-I MUST GET IT!
DIANA'S "BROKEN" ARM PROVES USEFUL.
IT'S GOOD YOU HAVE ONLY ONE HAND TO TIE - SAVES TIME!
I'LL HIDE THIS SHOE-PASTE BOX UNDER MY BAND-AGES AND OPEN IT LATER!
I'VE GOT YOU COVERED—WALK ALONG QUIETLY OR I SHOOT!
5
LEADING HER TO HIS CAR IN A DESERTED SPOT, THE NAZI PACKS DIANA INTO THE BAG-GAGE COMPARTMENT.
I BROUGHT THIS ALONG-YOU WILL NEED IT WHERE YOU'RE GOING—I DON'T THINK!
SOUNDS OMINOUS!
WITH GREAT DIFFICULTY IN HER CRAMPED QUARTERS, DIANA MANAGES TO OPEN THE SHOE-PASTE BOX AND EXTRACT THE PAPER.
THIS MAY BE ONLY A SHOE POLISH AD BUT I HAVE A FEELING IT'S SOMETHING IMPORTANT.

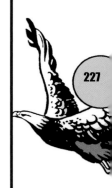

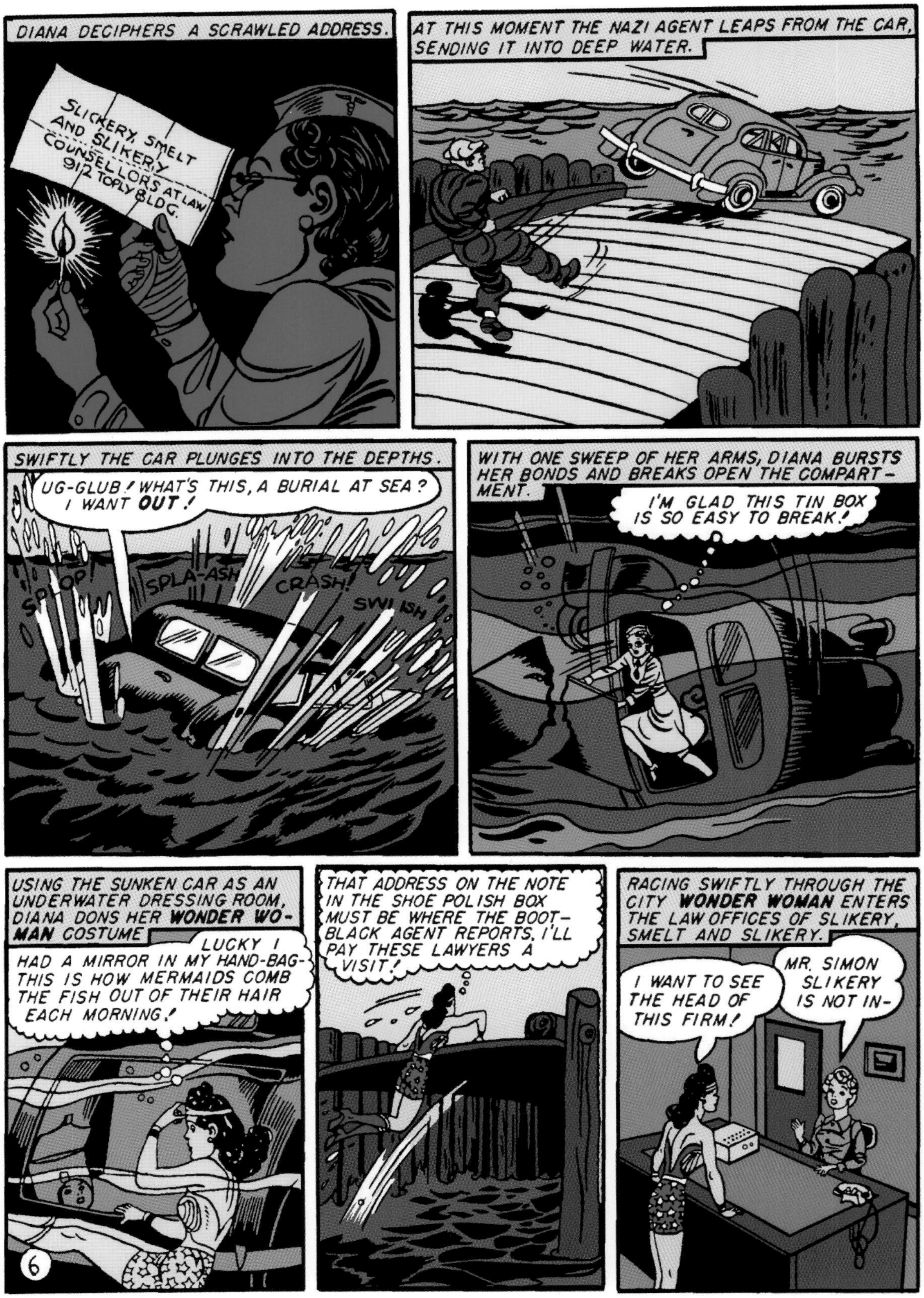
DIANA DECIPHERS A SCRAWLED ADDRESS.
SLICKERY, SMELT AND SLIKERY COUNSELLORS AT LAW 912 TOPLY BLDG.
AT THIS MOMENT THE NAZI AGENT LEAPS FROM THE CAR, SENDING IT INTO DEEP WATER.
SWIFTLY THE CAR PLUNGES INTO THE DEPTHS.
UG-GLUB! WHAT'S THIS, A BURIAL AT SEA? I WANT OUT!
SPLOP! SPLA-ASH CRASH! SWISH
WITH ONE SWEEP OF HER ARMS, DIANA BURSTS HER BONDS AND BREAKS OPEN THE COMPART-MENT.
I'M GLAD THIS TIN BOX IS SO EASY TO BREAK!
USING THE SUNKEN CAR AS AN UNDERWATER DRESSING ROOM, DIANA DONS HER WONDER WO-MAN COSTUME
LUCKY I HAD A MIRROR IN MY HAND-BAG- THIS IS HOW MERMAIDS COMB THE FISH OUT OF THEIR HAIR EACH MORNING!
6
THAT ADDRESS ON THE NOTE IN THE SHOE POLISH BOX MUST BE WHERE THE BOOT-BLACK AGENT REPORTS. I'LL PAY THESE LAWYERS A VISIT!
RACING SWIFTLY THROUGH THE CITY WONDER WOMAN ENTERS THE LAW OFFICES OF SLIKERY, SMELT AND SLIKERY.
I WANT TO SEE THE HEAD OF THIS FIRM!
MR. SIMON SLIKERY IS NOT IN-

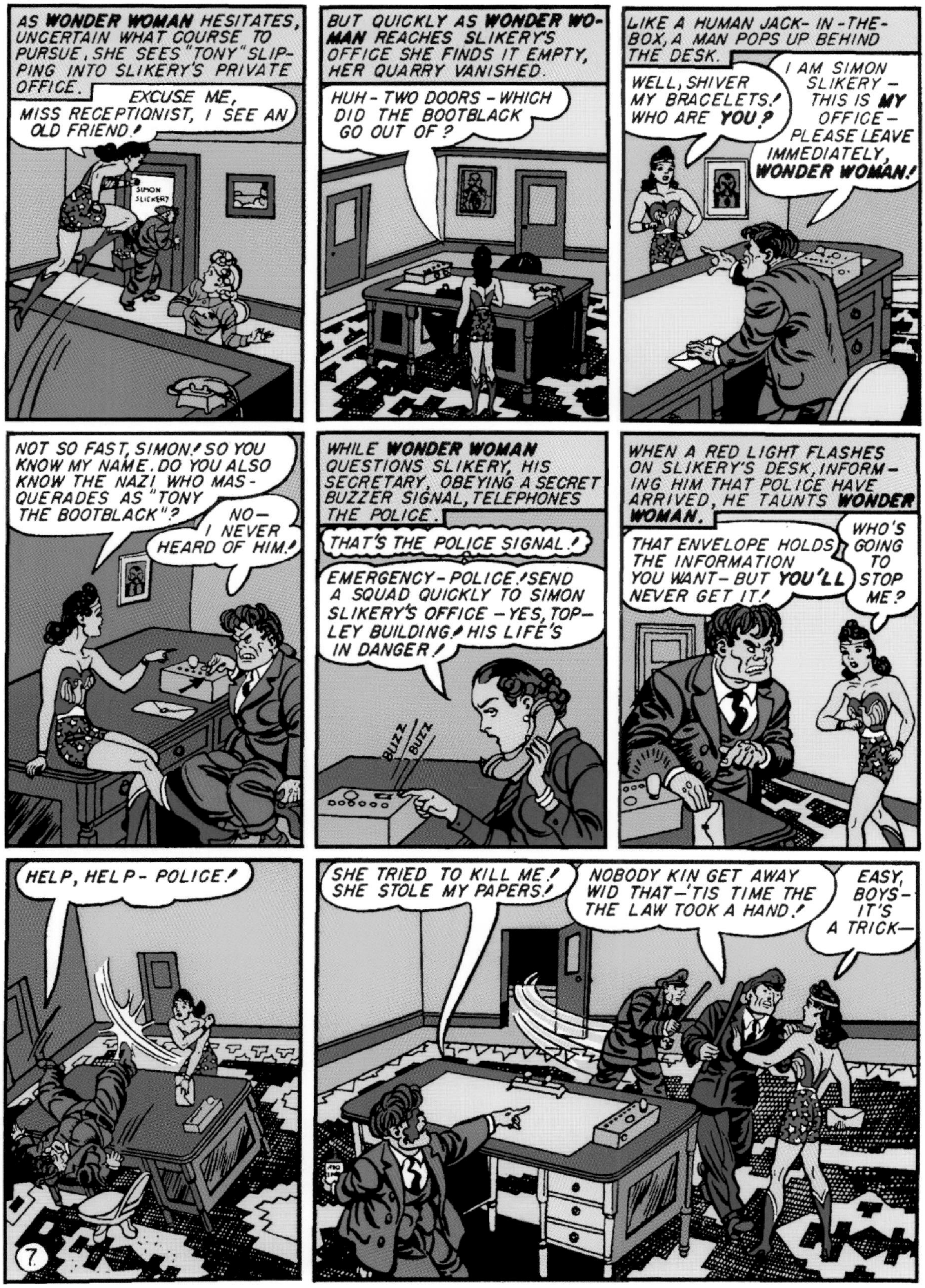
AS WONDER WOMAN HESITATES, UNCERTAIN WHAT COURSE TO PURSUE, SHE SEES "TONY" SLIPPING INTO SLIKERY'S PRIVATE OFFICE.
EXCUSE ME, MISS RECEPTIONIST, I SEE AN OLD FRIEND!
SIMON SLIKERY
BUT QUICKLY AS WONDER WOMAN REACHES SLIKERY'S OFFICE SHE FINDS IT EMPTY, HER QUARRY VANISHED.
HUH - TWO DOORS - WHICH DID THE BOOTBLACK GO OUT OF?
LIKE A HUMAN JACK-IN-THE-BOX, A MAN POPS UP BEHIND THE DESK.
WELL, SHIVER MY BRACELETS! WHO ARE YOU?
I AM SIMON SLIKERY - THIS IS MY OFFICE - PLEASE LEAVE IMMEDIATELY, WONDER WOMAN!
NOT SO FAST, SIMON! SO YOU KNOW MY NAME. DO YOU ALSO KNOW THE NAZI WHO MASQUERADES AS "TONY THE BOOTBLACK"?
NO - I NEVER HEARD OF HIM!
WHILE WONDER WOMAN QUESTIONS SLIKERY, HIS SECRETARY, OBEYING A SECRET BUZZER SIGNAL, TELEPHONES THE POLICE.
THAT'S THE POLICE SIGNAL!
EMERGENCY - POLICE! SEND A SQUAD QUICKLY TO SIMON SLIKERY'S OFFICE - YES, TOPLEY BUILDING! HIS LIFE'S IN DANGER!
BUZZ BUZZ
WHEN A RED LIGHT FLASHES ON SLIKERY'S DESK, INFORMING HIM THAT POLICE HAVE ARRIVED, HE TAUNTS WONDER WOMAN.
THAT ENVELOPE HOLDS THE INFORMATION YOU WANT - BUT YOU'LL NEVER GET IT!
WHO'S GOING TO STOP ME?
HELP, HELP - POLICE!
SHE TRIED TO KILL ME! SHE STOLE MY PAPERS!
NOBODY KIN GET AWAY WID THAT - 'TIS TIME THE THE LAW TOOK A HAND!
EASY, BOYS - IT'S A TRICK -
7

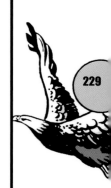

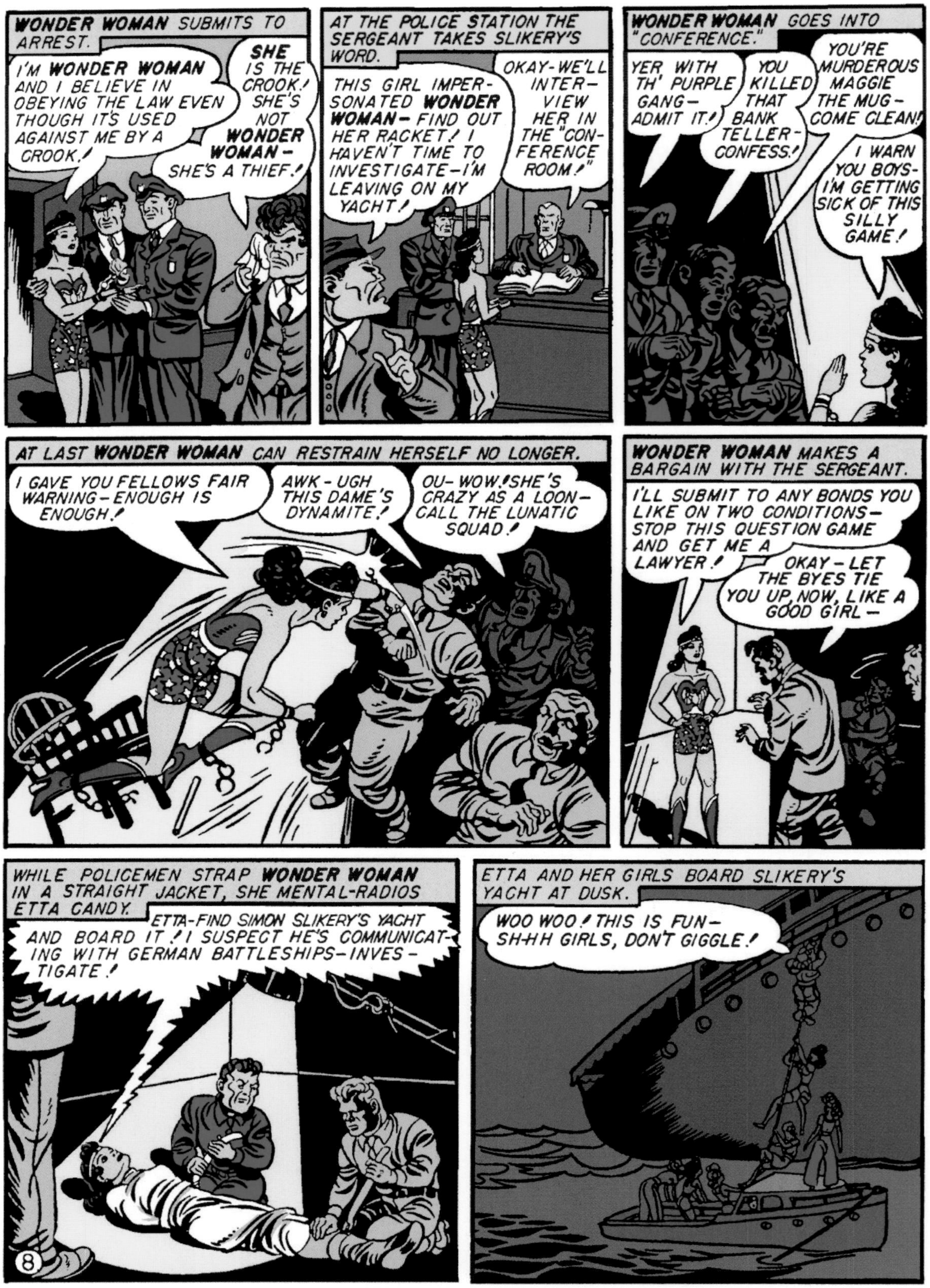
WONDER WOMAN SUBMITS TO ARREST.
I'M WONDER WOMAN AND I BELIEVE IN OBEYING THE LAW EVEN THOUGH IT'S USED AGAINST ME BY A CROOK.!
SHE IS THE CROOK.! SHE'S NOT WONDER WOMAN — SHE'S A THIEF.!
AT THE POLICE STATION THE SERGEANT TAKES SLIKERY'S WORD.
THIS GIRL IMPERSONATED WONDER WOMAN — FIND OUT HER RACKET.! I HAVEN'T TIME TO INVESTIGATE — I'M LEAVING ON MY YACHT.!
OKAY - WE'LL INTERVIEW HER IN THE "CONFERENCE ROOM.!"
WONDER WOMAN GOES INTO "CONFERENCE."
YER WITH TH' PURPLE GANG — ADMIT IT.!
YOU KILLED THAT BANK TELLER — CONFESS.!
YOU'RE MURDEROUS MAGGIE THE MUG — COME CLEAN!
I WARN YOU BOYS — I'M GETTING SICK OF THIS SILLY GAME!
AT LAST WONDER WOMAN CAN RESTRAIN HERSELF NO LONGER.
I GAVE YOU FELLOWS FAIR WARNING — ENOUGH IS ENOUGH.!
AWK - UGH THIS DAME'S DYNAMITE.!
OU- WOW.! SHE'S CRAZY AS A LOON — CALL THE LUNATIC SQUAD.!
WONDER WOMAN MAKES A BARGAIN WITH THE SERGEANT.
I'LL SUBMIT TO ANY BONDS YOU LIKE ON TWO CONDITIONS — STOP THIS QUESTION GAME AND GET ME A LAWYER.!
OKAY — LET THE BYES TIE YOU UP, NOW, LIKE A GOOD GIRL —
WHILE POLICEMEN STRAP WONDER WOMAN IN A STRAIGHT JACKET, SHE MENTAL-RADIOS ETTA CANDY.
ETTA-FIND SIMON SLIKERY'S YACHT AND BOARD IT.! I SUSPECT HE'S COMMUNICATING WITH GERMAN BATTLESHIPS — INVESTIGATE.!
8
ETTA AND HER GIRLS BOARD SLIKERY'S YACHT AT DUSK.
WOO WOO.! THIS IS FUN — SH-HH GIRLS, DON'T GIGGLE.!

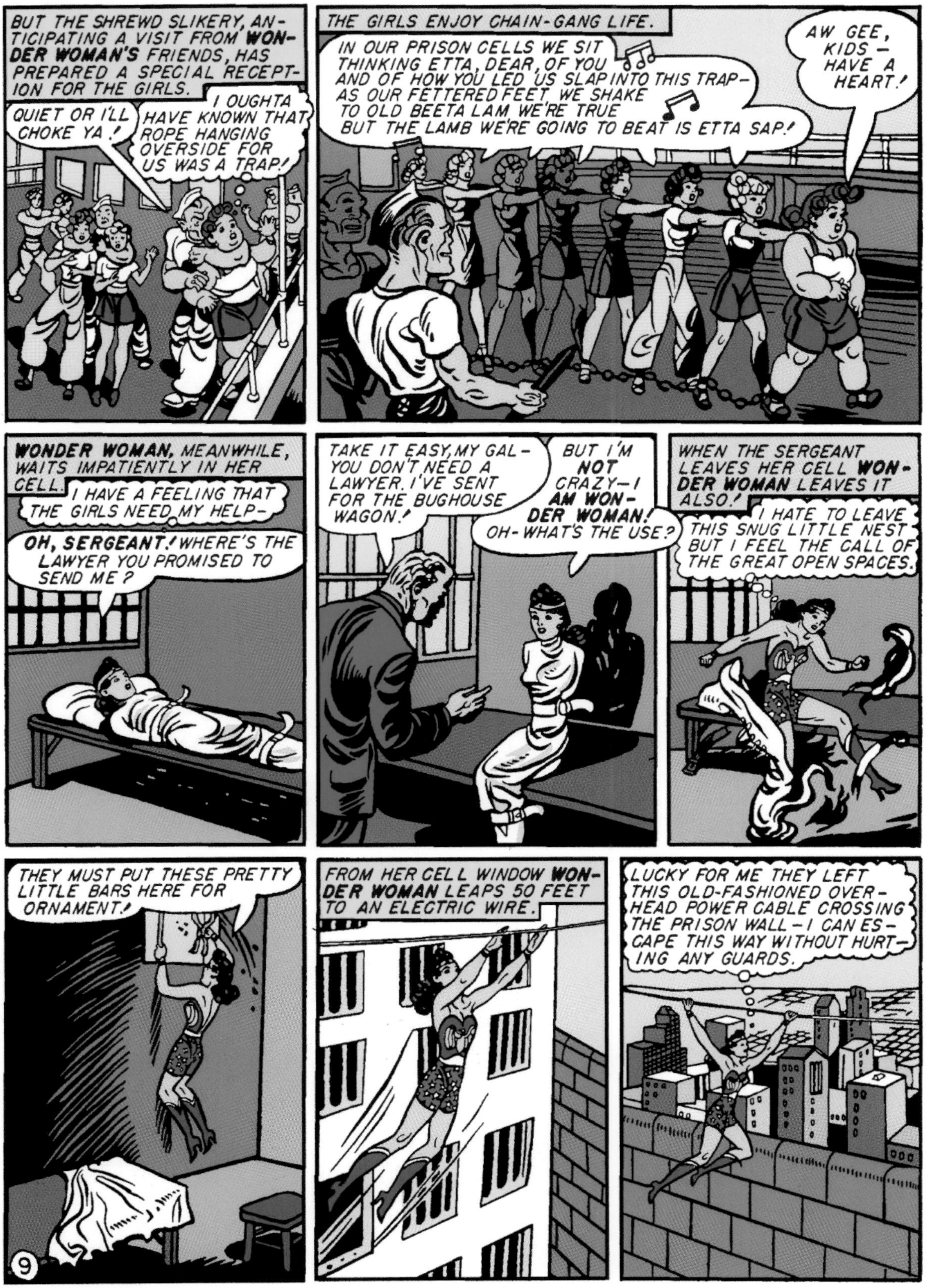
BUT THE SHREWD SLIKERY, ANTICIPATING A VISIT FROM WONDER WOMAN'S FRIENDS, HAS PREPARED A SPECIAL RECEPTION FOR THE GIRLS.
QUIET OR I'LL CHOKE YA!
I OUGHTA HAVE KNOWN THAT ROPE HANGING OVERSIDE FOR US WAS A TRAP!
THE GIRLS ENJOY CHAIN-GANG LIFE.
IN OUR PRISON CELLS WE SIT THINKING ETTA, DEAR, OF YOU AND OF HOW YOU LED US SLAP INTO THIS TRAP— AS OUR FETTERED FEET WE SHAKE TO OLD BEETA LAM WE'RE TRUE BUT THE LAMB WE'RE GOING TO BEAT IS ETTA SAP!
AW GEE, KIDS— HAVE A HEART!
WONDER WOMAN, MEANWHILE, WAITS IMPATIENTLY IN HER CELL.
I HAVE A FEELING THAT THE GIRLS NEED MY HELP—
OH, SERGEANT! WHERE'S THE LAWYER YOU PROMISED TO SEND ME?
TAKE IT EASY, MY GAL— YOU DON'T NEED A LAWYER. I'VE SENT FOR THE BUGHOUSE WAGON!
BUT I'M NOT CRAZY—I AM WONDER WOMAN! OH-WHAT'S THE USE?
WHEN THE SERGEANT LEAVES HER CELL WONDER WOMAN LEAVES IT ALSO!
I HATE TO LEAVE THIS SNUG LITTLE NEST BUT I FEEL THE CALL OF THE GREAT OPEN SPACES.
THEY MUST PUT THESE PRETTY LITTLE BARS HERE FOR ORNAMENT!
FROM HER CELL WINDOW WONDER WOMAN LEAPS 50 FEET TO AN ELECTRIC WIRE.
LUCKY FOR ME THEY LEFT THIS OLD-FASHIONED OVERHEAD POWER CABLE CROSSING THE PRISON WALL—I CAN ESCAPE THIS WAY WITHOUT HURTING ANY GUARDS.
9

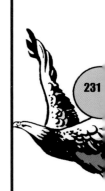

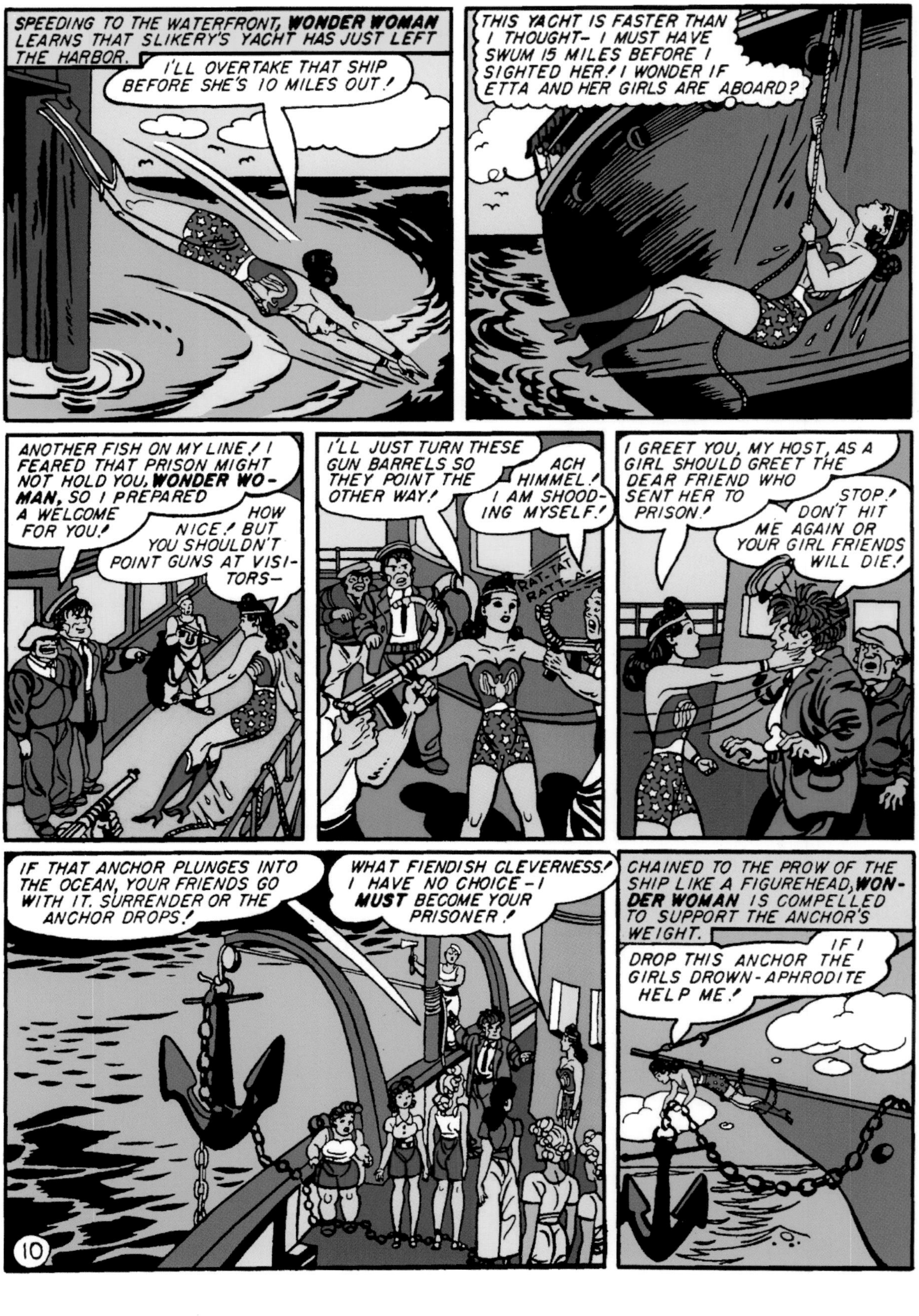
SPEEDING TO THE WATERFRONT, WONDER WOMAN LEARNS THAT SLIKERY'S YACHT HAS JUST LEFT THE HARBOR.
I'LL OVERTAKE THAT SHIP BEFORE SHE'S 10 MILES OUT!
THIS YACHT IS FASTER THAN I THOUGHT- I MUST HAVE SWUM 15 MILES BEFORE I SIGHTED HER! I WONDER IF ETTA AND HER GIRLS ARE ABOARD?
ANOTHER FISH ON MY LINE! I FEARED THAT PRISON MIGHT NOT HOLD YOU, WONDER WOMAN, SO I PREPARED A WELCOME FOR YOU!
HOW NICE! BUT YOU SHOULDN'T POINT GUNS AT VISITORS-
I'LL JUST TURN THESE GUN BARRELS SO THEY POINT THE OTHER WAY!
ACH HIMMEL! I AM SHOODING MYSELF!
RAT-TAT RATT-A
I GREET YOU, MY HOST, AS A GIRL SHOULD GREET THE DEAR FRIEND WHO SENT HER TO PRISON!
STOP! DON'T HIT ME AGAIN OR YOUR GIRL FRIENDS WILL DIE!
IF THAT ANCHOR PLUNGES INTO THE OCEAN, YOUR FRIENDS GO WITH IT. SURRENDER OR THE ANCHOR DROPS!
WHAT FIENDISH CLEVERNESS! I HAVE NO CHOICE - I MUST BECOME YOUR PRISONER!
10
CHAINED TO THE PROW OF THE SHIP LIKE A FIGUREHEAD, WONDER WOMAN IS COMPELLED TO SUPPORT THE ANCHOR'S WEIGHT.
IF I DROP THIS ANCHOR THE GIRLS DROWN - APHRODITE HELP ME!

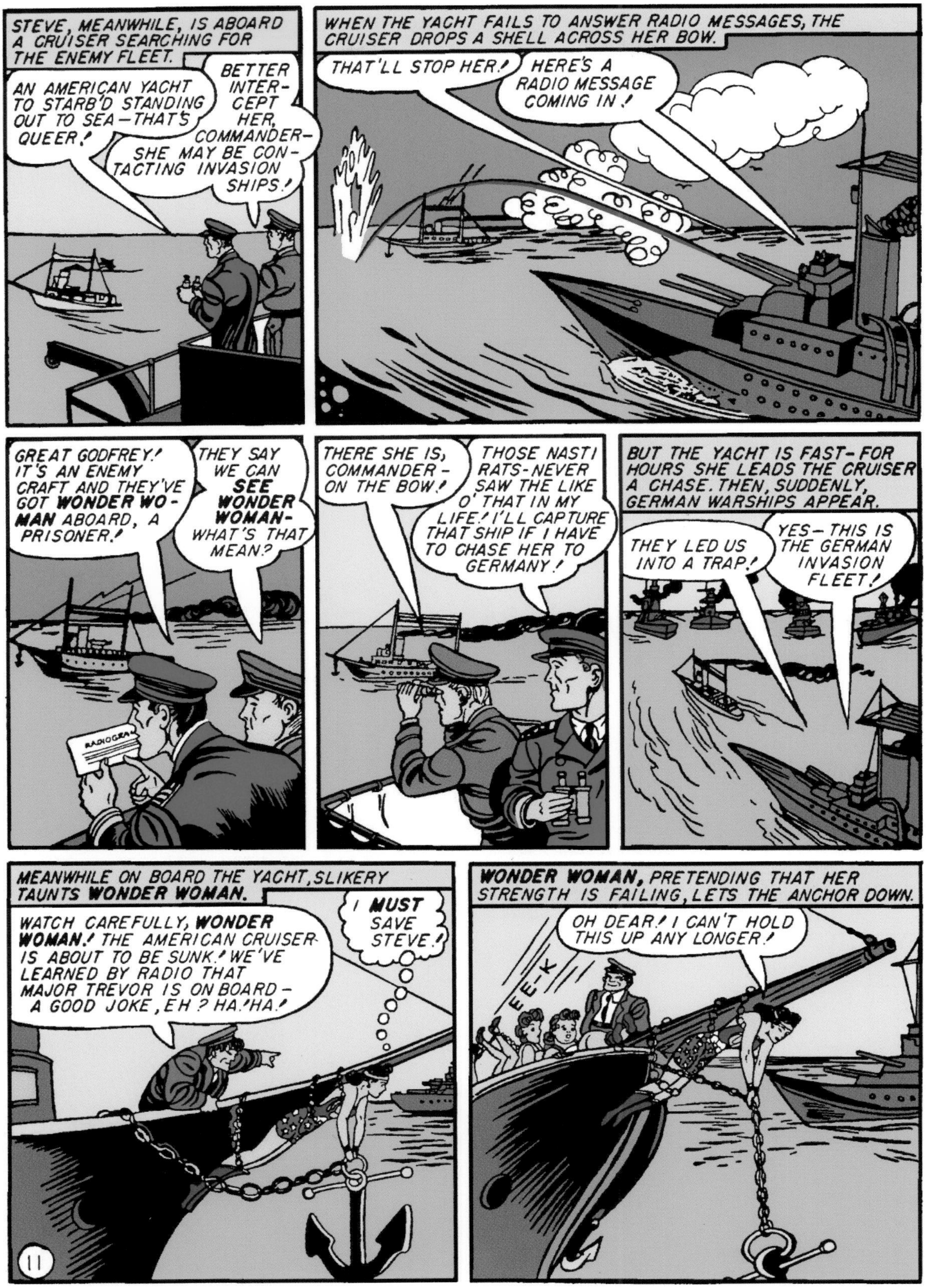
STEVE, MEANWHILE, IS ABOARD A CRUISER SEARCHING FOR THE ENEMY FLEET.
AN AMERICAN YACHT TO STARB'D STANDING OUT TO SEA—THAT'S QUEER!
BETTER INTERCEPT HER, COMMANDER—SHE MAY BE CONTACTING INVASION SHIPS!
WHEN THE YACHT FAILS TO ANSWER RADIO MESSAGES, THE CRUISER DROPS A SHELL ACROSS HER BOW.
THAT'LL STOP HER!
HERE'S A RADIO MESSAGE COMING IN!
GREAT GODFREY! IT'S AN ENEMY CRAFT AND THEY'VE GOT WONDER WOMAN ABOARD, A PRISONER!
THEY SAY WE CAN SEE WONDER WOMAN—WHAT'S THAT MEAN?
RADIOGRAM
THERE SHE IS, COMMANDER—ON THE BOW!
THOSE NASTI RATS—NEVER SAW THE LIKE O' THAT IN MY LIFE! I'LL CAPTURE THAT SHIP IF I HAVE TO CHASE HER TO GERMANY!
BUT THE YACHT IS FAST—FOR HOURS SHE LEADS THE CRUISER A CHASE. THEN, SUDDENLY, GERMAN WARSHIPS APPEAR.
THEY LED US INTO A TRAP!
YES—THIS IS THE GERMAN INVASION FLEET!
MEANWHILE ON BOARD THE YACHT, SLIKERY TAUNTS WONDER WOMAN.
WATCH CAREFULLY, WONDER WOMAN! THE AMERICAN CRUISER IS ABOUT TO BE SUNK! WE'VE LEARNED BY RADIO THAT MAJOR TREVOR IS ON BOARD—A GOOD JOKE, EH? HA! HA!
I MUST SAVE STEVE!
11
WONDER WOMAN, PRETENDING THAT HER STRENGTH IS FAILING, LETS THE ANCHOR DOWN.
OH DEAR! I CAN'T HOLD THIS UP ANY LONGER!
EE-K

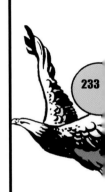

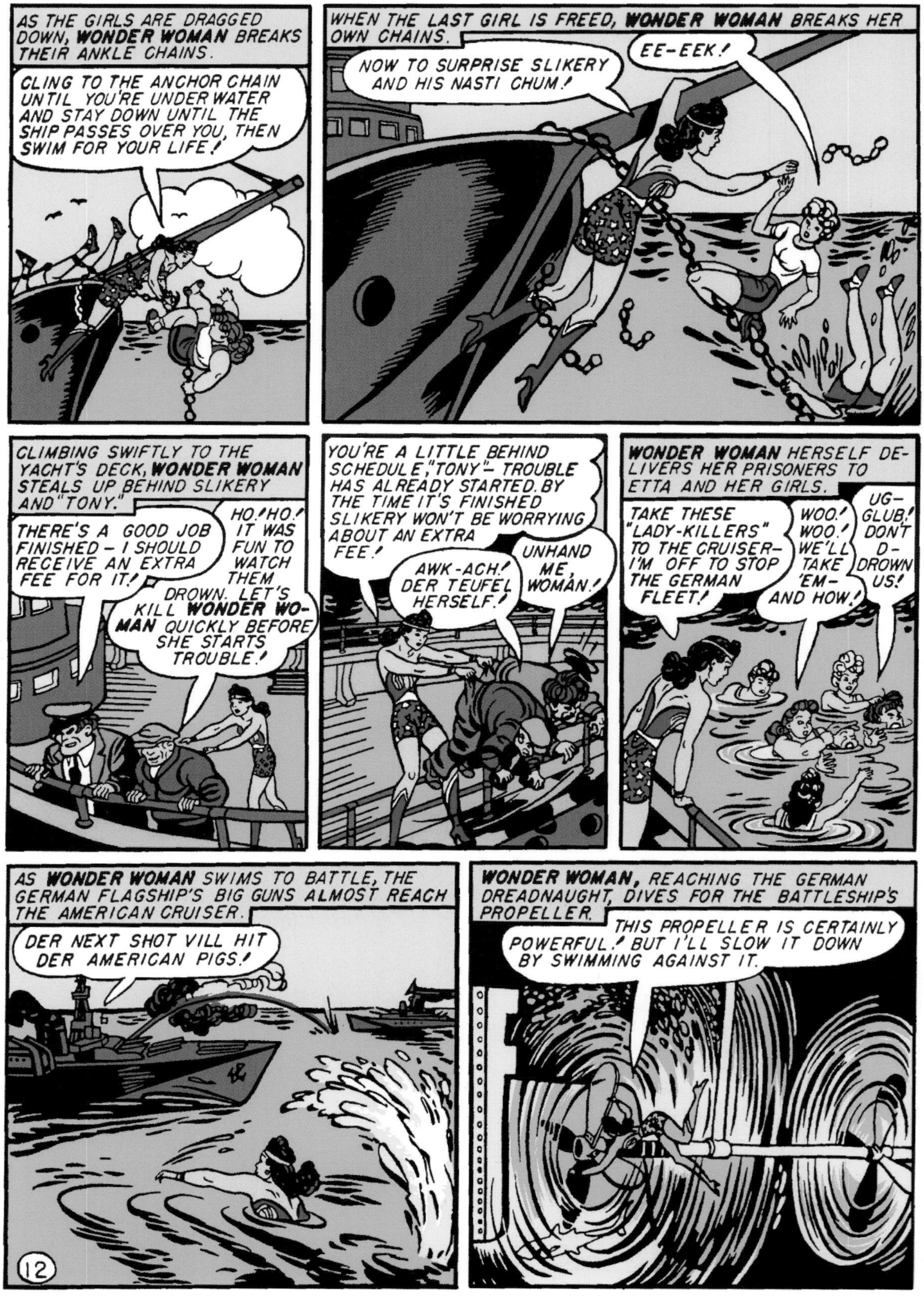
AS THE GIRLS ARE DRAGGED DOWN, WONDER WOMAN BREAKS THEIR ANKLE CHAINS.
CLING TO THE ANCHOR CHAIN UNTIL YOU'RE UNDER WATER AND STAY DOWN UNTIL THE SHIP PASSES OVER YOU, THEN SWIM FOR YOUR LIFE!
WHEN THE LAST GIRL IS FREED, WONDER WOMAN BREAKS HER OWN CHAINS.
NOW TO SURPRISE SLIKERY AND HIS NASTI CHUM!
EE-EEK!
CLIMBING SWIFTLY TO THE YACHT'S DECK, WONDER WOMAN STEALS UP BEHIND SLIKERY AND "TONY."
THERE'S A GOOD JOB FINISHED – I SHOULD RECEIVE AN EXTRA FEE FOR IT!
HO! HO! IT WAS FUN TO WATCH THEM DROWN. LET'S KILL WONDER WOMAN QUICKLY BEFORE SHE STARTS TROUBLE!
YOU'RE A LITTLE BEHIND SCHEDULE, "TONY"– TROUBLE HAS ALREADY STARTED. BY THE TIME IT'S FINISHED SLIKERY WON'T BE WORRYING ABOUT AN EXTRA FEE!
AWK-ACH! DER TEUFEL HERSELF!
UNHAND ME, WOMAN!
WONDER WOMAN HERSELF DELIVERS HER PRISONERS TO ETTA AND HER GIRLS.
TAKE THESE "LADY-KILLERS" TO THE CRUISER– I'M OFF TO STOP THE GERMAN FLEET!
WOO! WOO! WE'LL TAKE 'EM– AND HOW!
UG-GLUB! DON'T D-DROWN US!
AS WONDER WOMAN SWIMS TO BATTLE, THE GERMAN FLAGSHIP'S BIG GUNS ALMOST REACH THE AMERICAN CRUISER.
DER NEXT SHOT VILL HIT DER AMERICAN PIGS!
12
WONDER WOMAN, REACHING THE GERMAN DREADNAUGHT, DIVES FOR THE BATTLESHIP'S PROPELLER.
THIS PROPELLER IS CERTAINLY POWERFUL! BUT I'LL SLOW IT DOWN BY SWIMMING AGAINST IT.

I'VE STOPPED THE PROPELLER! NOW TO HOLD IT STEADY WHILE THE ENGINES TURN THE SHIP OVER.

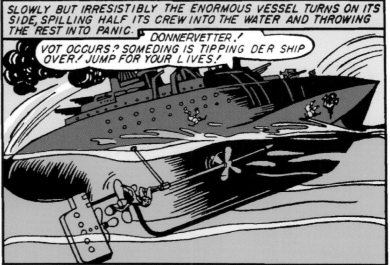

SLOWLY BUT IRRESISTIBLY THE ENORMOUS VESSEL TURNS ON ITS SIDE, SPILLING HALF ITS CREW INTO THE WATER AND THROWING THE REST INTO PANIC.

DONNERVETTER! VOT OCCURS? SOMEDING IS TIPPING DER SHIP OVER! JUMP FOR YOUR LIVES!

DESCRIBING A COMPLETE SOMERSAULT THE DREADNAUGHT TURNS UPSIDE DOWN, THEN RIGHTS ITSELF AGAIN ON THE OTHER SIDE.

VE ARE COMING UP, AGAIN!

DER SHIP'S GONE CRAZY!

WONDER WOMAN, CLIMBING SWIFTLY TO THE BATTLESHIP'S BRIDGE, CONFRONTS THE GERMAN ADMIRAL.

SO IT ISS YOU, VONDER VOMAN! VE GIF UP- YOU COULD DESTROY EFFERY SHIP! MIT DEMONS VE CANNOT FIGHT!

OKAY- RADIO YOUR FLEET TO SURRENDER!

235

AMERICAN PRIZE CREWS FROM THE CRUISER ARE PLACED ABOARD THE NAZI BATTLESHIPS, AND FOR THE FIRST TIME IN HISTORY AN ENTIRE ENEMY FLEET IS CAPTURED BY ONE INDIVIDUAL - WONDER WOMAN.

THE STAR-SPANGLED BANNER - OH LONG MAY IT WAVE-----

13

A FEW DAYS LATER DIANA PRINCE-WHOSE "BROKEN" ARM IS HEALING RAPIDLY-ASKS FOR LEAVE FROM THE OFFICE.

COLONEL, MAY I ATTEND THE MASS MEETING TO HONOR WONDER WOMAN?

CERTAINLY, DIANA- THERE'S A HEROINE FOR YOU!

YOU ARE ALL SO NICE TO ME I-I DON'T KNOW WHAT TO SAY! WHAT I'VE DONE PROVES THIS- THAT NOTHING IS IMPOSSIBLE IF YOU JUST GRIT YOUR TEETH AND TELL YOURSELF I WILL DO IT!

FOLLOW WONDER WOMAN'S ADVENTURES EVERY MONTH IN SENSATION COMICS-THEY'LL THRILL YOU AS NOTHING EVER DID BEFORE!

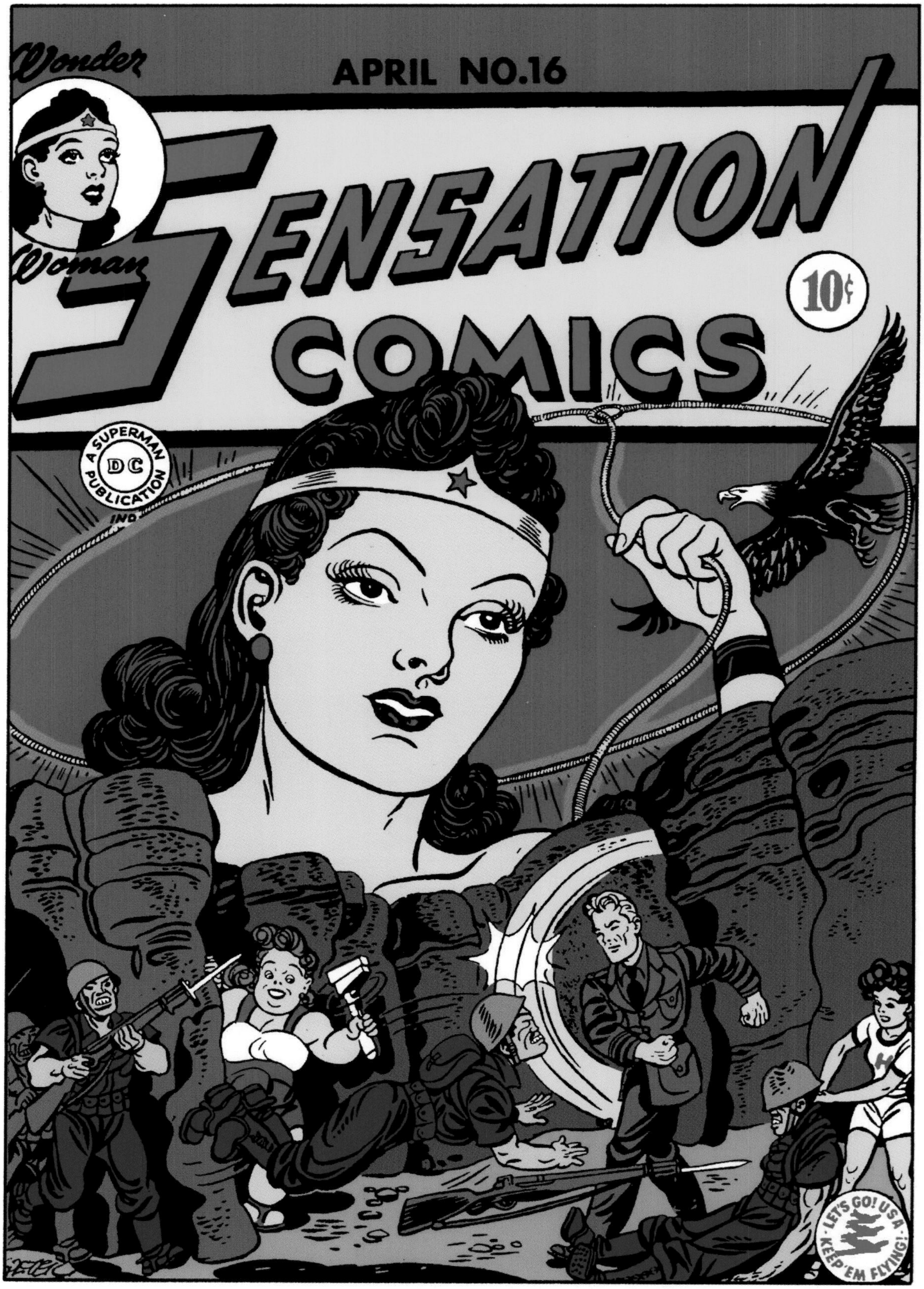
Wonder Woman
APRIL NO.16
SENSATION COMICS
10¢
A SUPERMAN DC PUBLICATION INC
LET'S GO! U.S.A. KEEP 'EM FLYING!

Sensation Comics #16 (April 1943) - art: H.G. Peter

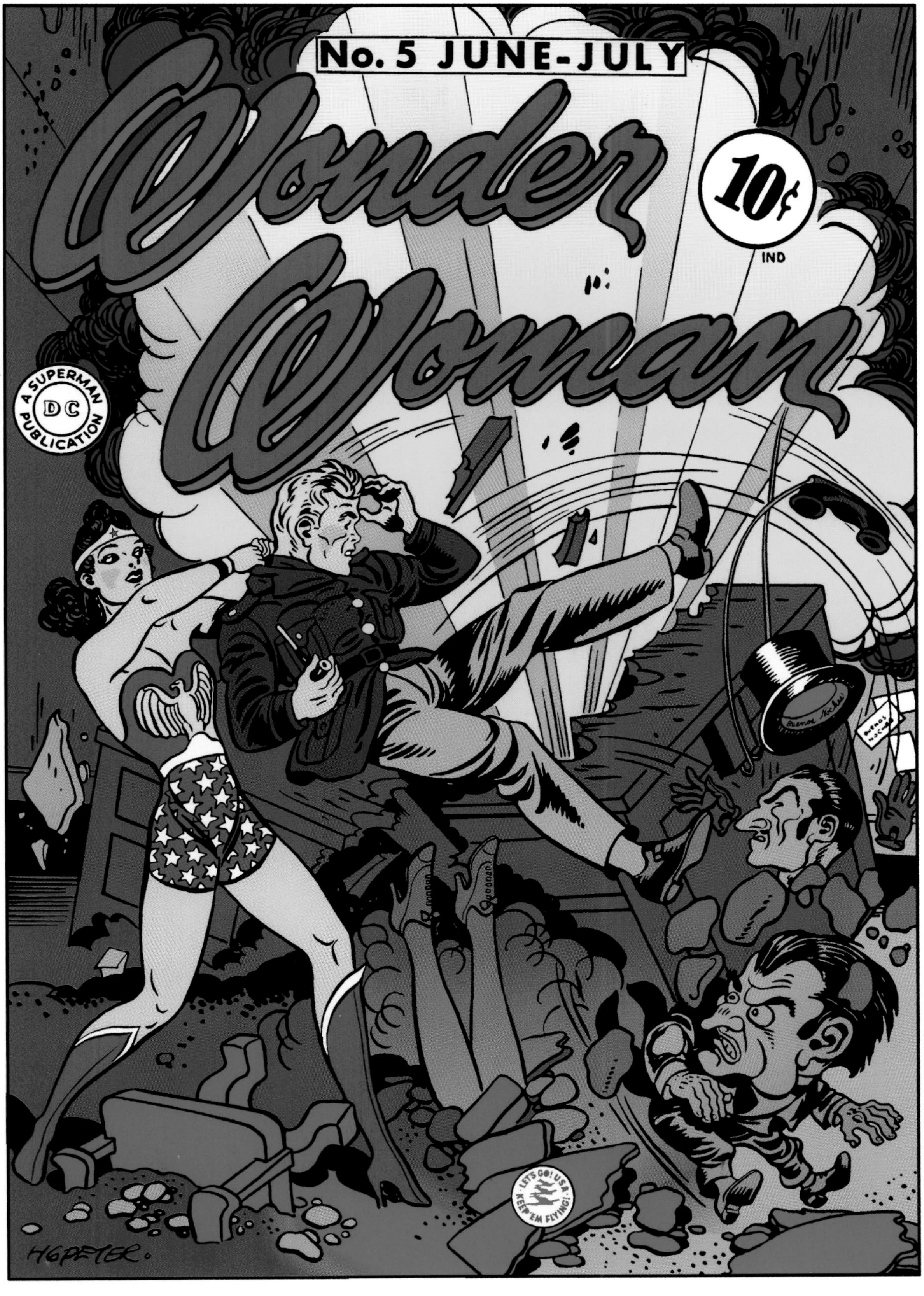
No. 5 JUNE-JULY
Wonder Woman
10¢
IND
A SUPERMAN DC PUBLICATION
LET'S GO! U.S.A. KEEP 'EM FLYING!
H.G. PETER

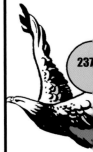

Wonder Woman #5 (June–July 1943) - art: H.G. Peter

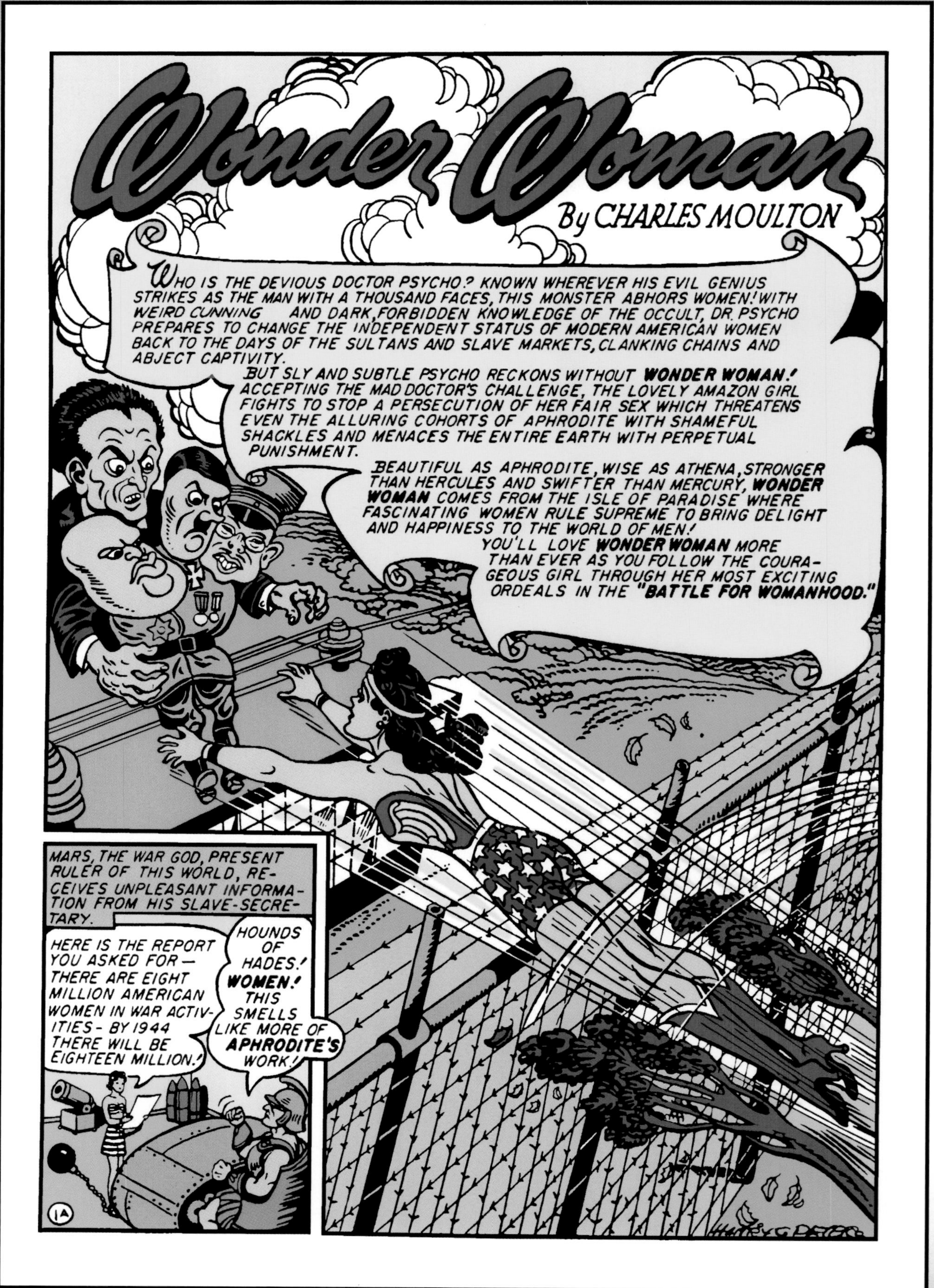

Wonder Woman
By CHARLES MOULTON
WHO IS THE DEVIOUS DOCTOR PSYCHO? KNOWN WHEREVER HIS EVIL GENIUS STRIKES AS THE MAN WITH A THOUSAND FACES, THIS MONSTER ABHORS WOMEN! WITH WEIRD CUNNING AND DARK, FORBIDDEN KNOWLEDGE OF THE OCCULT, DR. PSYCHO PREPARES TO CHANGE THE INDEPENDENT STATUS OF MODERN AMERICAN WOMEN BACK TO THE DAYS OF THE SULTANS AND SLAVE MARKETS, CLANKING CHAINS AND ABJECT CAPTIVITY.
BUT SLY AND SUBTLE PSYCHO RECKONS WITHOUT WONDER WOMAN! ACCEPTING THE MAD DOCTOR'S CHALLENGE, THE LOVELY AMAZON GIRL FIGHTS TO STOP A PERSECUTION OF HER FAIR SEX WHICH THREATENS EVEN THE ALLURING COHORTS OF APHRODITE WITH SHAMEFUL SHACKLES AND MENACES THE ENTIRE EARTH WITH PERPETUAL PUNISHMENT.
BEAUTIFUL AS APHRODITE, WISE AS ATHENA, STRONGER THAN HERCULES AND SWIFTER THAN MERCURY, WONDER WOMAN COMES FROM THE ISLE OF PARADISE WHERE FASCINATING WOMEN RULE SUPREME TO BRING DELIGHT AND HAPPINESS TO THE WORLD OF MEN!
YOU'LL LOVE WONDER WOMAN MORE THAN EVER AS YOU FOLLOW THE COURAGEOUS GIRL THROUGH HER MOST EXCITING ORDEALS IN THE "BATTLE FOR WOMANHOOD."
MARS, THE WAR GOD, PRESENT RULER OF THIS WORLD, RECEIVES UNPLEASANT INFORMATION FROM HIS SLAVE-SECRETARY.
HERE IS THE REPORT YOU ASKED FOR— THERE ARE EIGHT MILLION AMERICAN WOMEN IN WAR ACTIVITIES - BY 1944 THERE WILL BE EIGHTEEN MILLION!
HOUNDS OF HADES! WOMEN! THIS SMELLS LIKE MORE OF APHRODITE'S WORK!
1A
HARRY G PETER

Wonder Woman #5 (June–July 1943) - script: William Moulton Marston - art: H.G. Peter

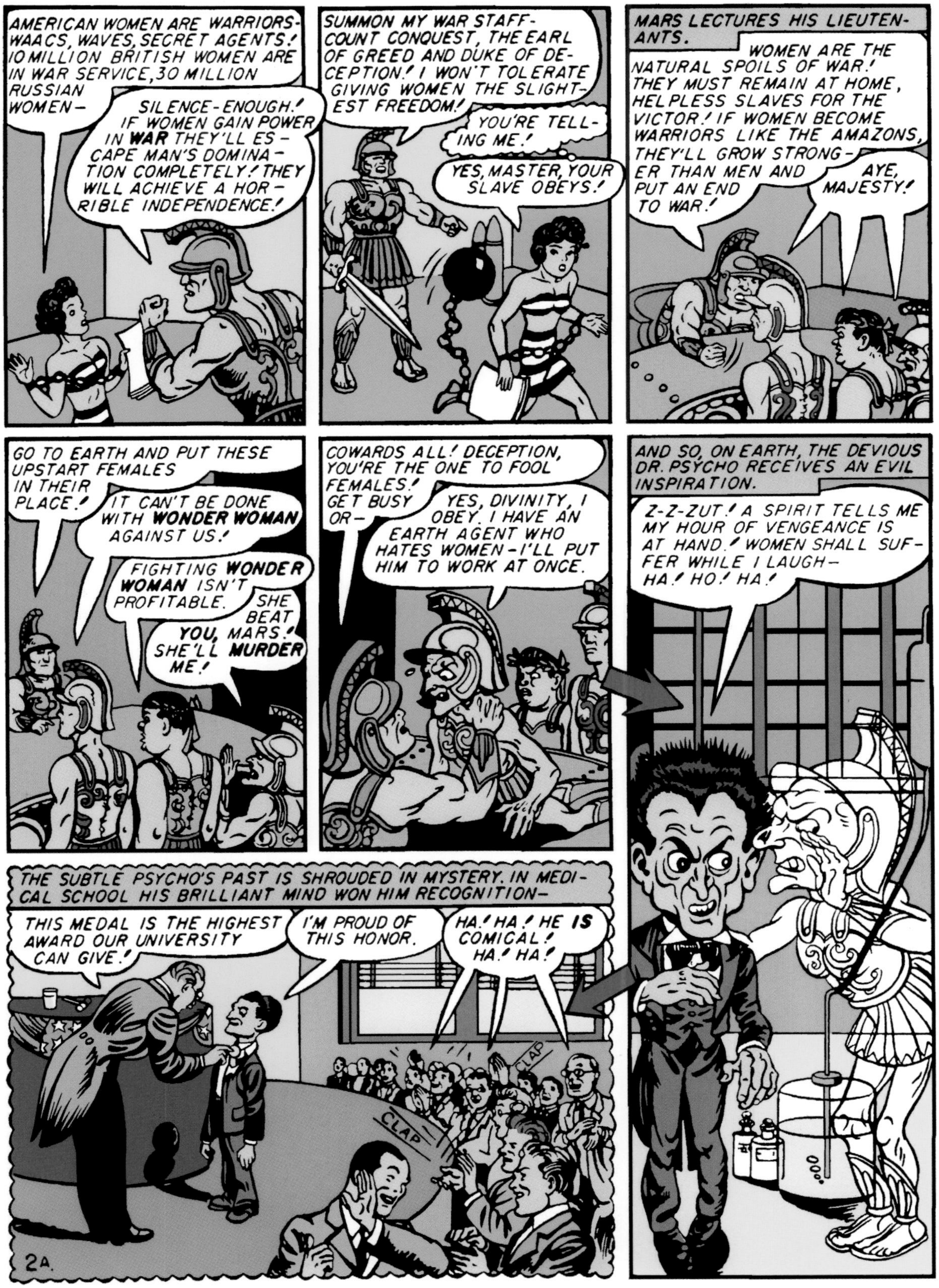
AMERICAN WOMEN ARE WARRIORS-WAACS, WAVES, SECRET AGENTS! 10 MILLION BRITISH WOMEN ARE IN WAR SERVICE, 30 MILLION RUSSIAN WOMEN-
SILENCE-ENOUGH! IF WOMEN GAIN POWER IN WAR THEY'LL ESCAPE MAN'S DOMINATION COMPLETELY! THEY WILL ACHIEVE A HORRIBLE INDEPENDENCE!
SUMMON MY WAR STAFF-COUNT CONQUEST, THE EARL OF GREED AND DUKE OF DECEPTION! I WON'T TOLERATE GIVING WOMEN THE SLIGHTEST FREEDOM!
YOU'RE TELLING ME!
YES, MASTER, YOUR SLAVE OBEYS!
MARS LECTURES HIS LIEUTENANTS.
WOMEN ARE THE NATURAL SPOILS OF WAR! THEY MUST REMAIN AT HOME, HELPLESS SLAVES FOR THE VICTOR! IF WOMEN BECOME WARRIORS LIKE THE AMAZONS, THEY'LL GROW STRONGER THAN MEN AND PUT AN END TO WAR!
AYE, MAJESTY!
GO TO EARTH AND PUT THESE UPSTART FEMALES IN THEIR PLACE!
IT CAN'T BE DONE WITH WONDER WOMAN AGAINST US!
FIGHTING WONDER WOMAN ISN'T PROFITABLE.
SHE BEAT YOU, MARS! SHE'LL MURDER ME!
COWARDS ALL! DECEPTION, YOU'RE THE ONE TO FOOL FEMALES! GET BUSY OR-
YES, DIVINITY, I OBEY. I HAVE AN EARTH AGENT WHO HATES WOMEN-I'LL PUT HIM TO WORK AT ONCE.
AND SO, ON EARTH, THE DEVIOUS DR. PSYCHO RECEIVES AN EVIL INSPIRATION.
Z-Z-ZUT! A SPIRIT TELLS ME MY HOUR OF VENGEANCE IS AT HAND! WOMEN SHALL SUFFER WHILE I LAUGH-HA! HO! HA!
THE SUBTLE PSYCHO'S PAST IS SHROUDED IN MYSTERY. IN MEDICAL SCHOOL HIS BRILLIANT MIND WON HIM RECOGNITION-
THIS MEDAL IS THE HIGHEST AWARD OUR UNIVERSITY CAN GIVE!
I'M PROUD OF THIS HONOR.
HA! HA! HE IS COMICAL! HA! HA!
CLAP
CLAP
2A.

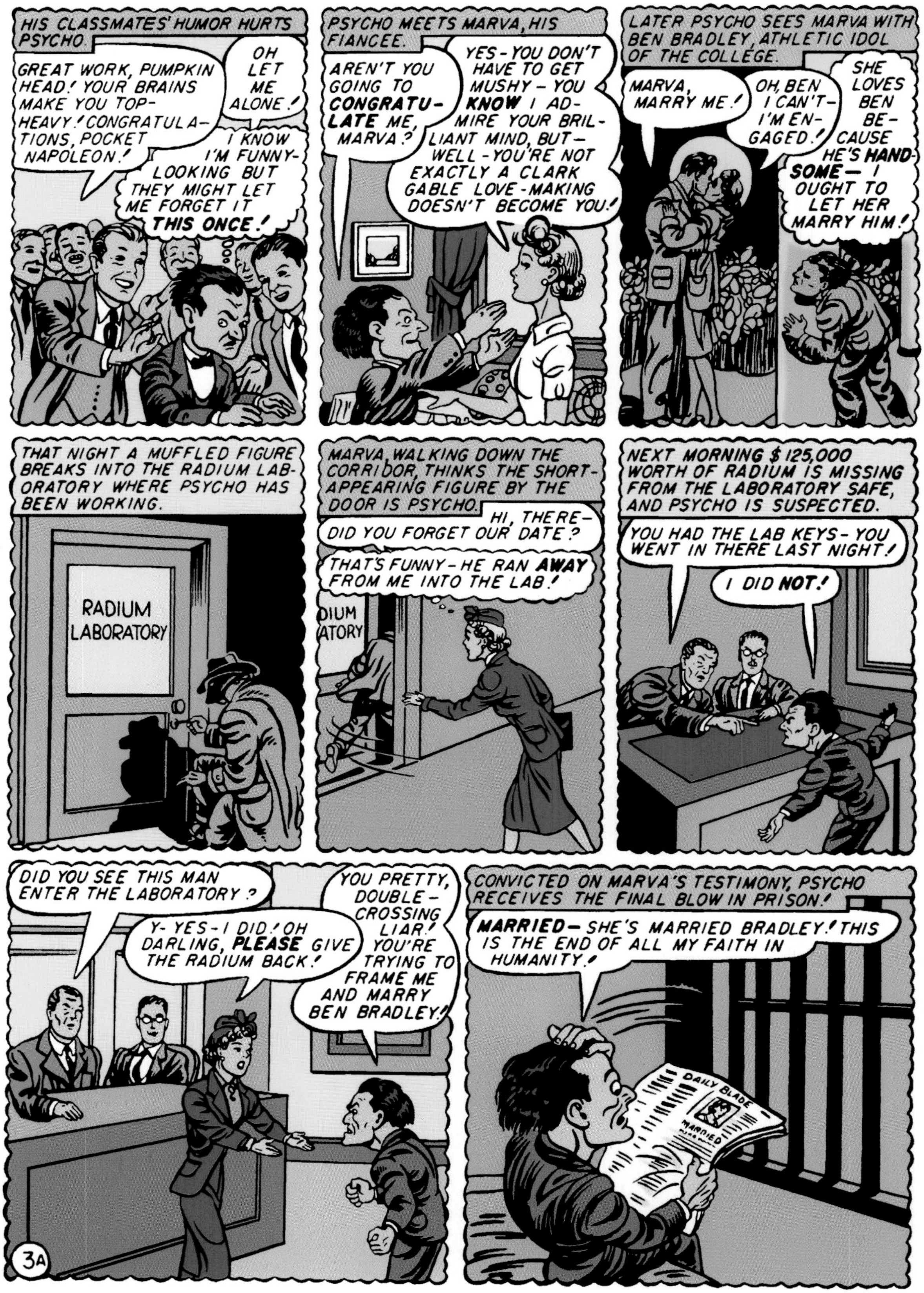

HIS CLASSMATES' HUMOR HURTS PSYCHO.
GREAT WORK, PUMPKIN HEAD! YOUR BRAINS MAKE YOU TOP-HEAVY! CONGRATULA-TIONS, POCKET NAPOLEON!
OH LET ME ALONE!
I KNOW I'M FUNNY-LOOKING BUT THEY MIGHT LET ME FORGET IT THIS ONCE!
PSYCHO MEETS MARVA, HIS FIANCEE.
AREN'T YOU GOING TO CONGRATU-LATE ME, MARVA?
YES-YOU DON'T HAVE TO GET MUSHY-YOU KNOW I AD-MIRE YOUR BRIL-LIANT MIND, BUT-WELL-YOU'RE NOT EXACTLY A CLARK GABLE LOVE-MAKING DOESN'T BECOME YOU!
LATER PSYCHO SEES MARVA WITH BEN BRADLEY, ATHLETIC IDOL OF THE COLLEGE.
MARVA, MARRY ME!
OH, BEN, I CAN'T-I'M EN-GAGED!
SHE LOVES BEN BE-CAUSE HE'S HAND-SOME-I OUGHT TO LET HER MARRY HIM!
THAT NIGHT A MUFFLED FIGURE BREAKS INTO THE RADIUM LAB-ORATORY WHERE PSYCHO HAS BEEN WORKING.
RADIUM LABORATORY
MARVA, WALKING DOWN THE CORRIDOR, THINKS THE SHORT-APPEARING FIGURE BY THE DOOR IS PSYCHO.
HI, THERE-DID YOU FORGET OUR DATE?
THAT'S FUNNY-HE RAN AWAY FROM ME INTO THE LAB!
NEXT MORNING $125,000 WORTH OF RADIUM IS MISSING FROM THE LABORATORY SAFE, AND PSYCHO IS SUSPECTED.
YOU HAD THE LAB KEYS-YOU WENT IN THERE LAST NIGHT!
I DID NOT!
DID YOU SEE THIS MAN ENTER THE LABORATORY?
Y-YES-I DID! OH DARLING, PLEASE GIVE THE RADIUM BACK!
YOU PRETTY, DOUBLE-CROSSING LIAR! YOU'RE TRYING TO FRAME ME AND MARRY BEN BRADLEY!
3A
CONVICTED ON MARVA'S TESTIMONY, PSYCHO RECEIVES THE FINAL BLOW IN PRISON!
MARRIED-SHE'S MARRIED BRADLEY! THIS IS THE END OF ALL MY FAITH IN HUMANITY!
DAILY BLADE
MARRIED

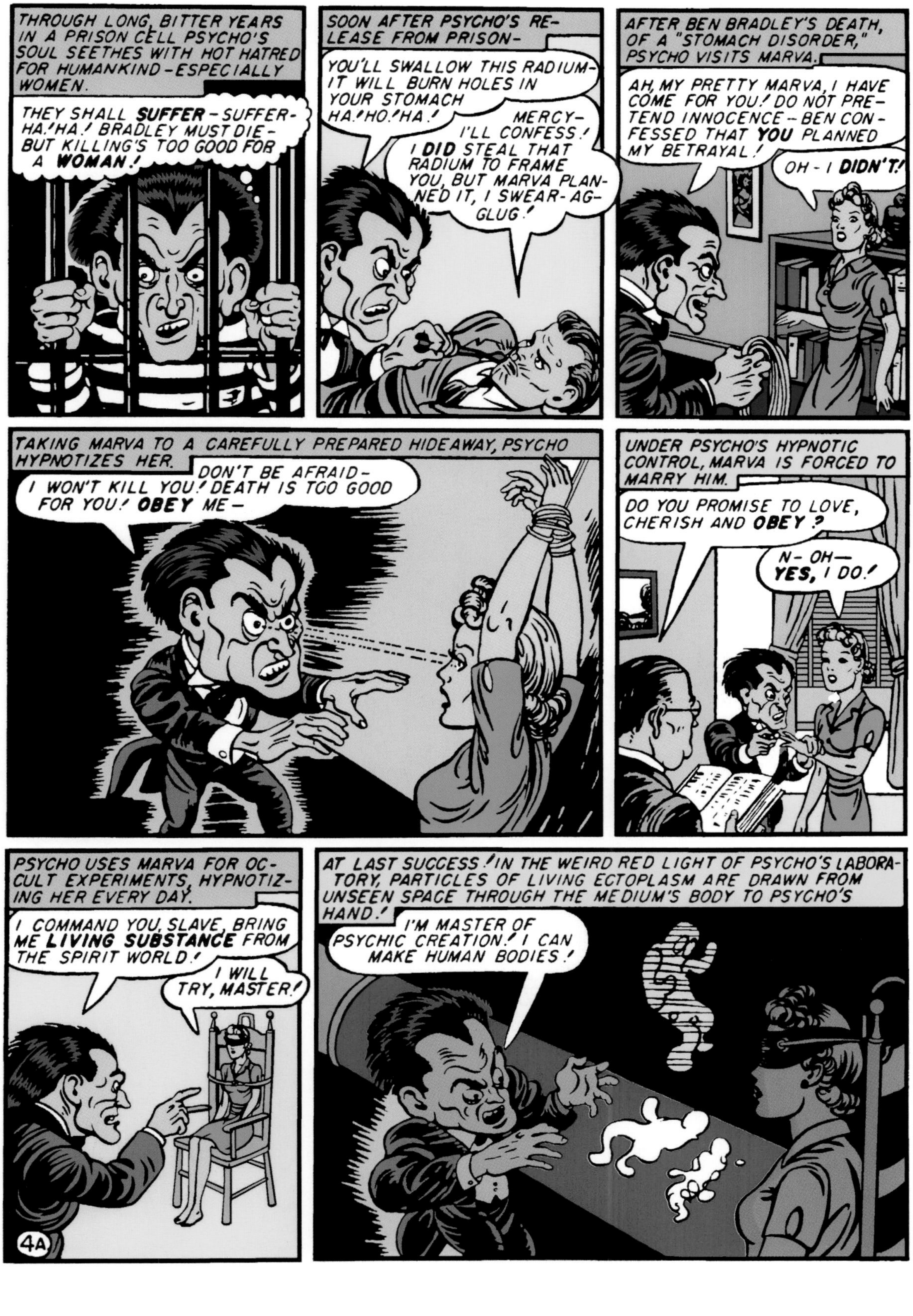
THROUGH LONG, BITTER YEARS IN A PRISON CELL PSYCHO'S SOUL SEETHES WITH HOT HATRED FOR HUMANKIND – ESPECIALLY WOMEN.
THEY SHALL SUFFER – SUFFER – HA! HA! BRADLEY MUST DIE – BUT KILLING'S TOO GOOD FOR A WOMAN!
SOON AFTER PSYCHO'S RELEASE FROM PRISON –
YOU'LL SWALLOW THIS RADIUM – IT WILL BURN HOLES IN YOUR STOMACH HA! HO! HA!
MERCY – I'LL CONFESS! I DID STEAL THAT RADIUM TO FRAME YOU, BUT MARVA PLANNED IT, I SWEAR – AGGLUG!
AFTER BEN BRADLEY'S DEATH, OF A "STOMACH DISORDER," PSYCHO VISITS MARVA.
AH, MY PRETTY MARVA, I HAVE COME FOR YOU! DO NOT PRETEND INNOCENCE – BEN CONFESSED THAT YOU PLANNED MY BETRAYAL!
OH – I DIDN'T!
TAKING MARVA TO A CAREFULLY PREPARED HIDEAWAY, PSYCHO HYPNOTIZES HER.
DON'T BE AFRAID – I WON'T KILL YOU! DEATH IS TOO GOOD FOR YOU! OBEY ME –
UNDER PSYCHO'S HYPNOTIC CONTROL, MARVA IS FORCED TO MARRY HIM.
DO YOU PROMISE TO LOVE, CHERISH AND OBEY?
N– OH– YES, I DO!
PSYCHO USES MARVA FOR OCCULT EXPERIMENTS, HYPNOTIZING HER EVERY DAY.
I COMMAND YOU, SLAVE, BRING ME LIVING SUBSTANCE FROM THE SPIRIT WORLD!
I WILL TRY, MASTER!
4A
AT LAST SUCCESS! IN THE WEIRD RED LIGHT OF PSYCHO'S LABORATORY, PARTICLES OF LIVING ECTOPLASM ARE DRAWN FROM UNSEEN SPACE THROUGH THE MEDIUM'S BODY TO PSYCHO'S HAND!
I'M MASTER OF PSYCHIC CREATION! I CAN MAKE HUMAN BODIES!

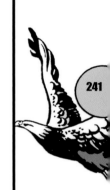

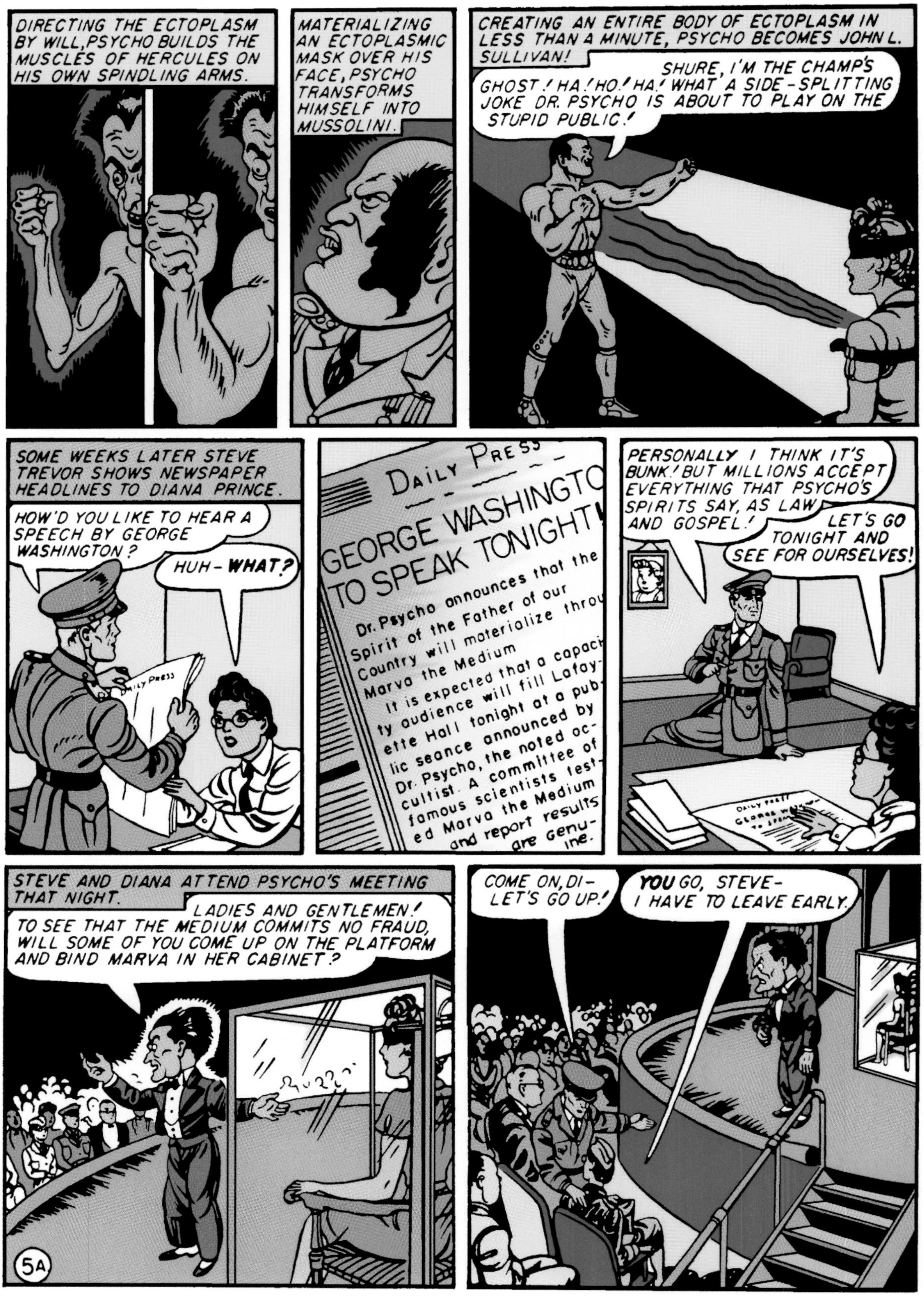
DIRECTING THE ECTOPLASM BY WILL, PSYCHO BUILDS THE MUSCLES OF HERCULES ON HIS OWN SPINDLING ARMS.
MATERIALIZING AN ECTOPLASMIC MASK OVER HIS FACE, PSYCHO TRANSFORMS HIMSELF INTO MUSSOLINI.
CREATING AN ENTIRE BODY OF ECTOPLASM IN LESS THAN A MINUTE, PSYCHO BECOMES JOHN L. SULLIVAN!
SHURE, I'M THE CHAMP'S GHOST! HA! HO! HA! WHAT A SIDE-SPLITTING JOKE DR. PSYCHO IS ABOUT TO PLAY ON THE STUPID PUBLIC!
SOME WEEKS LATER STEVE TREVOR SHOWS NEWSPAPER HEADLINES TO DIANA PRINCE.
HOW'D YOU LIKE TO HEAR A SPEECH BY GEORGE WASHINGTON?
HUH-WHAT?
DAILY PRESS
DAILY PRESS
GEORGE WASHINGTO
TO SPEAK TONIGHT!
Dr. Psycho announces that the Spirit of the Father of our Country will materialize throu Marva the Medium
It is expected that a capaci ty audience will fill Lafay- ette Hall tonight at a pub- lic seance announced by Dr. Psycho, the noted oc- cultist. A committee of famous scientists test- ed Marva the Medium and report results are genu- ine.
PERSONALLY I THINK IT'S BUNK! BUT MILLIONS ACCEPT EVERYTHING THAT PSYCHO'S SPIRITS SAY, AS LAW AND GOSPEL!
LET'S GO TONIGHT AND SEE FOR OURSELVES!
STEVE AND DIANA ATTEND PSYCHO'S MEETING THAT NIGHT.
LADIES AND GENTLEMEN! TO SEE THAT THE MEDIUM COMMITS NO FRAUD, WILL SOME OF YOU COME UP ON THE PLATFORM AND BIND MARVA IN HER CABINET?
5A
COME ON, DI-LET'S GO UP!
YOU GO, STEVE-I HAVE TO LEAVE EARLY.

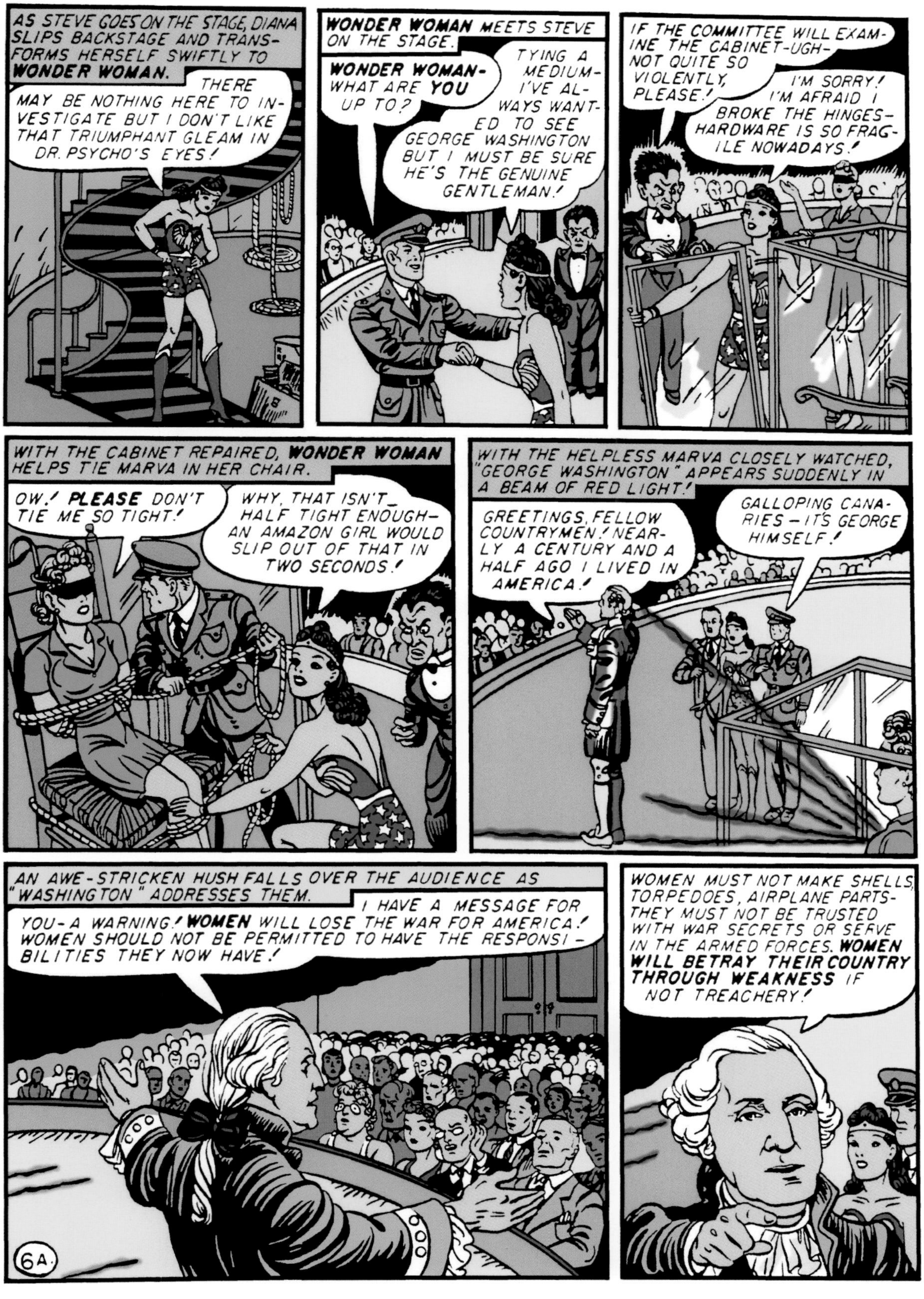
AS STEVE GOES ON THE STAGE, DIANA SLIPS BACKSTAGE AND TRANSFORMS HERSELF SWIFTLY TO WONDER WOMAN.
THERE MAY BE NOTHING HERE TO INVESTIGATE BUT I DON'T LIKE THAT TRIUMPHANT GLEAM IN DR. PSYCHO'S EYES!
WONDER WOMAN MEETS STEVE ON THE STAGE.
WONDER WOMAN- WHAT ARE YOU UP TO?
TYING A MEDIUM- I'VE ALWAYS WANTED TO SEE GEORGE WASHINGTON BUT I MUST BE SURE HE'S THE GENUINE GENTLEMAN!
IF THE COMMITTEE WILL EXAMINE THE CABINET-UGH- NOT QUITE SO VIOLENTLY, PLEASE!
I'M SORRY! I'M AFRAID I BROKE THE HINGES- HARDWARE IS SO FRAGILE NOWADAYS!
WITH THE CABINET REPAIRED, WONDER WOMAN HELPS TIE MARVA IN HER CHAIR.
OW! PLEASE DON'T TIE ME SO TIGHT!
WHY, THAT ISN'T HALF TIGHT ENOUGH- AN AMAZON GIRL WOULD SLIP OUT OF THAT IN TWO SECONDS!
WITH THE HELPLESS MARVA CLOSELY WATCHED, "GEORGE WASHINGTON" APPEARS SUDDENLY IN A BEAM OF RED LIGHT!
GREETINGS, FELLOW COUNTRYMEN! NEARLY A CENTURY AND A HALF AGO I LIVED IN AMERICA!
GALLOPING CANARIES – IT'S GEORGE HIMSELF!
AN AWE-STRICKEN HUSH FALLS OVER THE AUDIENCE AS "WASHINGTON" ADDRESSES THEM.
I HAVE A MESSAGE FOR YOU- A WARNING! WOMEN WILL LOSE THE WAR FOR AMERICA! WOMEN SHOULD NOT BE PERMITTED TO HAVE THE RESPONSIBILITIES THEY NOW HAVE!
6A.
WOMEN MUST NOT MAKE SHELLS, TORPEDOES, AIRPLANE PARTS- THEY MUST NOT BE TRUSTED WITH WAR SECRETS OR SERVE IN THE ARMED FORCES. WOMEN WILL BETRAY THEIR COUNTRY THROUGH WEAKNESS IF NOT TREACHERY!

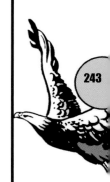

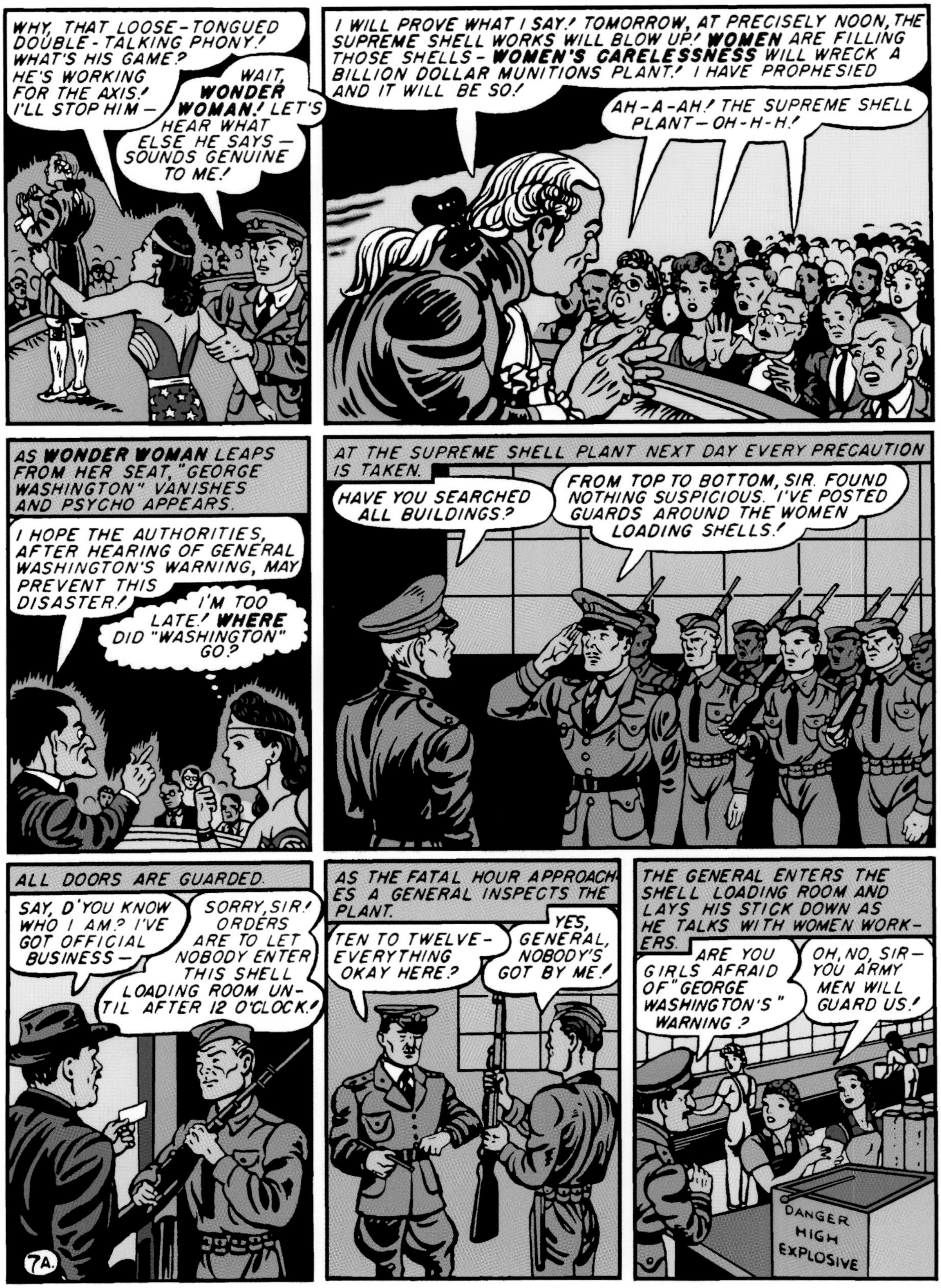
WHY, THAT LOOSE-TONGUED DOUBLE-TALKING PHONY! WHAT'S HIS GAME? HE'S WORKING FOR THE AXIS! I'LL STOP HIM —
WAIT, WONDER WOMAN! LET'S HEAR WHAT ELSE HE SAYS — SOUNDS GENUINE TO ME!
I WILL PROVE WHAT I SAY! TOMORROW, AT PRECISELY NOON, THE SUPREME SHELL WORKS WILL BLOW UP! WOMEN ARE FILLING THOSE SHELLS - WOMEN'S CARELESSNESS WILL WRECK A BILLION DOLLAR MUNITIONS PLANT! I HAVE PROPHESIED AND IT WILL BE SO!
AH-A-AH! THE SUPREME SHELL PLANT—OH-H-H!
AS WONDER WOMAN LEAPS FROM HER SEAT, "GEORGE WASHINGTON" VANISHES AND PSYCHO APPEARS.
I HOPE THE AUTHORITIES, AFTER HEARING OF GENERAL WASHINGTON'S WARNING, MAY PREVENT THIS DISASTER!
I'M TOO LATE! WHERE DID "WASHINGTON" GO?
AT THE SUPREME SHELL PLANT NEXT DAY EVERY PRECAUTION IS TAKEN.
HAVE YOU SEARCHED ALL BUILDINGS?
FROM TOP TO BOTTOM, SIR. FOUND NOTHING SUSPICIOUS. I'VE POSTED GUARDS AROUND THE WOMEN LOADING SHELLS!
ALL DOORS ARE GUARDED.
SAY, D'YOU KNOW WHO I AM? I'VE GOT OFFICIAL BUSINESS —
SORRY, SIR! ORDERS ARE TO LET NOBODY ENTER THIS SHELL LOADING ROOM UNTIL AFTER 12 O'CLOCK!
7A.
AS THE FATAL HOUR APPROACHES A GENERAL INSPECTS THE PLANT.
TEN TO TWELVE-EVERYTHING OKAY HERE?
YES, GENERAL, NOBODY'S GOT BY ME!
THE GENERAL ENTERS THE SHELL LOADING ROOM AND LAYS HIS STICK DOWN AS HE TALKS WITH WOMEN WORKERS.
ARE YOU GIRLS AFRAID OF "GEORGE WASHINGTON'S" WARNING?
OH, NO, SIR—YOU ARMY MEN WILL GUARD US!
DANGER HIGH EXPLOSIVE

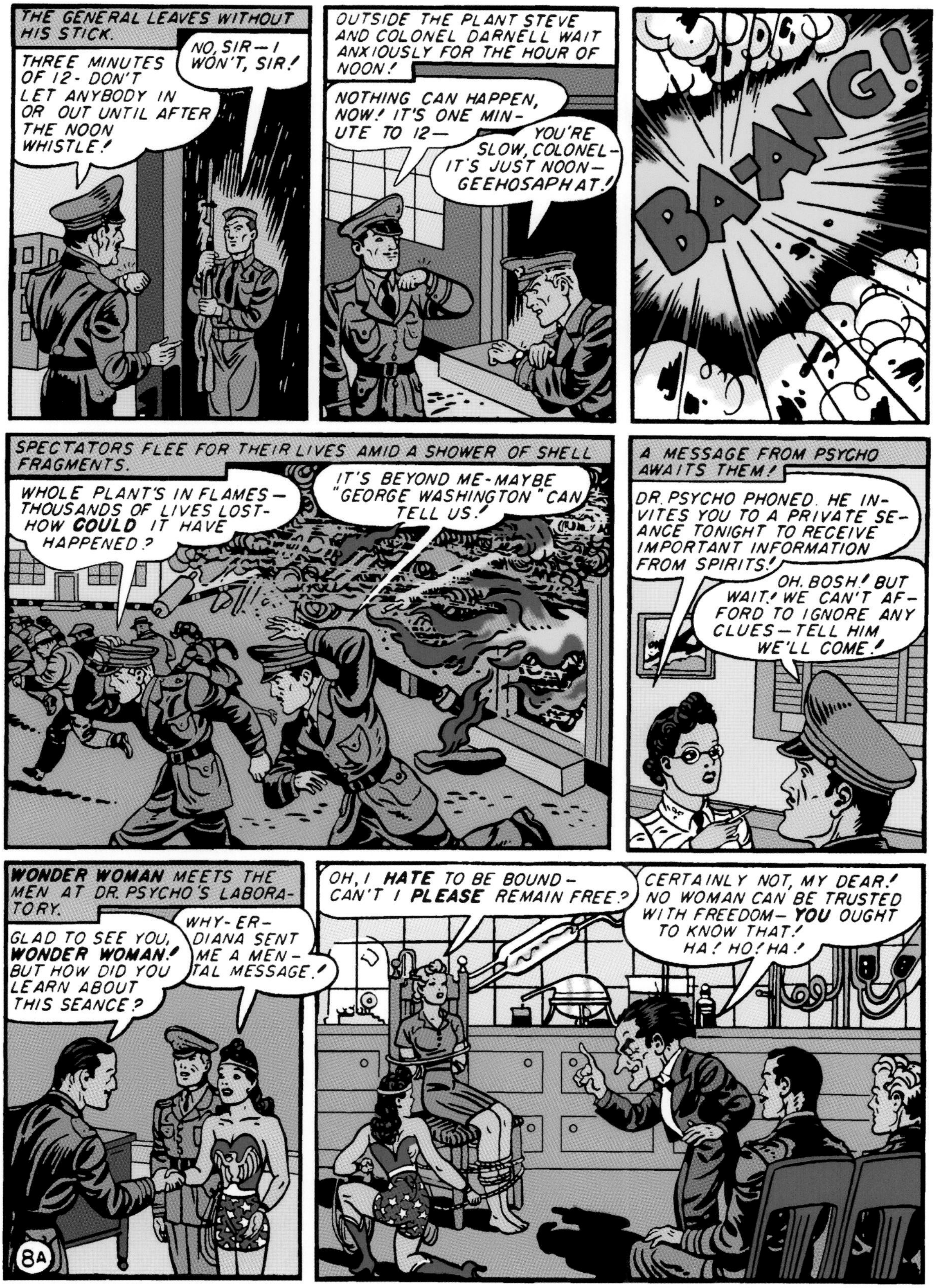
THE GENERAL LEAVES WITHOUT HIS STICK.
THREE MINUTES OF 12- DON'T LET ANYBODY IN OR OUT UNTIL AFTER THE NOON WHISTLE!
NO, SIR—I WON'T, SIR!
OUTSIDE THE PLANT STEVE AND COLONEL DARNELL WAIT ANXIOUSLY FOR THE HOUR OF NOON!
NOTHING CAN HAPPEN, NOW! IT'S ONE MINUTE TO 12—
YOU'RE SLOW, COLONEL- IT'S JUST NOON- GEEHOSAPHAT!
BA-ANG!
SPECTATORS FLEE FOR THEIR LIVES AMID A SHOWER OF SHELL FRAGMENTS.
WHOLE PLANT'S IN FLAMES— THOUSANDS OF LIVES LOST- HOW COULD IT HAVE HAPPENED?
IT'S BEYOND ME-MAYBE "GEORGE WASHINGTON" CAN TELL US!
A MESSAGE FROM PSYCHO AWAITS THEM!
DR. PSYCHO PHONED. HE INVITES YOU TO A PRIVATE SEANCE TONIGHT TO RECEIVE IMPORTANT INFORMATION FROM SPIRITS!
OH, BOSH! BUT WAIT! WE CAN'T AFFORD TO IGNORE ANY CLUES—TELL HIM WE'LL COME!
WONDER WOMAN MEETS THE MEN AT DR. PSYCHO'S LABORATORY.
GLAD TO SEE YOU, WONDER WOMAN! BUT HOW DID YOU LEARN ABOUT THIS SEANCE?
WHY- ER- DIANA SENT ME A MENTAL MESSAGE!
8A
OH, I HATE TO BE BOUND- CAN'T I PLEASE REMAIN FREE?
CERTAINLY NOT, MY DEAR! NO WOMAN CAN BE TRUSTED WITH FREEDOM— YOU OUGHT TO KNOW THAT! HA! HO! HA!

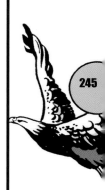

AS "GEORGE WASHINGTON" APPEARS, SEEMINGLY FROM NOWHERE, **WONDER WOMAN'S** KEEN EYES OBSERVE HIS ENTRANCE.

IN SOOTH, GOOD GENTLEMEN AND DAME, I GREET YOU KINDLY!

THAT'S PSYCHO'S VOICE, DISGUISED - HE CAME FROM BEHIND THAT SCREEN!

TOMORROW, AT NOON, IMPORTANT SECRET PAPERS WILL BE STOLEN FROM YOUR OFFICE SAFE. TRUST NOT **WOMEN!** EVEN NOW THEY ARE BETRAYING YOU—

I CAN'T STAND THIS AWFUL DRIVEL- I'VE GOT TO **ACT!**

WONDER WOMAN INTERRUPTS THE SEANCE.

YOU WILL FIND THE STOLEN PAPERS ON **THREE** OF YOUR OFFICE GIRLS - ULP - OUCH!

I'VE HEARD ENOUGH OF THESE LYING ATTACKS ON **WOMEN!**

TELL ME THE TRUTH — THIS "GEORGE WASHINGTON" BODY IS REALLY DR. PSYCHO, ISN'T IT?

NO, MADAM! THIS BODY IS LIVING ECTOPLASM MATERIALIZED THROUGH THE MEDIUM MARVA!

MAYBE YOUR MAGIC LASSO DOESN'T WORK ON GHOSTS, BEAUTIFUL!

YOU SHOULDN'T HAVE INTERRUPTED THE SEANCE, **WONDER WOMAN!** I MUST INSIST THAT IT CONTINUE!

OKAY COLONEL - I'LL ADMIT THIS ECTOPLASM STUFF HAS ME GUESSING!

9A

BUT "GEORGE WASHINGTON" RETIRES OFFENDED, REFUSING TO TALK FURTHER - THEY HURRY TO THE OFFICE AND SET GUARDS AT THE SAFETY VAULT.

YOU'LL BE RELIEVED AT 2 A.M. - A 4-HOUR SHIFT- KEEP ALERT!

YES, SIR!

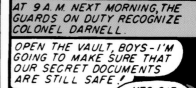

AT 9 A.M. NEXT MORNING, THE GUARDS ON DUTY RECOGNIZE COLONEL DARNELL.

OPEN THE VAULT, BOYS - I'M GOING TO MAKE SURE THAT OUR SECRET DOCUMENTS ARE STILL SAFE!

YES, SIR, COLONEL!

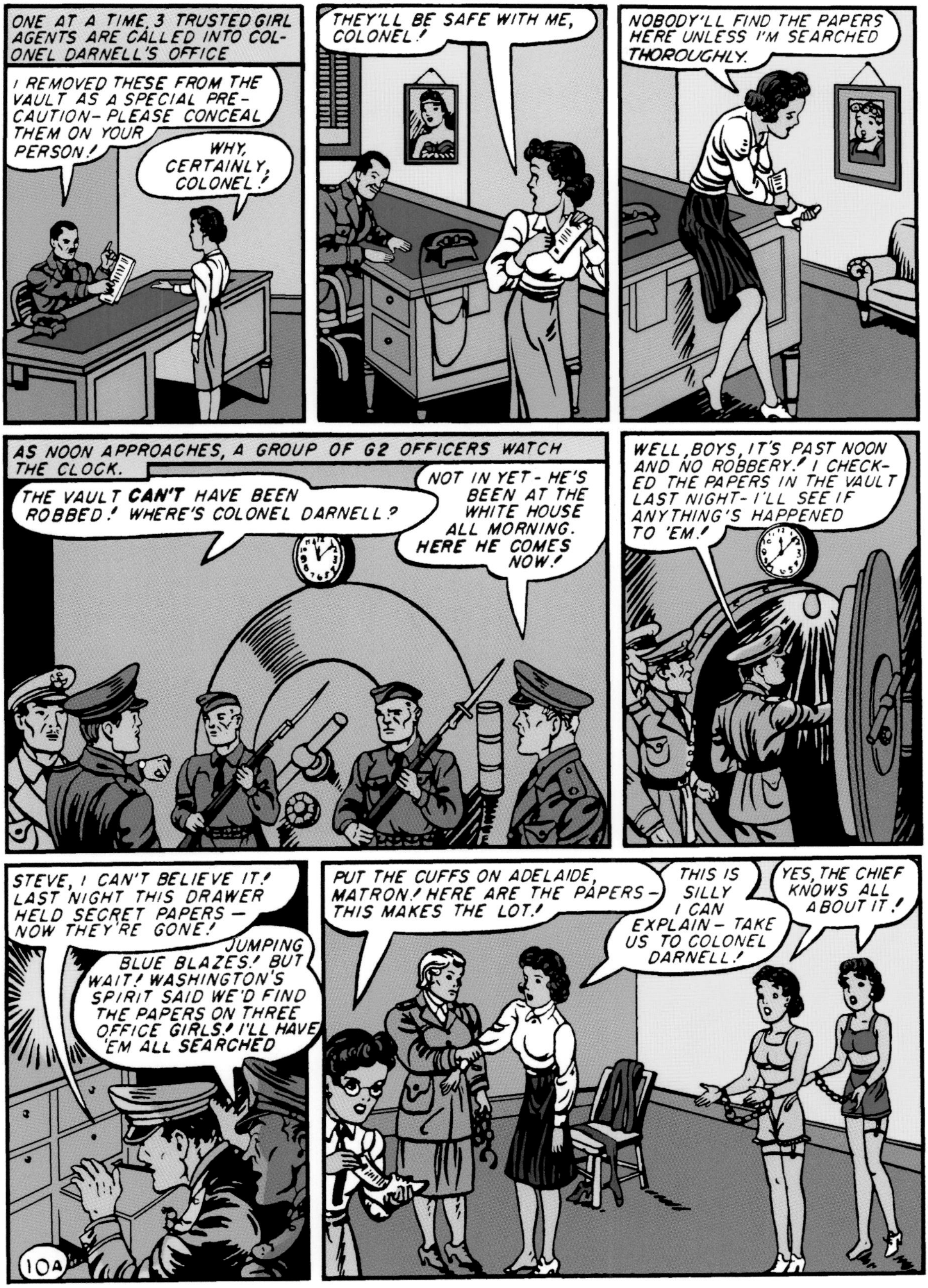
ONE AT A TIME, 3 TRUSTED GIRL AGENTS ARE CALLED INTO COLONEL DARNELL'S OFFICE
I REMOVED THESE FROM THE VAULT AS A SPECIAL PRECAUTION– PLEASE CONCEAL THEM ON YOUR PERSON!
WHY, CERTAINLY, COLONEL!
THEY'LL BE SAFE WITH ME, COLONEL!
NOBODY'LL FIND THE PAPERS HERE UNLESS I'M SEARCHED THOROUGHLY.
AS NOON APPROACHES, A GROUP OF G2 OFFICERS WATCH THE CLOCK.
THE VAULT CAN'T HAVE BEEN ROBBED! WHERE'S COLONEL DARNELL?
NOT IN YET - HE'S BEEN AT THE WHITE HOUSE ALL MORNING. HERE HE COMES NOW!
WELL, BOYS, IT'S PAST NOON AND NO ROBBERY! I CHECKED THE PAPERS IN THE VAULT LAST NIGHT- I'LL SEE IF ANYTHING'S HAPPENED TO 'EM!
STEVE, I CAN'T BELIEVE IT! LAST NIGHT THIS DRAWER HELD SECRET PAPERS — NOW THEY'RE GONE!
JUMPING BLUE BLAZES! BUT WAIT! WASHINGTON'S SPIRIT SAID WE'D FIND THE PAPERS ON THREE OFFICE GIRLS! I'LL HAVE 'EM ALL SEARCHED
10A
PUT THE CUFFS ON ADELAIDE, MATRON! HERE ARE THE PAPERS– THIS MAKES THE LOT!
THIS IS SILLY I CAN EXPLAIN – TAKE US TO COLONEL DARNELL!
YES, THE CHIEF KNOWS ALL ABOUT IT!

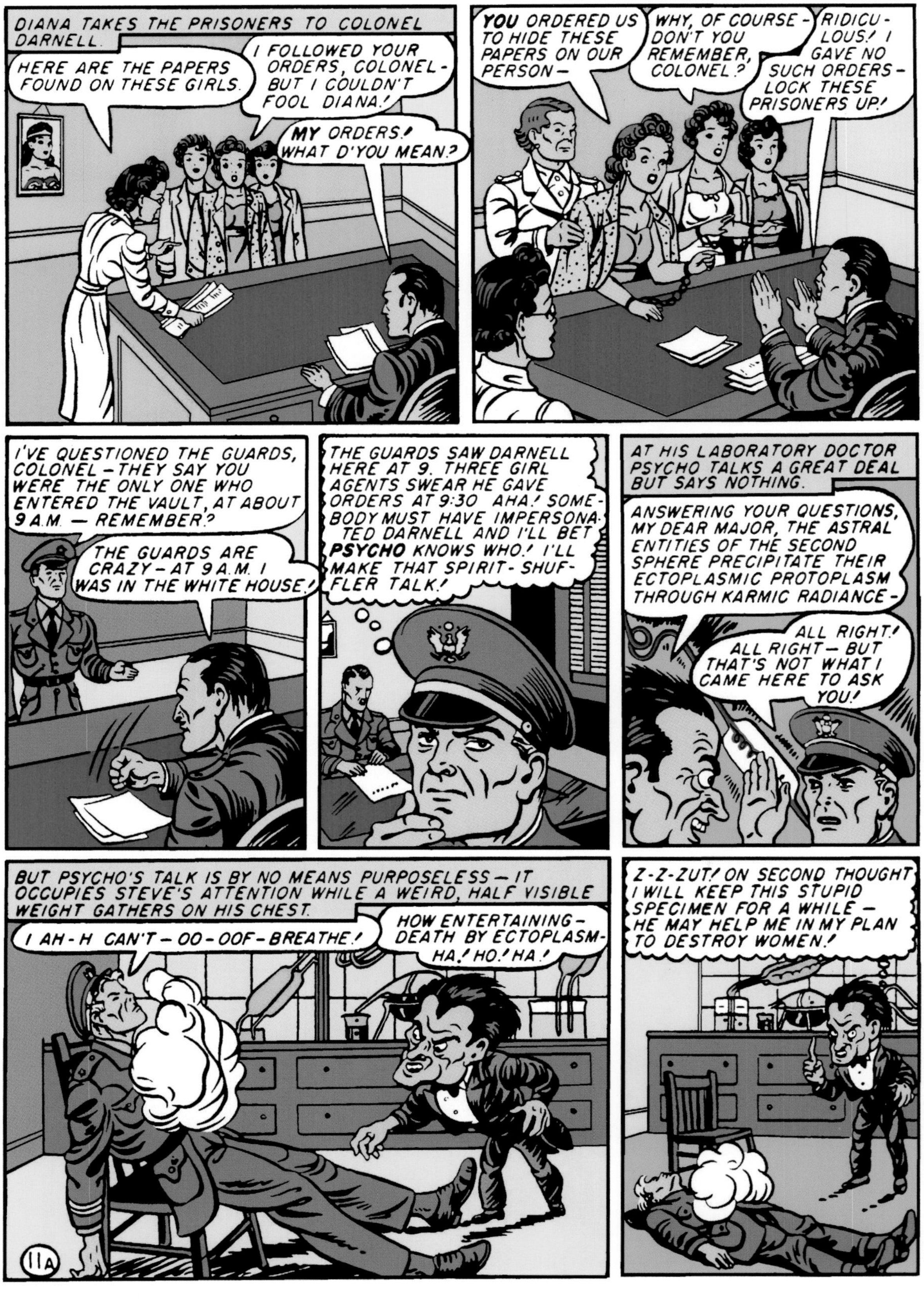
DIANA TAKES THE PRISONERS TO COLONEL DARNELL.
HERE ARE THE PAPERS FOUND ON THESE GIRLS.
I FOLLOWED YOUR ORDERS, COLONEL - BUT I COULDN'T FOOL DIANA!
MY ORDERS! WHAT D'YOU MEAN?
YOU ORDERED US TO HIDE THESE PAPERS ON OUR PERSON —
WHY, OF COURSE - DON'T YOU REMEMBER, COLONEL?
RIDICU-LOUS! I GAVE NO SUCH ORDERS - LOCK THESE PRISONERS UP!
I'VE QUESTIONED THE GUARDS, COLONEL — THEY SAY YOU WERE THE ONLY ONE WHO ENTERED THE VAULT, AT ABOUT 9 A.M. — REMEMBER?
THE GUARDS ARE CRAZY — AT 9 A.M. I WAS IN THE WHITE HOUSE!
THE GUARDS SAW DARNELL HERE AT 9. THREE GIRL AGENTS SWEAR HE GAVE ORDERS AT 9:30 AHA! SOME-BODY MUST HAVE IMPERSONA-TED DARNELL AND I'LL BET PSYCHO KNOWS WHO! I'LL MAKE THAT SPIRIT-SHUF-FLER TALK!
AT HIS LABORATORY DOCTOR PSYCHO TALKS A GREAT DEAL BUT SAYS NOTHING.
ANSWERING YOUR QUESTIONS, MY DEAR MAJOR, THE ASTRAL ENTITIES OF THE SECOND SPHERE PRECIPITATE THEIR ECTOPLASMIC PROTOPLASM THROUGH KARMIC RADIANCE -
ALL RIGHT! ALL RIGHT — BUT THAT'S NOT WHAT I CAME HERE TO ASK YOU!
BUT PSYCHO'S TALK IS BY NO MEANS PURPOSELESS — IT OCCUPIES STEVE'S ATTENTION WHILE A WEIRD, HALF VISIBLE WEIGHT GATHERS ON HIS CHEST.
I AH-H CAN'T — OO - OOF - BREATHE!
HOW ENTERTAINING - DEATH BY ECTOPLASM - HA! HO! HA!
11A
Z-Z-ZUT! ON SECOND THOUGHT I WILL KEEP THIS STUPID SPECIMEN FOR A WHILE — HE MAY HELP ME IN MY PLAN TO DESTROY WOMEN!

DIANA, WORRIED BECAUSE STEVE HAS NOT RETURNED TO THE OFFICE, GOES HOME EARLY.

THAT DR. PSYCHO IS FIENDISHLY CLEVER — HE MAY HAVE DONE SOMETHING TO STEVE THAT PREVENTS HIS SENDING A MENTAL MESSAGE!

OH, **THERE'S** STEVE NOW!

CALLING **WONDER WO-MAN!** WAS TAKEN PRISONER AT PSYCHO'S LABORA-TORY. AM IN CAGE — DON'T KNOW WHERE! LOOK OUT FOR BUR-GLAR ALARMS! THE LAB GROUNDS ARE COMPLETELY WIRED!

CHANGING SWIFTLY TO HER **WONDER WOMAN** COSTUME, THE AMAZON GIRL MAKES A QUICK EXIT.

SOMETHING TELLS ME THIS PSYCHO IS PLENTY DANGEROUS!

FROM A NEARBY HILL **WONDER WOMAN** SUR-VEYS THE PSYCHO LABORATORY GROUNDS.

IF ALL THE OPEN SPACE IS WIRED WITH BURGLAR ALARMS I CAN'T REACH THE LAB SECRETLY EXCEPT BY AIR — AH! THAT'S AN IDEA!

AT THE EDGE OF THE WOODS **WONDER WOMAN** BENDS DOWN A PAIR OF STRONG SAPLINGS.

THESE YOUNG TREES ARE TOUGH — THEY'LL GIVE A STRONG SNAP-BACK WHEN I LET THEM GO.

249

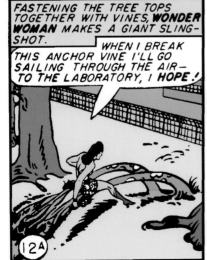

FASTENING THE TREE TOPS TOGETHER WITH VINES, **WONDER WOMAN** MAKES A GIANT SLING-SHOT.

WHEN I BREAK THIS ANCHOR VINE I'LL GO SAILING THROUGH THE AIR — TO THE LABORATORY, I **HOPE!**

12A

HURLED HIGH OVER PSYCHO'S GROUNDS BY THE TREMENDOUS POWER OF THE BENT TREES, **WONDER WOMAN** DESCENDS GRACEFULLY TOWARD THE LABORATORY ROOF.

I DON'T SEE HOW PSYCHO'S BURGLAR ALARMS COULD DETECT **THIS** APPROACH!

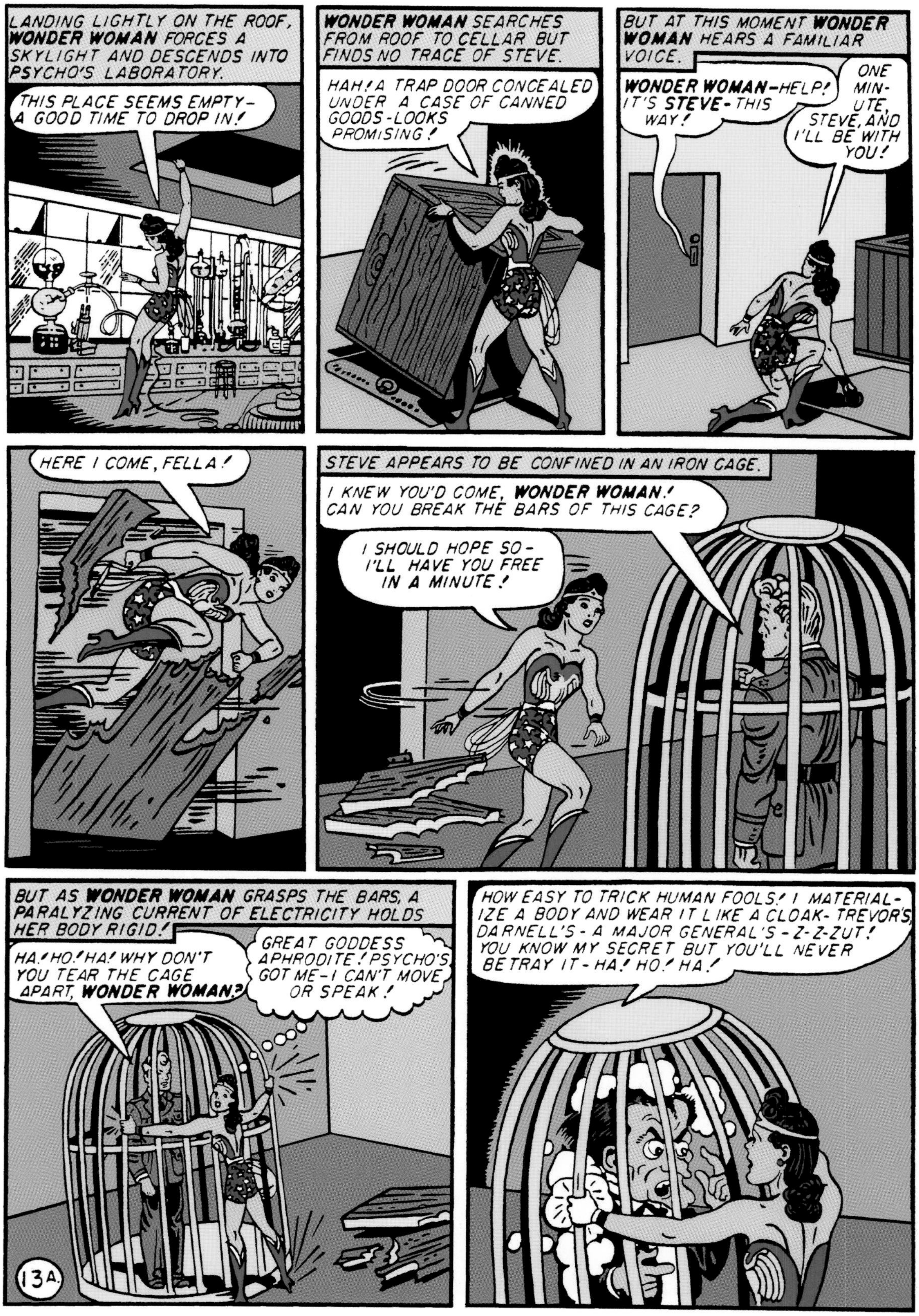

LANDING LIGHTLY ON THE ROOF, WONDER WOMAN FORCES A SKYLIGHT AND DESCENDS INTO PSYCHO'S LABORATORY.
THIS PLACE SEEMS EMPTY— A GOOD TIME TO DROP IN!
WONDER WOMAN SEARCHES FROM ROOF TO CELLAR BUT FINDS NO TRACE OF STEVE.
HAH! A TRAP DOOR CONCEALED UNDER A CASE OF CANNED GOODS-LOOKS PROMISING!
BUT AT THIS MOMENT WONDER WOMAN HEARS A FAMILIAR VOICE.
WONDER WOMAN—HELP! IT'S STEVE-THIS WAY!
ONE MINUTE, STEVE, AND I'LL BE WITH YOU!
HERE I COME, FELLA!
STEVE APPEARS TO BE CONFINED IN AN IRON CAGE.
I KNEW YOU'D COME, WONDER WOMAN! CAN YOU BREAK THE BARS OF THIS CAGE?
I SHOULD HOPE SO - I'LL HAVE YOU FREE IN A MINUTE!
BUT AS WONDER WOMAN GRASPS THE BARS, A PARALYZING CURRENT OF ELECTRICITY HOLDS HER BODY RIGID!
HA! HO! HA! WHY DON'T YOU TEAR THE CAGE APART, WONDER WOMAN?
GREAT GODDESS APHRODITE! PSYCHO'S GOT ME—I CAN'T MOVE OR SPEAK!
13A.
HOW EASY TO TRICK HUMAN FOOLS! I MATERIALIZE A BODY AND WEAR IT LIKE A CLOAK- TREVOR'S, DARNELL'S - A MAJOR GENERAL'S - Z-Z-ZUT! YOU KNOW MY SECRET BUT YOU'LL NEVER BETRAY IT - HA! HO! HA!

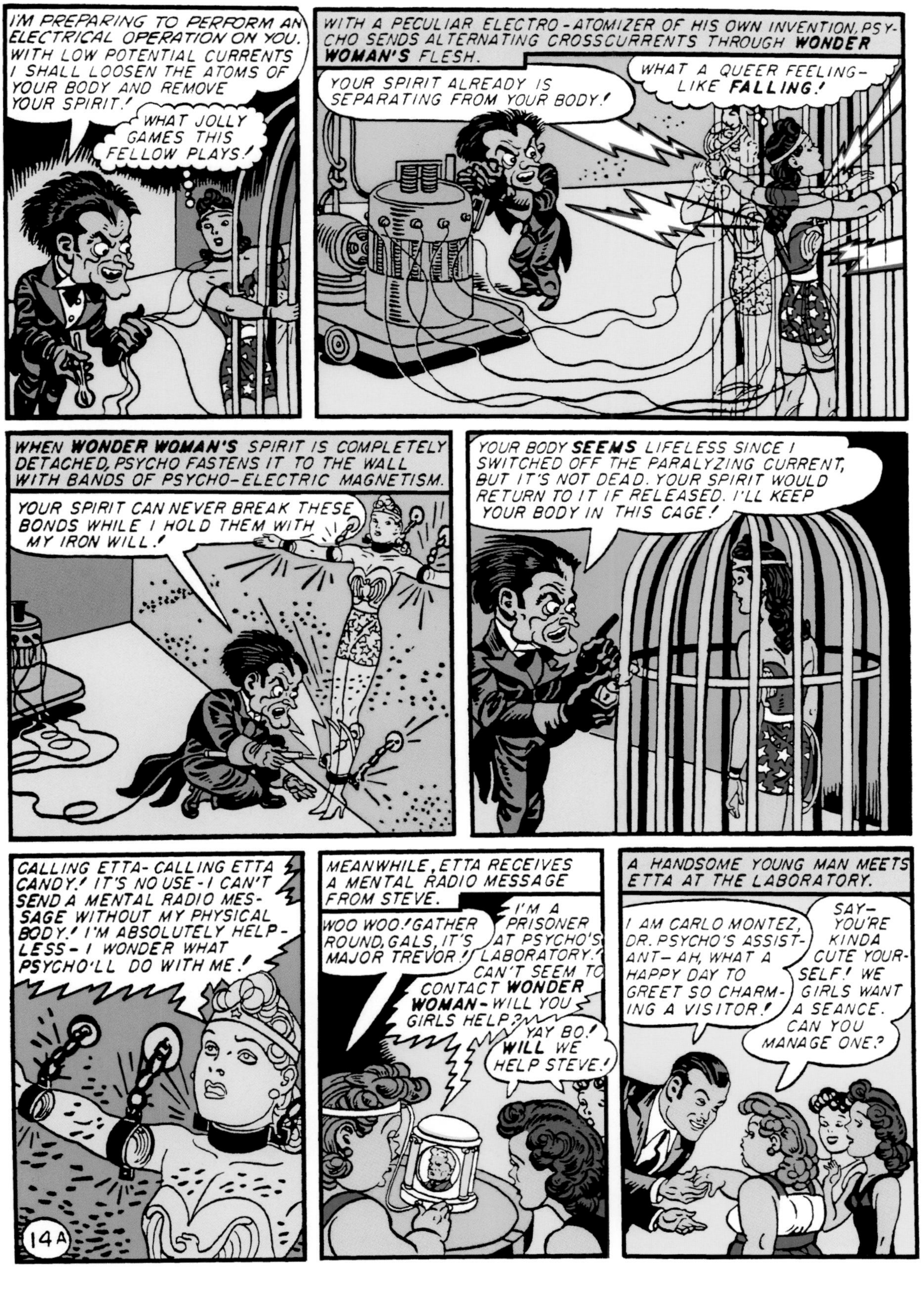
I'M PREPARING TO PERFORM AN ELECTRICAL OPERATION ON YOU. WITH LOW POTENTIAL CURRENTS I SHALL LOOSEN THE ATOMS OF YOUR BODY AND REMOVE YOUR SPIRIT!
WHAT JOLLY GAMES THIS FELLOW PLAYS!
WITH A PECULIAR ELECTRO-ATOMIZER OF HIS OWN INVENTION, PSYCHO SENDS ALTERNATING CROSSCURRENTS THROUGH WONDER WOMAN'S FLESH.
YOUR SPIRIT ALREADY IS SEPARATING FROM YOUR BODY!
WHAT A QUEER FEELING– LIKE FALLING!
WHEN WONDER WOMAN'S SPIRIT IS COMPLETELY DETACHED, PSYCHO FASTENS IT TO THE WALL WITH BANDS OF PSYCHO-ELECTRIC MAGNETISM.
YOUR SPIRIT CAN NEVER BREAK THESE BONDS WHILE I HOLD THEM WITH MY IRON WILL!
YOUR BODY SEEMS LIFELESS SINCE I SWITCHED OFF THE PARALYZING CURRENT, BUT IT'S NOT DEAD. YOUR SPIRIT WOULD RETURN TO IT IF RELEASED. I'LL KEEP YOUR BODY IN THIS CAGE!
CALLING ETTA-CALLING ETTA CANDY! IT'S NO USE-I CAN'T SEND A MENTAL RADIO MESSAGE WITHOUT MY PHYSICAL BODY! I'M ABSOLUTELY HELPLESS-I WONDER WHAT PSYCHO'LL DO WITH ME!
14A
MEANWHILE, ETTA RECEIVES A MENTAL RADIO MESSAGE FROM STEVE.
WOO WOO! GATHER ROUND, GALS, IT'S MAJOR TREVOR!
I'M A PRISONER AT PSYCHO'S LABORATORY! CAN'T SEEM TO CONTACT WONDER WOMAN-WILL YOU GIRLS HELP?
YAY BO! WILL WE HELP STEVE!
A HANDSOME YOUNG MAN MEETS ETTA AT THE LABORATORY.
I AM CARLO MONTEZ, DR. PSYCHO'S ASSISTANT– AH, WHAT A HAPPY DAY TO GREET SO CHARMING A VISITOR!
SAY– YOU'RE KINDA CUTE YOURSELF! WE GIRLS WANT A SEANCE. CAN YOU MANAGE ONE?

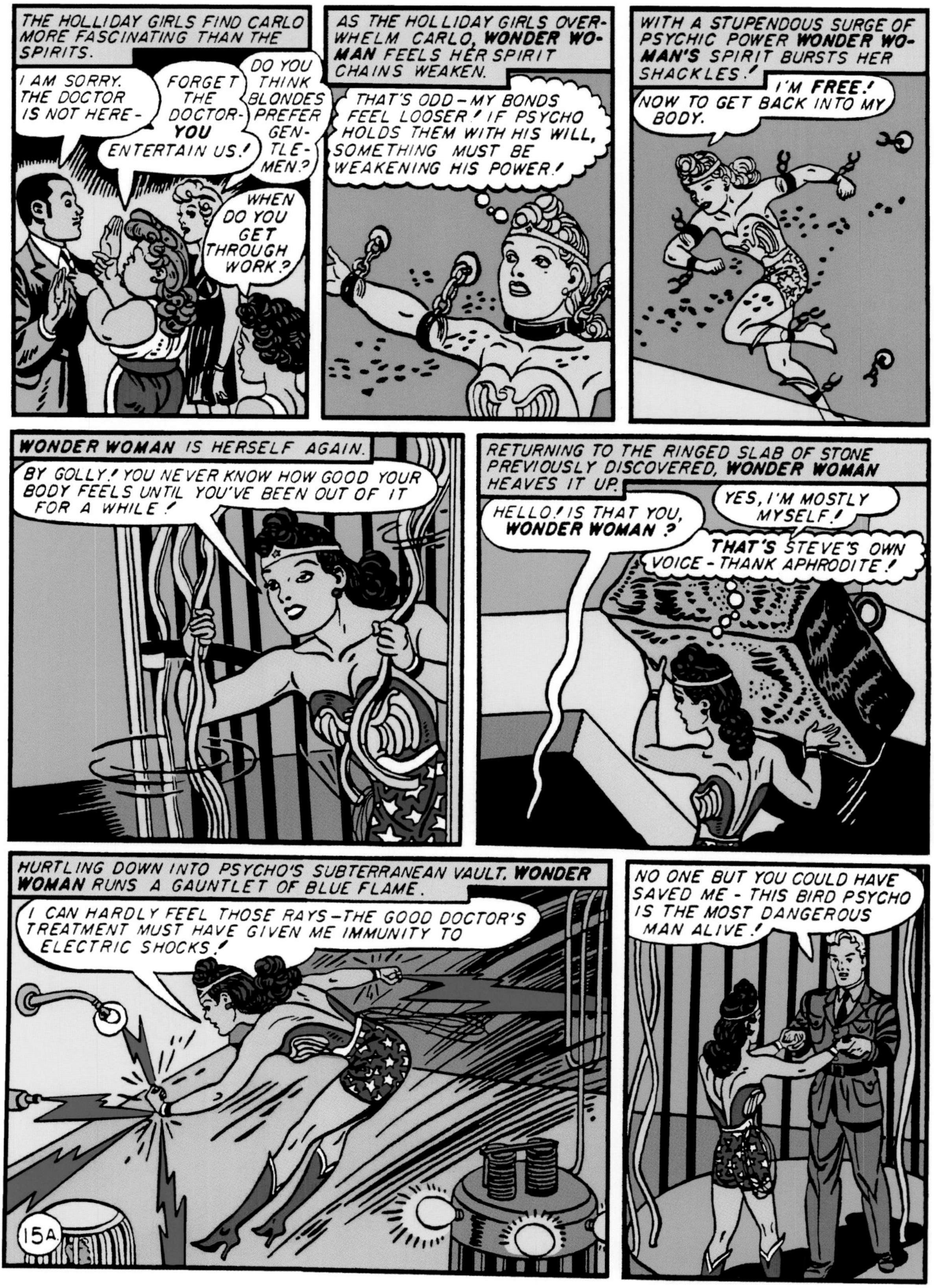
THE HOLLIDAY GIRLS FIND CARLO MORE FASCINATING THAN THE SPIRITS.
I AM SORRY. THE DOCTOR IS NOT HERE-
FORGET THE DOCTOR- YOU ENTERTAIN US!
DO YOU THINK BLONDES PREFER GEN-TLE-MEN?
WHEN DO YOU GET THROUGH WORK?
AS THE HOLLIDAY GIRLS OVER-WHELM CARLO, WONDER WO-MAN FEELS HER SPIRIT CHAINS WEAKEN.
THAT'S ODD - MY BONDS FEEL LOOSER! IF PSYCHO HOLDS THEM WITH HIS WILL, SOMETHING MUST BE WEAKENING HIS POWER!
WITH A STUPENDOUS SURGE OF PSYCHIC POWER WONDER WO-MAN'S SPIRIT BURSTS HER SHACKLES!
I'M FREE! NOW TO GET BACK INTO MY BODY.
WONDER WOMAN IS HERSELF AGAIN.
BY GOLLY! YOU NEVER KNOW HOW GOOD YOUR BODY FEELS UNTIL YOU'VE BEEN OUT OF IT FOR A WHILE!
RETURNING TO THE RINGED SLAB OF STONE PREVIOUSLY DISCOVERED, WONDER WOMAN HEAVES IT UP.
HELLO! IS THAT YOU, WONDER WOMAN?
YES, I'M MOSTLY MYSELF!
THAT'S STEVE'S OWN VOICE - THANK APHRODITE!
HURTLING DOWN INTO PSYCHO'S SUBTERRANEAN VAULT, WONDER WOMAN RUNS A GAUNTLET OF BLUE FLAME.
I CAN HARDLY FEEL THOSE RAYS - THE GOOD DOCTOR'S TREATMENT MUST HAVE GIVEN ME IMMUNITY TO ELECTRIC SHOCKS!
15A
NO ONE BUT YOU COULD HAVE SAVED ME - THIS BIRD PSYCHO IS THE MOST DANGEROUS MAN ALIVE!

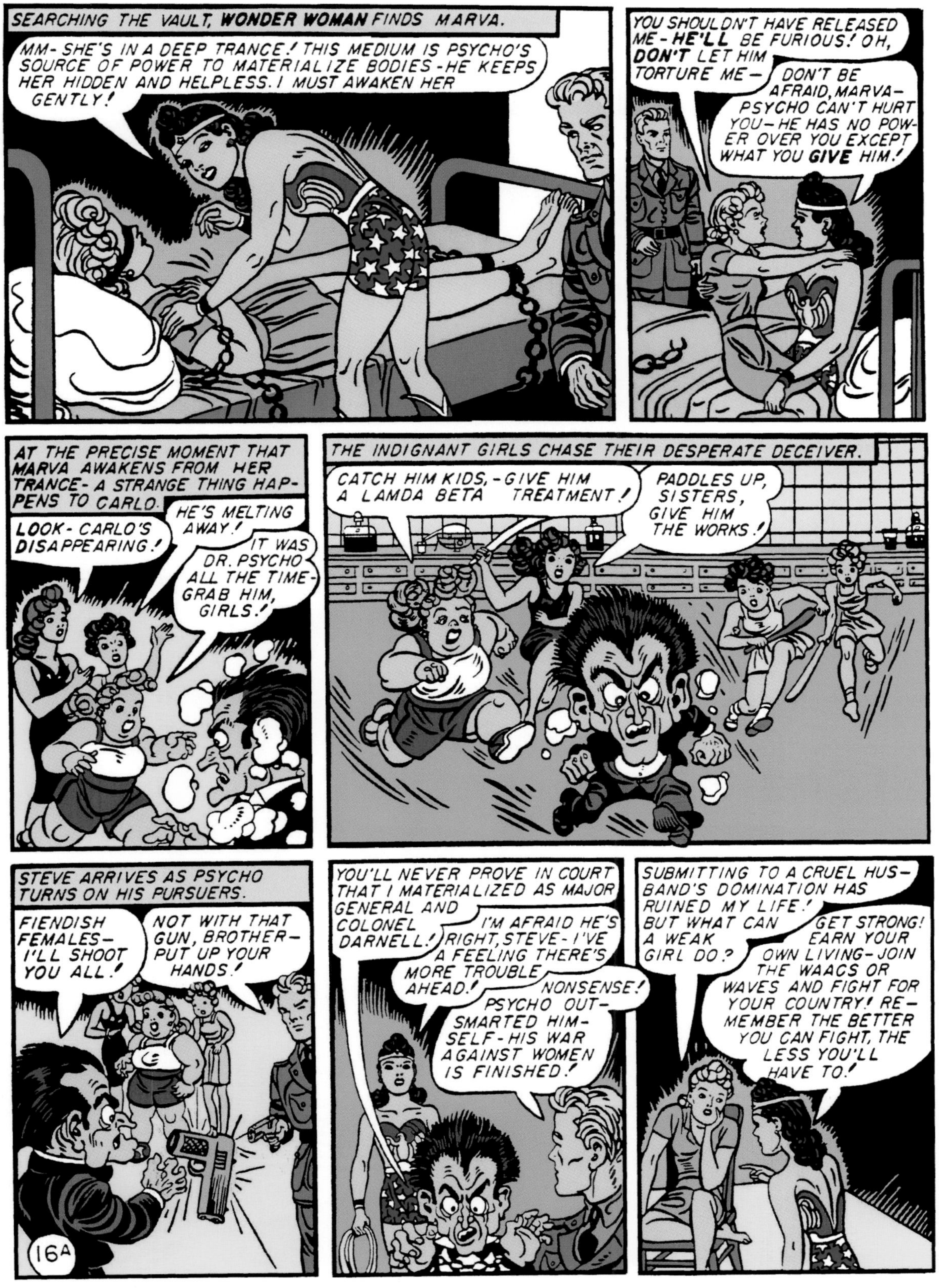
SEARCHING THE VAULT, WONDER WOMAN FINDS MARVA.
MM- SHE'S IN A DEEP TRANCE! THIS MEDIUM IS PSYCHO'S SOURCE OF POWER TO MATERIALIZE BODIES -HE KEEPS HER HIDDEN AND HELPLESS. I MUST AWAKEN HER GENTLY!
YOU SHOULDN'T HAVE RELEASED ME - HE'LL BE FURIOUS! OH, DON'T LET HIM TORTURE ME -
DON'T BE AFRAID, MARVA- PSYCHO CAN'T HURT YOU- HE HAS NO POWER OVER YOU EXCEPT WHAT YOU GIVE HIM!
AT THE PRECISE MOMENT THAT MARVA AWAKENS FROM HER TRANCE- A STRANGE THING HAPPENS TO CARLO.
LOOK- CARLO'S DISAPPEARING!
HE'S MELTING AWAY!
IT WAS DR. PSYCHO ALL THE TIME- GRAB HIM, GIRLS!
THE INDIGNANT GIRLS CHASE THEIR DESPERATE DECEIVER.
CATCH HIM KIDS, - GIVE HIM A LAMDA BETA TREATMENT!
PADDLES UP, SISTERS, GIVE HIM THE WORKS!
STEVE ARRIVES AS PSYCHO TURNS ON HIS PURSUERS.
FIENDISH FEMALES- I'LL SHOOT YOU ALL!
NOT WITH THAT GUN, BROTHER- PUT UP YOUR HANDS!
16A
YOU'LL NEVER PROVE IN COURT THAT I MATERIALIZED AS MAJOR GENERAL AND COLONEL DARNELL!
I'M AFRAID HE'S RIGHT, STEVE- I'VE A FEELING THERE'S MORE TROUBLE AHEAD!
NONSENSE! PSYCHO OUTSMARTED HIMSELF- HIS WAR AGAINST WOMEN IS FINISHED!
SUBMITTING TO A CRUEL HUSBAND'S DOMINATION HAS RUINED MY LIFE! BUT WHAT CAN A WEAK GIRL DO?
GET STRONG! EARN YOUR OWN LIVING- JOIN THE WAACS OR WAVES AND FIGHT FOR YOUR COUNTRY! REMEMBER THE BETTER YOU CAN FIGHT, THE LESS YOU'LL HAVE TO!

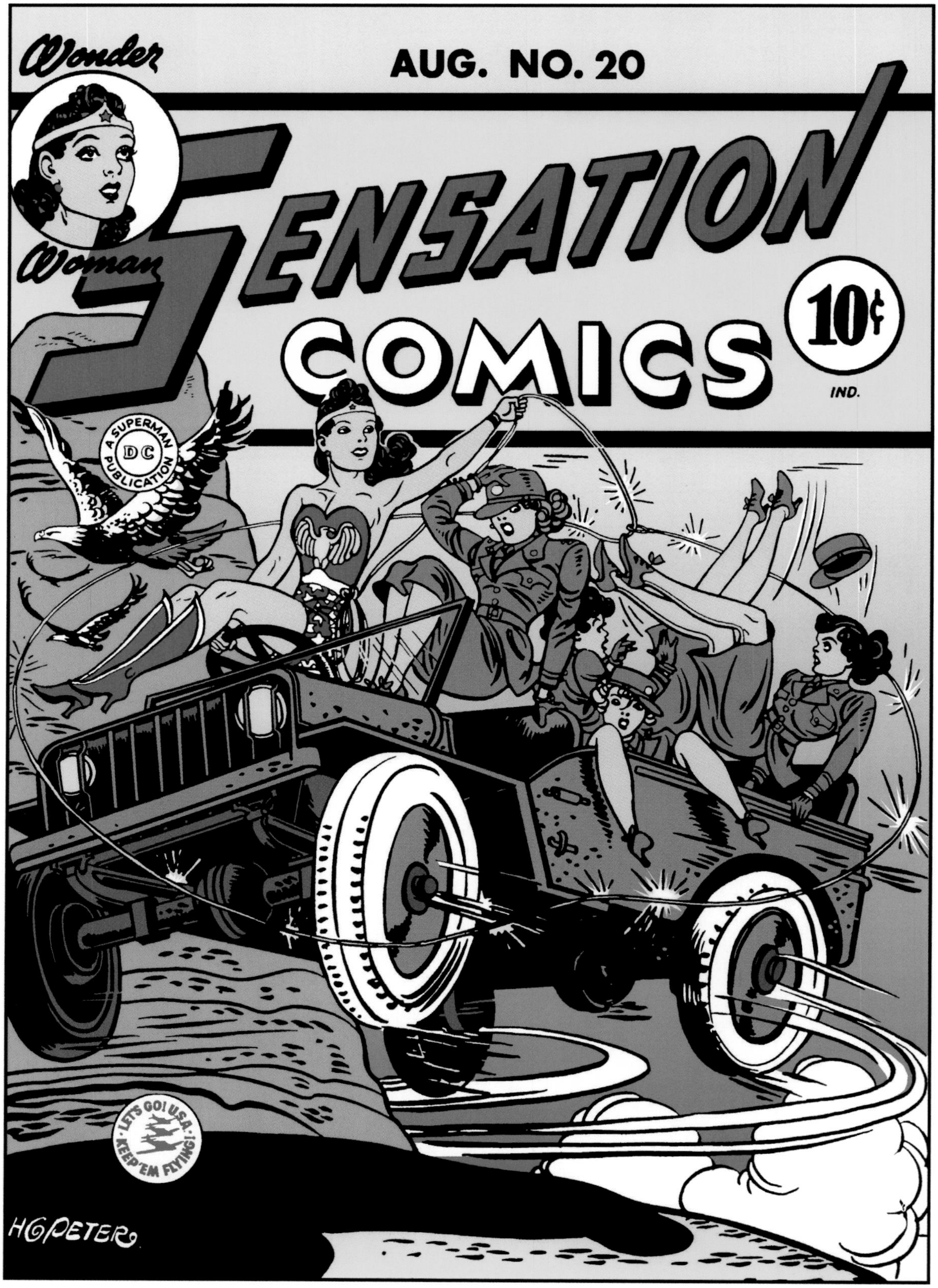
Wonder Woman
AUG. NO. 20
SENSATION COMICS
10¢
IND.
A SUPERMAN DC PUBLICATION
LET'S GO! U.S.A. KEEP 'EM FLYING!
H.G. PETER

Sensation Comics #20 (Aug. 1943) - art: H.G. Peter

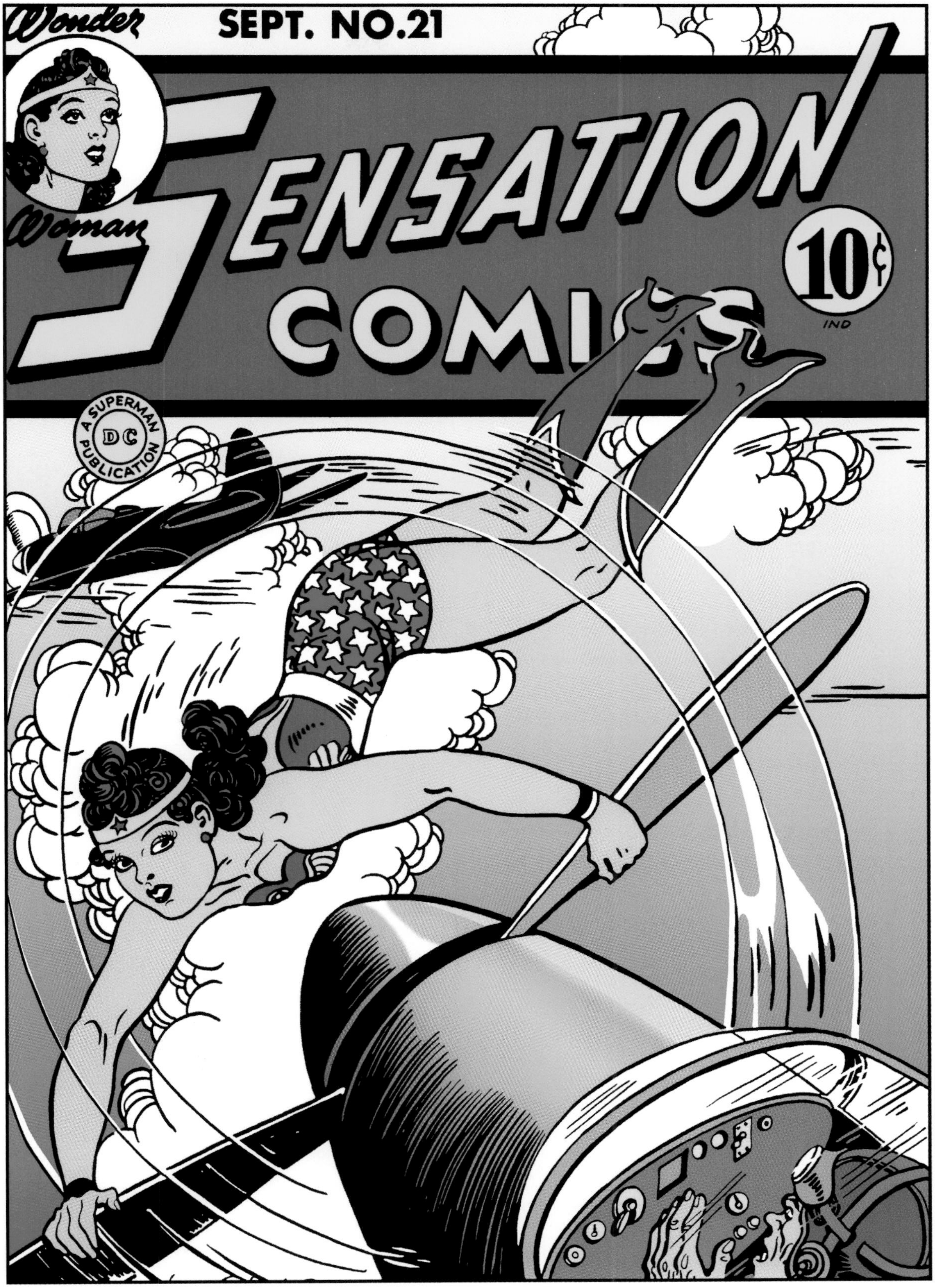
Wonder Woman
SEPT. NO.21
SENSATION COMICS
10¢
IND
A SUPERMAN DC PUBLICATION

Sensation Comics #21 (Sept. 1943) - art: H.G. Peter

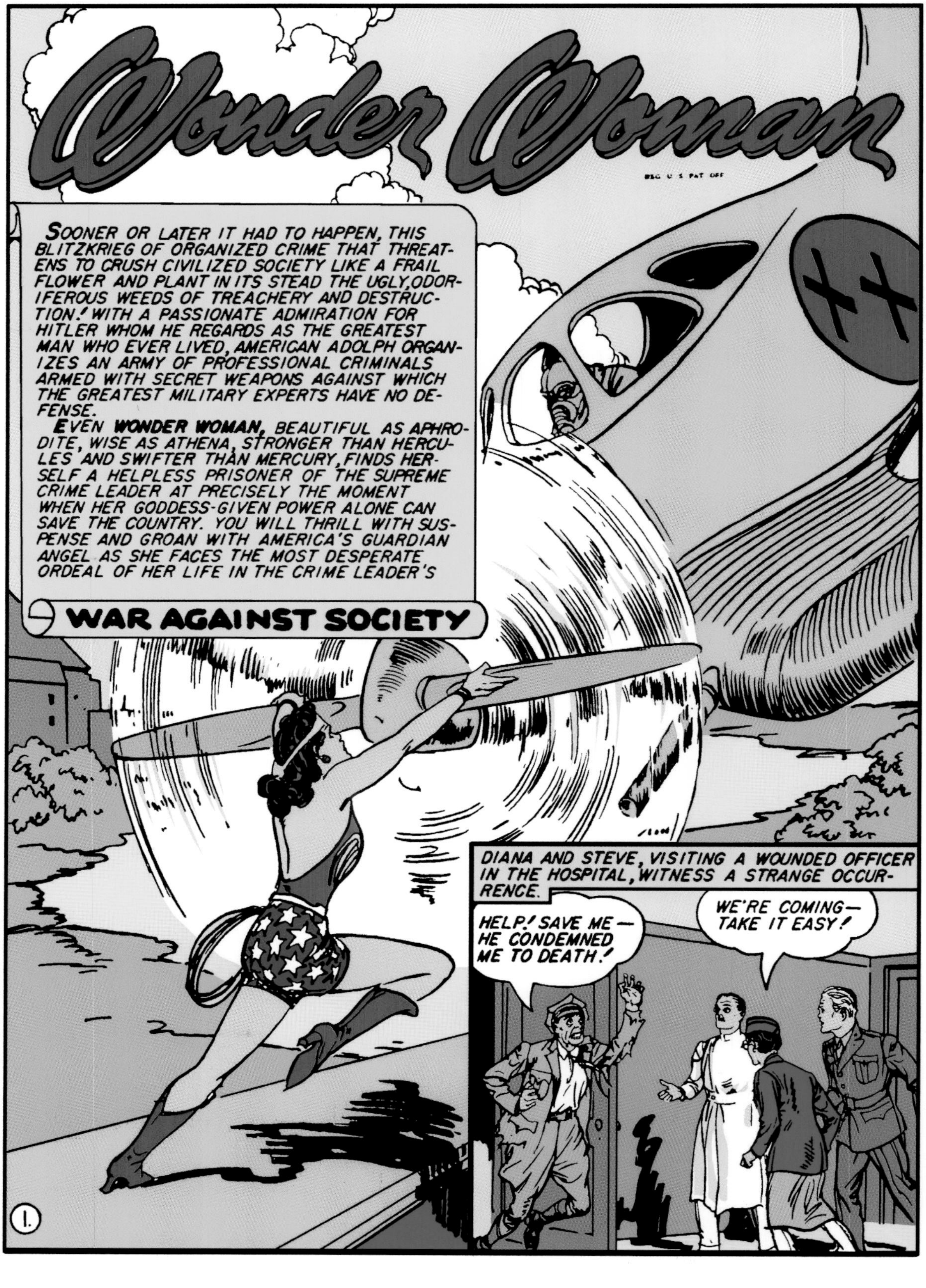

Wonder Woman
REG. U.S. PAT. OFF.
SOONER OR LATER IT HAD TO HAPPEN, THIS BLITZKRIEG OF ORGANIZED CRIME THAT THREATENS TO CRUSH CIVILIZED SOCIETY LIKE A FRAIL FLOWER AND PLANT IN ITS STEAD THE UGLY, ODORIFEROUS WEEDS OF TREACHERY AND DESTRUCTION! WITH A PASSIONATE ADMIRATION FOR HITLER WHOM HE REGARDS AS THE GREATEST MAN WHO EVER LIVED, AMERICAN ADOLPH ORGANIZES AN ARMY OF PROFESSIONAL CRIMINALS ARMED WITH SECRET WEAPONS AGAINST WHICH THE GREATEST MILITARY EXPERTS HAVE NO DEFENSE.
EVEN WONDER WOMAN, BEAUTIFUL AS APHRODITE, WISE AS ATHENA, STRONGER THAN HERCULES AND SWIFTER THAN MERCURY, FINDS HERSELF A HELPLESS PRISONER OF THE SUPREME CRIME LEADER AT PRECISELY THE MOMENT WHEN HER GODDESS-GIVEN POWER ALONE CAN SAVE THE COUNTRY. YOU WILL THRILL WITH SUSPENSE AND GROAN WITH AMERICA'S GUARDIAN ANGEL AS SHE FACES THE MOST DESPERATE ORDEAL OF HER LIFE IN THE CRIME LEADER'S
WAR AGAINST SOCIETY
1.
DIANA AND STEVE, VISITING A WOUNDED OFFICER IN THE HOSPITAL, WITNESS A STRANGE OCCURRENCE.
HELP! SAVE ME — HE CONDEMNED ME TO DEATH!
WE'RE COMING — TAKE IT EASY!

Sensation Comics #21 (Sept. 1943) - script: William Moulton Marston - art: Frank Godwin

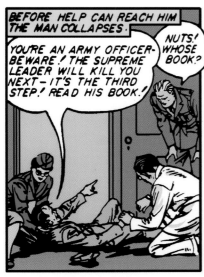

BEFORE HELP CAN REACH HIM THE MAN COLLAPSES.
YOU'RE AN ARMY OFFICER-BEWARE! THE SUPREME LEADER WILL KILL YOU NEXT-IT'S THE THIRD STEP! READ HIS BOOK!
NUTS! WHOSE BOOK?
AMERICAN ADOLPH'S BOOK-"MY WAR AGAINST SOCIETY!" HE'S DONE EVERYTHING HE SAID—COMPLETED STEPS 1 AND 2! THE GREAT HORROR'S COMING-STEP 3-THE RULE OF CRIME! LOOK FOR HIS MARK-THE DOUBLE CROSS!
HE'S DEAD-KNIFE WOUND-LOOKS LIKE MURDER!
THAT TATTOO WOULD INDICATE HE BELONGED TO A GANG. HE EVIDENTLY LIVED UP TO THEIR SYMBOL, DOUBLE CROSSED 'EM AND WAS EXECUTED-
THE POOR FELLOW WAS SCARED OUT OF HIS WITS! THERE IS NO SUCH BOOK AS "MY WAR AGAINST SOCIETY"-IS THERE?
I DON'T KNOW-BUT I'M GOING TO FIND OUT!
DIANA CALLS DIOGENES ARCHIVIAN, DEALER IN RARE BOOKS.
YOU REMEMBER ME-I'M YOUR AMAZON GIRL CUSTOMER. TELL ME-IS THERE A BOOK CALLED "MY WAR AGAINST SOCIETY" BY "AMERICAN ADOLPH"?
OH, YOU'RE WONDER WOMAN, WHO READS ALL LANGUAGES! "AMERICAN ADOLPH" IS THE PEN NAME OF A MASTER CRIMINAL. HE WROTE THIS STRANGE BOOK IN PRISON, AS HITLER DID MEIN KAMPF, DESCRIBING THE GREAT CRIME EMPIRE HE WOULD FOUND. THEY SAY HE HAS DONE IT!
THE BOOK IS HARD TO OBTAIN, BUT ARCHIVIAN GETS A COPY FOR WONDER WOMAN.
HOW AMAZING! THE DEDICATION READS-"TO ADOLPH SHICKELGRUBER, ALIAS HITLER-UNDOUBTEDLY THE GREATEST MAN WHO EVER LIVED!"
MY WAR AGAINST SOCIETY BY AMERICAN ADOLPH
2.
CHAPT. 1
MY CRIMINAL AIMS
Crime Pays! Every successful man in the world is a crook of one kind or another! The only way to become really successful is to be more crooked than others. Hitler was a great criminal. I shall be greater because my crime army will be professional criminals, not amateurs.
I shall proceed as follows:
Step no.1-Kill or conquer all rival Criminal Leaders.
Step no.2-Organize a national Crime army.
Step no.3-Murder important U.S. Army Officers, break Federal Prisons.
Step no.4-Take over the National Government.

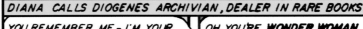

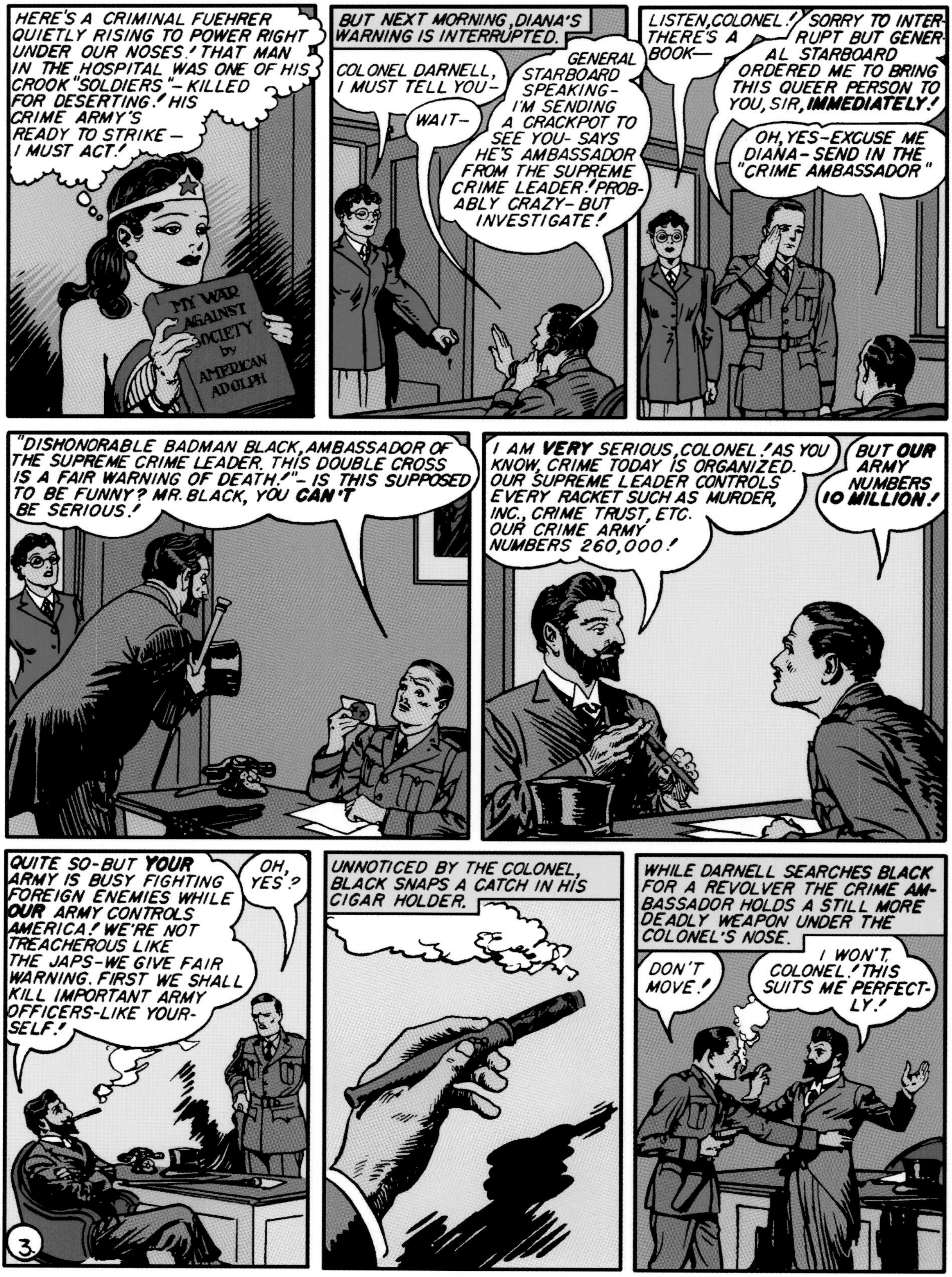
HERE'S A CRIMINAL FUEHRER QUIETLY RISING TO POWER RIGHT UNDER OUR NOSES! THAT MAN IN THE HOSPITAL WAS ONE OF HIS CROOK "SOLDIERS"—KILLED FOR DESERTING! HIS CRIME ARMY'S READY TO STRIKE—I MUST ACT!
MY WAR AGAINST SOCIETY by AMERICAN ADOLPH
BUT NEXT MORNING, DIANA'S WARNING IS INTERRUPTED.
COLONEL DARNELL, I MUST TELL YOU-
WAIT-
GENERAL STARBOARD SPEAKING- I'M SENDING A CRACKPOT TO SEE YOU- SAYS HE'S AMBASSADOR FROM THE SUPREME CRIME LEADER! PROBABLY CRAZY- BUT INVESTIGATE!
LISTEN, COLONEL! THERE'S A BOOK—
SORRY TO INTERRUPT BUT GENERAL STARBOARD ORDERED ME TO BRING THIS QUEER PERSON TO YOU, SIR, IMMEDIATELY!
OH, YES-EXCUSE ME DIANA- SEND IN THE "CRIME AMBASSADOR"
"DISHONORABLE BADMAN BLACK, AMBASSADOR OF THE SUPREME CRIME LEADER. THIS DOUBLE CROSS IS A FAIR WARNING OF DEATH!"- IS THIS SUPPOSED TO BE FUNNY? MR. BLACK, YOU CAN'T BE SERIOUS!
I AM VERY SERIOUS, COLONEL! AS YOU KNOW, CRIME TODAY IS ORGANIZED. OUR SUPREME LEADER CONTROLS EVERY RACKET SUCH AS MURDER, INC., CRIME TRUST, ETC. OUR CRIME ARMY NUMBERS 260,000!
BUT OUR ARMY NUMBERS 10 MILLION!
QUITE SO-BUT YOUR ARMY IS BUSY FIGHTING FOREIGN ENEMIES WHILE OUR ARMY CONTROLS AMERICA! WE'RE NOT TREACHEROUS LIKE THE JAPS-WE GIVE FAIR WARNING. FIRST WE SHALL KILL IMPORTANT ARMY OFFICERS-LIKE YOURSELF!
OH, YES?
3.
UNNOTICED BY THE COLONEL, BLACK SNAPS A CATCH IN HIS CIGAR HOLDER.
WHILE DARNELL SEARCHES BLACK FOR A REVOLVER THE CRIME AMBASSADOR HOLDS A STILL MORE DEADLY WEAPON UNDER THE COLONEL'S NOSE.
DON'T MOVE!
I WON'T, COLONEL! THIS SUITS ME PERFECTLY!

THE FUMES FROM BLACK'S CIGAR HAVE A STRANGE EFFECT.

AGGH—I'M CHOKING—UGH—AH—HELP—DIANA.!

HO, HO! MY FRIEND! NOBODY CAN HELP YOU NOW!

BUT THE CRIME AMBASSADOR DOESN'T KNOW THAT COLONEL DARNELL'S MEEK-APPEARING SECRETARY IS REALLY THAT LIVING THUNDERBOLT, WONDER WOMAN.

IF THIS IS YOUR "THIRD STEP," CRIME LEADER, YOUR FOOT IS SLIPPING!

UG—OW-W-W!

SUCH IS THE FORCE OF DIANA'S BLOW THAT BLACK CRASHES THROUGH THE WINDOW.

PLUTO SPANK ME, I HIT HIM TOO HARD! THIS HIRSUTE HITLER CAN'T TAKE IT.

SWIFTER THAN THE EYE CAN FOLLOW, DIANA FLASHES TO THE MEDICAL SUPPLY ROOM AND RETURNS WITH OXYGEN APPARATUS.

THIS'LL SAVE HIM IF I CAN GET OXYGEN INTO HIS LUNGS IN TIME!

SWIFTLY ADJUSTING THE OXYGEN MASK, DIANA APPLIES HER AMAZON METHOD OF ARTIFICIAL RESPIRATION.

HE'S PRETTY FAR GONE BUT I'LL MAKE HIM BREATHE THIS OXYGEN!

259

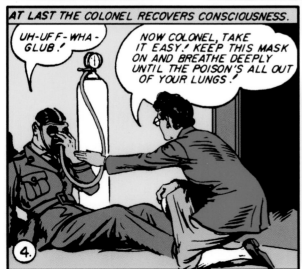

AT LAST THE COLONEL RECOVERS CONSCIOUSNESS.

UH-UFF-WHA-GLUB!

NOW COLONEL, TAKE IT EASY! KEEP THIS MASK ON AND BREATHE DEEPLY UNTIL THE POISON'S ALL OUT OF YOUR LUNGS!

4.

STEVE ARRIVES AS DIANA FINALLY REMOVES THE OXYGEN MASK.

GREAT CAESAR'S GHOST! WHAT HAPPENED, COLONEL?

CRIME AMBASSADOR—TRIED KILL ME!—MUST BEEN—POISON SMOKE—CIGAR—DIANA SAVED ME!

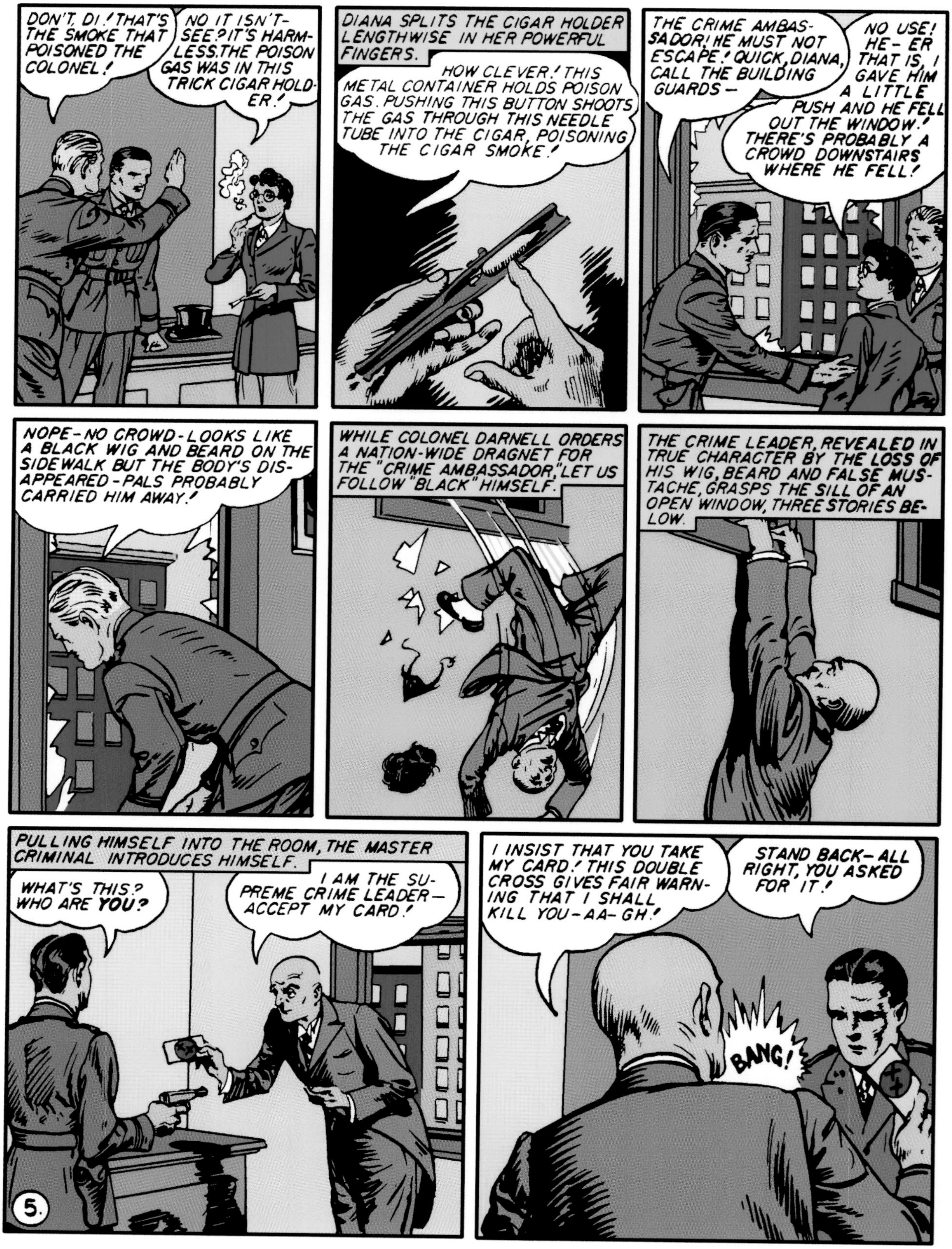
DON'T, DI! THAT'S THE SMOKE THAT POISONED THE COLONEL!
NO IT ISN'T- SEE? IT'S HARMLESS. THE POISON GAS WAS IN THIS TRICK CIGAR HOLDER!
DIANA SPLITS THE CIGAR HOLDER LENGTHWISE IN HER POWERFUL FINGERS.
HOW CLEVER! THIS METAL CONTAINER HOLDS POISON GAS. PUSHING THIS BUTTON SHOOTS THE GAS THROUGH THIS NEEDLE TUBE INTO THE CIGAR, POISONING THE CIGAR SMOKE!
THE CRIME AMBASSADOR! HE MUST NOT ESCAPE! QUICK, DIANA, CALL THE BUILDING GUARDS—
NO USE! HE— ER THAT IS, I GAVE HIM A LITTLE PUSH AND HE FELL OUT THE WINDOW! THERE'S PROBABLY A CROWD DOWNSTAIRS WHERE HE FELL!
NOPE-NO CROWD-LOOKS LIKE A BLACK WIG AND BEARD ON THE SIDEWALK BUT THE BODY'S DISAPPEARED-PALS PROBABLY CARRIED HIM AWAY!
WHILE COLONEL DARNELL ORDERS A NATION-WIDE DRAGNET FOR THE "CRIME AMBASSADOR," LET US FOLLOW "BLACK" HIMSELF.
THE CRIME LEADER, REVEALED IN TRUE CHARACTER BY THE LOSS OF HIS WIG, BEARD AND FALSE MUSTACHE, GRASPS THE SILL OF AN OPEN WINDOW, THREE STORIES BELOW.
PULLING HIMSELF INTO THE ROOM, THE MASTER CRIMINAL INTRODUCES HIMSELF.
WHAT'S THIS? WHO ARE YOU?
I AM THE SUPREME CRIME LEADER— ACCEPT MY CARD!
5.
I INSIST THAT YOU TAKE MY CARD! THIS DOUBLE CROSS GIVES FAIR WARNING THAT I SHALL KILL YOU-AA-GH!
STAND BACK— ALL RIGHT, YOU ASKED FOR IT!
BANG!

I **HAD** TO SHOOT— WHO **IS** THIS BIRD?

THIS BULLET-PROOF VEST I INVENTED IS A SUCCESS — THAT ARMY .45 AT 5 FEET ONLY KNOCKED ME OVER!

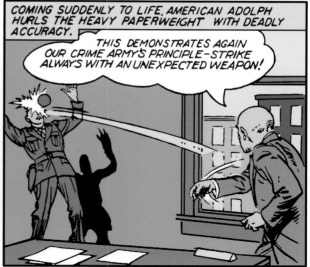

COMING SUDDENLY TO LIFE, AMERICAN ADOLPH HURLS THE HEAVY PAPERWEIGHT WITH DEADLY ACCURACY.

THIS DEMONSTRATES AGAIN OUR CRIME ARMY'S PRINCIPLE—STRIKE ALWAYS WITH AN UNEXPECTED WEAPON!

THE CRIME LEADER, ADEPT AT QUICK CHANGES, DONS THE LIEU-TENANT'S UNIFORM.

THEY WON'T FIND THE BODY IN THIS CLOSET FOR SOME TIME— I MUST GET THAT GIRL WHO PUSHED ME OUT THE WINDOW— SHE KNOWS TOO MUCH!

ADOLPH BOLDLY USES THE LIEU-TENANT'S PHONE, COVERING IT WITH HIS HANDKERCHIEF TO DISGUISE HIS VOICE.

MISS PRINCE? I'M QUICK-HUH? NOT FAST—**QUICK,** LT. QUICK! PLEASE COME TO MY OFFICE— I HAVE IM-PORTANT INFORMATION!

LT. K.L QUICK

DIANA, SUSPECTING TRICKERY, CHANGES QUICKLY TO **WONDER WOMAN,** HIDING HER NURSE'S UNIFORM IN A SECRET COMPART-MENT OF HER DESK.

THAT VOICE ON THE PHONE DIDN'T SOUND LIKE KEN QUICK'S—BESIDES HE'D NEVER CALL ME "MISS PRINCE"— IT'S TIME FOR **WONDER WOMAN** TO INVESTIGATE!

AS **WONDER WOMAN** ENTERS QUICK'S OFFICE, THE "LIEUTENANT" SPEAKS IN A MUFFLED VOICE.

ER— THAT YOU, MISS PRINCE?

6.

BUT THE CRIME MASTER, TURN-ING SWIFTLY ON HIS INTENDED VICTIM, MEETS A SURPRISE.

HANDS UP—WHAT! YOU'RE NOT DIANA PRINCE— YOU'RE **WONDER WOMAN!**

I WAS IN DIANA'S OFFICE WHEN YOU PHONED— I YEARNED TO MEET "LT. QUICK!"

THIS GUN IS NO USE AGAINST YOU, DEAR LADY! YOU REPEL ALL BULLETS WITH YOUR BRACELETS. I AM THE CRIME LEADER— MY CARD.

SORRY YOU WON'T PLAY BULLETS AND BRACELETS WITH ME—

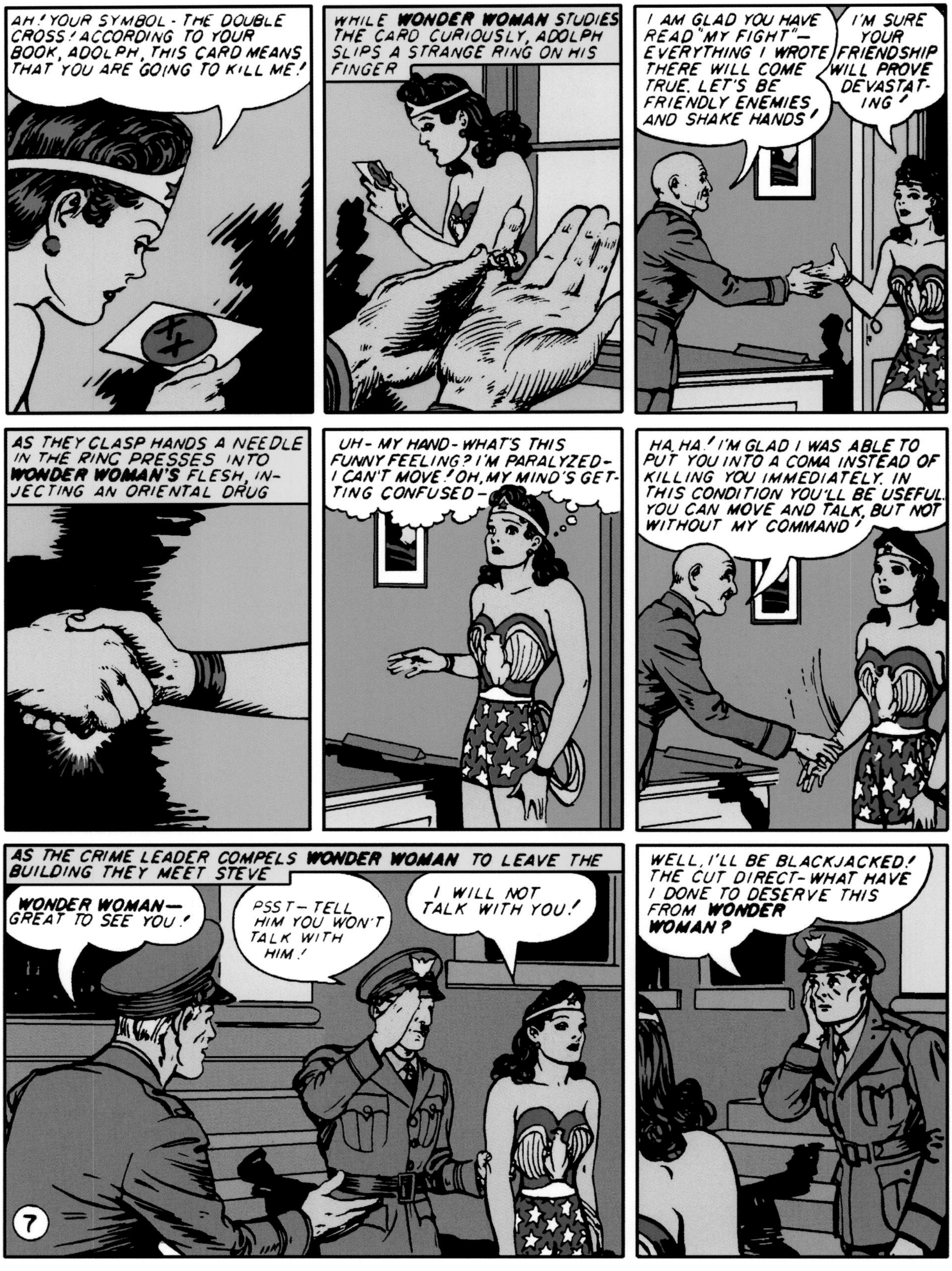

AH! YOUR SYMBOL - THE DOUBLE CROSS! ACCORDING TO YOUR BOOK, ADOLPH, THIS CARD MEANS THAT YOU ARE GOING TO KILL ME!
WHILE WONDER WOMAN STUDIES THE CARD CURIOUSLY, ADOLPH SLIPS A STRANGE RING ON HIS FINGER
I AM GLAD YOU HAVE READ "MY FIGHT"— EVERYTHING I WROTE THERE WILL COME TRUE. LET'S BE FRIENDLY ENEMIES, AND SHAKE HANDS!
I'M SURE YOUR FRIENDSHIP WILL PROVE DEVASTATING!
AS THEY CLASP HANDS A NEEDLE IN THE RING PRESSES INTO WONDER WOMAN'S FLESH, INJECTING AN ORIENTAL DRUG
UH- MY HAND- WHAT'S THIS FUNNY FEELING? I'M PARALYZED- I CAN'T MOVE! OH, MY MIND'S GETTING CONFUSED-
HA, HA! I'M GLAD I WAS ABLE TO PUT YOU INTO A COMA INSTEAD OF KILLING YOU IMMEDIATELY. IN THIS CONDITION YOU'LL BE USEFUL. YOU CAN MOVE AND TALK, BUT NOT WITHOUT MY COMMAND!
AS THE CRIME LEADER COMPELS WONDER WOMAN TO LEAVE THE BUILDING THEY MEET STEVE
WONDER WOMAN— GREAT TO SEE YOU!
PSST— TELL HIM YOU WON'T TALK WITH HIM!
I WILL NOT TALK WITH YOU!
7
WELL, I'LL BE BLACKJACKED! THE CUT DIRECT- WHAT HAVE I DONE TO DESERVE THIS FROM WONDER WOMAN?

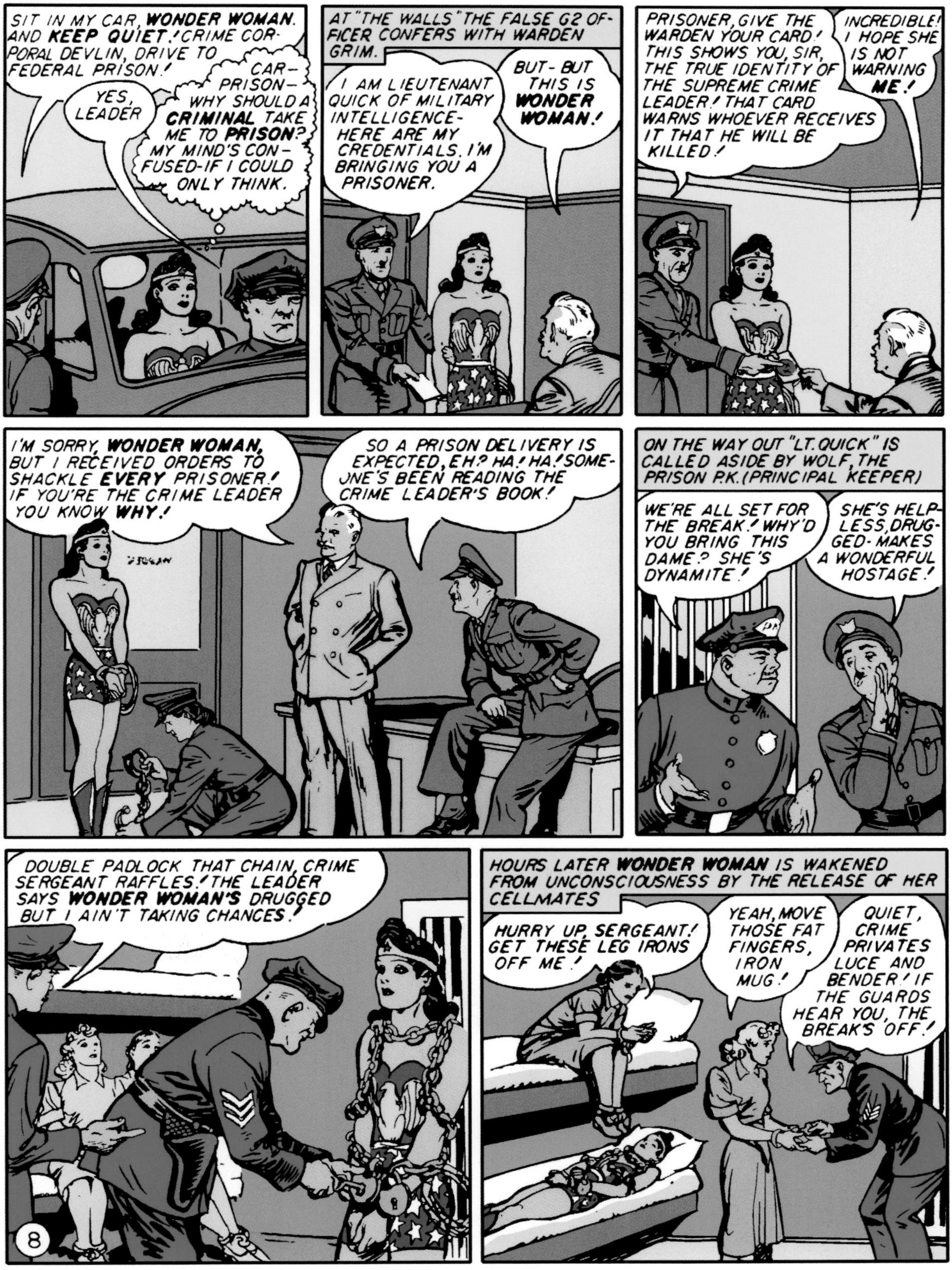
SIT IN MY CAR, WONDER WOMAN. AND KEEP QUIET! CRIME CORPORAL DEVLIN, DRIVE TO FEDERAL PRISON!
YES, LEADER
CAR-PRISON- WHY SHOULD A CRIMINAL TAKE ME TO PRISON? MY MIND'S CONFUSED-IF I COULD ONLY THINK.
AT "THE WALLS" THE FALSE G2 OFFICER CONFERS WITH WARDEN GRIM.
I AM LIEUTENANT QUICK OF MILITARY INTELLIGENCE- HERE ARE MY CREDENTIALS. I'M BRINGING YOU A PRISONER.
BUT- BUT THIS IS WONDER WOMAN!
PRISONER, GIVE THE WARDEN YOUR CARD! THIS SHOWS YOU, SIR, THE TRUE IDENTITY OF THE SUPREME CRIME LEADER! THAT CARD WARNS WHOEVER RECEIVES IT THAT HE WILL BE KILLED!
INCREDIBLE! I HOPE SHE IS NOT WARNING ME!
I'M SORRY, WONDER WOMAN, BUT I RECEIVED ORDERS TO SHACKLE EVERY PRISONER! IF YOU'RE THE CRIME LEADER YOU KNOW WHY!
SO A PRISON DELIVERY IS EXPECTED, EH? HA! HA! SOMEONE'S BEEN READING THE CRIME LEADER'S BOOK!
ON THE WAY OUT "LT. QUICK" IS CALLED ASIDE BY WOLF, THE PRISON P.K. (PRINCIPAL KEEPER)
WE'RE ALL SET FOR THE BREAK! WHY'D YOU BRING THIS DAME? SHE'S DYNAMITE!
SHE'S HELPLESS, DRUGGED- MAKES A WONDERFUL HOSTAGE!
DOUBLE PADLOCK THAT CHAIN, CRIME SERGEANT RAFFLES! THE LEADER SAYS WONDER WOMAN'S DRUGGED BUT I AIN'T TAKING CHANCES!
8
HOURS LATER WONDER WOMAN IS WAKENED FROM UNCONSCIOUSNESS BY THE RELEASE OF HER CELLMATES
HURRY UP, SERGEANT! GET THESE LEG IRONS OFF ME!
YEAH, MOVE THOSE FAT FINGERS, IRON MUG!
QUIET, CRIME PRIVATES LUCE AND BENDER! IF THE GUARDS HEAR YOU, THE BREAK'S OFF!

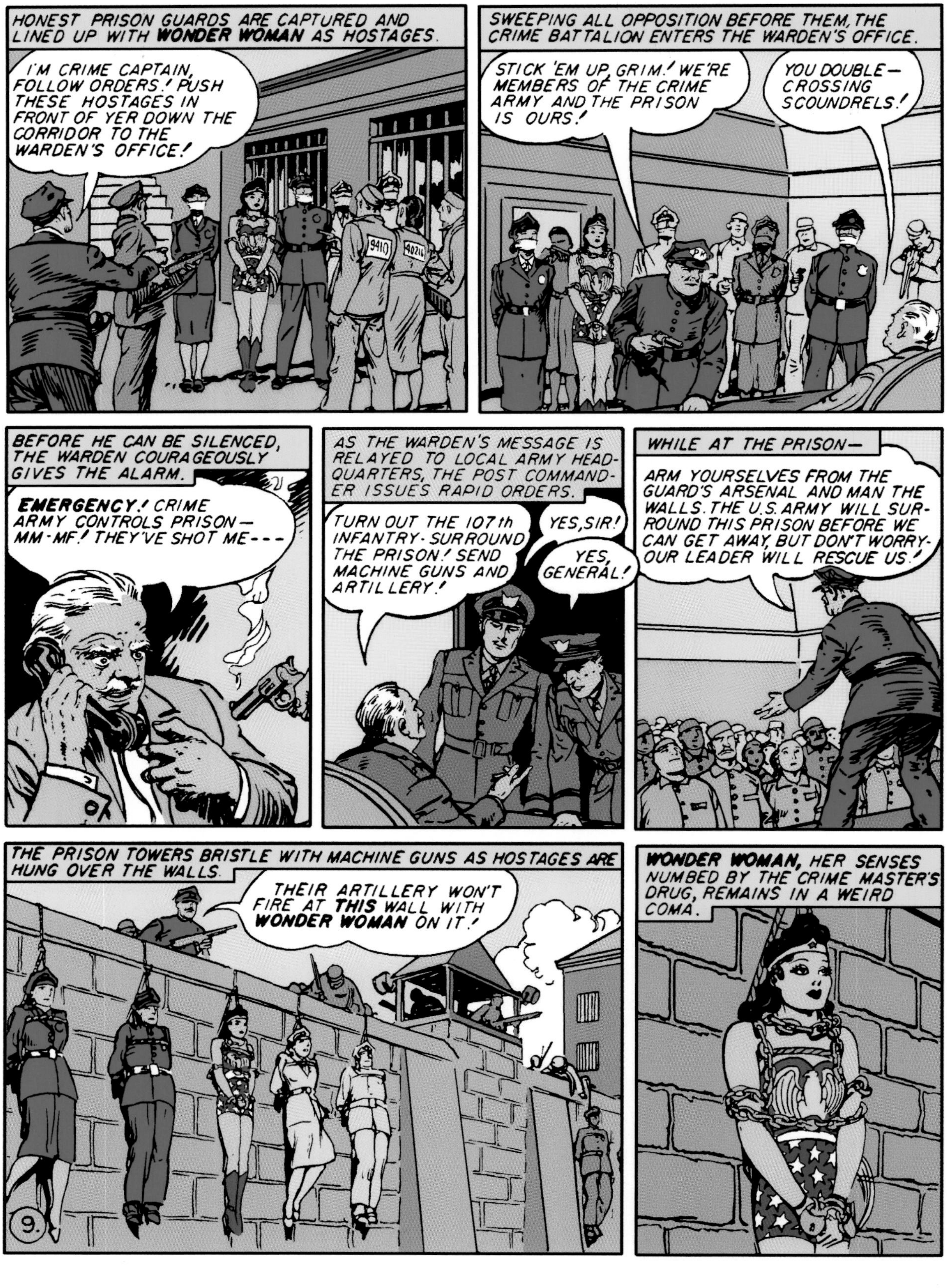
HONEST PRISON GUARDS ARE CAPTURED AND LINED UP WITH WONDER WOMAN AS HOSTAGES.
I'M CRIME CAPTAIN, FOLLOW ORDERS! PUSH THESE HOSTAGES IN FRONT OF YER DOWN THE CORRIDOR TO THE WARDEN'S OFFICE!
9410
4024
SWEEPING ALL OPPOSITION BEFORE THEM, THE CRIME BATTALION ENTERS THE WARDEN'S OFFICE.
STICK 'EM UP, GRIM! WE'RE MEMBERS OF THE CRIME ARMY AND THE PRISON IS OURS!
YOU DOUBLE-CROSSING SCOUNDRELS!
BEFORE HE CAN BE SILENCED, THE WARDEN COURAGEOUSLY GIVES THE ALARM.
EMERGENCY! CRIME ARMY CONTROLS PRISON— MM-MF! THEY'VE SHOT ME---
AS THE WARDEN'S MESSAGE IS RELAYED TO LOCAL ARMY HEADQUARTERS, THE POST COMMANDER ISSUES RAPID ORDERS.
TURN OUT THE 107th INFANTRY-SURROUND THE PRISON! SEND MACHINE GUNS AND ARTILLERY!
YES, SIR!
YES, GENERAL!
WHILE AT THE PRISON—
ARM YOURSELVES FROM THE GUARD'S ARSENAL AND MAN THE WALLS. THE U.S. ARMY WILL SURROUND THIS PRISON BEFORE WE CAN GET AWAY, BUT DON'T WORRY- OUR LEADER WILL RESCUE US!
THE PRISON TOWERS BRISTLE WITH MACHINE GUNS AS HOSTAGES ARE HUNG OVER THE WALLS.
THEIR ARTILLERY WON'T FIRE AT THIS WALL WITH WONDER WOMAN ON IT!
9.
WONDER WOMAN, HER SENSES NUMBED BY THE CRIME MASTER'S DRUG, REMAINS IN A WEIRD COMA.

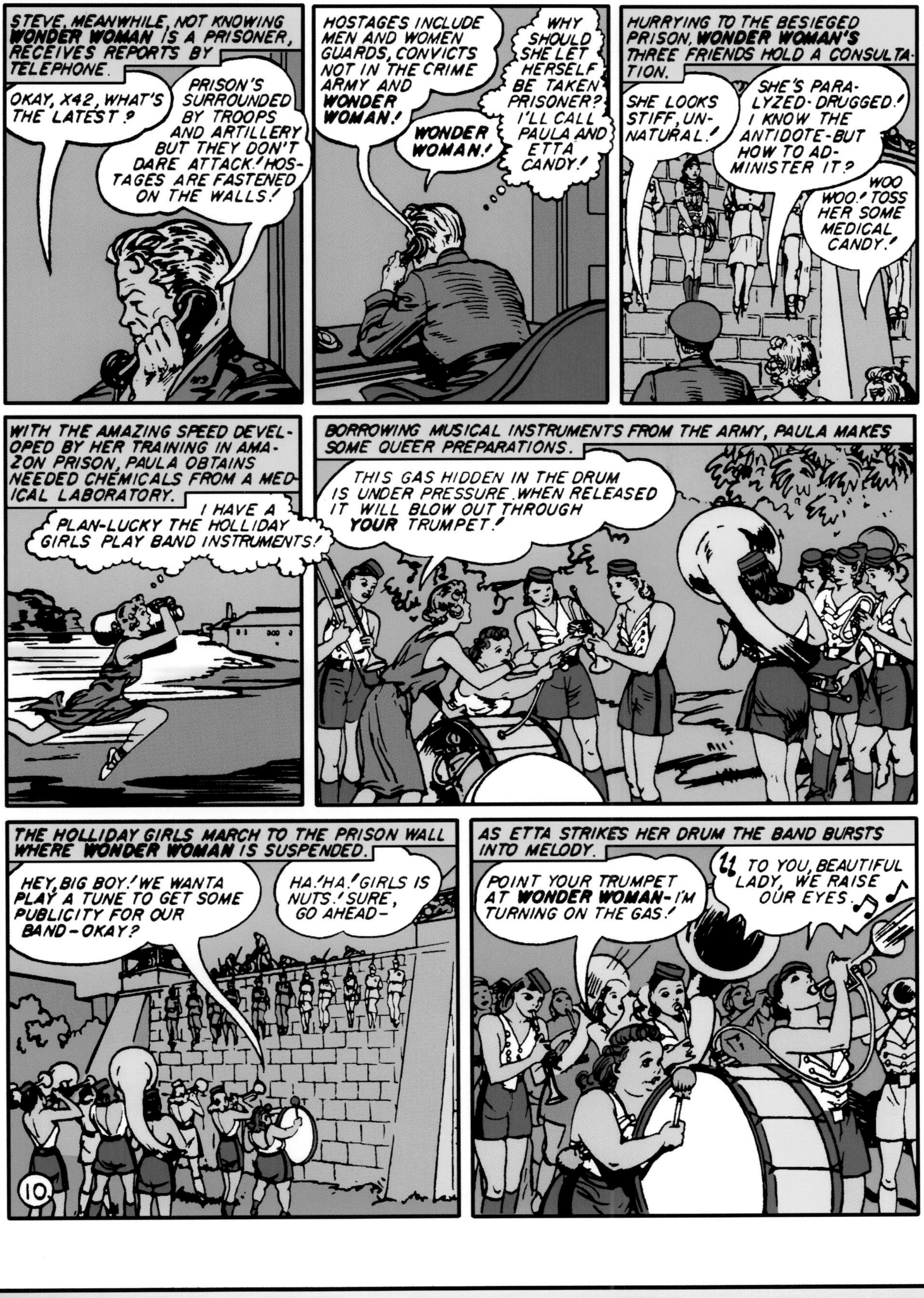
STEVE, MEANWHILE, NOT KNOWING WONDER WOMAN IS A PRISONER, RECEIVES REPORTS BY TELEPHONE.
OKAY, X42, WHAT'S THE LATEST?
PRISON'S SURROUNDED BY TROOPS AND ARTILLERY BUT THEY DON'T DARE ATTACK! HOSTAGES ARE FASTENED ON THE WALLS!
HOSTAGES INCLUDE MEN AND WOMEN GUARDS, CONVICTS NOT IN THE CRIME ARMY AND WONDER WOMAN!
WONDER WOMAN!
WHY SHOULD SHE LET HERSELF BE TAKEN PRISONER? I'LL CALL PAULA AND ETTA CANDY!
HURRYING TO THE BESIEGED PRISON, WONDER WOMAN'S THREE FRIENDS HOLD A CONSULTATION.
SHE LOOKS STIFF, UNNATURAL!
SHE'S PARALYZED-DRUGGED! I KNOW THE ANTIDOTE-BUT HOW TO ADMINISTER IT?
WOO WOO! TOSS HER SOME MEDICAL CANDY!
WITH THE AMAZING SPEED DEVELOPED BY HER TRAINING IN AMAZON PRISON, PAULA OBTAINS NEEDED CHEMICALS FROM A MEDICAL LABORATORY.
I HAVE A PLAN-LUCKY THE HOLLIDAY GIRLS PLAY BAND INSTRUMENTS!
BORROWING MUSICAL INSTRUMENTS FROM THE ARMY, PAULA MAKES SOME QUEER PREPARATIONS.
THIS GAS HIDDEN IN THE DRUM IS UNDER PRESSURE. WHEN RELEASED IT WILL BLOW OUT THROUGH YOUR TRUMPET!
THE HOLLIDAY GIRLS MARCH TO THE PRISON WALL WHERE WONDER WOMAN IS SUSPENDED.
HEY, BIG BOY! WE WANTA PLAY A TUNE TO GET SOME PUBLICITY FOR OUR BAND-OKAY?
HA! HA! GIRLS IS NUTS! SURE, GO AHEAD-
10
AS ETTA STRIKES HER DRUM THE BAND BURSTS INTO MELODY.
POINT YOUR TRUMPET AT WONDER WOMAN-I'M TURNING ON THE GAS!
TO YOU, BEAUTIFUL LADY, WE RAISE OUR EYES

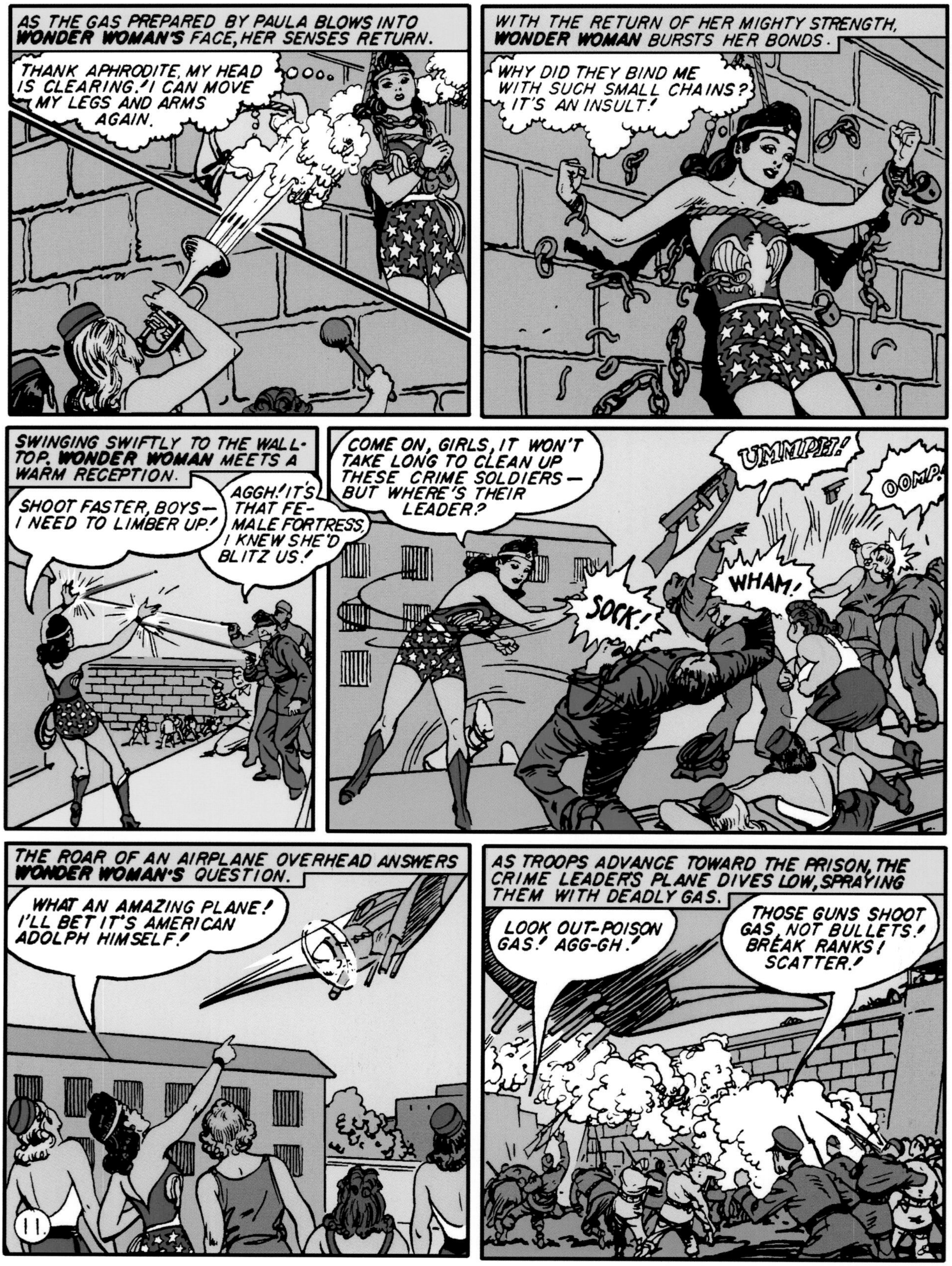

AS THE GAS PREPARED BY PAULA BLOWS INTO WONDER WOMAN'S FACE, HER SENSES RETURN.
THANK APHRODITE, MY HEAD IS CLEARING! I CAN MOVE MY LEGS AND ARMS AGAIN.
WITH THE RETURN OF HER MIGHTY STRENGTH, WONDER WOMAN BURSTS HER BONDS.
WHY DID THEY BIND ME WITH SUCH SMALL CHAINS? IT'S AN INSULT!
SWINGING SWIFTLY TO THE WALL-TOP, WONDER WOMAN MEETS A WARM RECEPTION.
SHOOT FASTER, BOYS— I NEED TO LIMBER UP!
AGGH! IT'S THAT FE-MALE FORTRESS. I KNEW SHE'D BLITZ US!
COME ON, GIRLS, IT WON'T TAKE LONG TO CLEAN UP THESE CRIME SOLDIERS— BUT WHERE'S THEIR LEADER?
UMMPH!
OOMP!
WHAM!
SOCK!
THE ROAR OF AN AIRPLANE OVERHEAD ANSWERS WONDER WOMAN'S QUESTION.
WHAT AN AMAZING PLANE! I'LL BET IT'S AMERICAN ADOLPH HIMSELF!
11
AS TROOPS ADVANCE TOWARD THE PRISON, THE CRIME LEADER'S PLANE DIVES LOW, SPRAYING THEM WITH DEADLY GAS.
LOOK OUT-POISON GAS! AGG-GH!
THOSE GUNS SHOOT GAS, NOT BULLETS! BREAK RANKS! SCATTER!

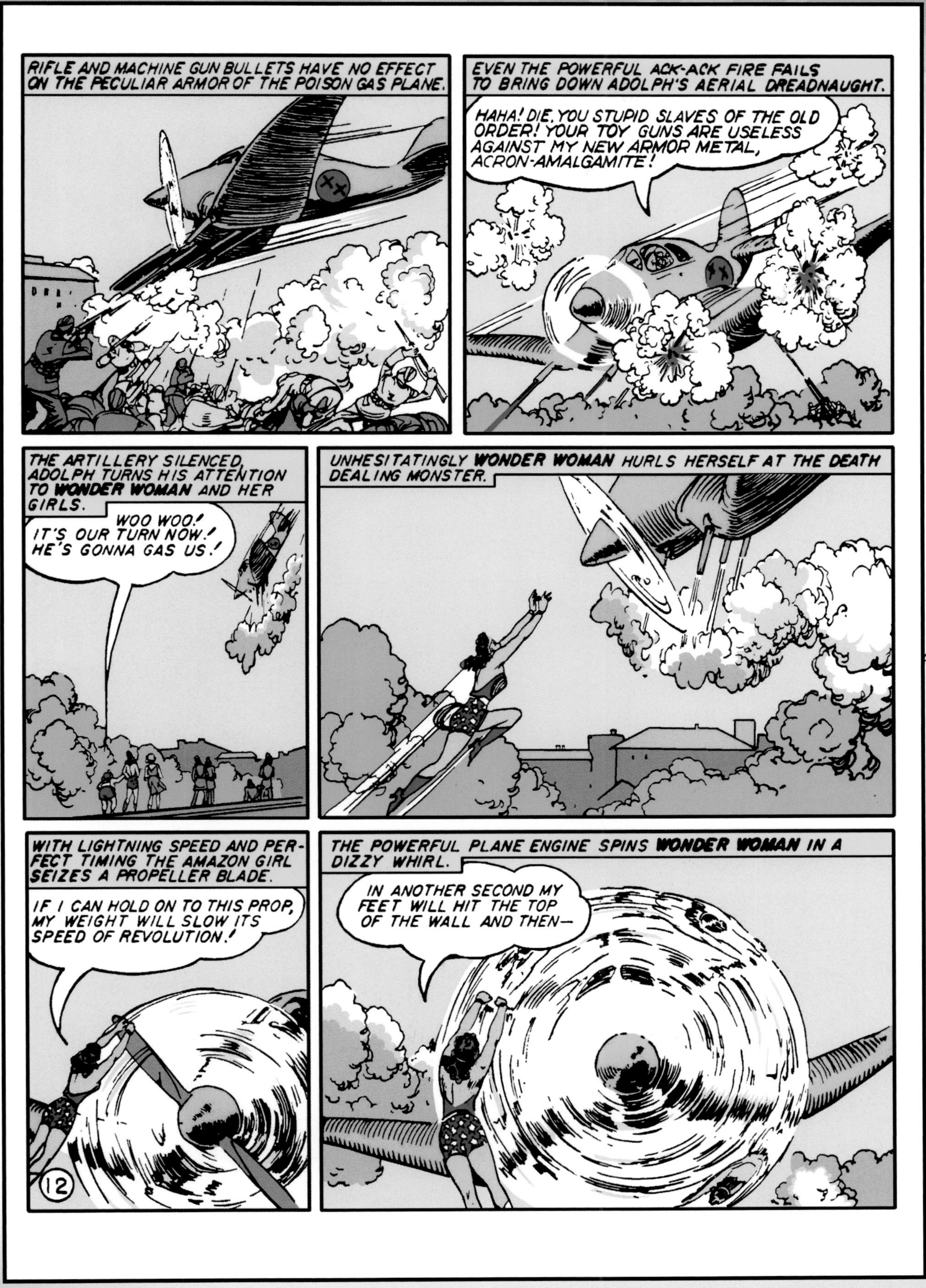
RIFLE AND MACHINE GUN BULLETS HAVE NO EFFECT ON THE PECULIAR ARMOR OF THE POISON GAS PLANE.
EVEN THE POWERFUL ACK-ACK FIRE FAILS TO BRING DOWN ADOLPH'S AERIAL DREADNAUGHT.
HAHA! DIE, YOU STUPID SLAVES OF THE OLD ORDER! YOUR TOY GUNS ARE USELESS AGAINST MY NEW ARMOR METAL, ACRON-AMALGAMITE!
THE ARTILLERY SILENCED, ADOLPH TURNS HIS ATTENTION TO WONDER WOMAN AND HER GIRLS.
WOO WOO! IT'S OUR TURN NOW! HE'S GONNA GAS US!
UNHESITATINGLY WONDER WOMAN HURLS HERSELF AT THE DEATH DEALING MONSTER.
WITH LIGHTNING SPEED AND PERFECT TIMING THE AMAZON GIRL SEIZES A PROPELLER BLADE.
IF I CAN HOLD ON TO THIS PROP, MY WEIGHT WILL SLOW ITS SPEED OF REVOLUTION!
12
THE POWERFUL PLANE ENGINE SPINS WONDER WOMAN IN A DIZZY WHIRL.
IN ANOTHER SECOND MY FEET WILL HIT THE TOP OF THE WALL AND THEN—

AS THE WHIRLING FORM OF THEIR LEADER COMES WITHIN REACH, THE GIRLS GRIP HER LEGS.
HOLD TIGHT, GIRLS! PULL ME DOWN ON THE WALL!
FIRMLY FIXED BY HER HUMAN ANCHOR, THE INVINCIBLE PRINCESS HOLDS THE PROPELLER MOTIONLESS WHILE THE PLANE ITSELF BEGINS TO WHIRL!
SWINGING THE PINIONED SHIP AROUND HER HEAD, WONDER WOMAN HURLS IT TO THE GROUND, A HEAP OF BLAZING WRECKAGE.
I HELD THE PLANE LONG ENOUGH FOR THE CRIME LEADER TO JUMP- HE CHOSE TO DIE RATHER THAN SUBMIT!
BANG!
CRASH!
YOUR STRENGTH AND COURAGE WERE MAGNIFICENT, MISTRESS, YOU SAVED US ALL!
AND YOUR BRAIN WORK WAS MAGNIFICENT, PAULA. YOU SAVED ME!
HEY YOU GALS, SKIP THE MUTUAL ADMIRATION- YOU BOTH NEED CANDY!
AS TROOPS POUR INTO THE PRISON, STEVE DRAWS WONDER WOMAN ASIDE.
I SHOULD HAVE KNOWN THERE WAS SOMETHING WRONG WHEN YOU CUT ME FOR ANOTHER MAN!
DON'T EVER LET ME DO IT AGAIN, STEVE!
13
AT G2 HEADQUARTERS COLONEL DARNELL IS IN A DITHER ABOUT DIANA.
SHE'S MISSING! YOU MUST FIND HER—DIANA! WHERE'VE YOU BEEN?
FINISHING THE CRIME LEADER'S CAREER—IT ENDED, LIKE THE DREAMS OF ALL CONQUERORS, IN BITTER DEFEAT!
MORE ADVENTURES OF WONDER WOMAN IN EVERY ISSUE OF SENSATION COMICS
FOR VICTORY BUY UNITED STATES WAR BONDS AND STAMPS

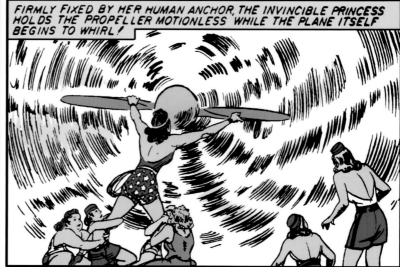

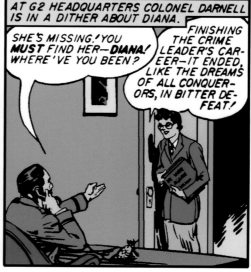

Part Five

*While many comic books,
just like Hollywood, produced less
war-oriented material after 1942 or '43,
Wonder Woman kept right at it.
She was determined to prove that her
star-spangled shorts and eagle-emblazoned
bustier weren't just for show!*

Victory in Sight

A potentially war-shortening invention was prominent in *Sensation Comics* #24 (Dec. 1943): a pilotless plane, something then definitely in the realm of science fiction. By mid-1944, though, the Germans were hurling V1 and V2 rockets at London—and what were they but pilotless aircraft? With jet engines, yet!

At this point, we couldn't resist tossing in the not specifically war-related cover of *Wonder Woman* #7 (Winter 1943), in which Princess Diana runs for President of the United States. As the cover blurb states, however, this tale occurs 1000 years in the future, by which time the U.S. Constitution has apparently been amended to allow someone not born in America to become President.

The covers of the multi-feature *Comic Cavalcade*, like those of DC proper's *World's Finest Comics*, featured symbolic scenes of the starring heroes. *WFC* sported several covers showcasing Superman, Batman, and Robin, on a battleship, tending a Victory Garden, and so on. Oddly, considering the number of Wonder Woman stories with a martial arc, there's only one truly war-connected cover on *Comic Cavalcade*: that of #6 (Spring 1944), where Wonder Woman, Green Lantern, and the Flash spearhead a paper drive. Paper was a scarce resource in wartime, since the government and the military depended on paperwork to keep track of everything. Publishing companies were allotted "paper quotas" and had to make do with less than in pre-war days. DC met this problem by issuing several of its "bimonthly" comics only four times

a year, and several "monthlies" only every second month. So popular was Wonder Woman, however, that Gaines kept *Sensation Comics* a true monthly.

She appeared in more than her share of so-called "public service" pages. In *All-Star Comics* #20 (Spring 1944), she's prominent in a comics-style Justice Society plea for the March of Dimes, a charity that fought polio by collecting coins from children and adults. In *All-Star* #24, she explains "waste paper salvage" to a rapt audience—namely, her mother! Nowadays, with that war far behind us, Diana needs to explain the wartime need for paper drives to *all* of us!

Fortunately, before we run out of book, we have one final full-blown war story, with true Axis villains! Sensation #37 involves a clever Nazi plan to conquer the Amazons' hidden Paradise Island . . . naturally involving a U-boat.

Fewer stories and covers dealt with the battle still raging overseas as the war wound down, although one would have been hard-pressed in December 1944 to convince embattled G.I.'s in Belgium that the war was "winding down." On the cover of *Wonder Woman* #11 (Winter 1944), she's again bending a weapon's barrel, but this time the villain is Hypnota, not an Axis agent, and the war involves the planet Saturn. The cover of #12 (Spring 1945) involves the winged maidens of the planet Venus; Diana riding a plummeting bomb reminds one of earlier covers on Superman.

Diana riding a plummeting bomb reminds one of earlier covers on *Superman*.

Thankfully, the war ended in 1945 . . . first in Europe, in May, with the defeat of the Nazis, and finally in the Pacific in August.

An *All-Star Comics* image closes this volume of Wonder Woman's World War II exploits. This cover—on which the Amazon stands farther in the background than the rest of the Justice Society, probably because she was added at the last minute by a different artist—appeared soon after the Japanese surrender document was signed in September. It depicts a serviceman, who is missing an arm, being saluted by the entire JSA. The story "A Place in the World!," was written by Gardner Fox after a national society for the handicapped asked DC (which had recently purchased the entirety of the AA line) to spotlight people with a physical handicap in one of their comics, to help acclimate America's civilian population to large numbers of injured veterans returning home, where it was necessary to re-integrate them into society. That issue of *All-Star* was later mentioned in the 1950 *World Book Encyclopedia*.

The story involves Jimmy, a pre-war football hero who shows courage in combat, but loses an arm in an explosion. He has always pitied his wheelchair-bound younger brother, but now he realizes that so-called "handicapped" people don't want (or need) to be pitied—they just want a chance to show what they can do. And he enlists the aid of the JSA to prove his point. The story may be a bit heavy-handed, like the later (1947) Oscar-winning film *The Best Years of Our Lives*, which also deals with returning veterans, one of whom is played by real-life soldier and amputee Harold Russell; but the comic's heart, like the movie's, is in the right place.

And so is Wonder Woman's. From 1941 until war's end—and far beyond—she has stood for equality for women, and she has fought for freedom for humankind everywhere.

Small wonder she's lasted nearly three quarters of a century, and is still going strong!

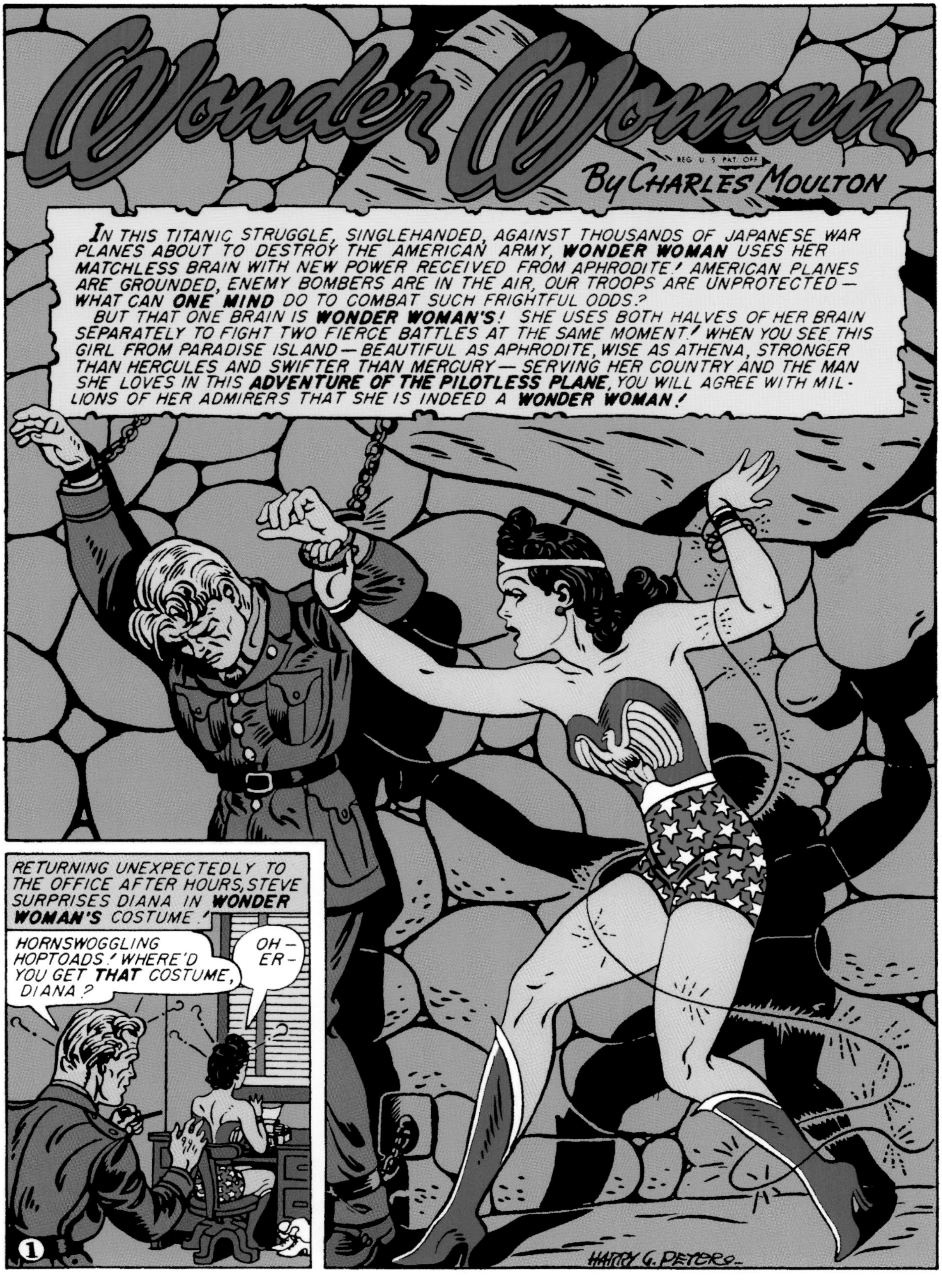
Wonder Woman
REG. U.S. PAT. OFF.
By CHARLES MOULTON
IN THIS TITANIC STRUGGLE, SINGLEHANDED, AGAINST THOUSANDS OF JAPANESE WAR PLANES ABOUT TO DESTROY THE AMERICAN ARMY, WONDER WOMAN USES HER MATCHLESS BRAIN WITH NEW POWER RECEIVED FROM APHRODITE! AMERICAN PLANES ARE GROUNDED, ENEMY BOMBERS ARE IN THE AIR, OUR TROOPS ARE UNPROTECTED — WHAT CAN ONE MIND DO TO COMBAT SUCH FRIGHTFUL ODDS? BUT THAT ONE BRAIN IS WONDER WOMAN'S! SHE USES BOTH HALVES OF HER BRAIN SEPARATELY TO FIGHT TWO FIERCE BATTLES AT THE SAME MOMENT! WHEN YOU SEE THIS GIRL FROM PARADISE ISLAND — BEAUTIFUL AS APHRODITE, WISE AS ATHENA, STRONGER THAN HERCULES AND SWIFTER THAN MERCURY — SERVING HER COUNTRY AND THE MAN SHE LOVES IN THIS ADVENTURE OF THE PILOTLESS PLANE, YOU WILL AGREE WITH MILLIONS OF HER ADMIRERS THAT SHE IS INDEED A WONDER WOMAN!
HARRY G. PETER
RETURNING UNEXPECTEDLY TO THE OFFICE AFTER HOURS, STEVE SURPRISES DIANA IN WONDER WOMAN'S COSTUME!
HORNSWOGGLING HOPTOADS! WHERE'D YOU GET THAT COSTUME, DIANA?
OH — ER —
1

Sensation Comics #24 (Dec. 1943) - script: William Moulton Marston - art: H.G. Peter

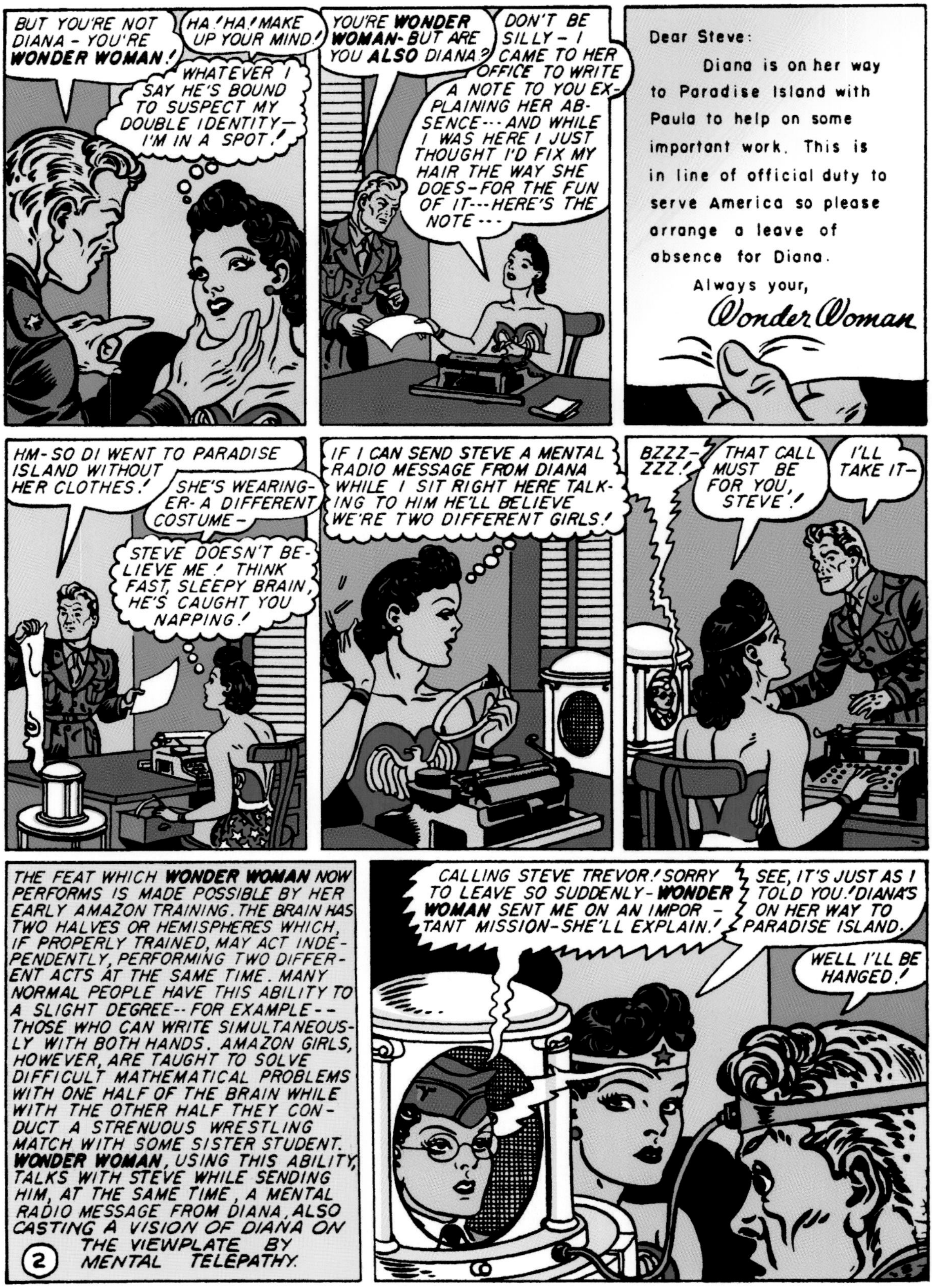

BUT YOU'RE NOT DIANA - YOU'RE **WONDER WOMAN**!
HA! HA! MAKE UP YOUR MIND!
WHATEVER I SAY HE'S BOUND TO SUSPECT MY DOUBLE IDENTITY— I'M IN A SPOT!
YOU'RE **WONDER WOMAN**- BUT ARE YOU **ALSO** DIANA?
DON'T BE SILLY - I CAME TO HER OFFICE TO WRITE A NOTE TO YOU EXPLAINING HER ABSENCE--- AND WHILE I WAS HERE I JUST THOUGHT I'D FIX MY HAIR THE WAY SHE DOES - FOR THE FUN OF IT---HERE'S THE NOTE---
Dear Steve:
Diana is on her way to Paradise Island with Paula to help on some important work. This is in line of official duty to serve America so please arrange a leave of absence for Diana.
Always your,
Wonder Woman
HM- SO DI WENT TO PARADISE ISLAND WITHOUT HER CLOTHES!
SHE'S WEARING-ER- A DIFFERENT COSTUME-
STEVE DOESN'T BELIEVE ME! THINK FAST, SLEEPY BRAIN, HE'S CAUGHT YOU NAPPING!
IF I CAN SEND STEVE A MENTAL RADIO MESSAGE FROM DIANA WHILE I SIT RIGHT HERE TALKING TO HIM HE'LL BELIEVE WE'RE TWO DIFFERENT GIRLS!
BZZZ-ZZZ!
THAT CALL MUST BE FOR YOU, STEVE!
I'LL TAKE IT-
THE FEAT WHICH **WONDER WOMAN** NOW PERFORMS IS MADE POSSIBLE BY HER EARLY AMAZON TRAINING. THE BRAIN HAS TWO HALVES OR HEMISPHERES WHICH, IF PROPERLY TRAINED, MAY ACT INDEPENDENTLY, PERFORMING TWO DIFFERENT ACTS AT THE SAME TIME. MANY NORMAL PEOPLE HAVE THIS ABILITY TO A SLIGHT DEGREE-- FOR EXAMPLE-- THOSE WHO CAN WRITE SIMULTANEOUSLY WITH BOTH HANDS. AMAZON GIRLS, HOWEVER, ARE TAUGHT TO SOLVE DIFFICULT MATHEMATICAL PROBLEMS WITH ONE HALF OF THE BRAIN WHILE WITH THE OTHER HALF THEY CONDUCT A STRENUOUS WRESTLING MATCH WITH SOME SISTER STUDENT. **WONDER WOMAN**, USING THIS ABILITY, TALKS WITH STEVE WHILE SENDING HIM, AT THE SAME TIME, A MENTAL RADIO MESSAGE FROM DIANA, ALSO CASTING A VISION OF DIANA ON THE VIEWPLATE BY MENTAL TELEPATHY.
2
CALLING STEVE TREVOR! SORRY TO LEAVE SO SUDDENLY- **WONDER WOMAN** SENT ME ON AN IMPORTANT MISSION- SHE'LL EXPLAIN!
SEE, IT'S JUST AS I TOLD YOU! DIANA'S ON HER WAY TO PARADISE ISLAND.
WELL I'LL BE HANGED!

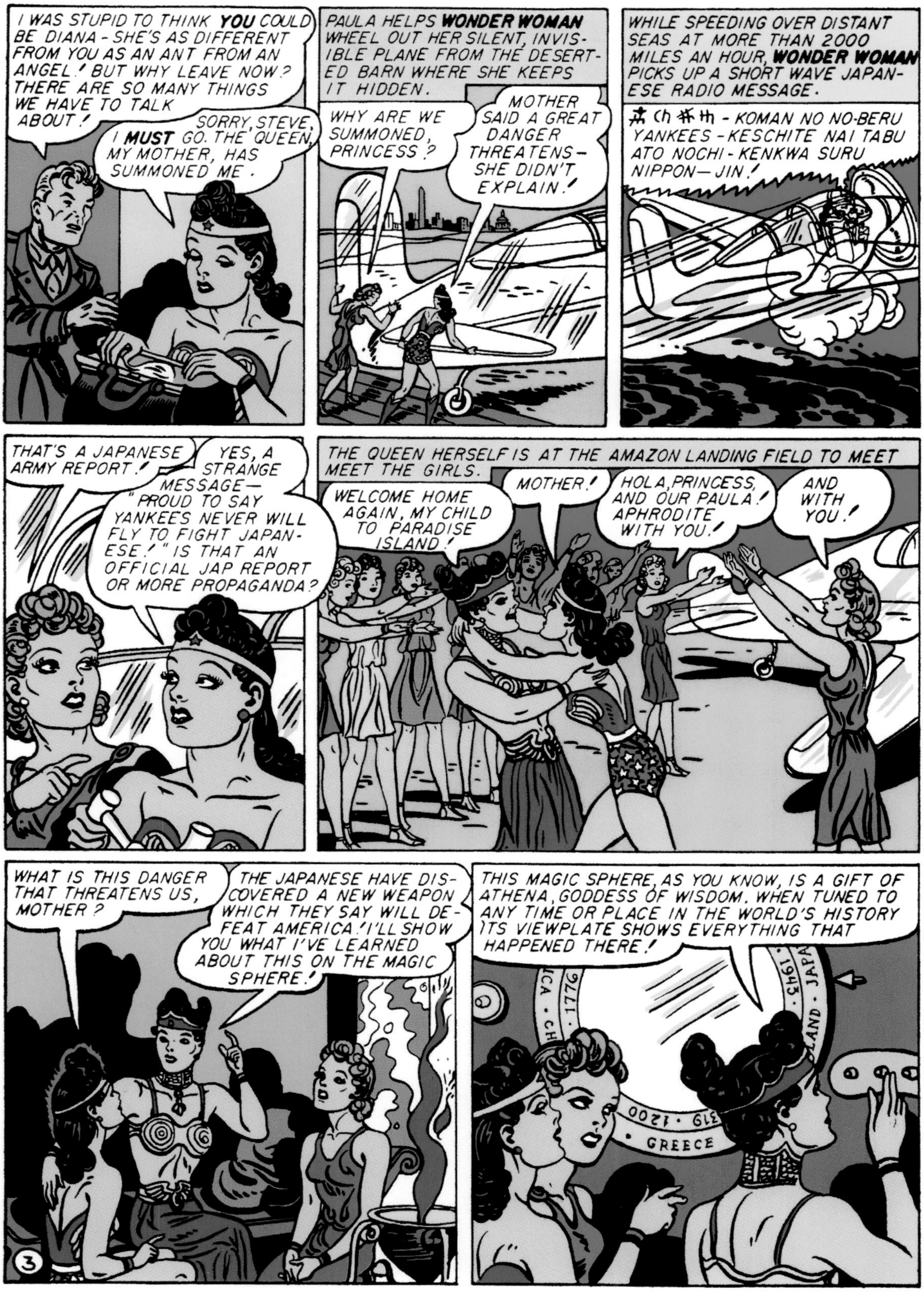
I WAS STUPID TO THINK YOU COULD BE DIANA - SHE'S AS DIFFERENT FROM YOU AS AN ANT FROM AN ANGEL! BUT WHY LEAVE NOW? THERE ARE SO MANY THINGS WE HAVE TO TALK ABOUT!
SORRY, STEVE, I MUST GO. THE QUEEN, MY MOTHER, HAS SUMMONED ME.
PAULA HELPS WONDER WOMAN WHEEL OUT HER SILENT, INVISIBLE PLANE FROM THE DESERTED BARN WHERE SHE KEEPS IT HIDDEN.
WHY ARE WE SUMMONED, PRINCESS?
MOTHER SAID A GREAT DANGER THREATENS - SHE DIDN'T EXPLAIN!
WHILE SPEEDING OVER DISTANT SEAS AT MORE THAN 2000 MILES AN HOUR, WONDER WOMAN PICKS UP A SHORT WAVE JAPANESE RADIO MESSAGE.
- KOMAN NO NO-BERU YANKEES - KESCHITE NAI TABU ATO NOCHI - KENKWA SURU NIPPON—JIN!
THAT'S A JAPANESE ARMY REPORT!
YES, A STRANGE MESSAGE— "PROUD TO SAY YANKEES NEVER WILL FLY TO FIGHT JAPANESE!" IS THAT AN OFFICIAL JAP REPORT OR MORE PROPAGANDA?
THE QUEEN HERSELF IS AT THE AMAZON LANDING FIELD TO MEET MEET THE GIRLS.
WELCOME HOME AGAIN, MY CHILD TO PARADISE ISLAND!
MOTHER!
HOLA, PRINCESS, AND OUR PAULA! APHRODITE WITH YOU!
AND WITH YOU!
WHAT IS THIS DANGER THAT THREATENS US, MOTHER?
THE JAPANESE HAVE DISCOVERED A NEW WEAPON WHICH THEY SAY WILL DEFEAT AMERICA! I'LL SHOW YOU WHAT I'VE LEARNED ABOUT THIS ON THE MAGIC SPHERE!
3
THIS MAGIC SPHERE, AS YOU KNOW, IS A GIFT OF ATHENA, GODDESS OF WISDOM. WHEN TUNED TO ANY TIME OR PLACE IN THE WORLD'S HISTORY ITS VIEWPLATE SHOWS EVERYTHING THAT HAPPENED THERE!
1776
1943
GREECE
1200

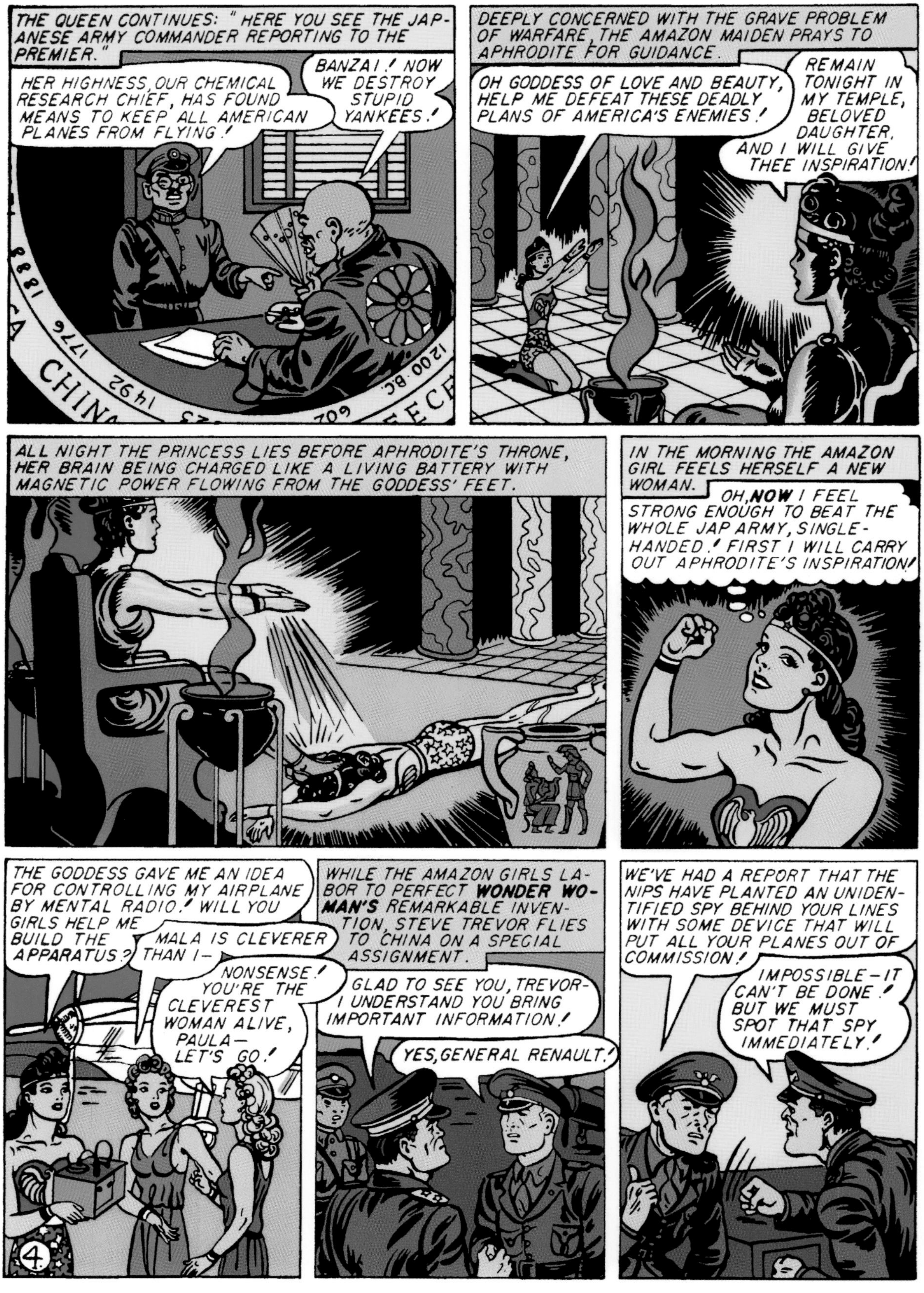

THE QUEEN CONTINUES: " HERE YOU SEE THE JAPANESE ARMY COMMANDER REPORTING TO THE PREMIER."
HER HIGHNESS, OUR CHEMICAL RESEARCH CHIEF, HAS FOUND MEANS TO KEEP ALL AMERICAN PLANES FROM FLYING!
BANZAI! NOW WE DESTROY STUPID YANKEES!
DEEPLY CONCERNED WITH THE GRAVE PROBLEM OF WARFARE, THE AMAZON MAIDEN PRAYS TO APHRODITE FOR GUIDANCE.
OH GODDESS OF LOVE AND BEAUTY, HELP ME DEFEAT THESE DEADLY PLANS OF AMERICA'S ENEMIES!
REMAIN TONIGHT IN MY TEMPLE, BELOVED DAUGHTER, AND I WILL GIVE THEE INSPIRATION!
ALL NIGHT THE PRINCESS LIES BEFORE APHRODITE'S THRONE, HER BRAIN BEING CHARGED LIKE A LIVING BATTERY WITH MAGNETIC POWER FLOWING FROM THE GODDESS' FEET.
IN THE MORNING THE AMAZON GIRL FEELS HERSELF A NEW WOMAN.
OH, NOW I FEEL STRONG ENOUGH TO BEAT THE WHOLE JAP ARMY, SINGLE-HANDED! FIRST I WILL CARRY OUT APHRODITE'S INSPIRATION!
THE GODDESS GAVE ME AN IDEA FOR CONTROLLING MY AIRPLANE BY MENTAL RADIO! WILL YOU GIRLS HELP ME BUILD THE APPARATUS?
MALA IS CLEVERER THAN I—
NONSENSE! YOU'RE THE CLEVEREST WOMAN ALIVE, PAULA— LET'S GO!
4
WHILE THE AMAZON GIRLS LABOR TO PERFECT WONDER WOMAN'S REMARKABLE INVENTION, STEVE TREVOR FLIES TO CHINA ON A SPECIAL ASSIGNMENT.
GLAD TO SEE YOU, TREVOR— I UNDERSTAND YOU BRING IMPORTANT INFORMATION!
YES, GENERAL RENAULT!
WE'VE HAD A REPORT THAT THE NIPS HAVE PLANTED AN UNIDENTIFIED SPY BEHIND YOUR LINES WITH SOME DEVICE THAT WILL PUT ALL YOUR PLANES OUT OF COMMISSION!
IMPOSSIBLE— IT CAN'T BE DONE! BUT WE MUST SPOT THAT SPY IMMEDIATELY!

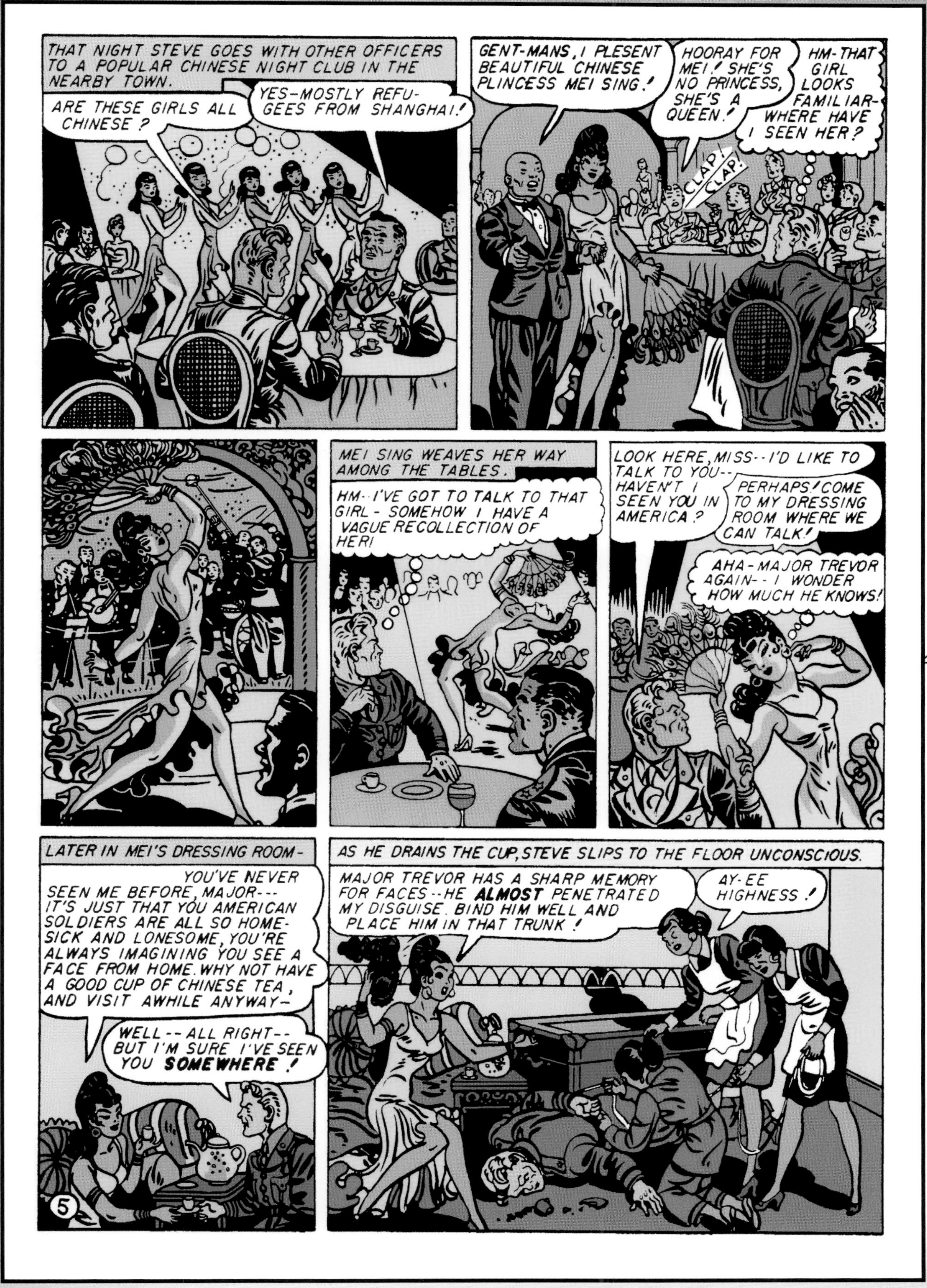
THAT NIGHT STEVE GOES WITH OTHER OFFICERS TO A POPULAR CHINESE NIGHT CLUB IN THE NEARBY TOWN.
ARE THESE GIRLS ALL CHINESE ?
YES—MOSTLY REFUGEES FROM SHANGHAI!
GENT-MANS, I PLESENT BEAUTIFUL CHINESE PLINCESS MEI SING!
HOORAY FOR MEI! SHE'S NO PRINCESS, SHE'S A QUEEN!
HM-THAT GIRL LOOKS FAMILIAR-WHERE HAVE I SEEN HER?
CLAP! CLAP!
MEI SING WEAVES HER WAY AMONG THE TABLES.
HM--I'VE GOT TO TALK TO THAT GIRL - SOMEHOW I HAVE A VAGUE RECOLLECTION OF HER!
LOOK HERE, MISS--I'D LIKE TO TALK TO YOU--HAVEN'T I SEEN YOU IN AMERICA?
PERHAPS! COME TO MY DRESSING ROOM WHERE WE CAN TALK!
AHA-MAJOR TREVOR AGAIN--I WONDER HOW MUCH HE KNOWS!
LATER IN MEI'S DRESSING ROOM-
YOU'VE NEVER SEEN ME BEFORE, MAJOR---IT'S JUST THAT YOU AMERICAN SOLDIERS ARE ALL SO HOMESICK AND LONESOME, YOU'RE ALWAYS IMAGINING YOU SEE A FACE FROM HOME. WHY NOT HAVE A GOOD CUP OF CHINESE TEA, AND VISIT AWHILE ANYWAY-
WELL--ALL RIGHT--BUT I'M SURE I'VE SEEN YOU SOMEWHERE!
5
AS HE DRAINS THE CUP, STEVE SLIPS TO THE FLOOR UNCONSCIOUS.
MAJOR TREVOR HAS A SHARP MEMORY FOR FACES--HE ALMOST PENETRATED MY DISGUISE. BIND HIM WELL AND PLACE HIM IN THAT TRUNK!
AY-EE HIGHNESS!

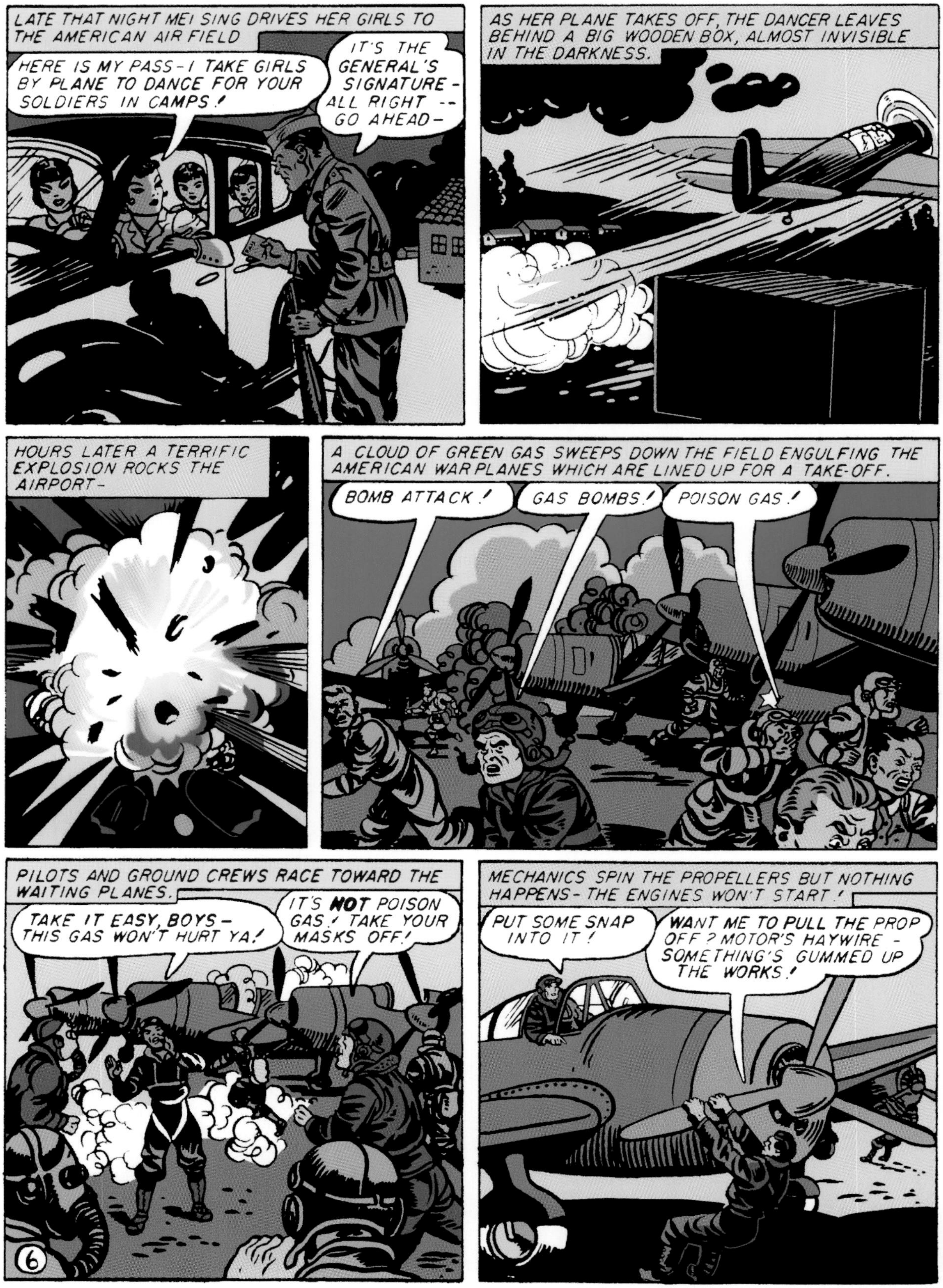
LATE THAT NIGHT MEI SING DRIVES HER GIRLS TO THE AMERICAN AIR FIELD
HERE IS MY PASS - I TAKE GIRLS BY PLANE TO DANCE FOR YOUR SOLDIERS IN CAMPS!
IT'S THE GENERAL'S SIGNATURE - ALL RIGHT -- GO AHEAD -
AS HER PLANE TAKES OFF, THE DANCER LEAVES BEHIND A BIG WOODEN BOX, ALMOST INVISIBLE IN THE DARKNESS.
HOURS LATER A TERRIFIC EXPLOSION ROCKS THE AIRPORT -
A CLOUD OF GREEN GAS SWEEPS DOWN THE FIELD ENGULFING THE AMERICAN WAR PLANES WHICH ARE LINED UP FOR A TAKE-OFF.
BOMB ATTACK!
GAS BOMBS!
POISON GAS!
PILOTS AND GROUND CREWS RACE TOWARD THE WAITING PLANES.
TAKE IT EASY, BOYS - THIS GAS WON'T HURT YA!
IT'S NOT POISON GAS! TAKE YOUR MASKS OFF!
6
MECHANICS SPIN THE PROPELLERS BUT NOTHING HAPPENS - THE ENGINES WON'T START!
PUT SOME SNAP INTO IT!
WANT ME TO PULL THE PROP OFF? MOTOR'S HAYWIRE - SOMETHING'S GUMMED UP THE WORKS!

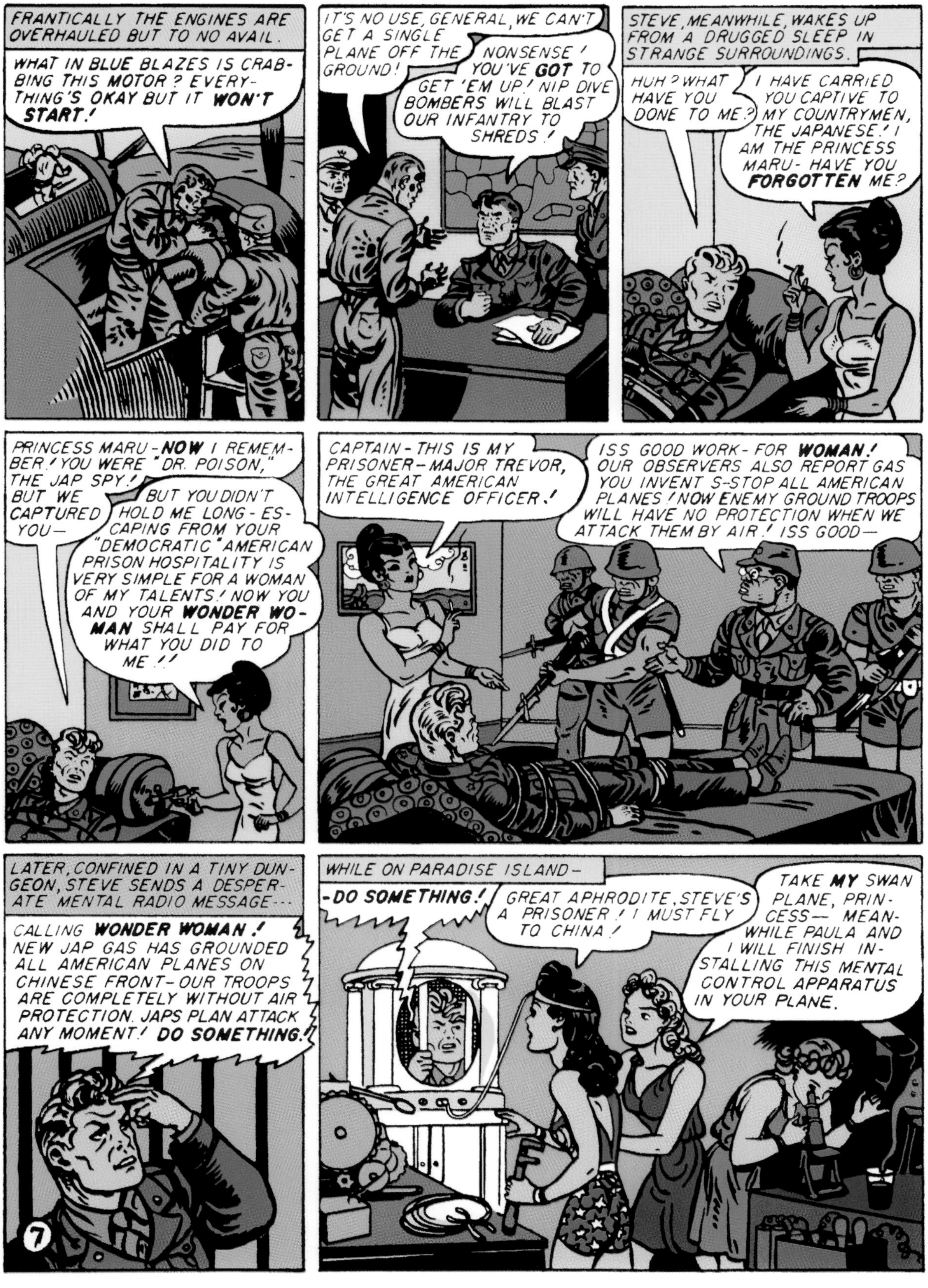
FRANTICALLY THE ENGINES ARE OVERHAULED BUT TO NO AVAIL.
WHAT IN BLUE BLAZES IS CRABBING THIS MOTOR? EVERYTHING'S OKAY BUT IT WON'T START!
IT'S NO USE, GENERAL, WE CAN'T GET A SINGLE PLANE OFF THE GROUND!
NONSENSE! YOU'VE GOT TO GET 'EM UP! NIP DIVE BOMBERS WILL BLAST OUR INFANTRY TO SHREDS!
STEVE, MEANWHILE, WAKES UP FROM A DRUGGED SLEEP IN STRANGE SURROUNDINGS.
HUH? WHAT HAVE YOU DONE TO ME?
I HAVE CARRIED YOU CAPTIVE TO MY COUNTRYMEN, THE JAPANESE! I AM THE PRINCESS MARU- HAVE YOU FORGOTTEN ME?
PRINCESS MARU-NOW I REMEMBER! YOU WERE "DR. POISON," THE JAP SPY! BUT WE CAPTURED YOU—
BUT YOU DIDN'T HOLD ME LONG-ESCAPING FROM YOUR "DEMOCRATIC" AMERICAN PRISON HOSPITALITY IS VERY SIMPLE FOR A WOMAN OF MY TALENTS! NOW YOU AND YOUR WONDER WOMAN SHALL PAY FOR WHAT YOU DID TO ME!!
CAPTAIN-THIS IS MY PRISONER-MAJOR TREVOR, THE GREAT AMERICAN INTELLIGENCE OFFICER!
ISS GOOD WORK-FOR WOMAN! OUR OBSERVERS ALSO REPORT GAS YOU INVENT S-STOP ALL AMERICAN PLANES! NOW ENEMY GROUND TROOPS WILL HAVE NO PROTECTION WHEN WE ATTACK THEM BY AIR! ISS GOOD—
LATER, CONFINED IN A TINY DUNGEON, STEVE SENDS A DESPERATE MENTAL RADIO MESSAGE...
CALLING WONDER WOMAN! NEW JAP GAS HAS GROUNDED ALL AMERICAN PLANES ON CHINESE FRONT-OUR TROOPS ARE COMPLETELY WITHOUT AIR PROTECTION. JAPS PLAN ATTACK ANY MOMENT! DO SOMETHING!
7
WHILE ON PARADISE ISLAND—
-DO SOMETHING!
GREAT APHRODITE, STEVE'S A PRISONER! I MUST FLY TO CHINA!
TAKE MY SWAN PLANE, PRINCESS— MEANWHILE PAULA AND I WILL FINISH INSTALLING THIS MENTAL CONTROL APPARATUS IN YOUR PLANE.

THIS PLANE IS FAST BUT IT'S NOT SILENT OR INVISIBLE LIKE MY OWN — IT'S AN EASY TARGET FOR THE JAPS!

FLYING LOW OVER THE ENEMY LINES TO RECONNOITER, THE SWAN PLANE'S WINGS ARE CLIPPED BY ACK-ACK SHELLS.

OH-OH! NOW I'M A SWOOSE — HALF SWAN BUT MOSTLY GOOSE! LOOKS LIKE MY LAST LANDING!

A JAPANESE ZERO ZOOMS ON TO THE TAIL OF THE HELPLESS, FALLING SWAN PLANE AND CRUELLY POURS BULLETS INTO IT!

HA! ISS ONE YANKEE PILOT WHO WILL NO MORE RESIST THE SONS OF HEAVEN!

BUT TO **WONDER WOMAN** THE NIP MURDERER IS A WELCOME VISITOR.

NICE OF YOU TO COME AROUND, JITSU — I'LL BE SEEING YOU!

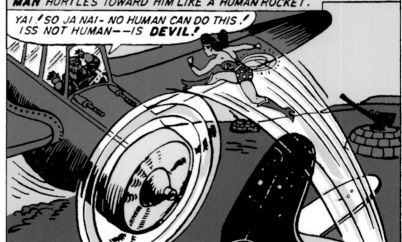

TO THE UTTER CONFUSION OF THE AMAZED JAP, **WONDER WOMAN** HURTLES TOWARD HIM LIKE A HUMAN ROCKET.

YAI! SO JA NAI — NO HUMAN CAN DO THIS! ISS NOT HUMAN — IS **DEVIL!**

THE AMAZON GIRL GIVES NIPPIE A RIDE.

LET'S PLAY I'M AN ORGAN GRINDER AND YOU'RE MY MONKEY — IF YOUR FRIENDS THROW ANY LEAD AT US, **YOU** COLLECT THEIR DONATIONS!

⑧

LANDING IN FRONT OF JAPANESE HEADQUARTERS, **WONDER WOMAN** REPELS BOARDERS.

YOUR WELCOME IS **TOO** WARM, MY FRIENDS! RELAX!

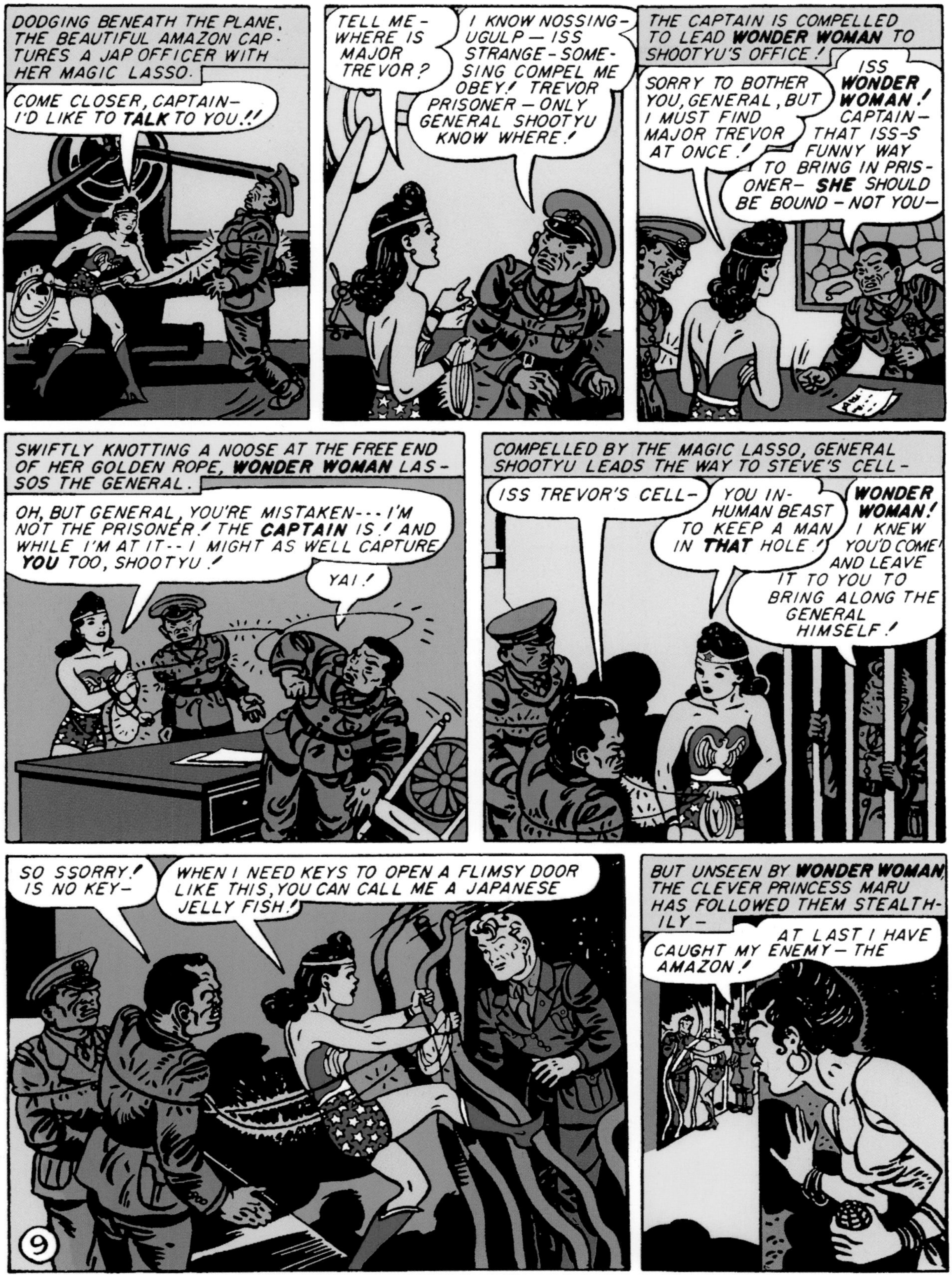
DODGING BENEATH THE PLANE, THE BEAUTIFUL AMAZON CAPTURES A JAP OFFICER WITH HER MAGIC LASSO.
COME CLOSER, CAPTAIN— I'D LIKE TO TALK TO YOU!!
TELL ME— WHERE IS MAJOR TREVOR?
I KNOW NOSSING— UGULP—ISS STRANGE-SOMESING COMPEL ME OBEY! TREVOR PRISONER—ONLY GENERAL SHOOTYU KNOW WHERE!
THE CAPTAIN IS COMPELLED TO LEAD WONDER WOMAN TO SHOOTYU'S OFFICE!
SORRY TO BOTHER YOU, GENERAL, BUT I MUST FIND MAJOR TREVOR AT ONCE!
ISS WONDER WOMAN! CAPTAIN— THAT ISS-S FUNNY WAY TO BRING IN PRISONER— SHE SHOULD BE BOUND—NOT YOU—
SWIFTLY KNOTTING A NOOSE AT THE FREE END OF HER GOLDEN ROPE, WONDER WOMAN LASSOS THE GENERAL.
OH, BUT GENERAL, YOU'RE MISTAKEN--- I'M NOT THE PRISONER! THE CAPTAIN IS! AND WHILE I'M AT IT-- I MIGHT AS WELL CAPTURE YOU TOO, SHOOTYU!
YAI!
COMPELLED BY THE MAGIC LASSO, GENERAL SHOOTYU LEADS THE WAY TO STEVE'S CELL—
ISS TREVOR'S CELL—
YOU INHUMAN BEAST TO KEEP A MAN IN THAT HOLE!
WONDER WOMAN! I KNEW YOU'D COME! AND LEAVE IT TO YOU TO BRING ALONG THE GENERAL HIMSELF!
SO SSORRY! IS NO KEY—
WHEN I NEED KEYS TO OPEN A FLIMSY DOOR LIKE THIS, YOU CAN CALL ME A JAPANESE JELLY FISH!
9
BUT UNSEEN BY WONDER WOMAN, THE CLEVER PRINCESS MARU HAS FOLLOWED THEM STEALTHILY—
AT LAST I HAVE CAUGHT MY ENEMY—THE AMAZON!

COVERING HER OWN FACE WITH A GAS MASK, THE JAPANESE CHEMIST HURLS A BOMB.

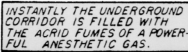

INSTANTLY THE UNDERGROUND CORRIDOR IS FILLED WITH THE ACRID FUMES OF A POWERFUL ANESTHETIC GAS.

BANG!

BOMB-SURPRISED ME-- I BREATHED GAS--

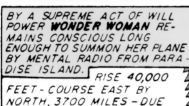

BY A SUPREME ACT OF WILL POWER **WONDER WOMAN** REMAINS CONSCIOUS LONG ENOUGH TO SUMMON HER PLANE BY MENTAL RADIO FROM PARADISE ISLAND.

RISE 40,000 FEET--COURSE EAST BY NORTH, 3700 MILES--DUE EAST 1250--FULL SPEED--

WONDER WOMAN WAKES TO FIND HERSELF AND STEVE PRISONERS.

OUR PLANES HAVE WAIT LONG FOR THE GENERAL'S COMMAND TO DESTROY THE AMERICAN ARMY!

HE IS NOW AWAKE--IT IS SAFE TO MOVE HIM!

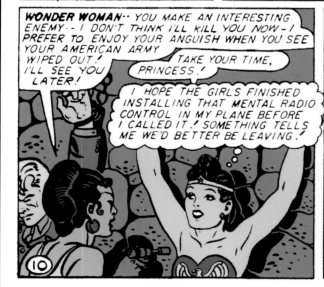

WONDER WOMAN-- YOU MAKE AN INTERESTING ENEMY--I DON'T THINK I'LL KILL YOU NOW--I PREFER TO ENJOY YOUR ANGUISH WHEN YOU SEE YOUR AMERICAN ARMY WIPED OUT! I'LL SEE YOU LATER!

TAKE YOUR TIME, PRINCESS!

I HOPE THE GIRLS FINISHED INSTALLING THAT MENTAL RADIO CONTROL IN MY PLANE BEFORE I CALLED IT! SOMETHING TELLS ME WE'D BETTER BE LEAVING!

⑩

SCARCELY HAS THE JAPANESE LEFT WHEN AN EXPLOSION SOUNDS OVERHEAD--WALLS AND CEILING BEGIN TO FALL--

CRACK! BOOOM!!!

OH-- SO MARU DIDN'T EVEN HAVE THE DECENCY TO ADMIT SHE'D PLANNED TO BLOW THIS PLACE UP AS SOON AS SHE LEFT--WELL--THIS MAY BE A LUCKY BREAK AFTER ALL!

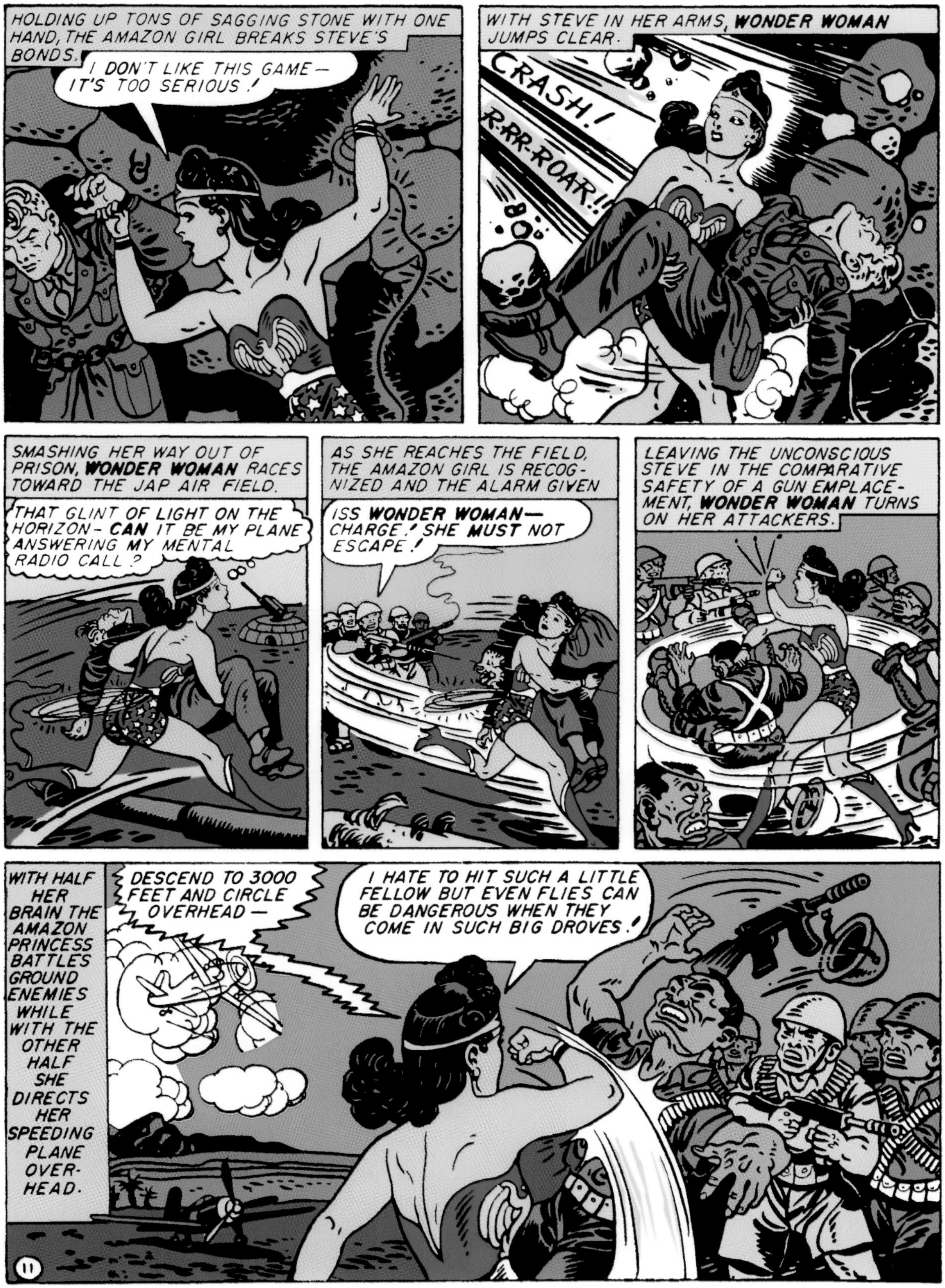
HOLDING UP TONS OF SAGGING STONE WITH ONE HAND, THE AMAZON GIRL BREAKS STEVE'S BONDS.
I DON'T LIKE THIS GAME— IT'S TOO SERIOUS!
WITH STEVE IN HER ARMS, WONDER WOMAN JUMPS CLEAR.
CRASH!
R-RR-ROAR!!
SMASHING HER WAY OUT OF PRISON, WONDER WOMAN RACES TOWARD THE JAP AIR FIELD.
THAT GLINT OF LIGHT ON THE HORIZON- CAN IT BE MY PLANE ANSWERING MY MENTAL RADIO CALL?
AS SHE REACHES THE FIELD, THE AMAZON GIRL IS RECOGNIZED AND THE ALARM GIVEN
ISS WONDER WOMAN— CHARGE! SHE MUST NOT ESCAPE!
LEAVING THE UNCONSCIOUS STEVE IN THE COMPARATIVE SAFETY OF A GUN EMPLACEMENT, WONDER WOMAN TURNS ON HER ATTACKERS.
WITH HALF HER BRAIN THE AMAZON PRINCESS BATTLES GROUND ENEMIES WHILE WITH THE OTHER HALF SHE DIRECTS HER SPEEDING PLANE OVERHEAD.
DESCEND TO 3000 FEET AND CIRCLE OVERHEAD—
I HATE TO HIT SUCH A LITTLE FELLOW BUT EVEN FLIES CAN BE DANGEROUS WHEN THEY COME IN SUCH BIG DROVES!
11

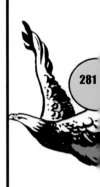

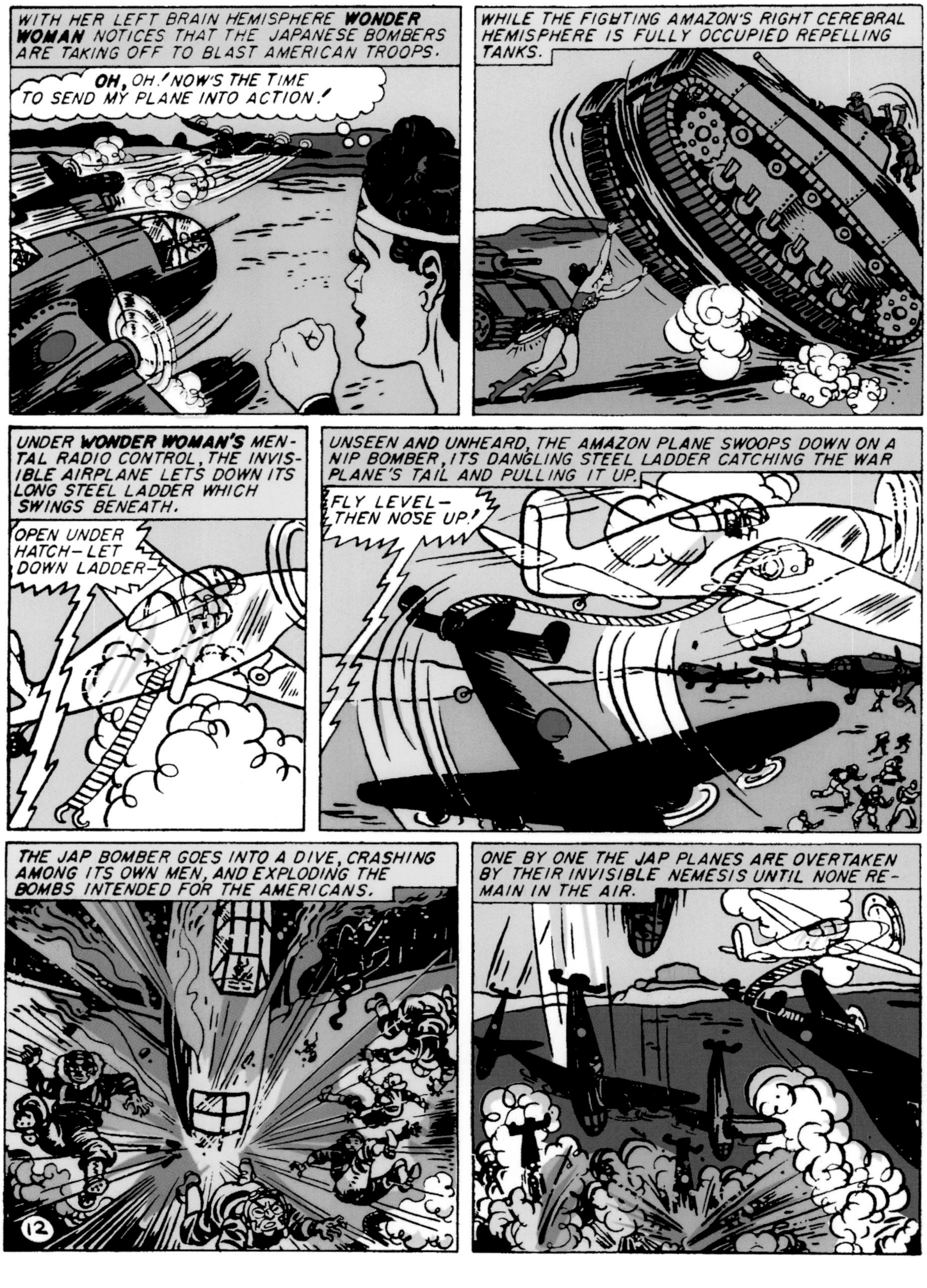
WITH HER LEFT BRAIN HEMISPHERE WONDER WOMAN NOTICES THAT THE JAPANESE BOMBERS ARE TAKING OFF TO BLAST AMERICAN TROOPS.
OH, OH! NOW'S THE TIME TO SEND MY PLANE INTO ACTION!
WHILE THE FIGHTING AMAZON'S RIGHT CEREBRAL HEMISPHERE IS FULLY OCCUPIED REPELLING TANKS.
UNDER WONDER WOMAN'S MENTAL RADIO CONTROL, THE INVISIBLE AIRPLANE LETS DOWN ITS LONG STEEL LADDER WHICH SWINGS BENEATH.
OPEN UNDER HATCH—LET DOWN LADDER—
UNSEEN AND UNHEARD, THE AMAZON PLANE SWOOPS DOWN ON A NIP BOMBER, ITS DANGLING STEEL LADDER CATCHING THE WAR PLANE'S TAIL AND PULLING IT UP.
FLY LEVEL—THEN NOSE UP!
THE JAP BOMBER GOES INTO A DIVE, CRASHING AMONG ITS OWN MEN, AND EXPLODING THE BOMBS INTENDED FOR THE AMERICANS.
12
ONE BY ONE THE JAP PLANES ARE OVERTAKEN BY THEIR INVISIBLE NEMESIS UNTIL NONE REMAIN IN THE AIR.

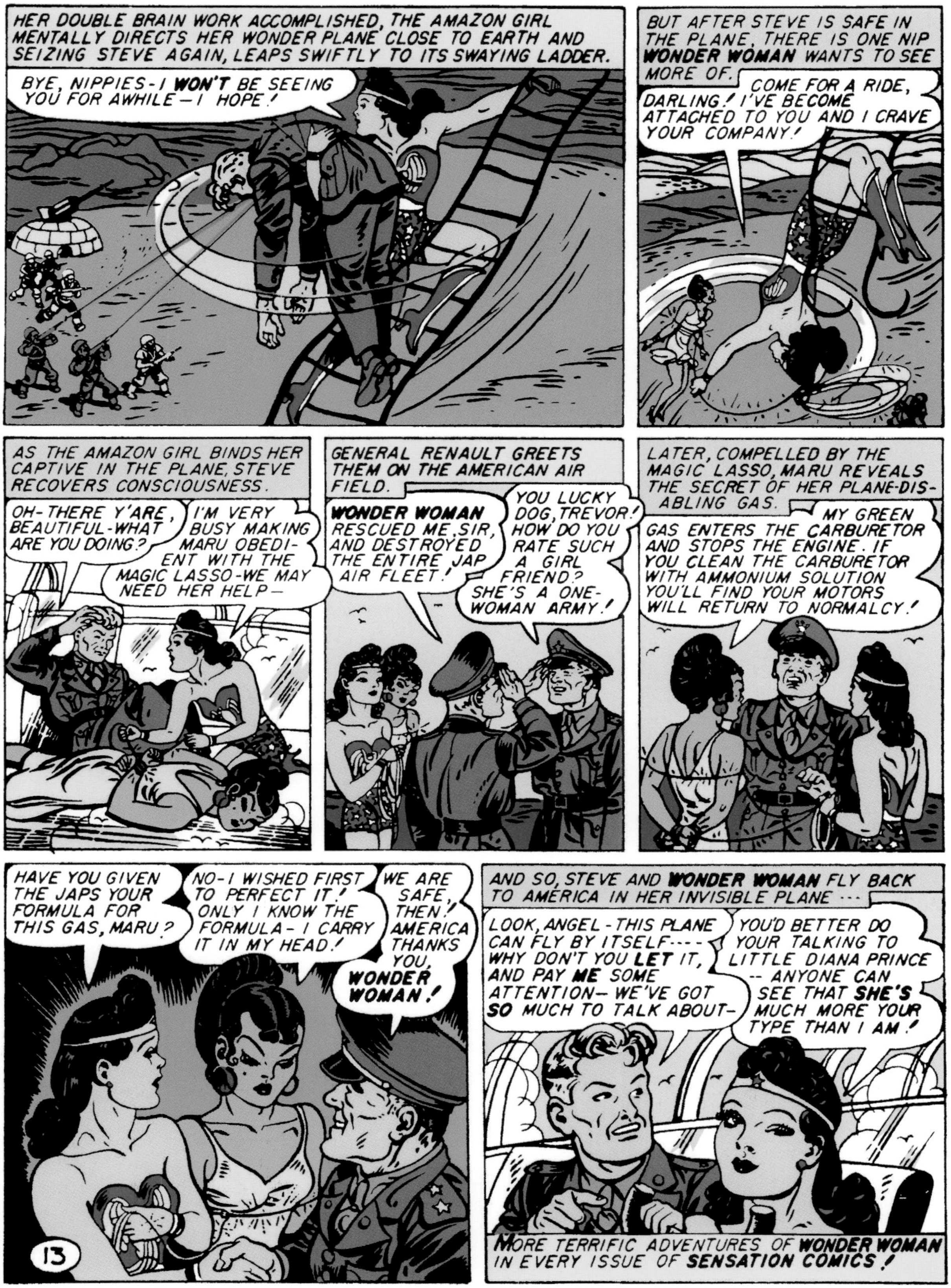
HER DOUBLE BRAIN WORK ACCOMPLISHED, THE AMAZON GIRL MENTALLY DIRECTS HER WONDER PLANE CLOSE TO EARTH AND SEIZING STEVE AGAIN, LEAPS SWIFTLY TO ITS SWAYING LADDER.
BYE, NIPPIES - I WON'T BE SEEING YOU FOR AWHILE — I HOPE!
BUT AFTER STEVE IS SAFE IN THE PLANE, THERE IS ONE NIP WONDER WOMAN WANTS TO SEE MORE OF.
COME FOR A RIDE, DARLING! I'VE BECOME ATTACHED TO YOU AND I CRAVE YOUR COMPANY!
AS THE AMAZON GIRL BINDS HER CAPTIVE IN THE PLANE, STEVE RECOVERS CONSCIOUSNESS.
OH - THERE Y'ARE, BEAUTIFUL - WHAT ARE YOU DOING?
I'M VERY BUSY MAKING MARU OBEDIENT WITH THE MAGIC LASSO - WE MAY NEED HER HELP —
GENERAL RENAULT GREETS THEM ON THE AMERICAN AIR FIELD.
WONDER WOMAN RESCUED ME, SIR, AND DESTROYED THE ENTIRE JAP AIR FLEET!
YOU LUCKY DOG, TREVOR! HOW DO YOU RATE SUCH A GIRL FRIEND? SHE'S A ONE-WOMAN ARMY!
LATER, COMPELLED BY THE MAGIC LASSO, MARU REVEALS THE SECRET OF HER PLANE-DISABLING GAS.
MY GREEN GAS ENTERS THE CARBURETOR AND STOPS THE ENGINE. IF YOU CLEAN THE CARBURETOR WITH AMMONIUM SOLUTION YOU'LL FIND YOUR MOTORS WILL RETURN TO NORMALCY!
HAVE YOU GIVEN THE JAPS YOUR FORMULA FOR THIS GAS, MARU?
NO - I WISHED FIRST TO PERFECT IT! ONLY I KNOW THE FORMULA - I CARRY IT IN MY HEAD!
WE ARE SAFE, THEN! AMERICA THANKS YOU, WONDER WOMAN!
13
AND SO, STEVE AND WONDER WOMAN FLY BACK TO AMERICA IN HER INVISIBLE PLANE ···
LOOK, ANGEL - THIS PLANE CAN FLY BY ITSELF---- WHY DON'T YOU LET IT, AND PAY ME SOME ATTENTION — WE'VE GOT SO MUCH TO TALK ABOUT -
YOU'D BETTER DO YOUR TALKING TO LITTLE DIANA PRINCE -- ANYONE CAN SEE THAT SHE'S MUCH MORE YOUR TYPE THAN I AM!
MORE TERRIFIC ADVENTURES OF WONDER WOMAN IN EVERY ISSUE OF SENSATION COMICS!

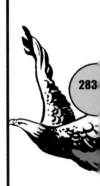

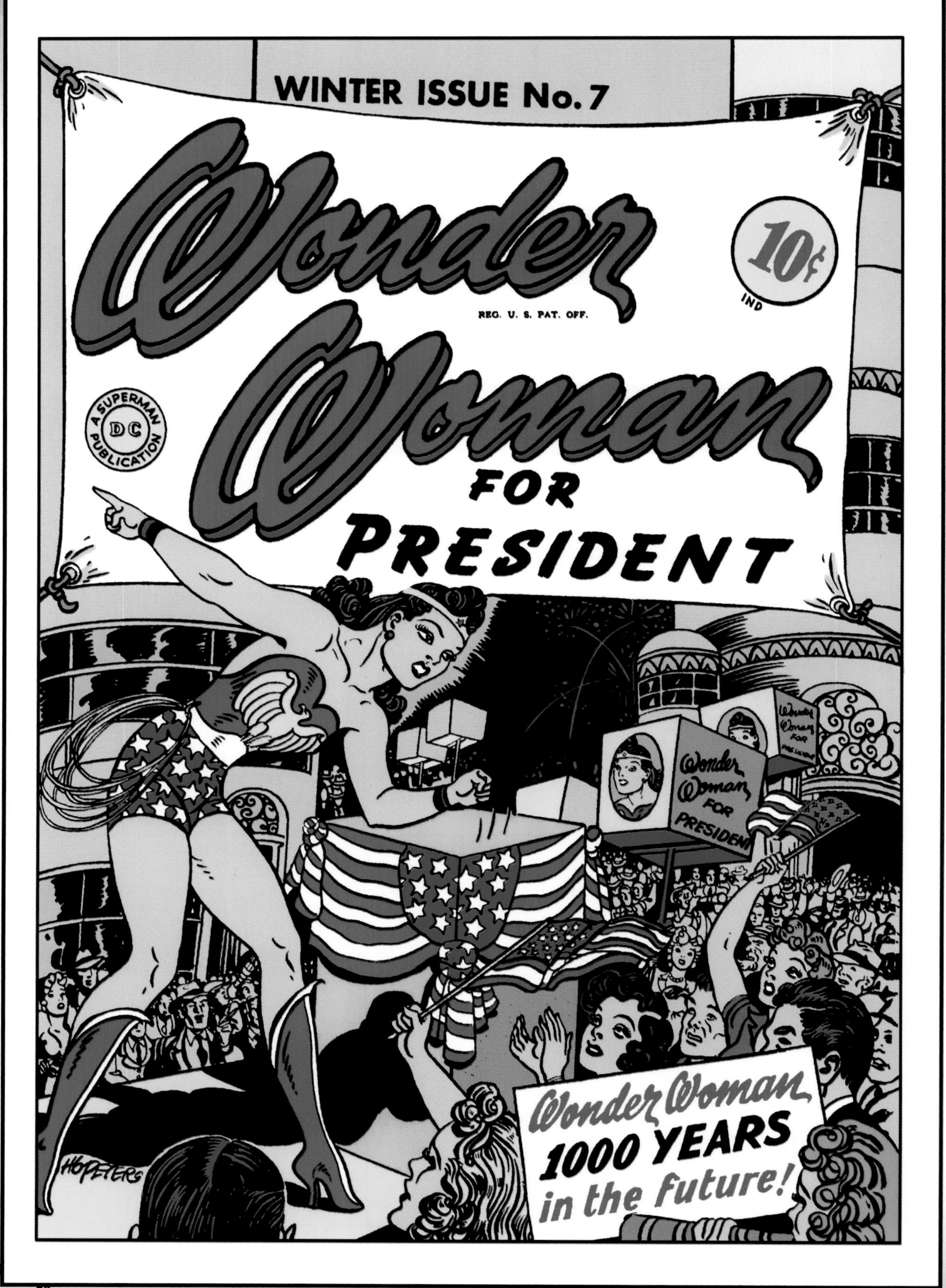
WINTER ISSUE No. 7
Wonder Woman
REG. U. S. PAT. OFF.
10¢
IND
A SUPERMAN DC PUBLICATION
FOR
PRESIDENT
Wonder Woman FOR PRESIDENT
Wonder Woman
1000 YEARS
in the future!
H.G.PETER

Wonder Woman #7 (Winter 1943) - art: H.G. Peter

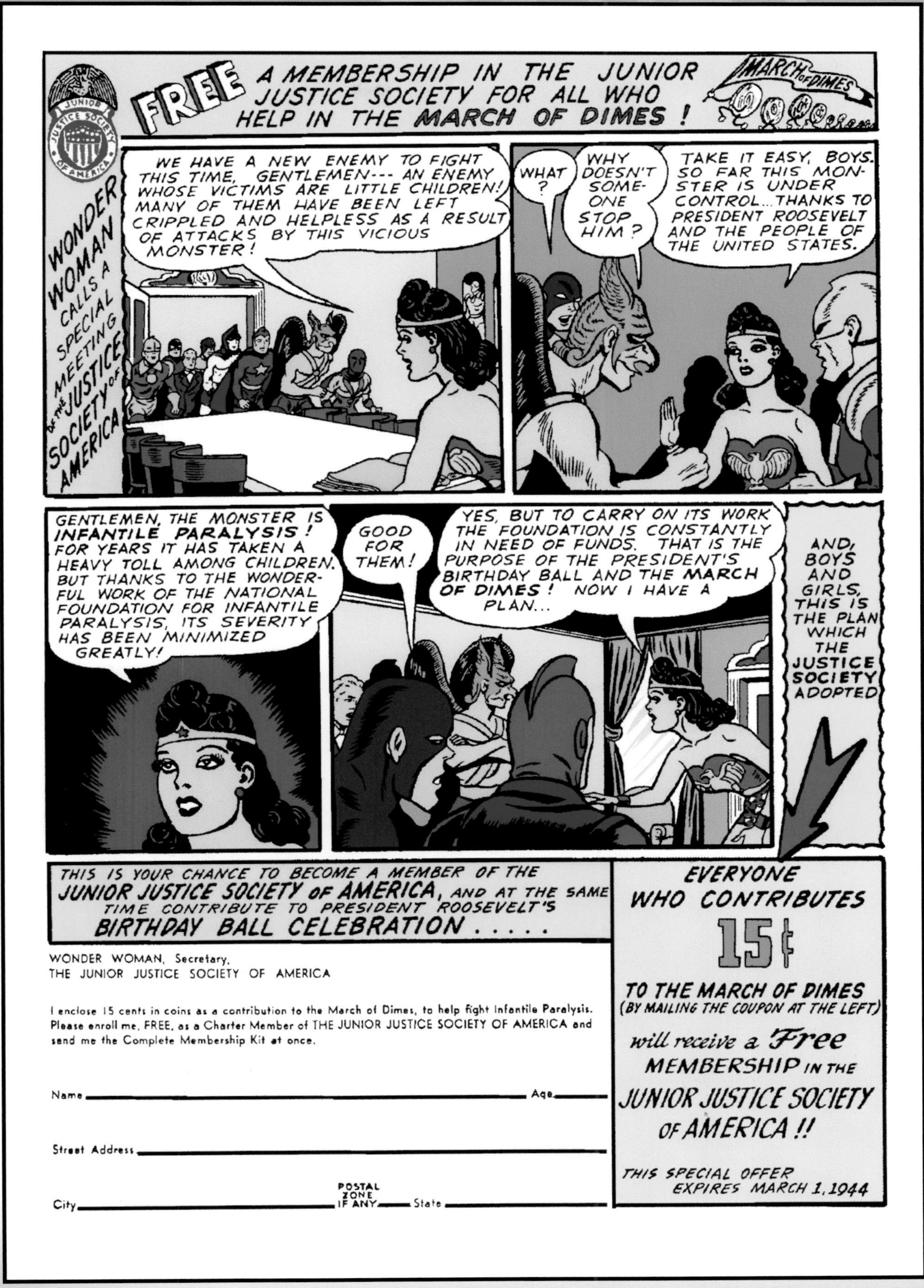
FREE A MEMBERSHIP IN THE JUNIOR JUSTICE SOCIETY FOR ALL WHO HELP IN THE MARCH OF DIMES !
MARCH OF DIMES
JUNIOR JUSTICE SOCIETY OF AMERICA
WONDER WOMAN CALLS A SPECIAL MEETING OF THE JUSTICE SOCIETY OF AMERICA
WE HAVE A NEW ENEMY TO FIGHT THIS TIME, GENTLEMEN--- AN ENEMY WHOSE VICTIMS ARE LITTLE CHILDREN! MANY OF THEM HAVE BEEN LEFT CRIPPLED AND HELPLESS AS A RESULT OF ATTACKS BY THIS VICIOUS MONSTER!
WHAT ?
WHY DOESN'T SOME-ONE STOP HIM ?
TAKE IT EASY, BOYS. SO FAR THIS MON-STER IS UNDER CONTROL... THANKS TO PRESIDENT ROOSEVELT AND THE PEOPLE OF THE UNITED STATES.
GENTLEMEN, THE MONSTER IS INFANTILE PARALYSIS! FOR YEARS IT HAS TAKEN A HEAVY TOLL AMONG CHILDREN. BUT THANKS TO THE WONDER-FUL WORK OF THE NATIONAL FOUNDATION FOR INFANTILE PARALYSIS, ITS SEVERITY HAS BEEN MINIMIZED GREATLY!
GOOD FOR THEM!
YES, BUT TO CARRY ON ITS WORK THE FOUNDATION IS CONSTANTLY IN NEED OF FUNDS. THAT IS THE PURPOSE OF THE PRESIDENT'S BIRTHDAY BALL AND THE MARCH OF DIMES! NOW I HAVE A PLAN...
AND, BOYS AND GIRLS, THIS IS THE PLAN WHICH THE JUSTICE SOCIETY ADOPTED
THIS IS YOUR CHANCE TO BECOME A MEMBER OF THE JUNIOR JUSTICE SOCIETY of AMERICA, AND AT THE SAME TIME CONTRIBUTE TO PRESIDENT ROOSEVELT'S BIRTHDAY BALL CELEBRATION . . . . .
WONDER WOMAN, Secretary,
THE JUNIOR JUSTICE SOCIETY OF AMERICA
I enclose 15 cents in coins as a contribution to the March of Dimes, to help fight Infantile Paralysis. Please enroll me, FREE, as a Charter Member of THE JUNIOR JUSTICE SOCIETY OF AMERICA and send me the Complete Membership Kit at once.
Name ______ Age ______
Street Address ______
City ______ POSTAL ZONE IF ANY ______ State ______
EVERYONE WHO CONTRIBUTES
15¢
TO THE MARCH OF DIMES
(BY MAILING THE COUPON AT THE LEFT)
will receive a Free MEMBERSHIP IN THE JUNIOR JUSTICE SOCIETY OF AMERICA !!
THIS SPECIAL OFFER EXPIRES MARCH 1, 1944

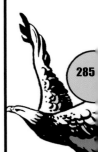

All-Star Comics #20 (Spring 1944) - script: unknown - art: Joe Gallagher & (perhaps) H.G. Peter

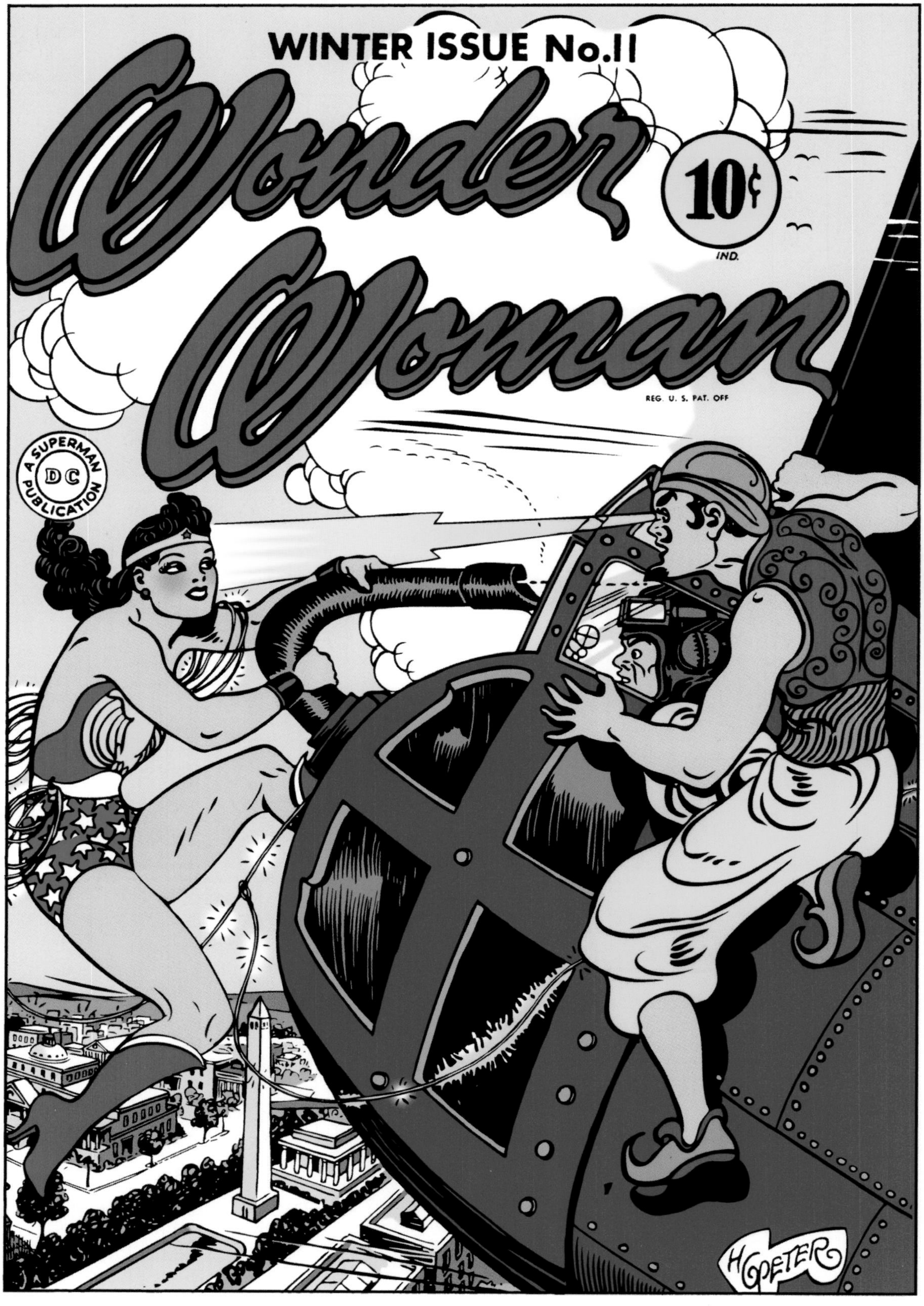
WINTER ISSUE No.11
Wonder Woman
10¢
IND.
REG. U. S. PAT. OFF
A SUPERMAN DC PUBLICATION
H.G. PETER

Wonder Woman #11 (Winter 1944) - art: H.G. Peter

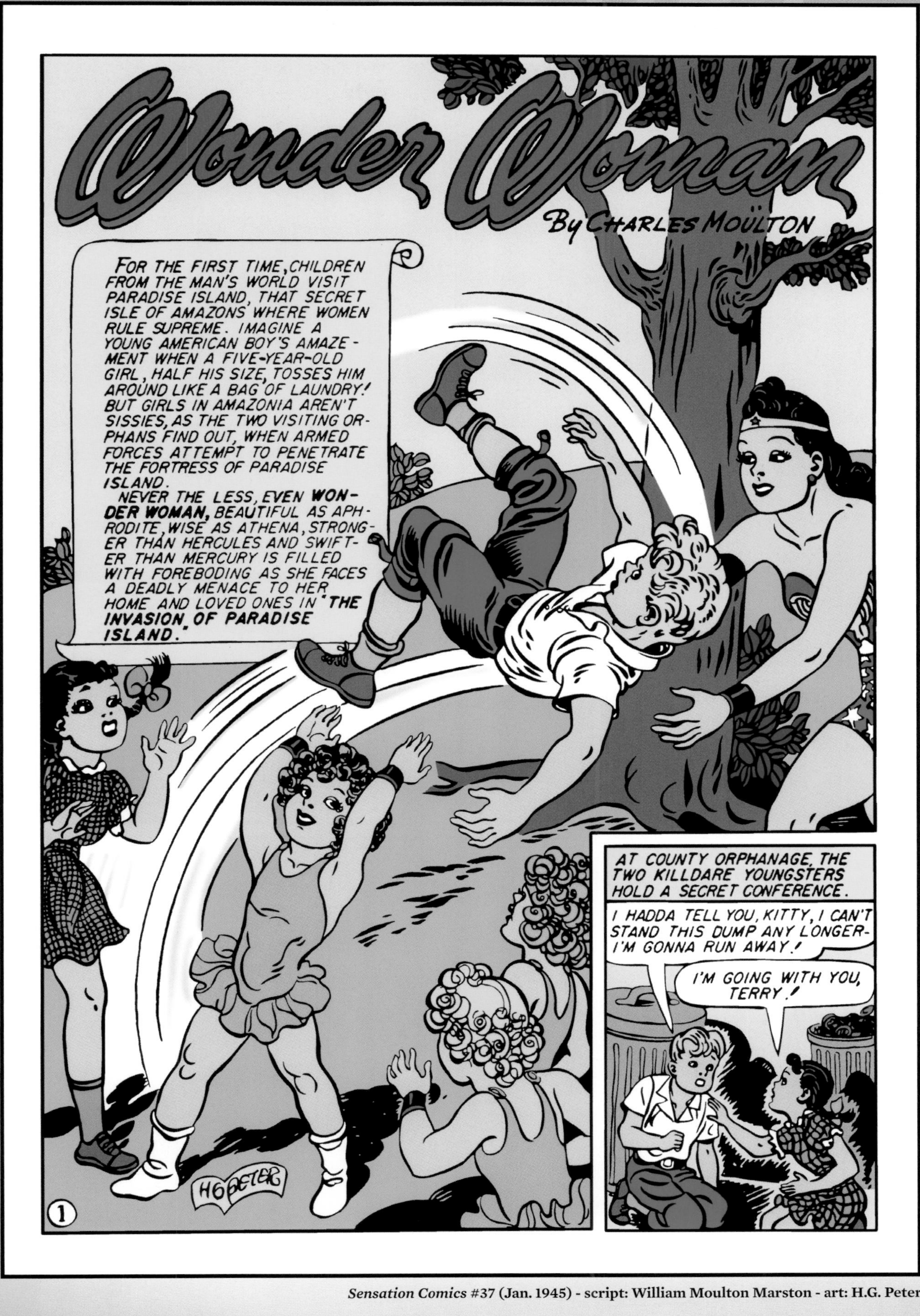
Wonder Woman
By CHARLES MOULTON
FOR THE FIRST TIME, CHILDREN FROM THE MAN'S WORLD VISIT PARADISE ISLAND, THAT SECRET ISLE OF AMAZONS WHERE WOMEN RULE SUPREME. IMAGINE A YOUNG AMERICAN BOY'S AMAZE-MENT WHEN A FIVE-YEAR-OLD GIRL, HALF HIS SIZE, TOSSES HIM AROUND LIKE A BAG OF LAUNDRY! BUT GIRLS IN AMAZONIA AREN'T SISSIES, AS THE TWO VISITING OR-PHANS FIND OUT, WHEN ARMED FORCES ATTEMPT TO PENETRATE THE FORTRESS OF PARADISE ISLAND.
NEVER THE LESS, EVEN WON-DER WOMAN, BEAUTIFUL AS APH-RODITE, WISE AS ATHENA, STRONG-ER THAN HERCULES AND SWIFT-ER THAN MERCURY IS FILLED WITH FOREBODING AS SHE FACES A DEADLY MENACE TO HER HOME AND LOVED ONES IN "THE INVASION OF PARADISE ISLAND."
HG PETER
1
AT COUNTY ORPHANAGE, THE TWO KILLDARE YOUNGSTERS HOLD A SECRET CONFERENCE.
I HADDA TELL YOU, KITTY, I CAN'T STAND THIS DUMP ANY LONGER- I'M GONNA RUN AWAY!
I'M GOING WITH YOU, TERRY!

Sensation Comics #37 (Jan. 1945) - script: William Moulton Marston - art: H.G. Peter

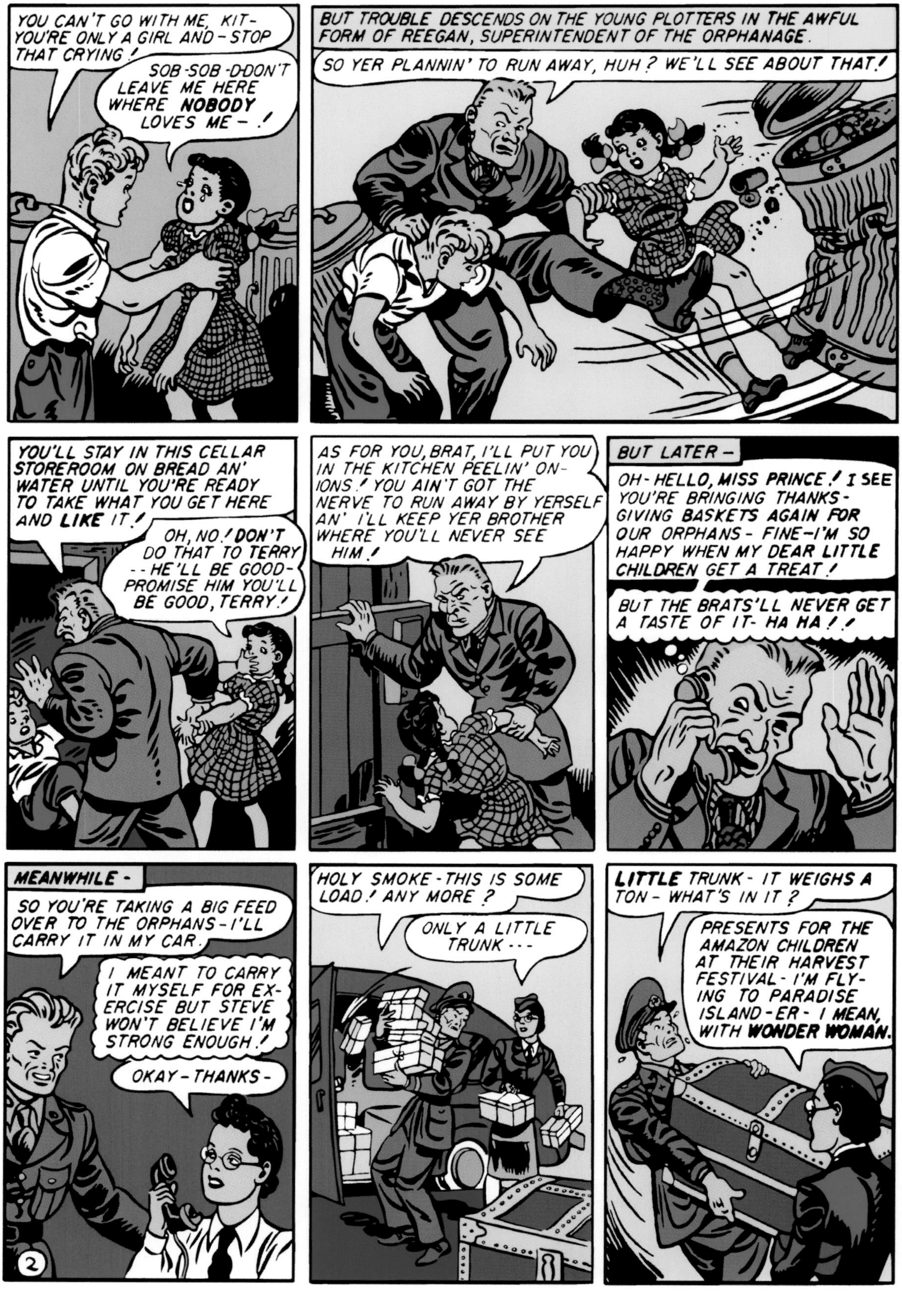
YOU CAN'T GO WITH ME, KIT- YOU'RE ONLY A GIRL AND-STOP THAT CRYING!
SOB-SOB-D-DON'T LEAVE ME HERE WHERE NOBODY LOVES ME-!
BUT TROUBLE DESCENDS ON THE YOUNG PLOTTERS IN THE AWFUL FORM OF REEGAN, SUPERINTENDENT OF THE ORPHANAGE.
SO YER PLANNIN' TO RUN AWAY, HUH? WE'LL SEE ABOUT THAT!
YOU'LL STAY IN THIS CELLAR STOREROOM ON BREAD AN' WATER UNTIL YOU'RE READY TO TAKE WHAT YOU GET HERE AND LIKE IT!
OH, NO! DON'T DO THAT TO TERRY--HE'LL BE GOOD-PROMISE HIM YOU'LL BE GOOD, TERRY!
AS FOR YOU, BRAT, I'LL PUT YOU IN THE KITCHEN PEELIN' ONIONS! YOU AIN'T GOT THE NERVE TO RUN AWAY BY YERSELF AN' I'LL KEEP YER BROTHER WHERE YOU'LL NEVER SEE HIM!
BUT LATER-
OH-HELLO, MISS PRINCE! I SEE YOU'RE BRINGING THANKSGIVING BASKETS AGAIN FOR OUR ORPHANS-FINE-I'M SO HAPPY WHEN MY DEAR LITTLE CHILDREN GET A TREAT!
BUT THE BRATS'LL NEVER GET A TASTE OF IT-HA HA!!
MEANWHILE-
SO YOU'RE TAKING A BIG FEED OVER TO THE ORPHANS-I'LL CARRY IT IN MY CAR.
I MEANT TO CARRY IT MYSELF FOR EXERCISE BUT STEVE WON'T BELIEVE I'M STRONG ENOUGH!
OKAY-THANKS-
2
HOLY SMOKE-THIS IS SOME LOAD! ANY MORE?
ONLY A LITTLE TRUNK---
LITTLE TRUNK-IT WEIGHS A TON-WHAT'S IN IT?
PRESENTS FOR THE AMAZON CHILDREN AT THEIR HARVEST FESTIVAL-I'M FLYING TO PARADISE ISLAND-ER-I MEAN, WITH WONDER WOMAN.

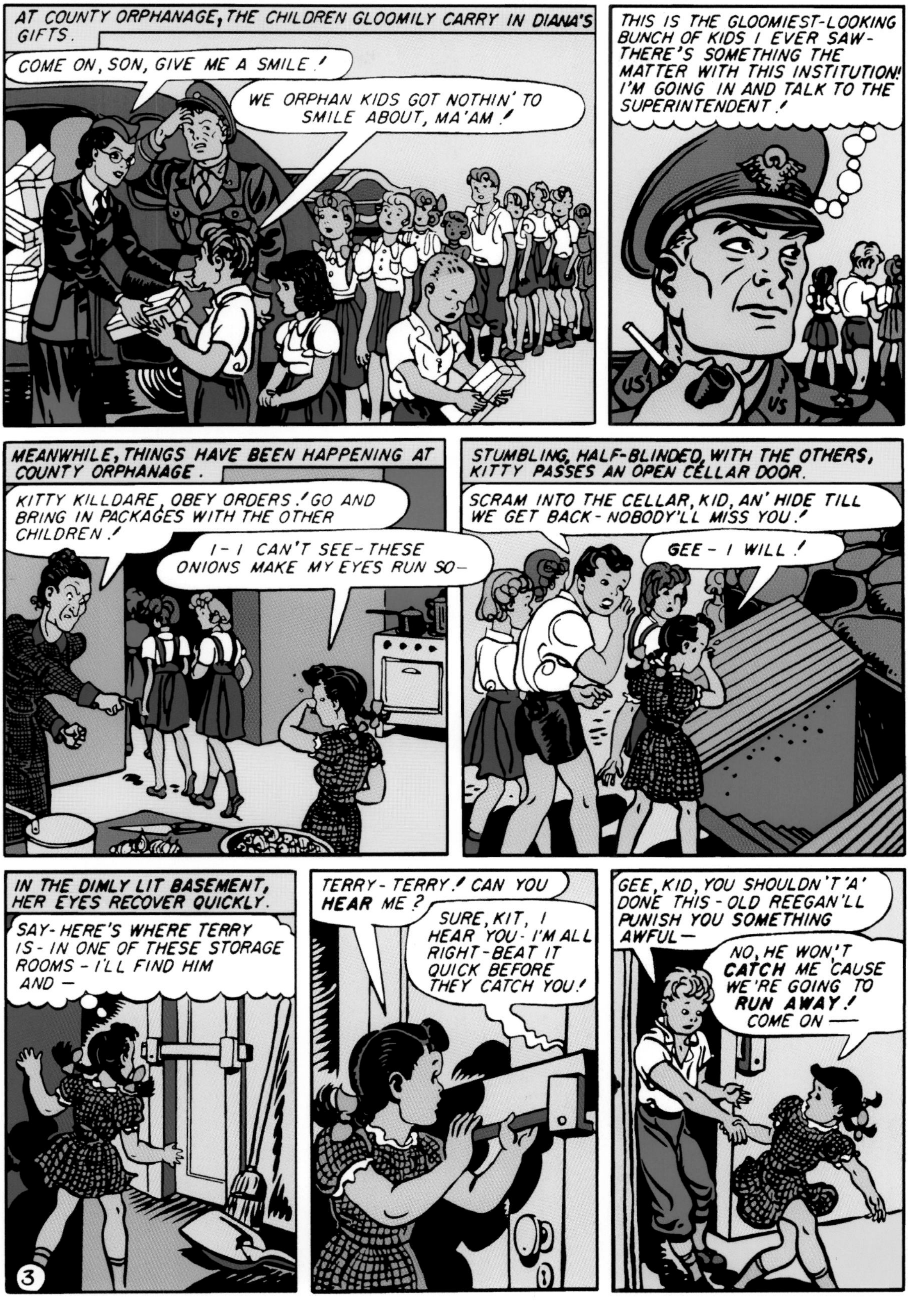
AT COUNTY ORPHANAGE, THE CHILDREN GLOOMILY CARRY IN DIANA'S GIFTS.
COME ON, SON, GIVE ME A SMILE!
WE ORPHAN KIDS GOT NOTHIN' TO SMILE ABOUT, MA'AM!
THIS IS THE GLOOMIEST-LOOKING BUNCH OF KIDS I EVER SAW- THERE'S SOMETHING THE MATTER WITH THIS INSTITUTION! I'M GOING IN AND TALK TO THE SUPERINTENDENT!
MEANWHILE, THINGS HAVE BEEN HAPPENING AT COUNTY ORPHANAGE.
KITTY KILLDARE, OBEY ORDERS! GO AND BRING IN PACKAGES WITH THE OTHER CHILDREN!
I- I CAN'T SEE- THESE ONIONS MAKE MY EYES RUN SO-
STUMBLING, HALF-BLINDED, WITH THE OTHERS, KITTY PASSES AN OPEN CELLAR DOOR.
SCRAM INTO THE CELLAR, KID, AN' HIDE TILL WE GET BACK- NOBODY'LL MISS YOU!
GEE- I WILL!
IN THE DIMLY LIT BASEMENT, HER EYES RECOVER QUICKLY.
SAY- HERE'S WHERE TERRY IS- IN ONE OF THESE STORAGE ROOMS- I'LL FIND HIM AND—
3
TERRY- TERRY! CAN YOU HEAR ME?
SURE, KIT, I HEAR YOU- I'M ALL RIGHT- BEAT IT QUICK BEFORE THEY CATCH YOU!
GEE, KID, YOU SHOULDN'T 'A' DONE THIS- OLD REEGAN'LL PUNISH YOU SOMETHING AWFUL—
NO, HE WON'T CATCH ME 'CAUSE WE'RE GOING TO RUN AWAY! COME ON—

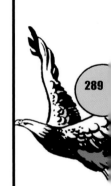

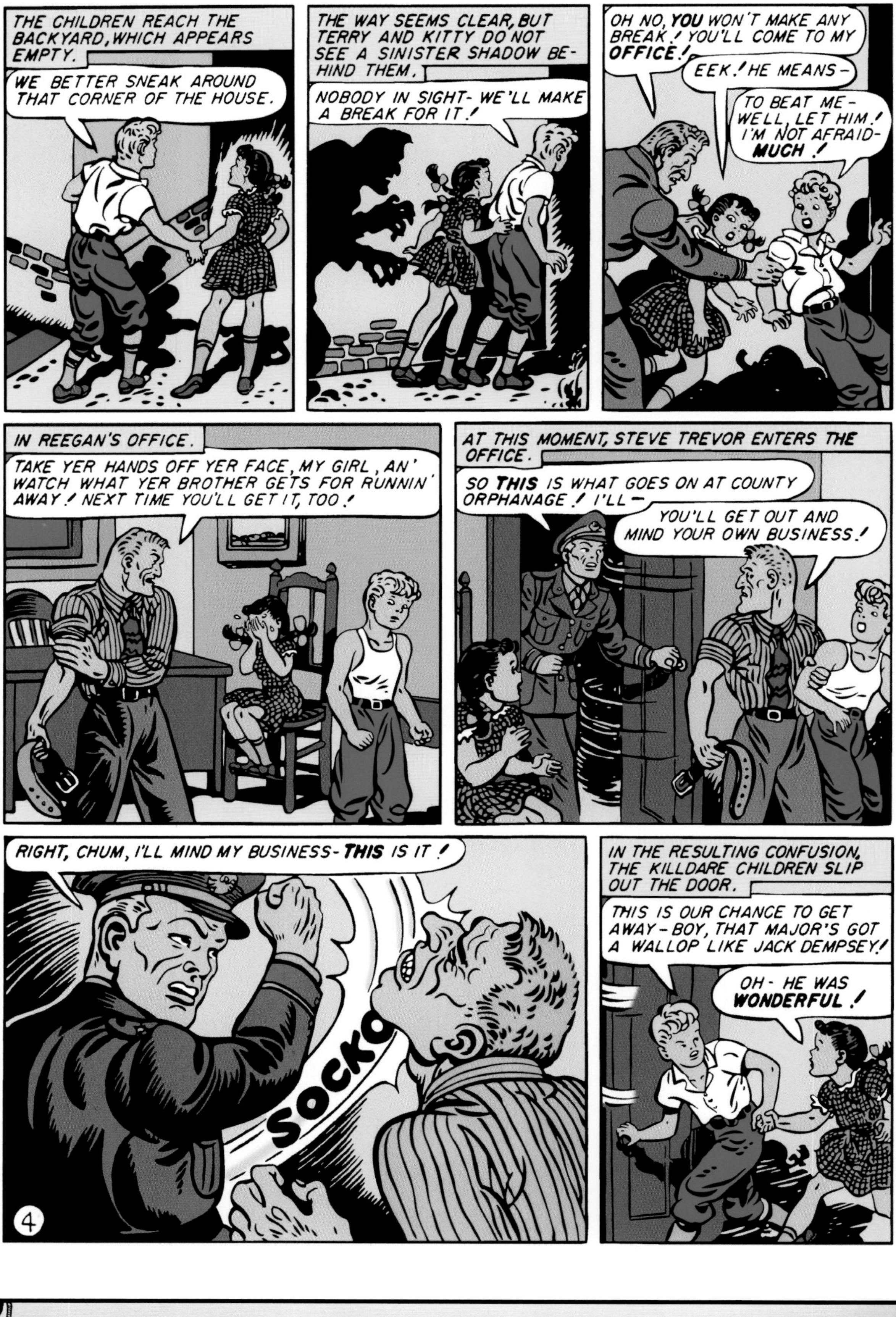
THE CHILDREN REACH THE BACKYARD, WHICH APPEARS EMPTY.
WE BETTER SNEAK AROUND THAT CORNER OF THE HOUSE.
THE WAY SEEMS CLEAR, BUT TERRY AND KITTY DO NOT SEE A SINISTER SHADOW BEHIND THEM.
NOBODY IN SIGHT- WE'LL MAKE A BREAK FOR IT!
OH NO, YOU WON'T MAKE ANY BREAK! YOU'LL COME TO MY OFFICE!
EEK! HE MEANS-
TO BEAT ME- WELL, LET HIM! I'M NOT AFRAID- MUCH!
IN REEGAN'S OFFICE.
TAKE YER HANDS OFF YER FACE, MY GIRL, AN' WATCH WHAT YER BROTHER GETS FOR RUNNIN' AWAY! NEXT TIME YOU'LL GET IT, TOO!
AT THIS MOMENT, STEVE TREVOR ENTERS THE OFFICE.
SO THIS IS WHAT GOES ON AT COUNTY ORPHANAGE! I'LL—
YOU'LL GET OUT AND MIND YOUR OWN BUSINESS!
RIGHT, CHUM, I'LL MIND MY BUSINESS- THIS IS IT!
SOCKO
4
IN THE RESULTING CONFUSION, THE KILLDARE CHILDREN SLIP OUT THE DOOR.
THIS IS OUR CHANCE TO GET AWAY- BOY, THAT MAJOR'S GOT A WALLOP LIKE JACK DEMPSEY!
OH- HE WAS WONDERFUL!

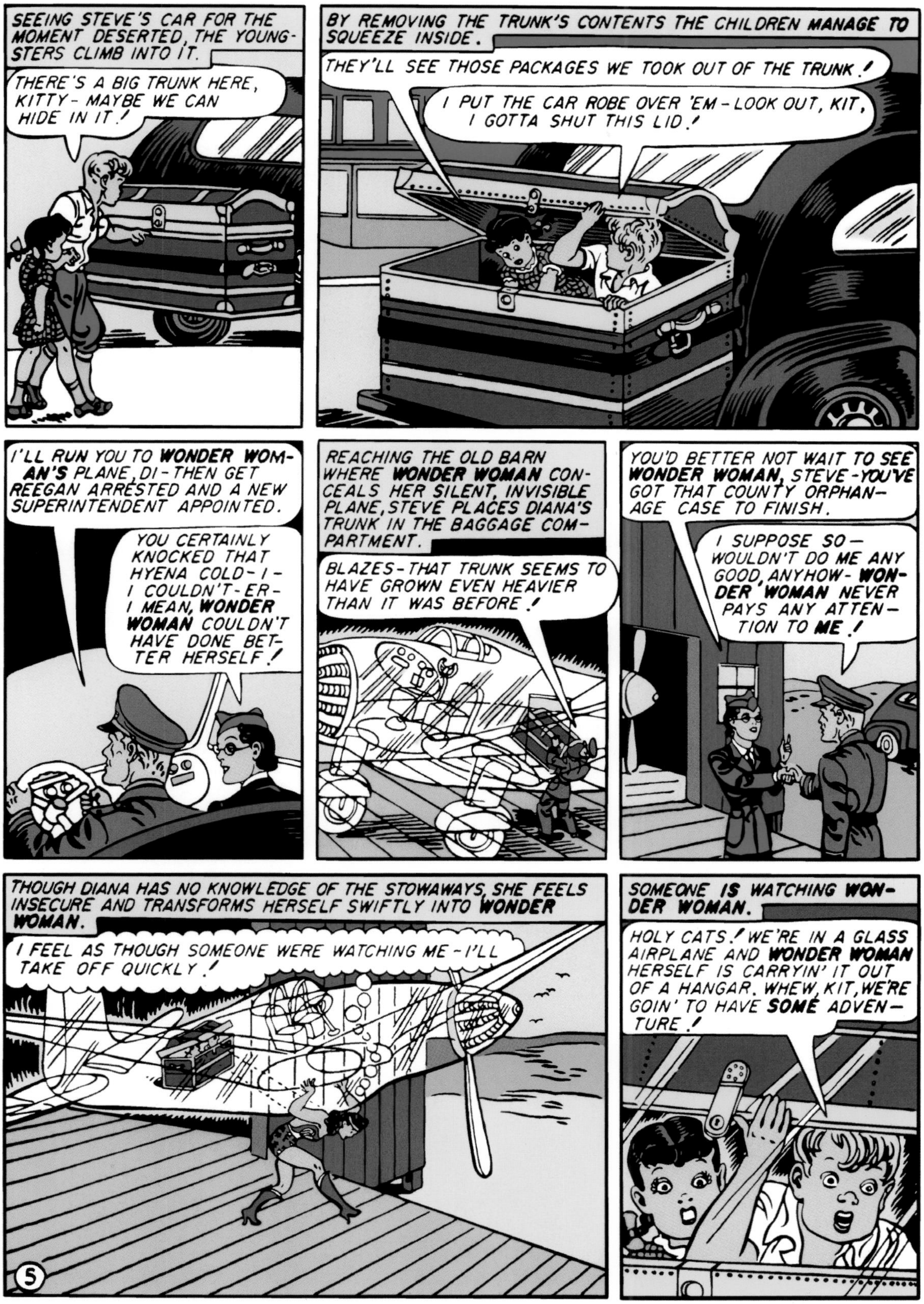
SEEING STEVE'S CAR FOR THE MOMENT DESERTED, THE YOUNGSTERS CLIMB INTO IT.
THERE'S A BIG TRUNK HERE, KITTY - MAYBE WE CAN HIDE IN IT!
BY REMOVING THE TRUNK'S CONTENTS THE CHILDREN MANAGE TO SQUEEZE INSIDE.
THEY'LL SEE THOSE PACKAGES WE TOOK OUT OF THE TRUNK!
I PUT THE CAR ROBE OVER 'EM - LOOK OUT, KIT, I GOTTA SHUT THIS LID!
I'LL RUN YOU TO WONDER WOMAN'S PLANE, DI - THEN GET REEGAN ARRESTED AND A NEW SUPERINTENDENT APPOINTED.
YOU CERTAINLY KNOCKED THAT HYENA COLD - I - I COULDN'T - ER - I MEAN, WONDER WOMAN COULDN'T HAVE DONE BETTER HERSELF!
REACHING THE OLD BARN WHERE WONDER WOMAN CONCEALS HER SILENT, INVISIBLE PLANE, STEVE PLACES DIANA'S TRUNK IN THE BAGGAGE COMPARTMENT.
BLAZES - THAT TRUNK SEEMS TO HAVE GROWN EVEN HEAVIER THAN IT WAS BEFORE!
YOU'D BETTER NOT WAIT TO SEE WONDER WOMAN, STEVE - YOU'VE GOT THAT COUNTY ORPHANAGE CASE TO FINISH.
I SUPPOSE SO - WOULDN'T DO ME ANY GOOD, ANYHOW - WONDER WOMAN NEVER PAYS ANY ATTENTION TO ME!
THOUGH DIANA HAS NO KNOWLEDGE OF THE STOWAWAYS, SHE FEELS INSECURE AND TRANSFORMS HERSELF SWIFTLY INTO WONDER WOMAN.
I FEEL AS THOUGH SOMEONE WERE WATCHING ME - I'LL TAKE OFF QUICKLY!
5
SOMEONE IS WATCHING WONDER WOMAN.
HOLY CATS! WE'RE IN A GLASS AIRPLANE AND WONDER WOMAN HERSELF IS CARRYIN' IT OUT OF A HANGAR. WHEW, KIT, WE'RE GOIN' TO HAVE SOME ADVENTURE!

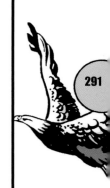

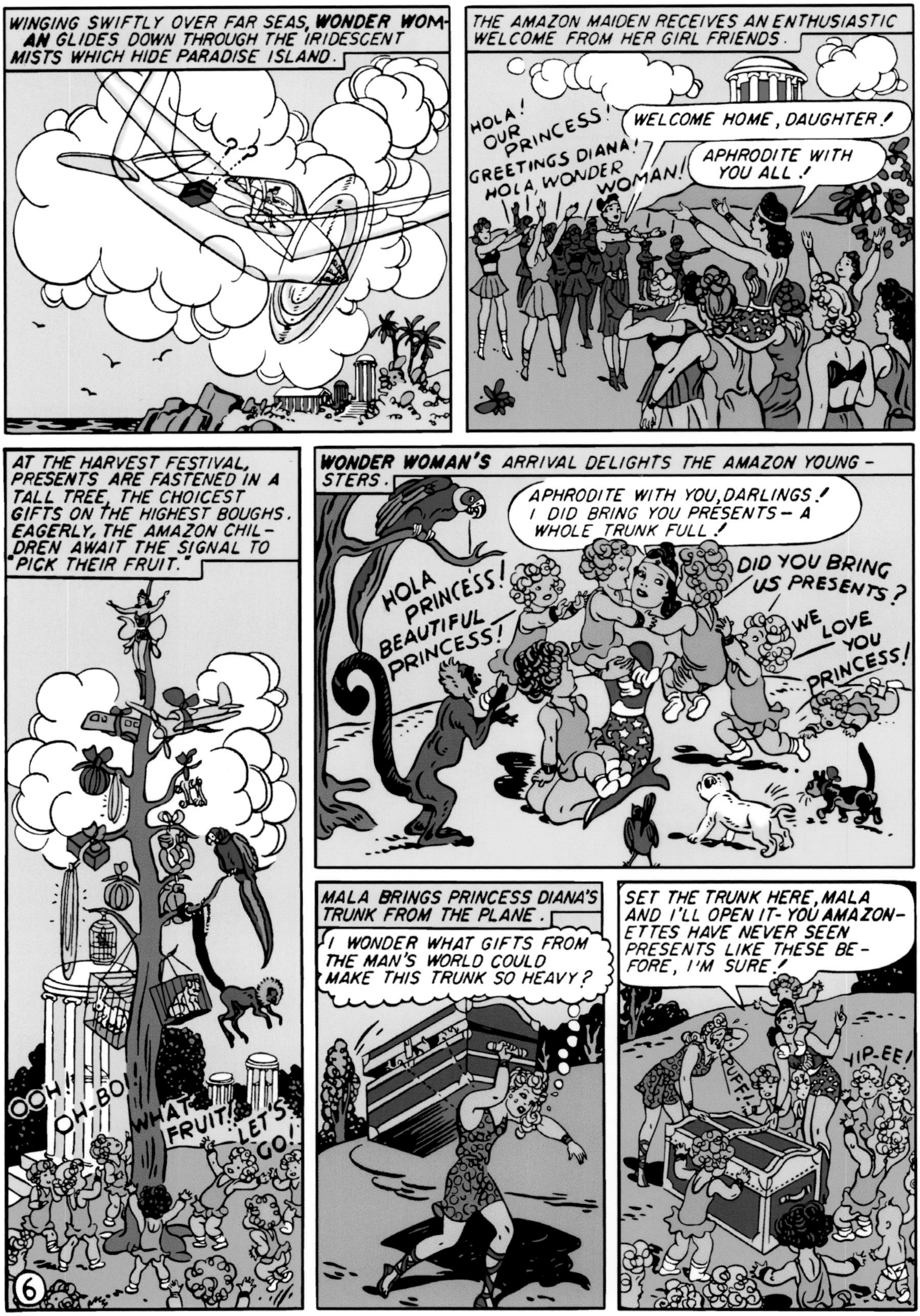

WINGING SWIFTLY OVER FAR SEAS, WONDER WOMAN GLIDES DOWN THROUGH THE IRIDESCENT MISTS WHICH HIDE PARADISE ISLAND.
THE AMAZON MAIDEN RECEIVES AN ENTHUSIASTIC WELCOME FROM HER GIRL FRIENDS.
HOLA! OUR PRINCESS!
GREETINGS DIANA!
HOLA, WONDER WOMAN!
WELCOME HOME, DAUGHTER!
APHRODITE WITH YOU ALL!
AT THE HARVEST FESTIVAL, PRESENTS ARE FASTENED IN A TALL TREE, THE CHOICEST GIFTS ON THE HIGHEST BOUGHS. EAGERLY, THE AMAZON CHILDREN AWAIT THE SIGNAL TO "PICK THEIR FRUIT."
OOH!
OH-BOY!
WHAT FRUIT!
LET'S GO!
6
WONDER WOMAN'S ARRIVAL DELIGHTS THE AMAZON YOUNGSTERS.
APHRODITE WITH YOU, DARLINGS! I DID BRING YOU PRESENTS — A WHOLE TRUNK FULL!
HOLA PRINCESS!
BEAUTIFUL PRINCESS!
DID YOU BRING US PRESENTS?
WE LOVE YOU PRINCESS!
MALA BRINGS PRINCESS DIANA'S TRUNK FROM THE PLANE.
I WONDER WHAT GIFTS FROM THE MAN'S WORLD COULD MAKE THIS TRUNK SO HEAVY?
SET THE TRUNK HERE, MALA AND I'LL OPEN IT- YOU AMAZONETTES HAVE NEVER SEEN PRESENTS LIKE THESE BEFORE, I'M SURE!
PUFF!
YIP-EE!

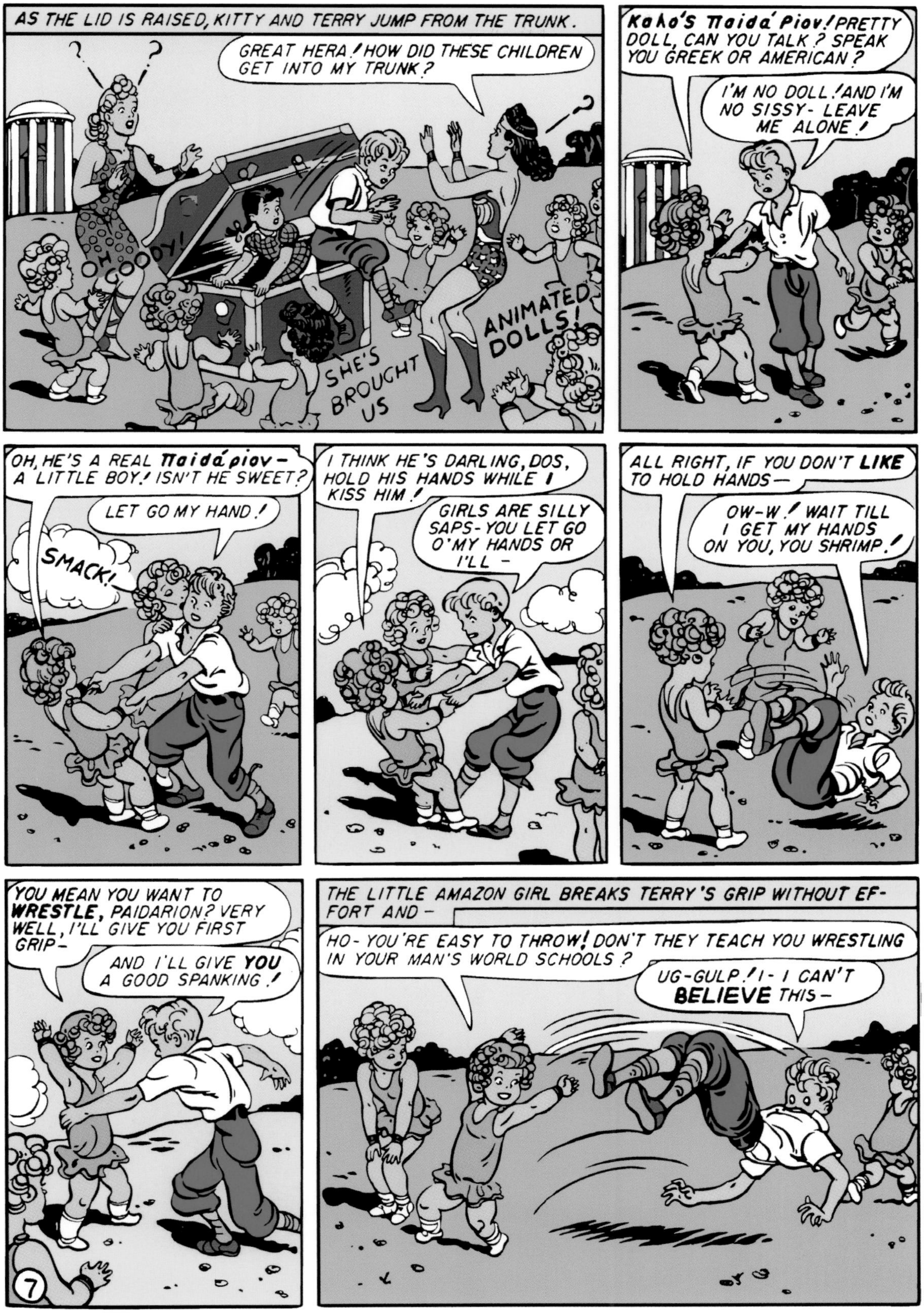
AS THE LID IS RAISED, KITTY AND TERRY JUMP FROM THE TRUNK.
GREAT HERA! HOW DID THESE CHILDREN GET INTO MY TRUNK?
OH GOODY!
SHE'S BROUGHT US
ANIMATED DOLLS!
Καλό'ς Παιδά'ριον! PRETTY DOLL, CAN YOU TALK? SPEAK YOU GREEK OR AMERICAN?
I'M NO DOLL! AND I'M NO SISSY- LEAVE ME ALONE!
OH, HE'S A REAL Παιδάριον – A LITTLE BOY! ISN'T HE SWEET?
LET GO MY HAND!
SMACK!
I THINK HE'S DARLING, DOS, HOLD HIS HANDS WHILE I KISS HIM!
GIRLS ARE SILLY SAPS- YOU LET GO O'MY HANDS OR I'LL –
ALL RIGHT, IF YOU DON'T LIKE TO HOLD HANDS—
OW-W! WAIT TILL I GET MY HANDS ON YOU, YOU SHRIMP!
YOU MEAN YOU WANT TO WRESTLE, PAIDARION? VERY WELL, I'LL GIVE YOU FIRST GRIP–
AND I'LL GIVE YOU A GOOD SPANKING!
7
THE LITTLE AMAZON GIRL BREAKS TERRY'S GRIP WITHOUT EFFORT AND –
HO- YOU'RE EASY TO THROW! DON'T THEY TEACH YOU WRESTLING IN YOUR MAN'S WORLD SCHOOLS?
UG-GULP! I- I CAN'T BELIEVE THIS –

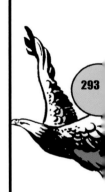

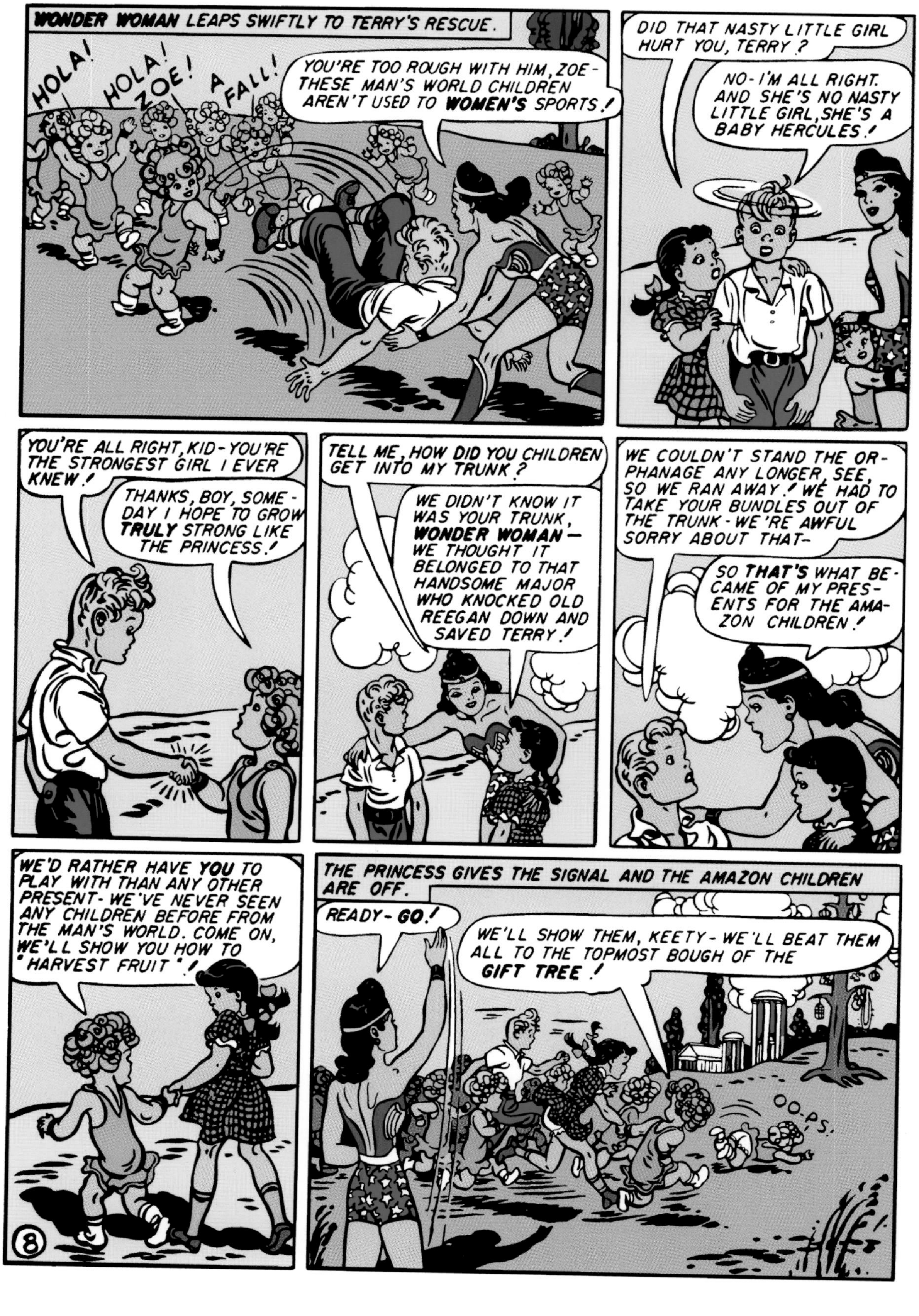
WONDER WOMAN LEAPS SWIFTLY TO TERRY'S RESCUE.
HOLA!
HOLA! ZOE!
A FALL!
YOU'RE TOO ROUGH WITH HIM, ZOE - THESE MAN'S WORLD CHILDREN AREN'T USED TO WOMEN'S SPORTS!
DID THAT NASTY LITTLE GIRL HURT YOU, TERRY?
NO - I'M ALL RIGHT. AND SHE'S NO NASTY LITTLE GIRL, SHE'S A BABY HERCULES!
YOU'RE ALL RIGHT, KID - YOU'RE THE STRONGEST GIRL I EVER KNEW!
THANKS, BOY, SOME-DAY I HOPE TO GROW TRULY STRONG LIKE THE PRINCESS!
TELL ME, HOW DID YOU CHILDREN GET INTO MY TRUNK?
WE DIDN'T KNOW IT WAS YOUR TRUNK, WONDER WOMAN - WE THOUGHT IT BELONGED TO THAT HANDSOME MAJOR WHO KNOCKED OLD REEGAN DOWN AND SAVED TERRY!
WE COULDN'T STAND THE OR-PHANAGE ANY LONGER, SEE, SO WE RAN AWAY! WE HAD TO TAKE YOUR BUNDLES OUT OF THE TRUNK - WE'RE AWFUL SORRY ABOUT THAT-
SO THAT'S WHAT BE-CAME OF MY PRES-ENTS FOR THE AMA-ZON CHILDREN!
WE'D RATHER HAVE YOU TO PLAY WITH THAN ANY OTHER PRESENT - WE'VE NEVER SEEN ANY CHILDREN BEFORE FROM THE MAN'S WORLD. COME ON, WE'LL SHOW YOU HOW TO "HARVEST FRUIT"!
8
THE PRINCESS GIVES THE SIGNAL AND THE AMAZON CHILDREN ARE OFF.
READY - GO!
WE'LL SHOW THEM, KEETY - WE'LL BEAT THEM ALL TO THE TOPMOST BOUGH OF THE GIFT TREE!
OO-PS!

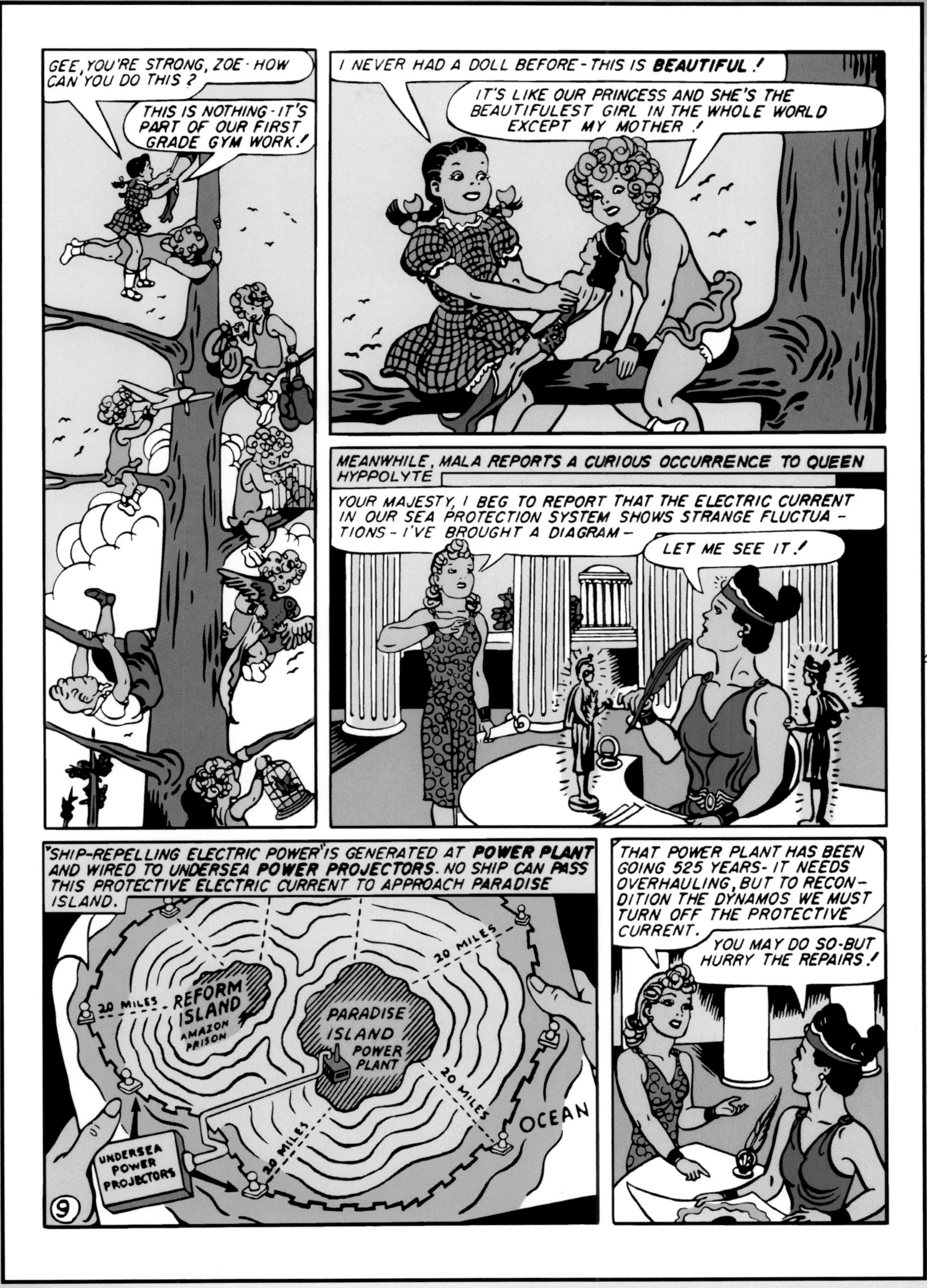
GEE, YOU'RE STRONG, ZOE - HOW CAN YOU DO THIS ?
THIS IS NOTHING - IT'S PART OF OUR FIRST GRADE GYM WORK !
I NEVER HAD A DOLL BEFORE - THIS IS BEAUTIFUL !
IT'S LIKE OUR PRINCESS AND SHE'S THE BEAUTIFULEST GIRL IN THE WHOLE WORLD EXCEPT MY MOTHER !
MEANWHILE, MALA REPORTS A CURIOUS OCCURRENCE TO QUEEN HYPPOLYTE
YOUR MAJESTY, I BEG TO REPORT THAT THE ELECTRIC CURRENT IN OUR SEA PROTECTION SYSTEM SHOWS STRANGE FLUCTUA - TIONS - I'VE BROUGHT A DIAGRAM -
LET ME SEE IT !
"SHIP-REPELLING ELECTRIC POWER" IS GENERATED AT POWER PLANT AND WIRED TO UNDERSEA POWER PROJECTORS. NO SHIP CAN PASS THIS PROTECTIVE ELECTRIC CURRENT TO APPROACH PARADISE ISLAND.
20 MILES
20 MILES
REFORM ISLAND
AMAZON PRISON
PARADISE ISLAND
POWER PLANT
20 MILES
20 MILES
OCEAN
UNDERSEA POWER PROJECTORS
9
THAT POWER PLANT HAS BEEN GOING 525 YEARS - IT NEEDS OVERHAULING, BUT TO RECON - DITION THE DYNAMOS WE MUST TURN OFF THE PROTECTIVE CURRENT.
YOU MAY DO SO - BUT HURRY THE REPAIRS !

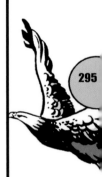

TURNING OFF THE ELECTRIC CURRENT WHICH HAD PROTECTED PARADISE ISLAND FOR 5 CENTURIES CAUSES STARTLING CONSEQUENCES. TO UNDERSTAND THE TERRIBLE MENACE WHICH NOW THREATENS THE AMAZONS, LET US GO BACK 9 MONTHS AND OBSERVE WHAT HAPPENED ON A NAZI SUBMARINE LOST IN AN UNCHARTED OCEAN----

DIS CHARDT IST NO GOOT- VE DUNT KNOW VERE VE ARE !

BUT HERR KOMMANDANT, DER SHIP VILL NOT ANSWER DER HELM- VE ARE GOING IN CIRCLES !

SUDDENLY, EVERY MAN ON BOARD THE U-BOAT DROPS UNCONSCIOUS.

IN CIRCLES !! VAS MONKEY PIZNESS IS DAS -URRRRRR -UMP-

AND SO FOR 9 LONG MONTHS, A GHOST SUBMARINE, MANNED BY UNCONSCIOUS NAZIS IN A STATE OF SUSPENDED ANIMATION, CIRCLES PARADISE ISLAND, PROPELLED BY A FORCE OF THE ELECTRIC CURRENT NOT KNOWN TO THE AMAZONS THEMSELVES.

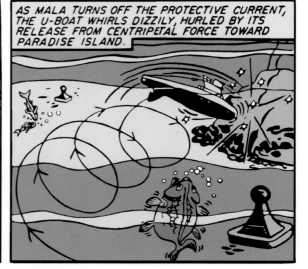

AS MALA TURNS OFF THE PROTECTIVE CURRENT, THE U-BOAT WHIRLS DIZZILY, HURLED BY ITS RELEASE FROM CENTRIPETAL FORCE TOWARD PARADISE ISLAND.

AS THE PIG-BOAT HITS SHORE, THE SHOCK OF GROUNDING ROUSES THE NAZI CREW TO RENEWED LIFE.

DONNERWETTER -NOCH MAL- WEIS NICHT- HEIL HITLER ! VAS IST DAS? VY ARE VE VERE ?

THE NAZI CREW, ARMED WITH RIFLES AND MACHINE GUNS, LAND ON PARADISE ISLAND.

VORWAERTS-HUP ! VE VILL ADVANCE SECRETLY THROUGH DER VOODS UND SURVEY DER ISLAND ! IT MAY BE ENEMY TERRITORY !

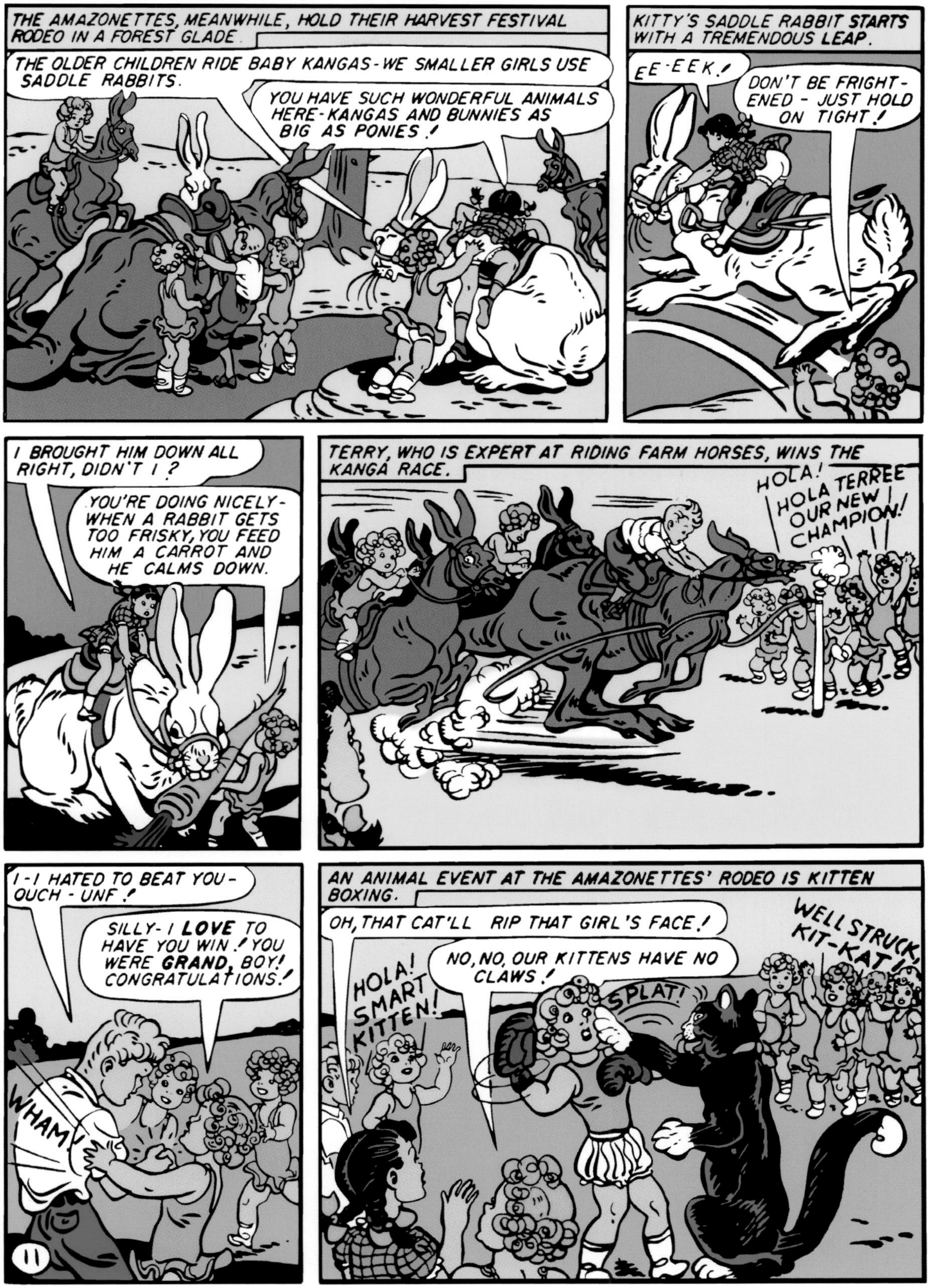
THE AMAZONETTES, MEANWHILE, HOLD THEIR HARVEST FESTIVAL RODEO IN A FOREST GLADE.
THE OLDER CHILDREN RIDE BABY KANGAS - WE SMALLER GIRLS USE SADDLE RABBITS.
YOU HAVE SUCH WONDERFUL ANIMALS HERE - KANGAS AND BUNNIES AS BIG AS PONIES!
KITTY'S SADDLE RABBIT STARTS WITH A TREMENDOUS LEAP.
EE-EEK!
DON'T BE FRIGHT-ENED - JUST HOLD ON TIGHT!
I BROUGHT HIM DOWN ALL RIGHT, DIDN'T I?
YOU'RE DOING NICELY - WHEN A RABBIT GETS TOO FRISKY, YOU FEED HIM A CARROT AND HE CALMS DOWN.
TERRY, WHO IS EXPERT AT RIDING FARM HORSES, WINS THE KANGA RACE.
HOLA! HOLA TERREE OUR NEW CHAMPION!
I-I HATED TO BEAT YOU - OUCH - UNF!
SILLY - I LOVE TO HAVE YOU WIN! YOU WERE GRAND, BOY! CONGRATULATIONS!
WHAM!
11
AN ANIMAL EVENT AT THE AMAZONETTES' RODEO IS KITTEN BOXING.
OH, THAT CAT'LL RIP THAT GIRL'S FACE!
NO, NO, OUR KITTENS HAVE NO CLAWS!
HOLA! SMART KITTEN!
SPLAT!
WELL STRUCK, KIT-KAT!

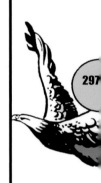

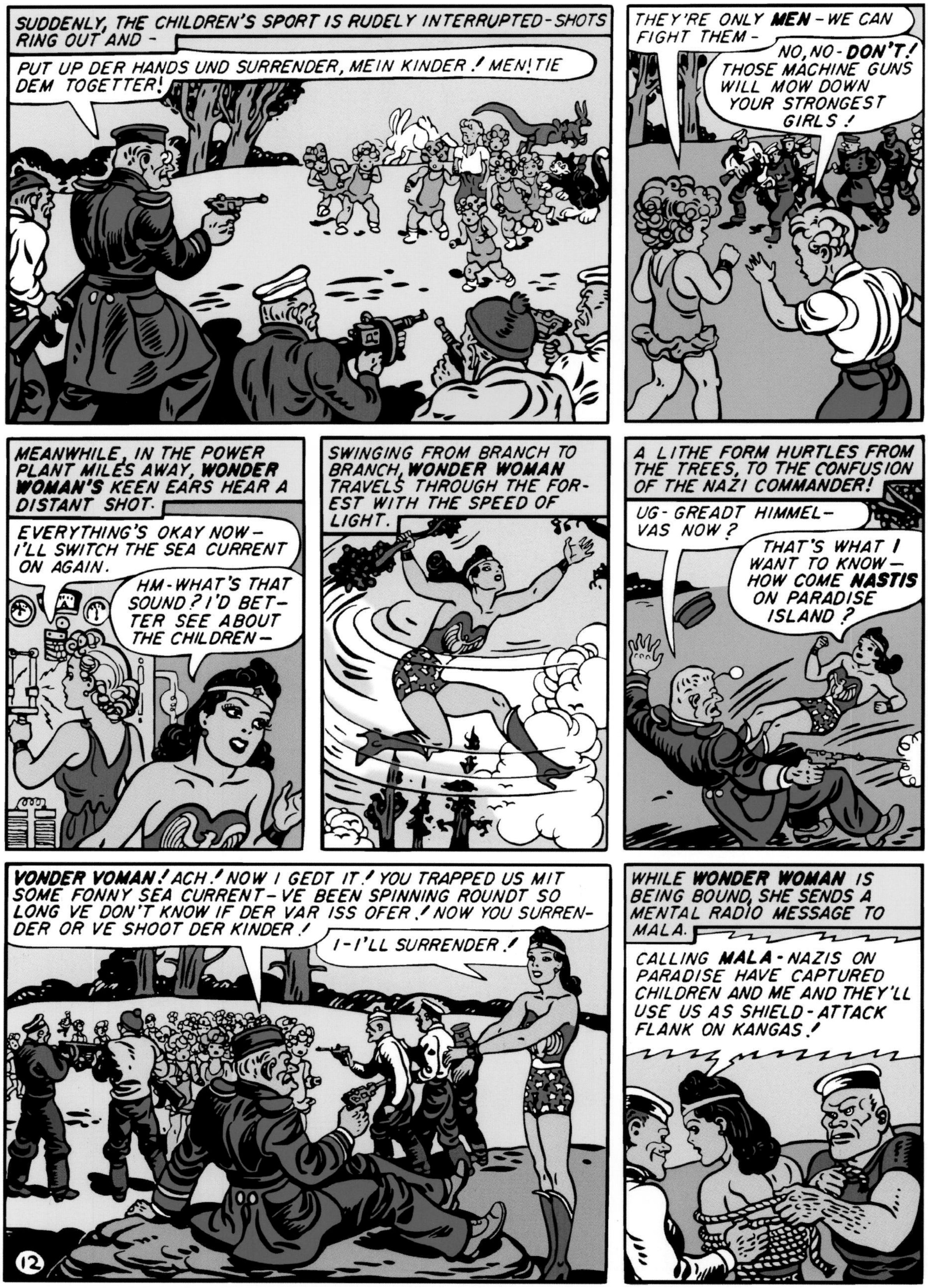
SUDDENLY, THE CHILDREN'S SPORT IS RUDELY INTERRUPTED-SHOTS RING OUT AND -
PUT UP DER HANDS UND SURRENDER, MEIN KINDER! MEN! TIE DEM TOGETTER!
THEY'RE ONLY MEN - WE CAN FIGHT THEM -
NO, NO- DON'T! THOSE MACHINE GUNS WILL MOW DOWN YOUR STRONGEST GIRLS!
MEANWHILE, IN THE POWER PLANT MILES AWAY, WONDER WOMAN'S KEEN EARS HEAR A DISTANT SHOT.
EVERYTHING'S OKAY NOW - I'LL SWITCH THE SEA CURRENT ON AGAIN.
HM-WHAT'S THAT SOUND? I'D BETTER SEE ABOUT THE CHILDREN-
SWINGING FROM BRANCH TO BRANCH, WONDER WOMAN TRAVELS THROUGH THE FOREST WITH THE SPEED OF LIGHT.
A LITHE FORM HURTLES FROM THE TREES, TO THE CONFUSION OF THE NAZI COMMANDER!
UG- GREADT HIMMEL- VAS NOW?
THAT'S WHAT I WANT TO KNOW- HOW COME NASTIS ON PARADISE ISLAND?
VONDER VOMAN! ACH! NOW I GEDT IT! YOU TRAPPED US MIT SOME FONNY SEA CURRENT-VE BEEN SPINNING ROUNDT SO LONG VE DON'T KNOW IF DER VAR ISS OFER! NOW YOU SURRENDER OR VE SHOOT DER KINDER!
I-I'LL SURRENDER!
12
WHILE WONDER WOMAN IS BEING BOUND, SHE SENDS A MENTAL RADIO MESSAGE TO MALA.
CALLING MALA - NAZIS ON PARADISE HAVE CAPTURED CHILDREN AND ME AND THEY'LL USE US AS SHIELD - ATTACK FLANK ON KANGAS!

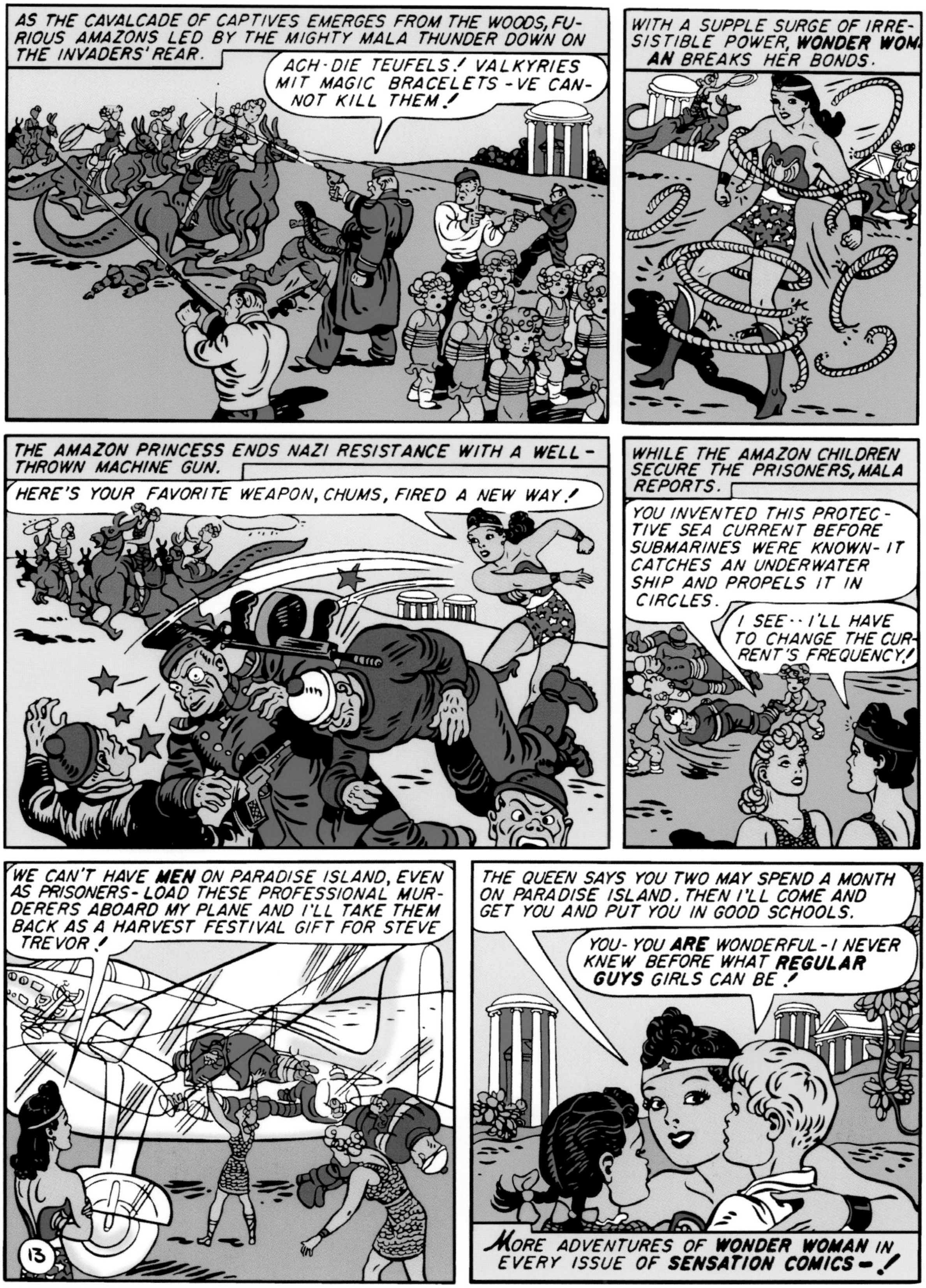

AS THE CAVALCADE OF CAPTIVES EMERGES FROM THE WOODS, FURIOUS AMAZONS LED BY THE MIGHTY MALA THUNDER DOWN ON THE INVADERS' REAR.
ACH-DIE TEUFELS! VALKYRIES MIT MAGIC BRACELETS -VE CANNOT KILL THEM!
WITH A SUPPLE SURGE OF IRRESISTIBLE POWER, WONDER WOMAN BREAKS HER BONDS.
THE AMAZON PRINCESS ENDS NAZI RESISTANCE WITH A WELL-THROWN MACHINE GUN.
HERE'S YOUR FAVORITE WEAPON, CHUMS, FIRED A NEW WAY!
WHILE THE AMAZON CHILDREN SECURE THE PRISONERS, MALA REPORTS.
YOU INVENTED THIS PROTECTIVE SEA CURRENT BEFORE SUBMARINES WERE KNOWN- IT CATCHES AN UNDERWATER SHIP AND PROPELS IT IN CIRCLES.
I SEE-- I'LL HAVE TO CHANGE THE CURRENT'S FREQUENCY!
WE CAN'T HAVE MEN ON PARADISE ISLAND, EVEN AS PRISONERS- LOAD THESE PROFESSIONAL MURDERERS ABOARD MY PLANE AND I'LL TAKE THEM BACK AS A HARVEST FESTIVAL GIFT FOR STEVE TREVOR!
13
THE QUEEN SAYS YOU TWO MAY SPEND A MONTH ON PARADISE ISLAND. THEN I'LL COME AND GET YOU AND PUT YOU IN GOOD SCHOOLS.
YOU- YOU ARE WONDERFUL- I NEVER KNEW BEFORE WHAT REGULAR GUYS GIRLS CAN BE!
MORE ADVENTURES OF WONDER WOMAN IN EVERY ISSUE OF SENSATION COMICS-!

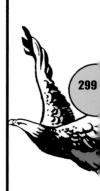

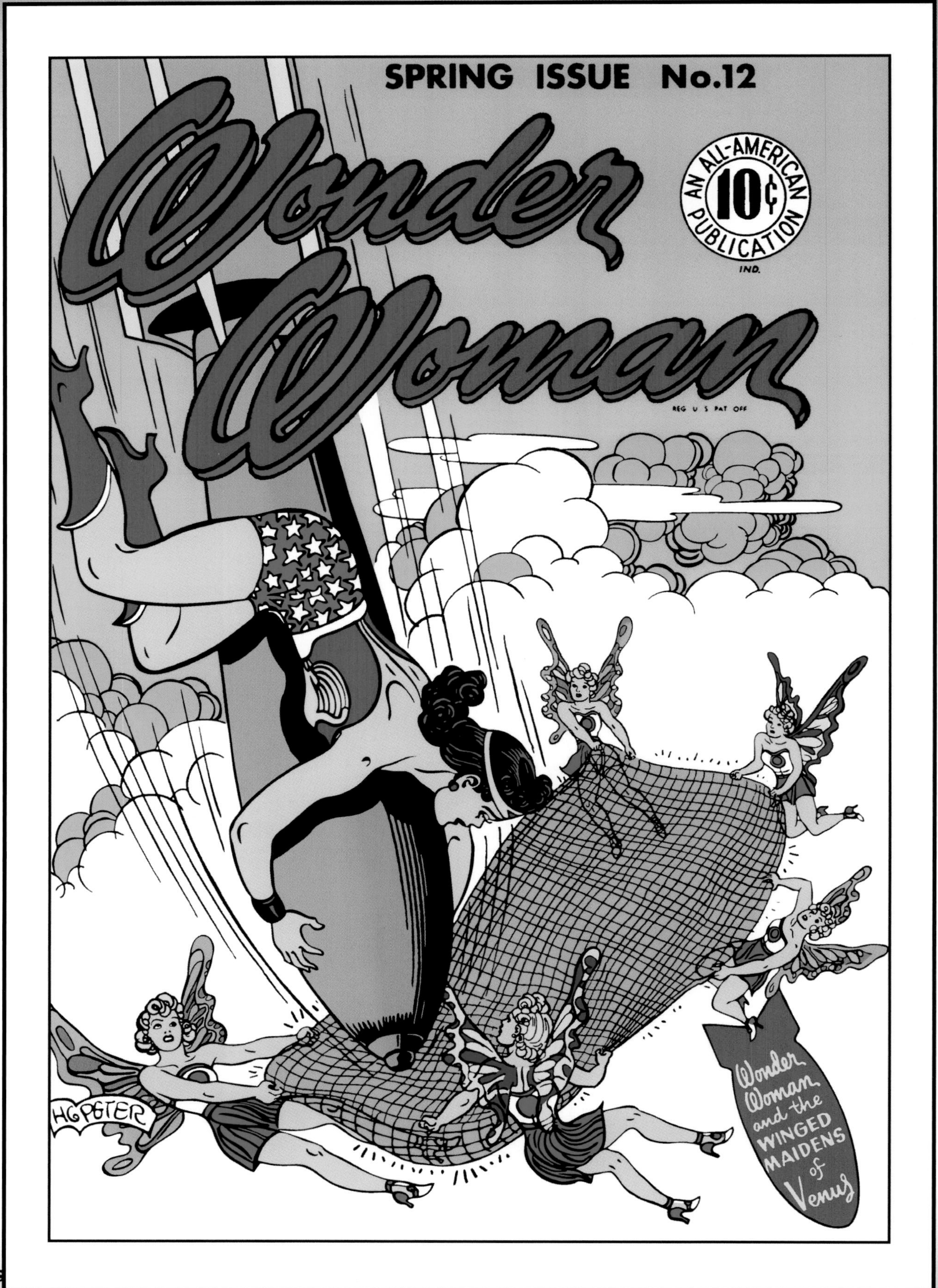
SPRING ISSUE No.12
Wonder Woman
AN ALL-AMERICAN PUBLICATION 10¢
IND.
REG U S PAT OFF
H.G. PETER
Wonder Woman and the WINGED MAIDENS of Venus

Wonder Woman #12 (Spring 1945) - art: H.G. Peter

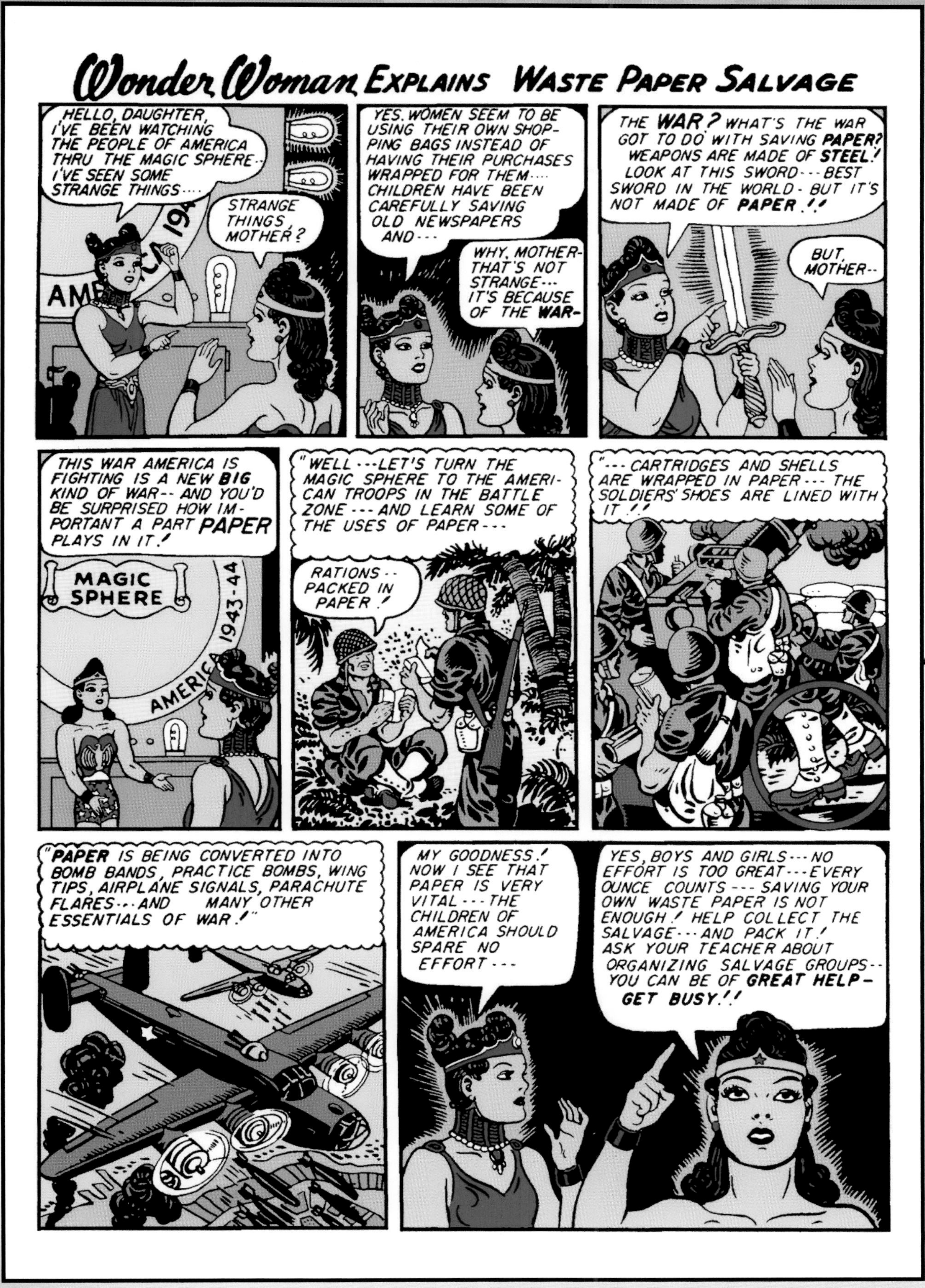
Wonder Woman EXPLAINS WASTE PAPER SALVAGE
HELLO, DAUGHTER, I'VE BEEN WATCHING THE PEOPLE OF AMERICA THRU THE MAGIC SPHERE.. I'VE SEEN SOME STRANGE THINGS....
STRANGE THINGS, MOTHER?
YES. WOMEN SEEM TO BE USING THEIR OWN SHOPPING BAGS INSTEAD OF HAVING THEIR PURCHASES WRAPPED FOR THEM.... CHILDREN HAVE BEEN CAREFULLY SAVING OLD NEWSPAPERS AND---
WHY, MOTHER-THAT'S NOT STRANGE--- IT'S BECAUSE OF THE WAR-
THE WAR? WHAT'S THE WAR GOT TO DO WITH SAVING PAPER? WEAPONS ARE MADE OF STEEL! LOOK AT THIS SWORD---BEST SWORD IN THE WORLD-BUT IT'S NOT MADE OF PAPER!!
BUT, MOTHER--
THIS WAR AMERICA IS FIGHTING IS A NEW BIG KIND OF WAR-- AND YOU'D BE SURPRISED HOW IMPORTANT A PART PAPER PLAYS IN IT!
MAGIC SPHERE
AMERICA 1943-44
"WELL---LET'S TURN THE MAGIC SPHERE TO THE AMERICAN TROOPS IN THE BATTLE ZONE---AND LEARN SOME OF THE USES OF PAPER---
RATIONS-- PACKED IN PAPER!
"---CARTRIDGES AND SHELLS ARE WRAPPED IN PAPER---THE SOLDIERS' SHOES ARE LINED WITH IT!!
"PAPER IS BEING CONVERTED INTO BOMB BANDS, PRACTICE BOMBS, WING TIPS, AIRPLANE SIGNALS, PARACHUTE FLARES---AND MANY OTHER ESSENTIALS OF WAR!"
MY GOODNESS! NOW I SEE THAT PAPER IS VERY VITAL---THE CHILDREN OF AMERICA SHOULD SPARE NO EFFORT---
YES, BOYS AND GIRLS---NO EFFORT IS TOO GREAT---EVERY OUNCE COUNTS---SAVING YOUR OWN WASTE PAPER IS NOT ENOUGH! HELP COLLECT THE SALVAGE---AND PACK IT! ASK YOUR TEACHER ABOUT ORGANIZING SALVAGE GROUPS-- YOU CAN BE OF GREAT HELP-GET BUSY!!

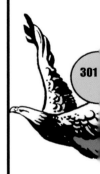

All-Star Comics #24 (Spring 1945) - script: William Moulton Marston - art: H.G. Peter

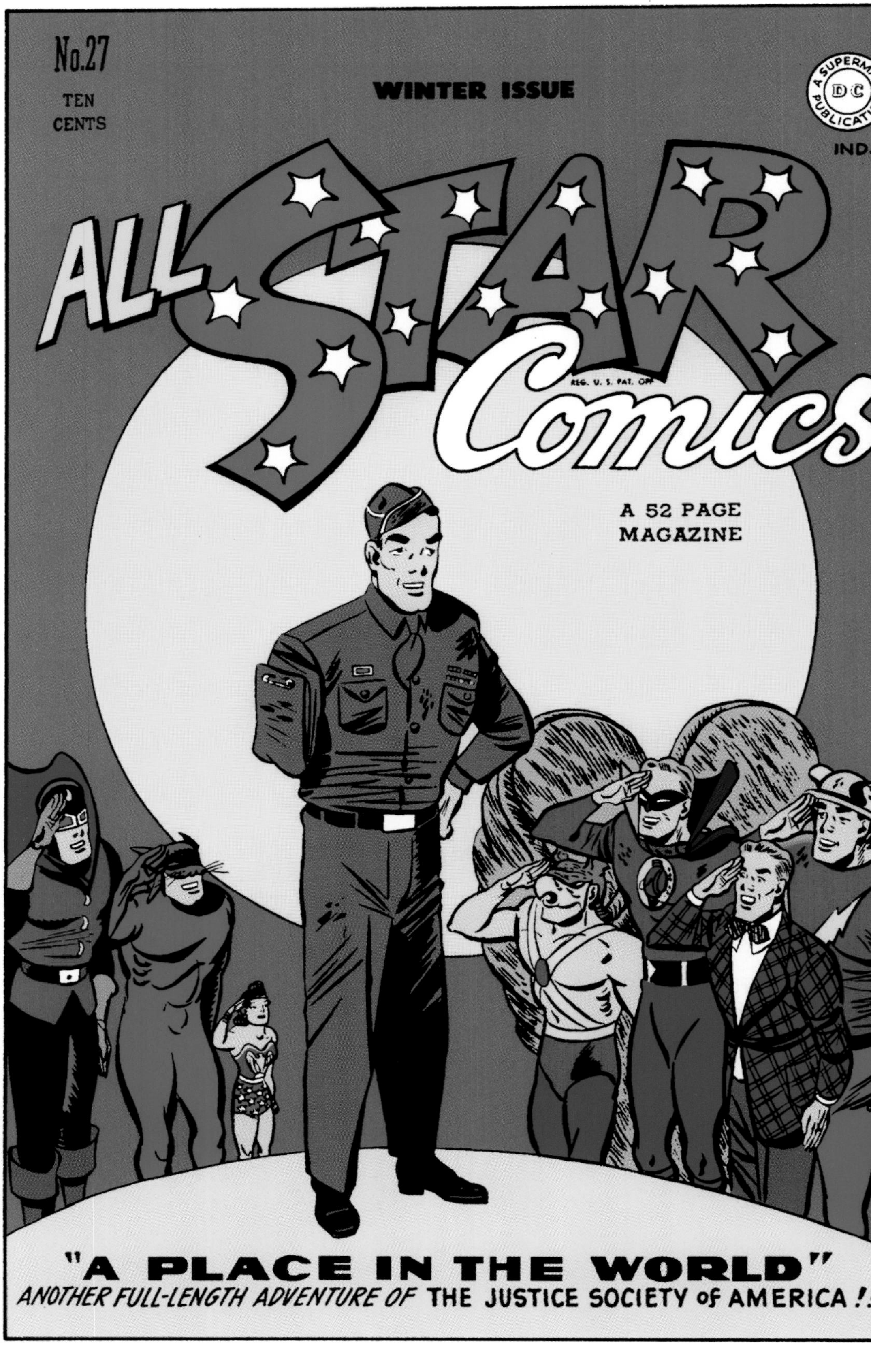
No.27
TEN CENTS
WINTER ISSUE
A SUPERMAN DC PUBLICATION
IND.
ALL STAR Comics
REG. U. S. PAT. OFF
A 52 PAGE MAGAZINE
mn
"A PLACE IN THE WORLD"
ANOTHER FULL-LENGTH ADVENTURE OF THE JUSTICE SOCIETY of AMERICA !!

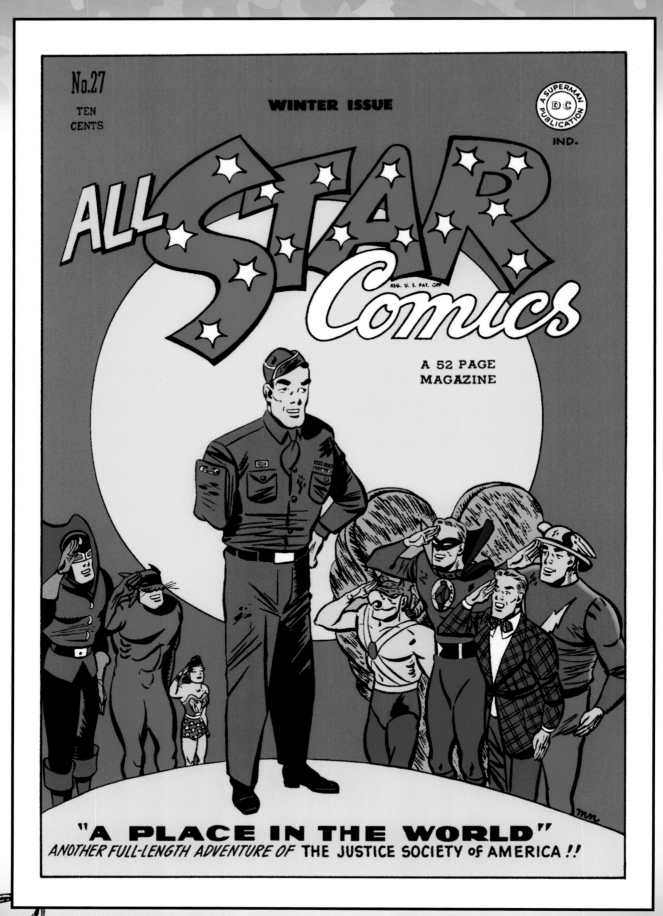

All-Star Comics #27 (Winter 1945) - art: Martin Naydel